Faraway...
the Candle Softly Flickers

by

Edy Elfring

To
Tina Rose

Oh those sweet memories !

Edy 2013

Faraway...the Candle Softly Flickers

Copyright 2009
by
Edy Elfring
front cover art by Edy Elfring

ISBN (10 digit) 1-934335-32-0
ISBN (13 digit) 978-1-934335-32-1

Special Delivery Books
WordWright Business Park
46561 State Highway 118
Alpine, TX 79830

Printed in the United States of America

To my daughter
Sheila Undine Ratliff
With love

Acknowledgements

I'd like to thank all my family and dear friends who encouraged me to write this book.

Thanks to my neighbor, Diane Frasier, for believing in me and her many special ways of telling me that I could write.

Many special thanks to Nancy Lee Blosser Schlender and Pat Jett for editing my book.

I'd also like to thank my friends in the West Texas Mountain Trail Writers club for their support.

And thanks to my editor and publisher at WordWright.biz, Joan R. Neubauer, for all her patient, knowledgeable help with the English language.

I love you all.

Edy Elfring

Introduction

Hi, my girl!

For so many years, my mind has drifted back in time as I wondered about my ancestors. I wanted to know where they lived and especially about their lives. I wish that my mom, my grandma and all the grandmas before had written down and passed on something about their life experiences.

I thought that perhaps you too would wonder some day, so I wrote this book for you, about my young life, both the perils and the easy, wonderful times. The things I really shouldn't have done and the things we didn't have.

Perhaps it will seem to you that we did without a lot that makes your life happy today. I count myself lucky though to have grown up at that time and place. I didn't have to spend my young years in fenced-in backyards or crowded nurseries. I was not held back from becoming independent by pampering, smothering parents. My playground included our whole island. Right after I learned how to walk, swim, and understand the meaning of danger, I could go anywhere on my own. Mothers didn't have to worry about someone stealing their children. Everyone had too many already.

My mom raised me to be independent at an early age so I could enjoy my tender years to their fullest, for which I'm thankful. I grew up in a time and place where that was still possible. Very early in my life, I learned a few rules which you might find ridiculous in today's world.

If I misbehaved, any adult could punish me. If my mom found out, which she usually did, she punished me again. Hitting unruly children was still the normal punishment.

Never, ever disagree with, or speak back to an adult in anger.

Always show respect to our island witch. Don't look her in the face unless she has blessed you. Whatever she asks you to do, you'd better smile and do it right away.

Your teacher is always right, no matter what he says.

Be thankful for the sea and the bounty that lives in her. Without her, we couldn't survive here.

Don't enter your grandma's cellar unless she asks you to.

Stay out of the church's bell tower where the old ghosts live.

Help any person or animal that you see in need.

Don't sell your soul or body to the devil disguised as sweet talking men.

Don't ever enter the sea burial grounds except for a funeral.

Stay away from the mean, old ghost who watches over the ancient mound graves.

Never enter the frozen bay where our people ice fish.

Don't enter the cemetery at midnight or look at the graves on sinners' row.

Respect all that grows on our island, for it nourishes you.

I never had to worry about making up a realistic lie to tell my mom or my grandma after I did something wrong. They almost always knew what I did before I got home and that without a single telephone on our island.

My mom and dad in 1942.

No peanuts, Hot Pockets, yogurt or sponges.

How it All Began

The Vikings are coming.

The hail pounded our roof while my best friends and I sat in Grandma's room waiting in anticipation of hearing tales of our heritage that have been passed on for generations. After a brief moment of collecting her memories, my grandma's eyes began to sparkle and she told us this story.

"Many centuries ago, word came to our small island from a reliable source, that the Wild Vikingers, an estranged band of the king of Norway, sailed southward. People said that they robbed, burned, and killed everything in their path, even the women and children. Rumor had it that those pirates had many big ships and could arrive at the island before winter set in.

"The islanders, though brave pirates themselves, worried. Everyone buried their precious belongings deep in the dark earth, to keep them safe from the robbers. In the very big church, work began to cover all the pure gold and silver statues and the ivory altar, with all its inlaid precious stones, with plaster. After they completed that task, they painted everything over nicely to give the impression of originality.

"The men dug big caves in the steep banks around the island to hide their women and children in at night. Many people dug deep holes in front of their houses and covered them with thin wood or cloth as a trap. The men kept whatever they had to fight

4

with close by them at all times.

"They wrapped the huge church book, which recorded the history of important events on the island, in leather, and placed it inside a tin box with a note that told of the reason for their worries. They then buried the box in the graveyard, which enclosed the old church.

"Since all the rich, important pirates lay buried with their worldly belongings inside the church, the people removed all the flat headstones and buried them with the church book among the poor and sinners, where no one thought to look for those very precious belongings. The islanders placed guards all along the coast of the island to keep watch for the murdering Vikingers.

"Time passed, and the sea slowly began to freeze over. The people of the island relaxed because no one had ever heard of ships or boats that could break the ice without destroying themselves.

"The women and children moved back into their houses and spent the nights there in comfort. The guards no longer watched the coast, but slept inside their houses again with their women. Since the ground was also frozen at this time, people waited to recover the church book and the other buried treasures.

"Then, once icy morning before the sun rose, the bloodthirsty Vikings came in masses. Before the islanders knew what happened, they found themselves drowning in their own blood, or burning to death on poles. The Vikings murdered young children in front of their parents. Amidst wild laughter, the invaders cut their heads off and tossed them into sizzling fires, while the tied up parents watched, pleaded and screamed to the heavens. The outraged, desperate loud screams of the helpless, dying people in the cold dark night must have been heard far out to sea."

Grandma quit talking for a moment, folded her hands and took a deep breath before continuing.

"Some of the islanders fought back, but not for long. Before the sun rose, the pleading cries of the burning and dying people ended. They would never hurt again. The island lay eerily silent until the Vikings awoke, when the wings of morning shed light on the massacre.

"They had celebration on their mind. They slaughtered some animals, then cooked them over an open fire inside the unfinished church, using the church benches as firewood. The search for precious items began.

"Stumbling and kicking away the dead bodies, they searched through the ruins of the burned out houses. They even ripped the clothing off the dead to gain some riches. They found very little since just about everything of value remained buried.

"After the Vikings gorged themselves all day long, they declared that the island of Fehmarn belonged to them, since no one remained alive to claim it. In the late afternoon they walked, rowdily celebrating, killing an innocent animal or two on their way to the northern coast of the island where their big ships lay anchored. Soon they heaved their red sails, and the ruthless, murdering, Wild Vikings left for more prosperous grounds to plunder.

"Low down in a nearly finished grave, a man huddled with his small son in his arms. He had just lost his wife in childbirth, and now these Vikings had killed the remainder of his family.

"Both, very hungry and cold, clung to each other for warmth and life. When the complete silence of the island assured him they could safely emerge from the grave, he picked up his small, frightened son and ever so slowly crawled from the freshly dug grave that hid them so well.

"Still bleeding from a Vikinger spear embedded in his leg, he warily left the graveyard and headed for the altar of the small chapel which adjoined the big church. There he left a lengthy note of the gruesome ordeal scratched into the mud near the altar.

"Workers had just begun to even out the dirt inside the chapel to lay small cobblestones down into ground. That part of the church had a roof on it already, and so it protected his writing from the rain. He left drawings of the murdered people and children on the walls all around the church.

"One drawing near the end showed him in a grave lying atop a woman with a tiny infant in her arms. The last drawing showed a man with a small boy. The man had blood running from his leg. Then the story ended with no way of telling what happened to the man and the little boy. He didn't mention the hidden treasures of the church or of the people in his wall drawings, or in his writings.

"No one knows how he died, or if he and his son sailed away. For the next centuries, the island lay empty and quiet. Then a group of pirates from Finland discovered the island. With their leader Stoertebaecker, they established new villages and worked on the huge church building. The first entry into their new church book told of the gruesome raid on the island by the Wild Vikings, just as they found it described in the dried mud by the altar and on all the walls of the huge, unfinished church.

"The pirates, with Stoertebaecker in command, prospered. They raided, plundered and murdered the people on the big ships that used the important trade route past our island to the northern countries. They managed to build castles and forts all around the island. The sea had swallowed most of them by the time you kids came along, but you can still reach a few by a short swim. One of them, named Plambeck, had partially fallen into the sea, but you can still reach it with a big jump over a seaweed filled ditch. As a young woman, my friends and I used to dive down into the sea to explore those castles and forts. They contained lots of human bones, pottery, iron chains, old spears of many different sizes and things we couldn't identify. Have any of you dived down there?"

Most of us nodded.

Grandma smiled. "At some time, the king of Denmark heard about the island and the pirates and decided to own the island of Fehmarn for himself. He sent out a group of very loyal, well-equipped men of his army to overtake the island.

"They came on a stormy night, captured the leader and all of his twenty-seven important followers. The Danish king's men

ined the pirate gang up in a straight line inside the church. They told the leader, Stoertebaecker, that they intended to chop his head off, but that they'd spare the lives of any of his men that he could run past without his head.

"The church book reads that right after Stoertebaecker's head got chopped off, he fell without rescuing even one of his loyal followers. Therefore, twenty-eight heads rolled down the aisle of the church. The Danish king, who came on his royal ship to claim his new island, named her Fembre.

"Still, after the death of that pirate group, many entries in the church book showed hangings, killing witches, drowning a few devils, and many wars. Somehow, the population of the island survived. Ever so slowly over the next centuries, life on the island grew more civilized.

"All the precious stones on the ivory altar and the golden and silver statues inside the church remained hidden for a very long time to come.

"In 1893, at the age of six, I attended a funeral service in the now long completed, beautiful church. Suddenly, the ground of our island trembled. At that precise moment, a statue of one of the old saints fell off its pedestal and smashed onto the cobblestone floor, right next to me, and all the plaster fell off the statue.

"People gathered around the lovely, shining statue and stared at it in awe, especially at the eyes made from pretty light blue stones. The sun's rays, shining through the colorful, stained-glass windows, made them sparkle ever so lovely. Amazed, but frightened, the people didn't know what to think about the tremor and the falling statue. Was it a sign from God, or perhaps the devil? Was the island about to fall apart and everyone condemned by the Lord Almighty Himself?

"The people of the funeral mass huddled together in the church, waiting in great fear. After everything quieted down and neither the devil nor an angry God arrived, they completed the funeral service.

"After the burial, everyone walked back into the church and began to remove the plaster from the statues. Eventually, they cleaned and restored everything to its original beauty.

"Everyone stared amazed at all the beautiful, statues and the most gorgeous altar with all the shining precious stones. You all know what that feels like, especially when the sunlight touches the inside of our church."

We all agreed with her.

"While the people restored the church, no one had yet discovered the buried church book or the headstones."

Grandma stood up, walked to the window and stared out into the wild storm as though she saw what had happened so long ago. We waited for her to tell us more. Then, with one big sigh, she turned around and sat back down in her worn out chair.

Slowly, she looked at each of us with a proud smile. Then her eyes seemed to wander and she began to speak.

"In 1903, when I turned sixteen, I fell head over heels in love with your grandpa. The only place to get married was in the church but it cost a lot of money. Since neither of us had any money to get married right away, your grandpa took on extra work to save up the money for our wedding and worked as a gravedigger.

"Legend had it that if a grave got dug during the daytime, the evil spirits who served the devil, would sneak inside it and wait there to snatch up the soul of the dead person who shortly would be buried there. Since evil spirits slept at night, graves were only dug at night. That fit in fine with your grandpa's other job as a builder of dirt roads and houses.

"On this dark night, your grandpa and another man, after digging for hours, suddenly hit something that sounded like metal. Eagerly they kept on digging. In great surprise, they discovered a big metal box and many small, flat headstones. Hurriedly, Grandpa ran to the preacher's house. He hammered on the door with his fist until a sleepy preacher answered.

After hearing the news about the box and the headstones in the

shly-dug grave, the preacher, still in his nightclothes, quickly
llowed Grandpa to the grave site. The very heavy preacher
rrived at the grave breathlessly coughing and sneezing. He sat
down at the edge of the grave and looked into it in disbelief. After
he caught his breath, he realized that he couldn't physically get
inside the grave to help lift the big box out. He asked Grandpa to
hurry and get the tavern keeper to help.

"Grandpa found the tavern keeper cleaning up his little place
from a good night's business. When the tavern keeper heard about
what they had found, he quickly grabbed a few bottles of his best
concoction and closed his tavern. Excited, the two of them nearly
ran to the cemetery."

Grandma stopped talking and laughed out loud before
continuing. "Together, the men lifted the heavy metal box and all
the gravestones out of the grave. They took everything inside the
church and lit all the candles on the altar to investigate their
findings. After a good stiff drink from the tavern keeper's bottles,
they broke the heavily damaged box open with brute force.
Surprised, they stared at a very old book with many drawings and
pages of text inside the box.

"Carefully, after another drink, the men took everything out of
the box and laid it on the cobblestone floor of the church. They
soon found the words in the church book had been written in
languages they could not understand. They found numbers on the
back of the flat gravestones and names on the other side with a
sketch showing where to place the headstones.

"They found many gruesome drawings on some kind of dry
brittle skin, showing ships that carried men with big spears in their
hands, and some of those spears acted as spits for human heads.
Some drawings showed humans cut in half, bodies burning, people
screaming, and running children, some with their arms cut off. One
drawing showed a figure half covered up, which seemed to lay
inside the church.

"Many pages just fell out of the church book and

disintegrated, as if made of flour. There the three men sat, among all the discovered history, drinking the tavern owner's strong concoctions and trying to piece together the story of their findings. Somehow, none of the men made it home that night.

"A woman who played the mighty pipe organ in our church, woke them the next morning just before the funeral Mass was about to begin. Startled from the loud sound of the pipe organ, the men jumped to their feet. They escorted the preacher to the altar to give his funeral service. Your grandpa faithfully held him up throughout the service," so my grandma said with a proud smile on her face.

"Between those findings in that freshly-dug grave and the entries inside the first pages of the next church book, people concluded that certainly the Vikings had cruelly raided the island very long ago. They placed the small, flat headstones back into the church's floor where they belonged."

Grandma then closed her eyes. Her head slowly fell forward and she started to snore.

So let me take you there!

I was born when the world still occupied itself with the Second World War. On October 12, Columbus Day, in 1943 at four a.m., nature decided I should come into the world. My grandma delivered me right there in the house my grandpa built on the small island of Fehmarn.

Fehmarn lies in the Baltic Sea, the part called the East Sea, right between Germany and Denmark. Looking at a European road map one could not find Fehmarn, it's just too small and at that time too unimportant to appear on a road map.

The actual war did not reach my island. Still, so many young men had to go away and join Hitler's army. Some came back after the war ended, but many did not.

Our island had a very short growing season, fertile black earth and we had plenty of fish in the sea to help nourish us in the short, mild seasons.

My ancestors started out in Finland and with every generation or so they migrated a little further south. I don't know for certain how many generations back they settled on this island, but I'm sure it was quite a long time ago. In fact, I remember two pirate's graves, inside our huge church that bear my family name.

At the time, I grew up on my island, only a handful of families lived around each farmer's house, and that made up a village. I remember eight of them. The biggest village sat on the highest point of my island, nestled around our huge church. A graveyard embraced the church, and a clapboard two-story schoolhouse stood close by. A few small houses huddled around a very tall, old oak tree across from the church. A small, but very important tavern and a tiny store where people mostly bartered for items also stood directly across from the church. This village is called Burg, translated castle or fort.

My small fishing village, where I was born and grew up, sat at the south bay, is called Burgstaaken and I lived there for the first fifteen years of my life.

A staaken consists of a piece of wood about a yard wide and long, and sawed in half with a hole cut out in the middle just big enough to fit around a sinner's, thief's or crazy person's neck. The magistrate, or person in charge then locked it around the guilty person's head and tied him to a tree in front of our church. The length of the punishment depended on the severity of the crime. No one gave him food or water and anyone who wished could throw trash at him, spit, kick, or urinate on him. In extreme cases, the injured person had the right to kill the guilty party any way he wished.

However, that was so very many generations ago and I did not have to witness such cruelty.

At the time I grew up on my island, I only had to worry about the pain my mom's wooden paddle inflicted, our island witch,

God, the devil, a handful of ghosts and my grandma's slipper.

My grandma had a habit of throwing her slipper through the air at someone who had done wrong, and when the leather sole hit me, it packed quite a stinging pain. I remember it so very well. My grandma never missed. She'd have made a great basketball player!

Other children tried to make my life miserable by teasing me because my mom had red hair, a trait some - considered made her a loose woman. They picked on me because my little sister had a lazy eye, and they connected that with stupidity. Then, of course, we had no father who lived with us, which gave them another reason to pick on me.

I took on each child, one at a time, sailing my fist into their faces. Strong, quick, and fearless I quickly established peace and made sure that it stayed that way!

Chapter 1

Come on in!

Let me show you the house I lived in for the first fifteen years of my life. Compared to today's standards, I'm sure you wonder how so many people could live in such a small house. My grandpa built this house with his own hands out of strong, red brick.

Just inside the front door, you stood in a short hallway with my grandpa and grandma's room to the right. This small room served as their kitchen, living room and bedroom. To the left stood a door that led down to my grandma's cellar where she tended to her business, a first class production of fine liquors, brandy and a few other things in the medicinal field. I liked that sweet smell which always drifted up from her cellar.

The door straight ahead led to Uncle Fred and Aunt Hilde's place. They had two small rooms to share with their three children. People whispered that Aunt Hilde was crazy, probably because she screamed an awful lot. I stayed out of her way as much as I could. I did like her husband, Uncle Fred, because he was so much fun and so very smart.

On the left, over the cellar door, a staircase led up to where my mom, my smaller sister, Uschi, and I lived. At the top of the stairs and to the left, you'd find a window which we used to climb through to get to the chimney. My mother always cleared the chimney of snow early in the still dark mornings so everyone could start their little iron stoves. To the right and left side of the window was attic space.

In the middle stood my mom's tiny room where she cooked our meals, washed our clothes, and slept on a small couch. We all lived here, but since that room was too small for our bed, my sister and I slept in a bed in the attic to the right. We used the attic space to the left side as a common area to hang the laundry in winter and for us kids to play in. My cousins, sister, and I often played hide and seek among the frozen laundry.

I can still hear my mother shout to me as I walked down the stairs, "Take your sister with you!"

The house had no central heat or inside plumbing. We had an outhouse in the backyard, close to the house, so we could more easily reach it in the harsh winters. Also near the house, we had a deep, sweet well with a hand pump.

The whole family maintained and shared the huge garden, chicken coop, animal stall, and lean-to. Though this may seem an odd way to live, it was very common in that time and place.

Edith and Mutti (Mother) 1944

No baby formula or maternity care yet.

Chapter 2

Why did we sing at funerals?

I barely remember the day my mom told me that my father had died in the fight of the Second World War. She handed me a picture of him which had words written on the back. I stared at the man in the picture and the words on the back of that picture. I couldn't read yet and really didn't comprehend what my mom had tried to tell me.

I had no idea what a father was or what the word *war* meant. I did know though that we buried dead things. My mom gave my little sister a picture of her father and told her that he had survived the war, but most likely, wouldn't come to see her.

Slowly I walked to the corner of our garden where we buried small dead things. Right next to the grave of the dead snail, which I had accidentally stepped on and killed early that morning, I dug a hole in the soft black earth with my hands. After another look at the picture, I buried my father in the cold, black dirt. I sang part of a song I remembered from funerals. Then I put a flower on his grave, wondering what a father was, what war meant, and why we sang at funerals.

And so, life went on, on our island.

Without television, vending machines, Kleenex, fathers,
bologna, microwave ovens, CDs, calculators,
birth control, toothbrushes or computers.

No licorice, speed limits, VCR or turkeys.

Chapter 3

So many children.

After my grandma gave birth to twenty-four children, she told my grandpa, "I'm worn out and refuse to have any more children. I'll sleep here in our room, and you need to find another place to sleep."

Grandpa's face grew sad and bitter. He slammed his fist on the table and said, "All right old woman, I'll move out of our bed and will find a girlfriend to comfort me!" He stomped out of the room and walked out of the house.

My grandma wiped a tear from her face and smiled a sad smile. That same evening grandpa fixed up the lean-to and moved in. He took his meals with grandma inside their room, but they never talked to each other anymore.

Soon my grandpa had two women visiting him now and then, which seemed fine with my grandma, until the day he demanded that she should cook and clean for him and his girlfriends. That's when my grandma changed her mind about that situation!

With her face red with anger, she steamed like a teakettle and said words I'd never heard before. She stomped her foot on the floor, grabbed her broom, and slammed the door shut on her way out. With a voice likely heard all over our island, she walked toward my grandpa's lean-to.

I hurried outside to watch. With a strength I never knew she had, my grandma ripped the locked lean-to wooden door off its hinges, set it aside, and marched inside with her broom held high, as if to kill someone. I couldn't believe all the commotion!

I heard all sorts of screaming and yelling from my grandpa's place like I never heard before. Not even Aunt Hilde screamed that loud, even though she had a tremendous voice.

Peeking through a hole in the lean-to, I saw my grandma beating up both of the visiting women. In no time at all, my grandma had cleared out the girlfriends! My, could they run fast! One of the women didn't even have enough time to put her shoes and girdle on. She carried them in her hands.

Then my grandma swung her broom up high again and with great force hit the bedcover where my grandpa had taken refuge. His long pants slowly slipped off the chair and fell to the ground. I immediately had a fear of my grandma's temper and swore to myself never to make her mad at me!

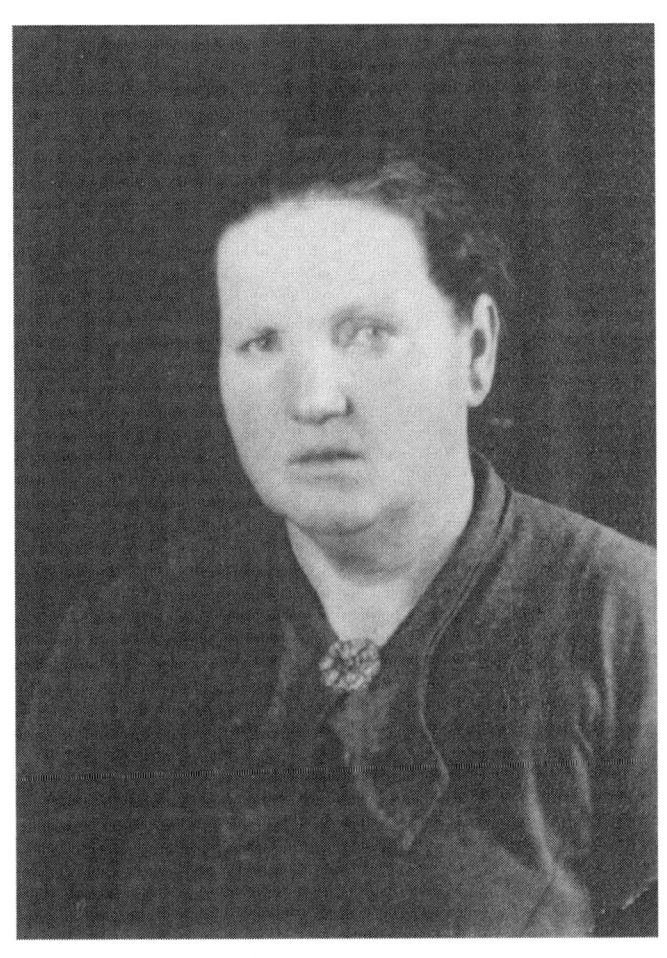

Grandmom
Elise Dorothea Wilhelmine Navers Siebert
November 17, 1887 – 1962

Grandpop
Franz Ludwig Oskar Siebert
February 14, 1880 - 1948

No hairdryer, coloring books, or crackers yet.

Chapter 4

The silence

One bitter cold day, my grandma and I played marbles in the attic of our house when all of a sudden my grandma's old closet door opened. With a slow moaning noise and a short squeak, it stopped. I recognized her other dress that hung inside, but not the new outfit.

"Grandma, whose outfit is that?" I asked.

"Edith, your mother and I sewed it so that your grandpa will have a nice outfit to wear at his funeral." She looked me in the eye and said, "You know, the cancer will kill him soon."

I didn't know anything about cancer but figured it had to be huge to kill my big grandpa. I asked my grandma, "What does that cancer look like? I want to hide from it when it comes into our house."

Surely, it couldn't find me under my bed, in my dark, safe place. Even my mom couldn't see me under there most of the time. I needed to tell my grandpa that he could hide under there too when the cancer came into our house to kill him.

Slowly my grandma answered, "I'm not sure what the cancer looks like."

Her answer caused me to think I should look out for strangers who might come close to our house. When I saw one, I'd run home as fast as I could, tell my grandpa the bad news, and both of us could quickly hide under my bed.

Then Grandma announced, "It's time to go downstairs to eat."

I hurried and gathered up all our marbles. I tried to close the closet door, but it fell to the floor with a loud bang. All the dust, the result of woodworms that had feasted on this old closet for many years, flew into the air.

My grandma heard the noise and came running back to ask, "Edith, are you hurt?"

"No, I'm fine," I said coughing from inhaling the dust as I followed her down the stairs.

Entering my grandma and grandpa's room, I noticed my grandma stirring a pot on her little iron stove. I sat down in my chair, which had a pillow on it, so I could see the food on my plate better. Soon my grandma put two cups of soup on the table, one for her and one for me.

Then she walked over to my grandpa, who lay in their bed. She gave him morphine and a big glass of brandy, my grandpa's diet now.

He used to smoke one cigar after the other, sometimes filling their room so full of smoke that stepping into their room felt like stepping into a cloud.

My grandma no longer let him smoke since he nearly burned himself to death. Grandpa had dropped his lit cigar in his bed and couldn't move his weak body away from the burning sheets.

My grandpa used to work hard in his beloved tobacco field. He rolled and sold cigars. But now that he was so sick, my grandma and mom did all the work and I delivered the cigars to our neighbors.

Soon my grandma sat down next to me. As she began to slice off a piece of her freshly baked black bread, the huge grandfather clock began to chime the midday hour.

My grandpa raised his head and yelled at my grandma, "Silence that big clock!"

Grandma paid him no mind.

Slowly my grandpa took his big gun, which I thought he kept beside him to shoot the cancer when it came to kill him, sat up a little, pointed the shaking gun at the huge grandfather clock and pulled the trigger. For a brief moment, I couldn't breathe and my body shook violently while I watched all sorts of pieces leak out of the clock's brain.

When the clock fell silent, I took in a huge breath and screamed in panic, but could barely hear myself. My ears hummed and I reached out for Grandma for help. She rose from her chair and took me into her arms. I clung to her in desperation, still screaming with fear.

Grandma waved her fist at Grandpa and yelled something at him, but I couldn't hear what she said. I just saw her angry face and her lips moving.

Still clinging to my grandma and with tears streaming down my face, I barely heard the second shot. Suddenly, Grandma firmed her grip around me, and I looked over to Grandpa.

Blood and other strange things leaked out of his brain. His big gun slid out of his bed onto the floor with a bang and my grandpa was silent now too. When the door opened, my mom and uncle rushed into the room, and I could finally hear again and quit screaming.

Mom took me from Grandma's arms and sat me back in my chair. Ashamed, I realized that I had wet the pillow.

When the adults covered up Grandpa's bloody face, I realized that the cancer didn't need to come to kill my grandpa anymore.

No peanut butter, or Brillo pads.
No man made fertilizer, just the real stuff.
At fertilizing time, it was best to stay way up wind!

Chapter 5

Flour Power

I remember seeing my mom putting a tiny pinch of our precious flour around our windowsill and her door at night.

I was only six, and when I asked her why she did that, and she said, "So the stork won't be able to come inside to bring me another baby."

It scared me to think that the stork could also visit me. I liked babies all right, but I didn't want to have one yet! I thought my sister was enough to take care of, and we really didn't have any more room in our bed for another child!

That night, I decided to watch my mom closely to learn exactly what she did with the flour. Nighttime came quickly and mom hugged us both and sent us to bed. I helped my little sister into our bed and told her to stay very quiet. Then I carefully walked back to mom's door and kneeled down in front of it so I could watch her through the slits of the clapboard door.

Soon my mom started to undress and slipped her nightgown on. Then she walked toward our precious flour can. She carefully lifted the lid off the rusted old can, lowered her hand inside, and lifted it back out. She had just a tiny pinch of flour between two fingers, as she usually did. Then mom walked to the window, looked up to the ceiling of the little room and mumbled something. After a moment, she looked down and placed just a very small part of the pinch of flour on the windowsill.

I couldn't understand even one of the words she mumbled and I worried about it. I hoped to understand the words when mom did her ritual by the door because it was so important to me not to have a baby yet.

When I saw her coming toward the door, I quickly put my ear onto the wood, hoping to understand the words she mumbled. Sure enough, I heard my mom clearly.

She said, "Please, Ola, help me through this month! Please do not let me be with child!" Then my mom walked away from the door and sat on her couch, which also served as her bed. I peeked beneath the door to see if she put flour on the floor. I saw just a small sprinkle of it lying on the floor.

Careful not to step on the creaking floorboards, I walked over to our bed and crawled inside, next to my little sleeping sister. Even though I didn't know yet who Ola was and had no flour, I repeated my mom's words and hoped for the best.

In my simple mind, I figured that Ola must be the person who tells the stork where to deliver the babies. How happy I felt the next morning when I found no baby lying in my arms.

That afternoon, when my mom went downstairs to visit with my grandma, I opened our flour can, took out a small handful of our precious flour, and hid it inside my small cardboard box which contained all my worldly possessions. At night, after mom had gone to bed, I silently performed the stork ritual just as she did. Every morning I felt relieved not to see a baby in our bed. When my mom stopped the nightly stork ritual, I figured it safe for me to quit too. I wondered for a long time about the power of a pinch of flour.

No chainsaws, candy apples or aspirin yet.

Chapter 6

Winter of 1949

One cold winter night, my mom shook me awake. "Get up, Edith. Dress warmly. I need your help to get firewood."

I felt proud that she had asked me and dressed hurriedly. Mom stuck a bread knife in her coat sleeve and a small sack in her coat pocket. She took my hand and held it as we walked silently through the deep snow. We stopped at a stand of young trees on the outside of our village. She positioned me near a bush from where I could see the road and the only nearby house.

"Just watch, Edith. Whistle if you see someone coming," she whispered.

I nodded. I could do that. I knew how to whistle with the best of them. My Uncle Fred taught me well long ago.

Then my mom walked inside the small stand of young trees. She tried to cut off some of the small branches with her bread knife. Our lumberyard that sold coal and wood had long run out of goods to sell or barter for. The winter ration of coal never arrived. Most likely, some desperate people had stolen it.

At that moment, I realized that my mom was about to steal too. I started to shiver and got scared. I knew that someone else owned that stand of young trees. I also knew that stealing was against the law!

Suddenly the door of the house across the road from me opened. The bright light floating out of the house made the snow in front of it sparkle with thousands of small, silvery pieces. I quickly lay down in the deep snow under the bush closest to me. The man looked toward my mom. I tried my best to whistle, but my cold, shaking lips refused to produce a sound.

The man stepped out of the door and walked toward us. He recognized my mom and shouted her name.

I lay shivering with fear. My tears froze to my cheeks. Lifting my head just a little, I could see that the man had reached his trees. He called my mom by her name again.

Oh, how I hoped that my mom had run away from there.

Still lying under my bush, I saw the man come out of the trees. He turned and looked around one more time then walked back into his house.

After he closed his door, I slowly crawled out from under the bush, wiped the snow from my face and stood up. I felt so bad that I let my mom down. I couldn't understand why I couldn't whistle. Feeling scared and guilty, I started to walk home and wondered where my mom went. With my tears still running down my cheeks I stumbled.

Someone grabbed my hand and nearly scared me to death. I thought the owner had snuck around behind the trees and had trapped me. Then I realized that my mom helped me up. She held my hand, and in silence, we walked home. My cheeks began to hurt from all the tears that had frozen onto my skin.

At home, between sniffles and sobs, I told my mom just how sorry I was that I had let her down.

She hugged me. "That's all right. Everything will be just fine."

She helped me get my snow-covered clothes off, and I crawled into my bed next to my warm sister. Slowly, trying not to wake her, I moved real close to her to get warm.

Before noon on the next morning, our only lawman and the owner of the stand of young trees arrived at our house. I heard them talking to my grandma. When they came upstairs to talk to my mom, I quickly hid underneath my bed.

The owner of the little stand of trees sounded very angry, but our lawman stayed calm. They searched our little place for the evidence. Even though my mom had hidden the few tiny sticks of wood she took, they found them and her weapon, the bread knife.

"Put on your coat and come with us," they told my mom.

They took the wood and the bread knife with them. That knife was the only cutting tool she had not yet bartered for food. When they left the house, I started to cry. If only I had whistled! Even just a little whistle would have helped. I felt awfully guilty again and didn't know what to do.

Shaking with fear and from the bitter cold in our unheated attic, I crawled back into bed with my sister. Covered warmly, we both counted the icicles that hung down from the brick shingled roof inside our attic. I found no fun in this pastime because I worried about my mom, but it occupied my sister.

Before long, Grandma came upstairs with two cups of steaming hot soup. I was so glad to get something warm to eat.

She talked calmly to us and said, "Your mom will return soon." She asked us to get dressed and come downstairs to her room where we could play some card games.

After we ate, I held our feather cover down to keep the warm air in while my sister dressed beneath it. I had taught her long ago how to dress like this so we could stay warm.

The moment the two of us walked down the stairs, the front door opened and in walked our mom. She didn't see us standing on the stairs, and headed straight for my grandma's room.

My sister and I sat down on the stairs and listened.

Our mom said, "Our lawman kept the sticks I stole and my precious bread knife." She started to cry in anger and screamed at my grandma.

My grandma now started to scream at my mom, and the whole situation made me very sad, to see the two people I love most in an argument that I considered all my fault. If I had only whistled, none of this would have happened.

Sadly, I took my little sister by the hand, walked down the stairs, grabbed our coats and walked outside to play in the snow.

A short while later my Uncle Fred came around the corner of our house with a bucket full of fish. I ran toward him crying. He lifted me into his arms and I hurriedly told him what had happened.

He dried my tears. "Now, Edith, it's not your fault. It's the war."

I didn't understand what the war had to do with my inability to whistle, but I felt relieved to hear that it wasn't my fault. Then my Uncle Fred let me down.

He handed me the bucket with some good looking fish inside of it and said, "Take this to my wife. Take your sister along and stay to help clean the fish."

Then my uncle hurried in front of us into our house. In no time at all, he had calmed my mom and my grandma.

While cleaning the fish, I saw my grandma coming out of her cellar with a bottle of her fine liquor. She wrapped the bottle up in a towel, stuck it in her coat pocket and left the house. Mom meanwhile skinned some onions and peeled potatoes while she still cried.

Soon a great smell drifted through our house. The fish fried. The potatoes and onions boiled, and the small room grew warm. We took off our winter coats and played marbles with our cousins beneath the kitchen table. Still feeling very guilty about letting my mom down, I played an honest game and lost all ten of my marbles.

The moment I crawled from beneath the table, my grandma walked in the door wearing a big smile. She took my mom's bread knife out of her coat sleeve and unwrapped a bundle of wood twice as big as what mom stole the night before. She handed both to my smiling mom. I noticed that my grandma didn't bring the bottle of liquor back. They hugged each other for quite some time, and a few happy tears ran silently down my cheeks.

My mother told me to pour the steaming water into the big teapot to brew some dandelion tea. Soon we had a great, warm meal in the cozy kitchen. How lucky we were today.

In this harsh winter of 1949, I spent a lot of time with my sister on my mom's couch under her feather covers. We learned how to knit, read, add numbers, and play games. Even with three families in this house, because of fuel shortage, only one family could light their iron stove once a day to cook a warm meal for everyone.

All of us gathered around that stove to enjoy the short-lived warmth of a crackling fire and ate a hot meal that we looked forward to all day. We stayed there together talking and laughing until the fire died and the biting cold forced us back under our feather covers.

No fruit juices, tomatoes or mailboxes.

Chapter 7

A good laugh.

Our mail carrier came to our island faithfully, once a week, whenever the sea was kind.

He came by boat in the summer and by dog sled in the winter. In the middle of our harsh winters, when the temperature dropped too much for even the animals, or if the snow was too deep, he didn't come to our island. Some winters, we did not see him for months at a time.

He always wore a gun to scare away the pack of village dogs that threatened him. The sound of his gun scattered the dogs in all directions. It also served as our signal for us to come down to the pier to pick up the mail.

Most of us children ran to the pier in great excitement, perhaps even with a letter to mail. When we arrived at our pier, the mail carrier might hand us a letter, or a newspaper or two to bring to our neighbors. He then took the rest of the important newspapers and letters addressed to people on the other side of our island to our little store. There they sat until someone came to pick them up.

On this early fall day, things went badly. I sat on a big stone near the pier, dangling my naked feet in the salty sea, when I saw the mailman's small boat gliding into our harbor. Quickly I ran over to the pier to greet him.

The sea, a little rough today, had splashed the planks of his boat. As soon as he tied his boat to the pier, the herd of village dogs came running toward him ready to kill him, as though he were the biggest threat in the world.

The mail carrier got ready to shoot his gun to scare the rowdy dogs away, but he slipped and fell into his little boat. The little boat capsized, dumping the mail carrier, the mail, and the important newspapers into the cold seawater.

The herd of dogs furiously jumped into the sea, trying to reach him. Seeing the dogs coming after him, the mail carrier quickly climbed on top of his capsized boat. He tried to shoot his wet gun, but it didn't work.

Some fishermen came running with a big fishing net and threw it over the wildly barking herd of dogs and slowly dragged them to the other side of the pier, where the dogs could easily get out of the water.

One little black dog, not caught in the net, continued swimming toward the mail carrier. All of a sudden, this little dog realized that his comrades had left him, and for a brief moment didn't know what to do. It looked once more at the mail carrier with his big gun in his hand, turned around and hurried up to catch up with its comrades.

A man threw a rope down to the mailman and heaved him up to dry land. Two of the boys from our island jumped in the water and turned his boat upright.

No one got any mail or newspapers that week. All of it had sunk to the bottom of the murky water, but we had clean dogs and a good laugh!

No pancakes, balloons or duct tape.

Chapter 8

Changing

We children always thought it a special treat to spend the night in our grandma's room. We brought our old blankets and spread them out beneath her bed which stood high off the floor, about three feet. That space was high and wide enough for four of us to crawl beneath and closely snuggle together. Two very small children could sleep on my grandma's old, red sofa. One on each end fit fine if they didn't stretch out their legs too much. I preferred to sleep under my grandma's bed, instead of on that old, worn out, bumpy sofa.

After all of us bedded down, my grandma gave us a sweet drink from her bottles in her cellar. She based the amount she gave us on our age. My grandma of course, very old by now, poured herself a big glass of the sweet tasting, warming treat.

Then she lit a small, white candle and turned off the lantern. She put on her long, white nightgown and let her grey hair fall to her shoulders. Then she slowly started to tell us a good night story.

Grandma never read us a story, but always made them up and acted them out with fire in her eyes. Her long hair flew around her neck as she moved through the small room. Now and then, she took another sip from her glass. Soon the story got scary and wild.

By that time, my grandma waved her arms in the air as she waltzed through the room. To me it seemed that she floated in the air with her long nightgown dragging behind her. Sometimes her hair glowed in the candle light, just enough to make it look like the angels in my dreams. At other times, while telling her stories, her laughter reminded me of the witch's laugh, which I often heard whenever I walked past her house. She had an eerie, scary laugh. At those times, I believed that my grandma actually became part witch, though a good witch of course. The story always involved all of us in her room on that particular night. Often we held hands and huddled a little closer to each other when my grandma's story came to its end. We waited, scared to hear which one of us would die in her story. Amazingly, she always pulled all of us out of the scary ending we just knew had to come.

With relief, we crawled under our blankets and went to sleep, still holding tightly to each other, just in case one of those monsters in her story came to get us.

Then my grandma blew out the small, white candle, leaving the room in pitch darkness. I wondered if my grandma would turn back into herself when the darkness of the night left us!

No Ben-Gay, candy, cars or childhood immunizations.

Chapter 9

The day I met our witch.

Smallpox invaded our island, and my little sister and I both fell ill to the infection. Our church filled with sick people crying, praying and pleading to God for help, and I sat among those desperate people.

For days, my grandma dragged me to our church so we could ask God together to please end that awful sickness. In the beginning, my sister came with us, but soon she grew too weak to get out of bed. I sat on a bench in our beautiful church, with my clothes sticking to the pus of the smallpox. Shivering with fever I began to wonder what I had done so very wrong to deserve this terrible sickness.

I didn't know much about God but I surely was mad at Him for not coming to our rescue. Almost every day a child or an adult died. I once heard people talking about liking to go on a vacation faraway, and I thought that maybe that's where God was.

Quickly I too grew too ill to get out of bed to go to church. My younger sister, even sicker than I, no longer talked to me. Downstairs, the adults cried over the recent death of a young girl. I wondered what dead would feel like when it came to get me.

Our doctor, who came to our island once a month or so, had

long been notified but had not arrived yet. The many wild storms at this time of year most likely prevented him from seeing us. That afternoon I heard people talking in my grandma's room.

With sad, desperate voices they said, "It's time to beg our island witch for a miracle."

I was very scared of her, and believe me, I wasn't the only one. No child that I knew dared to look into her window or walk close by her house. Out of fear for her great, strange power, we always crossed over to the other side of our dirt road to pass her house. People whispered that she spent some nights at the cemetery and often danced there with the devil at sinners' row. I wanted to watch them dance there someday when I got a little braver.

That night, in my feverish dream, three white horses flew down to me. Steam came out of their nostrils. The very long, white manes of the beautiful horses floated wildly above their bodies. Their skin, sweaty from a long, hard ride, glistened in the dim light. All three of them softly whinnied and threw their heads up in a playful manner as they came closer toward me.

Then the one closest to me stood still and looked at me with its dark, inviting, endless eyes. I felt his hot, restless breath in my face. When I touched his soft wet nose, the beautiful white horse stood up on his hind legs and danced around me. He then whinnied loudly and galloped just a little past me toward the other two white horses. Suddenly, all three of the beautiful horses turned around and gracefully galloped back to me. They stopped in front of me and nodded their heads as if to invite me to go along with them.

Oh, yes, I wanted to go! I grabbed the long, white, floating mane of the horse nearest to me. All three horses began to float gently upward. I held onto the soft, wet mane with all my strength, but ever so slowly, it slipped out of my hands. The beautiful white horse must have noticed that I slipped off. He looked around at me with his shiny, deep, dark eyes. I held both of my hands out, asking him to please come back. He stood still, turned around, and came back to me.

The other two white horses waited in the distance. Their silver hooves sparkled in the moonlight. Soon my beautiful white horse bent down in front of me. Happily, I climbed on top of him. Excited, he flew upwards in a gentle gallop. I desperately clung to his wet mane again with all the strength my sick body had left to give me.

With great disappointment, I noticed that I slipped off him and just hung there in the endless, star-filled night. Again I begged him to come back. The beautiful white horse with the endless, dark eyes and silver hooves looked back at me with a sad face. Then he gently galloped on to join the other white horses that waited for him in the distance. Together they drifted upward and out of sight. I cried out for them to come back, but the stars disappeared and as the night grew completely black, I felt as though something pulled me down.

Someone shook me fiercely. When I opened my tear-filled eyes, I realized that my mom had shaken me awake and I saw that my grandma had my wrapped up sister in her arms. I wondered if she had died.

Mom said, "Come on child, we need to leave."

She helped me out of bed and wrapped a blanket around me.

While walking down our stairs, I asked my mom, "Where are we going?"

She said, "We're going to see our island witch."

That immediately woke me up. Downstairs, the rest of our family joined us, holding the smaller children in their arms.

Together we walked through our garden and down toward the field where our ducks and geese spent a lot of time inside the pond. I shivered with fear in this dark, cold night. I stumbled along besides my mom. My body hurt from the movement of my nightclothes, which had stuck to the pus of my open wounds. At that moment, I wished I could have hung on to that beautiful white horse.

Finally, we arrived at the pond. My mom and my grandma sat down in the dry grass. They laid my little sister between them. She had her eyes closed. Though she looked dead, she moved her lips. To me it seemed that our whole village had gathered around the pond in hope that our island witch could help them.

In this moonless night, billions of stars sparkled in the sky. Their twinkling made me feel as though the heavens smiled down on all the sick and worried people. Even though the night wind blew slightly, the water in the pond never moved; and it looked like a big mirror in which the stars sparkled back up to the heavens.

Though I didn't know what our island witch looked like, I searched around for someone who looked like the bad witch in the storybook of *Hansel and Gretel*. You can imagine how strange and eerie that night was for me. Scared to death, I clung to my mom.

Suddenly, from the tall trees behind the pond, a small figure appeared to float toward us. A hush fell over the people.

Grandma whispered, "There she is!"

Everyone knelt on the grass.

Our island witch floated closer and stepped onto the grass beside the pond. A tall person, she wore a long, black coat and her long, white hair hung loosely to her hips. Silently she stood at the edge of the pond with her hands raised.

Grandma and a few other people rose up out of the grass and walked toward her. Each of them carried a small sack. They opened the sacks in front of our witch and handed her the requested eleven killed chickens. Our witch, with amazing power, threw all the chickens high up in the air at once. Those dead bodies hung up there for a moment, which I found amazing. After I threw my ball up into the air, it always fell to earth quickly.

I saw our witch look up to those dead chickens and mumble something at them. Slowly, they fell into the pond one by one. That seemed like a miracle to me and completely convinced me that she could take the smallpox from us.

Her voice grew louder and louder. She counted numbers in a strange fashion, and she screamed words I couldn't understand. Madness grew stronger in her voice. I wondered how such a normal-sized person could scream so loud.

The sound of her voice disturbed flocks of sleeping birds and they soared to the sky. The village dogs awakened and started to bark, but they quieted quickly when our witch turned in their direction and lifted her hand. In awe, I stared at her and wondered how she accomplished this second miracle.

Then the witch went silent. She knelt and shivered wildly. Big ripples appeared on the pond for a moment. Then the wind blew very hard. She turned, looked at the pond, and raised her hand. The beautiful image of the sparkling stars returned to it more brightly than before, almost as bright as the moon, but I couldn't see him in the sky.

Calm now, our island witch stood up. She looked up to the heavens and talked to someone. I looked up too, but saw no one. Suddenly, a lightning bolt flashed through the sky and lit up the pond. The trees and bushes around the pond moved violently. Tall ripples appeared on the pond, destroying the beautiful sparkling star image. Scared to death, I hid behind my mom, just barely looking at our island witch with one eye.

Calmly, she fetched a bucket of water from the pond. She put both of her hands inside of the bucket and a big flame escaped. Frightened, people got up and readied themselves to run, but she calmed them down by pointing her left hand to the ground. Slowly, she walked to each person mumbling numbers and putting a little warm water from the bucket on each one's head. She showed no fear in touching the infected people and children.

As she came closer to us, my mom made me kneel next to her and told me to look down at the ground, because without being blessed by our island witch, one could not look into her face, no matter what. I often heard the old people whisper that if an unblessed person looked into her face, our witch could at that moment send one's soul right to hell.

Too scared to let go completely of my mom, I desperately clung to her arm. Somehow, I felt the need to see what our witch did. I moved my head up just a little and partially opened one eye, figuring I could get away with that.

I saw her touching everyone's head with her wet hand and little droplets of water ran down from the people's heads. After she touched a person's or child's head, she mumbled something with numbers and dipped her hand back into the bucket of pond water. The thought of the witch touching me scared me to death. Again, I thought about her dancing with the devil on sinners' row. When she came closer to us, I decided to leave.

When I started to stand up to run away, my mom grabbed my arm and harshly pulled me back down. Our island witch looked over toward me, and for some unknown reason, I calmed completely. When she came to us, I knelt there frozen stiff, but without fear. When she touched my head, my chattering teeth quit moving and a warmth suffused my body.

Without fear, I looked straight into her face. She looked old with many wrinkles, had red eyes and very white skin. She had a surprisingly huge set of white teeth in her mouth. She looked back at me and slapped me hard across my face. I fell over onto the grass. I knew that I was in big trouble now. I wanted to beg God for help, but mentioning His name in the presence of a witch could cause huge disasters, so my grandma told me.

Very angry, Mom reached down to me, apologized to the witch, and promised that she would punish me properly. Then my mom picked me up and we started to walk home. Through my tear filled eyes, I saw our island witch disappear into the air above our pond. The water rippled briefly, making the sparkling star images in the pond disappear again.

I heard water splashing and people's voices, but I was too scared to look around. Grandma caught up with us. She carried my sister in one arm and two dripping wet chickens in the other. Other people had recovered their chickens from the pond also.

The next day my smallpox dried up and my fever left my body. My little sister opened her eyes and talked to me for the first time in many days. Only two more children in our village died that night and the terrible epidemic ended.

We had delicious chicken soup for the next few days. With my grandma's help, I wrote a note of apology to our witch. I drew pretty flowers on the other side of the paper in the hope that she'd like them and would forgive me. Still too scared to do it myself, I gave my little sister a penny and told her to put the note under the witch's door. At our next Sunday church service, our preacher ranted and raved as never before. He found out that we had asked our island witch for help. He steamed up his pulpit and thundered his sermon down to us sinners. He had all of us going to hell twice in the first ten minutes of his service.

His fat face turned purple with anger and steam drifted up from his bald head.

When he finally took a long, deep breath, I stood up and asked him, "What else were we supposed to do since God was on vacation and unwilling to help us?"

A complete silence followed my question. I wondered if I had said something wrong. Our preacher gave me an awful, stern look, which I will never forget! Without finishing his thundering sermon, he descended from his pulpit. On his way out of the church, he briefly stopped in front of me. With a bitter face, he called me a devil's child, which sent a jolt of fear through me, then he walked out of the church.

All of the women and children gathered at the big church door to see where our preacher was going. In disbelief, we watched him walk across the road toward the small tavern, which my grandma supplied with her fine liquors. A surprising hush settled over us as we saw him walk into the tavern where all the village men held their Sunday service. Our village men considered the tavern close enough to our church and to God. I don't know what happened but we heard some loud voices coming from the tavern.

In time, the fear that troubled me at the preacher's words slowly disappeared, as did the scars from the smallpox.

No mustard, Listerine, Crisco or fruitcake.

Chapter 10

The God-Fearing People

We didn't study much world history in our little school, but we learned a lot about the history of our island.

Quite a long time back, pirates settled on our island. They only feared God and the devil. In order to please God and avoid confrontations with the devil, they built God a huge church.

To get the supplies and money for such a huge task, they built themselves small, fast boats, which they moored close to the route the trade ships traveled. As soon as a merchant ship came into view, the pirates sailed their little fast boats out to sea to plunder the merchant ship.

They first boldly murdered everyone on board the ship, then loaded all the gold, silver, precious stones and whatever else they found useful into their boats. They tied planks from the merchant ships behind their small boats and towed them to the island. If by any chance the pirates found a woman on board, they spared her life and most likely kept her as a maid. If she was young and pretty, the men sold her at auction for a good price. These auctions always took place on the church ground, a manmade hill and the highest point on the island.

According to our church book, the work on our huge church started near the end of the eleventh century with slave labor. Builders first finished the small chapel. After that, they began the big task of building our huge church.

They built the church with boulders and bricks made on the island. We don't know for certain when they finished the big building because wars raged on the island, and part of the church books, which contained that information, were destroyed.

Centuries later, the congregation added a very tall and wide bell tower with many bells. Each bell had a different meaning and still does today.

All the life-sized statues were made from pure gold and silver. To please God absolutely, they built Him a very big altar out of stolen ivory. An artist carved religious scenes into the ivory and inlaid it with precious stones of many colors.

The pirates had the earth inside the church pounded down and hammered small, gray cobblestones into the floor. They could easily remove and replace these stones when it came time to bury a deserving soul of their violent group. They buried the mighty leaders of the pirates closest to the altar, since the men felt they deserved to be closest to God.

They filled the next rows by how much stolen goods and killed people one had registered. Undeserving souls, the common people, were buried outside in the graveyard, since the pirates didn't consider them worthy enough to lie near God.

Much later, the congregation added a tremendous pipe organ. The loud, echoing sound of the pipe organ grabbed everyone's immediate attention. At times, the low notes sounded as though they came from way beneath the floor. Goose bumps often rose on my neck when I heard the organ play, and I wondered if the floor would cave in beneath me. Perhaps one of the dead pirates, a vicious relative of mine, would grab me and brutally drag me into his grave!

Still, today, our mighty church stands on her man-made hill
Overlooking our island, as proud as can be
Her many different sounding bells clearly announce:
The time or warning of a disaster
A wedding taking place or the end of one's life
The beginning of church service or the end of it
And the high sound of the little silver bell
Will sound happily to welcome a new life.

Our beautiful church stands mostly empty now. I guess all the God-fearing people lie beneath her floor.

Our Church

No bananas, deodorant or chocolate Easter eggs.

Chapter 11

Grandma's remedies cured many.

My grandma always stayed very busy. In the warm seasons, she smoked delicious fish in her big barrels in our backyard, tended to her gardens and took care of her animals. She also took care of many scraped knees and bloody noses of her many grandchildren. In the colder seasons, she knitted socks like a mad machine for the whole population of our island and brewed her fine liquor in her earthen cellar. At that time, she also prepared large quantities of her secret remedies to cure the cough.

I often helped her slice the onion and fetch the honey from the beekeeper to prepare her specially-sought-after cough remedy. Grandma put the honey and onions in her old iron cook pot and let it boil for a while. She sat in front of the little stove knitting away on a sock, talking to me and keeping an eye on her concoction.

When the whole room started to smell absolutely great, she took the pot off the stove and let it cool on her table. After it cooled to her satisfaction, she added a copious amount of her slightly brown liquor to the pot. She gently stirred the ingredients and stuck her finger inside of the pot often to taste her concoction.

After adding a little more liquor and tasting the concoction a few more times, she smiled and asked me to get that special can out of her food box. I knew which one she meant and hurried to fetch it for her.

Every time I helped her to prepare her remedy, I asked her, "Grandma, what's inside this can?"

She smiled and said, "Child, this is snail witch powder."

When I grew older, I asked her, "Grandma, where does it come from?"

"From the snails, of course!" and she laughed out loud.

The whole thing confused me because I never saw snails making red powder, but I laughed with her.

If any one of us children coughed in front of my grandma, she gave us three spoonfuls of her great, sweet cough remedy. We then had to wear our dirty left sock, fastened with a scarf, around our neck for the next three days. The cough remedy made us tired and made us want to take a nap. If it weren't for the darn stinking sock around my neck, I'd have coughed a lot more often around my grandma. I loved that fine, sweet taste of her concoction.

Our mailman had bad coughs around every Christmas. When he came to our village with his dog team pulling his sled over the frozen ocean, he'd come straight to our house, coughing and complaining about the cold weather.

Grandma coughed too and invited him inside with a great smile on her face. He led his dogs into the lean-to and always asked me to feed the big dogs the food he brought with him and to offer them water.

I happily took care of his gentle dogs because I loved animals and he always handed me five pennies. At that time and place, I could get ten fine sugar cookies or a beautiful ribbon for my braids at our small store for those five pennies.

Happy and somewhat dancing, our mail carrier walked inside our house and hugged my grandma in the hallway. She put her arms around him and they walked into her room. When I finished taking care of the dogs, I walked back to our house and went directly to my grandma's room to tell our mailman that I fed and watered his dogs.

I found both of them sitting on grandma's old red couch. She poured a good amount of her cough remedy into the cups, which stood on the table in front of them, and then she added some of the brown liquor from her cellar to both of their cups.

The mail carrier handed me the five pennies and my grandma said to me, "It's time to see your mother."

I didn't know why I had to see my mother. She hadn't called for me, but I obeyed and left my grandma's room.

Later that afternoon I looked through one of the holes in her wooden door to see what the two of them were doing. I saw them sitting close together on the sofa, talking, laughing and still drinking my grandma's concoction. I figured they both must have had really bad colds because they sure had to drink a lot of my grandma's remedies. It took all afternoon before they went to sleep in my grandma's bed. I sure hoped they'd get well soon.

Sure enough, by the next morning both woke up completely cured. Our mailman left our house smiling and my grandma sang happy songs all morning long. She asked me to take the few letters and papers our mail carrier left at our house to our village neighbors, which I gladly did. I was very happy that my grandma's cough remedy worked.

Chapter 12

I killed him.

My little sister and I slept in the same bed in the attic beneath the eaves of our house. At times, we found it a very scary place.

In the deep winter, the brick shingles and the brick itself cracked and moaned under the extreme cold, sounding as if some strange, huge creature was about to eat our house.

The icicles that hung from the shingles grew quite large, and in my dreams, they grew even larger, fell, and the sharp spikes would pierce my body. I often awoke screaming from that painful dream, but knowing it was only a dream, I quickly forgot about it.

However, at the age of seven, I believed the devil lived inside the electrical meter box. He was real for me for many years. The huge box hung in the darkest corner of our house, not far from our bed. We needed to feed it coins to keep the power flowing to the few naked light bulbs that hung from the ceilings of our house. The moment it swallowed the coins, the devil got loose inside of it. He hissed and sent out sparks. I feared he'd electrocute me.

Sometimes he made high, loud shrills, which I took for his laughter. I believed that before long, he'd kill me. I often pleaded with my mom to let me move our bed away from the corner so the devil couldn't kill me, but my mom wouldn't hear of it.

When I begged my grandma to convince my mom to let me move our bed, she smiled and said, "Child there's no way the devil could get into that box. You just hear the normal operating noise of

49

that big meter box."

Neither of the people closest to me would help. One day while my mom and grandma left the house, I told my sister to help me move our bed across the floor to the other side of our attic. We pushed and pulled hard until we succeeded. How relieved, glad and proud I felt. I walked over to the sleeping box and laughed right into its face. I called the devil inside of it a loser and spat at him. Relieved at leaving the possibility of electrocution behind me, I jumped and danced around our attic.

My mom's loud, angry voice interrupted my celebration. With her hand reaching towards me and an angry face, she grabbed my ear, pulled on it and yelled, "Did I say you could move your bed?"

Afraid she'd rip my ear off, I quickly answered, "No, Mom."

She let loose of my ear and moved our bed right back into the corner where the scary electrical box hung on the wall.

Angry and scared I sat down on our bed and cried. I hoped night and therefore bedtime would never come. To my great relief, no one fed the monster box for quite a while. Money was scarce in our house and candles were more affordable.

One night though, when Aunt Hilde gave birth to her fourth child, my grandma fed that meter box some coins. Sure enough, the devil went wild again. All night, he hissed exceptionally loud.

I hid under my bed cover for a while, shivering with fear that he would definitely kill me that night. When I lifted my bedcover a little, the devil spit sparks at me. That did it. I refused to stay in my bed and get fried. Quickly, I jumped out of bed, ran downstairs, and outside.

Slowly, I walked to our lean-to, thinking how I could get rid of that scary box. Though cold and uncomfortable, I felt safe from the devil and those flying sparks. I didn't get much sleep that night, but I made a decision to kill the box with the devil inside of it.

The next morning, after everyone left the house, I checked the huge breaker box to see if it had power. Happily, I noticed that it had run out of money and hung there like a sleeping bat. Now the devil was vulnerable.

I ran for my mom's big broom and with all the strength and anger I had, I hit that huge box repeatedly. Pieces of all sorts of metal fell out of the box, even coins! With my last angry hit, the rest of the huge box fell off the wall and onto the floor. At that moment, I felt so relieved that I started to cry. I believed I killed that darn devil!

A thunderstorm rolled onto our island that morning, and lightning struck with such force that it frightened me. I wondered if the devil's mad soul brought the storm to our island to punish me. By midday, however, the storm had passed over and my mom came home.

When she came up into our attic and saw all the metal pieces of the electric box lying on the floor, she opened her mouth in astonishment.

She looked at me and asked, "Did you get hurt, girl?"

I shook my head and mumbled, "No, Mom." I sincerely hoped she wouldn't think that I had killed the box.

Then my mom shouted downstairs, "Mother, lightning hit the electric box."

Grandma ran upstairs. "My goodness, are we ever lucky our house didn't burn down!"

I just breathed a sigh of relief that no one knew I had destroyed our electric meter box.

That night, for the first time in quite a while, I went to bed without fear of death. How happy I was! I fell asleep looking and smiling at the wall where the huge box once hung.

About a year passed before a man came and installed a quiet, new electric box, and no devil lived inside of this one.

No toilet paper, gravy in a bag or Sears Catalog.

Chapter 13

The outhouse.

Our clapboard outhouse stood in our backyard, very close to our house and our water well. The bottom parts of its wooden sides rotted away long ago, and the roof leaked when it rained. Our harsh winter storms blew snow inside it through the slits of the wood siding. As bad as this place looked and stank, it served a very important function for our family and many animals.

A big stick stood by the door to cancel the meetings of the rodents inside of our outhouse. A few good knocks on the door and those creatures canceled their meetings in a great hurry and ran outside of our important place. Dogs and cats learned that the knocking on the outhouse door signaled them to come and catch fresh meat. You can imagine how wild it was at times.

Though used to this, one day I noticed strange little pieces of newspaper inside our outhouse and I wondered about them. The next time I used the little house the small pieces of newspaper were gone. I didn't think about the strange paper again until I saw my grandma ripping our weekly newspaper.

There she sat on her worn out sofa with the bucket beneath it to hold it up, seriously humming a church tune and ripping apart the two pages of newspaper.

I asked her, "Why are you ripping the newspaper into such small pieces?"

She smiled. "Everyone in our house has read the paper, now we'll use these small pieces in our outhouse."

While reading a small piece of a story inside the outhouse which everyone had already read, I began to wonder if my grandma was getting sick, and doing strange things like a lot of old people did on our island. Soon she left the room with her small pieces of newspaper in her hand. I walked outside with her and watched her place those little pieces inside the outhouse while she still smiled and hummed away the same song.

With nine people to our outhouse, I never saw those little pieces of paper often. I really didn't want to read a small part of a story inside that stinking outhouse. I just wondered where they went.

No Frisbees, nylon, credit cards or Ajax cleaner.

Chapter 14

A luxury feast.

We had just enough cows on our island to provide us with milk throughout most of the year. In the short summer months, when our grass grew tall and fast, we had plenty of rich milk to make cheese and butter and to drink. During winter months, it was scarce indeed.

Our small island couldn't grow enough grass to support cattle just for stilling our hungers. In order to buy or barter for a piece of beef, which the adults got ever so excited over, one had to register with the island butcher. When an old milk cow dried up or was about to die of unknown reasons, she was slaughtered. The butcher then notified the people at the top of his list to come and purchase the precious meat. He always had a long waiting list.

On one lucky day, our family name reached the top of the butcher's list. In a hurry, my grandma walked down to her cellar and fetched two bottles of her best liquor. Mom called me and we ran downstairs. She told me to sit in the little wagon, and the two of them, with broad smiles, hurried to our island butcher. I never saw the two of them so excited together.

At the butcher, my grandma bartered for the beef meat. The butcher took us in the back of his house where the meat of the slaughtered cow lay on a large table. I never saw such a huge piece of meat before in my whole life! I wondered what it would taste like. The butcher chopped off a big piece of the meat and handed it to my grandma. She almost fell over under the heavy load. Mom helped her carry it to our little wagon.

After folding the huge piece of meat over and placing it inside the wagon, my mom told me to sit next to it and then handed me a towel. She then told me to place the towel over the meat and hold onto it so the flies wouldn't bother it.

On our way home, we caused quite some excitement. People stopped to have a look at our huge piece of beef, and I could see the envy in their eyes. At home, the adults in our house excitedly cut that huge piece of meat into smaller pieces. They busied themselves all afternoon in Uncle Fred's kitchen. Soon it began to smell great inside the whole house. Grandma fried some of the meat then poured a lot of water into the pot, which made hissing sounds and sent steam high up into the air. Then she added a big bowl of vegetables to the pot. The pot, now full to its rim, made my mouth water. I was hungry, very hungry, as I had often been, and hoped that the big pot started to boil soon.

After what seemed like forever, Grandma announced, "The stew is ready."

She turned to me and asked me to set the table. I did it as quickly as I could and sat down in anticipation of a good portion of food tonight.

Proudly, my grandma placed the big pot of delicious smelling food on the wooden table. Still smiling, she ladled a big portion of the beef stew onto our plates. I could barely believe how much food I had on my plate!

Potatoes, carrots, onions, and real pieces of meat swam in brown gravy to the rim of my plate. I desperately hoped I could start eating, but couldn't until everyone sat down and my grandma looked up at the ceiling to say a few words. When she said, "Amen," I quickly picked up my spoon and started to eat. Perhaps I could have more if I finished my plate first.

The potatoes, vegetables and gravy tasted absolutely great, but though I tried hard, I couldn't chew the pieces of this luxury meat down to swallowing sizes. I needed much stronger teeth for this tough meat! So as not to disappoint my grandma and avoid getting disciplined by my mom for not eating everything on my plate, I sucked the gravy off the pieces of tough meat and carefully stuck them into my pants pocket. The adults were too busy celebrating this special meal to notice anything I did.

Later, out of sight of everyone, I ripped the chunks of meat apart and fed them to my grandma's cat Zissie. She liked the luxury meat and followed me around for the rest of the day.

No drip dry clothes, ice cream or washing machine.

Chapter 15

A daily bath or shower?

Oh my, we lived far removed from daily bathing. Since we had no inside plumbing, a shower was completely out of the question. I didn't see a bathtub until my mother sent me to a children's home, away from our island.

In the bitter cold winters, we seldom washed our bodies. Mom couldn't usually heat our little room properly to even get undressed. We only had driftwood and tree limbs to feed to our stove.

We really needed coal to feed that little iron stove to warm our small room, but mom didn't have enough money to purchase much of it. We usually stayed fully dressed and mostly under our feather bedcovers. Besides having little or no fuel for our iron stove, there was always the question of getting enough precious water to waste on washing.

My Uncle Fred had the responsibility of thawing the hand pump every other morning. He wrapped straw tightly around the pump and set it on fire. When the straw burned away, he'd try to move the pump's handle. If it moved, we were lucky. Then he only had to pour a kettle of steaming water into the top opening of the pump, and the pump worked. However, I remember many days when my uncle couldn't thaw it out.

If the pump stayed frozen, we'd take our bucket and check

with the neighbors to see if they had luck in thawing their pump out. If we didn't have any luck, we brought buckets of snow into the house to use. If we had a fire going in the stove, it would thaw quickly. Either way, my mom made sure that we always had enough to drink.

If we had fuel for our little iron stove and water, my mom occasionally got out the small wash bucket and filled it with about a half gallon of warm water. She then handed me our piece of soap. With a stern face and a strict voice, she told me, "Get every inch of your body washed."

I didn't like that idea at all. I always tried at first to tell Mom, "I'm cold."

My mom's look told me that she didn't care.

Then I tried, "I have to go to the outhouse now, Mom."

She usually said to go on. There I sat in the stinking outhouse, freezing bitterly, hoping my mom would forget the idea about me washing my whole body.

The bitter cold soon made me leave the outhouse and I walked back into our room. Mom's angry look said, "Get with it," and I started to undress. Before I fully undressed, I used my last excuse not to get washed up.

I stuck my finger in the bowl filled with water and said, "Mom, the water's cold."

My mom didn't say a word. She got up and reached for her large, hard brush, with which she cleaned the wooden floor in our little room. I remembered from a while back how that brush hurt and quickly undressed.

Since we didn't wash our hair in the harsh winter months, I started by washing my face and ended with my feet, all in that half gallon of water. By the time I reached down to wash my feet, I had used all the water in the small washbowl. I just took the wet rag and pretended to wash my feet thoroughly since my mom kept her eyes on me. I was so glad we didn't have to do that every day.

In early summer, when all the ice had melted in the sea, my

mom handed me a piece of soap and sent me to the sea to wash up. In spring, I found it a challenge to stay in the water more than a few minutes because it was still awfully cold. Later on in the season, we stayed in the ocean for as long as possible. We had so much fun swimming, diving and playing games in the salty water.

Throughout the summer and into late fall, we children on our island were most likely the cleanest children on this earth even though we never used our mom's soap.

No bleach, milk shakes or typewriters yet.

Chapter 16

Thank you, Grandma!

Early on in my young life, I cried for days over every dead animal, bird or other body I stumbled upon. Life was very precious to me and I couldn't understand why things had to die. On one exceptionally bad day, I came home with one dead cat, two dead birds, and a frog that had lost its head. I sat down on the front steps of our house and cried my heart out.

When Grandma heard me crying, she came outside to investigate. She looked at all the dead bodies in my lap and sat down next to me. She put her arms around me and said, "Let me tell you what most people on our island believe. You know, we bury the young children at sea because they're still innocent and didn't have time enough on this earth to sin. Therefore, they'll go back to the birthplace of all life. The sea will take them gently on their journey. Before long, they'll be born again and have another chance at life. That goes for all young life.

"Now go and take these young dead bodies to the sea so they won't miss out on another chance of life. Take them out to the end of the boulder walk, way out to sea where the lighthouse stands. There, the strong currents will take everything out to the mighty sea."

She dried my tears with the end of her big apron and gently touched my head. Then she took a rag from her apron's pocket and handed it to me. While I held the rag, she ever so carefully took the dead bodies from my lap and placed them on the rag.

Then my wise grandma said, "Hurry on, girl, and take these young bodies to the sea to be born again, before they lose their chance."

I gave my grandma a big hug, held my rag of dead animal bodies to my heart and ran barefooted down to the ocean.

Reaching the big boulder walk, which protected our harbor from the very tall waves of the angry ocean, I slowed down and carefully walked down to the very end of it. There I sat on one of the wet boulders, slippery with sea moss. The gentle waves licked at my naked, hot feet and soothed them. The excitement within me built. I would give these dead bodies back to the powerful sea to live again!

Shedding happy tears, I unfolded the rag and gently let the dead animals slide into the life giving, salty ocean. While their little bodies floated and swirled around in the strong current, I waved farewell and wished them a better and longer next life.

In moments, the dark, ever so mysterious waters of the wide ocean took their bodies down into their arms to guide them toward the birthplace. I felt so relieved and happy!

What a smart grandma I had!

She surely made my life a lot easier for many years to come.

No margarine, cheesecake or bleached flour.

Men still urinated outside, behind a bush, so the can in the outhouse wouldn't fill up so quickly.

Chapter 17

What a disaster!

In spring of 1950, at the age of six-and-a-half years, I had to start school. For this big occasion, my mom made a new dress for me. She took the still good parts from her brown skirt and sewed a new skirt for me. Then she knitted a green top and sewed it onto the skirt. With a proud smile, she asked me to try my new dress on. Oh, how pretty it looked on me. I just knew that I'd be the prettiest girl in school. I thanked my mom with a big hug.

Four days after the Easter holidays, the new school year started. I will never forget my first day of school. After my mom braided my hair and talked to me how important it was to learn a lot in school, my grandma and Uncle Fred came upstairs. With a twinkle in his blue eyes, my uncle handed me a backpack which he had made out of brown leather. Grandma patted my head and gave me a small slate and two pieces of white chalk, which I put into my brand new backpack. I thanked them for their gifts.

With an almost tearful smile, my mom handed me the customary Easter cone, about two feet long and made out of reed. My mother had covered its cone shape with shiny paper. Though borrowed, and a bit banged up from years of use, it was very special to me. I knew that the Easter cone held a surprise for me to help make the start of school a little easier. A note with my name hung on the outside of the cone, but I couldn't open it until the end of my first day of school.

Ever so proudly, like most other moms, my mom walked me to the school in the village of Burg. On our way, people smiled and waved at us. I wondered why everyone looked so happy. This going to school idea didn't sound good to me at all. The older children told me we'd have to sit there for half a day and listen to the teacher. I wanted to roam around our island. When we arrived at the schoolyard, a few other mothers with their small children already stood in the yard talking to each other while the older children went inside the school.

I clung to my mom's hand and stared at the old two-story clapboard building. I didn't like the idea of spending so much time inside that sad looking building and tried to figure out how to sneak out of it.

To my surprise, a young girl opened the door of the schoolhouse and waved for us to come inside. The mothers of the small children smiled and gently gave their children a slight push to get them on their way into the schoolhouse. The adults then waited outside for that short first day session and eagerly exchanged the newest gossip.

Tempted to run away instead of going into this sad building, I told my mom, "I have to go to the outhouse."

She gave me a stern look and said, "Get inside that schoolhouse now."

Reluctant and scared, I walked toward that worn out building just short of crying.

Once inside the dark schoolroom, I saw a few rows of long benches with long, narrow tabletops. The older children had already taken their seats and watched us while we younger ones stood bewildered at the entrance.

The friendly young girl who had asked us to come inside

greeted us, showed us to an empty bench and asked us to sit down. She then showed us where to put our slate, chalks and backpacks and told us that we could put our Easter cone right next to us.

I took one look around that stark room and knew school was not for me. I wanted to go outside to run around and check on my friends, the birds on the tiny islet, which I named Fillalilla and claimed for my own. I wanted to wade in the water or climb a tree, anything but sit in this classroom. With my mind made up, I took my belongings and walked out of the building.

Well, I didn't get far. Mom saw me, grabbed my hand, and promptly marched me back inside with a few promises to whip my behind if I didn't stay in the classroom. Back inside, I stood near the door, waiting for a good moment to escape again, thinking I could sneak past my mom.

Suddenly, the classroom door opened. In came a tall old man with a long stick in his hand. With loud steps, he walked through the rows up to a small table. There he stood like God himself and said, "My name is Herr Von Osten and I'm your teacher." He hit his big stick on his table and told us to sit down.

In a hurry, scared he'd use his long stick to hit me, I sat down in the last bench closest to the door.

I knew our teacher and where he lived. Someone had painted nasty, hateful words in huge letters on the front of his fine, big brick house. When I asked my mom or my grandma what the letters meant they answered, "Never mind, child," and grinned when we walked by his house. People whispered that he once served in Hitler's army and did some terrible things. As soon as our teacher turned his back to write something on the blackboard, I ran out the door.

I didn't get far. Before I could take off running down the short hall, my mom grabbed my arm and pulled me toward her. She scolded me again, this time with a loud angry voice. Still holding on to me, she opened the classroom door and pushed me back inside.

All the older children laughed out loud at me.

The teacher walked toward me waving his stick and shouted, "Sit down!"

I sat down in a great hurry on the seat closest to the door again. Some of the small children had started sniffling, and others cried.

Our teacher hit his stick on his table again and with his angry, red face yelled at us. "Be quiet now or get a whipping!"

That ended the disruptions in the room except for a barely noticeable sniffle from a little boy who hid beneath the bench I sat on. Tears rolled down his face and he desperately tried to get rid of his snot by wiping it away with the sleeve of his sweater.

Now the teacher started to talk about basic letters, which my mom had taught me long ago. I could already read simple words and add numbers. I began to get bored and tired. Slowly, I drifted off to a better place where the sun smiled down at the mighty ocean.

Just before I fell asleep completely, the teacher announced, "Go outside and play for a little while."

I couldn't believe his words, but everyone stood up to go outside. What a perfect time to leave this school!

Before I could get out the door, the teacher said, "Leave all your belongings inside the schoolroom."

Oh, how disappointing. I couldn't leave without my backpack, Easter cone, or slate. Mom would get very angry with me if I left such fine things behind.

Outside in the small schoolyard, the adults still stood together laughing and talking. Some children ran to their mothers crying and begging to go home. Since I knew I'd never come back to this school after today, I didn't disturb my mom while she enjoyed visiting with the other women. Instead, I sat on the stone step and thought hard about how I could avoid ever entering this building again.

Too soon, the teacher blew a whistle and waved us back inside the schoolhouse. Reluctantly, I followed the other children who started a fight over who was supposed to sit where. As I sat closest to the door, the teacher blew the whistle again and told us to go home. I grabbed my belongings and ran out the door before anyone else.

Ever so happy to get out of that old, dark schoolroom, I walked home beside my mom humming a happy song.

She asked me how I liked my first day of school.

Since she had taught me to be honest, I said, "I'm never going back to school again."

It felt great to get that off my mind. It was over! I felt free again to enjoy the warm, sunny days outside of that dark schoolroom, faraway from that old, mean teacher.

My mom stopped abruptly, picked up my head and looked me square in the eyes. "You will go to school for many more years to come!"

Her words thoroughly shocked me. "Please, mom don't send me back to school!" I begged. "It's scary inside and the teacher is mean."

Mom didn't say a word, she just walked faster with a strange look on her face. At home, she said, "You can't have the surprise inside the Easter cone until you're ready to go to school and stay there until the teacher tells you to go home."

Talk about disappointment. I so seldom received a sweet treat. Sadly, I took my cone and placed it beneath my bed.

That night, after my sister lay fast asleep next to me and my mom turned off her light, I quietly slipped from our bed and crawled beneath it. Careful not to awaken anyone I opened my Easter cone and took out a sweet cookie and a dried plum. Oh, how fine they tasted! Under that bed, I slowly made a plan to get out of going back to that school.

By the next morning, I felt absolutely sure about my plan.

I lied to my mom and said, "I'll be happy to go back to school today."

She looked at me with great surprise and answered, "Good, I'm glad you came to your senses." She handed me my backpack and a pig lard sandwich to eat on my way to school.

With a smile, I said goodbye to my mom and left the house. She watched me walk toward the school for a little while, and as soon as I saw her go inside our house, I walked across the dirt road and through the fields.

Oh, happy day! Freedom! The fields had new, green grass all the way down to the bay. By the bay, I took my shoes and socks off and waded through the cool, shallow water to reach my favorite sandy spot on my little isle Fillalilla.

How wonderful to have the sun smiling down at me, instead of spending my day inside that dark, musty schoolhouse. I enjoyed sitting in the soft, warm sand, instead of on the hard bench in the classroom.

The moment I unwrapped my lunch sandwich, my friend, Lola the seagull, landed in front of me. She had two legs but only one had a webbed foot attached to it. Though she had one wing bigger than the other, she seemed to fly and swim all right. The other seagulls, much faster than she, always tried to steal the small fish from her.

She mostly tried to keep to herself, but I felt sorry for her and often brought her a morsel to eat. Lola wobbled up to me and sat next to me, eyeing my sandwich. I shared my food with her and told her my nifty plan of never going back into that schoolhouse again. I believe she smiled at me.

After we finished the delicious sandwich, I lay down next to my friend, closed my eyes and drifted away into a daydream. The little white clouds above me took me faraway where no one ever heard of going to school.

All of a sudden, in the middle of a wonderful dream, someone rudely awakened me. Someone had a hold of my hair and shook my head with great force. Lola, my dear friend, flew away while shrilly screaming at whoever had pulled on my hair.

Looking up at my attacker, I saw my very angry mom standing over me. She screamed at me and gave me a harsh whipping, which I can still almost feel. Then she picked a switch from the young willow bush and shouted, "Start walking back to school!"

My so absolutely perfect plan failed! If I stopped walking or complained about the smallest thing, my mom hit me on my naked legs with that thin switch. I can tell you it hurt quite a bit. Suddenly, I didn't like my mom any longer. I thought she was just being mean.

When we reached the school, she walked me inside, handed the teacher her switch and said, "If she moves off her seat, hit her good!"

That somehow made it clear to me that I had lost my freedom and had to accept sitting inside this dark, boring schoolroom.

When I got home and looked beneath our bed, I sadly realized that my Easter cone had disappeared.

When I asked my little sister what happened to it, she smiled and said, "Mom and I ate all the good, sweet stuff."

I wanted to hit her, but didn't since I was in big trouble already.

Faithfully, but so unhappily, I dragged myself to school every day that I had to be there. I'd lay my head on the top part of the bench, look outside the small window, and go to sleep or daydream away the boring hours.

One day my teacher threw a children's storybook right at my head. He then asked me to read it aloud. I read the whole story without hesitation. He then handed me a slate with numbers on it and asked me to work the problems out and write them on the blackboard. I did it easily. After all, they were just simple numbers to add. I could do them in my head.

When I handed that slate back to him, he said, "You're in second grade now."

From that day on, he gave me work at that grade level and I

found it far more interesting. He let me leave school as soon as I finished my work, which I really liked. I worked hard and hurried so I could roam freely around our island. That ended the disaster.

Edy with her Easter cone.

No fire alarm, cornbread or cake mix in a box.

Chapter 18

The difference.

One late summer afternoon, the day we waited for our mailman to come to our small harbor, I walked there with a handful of our village people to watch the excitement. We gathered on the pier, anxiously looking out to sea. The calm ocean had only small, white combs dancing on the slowly moving waves. In some places, the salty water reflected the bright sunlight like a mirror.

Before long, we saw a boat in the distance. As it came closer, I realized that it wasn't the small boat in which our mail carrier usually came. Everyone quit talking and stared out to sea. Excitedly I wondered who had come to visit us. Soon the boat entered our bay. At that moment, I recognized the man steering the big boat as our mailman and he had many packages loaded on that boat. I never saw so many packages in all my life. I wondered who they were for. It wasn't even near Christmas.

Everyone watched in awe as the big boat drew closer and docked on our pier. I didn't think all those packages could be for us. I figured that our mailman was on his way to somewhere else and just stopped here to repair something.

Our harbormaster came dragging his big cart behind him and parked it next to the big boat. With a warm smile, he greeted the mail carrier who smiled in return and greeted the harbormaster with a hefty handshake and a tap on the shoulder. Then he introduced the fine looking young man who still stood on board the loaded boat.

The mailman said, "Meet my helper, Otto."

Otto grinned broadly, waved at us and loudly announced that all the packages were for us. I couldn't believe it.

Our mailman then announced, "All those packages came from America."

At the age of around seven or so, I didn't know who America was. I figured him for a very rich man who could send all those packages to us. I wondered how he knew about us and where he lived.

The mailman began reading names from a list he held in front of him. The helper handed out packages to the people whose names he called. If someone had not come to the dock, the harbormaster put the package in his cart. I couldn't believe how many people this America person knew on our island.

My biggest surprise came when our mailman called out our last name three times. Stunned, I just stood there. The harbormaster waved at me to go to the big boat. Like in a dream, I hurriedly walked closer to the boat. The helper asked me if I could deliver all three packages.

Loud and clear, I said," Yes, I can."

He handed me three packages. I thanked him and ran home as fast as my legs could take me. My heart jumped with excitement.

When I entered our house, I screamed, "Packages, packages!"

Grandma opened her door, Uncle Fred looked out from his, and my mom came downstairs to see why I screamed. Everyone wore a surprised look. Between gulps for air, I quickly told them what happened at the harbor.

"They're from Mr. America!"

All the adults laughed, and I wondered at what I said.

Mom put her arm around me. "Edith, America is a big country very faraway. Some nice people over in that country have sent those packages to help us out, since the war has left us with very little."

Now totally confused, I wondered how all those packages got here. Then I figured that now since our mail carrier had a big boat, he could sail faraway to America and bring back those packages. I thought maybe I could go with him on his next trip there so I could thank all those people.

Uncle Fred waved us into his kitchen and I placed the packages on his table. Since the packages had only our last names on them, the adults could choose which package they wanted.

Grandma came first. With a happy twinkle in her eyes, she selected the smallest. Mom chose her package carefully, and Uncle Fred pulled the last one toward him. At that moment, finished with their chores, my little sister and cousins came inside. Seeing the three packages on the table truly surprised them.

Then the adults opened the packages with all of us children watching in awe. How exciting! Those packages came from a faraway place. I wondered what we'd find inside of them.

The adults pulled bags with labels on them from the package. Some bags had no labels on them because they had fallen off. Finally, with everything laid on the table, the dividing began.

Mom right away recognized the clear bag with cocoa in it and spoke to have it. Grandma pointed at the coffee beans. She was ready to trade for them. She loved her coffee. Aunt Hilde figured out quickly which bags contained tea and asked to have them.

My mom bit into one of the small, white pills in an unmarked bag and made a terrible face.

"Aspirin," she announced and reached for them.

All of us children received a chocolate candy bar, the first one in our young lives. My, did I like the taste of that chocolate candy bar! The small, sweet bite melted in my mouth. I decided to hide the rest and enjoy just a little every day to make it last a long time.

We still had many bags left on the table, which nobody could identify. The tags were in a language different from ours. Uncle Fred, our world traveler, had sailed on a big oil tanker before his accident, and had learned a little of that language, so he translated some words.

The adults opened, smelled, or tasted the ingredients of the rest of the bags to identify them. Sugar was easy. We had enough bags of precious white sugar so that every adult received one.

Everyone wondered about the bag labeled as cornstarch. We didn't know what corn or starch was. After the adults tasted it, they laid it in the pile of unidentifiable items.

When my grandma opened a bag with pepper on the label and took a good sniff of it, she started to sneeze like crazy. What an exciting, happy group we were! We tasted, laughed, guessed and wondered. We identified a few more items, but still had many which were totally foreign to us.

Mom made soups out of the unidentified items. Some tasted very good while others didn't. She just added a spoonful of sugar to the less flavorful soups and we ate them that way, glad to fill our constantly hungry bellies.

For many days, everyone on our island exchanged the printed newspaper parts and pages to look at them. We shared a common alphabet, but put together they made different words. I really enjoyed the black and white pictures on those printed sheets. I stared at each of them for a long time. What a different world this America was.

One page showed people with black faces and others with white faces on another picture. The people with white faces had guns in their hands and they stood before a burning shack. Everyone had their fist up in the air and hate in their faces. For some reason, that's the only picture I remember clearly today.

If only we had had a German/English dictionary on our island, what a difference it would have made! We could have used that fine food those nice people sent us properly and perhaps understood what it said below those pictures on the printed paper.

No jail, lawn chairs, corn or checkbooks.

Chapter 19

A heavenly treat.

The day after our care packages from America arrived, it rained all day.

By late afternoon, we were all bored, so my mom said excitedly, "Since we have white sugar now, let's make a sweet egg."

She took a chicken egg out of the basket on the windowsill and asked me to fetch a bowl and a cup. I didn't know what a sweet egg was, but since the thought of it made my mom so excited, I hurried and placed the requested pieces of dinnerware on the table.

Then my mom said, "Now sit at that table and learn how to prepare this heavenly treat."

We both sat quickly, wondering what mom was going to make.

Carefully, she cracked the egg on the rim of the bowl and let the white run into it. Then she let the yolk slide into the metal cup. I wondered what came next to make it sweet.

Then my mom took two heaping spoonfuls of the white sugar, which came all the way from America, and added them to the cup with the egg yolk. Then she added the same amount to the egg white. Now I understood how the egg got sweet, and my mouth started to water in anticipation.

Mom stuck the spoon inside the cup, handed it to my little sister and told her to stir until completely smooth. With a smile, my sister stirred the yolk and sugar together. My mom handed me the bowl and a fork and told me to whip the egg white until it turned stiff.

I gladly obeyed. Mom started to knit and hummed a happy song along with the raindrops pounding on our roof. Perhaps it made her happy to give us something special today.

I had seen my grandma and my mom whipping eggs before and it seemed so easy, so I started to whip in a hurry, but I found it much harder than it looked! The fork kept falling into the mix, and I couldn't get the white to stiffen and got very frustrated.

Angry tears welled in my eyes. At that moment, mom walked over to stand behind me. She held my hand, turned the fork sideways and gently moved my hand back and forth. Slowly the egg white stiffened and a great excitement surged through me.

I turned a little sideways so no one could see me and stuck my finger in the bowl to taste the egg white. Oh, how wonderful!

I looked into my sister's cup and asked, "Are you finished?"

She nodded.

Mom checked both of our containers and announced, "It's ready!"

She sprinkled a small spoonful of cocoa over the stiff egg white and told me to stir it gently until well mixed. I had never seen the dark cocoa powder in my life. I hoped it wouldn't make the sweet egg taste bad.

I volunteered to divide our treats, but my mom refused my generous gesture. She knew when I had to share a sandwich with my sister and cut or ripped it in half, that my half always ended up bigger than my sister's. I couldn't convince her that since I was bigger than my sister, I needed the bigger part of the sandwich.

Instead, Mom took two small bowls from our wooden dish box and divided the sweet treats in half.

Finally, the moment of extreme pleasure could begin. First, I tasted the egg white with the cocoa in it. The wonderful taste overwhelmed me. I liked it even better than that fine chocolate candy bar. Then I tasted the egg yolk, and it left me speechless. While my mom slowly cleaned out the cup and the bowl with her fingers, my sister and I ate every bit of the heavenly treat. We licked our plates to leave not even the smallest morsel behind. What a wonderful treat! Soon, the time came to go to bed. With the lullaby of the raindrops' song on our roof, I told myself that I'd definitely have this heavenly treat all the time when I grew up, even if I had to walk to America to get the white sugar.

No cottage cheese, trash pickup or baseball.

Chapter 20

We received only one radio station on calm days, a Russian station that only broadcasted between 8 and 10 in the morning. After I wound up the radio, my grandma and I often sat in front of it, hoping the station would come in clearly. When it did, Grandma turned the big volume button up to high and the two of us danced around her table a few times. We couldn't understand the Russian language, but they sure aired some fine music. We made up words to certain songs and sang along with the singer loud and clear. We may not have been in tune with the singer, but my, did we have fun.

Fire

In my early childhood, I had to take my little sister along with me most of the time, and that made me very angry. What a burden!

She couldn't run as fast as my friends and I could. She couldn't even jump over a ditch. She always fell into it. She was afraid to paddle around our bay in our makeshift raft, and she wouldn't even crawl into the old castle ruins with us to play war among the many human bones scattered around the cellar.

She cried a lot and always told my mom about the forbidden things we did. So, I decided to get rid of my little sister. I planned to tie her to a tree and burn her, just as the old people said the Vikings had done to so many islanders so long ago.

I rounded up my friends and told them about my plan. Together we gathered a big bundle of sticks and piled them around our big tree right in front of our house. Someone brought a little paper, and I stuck it beneath the sticks to get the fire started.

Quickly, I ran into the lean-to to fetch a rope and some matches. Oh how excited I was to get rid of my little sister!

Back at the tree, I called my sister in my sweetest voice. She came running out of the house.

I said to her, "Go stand by the tree among the branches."

When she did, I tied her to the tree, then I lit the match and held it under the paper.

Flames immediately licked up toward the sticks.

My friends and I started yelling and dancing around the tree with great excitement.

All of a sudden, my sister screamed like hell. "Mom!"

Such a loud scream from such a little kid astounded me. As I looked up to our window, I saw Mom's angry face. I swear she flew down from the second story for her to get to us as quickly as she did. Something told me that I was in big trouble. All my friends ran away in a hurry.

When my mom untied my sister from the tree, I figured I'd better hide somewhere in a hurry from my screaming, very angry mother.

I started to run, and quickly thought of hiding in our outhouse because it locked from the inside. I hoped to lock myself in there until my mom got over her tremendous anger.

With all the speed I had in my young legs, I managed to reach the outhouse before my mom could get a hold of me. With shaking hands, I quickly locked myself inside. For a second or so I felt safe inside the stinking place and hoped my mom hadn't seen me.

As soon as I sat down on the toilet seat, my shouting mom drew closer. I kept quiet, thinking she wouldn't find me. Within the next few seconds, my very angry mom tried to open the locked outhouse door. When the door didn't open, she took both fists and hammered on the door.

She screeched, "Open this door immediately!"

My short-lived feeling of safety changed in a hurry. Frightened of my mom and what she might do, I didn't answer her.

Another strong, loud banging on the outhouse door sounded, and in a shaking, bitterly angry voice, my mom clearly said to me, "If you don't come out of this outhouse immediately, I'll burn it down with you inside of it!"

Silence followed.

I began to shake with fear. I knew my mom as a woman of her word, but I tried to convince myself that she'd never do it. The outhouse was too important.

Suddenly, the eerie silence ended. I clearly heard the rustle of paper. Then someone actually stuck paper beneath two sides of the building where the wood had rotted away.

While peeking through a missing wood knot, I saw my angry mother sticking the paper beneath the outhouse walls. I quit shaking and grew stiff with fear. Tears began to flow, but somehow I didn't get off the seat to open the door and take mom's whipping.

Then came Mom's slow, spoken command. "Get out now or die in there."

After a brief moment, I heard her strike a match. My heart beat wildly. I saw my mom hold the lit match against the paper. Quickly, small flames started to consume the paper and began to lick the sides of the outhouse.

Soon the rotted wood started to burn, making lots of smoke. I desperately hoped for a miracle to get me out of the burning outhouse.

The flames had reached the dry planks now. They grew bigger and began to eat away at them quickly. Smoke filled the small room, and it grew hotter and hotter.

I still sat on the seat as if glued to it and started to cough. I found it hard to breathe. I wondered what would hurt more, burning to death or being whipped to death by my mom. I had never seen her angrier.

The moment I decided to run from the burning outhouse and take the beating, I heard many shouting voices, among them my grandma's.

When I unlatched the outhouse door to escape the flames, our neighbors stormed into our backyard. With stinging, smoke-filled eyes, and a deep, wild cough, I ran into my grandma's arms.

The adults exchanged many angry words. They pointed and fiercely shouted at my mom while they extinguished the fire. I held tightly to my grandma and cried the stinging smoke out of my eyes.

After they had put the fire out and our upset neighbors left our backyard, my grandma handed me over to my mom. Mom didn't kill me, but for many days I had quite a hard time sitting down.

Both sides of our outhouse burned down. The roof, the door, the backside and the most important part, the seat, still stood. We had a fresh air outhouse until the first snow fell. Uncle Fred and Mom repaired the damaged sides just before the harsh winter storms reached us. I liked the open-air outhouse much better because it didn't stink so badly.

Never again in my life did I try to burn my sister, anyone else, or set something on fire not meant to be burned.

To this day, I'm absolutely sure that Mom could have kicked in the flimsy door of the outhouse, broken through the small hook, and taken me out safely. She wasn't a killer, just awfully darn mad at me.

No flu vaccine, oatmeal or potato chips.

Chapter 21

No prejudiced minds here.

What a beautiful, warm spring we had! The sun smiled down on our island and the mighty ocean calmly whispered onto shore. Flowers bloomed all around us and the migratory birds had already returned. They sang their love songs now and kept busy building their nests.

Grandma collected driftwood from the beach to feed to her little stove to cook tomorrow's meal. I picked dandelions and fresh greens for the chickens and the geese to enjoy that evening.

My grandma's favorite goose sat on her well made nest, now full of eggs she had laid. They would hatch soon. One of the hens sat on her nest as well, with plenty of eggs beneath her. Grandma worried about the hen.

She said, "That hen is old and should have been in the soup pot long ago. But she has patience and never abandoned her nest, or broke a single egg."

Suddenly, before I filled my big basket with those fresh greens, I saw Grandma stand still, turn toward our house and listen to something. I turned and listened too, but heard nothing more than the singing birds and the small waves gently leaping onto shore.

With a brisk voice my grandma said, "Something's wrong. Come on, girl, let's go home in a hurry."

Quickly I picked up my basket and we walked home as fast as we could. I had a hard time keeping up with my grandma. At times, I had to run to stay by her side. I wondered what could have gone wrong at home that we had to get there so quickly.

When we arrived, Grandma walked right into the stall, and I followed. The goose sat there on her nest just fine. Next, we checked on the hen and found her lying sideways in her nest. Grandma lifted her up, and sure enough, her favorite hen lay dead. Three of her eggs had fallen out of her nest while she stretched out on her deathbed. They fell onto the floor, and the eggshells broke into many pieces.

The chicks' small bodies lay motionless among the broken pieces. They had not yet grown any plumage and they didn't breathe. They lay with their eyes closed and their small beaks wide open. Their little red tongues hung out slightly, as though they had yelled for help.

I wondered if my grandma heard them. I was so sad and just about to cry, when I remembered what she had told me: "Take the young dead ones to the sea, child, so they may be born again!"

I reached down, picked up the three lifeless bodies and placed them in my basket on top of the freshly-picked greens. I planned to take them to the sea in a little while so they could have another chance at life.

My grandma took the five remaining, warm chicken eggs, and gently placed them in her apron which she had gathered up like a basket. Then both of us walked over to the goose. Grandma bent over slowly and showed the goose the chicken eggs. The goose took a good long look at the eggs, then with her beak, she softly touched each one as though smelling them. Then she raised her head up, looked at my grandma and whispered something to her. The goose lifted her wings, stood up and gently moved her eggs a little closer together with her beak. Carefully, she sat back down. Once more, she lifted her wing, the one closest to my grandma.

Grandma took the chicken eggs and carefully placed them

beneath the goose, in the space the bird had made for them. Gently, our goose retrieved her wing and covered the eggs. She looked up at my grandma and it looked as though she nodded her head.

My grandma smiled, but she said, "She'll hatch those eggs, but I worry that goose will reject the chicks once she sees them, maybe even kill them, because they won't look like her own brood."

While I gently cleaned the three tiny dead chicks beneath our water pump, I asked my grandma, "Did you hear the chicks cry for help, or did you hear the hen begging for help?"

With distress she said, "I didn't really hear them with my ears, but I felt their need inside."

Though still too young to understand what Grandma meant, I nodded. After I had cleaned the little bodies, I held them to my chest and walked down to the sea. At the end of the long stone walk which reached far into the sea stood a small lighthouse. Its blinking light warned boats not to come too close to the strong, strange undertow in this part of the ocean. There I sat down near the salty water and let the cooling waves caress my feet.

I always found this place strange and a little scary. Huge boulders stuck out from the very deep, dark ocean's bottom, and the water curled around them in gurgling circles. Here the current took things out to the vast ocean instead of onto our shores.

Ever so gently, I let the three little chicks slide into the cold sea. The strong current swept the bodies away. I wished them well. After a tear or two of mine fell into the salty water, I walked home. I hoped that the goose would give life to the surviving chicken eggs.

At home, my grandma prepared the dead hen for the soup pot. I didn't feel bad about that because she wasn't butchered but died on her own. She lived a good, long life. We always cared well for our animals.

Grandma could make some great chicken soup, and because I was very hungry, I hoped the soup would be ready soon.

Sometimes, on special occasions, she even made dumplings and dropped them by spoonfuls into the soup pot. Once, on the second Easter holiday, what we called Easter Monday, my grandma made dumplings, fried them in pork grease, and poured a little dark beet sugar over them. What a special treat. I hoped she'd make them again soon.

Many times a day I checked on the goose. I brought her special fresh greens and fresh, cool water. After a week or so when I went to check on her, she grew very excited. She lifted her wing and let me see the first gosling that had just hatched. It was still wet, but so cute.

Within the next few days, all the ducklings hatched and began to explore their surroundings. Grandma and I began to worry if the chicken eggs would hatch before the goose gave up on them and left the nest to look after her brood. We never expected her to raise them. We'd be happy and thankful if she'd just hatch those chicks, then we'd raise them.

We watched her very closely now, and I gave her more special greens and grain than usual. I sat beside her most of the day, played with the goslings, talked to her and did my schoolwork next to her. She gently talked back to me, and moved only now and then to look beneath her at the chicken eggs.

One late afternoon when the darkness slowly took hold of our island, I touched her long, soft neck gently and told her that I had to leave. At that moment, she stood up and slowly put her head down on the chicken eggs as though listening to them.

After she inspected them, she let out a loud scream, flapped her big wings, and sat back down on her nest. That loud scream scared me for a moment and brought my grandma running into the stall.

Before my grandma could asked me what happened, I quickly told her what the goose did. Grandma walked beside the goose and asked for a look at her eggs. Excitedly, the goose stood up again.

Grandma and I quickly knelt beside her. What a surprise! The eggs moved slightly, and we noticed that on two of them, the shell had broken open a little.

With one more scream, the goose sat back down and all her little ones came waddling over to her to find a warm spot to spend the night.

Grandma happily announced, "The chicks will hatch during the night."

Sure enough, by the next morning, all the chicks had hatched. Their feathers, so far, were about the same yellow color as that of the goslings. The goose stood proudly among her strange looking brood and talked up a storm. After she said all that she had wanted to, she pushed all the eggshell pieces out of her nest and sat down.

Quickly, all the little birds climbed underneath her or snuggled next to her. She then slowly began to eat the eggshell pieces. The fine goose took good care of her fluffy, yellow brood regardless of their race. We had worried about her rejecting or killing the young chickens for nothing. Soon all those cute, yellow hatchlings began to grow their adult plumage. The difference between her goslings and the chicks would soon become very noticeable. The goslings' feathers would turn all white, but the chicks would develop darker feathers. Again, we worried and watched her closely. Grandma thought that we should separate them, but the goose showed no prejudice, even when the differences became very visible. Over the next few weeks, she kept her whole brood warm and safe.

When all of the goose's brood had their adult feathers, the goose grew restless. She looked toward the pond, longing to take her brood for a swim. Grandma decided the time had come to let them go, but she told me to gather up the chicks first.

With no problem, I picked up the little chicks and put them in my basket. I sat down in our backyard with them on a bench, just a little way down toward the pond, to watch our goose take her brood to the water.

The basket with the chicks stood right next to me on the bench. Out of her outside enclosure, the mama goose walked with her wings spread very wide. She flapped them fiercely and lowered her head in an attack mode.

She gave a loud, high-pitched warning noise, which drove our cat, Zissie, up the nearest tree. That cat had its mind set on eating one of the goslings a year ago. She had quickly learned how strong and fierce a mama goose could get. That cat lost half of an ear in that fight, but gained a great respect for the goose. With one more good look to see if it was safe, the goose called her goslings to come and join her.

Here came the goose with all her goslings behind her, still putting on a warning display of great power. The little ones walked one after the other in a straight row behind their mama. The goose kept a close watch on her brood.

When she reached me, she stopped. She looked around, picked her head up and listened. The chicks in my basket peeped. The goose drew closer to me. She stretched her long neck and looked into the basket.

She flapped her wings with great power and tried to get into the basket to get her chicks back. I held on tight, but the very strong goose bit my hand with her sharp, needle-like teeth. In pain, I let go of the basket and it fell.

All the chicks survived the ordeal and mixed in with the goslings. The goose gave me one more bite on my leg, which also hurt very much. Then, knowing she had all of her brood together, she settled down.

On toward the pond she walked, with everyone in tow. The chicks didn't follow in a straight row. They ran and tried to fly all over and around the goslings. Behind them walked my grandma with her crab net in her hand. What a funny parade. With my hand and leg bleeding, I followed them to the pond.

When we arrived, the goose gave one more great display of her power, with loud screams, stretching up high and flapping those big, very powerful wings in a great hurry. With that, all the visitors cleared out of the pond.

Slowly, and very alert to her surroundings, the goose walked into the water. All of the goslings followed her. The chicks just stood there, a little unsure of what to do. I walked closer to the chicks to gather them up and take them home with me. One more peep and a look at their mama goose, and the chicks jumped, flew and fell into the water.

Grandma hurried closer to the pond, crab net in hand, to rescue the chicks from a sure drowning death. To our huge surprise, the chicks had no intention of drowning. They floated just like the goslings! Both of us had a great, relieved laugh! Suddenly, the neighbor's gander, the father of the brood, came back into the pond. With her wings spread wide and a loud, high-pitched scream, the goose went after the gander. He wisely left the pond.

I guessed that since they had been kept separated, they didn't know their relation to each other. That seemed sad to me. After a while, the goose felt more secure. Slowly, the mother goose allowed the other feathered visitors to come back into the water, but they kept a careful distance from the goose and her brood.

Soon the chicks grew up. They didn't go into the pond any longer. They just nibbled on the fresh grasses that grew on its edge. When let out of their enclosure to go to the pond with the goose, they always stopped at the big chicken cube. The old rooster stood up all excited from his favorite resting place beneath the tall tree and did a strange dance in front of them. He slowly walked closer to the young chicks with his wings flapping. With all his feathers fluffed up, he looked twice his size, and he crowed and crowed. The young chicks, all girls, watched him with great interest. They seemed very attracted to him.

The day the young chicks didn't follow the goose to the pond, Grandma opened the door to the chicken cube. In walked the five half-grown chicks. The old rooster danced his wild love dance and crowed his heart out all morning long.

No donuts, chocolate milk or lawnmowers.

Chapter 22

God and the devil.

At the age of eight, I firmly believed that our beautiful church was God's house, His alone! I believed that the devil could absolutely not come inside our church even though our preacher said otherwise.

That year at our annual Christmas cantata, I played the part of an angel, the one that held up the big, important star over the scene. The star, made out of parchment paper, had a fat candle inside to brightly light up the star. The candle's softly moving flame made the pattern of the parchment paper dance around in a pretty way. I made sure to hold the star very still so the flame wouldn't reach the paper.

Other children, also dressed as angels, walked around the scene in a circle with their lit candles. We all sang the songs we had practiced for so long. What a festive setting. The girls dressed as angels in white nightgowns. We all wore our hair loose, and mine hung down my neck and over my shoulders to my waist. The movements of the walking angels around me made my hair sway a bit in the air.

Just as I proudly ended my solo, I noticed a strange odor. Before I could look around to see where that strong, strange odor came from, someone took the star from me. Someone else threw a blanket over me and pulled me down onto the cold cobblestone floor.

Scared to death, I screamed for help. Someone grabbed me,

pulled me down, and rolled me around on the stone floor. I fought back with all my strength but couldn't get away.

At that moment, I instantly believed our preacher's words: "The devil sits among you!"

I knew it! He had come to kill me right here in our church! I smelled his foul breath. I felt the heat from it on my body. I had no idea what I had done so terribly wrong that I would die in the devil's hands.

Okay, so last Sunday I took a coin out of the offering plate. I needed it to buy my mom a new milk can. The old one had slipped out of my hands a few days before and had broken into a thousand pieces.

My mom said sadly, "I don't have the money to buy a new one." Then she sat down on her couch and cried.

Seeing my mom cry made me feel awfully bad. I needed to borrow money to buy her a new milk can, but from whom? Then I came up with the great idea of borrowing from God since He had so many coins in his Sunday offering plate. I asked God first though, if I could borrow that coin. I promised Him to pay it back as soon as the fieldwork began and I made some money. He hadn't disagreed. With those thoughts swirling in my head, I screamed to God with all my might. "Get the devil off me!"

But He didn't answer. Maybe he hadn't even come for His birthday celebration!

Someone hit me and continued to roll me around on the church floor. I choked and coughed a lot, and breathing got hard. I heard people yelling and heard many voices close by. Maybe someone came to help me!

Stars appeared before my eyes and I grew dizzy, but I still tried to escape the stinking, hot darkness.

Suddenly, water drenched me. What a cool relief, but I thought the devil was trying to drown me now.

Then I heard someone say, "You're all right now," and whoever it was sat me up.

I took a deep breath, perhaps my last one, but determined to meet the devil head on and fight for my life. My grandma had told me long ago to fight the devil off one must look him straight in the face and scream with a mighty voice. I prepared to do just that.

No longer held down and with the blanket removed from me, I screamed as loud as I could at the devil. My scream echoed on and on in our huge church. My grandma's advice worked! I didn't see a man near me dressed in red with horns, pitchfork, and a long tail.

Perhaps he wore a disguise. Our preacher often shouted from his pulpit to us sinners, "The devil will come to you in disguise! He sits among you and waits for a chance to grab your soul!"

Either way, I felt sure my scream had chased him away. There I sat, right in front of our mighty altar in a puddle of water, coughing and crying. My special white nightgown that my mom proudly sewed for me from an old sheet, had burned behind repair. I shivered with fear and felt awfully angry at the devil. I reached up to the left side of my head and found that my long hair had completely burned away on that side and my ear hurt.

My grandma came to my rescue. She wrapped her arms around me and helped me up. She took me inside the little chapel and helped me take off my burned, wet clothes. She wrapped me in her thick winter coat and told me, "Your hair caught on fire."

"Did the devil set it on fire?" I asked.

She smiled, but I saw the worry in her face. Grandma picked me up and carried me back into the church to watch the rest of the evening performance. The beautiful show continued without me, the important paper star holder.

From that day on, I believed what our preacher had said about the devil. He could come into God's house, sit among us in disguise, all the while making himself ready to reach out and grab a soul.

No lipstick, diet drinks, diet food or flashlights.

Chapter 23

The mink's great escape.

My Aunt Annie had a mink farm just across the dirt road from us. Four rows of small wire cages stood in her barn. And each row had ten cages. Inside each of those cages lived a pair of pure, black mink.

Since we had bitter cold winters, the minks grew a thick, shiny fur coat for warmth, and my aunt raised them for their beautiful coats. She killed some of the older ones in the middle of the winter before they started to shed, and sold the precious coats to a buyer who came to our island in spring.

Uncle Paul, her husband, had his own fishing boat and fed the minks healthy seafood meals. Each mink could easily eat a pound of fresh fish a day. I often helped my aunt feed all those creatures. They sure jumped and ran from one end of the cage to the other in no time at all. I had to be careful not to let them escape their cages at feeding time or bite me with their sharp teeth. A loose mink was a gone mink with the potential of doing great harm to many creatures. I always made sure to close the latch tightly on their door when I finished feeding them.

The minks feared loud noises, especially when they had young ones to care for. Whenever they heard loud noises, they desperately killed their litter and tried to get out of their cages to go underground where they naturally lived and felt safe.

One late spring day, a violent thunderstorm raged over our island all afternoon. Right after the storm moved away, someone banged on our door with both fists and yelled for my grandma to come outside. Quickly I jumped downstairs to investigate.

In an unsteady voice, my worried Aunt Annie said, "A dozen minks escaped. Get your animals in a safe place." Then she ran on to warn other neighbors in our small village. Grandma sent my little sister and cousins with her to help warn people.

Hurriedly, my family started to get our animals inside the house. Mom told me to spread the old tarps and blankets in the usual corner of our attic where the animals had spent brutally cold days many times before. I hurriedly followed Mom's order, then I ran downstairs to help bring some of the animals upstairs.

There I saw my grandma fetching a bowl of grain from the sack in our stall. She walked over to the chicken enclosure, opened the door, rattled the bowl of grain and showed them the special food. Without hesitation, all the chickens followed her into our house and up the stairs.

I gently picked up our pair of old ducks. They were used to being picked up and carried inside the house. At the top of our stairs, I put them down on the wooden floor and they peacefully waddled over to their familiar corner.

The old geese, though, never got used to us handling them. Only my grandma could touch them. Both gave her a hard time, though. She had to hold their beaks closed with one hand so they wouldn't bite her. With the other hand, she professionally picked up the rest of the goose and, under great protest, carried one at a time upstairs.

They both loudly complained for a while but eventually settled in next to the peaceful ducks. Uncle Fred brought up enough straw and feed for them, and I filled the old, banged-up tin bowl with water and placed it on the floor among the animals. My mom set up a barricade of old, rusted cans and such from our lean-to at the edge of the tarp and the old, discarded blankets.

Grandma's cat had to sleep inside her room that night. Otherwise, my grandma felt sure that cat would make a fine dinner of one of those young, half-grown chickens. The little piglet, given to us by a farmer because it was born too early and needed to be fed every few hours by hand, spent the night in Aunt Hilde's baby carriage in her kitchen.

Grandma and Uncle Fred loaded their guns. Aunt Annie came back and set some traps around our place in the hope of catching some of her minks. Sadly, she apologized for all the trouble.

Needless to say, the house sounded a bit noisy that night, but I enjoyed having the animals in a safe place with us beneath the eaves of our house. I sat on the floor next to them and told them stories.

The geese and ducks sat quietly and listened to my stories. They moved their heads from side to side and looked straight at me. The chickens didn't pay any attention, but kept talking to each other softly, picked at their plumage and walked around.

Before I finished my stories, Mom opened her door and waved a warning finger at me. "Go to bed right now!" Quickly, but in silent protest, I climbed inside our bed next to my sleeping sister.

Morning came and people gathered in front of Aunt Annie's place. Someone handed her a dead mink, and someone else gave her a live one inside a cage. However, she still missed ten minks.

One of the escaped minks killed my aunt's huge, tough gander overnight, even though she had taken him and her goose into the attic of the barn. She found the dead gander with the goose sitting next to him, her head bent over his body.

She seemed to gently whisper to him as she grieved. Together the two of them had raised over a hundred goslings in the eight years they lived together. Sometime later that year, Aunt Annie got the goose a new partner, but she didn't like her young, new partner at all. She didn't lay another egg. The next year she served as Christmas dinner.

Everyone kept their eyes open for the missing minks. That evening someone saw two of them on the pier stealing fish, but they couldn't catch them. One man reported a handful of dead seagulls with missing heads, and an infant got badly bitten on her small legs and hands. My grandma shot one mink as he tried to enter our outhouse, but we never found the others again.

A few days later, my grandma declared the danger over. She said, "It's time to get all our very restless feathered friends out of the attic and back inside their living quarters."

A little sad to lose the closeness of my feathered friends, I removed their barricade. I heard Grandma downstairs rattling the can with the chicken feed. That got the chickens out of the house in a hurry. They flew and trampled over each other down the stairs as if a fox were after them. I found it hilarious.

I carried the ducks downstairs, while they softly nibbled on my arms, and set them outside on the ground. They walked straight toward the nearby pond. My grandma picked up her broom and gently pushed the geese down the stairs one step at a time. They complained fiercely and pooped on every stair.

Uncle Fred put the tiny piglet back into its warm straw bed. It looked so cute all snuggled up inside its box with fresh straw. He handed me a bottle filled with milk and asked me to feed it. Very gladly I did it because it saved me from having to help the adults scrubbing the attic and the stairs.

After the little rosy piglet finished its bottle of warm milk, I talked to it until I could hear no more scrubbing inside our house. Then I casually walked back inside. My mom gave me a disapproving look, handed me a bucket with filthy rags inside of it and told me, "Rinse them out well underneath our pump and hang them on the clothes line to dry!"

No fire department, Pledge furniture polish or
macaroni and cheese.

Chapter 24

Sinners' row

Every Saturday evening when it didn't rain or snow, my grandma and I walked to our island cemetery. We took fresh flowers from our garden, or wildflowers that we picked along the way and placed them in the vases on our family's graves. We ripped out weeds and perhaps watered all the newly-planted flowers if they needed a drink.

I liked to go to the small pond and fetch the water for the flowers. The biggest frogs of our island lived in that pond. Whenever they heard me coming, they began their warning concert with deep guttural sounds and puffed out their chests. The moment I reached the pond's edge, they all jumped into the pond.

From beneath the surface, they watched me carefully with their dark eyes. Sometimes I hid behind a bush and stood absolutely still to watch them emerge from the water. The biggest ones always came out first. I figured those were the grandparents because my grandma was the biggest person in our family.

Our cemetery had two sections. In the first and larger section we buried regular people, those God-fearing souls with hope of going to heaven. The other section, the last row, we called "Sinners' Row." There we buried the sinners, those who became devil's food.

Their graves bore no headstones, and no one planted flowers, or greenery on them. All, with the exception of one grave, looked like tiny jungles, overgrown with weeds. Though this one grave had no headstone, it didn't have any weeds either. Instead, a vine of small-leafed creeping ivy graced that lone site. A bunch of forget-me-nots grew in place of a headstone. Those plants had a beautiful blue color and bloomed all through the fair seasons.

Each time we finished taking care of our family graves, my grandma sent me to the front gate with a set of instructions.

"Edith, watch for anyone coming close to the cemetery. If you see someone coming, pretend to call your dog."

"But, Grandma, I don't have a dog," I protested the first time.

"This is a game of pretend. Pretend you have a dog and his name is Dome."

This all sounded like a fine game to me, so I went and did as she said.

One day, I wondered what my grandma did that she didn't want other people to know. So, I walked a little bit away from the front gate, but still able to see if someone should come, and peeked around a bush. There, to my great surprise, I saw Grandma in Sinners' Row.

Bent over, she picked weeds and cared for that single grave. I immediately became very worried about her. People whispered that the devil would snatch you for sure if you take care of one of his soul's graves. Just walking through that row presented a certain amount of risk. Some people whispered that they saw the devil there at Sinners' Row, dancing away the nights with our island witch.

I worried about the danger to my sweet grandma. Afraid that something bad would happen, I wanted to run to her and get her out of Sinners' Row, before the devil saw her there.

At that moment, my grandma stood up, wiped her face with her big white handkerchief, and stood a moment, just looking down at the grave, in deep thought. Then she turned and walked toward me. I hurriedly went back to my lookout place.

When she reached me, she gave me a hug and said, "Let's go

home, girl."

As we walked home hand in hand, I asked my grandma, "What can the devil do to people that care for graves on Sinners' Row?"

The look on her face told me she realized that I saw her there.

After a long, deep breath, my grandma stopped walking. "The man in that grave that you saw me caring for shouldn't have been buried there. Someone lied, and that someone is dead now too. They should have buried him on Sinners' Row. Instead, they buried the man guilty of killing his own wife with an ax in the regular part of our cemetery. If you'll notice, nothing ever grows on his grave, not even the weeds. The headstone on that grave always tips over no matter how often people pick it back up. Only the dead, God, the devil, and I know the truth."

I knew that grave. It always looked like some animal had tried to dig its way inside.

Then my grandma said, "Don't worry about me when I go and take care of that grave on Sinners' Row. Since it's not the grave of a sinner and doesn't belong to the devil, nothing will happen to me. We need to keep this our deep secret forever. Promise me to never tell anyone."

With wide eyes I nodded, then I asked her, "Who's inside that grave?"

She stopped walking again and smiled at me. A tear fell from her twinkling green eyes, but she didn't answer me.

Walking home in silence, I thought about that grave. I knew my grandpa wasn't buried on Sinners' Row, but I wondered if my grandma had a secret lover.

No movie house, Cool Whip, or sterile bandages.
We didn't know what a psychiatrist did.

Chapter 25

He was so smart!

My Uncle Fred, my mom's brother, could explain many things to me. We had some great times together. He often gave me money to go to our small store to buy him a beer or two and a cookie for me. The two of us then walked to my uncle's favorite spot, down to the sea where the big boulders had recently fallen down from the coast.

From that vantage spot, we could clearly see all the huge, ships from all over the world, on the horizon. My uncle had eyes as green as the sea, and they looked so sad in the moments we saw those ships.

He used to work in a big oil tanker's machine room. One day while he repaired a part of the big machines, something went terribly wrong. The huge machine caught his left leg and it had to be partially amputated. That brought an end to his fine traveling job at sea. After he healed, he walked slowly with a stick tied from his knee down on his left leg and a walking stick in his hand.

He supported his family by doing odd jobs, but I always saw a sadness in him that he no longer could see the world from the decks of those big ships. Each time we saw a big merchant ship on the horizon, he smiled. His eyes lit up and often a tear or two ran silently down his face, which he quickly wiped away. I felt so sorry for him.

On this particular day, sitting out there with him, I worried about the big, red apples I had stolen early in the morning. I hid them well in the henhouse so my mom wouldn't find them. Then I wondered about God. Could He find them? And what if He did?

Finally, I bravely asked my uncle, "Do you know how all that works with heaven and hell? Can I go to hell for stealing apples if God finds them?"

He put his arm around me. "No my child, if there is a God, he has more important things to do then to look for your apples. A very, very long time ago, a smart person told all the stories about Jesus. Eventually someone wrote them down in a big book called the Bible. That book, as you know, talks about heaven and hell. If all those stories really happened, as they were written down, no one knows.

"Some of the stories your grandma tells you really happened, others she makes up. Perhaps someday someone will write all her stories in a big book too. If your mom finds your stolen apples though, all hell will break loose here on earth!"

I felt very relieved because I figured I could live through my mom's hell.

Since I often heard people whispering that my uncle's wife, Aunt Hilde, was crazy, and I heard her mad screams, I finally got brave enough and asked him about her.

My uncle took a deep breath and slowly answered with a sad voice. "Yes, many times I believe so!"

He looked so sad and frail. He looked down and touched the sand. I felt bad for asking that question.

I put my small hand in his big, strong hand. "Uncle Fred, as soon as I'm big enough, I'll marry you. You could give your old wife away and we could keep your children. We'll sit at the sea together all day long and drink beer."

Uncle Fred laughed hard and long, and gave me a huge hug. "Sure, Edith. That sounds great."

Well, since I would soon have a husband, I figured I needed to learn how people made babies. Last year, I asked my grandma that question and she said, "That's pretty simple. A man and woman get on top of each other and there come the babies, but you're too young to worry about such things."

Her explanation didn't completely convince me because I sat on top of boys many times to beat them up and didn't get a baby out of the fight. Since my Uncle Fred would become my husband some day, I figured I should ask him.

I looked at him and seriously asked him, "How do we make babies when we get married?"

After a short moment of complete silence, he answered, "Now that's absolutely women's stuff. Only they alone know how that works! You need to ask your mom about those things."

Oh, how smart he was!

Neither God nor my mom found my stolen apples. The darn chickens did. They picked every apple apart, leaving not one for me to enjoy.

No dictionary, mammogram or a way to neuter the animals.

Chapter 26

The big, sad lie.

Our old female cat, Zissie, gave birth faithfully twice a year to many pretty kittens. One fall her litter of six looked all like her, with black and white marks all over their bodies. Grandma let her take care of them for a few days, then, as usual, she took all of the kittens and placed them in her apron.

Grandma said, "Our neighbor, Mr. Willer, will take these cute little kittens to a farmer who has many mice in his place for the kittens to eat."

She always assured me that we didn't have enough food or mice for them to survive in our place. Each time my grandma took the kittens over to our neighbor, I grew sad, but I didn't really feel bad because I thought the kittens would have a good life at that farmer's place.

Again, the day came when my grandma gathered up all the kittens in the early evening and placed them in her apron. She let me stroke the small creatures for the last time.

Before she walked out of her room, she said, "Keep the mama cat inside with you until I get back." Then she walked out of the house with the tiny, crying kittens cuddled in her apron.

Zissie, the mama cat, cried bitterly for her kittens. She scratched on the door to get out to run after them. I felt so awfully sad for her.

I tried to soothe her. "Now, Zizzie, Grandma will make sure your kittens go to a fine place with many mice for them to eat."

She cried even louder. She climbed up the windowsill and clawed the glass to run after her kittens.

I could no longer stand to hear the painful begging of the mama cat for her litter. Disobeying my grandma's orders to stay inside, I ran from the house with tears rolling down my face.

Outside, I caught sight of Grandma and our neighbor standing together in his backyard. He had a shovel in his hand and she still had the kittens in her apron. I crawled a little closer and hid beneath a bush so I could see better in the twilight.

Grandma put the mewing kittens on the ground. Too young to do much of anything, they just lay there. Then she abruptly left the neighbor's yard while wiping her cheeks with her apron.

Completely confused, I watched our neighbor dig a shallow hole in the soft, black earth. I couldn't figure out what was going on. Something was wrong here!

Fear crept through me. I began to worry for those tiny, innocent kittens. Driven by sheer madness, I jumped out of the bush and screamed. "No! No! No!"

I jumped over the hedge to rescue the kittens. The second I reached our neighbor, he lifted his shovel and smashed it down on the huddled, whining kittens.

Before he could lift his shovel again, I jumped at him and knocked the old man down. I hit him as hard as I could with my fists and kept on screaming.

"Grandma! Grandma!"

I saw some of the tiny kittens lying motionless in their own blood. Others still moved and desperately cried out with their little voices. One bloody, mostly black kitten tried to crawl away, unable to even see where it headed. I cried. I screamed. I hit the murderous neighbor as hard as I could.

Suddenly, someone grabbed me from behind. A quick look around told me my grandma had come back. I quit screaming and climbed off our neighbor.

In so much pain and outrage over the cruelty of killing tiny, innocent kittens, I fell into my grandma's arms. How could God let His people murder His sweet, blameless animals? Where was He anyway?

Between an outburst of screaming and crying, I told both our neighbor and my grandma just what I thought of them. "I hate you! I hate you both! You're cruel, and I hope you both go to hell tonight!"

Grandma held me tightly as I sobbed into her breast. She let me scream and go on with my rage while she slowly walked me home. In her room, she sat me down on the couch.

After I quit screaming I asked, "Did our neighbor kill all the other kittens that you took over to him before also?"

With a tear in her eyes, Grandma said, "Yes, he did."

"So why did you lie to me?" I asked between gulps for air.

"Child, I tried to save you from seeing or hearing the cruelty of such an act." Gently my grandma tried to soothe me. "Edith, our island doesn't have enough space for all the kittens to grow up and live. In a short time, they'll all starve to death, a horrible way to die."

I thought that over for a short while. "Grandma, I want to take the tiny, dead kittens to the sea. That way they may be born again in another place." She smiled and smoothed my hair. "That sounds fine. Tonight, when the neighbor's lantern goes out, I'll help you dig them up."

We walked outside, sat down on the bench in our backyard and watched the neighbor's house. I clutched my small willow basket to carry the tiny bodies to the sea. I had placed a little fresh straw on the bottom of it so the kittens could travel with me in comfort to the sea.

Night moved in quickly with heavy clouds hanging low. The moment the neighbor's light went out, my grandma took her spade and we snuck into our neighbor's backyard. We found the terrible, bloody spot where the kittens were so easily killed. Carefully my grandma pushed her spade into the soft dirt next to the bloody spot. Quickly, she brought up the spade filled with dirt and five dead kittens. Gently, I placed them in my basket. One was missing, but I found it lying right next to me under a small, bushy weed. I placed it in my basket too, and hurriedly we left the neighbor's yard.

Grandma walked back to the house, but I walked down to the sea, out on the stone walk where the little lighthouse stood, to my sea burial spot. There I sat on a boulder and touched the swift, cold current.

In the blinking light of the lighthouse, I gently took one tiny body out of my basket at a time. I washed each carefully and gave them to the sea so they might be reborn in a better place, with enough food and where they could live a happy life.

Still crying, I picked up the last body, the one I found beneath the weeds. When I dropped a little cold water over its tiny body, the front paws moved just a little.

Slowly, I lifted its tiny body to my ear and listened for a heartbeat. Yes! I heard a faint, slow heartbeat! This kitten was alive! Something hard to explain shot through me, something more than happiness, excitement and thankfulness all put together.

I held the little body to my face and cried out loud. Though full of dried blood and salt water, I kissed this little kitten all over. Then I carefully tried to clean the little body. I held the kitten high enough above the water so the strong current couldn't snatch it away from me.

With one hand, I dripped water over the kitten to rinse off the blood and dirt. Then I took off my knitted jacket and wrapped it around the wet little body, just leaving its tiny face out so it could breathe. Excited, I grabbed my basket and ran home.

On my way, the heavy, low clouds moved away and the bright moon lit our way. I looked up at that silver moon and wondered what I could do to keep this kitten alive. The answer came quickly: Let its mama nurse and care for it. But where? I needed to find a place where no one would find the kitten. Breathlessly, I reached home. I found Zissie, the mama cat, sitting in front of our house. She lapped up the milk that freely dripped from her swollen tits onto the ground.

When she saw me, she ran toward me. She still cried that hurtful cry until she reached me. I stopped to greet her. She got up on her hind legs, and I bent down to let her have a close sniff of the tiny, wrapped kitten. She immediately recognized her kitten and stopped crying.

Excitedly, Zissie walked beside me into our backyard. Our house was completely dark, but just in case someone needed to use the outhouse, I walked down to the corner of our yard where I could clearly see someone coming. I sat on the cool earth and gently uncovered the kitten and handed it to its mother. Zissie took her tiny kitten from my hands. She laid it in front of me and licked it all over. The kitten didn't move a muscle. It seemed to me that she licked that kitten awfully hard, but I guessed as the mother, Zissie must know what she was doing.

Soon, I heard a weak, barely noticeable meow, and I became the happiest child on earth. I'm sure Zissie was even happier. She gently picked up her kitten by the scruff of the neck and she looked at me as if to say, "Now what are we going to do?"

I had to find a place for her where no one would find her. After the kitten grew big enough to kill its own food, I'd set it free faraway from here.

Then I remembered we didn't have a pig this year, but we still had two bales of straw on the loft above the pig's enclosure. Perfect!

Zissie followed me with her kitten in her mouth. I crawled up to the loft and made a soft nest out of the straw for them back in the corner where no one could see it. Then I called Zissie and she climbed up with ease, still carrying her kitten in her mouth.

She looked at the nest I made for her and then at me. She then laid her tiny kitten in the nest and began to lick its fur again.

I softly stroked Zissie's fur and said, "You have to keep your kitten here all the time so no one will find it."

She came over to me and licked my hand.

"I promise I'll bring you food and water, Zissie." I sighed, hoping she'd understand.

I hated to leave her, but the sun would rise soon. Grandma would look for eggs and the outhouse would get busy. I needed to get out of here before someone saw me. I stroked Zissie one more time and reluctantly slid down from the loft. On my way down, I saw the little kitten hungrily suckling on its mama's tit. Quietly, I walked into our house.

On this Sunday morning, mom fried slices of bread in pork lard, and it smelled so delicious. I ate half of my piece of the tasty bread and drank part of my warm milk. Then I snuck the rest of my bread and the precious milk, which we only drank on Sundays, out of the house. Inside the lean-to, I found two small, old cans, which I cleaned under our outside pump. One of them I filled with clean, cool water, and in the other, I poured the warm milk.

After my grandma gathered her eggs and the outhouse saw its last customer for a while, I walked back inside our stall, placed the water in one corner where no one would notice it, and climbed up to the loft where I found Zissie sleeping peacefully in the straw. Her kitten slept curled up against her body.

I felt tremendously happy and couldn't understand why tears streamed down my cheeks. As I walked closer to her, Zissie opened her eyes and greeted me with a long yawn. I handed her the can of warm milk. She stood and eagerly licked up the warm milk. After that, I tore the fried bread into small pieces and handed it to her. She ate all of it, licked her whiskers clean and lay back down next to her kitten.

Right away, the kitten started to nurse again. I lay down next to them, and before I even realized that I was tired, I fell asleep.

When I awoke, I only saw the kitten. I wondered where its mama went, but I felt very relieved that she had left the kitten here.

Ever so gently, I stroked the kitten's soft fur, and it quietly meowed.

What a beautiful kitten she had given birth to. Its black fur was darker than its mama's, and I wondered about the color of the kitten's eyes. I didn't know if it was a boy or a girl, so I named it Peter for now. I figured I could easily change it to a girl's name if I had to.

On my way out, I left the little window by the straw shelf half open so Zissie could come and go easier without someone seeing her. For many weeks, I spent hours in the straw playing with the kitten. I only needed a little stick or a short string to entertain Peter.

Soon he began eating solid food. His mama brought him fresh mouse and rat meat, and I made sure that he had enough food too so he'd stay in the stall until he grew big enough to catch his own food. Since I shared my own food with him, I stayed pretty hungry most of the time, but I happily did so. Seeing him grow made me feel so good.

Soon his mama brought him live mice so he could learn how to kill them, but he saw them as entertainment and had a lot of fun chasing them around on the loft. Too soon he grew big and strong. I had to let him go. I hated to think about losing my special, secret friend whom I loved so much. Since we had no school the next day, I decided to take him to the other side of our island in the early morning.

Late that afternoon, my grandma and I sat on our backyard bench stripping spinach leaves off their long, tough stalks. Out of the stall, through the half open window, strolled Zissie with Peter right behind her.

I quickly glanced at my grandma to see if she had noticed him yet, but it didn't seem that she had. I silently begged Peter to go back inside the stall. Instead, he continued to follow his mama. I desperately hoped that they'd go in the direction of our garden, away from us. But no, Zissie came straight to us with Peter. I worried so much for his safety, but could think of nothing to do but sit there and hope for the best!

Ever so proudly, Zissie presented her much grown up kitten, Peter, to us. With no effort whatsoever, he jumped up onto the bench where we sat. My grandma gave me an astounded look. My heart froze with fear. I hoped for the ground to open up and swallow me so I wouldn't have to see my grandma take Peter to the neighbor to have him killed. Perhaps someone nearby could grant me a miracle. God, the devil, our island witch, anybody please let nothing happen to my dear friend, Peter, the cat!

I felt dizzy. Grandma picked Peter up by the neck. Would she take him to the chopping block and with one easy hit chop off his head, as she did with the chickens? Silver spots danced around in front of me and my stomach turned inside out. I tried to get up from the bench, but sat frozen.

Grandma thoroughly inspected Peter. "He's a fine looking boy cat and looks just like his mama." Looking at me, she asked, "So what's his name?"

Her words barely reached my spinning head. "Peter," I murmured.

She gave me an amused look and I barely heard her say, "Okay, he can stay."

The next thing I knew, I felt very cold and wet. My laughing grandma pulled me out of the bucket of cold water in which we had put the spinach leaves. I didn't remember falling into the bucket.

Just to make sure I had heard her right, I asked, "Did you say that Peter can stay?"

She smiled and said, "Yes."

Relief washed over me. I'm sure my grandma figured out, or perhaps had already known long ago, that Peter was Zissie's kitten from the litter that I had witnessed being so cruelly killed. Grandma never mentioned it though. Maybe she didn't want to bring that horrible memory back for both of us.

Peter grew into a fine looking cat, but was different from most housecats. He liked to lie inside my grandma's oven. After she finished baking her bread, she put a small amount of kindling in the oven to dry so she could start the next morning's fire easier. Peter preferred to lie on that wood all afternoon long. Of course, Grandma left the oven door open to spread the precious warmth out into her room.

Often he sat on top of the lean-to and had a serious conversation with the moon and long-gone ancestors. In early spring and late summer, he sat there and sang ever so loudly to all the neighborhood lady cats. He often lay in my aunt's front yard and let that mean gander rip out his fur one little piece at a time, seeming to enjoy it.

I don't believe he ever thought about catching mice and rats. He caught butterflies and walked with Grandma and me to the cemetery to tend to our family's graves. When Grandma smoked her delicious fish, he sat right next to the smoking barrel all day long. If a tail or a fin fell off, he reached inside the barrel and pulled the morsel right out of the hot, smoking sawdust. He always walked a little sideways. Well, what can one expect from someone who was hit over the head with a shovel at a very early age in his life?

Peter's mama cat, Zissie, got shot at the fall rabbit hunt. On her way home with a mouse in her mouth, some ignorant person spotted her and didn't know the difference between a big black and white cat and a small, grey rabbit. I wonder how he made it through life.

A long time passed before I forgave my grandma, our neighbor, and especially the world we lived in, for such cruelty.

No Baskin-Robbins, powdered sugar, penicillin
or minimum wages.

Chapter 27

A handful of change.

At the age of eight, I had to say farewell to my easy, lazy summer days. By custom, all the children started working in the fields at that age. We had no child labor laws.

During the planting, growing, and harvesting, school started at seven a.m. and ended at noon. The farmers waited for us right outside our schoolhouse, with their horse-drawn wagons, to pick us up. They took us to the fields that we had to work on that particular day. For the first few days, the young children worked beside their parent or some other adult to learn fieldwork.

On my first day of fieldwork, my mom worked at planting cabbage with a handful of other women. The farmer took me over to her and told me to work the row next to my mom, and I did so proudly.

I knew how to plant cabbage. I had done it many times before in our garden. My grandma taught me how to plant many different plants over the years. While we children worked in the fields, the adults practiced addition, subtraction, and multiplication with us. Every day we learned how to spell a new word or two and what they meant, which I thought was actually fun.

The farmer's wife came at three o'clock with a big basket full of food. We all gathered at the end of the field near a pond or under a tree and sat in the soft, green grass.

The farmer's wife handed each of us a huge sandwich and a cup of cool buttermilk. The sandwich consisted of two pieces of freshly baked black bread and had the biggest, thickest piece of smoked ham in the middle that I had ever seen. Then the woman handed all the children a good size carrot. For the first time in my life, I actually couldn't finish the food handed to me. I barely ate half of that huge, very delicious sandwich before I felt full.

I noticed that my mom only ate half of hers too. She took a can out of her bundle and put both of our leftover sandwiches inside of the can. She said, "This will make a fine evening meal for all three of us."

I stuck the carrot in my pocket in case I got hungry before we finished work.

At 6 p.m. we quit and the farmer paid everyone with cash. He handed me a handful of change. Proudly, I showed it to my mom. She smiled at me and told me that I did well. I don't remember how much money I held in my hand, but to me it meant more than a million dollars. I proudly clung to the handful of change as we walked home.

At home, Mom and I dropped our day's pay into our money jar. We saved our money for the lean, long winter months when we could find no work, and therefore could earn no money. And no one on our island offered any financial help.

Happily, I ran down to the bay to take a long swim in the cool, refreshing water. I played and talked to my friends until hunger drove me homeward. Tired and hungry, but so proud of myself for the pay of my first day's work, I walked home in the moonlight.

My mom had cut the leftover sandwiches into smaller pieces for the three of us for our supper. She made hot tea, and to celebrate my first day of work, she baked an apple flat cake, which stood in the middle of our small table. What a surprise!

After we finished our great smoked ham sandwiches, my mom cut the apple cake and gave me the first, biggest piece.

She smiled at me with a tired face and said, "Girl, I'm very proud of you!"

I felt mighty proud of myself too, to contribute to the support of my small family. Exhausted, but smiling, after a last look at our money jar, I gladly went to bed.

What a big difference a handful of change made that day!

No pumpkins, oranges or folding chairs.

Chapter 28

A bitter shock.

On this warm, early fall day, just about everyone in our village worked in a nearby bean field that we had already harvested for the farmer. Now we could rip out the bean plants themselves, with their second, much skimpier crop for our own use. We hung them up to dry, and when the bean pods completely dried out, we shelled them and placed the big ones in a sack to save for spring planting. The rest wound up in our soup pot. My mom often cooked a big pot of bean soup which lasted us all week long. She just added some water to it every day.

The small children played peacefully at the nearby pond while the adults talked and laughed. About halfway into the afternoon, we heard a shrill, loud scream, then another. The small children ran toward us screaming and pointing at the pond. Everyone in that field dropped their bean plants and ran toward the pond. Mom took my sister and me by our hands and we ran together toward the pond.

There, near the pond's edge, stood the old farmer who owned this field. He had both of his arms around Albert's neck. Albert, about thirteen years old, had long been declared dangerous and crazy. The authorities had told his parents to always keep him locked up. Albert, naked from the waist down, fought to break the farmer's hard grip.

Below him in the grass, lay Rosie, a little girl of five years old. She was tied to the old cottonwood tree and her skirt had been torn from her. She shivered and cried while her father untied her.

In outrage, people screamed. A few men fell upon the boy and started beating him up. I felt terribly afraid. Albert fell to the ground. Blood came from his nose and he screamed like a wild, injured animal. Some people threw stones at him.

Some shouted, "Get a rope!"

Just about all the men yelled back, "Yes, get a rope!"

A few young men ran toward our village. My mom, little sister and I sat down in the green grass near the pond's edge, opposite the angry mob, near other women with their children. I wondered why the men needed a rope.

Rosie's father knelt atop Albert now and pummeled him. Some of the women spit on him and kicked him.

I asked my mom, "What are they doing? Will they kill him?"

Mom held my hand, looked at me and answered, "He's a very bad boy and either raped, or was about to rape Rosie. Most likely, our men will hang him."

I neither understood rape nor what happened when someone got hung. At the moment I tried to ask my mom about those words. I saw men running back toward us from our village with a rope. The outraged people loudly welcomed the men back with excited screams and angry faces.

One young man from our village climbed up the old cottonwood tree with a long, thick rope in his hand. He swung the rope over a thick limb and let both ends fall back to the ground. Some of the other men held Albert down and strung one end of the rope around his neck.

Rosie's father and two men from our village took a hold of the other end of the rope. Albert screamed even louder now.

I asked my mom, "Are they going to hang him in the tree?"

She quietly answered, "Yes."

Then I asked her, "For how long, Mom?"

My mom plainly said, "Until he's dead."

Her answer shocked and scared me. I quickly held on to her arm tightly with both hands. I surely knew what the word death meant!

With loud, satisfied screams, the furious men heaved Albert up off the ground. The rope tightened around his neck. He still screamed like a wild, wounded animal. His whole body and his legs twitched around in the air. Blood ran down from his face over his body.

The rowdy crowd yelled, "Go to hell, Albert!"

Then the two men who heaved Albert up jerked on the rope hard and Albert no longer screamed. His body hung motionless.

Then the men let him down quickly. His body fell onto the ground with a hollow thump. I hoped against hope that Albert still lived and that the men had just wanted to teach him a lesson.

Filled with great fear, I stood and stared at Albert. My hope, that he still lived, vanished quickly. He just lay on the ground, neither moving nor screaming.

Some people whispered, "He's dead."

I wondered if dying hurt and what about after that? Did death itself hurt? At the age of eight, I had a lot of fear and confusion about life and death.

I stared across the pond in shock. I felt stuck to the ground, not quite on earth but neither in a dream. My teeth chattered out of control. Somehow, I felt very ashamed and guilty of what I had just witnessed.

Through wet eyes, I saw our only man of the law coming onto the field. I always called our lawman "Uncle" since we were related somehow, but so were most of us on that small island. Someone must have notified him, or perhaps he had heard the wild screams of the people. He rode his huge plow horse. The horse pulled a two-wheeled cart. An immediate silence fell over the villagers.

Mom called him a fair man and he handled whatever problems

arose all by himself, though not always to the liking of all the people.

After our lawman briefly looked the situation over, he climbed down from his huge plow horse. Rosie's father told him loudly what had happened and all the people agreed with him. Then all the people wanted to tell him their own opinion at once. They talked louder and louder. Soon just about everyone screamed to be heard.

At that time, our lawman shot his big gun off into the air to quiet everyone and he established silence immediately.

Then, our lawman said, "As all of you know, Albert should have been locked away somewhere around three years ago, when he burned down his parent's barn with his sister inside of it. His parents pleaded with me not to send him away. They asked me to let them keep him locked up in their house. I told them they could do that." He shook his head sadly. "I guess Albert had three more years of life at home than he would have had otherwise."

He slowly walked over to Albert, took the rope from his neck, picked him up, and dropped him into the cart. He landed with a dull sound and I wondered if the fall had broken some of Albert's bones and if he hurt.

Grandma had told me long ago, "Child, believe me, dying might hurt, but being dead doesn't."

I wasn't so sure yet and wondered how my grandma knew this.

Our lawman climbed back on his huge plow horse and rode away with Albert inside of his cart.

I looked up at my mom. "Where's he taking him?"

"To the cemetery."

After a few more moments of talking, everyone went back to work ripping out the bean plants. After we cleared the field of all the precious bean plants and hung them up at home to dry, I walked to the cemetery. I wanted to see if Albert was laid out in the small, old chapel. I wanted to tell him how sorry I felt that he had to die so young.

Quietly and filled with shame, I walked into the almost dark chapel but found it empty. I walked back outside and looked around to see if I could find a new grave. Soon I saw two men digging a grave on Sinners' Row. I wondered if they were digging that grave for Albert. He did do much wrong in his short life. He killed his little sister and did harm to Rosie.

When I walked closer to Sinners' Row, I saw a body wrapped up in a blanket lying next to the new grave. A woman came into the cemetery and held her head low, as though crying. The woman walked over toward Sinners' Row. As she came closer, I saw her grieving face. I recognized her as Albert's mom.

She slowly walked over to the grave. Both gravediggers came out of the freshly dug grave. They stood still while Albert's mom bent down beside her dead son. I didn't know if people usually prayed or sang on the graves in Sinners' Row. I didn't hear his mom singing our funeral song but I hoped she prayed for his forgiveness.

When Albert's mom stood up, the gravediggers took Albert's wrapped body and lowered it into the grave. His mom shook with grief. She turned around and saw me. Her tears ran freely. I felt so sorry and sad. I wanted to go over to her. Perhaps hold her hand, maybe say a kind word to heal her pain, but the guilt and shame froze me to the spot. She just turned and left.

After Albert's mother left the graveyard, I went inside the small chapel and cried my heart out. Relieved, I walked home that evening with the moon keeping watch over me.

Very early the next morning, I picked a red rose from my grandma's big rosebush. I took it to the cemetery and quickly laid it on Albert's grave on Sinners' Row. It was the only flower on his grave. Then I quickly ran home before the devil could catch me.

No magazines, spices for our food and most of the time we had no coals to feed our little iron stove.

Chapter 29

Big trouble!

Winter had arrived again. The red shingles of our roof froze white on the inside of our house, and icicles hung down from them. My sister, Uschi, and I lay in our bed beneath the shingles, trying to see who could count the rows of icicles the fastest.

Each time our house moaned or cracked in the bitter cold, we tried to say a word that sounded closest to the sound the house made. If the cracking or moaning sounds grew very loud, we pulled our bedcover over our heads. We pretended to be completely safe beneath our thick cover, even if our house broke under the heavy burden of winter and tumbled down on us.

In the mornings when we had to get out of bed, we'd stick our day clothes under the covers to warm them. One at the time, so as not to let too much of the icy air under our covers, we dressed without leaving the warmth of our bed.

I never understood why we had to put nightgowns on in our bed. I always thought it would be a lot easier to go to bed in our day clothing. That way, we wouldn't have to go through the dressing and undressing ceremony every day. When I shared my great idea with my mom, the thought scandalized her.

If mom had coal to feed our little stove, it would have warmed her small room by the time we got out of bed. Mom didn't always find coal available to buy, but when she did, she always complained that it cost too much. Most of the time we only had driftwood and limbs from bushes or dead trees.

On that diet, our iron stove refused to heat the room properly. On such days, we crawled on mom's couch under her bedcover. There we ate our breakfast, usually hot tea and a pork grease sandwich. Sometimes the sandwich even had sweet marmalade or honey on it.

After breakfast, when too cold to walk to school, we stayed in Mom's bed and did schoolwork for a while. When we finished that to Mom's satisfaction, she taught us how to knit and sew by hand. If the sun had come out by noon to warm the air a bit, Mom allowed us outside to play in the snow.

On this particular day, we were lucky! The sun shone brightly and not a cloud drifted in the clear blue sky.

Hurriedly we bundled up by putting on all the clothes we had. Excited to get out of the house, we grabbed our fine wooden sled which Uncle Fred had built for us, and ran out the door. We barely heard our mom's warning not to go sledding in the bay where the men ice fished. Happiness rushed through me as I ran outside. I looked forward to a fun afternoon. I let my sister pull the sled with me on it down toward the dike by the bay, the favorite spot for all the children of our village to go sledding. There the dike stood at its highest, which gave our sleds a lot of speed to run fast and far out onto the frozen bay. Full of excitement and stored-up energy, we arrived at the favorite spot and found it a very busy place. Seemingly, all the children from our village had already gathered with their homemade configurations of sleds. They laughed, talked, sledded, and threw snowballs.

Actually remembering my mom's warning about not to sled where the men went ice fishing, I looked down at the bay below me to find a safe spot to speed down off the high dike and then onto the frozen bay. I noticed many men and some women down there ice fishing. Luckily, they all fished to the right side of the runway for the sleds. So, I only needed to steer the sled slightly to the left, like all the other children did, when I hit the ice.

The danger in sledding where people went ice fishing was that the holes they hacked into the ice froze over quickly when the water no longer moved. However, it took a few hours before the ice froze thick enough to hold the weight of a person. Since all the fishing boats wintered on land to prevent damages from the frozen sea, this method provided the only way for many village people to put a meal on their tables, or barter for other goods.

Since my sister pulled me all the way to our dike, I figured I owed her the first ride down on the sled. I placed her in position to push her down the dike. I showed her when and how to pull the sled to the left a little to miss the ice fishers, and then I gave her a big push.

Down the dike, she slid gathering speed. When she should have pulled slightly to the left, she pulled to the right!

I screamed at her. "Pull to the left!" but she slid too faraway from me to hear my desperate screams.

Everyone around me stood still, watching in awe at how my little sister slid among the ice fishers' holes. Finally, her sled slowed. I took a deep breath of relief, but a bit too early. She slid right into the next hole in the ice. A little burst of water came out of the hole.

All the children screamed to the adults on the ice, pointing toward the ice holes. By the time I sped down the dike on someone else's sled, I felt so scared, I couldn't even think straight.

After the very few seconds it took me to slide down the dike and hit the ice, I saw all the adults running toward the hole into which my sister had disappeared. Somehow, I reached that hole in the ice first. I almost slid into it myself.

Panic stricken, I jumped off the sled and bent down on the ice at the edge of the hole. Our sled floated in the hole. Hurriedly, I pulled it out of the water. Then my sister's hand came up out of the water. I grabbed it and pulled on it as hard as I could. Her head came above the water and she took a deep breath.

Excited and relieved I cried, "She's alive! She's alive!"

I pulled and tried to get her out of the water while I screamed for help. When the first adult reached me, I slipped on the ice and let her hand loose. My little sister slipped back into the ice-cold water. By the time I got back up on my feet, many adults knelt at the edge of the hole with their hands in the water, ready to grab her when she came back up.

By now, I shivered with fear for the life of my sister. Stars danced before my eyes. My sister came back up, but not in the open water of the hole. She hit her head beneath the ice just a few feet away from the hole. A young man hurriedly took off his coat and boots and jumped into the icy water. Very quickly, he came back up and out of the water with my sister.

She hung like a limp rag in his arms. Someone bent her over. Lots of water ran from her mouth. People took off some of their outer clothing to give to the brave young man who rescued her. An elderly woman wrapped my sister up in her coat. Another woman pushed heavily on her chest. A third person breathed into her mouth.

I grew very dizzy and got sick to my stomach. The frozen tears bit sharply into my face. Someone brought a horse, pulling a sled. Suddenly, my little sister coughed and spit out water. She was alive! A hot flash of relief sped through my body.

Dizziness blurred my vision and I no longer heard a sound. My legs weakened and everything whirled dark around me. I never felt falling onto the ice.

I awoke at home on my mom's couch with my mother feeding my little sister hot soup from a cup while she lay next to me. I felt so happy to see her alive. I saw my mom wiping tears from her face.

Wet clothes hung all over the table and chairs inside the little room. My grandma fed mom's iron stove a lot of wood to get this little room warm and things dried out. When my grandma finished feeding the stove, she came over to me with a cup full of hot, steaming soup. It tasted delicious and warmed my insides. Quickly, I fell asleep. My sister and I both slept on mom's couch until late the next day.

While we ate breakfast, my mom, with a strange calmness, said, "Edith, you're older and therefore responsible for this terrible ordeal. You should have known better than to let your little sister slide down the dike in the wrong direction. You'll have no playtime at all this winter. You'll do many extra chores around here. After that, you'll sit in this room and knit a sweater for the brave man who rescued your sister!"

I couldn't believe what my mom had said, especially since it was only January. Winter would stay for at least four more months. Mom sure dished out a hard sentence. I knew she'd never ease up once she announced a sentence and if I complained, my punishment only increased. I felt guilty for what happened, but not that guilty since my sister pulled the sled to the wrong side by herself.

I worked hard all winter chopping wood, shoveling snow, and cleaning out the animals' stalls. After I finished those chores, I knitted until daylight slipped away. I had no fun at all.

Finally, the sun scared away the winter. Crocuses reached through the snow to announce spring's arrival. They turned this still white world into a pretty, colorful one. When I finished knitting the sweater, my mom complimented me on my good work. She said, "Go on, child, and take the fine sweater to the man who rescued your sister. And don't forget to thank him."

Gladly I walked out of our house and down the road for the first time since my punishment started. How great it felt to walk away from our house. I wished I could just keep on walking and never return, but where could I go in this awful, cold world? Perhaps I should wait until summer to just walk away from home and never return. With the sweater neatly folded, and feeling somewhat nervous, I knocked on the door of the house where the young man lived. By the second knock, he answered and opened the door. Surprised to see me, he smiled and asked me to come inside his house. I stepped inside and after he closed the door, I thanked him for saving my sister and told him that I had made a sweater for him, which I handed to him at that moment.

Very surprised, he admired the sweater and thanked me. Then he asked me to come inside his kitchen to have some hot tea and fresh bread with honey. I gladly accepted his offer.

In his small, warm kitchen, his big dog greeted me with a friendly lick. The bread tasted great and I liked that young man a lot. I played with the idea of asking him if I could live with him, but I was too shy. Reluctantly, I left his house and walked back home.

When I got home, my mom declared that spring had come and therefore my punishment ended, and that made me very happy.

No cotton candy, Crock Pot or Slurpies.
We did not know what ICU or IUD meant,
but we sure know what TB was!

Chapter 30

TB

Tuberculosis crept onto our island early in 1952, and many fell ill, including my mom. She lay in bed most of the time and had a hard time breathing. By late fall, she could no longer walk down the stairs to use the outhouse. And during these months, she unwillingly infected my little sister and me.

Finally, someone sent a doctor to check out our situation. He found the conditions on the island shocking, and it worried him that so many people had died. Right away he organized all the sick for transport to a sanatorium, including my mom.

Early the next morning, my mom stepped out of bed and fell onto the floor. She then crawled to the top stair of our staircase, sat down next to us, and held us close. She tried to say goodbye to my sister and me without crying, but couldn't quite hold back the tears. Her red, swollen eyes told me that she had already cried quite a bit.

Then my grandma came upstairs and said, "Erna, it's time to leave."

Very slowly, and in a strange, scary way, my mom hugged my sister and me for a long time and tearfully whispered her goodbye into our ears. Her tears ran down my cheek.

"I want you two to be good and do whatever Grandma tells you to. Do you understand?"

We both nodded as we held back our own tears.

My mom never hugged us that long or cried that much before and I thought that maybe she'd never come back to us, or die as so many other people had.

She turned to my grandma and said, "You know what to do with my children in case..."

She never finished that sentence, but I saw what she meant in my grandma's tearful eyes.

I felt so helpless and so scared during what seemed a final goodbye. I wondered if this would be the last moment, the last hug, and the last tear I saw my mom cry.

Someone knocked at the door and Grandma said, "Please come inside."

Two strong men with white masks over their mouth and nose entered our house.

They said, "We've come to pick up Erna."

My mom, as weak as she was, tried to stand and walk down the stairs, but she didn't have enough strength. When she started to slip, my grandma and I held her back and the two strong men hurried up the stairs.

They picked her up and carried her outside.

Gently, they lifted my mom up into the horse-drawn wagon. I walked over to the wagon and handed my mom her small bundle she had asked me to pack for her. I had made sure to add the nice picture with the writing on the other side saying that I loved her.

Eight people barely sat up in the wagon, wrapped in heavy blankets. They all coughed up blood, just like my mom. They leaned against the wooden planks of the wagon. Their horrible suffering frightened me.

One of the men with the white mask over his mouth said, "We're taking them all into quarantine to a sanatorium."

I could only numbly nod my head as I wondered if any of them would return alive. None of them looked like they would.

Ever so slowly, the wagon pulled away. As I watched my mom roll away in that wagon, I realized it had two black horses towing it, and it reminded me of a funeral. Somehow, my frightened mind changed the picture, and in utter grief, I faintly saw the horse-drawn wagon disappear around the bend in the dirt road with eight coffins on it, one piled on top of the other.

Dazed, I walked inside, crawled into my grandma's lap and quietly cried my heart out.

Before long, my grandma said, "Now, child, you and your sister must also pack a bundle, because a wagon will come for you in the morning to take you to a sanatorium as well."

Somehow, the words didn't frighten me as much as I thought they would have. I didn't want to leave home. In fact, I had never even left our island, but if someone took me to the sanatorium, that would be fine. I could stay with my mom then, and perhaps take care of her, so she wouldn't die. But that feeling of resignation didn't last long.

Early the next morning, the same horse-drawn wagon came to pick us up to take us away. This time, the wagon had only one driver, and he didn't wear a strange, white mask over his mouth.

I desperately clung to my grandma and hoped that she'd let me stay at home with her. As we reached the wagon, the driver stepped down. He helped my sister into the wagon. I still clung to my grandma with all my strength.

The driver bent down and calmly and kindly explained, "I know this is hard, but if you stay here, you'll soon be as sick as your mother. Then you'll most likely infect your grandma, and before long, your whole family will die."

Tears streamed down my face. My fears grew. I clung more tightly to my grandma.

The driver reached for my hand. "I promise. It'll only be for a little while. It's a very nice place, really, and you'll be with eleven other children from the island." Though I absolutely did not want to leave, I didn't want my grandma to get sick and die either. Slowly, but not willingly, I let loose of my grandma's strong arms. The driver picked me up and sat me down in the wagon. Grandma tearfully handed me our bundles.

At that moment, I knew something felt very wrong, but didn't know exactly what. I only knew that I had to stay strong so that my sweet grandma would quit crying. I stood up in the wagon, smiled and waved goodbye. When I could no longer see my grandma, I sat on bales of straw and cried.

I wondered if I'd ever return alive to my home. I thought perhaps the tuberculosis would kill all three of us. Maybe my mom and I could die together and go to heaven together. I hoped my mom knew the way. I surely didn't and my little sister had no idea about those things yet.

My mom was a good mom. Surely, she'd go to heaven. My little sister was too young yet to go to heaven. Grandma could bury her at sea so she could be born again and have another chance at life. I was sure about my mom going to heaven, but I wasn't so sure about myself because I wasn't very good. I stole many apples. I hit instead of loved my neighbor, and yes, I had lied plenty of times by now, to get out of trouble. I hoped that God had stayed busy in other places and didn't see or hear my sins.

Before long, we arrived at our little ferryboat. I had thought the driver would take us to someone's house on our island, but I learned differently when the driver escorted us to the little ferryboat. Slowly, we walked toward the ferry.

More children arrived at the landing, bringing our group to eleven sick, frightened children with red and swollen eyes. We had all left our homes and all we had known.

Silently, our little group of sad souls and the driver walked onto the little ferryboat on that fall day of 1952. At nine years old, I left my little island for the first time.

All of us children huddled together at the back of the little ferryboat, as if to protect one another. With silent, frightened tears, we watched our island grow smaller and slowly disappear in the low haze.

Suddenly, huge, beautiful snowflakes drifted down from the

sky. What a welcome sight. We dropped our bundles and tried to catch a few of the prettiest, biggest snowflakes we had ever seen. What a relief to our stressed-out, sick little group, running around catching the big snowflakes, forgetting for a moment the huge problems of our young lives

Soon, the ferry landed on the mainland of Germany. A train waited for us patiently. On clear days, I saw the train from our island, but I never imagined it so big.

A huge, black engine made lots of noise and shook, full of power. Dark grey steam rose way up into the sky, melting away in the snow clouds. The locomotive had a wagon full of coal behind it. If Mom had that much coal to feed our little stove in our brutal winters, we'd have stayed snugly warm all winter long!

Behind the wagon of coal, I saw two passenger cars. Our escort led us to the last passenger car with the letters TB on it in big, bold, white letters. I climbed inside, holding my little sister's hand, so I wouldn't lose her.

Inside, we saw many children and a woman welcomed us. She told us where to sit and she attached little nametags to our coats and our bundles.

I scooted over to the window so I could enjoy the view better. My little sister laid her head down in my lap and fell asleep. I held onto her so she wouldn't fall off the bench. The car felt warm, even though I didn't see a stove.

Then I heard one very loud, deep blow from the locomotive. A quick jerk followed, and the engineer let the powerful, shaking engine loose. With squeaks and rattles, we moved forward.

My first time on a train was so exciting. I watched as the world passed by. For the moment, I forgot all my trouble, glued my face to the window, and, in amazement, took in all the scenery.

I saw so many cows and horses out in the snow-covered fields. I also noticed smaller animals that I had never seen before.

The woman in our car said, "Those are sheep and goats."

What thick fur the sheep had. Surely, that kept them warm in the winter.

The train stopped in every town that we passed, and I thought that was very special. Those towns had many houses, and they looked so different from ours. Cars of all kinds drove all over the streets. So many people stood at the railroad stations. Some got on and some got off, but none came or went from our railroad car.

I saw children who had dogs tied to a leash. I felt sorry for the dogs. We never tied ours like that. I thought it must feel terrible to have a rope around your neck. The leashes reminded me of the day they hung Albert.

At the next stop, a big woman came into our car. She brought us a big box full of wonderful smelling sandwiches and a can of milk, then she quickly left. I saw her drive away in a big automobile with an open back. That car looked a lot like the one the men drove that came to buy fish from our fishermen on our island. A lot of blue smoke came out of the tail end of that car too.

I looked for my mom each time the train stopped, but I never spotted her among the people I saw. I figured she had already arrived at the sanatorium. My spirits lifted at the prospect of seeing her again soon.

Our escort handed out the sandwiches to us and ladled milk into metal cups for us. I woke up my sister. She sat up and we ate our delicious meal together. The sandwich had fried liver with cooked apple slices on top of it between two big pieces of almost warm, dark bread. The milk still had the milk fat in it and tasted much better than the kind we drank at home which had the milk fat removed to use for other purposes. How I wished this ride could go on forever.

This train's passenger car even had an outhouse, but it didn't have a bucket beneath the seat. Things just fell onto the railroad tracks. What a funny outhouse. I could barely wait to tell my grandma about this, a much easier way than having to empty the bucket constantly.

When we stopped again, a big, wooden sign at the railroad

station had the name Niendorf on it. The woman asked us to grab our bundles, put on our coats and slowly get out of the train.

I still stared out the window at the big city with its two churches, many houses, and stores with big glass windows on the front. I hoped to take a long walk around this city soon to see all the different sights.

Someone grabbed my arm and said, "Let's go, girl!"

I took my sister's hand and we walked out of the train.

Two open trucks waited to take us to the institution. Someone started to separate us, boys on one truck and girls on the other. I held on tight to my little sister so she wouldn't get lost in the commotion. I wasn't even sure if she knew yet that she was a girl.

The train lumbered away from the station with the woman who helped us still on board. She stood at the small platform, looked at us and waved. I waved back. She waved with both hands now and smiled very nicely. I wished I could have ridden with her on that train.

We were separated quickly, except for one little child that lost its nametag.

A woman asked, "Are you a boy, or a girl?"

The child said, "Yes."

The woman decided to put that child in the girl's group for now.

Heavy snow began to fall. Quickly, we all climbed up into the trucks. They gave us blankets to wrap around ourselves and told us to sit down. I wrapped myself in a blanket and knelt so I could still see where we were going. Perhaps someday I'd have to find my way back to the train station to ride home. My little sister lay down and cried. I covered her with the last two available blankets. The snow fell even harder. The wind bit my face and I missed home so much. Too dark to see anymore, I decided to sit down next to my sister. At that moment, the truck made a sharp left turn. In the distance, even through the heavy snow, I saw faint lights.

Before long, the lights shone more clearly I could make out

three huge houses with lights in every window. The light glowed much brighter than our lantern at home, even brighter than the light bulb that hung from the low ceiling in Mom's room. I wondered what could make all that light in these huge houses. Did they have a huge electric box and thousands of coins to feed it?

The sharp wind made my eyes tear, but I refused to sit. The truck slowed and the size of the houses amazed me. They each stood four stories high.

Abruptly our truck stopped. The other truck went on to the next building.

Our chaperone said, "Climb down off the truck, girls!"

She then guided us inside one of the huge buildings with the name Searose painted on the door and a smiling girl's face painted next to it. I could hardly believe such huge buildings existed, except for our church, which was even bigger than this building.

I held my sister's hand and hoped that we could stay together. A few women in light blue outfits came over to us, smiled and welcomed us. What a place! The warmth made me feel good, and I saw many nice light fixtures hanging from the ceilings, not just the light bulb itself.

Many children of different ages played and ran around the large room. I stood in awe, staring around the brightly lit room, thinking what my grandma would say if she saw this room. Then I wondered how these people could have enough food and beds for all the children, even if two children slept in one bed as we did at home.

My sister's pull on my hand ended my moment of bewildered gaze. One of the women in the light blue outfits waved her hand for us to follow her up the stairs. We climbed three flights of steps, a lot of work for me, especially since I had my little sister in tow.

The only place that I knew of that had more stairs than this house was our church's bell tower on my island. Exhausted and out of breath, I wanted to sit down on the last step, but the woman waved us on to follow her into an even bigger room than the one downstairs.

Many rows of small beds filled this room. The nurse called them cots. She told us to pick an empty cot and store our belongings underneath it in the small cardboard box.

I hurried over to the empty cots by the big windows, dragging my little sister behind me. There I picked the two cots closest to the big window for us and quickly unpacked my little bundle.

When I reached the partially open window to look out, it surprised me to see that the window was really a door made out of glass. I had never seen a glass door.

Carefully, I stepped outside onto a wooden deck with a little fence surrounding it. Many small benches and tables stood there in the snow. On one side, a long flight of stairs led all the way downstairs to a playground that looked so pretty with all the snow on it.

Forlorn and hungry, I stood on the snow-covered deck wondering in which direction lay my home. All of a sudden, I heard the sea gently rolling on land. That made me so happy. Now I knew I wasn't so very far from home and perhaps I could even see our island when the wings of morning hushed away the snow clouds. A few tears, the ones that really matter, ran down my cheeks. In the dark, snowy night, I waved toward the whispering sea and said, "Good night"

Someone blew a whistle. I quickly wiped away my tears on my sleeve and walked inside.

The nurse announced, "I'd like all of you to go to the other end of the hallway into the bathroom and wash your hands. After that, go back downstairs to meet all the other children in the dining hall."

I wondered why we had to wash our hands before we ate. Perhaps they didn't have enough flatware for all of us to use.

The bathroom totally amazed me. Four long rows of bowls stood ready for us to wash our hands in. Someone showed us how to turn the faucet on and off. I couldn't believe that water ran right out of the wall.

Soap sat in every small bowl, and towels hung right next to the bowl on the wall. I bent down to see where the water went. At the bottom of the bowl, I found a pipe into which the dirty water ran right back into the wall. I laughed out loud in disbelief.

On the other side of that room stood a row of huge, oblong, deep bowls filled with water, and two children sat in each. Older children washed their hair.

One of them looked at me while I stared and said, "These bowls are called bathtubs."

Now that looked like fun to me. "Could I come in?"

She smiled. "You'll get to take a bath very soon. I'll let you know when."

Then, as politely as I could, I asked where the outhouse was because I really had to go. She pointed to a row of what looked like closets. I looked at her in disbelief.

"Maybe you didn't understand," I said. "Outhouses stand outside."

She smiled, dried her hands, took my hand, and walked me over to the row of closets. As we walked, I saw children going in and coming out of those closets. The friendly young woman opened one of the doors and told me where to sit and that I needed to pull the string when I finished.

Now that completely flabbergasted me! My grandma would never believe this. Besides that, the bucket I needed to sit on had water inside of it. Way above it hung a square bucket with a metal string hanging down to pull when I finished.

While I sat down on the strange bowl, I heard water rushing down in the closets next to me, and I wondered why. As soon as I finished, I pulled the string and water rushed down out of the square bucket into the bowl I had sat on and flushed everything away.

I hoped that nobody stood beneath the floor. What a mysterious place I found myself in. They sure had plenty of water.

I wondered where it all came from and where it went.

I couldn't wait to tell my mom and my grandma. Then I wondered about my mom. I had only seen children in this huge building. Perhaps I could find my mom in the building across the street. I decided to go over there and check on her early in the morning.

The nurse came inside the mysterious bathroom and reminded me to go to the dining hall downstairs. I found it a lot easier walking down all those stairs than up.

I finally found the dining hall, also a very large room with many long, narrow tables and benches. Twenty children fit at one table. Ten sat on each side on a long bench. The evening meal of a thick vegetable soup with big chunks of real meat in it tasted great. To my great surprise, these people even had enough food for all the children. We could even have seconds.

The pills the nurse gave us seemed not so hard to swallow when stuck in a piece of the vegetables. The spoonful of cod liver oil she put in my mouth tasted horrible and I spit it out right away. She took another spoonful and added it to my delicious soup. Now my soup tasted horrible and I felt so very hungry.

Since everyone had made clear to us at the beginning of our first meal that we had to eat all of the food set in front of us, I found myself in a dilemma.

Slowly the dining hall emptied and most of the children had gone into the next room to play, leaving just a handful of us newcomers stirring our soup around. If the nurse hadn't kept a constant eye on us, I'm sure we'd all have left the dining hall long ago.

I tried to swallow that horrible tasting soup again. At the next spoonful, my stomach refused to accept that mess. I spit up with great force. Things flew all over the table, even into some of the other children's plates. With great relief to all of us still at the table, the nurse announced that we could go and play. On our way out, she said that she'd teach us how to swallow that cod liver oil the next day.

Bedtime came soon. After I tucked my sister in and gave her a good night hug, I snuggled into my blankets on my cot with the doll my mom had made for me years ago.

I listened to the sea softly washing her waves onto the shore. Slowly I drifted away into a place without cod liver oil in my soup. I sat on the shore by the softly whispering sea and told her all my problems. She rocked me in her soothing arms and promised me that all would end well.

That ended my very first day away from my island.

Early the next morning, before the sun warmed the day, I dressed, quietly snuck out of the huge house and walked across the road to the other big building.

A friendly nurse greeted me and asked, "Who would you like to see?"

I answered, "Please let me see my mom. Her name is Erna Siebert, and she has red hair and is very sick."

The nurse looked through a long list of names, and then looked at me with a confused expression. "I don't have your mother on my list."

Frightened, I asked, "Please check if she died."

After a short while, the nurse looked at me and with a smiling face told me, "She did not die."

Though relieved, I felt sad at not finding my mother here. I thanked her and walked outside.

I saw only one more of these huge buildings, and it stood at the end of the road. Excited, I walked toward that building, figuring my mom must be there. How great it would feel to see and hug her.

I found the door of this building locked, but it had the word sanatorium written on a small tag which had a knob on it. I pushed the knob in and heard a bell ringing inside. I thought that was strange.

A big man came and opened the door. With a deep voice, he

asked, "What do you want?"

Politely I answered, "I'd like to see my mom."

He looked down at me. "Only men and boys live in this building." Then he slammed the door closed.

I stood shocked and bewildered in the cold morning. I had no idea that other institutions like this existed in different places. I worried that my mom got lost somewhere on the way to this place, or that she died and someone buried her beside the road somewhere.

In dismay, I slowly turned and walked toward the sea. There I brushed the snow off a boulder, sat down, and cried. Maybe when the sun rose and lit up the world I could see my island and walk home to tell my grandma that my mom disappeared. She would help me look for her.

Soon the sun greeted the world with all her glory. She sent her pink and orange rays out first to chase the night away, then she came out of her seabed inch by inch, a fiery, glowing, orange ball. She looked the same as she did on my island. Where was my island?

I desperately scanned the horizon from one side to the other side, but I couldn't see it. Way back to the left of me, heavy fog still lay over the sea. I figured that's where my island was. I needed to come back a little later and check on it. At that moment, I felt too cold and hungry to wait for the fog to lift. Sad, and wondering about my mom, I slowly walked back to the building I now called home.

On my way back, the friendly nurse from the first building came to me. She bent down a little, put her arm around me and asked, "How are you doing?" She took her handkerchief from her pocket and wiped the tears from my face. "There are many institutions like this in this country. Some nearby, and others very faraway. Your mom surely lives in one of them. I'll check if I can find out where she is and let you know."

I thanked her with a big smile and a hug. She held my hand

and walked with me to the door of the Searose building.

Once inside, a nurse took me to the office.

In the small room, a man who sat behind a table spoke harshly to me. "Do not ever leave this building by yourself again! Go to the dining hall and see if they saved any breakfast for you."

I left immediately, very glad to get out of that room. I worried that he'd whip me. He looked very strong too. Surely he could dish out a hard whipping.

I took off my coat, hung it on one of the big wooden nails on the wall and entered the dining hall. I had grown very hungry and thirsty by now. I had last eaten that liver sandwich about noon the day before.

Then I spotted her, the nurse with her big bottle of cod liver oil and a spoon in her hand, dishing out that awful concoction. Oh no, not again. I felt so terribly hungry. I sat down and hoped she didn't see me. Eagerly I bit into a jelly sandwich my sister had saved for me and drank a little of the warm milk she handed me.

Then came the nurse, swinging that big spoon in her hand. I slid beneath the table clinging to my sandwich and hoped she didn't see me.

A loud voice demanded, "Edith, get out from beneath the table now!"

How I dreaded what would happen, but slowly I crawled up and sat back on the bench.

Smiling, the nurse said, "I know all of you want to go home, but first you need to get well. Therefore, you need to swallow this medication every time I bring it to you. Today I'll teach you how to swallow one spoonful of cod liver oil without too much trouble."

She took the cup of warm milk from my sister and placed it closer to her. Then she filled the spoon full of that gross tasting stuff, lifted her head up and tilted it a little backwards. Then she pinched her nose closed, brought the spoon to her mouth and hurriedly swallowed that disgusting cod liver oil.

Quickly, she took the cup of warm milk and took a few swallows of it. My little sister came next. She swallowed it, but gagged afterwards. She kept that darn stuff inside her though. Then came my turn. I did exactly what the nurse said.

After I swallowed that horrible stuff, I hurriedly drank all my milk. I made it without spitting it back up, but it was a terrible procedure. I hoped that taking that spoonful of cod liver oil would get a lot easier in time. Better yet, I hoped to get out of here soon, very soon.

Our homesickness grew. We all cried a lot, except at bath time. I had so much fun in the tub of warm water playing with my bath partner. I often closed my eyes and pretended to float home. Other times we flipped pieces of soap high up into the air and watch them splash down hard, splashing some water out of the tub.

Best of all, I liked to take a real deep breath, then put my head under water and pretend I was home bathing in our sea. Most of my bath partners seemed scared to put their heads beneath the surface though. I wished we had a big bathtub like this at home. I'd stay in it all day long. Even here, with all the tubs available, we couldn't stay in the water very long, and many days passed between baths.

We didn't wash our hair with every bath, but a nurse checked us for lice every time. Sure enough, one day I had lice. After dressing, the girl sent me downstairs to the nurse's room. She powdered my head and wrapped a big, white towel tightly around my head. She told me to leave the towel on my head until she called for me.

Her little room stayed very busy that afternoon. Before long, I noticed more of us children wore those towel turbans than those who didn't. Somehow, all of us turban heads grouped together. We formed a long line and walked through every room and hall with our heads hung down, our hands behind our backs, stomping our feet in rhythm to a funeral song we knew the first verse of. Everyone, even the adults, laughed out loud. When all the fun ended, the intense hurt crept up again, like a never-ending homesickness.

A doctor checked our lungs twice a month. We had to take off our clothing above our waist and step behind a very huge machine. The only light in the room came from the screen where the doctor looked at our lungs. The procedure, called *Durchleuchten,* preceded the use of x-rays, and it gave the doctor a vague look inside our bodies. This doctor seemed like God to me. He had the power of so many children in his hands. He decided who would go home and who would stay. I always entered his room with so much hope of going home, but so far he had only said no. How deeply it hurt me each time he said that word. I had to find a way to get out of here. Homesickness was tearing me apart.

Soon, the deep winter gripped our part of the world. The daylight hours grew short. Day and night, the sky hung full of heavy, grey snow clouds. As far as I could see, the sea had frozen over. I figured this as the perfect time to walk home over the frozen ocean, if I just knew where my island was.

One afternoon, I saw a big girl from our island who came here the same time as I did. I walked up to her and asked her, "Can you see our island from here?"

She said, "Sure, but I can only identify it at night when the lighthouse blinks."

I asked her, "Would you please show it to me when it gets dark?"

She said, "Sure."

That same evening, when darkness covered our world, the two of us stood at the big window upstairs in our huge sleeping room. She pointed slightly to the left. On that clear night, a billion stars twinkled in the sky. Yes, I could see a faint, barely visible, blinking light. With great joy, I thanked her. I decided to go home tonight.

At our evening meal, I stuffed my pants pockets full with sandwiches and apples to sustain me on my long journey. I didn't need to take something to drink since plenty of snow covered the ground. That night I told my little sister, "I'm going home. Please promise not to tell anyone."

She said, "Please take me along. I want to go home too."

I shook my head. "I can't. You're too small for such a long walk."

When she started to cry, I lied. "Don't cry. Listen, I'll come back for you."

I hoped God didn't hear my lie. Most likely He never came here anyway. I had prayed and prayed for His help to get me out of here, but He did nothing to help me. I hoped He at least helped my mom, whom I had also kept in my prayers. At this point in my life, I wasn't sure anymore if God existed.

When the nurse wished us good night, turned off the big light and left, I put on all my clothes, gave my little sister my much loved doll to keep for me, hugged her, and whispered goodbye into her ear. I rolled up both of my blankets, tucked them under my arms and quietly left my sleeping room through the glass door.

Holding onto the handrail, I carefully walked down all those snow-covered stairs. I felt so excited at the prospect of finally going home. Goose bumps crept all over my body. I wanted to jump up and scream with joy, but that had to wait until I put some distance between me and the sanatorium.

Though the wind had died, the bitter cold cut through me on that clear night. The snow crunched beneath my feet. The small sliver of moonlight and the brightly shining stars lit my way well down to the sea.

In no time at all, I stepped onto the frozen ocean. With so much happiness, I lifted my head high in excitement and looked toward the dimly blinking, faraway light. Then I lifted my hands up high and whispered into the completely still night, "I'm going home!"

After I wrapped both of my blankets around me, I marched on toward the faint, blinking light. I knew I'd find my grandma there for sure, and hoped to find my mom at home also. If I still had tuberculosis, I could live in the lean-to. That way I wouldn't make anyone else sick.

After a while, I grew exhausted and stopped to rest just a moment. I sat down in the snow and ate part of one of my sandwiches. Though it had fallen apart in my pants pocket, it still tasted great. Then I took a handful of snow and slowly licked it away. On I went, marching homeward happily. After a while, I could no longer see the lights from the institution or the town. The faint, blinking light before me shone more clearly.

Now, since no one could hear me any longer, I shouted, "Grandma, I'm coming home!"

Now and then, I heard the ice moan under the pressure of the slightly rising sea. At times the ice cracked partially, but I knew it had frozen so thick at this time of the year that it did no harm to walk on the narrow cracks.

Soon, to the right of me, I saw another light. The blinking, reddish light slightly bounced up and down in the distance. I recognized it as the border light between our island and the Soviet Union. Those lights, attached to a very big buoy, warned people not to escape from the Soviet Union. That bolstered my confidence that I headed in the right direction. Soon I'd arrive home. How happy and tired I was.

After another sandwich break, I resumed my trek toward the blinking light, but walked more slowly now. I often stumbled and fell onto the snow covered ice shell. Though tricky to stand back up on the slick ice, I made it. The small sliver of the moon had long left this part of the earth. Way in the distance, a faint thin line of light emerged from the horizon. The wind woke me up and kissed my face with its sharp needles.

Suddenly, I heard waves rolling up onto the ice. As I walked closer toward my island, I realized that the sea had not frozen over completely. A flock of seagulls emerged from the open water. With shrill screams, they flew up into the sky as though laughing at me.

Soon, the thin line of light on the horizon expanded into a wider band. Through tired eyes, I clearly saw my island and the narrow channel of fast moving open sea between my island and me. I had come so far. My island lay so near, but I had no way to reach home. The water was too cold to swim across this time of the year.

So greatly disappointed, I stood on the slightly swaying ice, gazing bewildered at the fast moving current. The light on the horizon spread out wider. Soon the sun would take over this world. Forlorn, freezing and so very disappointed, I sat on the frozen sea.

I could have easily found my way back to the sanatorium by tracking my footprints in the snow, but fatigue overcame me. I covered myself with my blankets. Through a small open spot in the blanket, I watched the beautiful sunrise over my beloved home, my island.

The sun rose from her seabed in a golden dress, setting the surrounding sky on fire with deep, bright, and flaming red colors. The outside edges turned a pale pink. A few dark purple clouds hung in the sky among the flaming red colors. The ever so slightly swaying ice shell rocked me gently into a land that did not know homesickness or a freezing body. Perhaps God would pick me up and drop me off on my island. Sometime before I sank into deep sleep, I thought I heard the wind whisper my name, or did the seagulls call me?

A big, rocking movement woke me. In my first, not completely conscious moment, I thought the ice beneath me had broken apart. I tried to get up, but something very heavy lay on top of me and I found myself in complete darkness. I moved my hands up to my face and pulled away a part of the very heavy rug which I had wrapped around me. The bright sun blinded me for a second. Then I noticed that I sat on a horse drawn sled.

A man sat beside me and held on to me, so I wouldn't fall off the sled. Had God picked me up and dropped me onto my island?

When I looked around, I sadly realized that I was not on my island. In the not too far distance, I saw the big houses of the institution. My disappointment in God grew again.

Back at the sanatorium, they took me to the sick ward. A nurse looked me over and ordered a week of bed rest for me. They kept the only door into and out of that ward locked. My frostbite healed in time, but my homesickness did not.

Before long, I heard the older children practicing Christmas songs. A week before Christmas, the same children presented a Christmas play in our dining hall. Though a far cry from our Christmas performance in our huge church on our island, I liked it.

A few days before Christmas, children occupied themselves with a lot of bathing and packing. I wondered if I had missed the going home announcement. Had the doctor said yes at my last check up, or were all of us children going home for Christmas? I quickly packed our bundles.

Early the next morning, two big trucks parked in front of our building. In excitement, I took my little sister's hand, grabbed our bundles and walked over to the checkout line.

The line moved quite quickly. I noticed that each child gave his name. The nurse then crossed the name off her list and said goodbye to that child. Very simple. I thought I'd finally go home! No more cod liver oil with every meal, no more painful homesickness for me. What a happy Christmas it would be!

Soon my little sister and I came to the front of the line. With a relieved, bright smile, I told the nurse our names.

She looked at her list, shook her head and gave us a stern look. "You're staying!"

Angry and sad, I walked back upstairs with my crying sister in tow. From the big windows of our sleeping hall, we watched the lucky, excited children climbing on the trucks to leave for home. When the trucks started to move, the lucky children laughed, screamed and waved goodbye.

I took my sister's hand. We crawled under my blankets, held

onto each other, and cried our hearts out.

Christmas Eve arrived and the nurses placed small packages on many of the children's cots, but we found none on ours. I wondered if my mom and my grandma had forgotten us by now, or if they had died.

When it came time to open packages, the nurse came to each child who had not received a package and handed them a pretty bag. The bag, full of Christmas cookies and sweet treats, helped us feel a bit better.

My sister and I walked over to the glass door, now locked since my escape, and ate our sweet surprises. Big snowflakes tumbled down onto the already white world. My thoughts flew home to my family. I closed my eyes and saw the little evergreen twigs inside a can on our table. They had silver tinsels hanging on them in my imagination and a fat, white candle stood next to the can. I imagined a warm room and something good smelling simmered on the little stove. The loud voice of the old night nurse brought me back to reality. The time had come to lie down on our cots and go to sleep.

Just before noon the next day, Christmas day, the nurse called my sister and me to the office. Usually we had to go to the office only when we misbehaved, where the director of this place dished out punishment.

Those times I was called to his office, he never whipped me, but made me sit on a chair in the corner of his room and write down, for what seemed forever, what I did wrong. I always thought it a waste of good paper. If I had hit someone, even if they deserved it, I had to wash all the stairs. That took almost all day for me to get that job done.

As we walked down the stairs on this day, I tried to think of what I had done wrong. I wondered why my little sister had to go to his office too. She never did anything bad. I figured it was about standing in line to go home. Slowly, filled with guilt, I opened the director's office door.

I couldn't believe my eyes. There stood my grandma! I ran to her and jumped into her open arms. I think these were some of the first happy tears I cried in my young life. I just knew that I was going home now.

I clung to my grandma while my happy tears ran down her face. Soon my grandma peeled me from her and stood me on the floor. She then greeted my little sister. A young woman, who worked at the sanatorium came into the office. She invited all of us to go into the visitors' room. My grandma took us by the hand and we walked into the fine room which I never had seen before.

Inside the room stood many tables and chairs, and a pretty, decorated Christmas tree. Pictures drawn by children hung all over on the walls. Adults, visiting their children, occupied some of those tables. Grandma took us to a table which stood right next to the pretty Christmas tree.

The young woman who invited us into this room, helped my grandma out of her heavy coat and hung it on the coat rack. She smiled and said, "I'll bring your Christmas meal soon. Your grandma is invited to eat with you."

My grandma smiled and thanked her.

After we sat down, she opened her handbag and pulled out presents for us. She had knitted me a pair of dark blue socks and a pair of red mittens with many other colors knitted into them. She gave my little sister a pair of red socks and blue mittens with many different colors knitted into them. They were absolutely beautiful. Then my grandma handed us each a bag full of apples, dried plums and sugar cookies. What fine presents! Both of us clung to her, hugged her, and thanked her.

Soon the young woman brought our delicious, Christmas noon meal of fried potatoes, a fat piece of sausage, and a big slice of warm, black bread with honey on it. She also brought us a whole can of hot, sweet tea. The best part of this meal though, was that I thought our grandma had come to take us home. The next best part was that we didn't have to take our spoonful of cod liver oil.

Grandma told us, "Your mom is still very sick and needs to stay in the sanatorium in Bavaria for some time to come."

Then she handed us an envelope with my mom's address on it and two pieces of paper to write to her. She had even put a stamp on the envelope.

Grandma said, "Don't write sad or bad things in that letter. We don't want to upset your mom and make her even sicker."

I promised to write just fine things. I wondered though why she brought the envelope and paper to us here, since we were going home with her.

When we finished our fine meal, my grandma stood up from the table and announced, "Let us go take a walk and see the nice town."

That sounded like great fun. I wanted so much to see the town when we first arrived here, but we couldn't visit it.

I told my grandma, "I'll run upstairs very quickly to pack and fetch our bundles. That way we won't have to come back to this place. We could just go home."

My grandma took a moment before she answered. She didn't look at me when she said, "All of us have to come back here. I'll need to spend the night here, because the next train going back to our island won't leave until early tomorrow morning."

That sounded all right to me. One more night here was not so bad. Tomorrow would come soon.

A short, fun walk took us to town, and what a pretty town it was. The stores had windows in front of them, and were decorated for Christmas with pine tree branches, and round, silver and gold ornaments hung from the branches. Some windows had tinsel hanging inside of them. The display windows held so many different candies and things I had never seen before.

Grandma pointed to a beautiful display of shiny items and said, "Those are toys to play with."

In one of the windows sat the most beautiful doll I had ever seen. I barely could believe that she was real. She had golden, curly hair and a real looking face with blue eyes. Her arms and legs, not sewn out of cloth like my doll, looked like they were made of the same material as her face.

"That doll is made of ceramic," Grandma told me.

And her dress, oh my, how pretty it looked. The dress of light pink material had many white ruffles sewn into it. Her little feet even had little red shiny shoes on. What a wonderful sight. How I wanted that doll, but somehow I knew it was not possible.

Our family didn't buy toys at all. I didn't think it was even possible to buy such things in our tiny store on our island. I never saw such dolls or toys in that store. At least I could have this beautiful doll in my dreams.

All the houses in the middle of the town huddled together, as if to warm themselves on each other on this cold winter day. Children of all ages played in the snow. Some rode their sleds. Others threw snowballs at each other. Dogs joined them in the fun. This town had two churches. Though not half as big as our church on our island, I wondered why a town needed two churches. I thought all the people in this town could easily fit into one of their churches.

Christmas music came out of a place that had the name Café written on the door in big letters. I wondered if that was another church. On the other side of this Café I saw the railroad station. A sleeping train waited on the tracks. Oh yes, I firmly believed that the train would take all of us home tomorrow morning, to take me faraway from all the pain and misery I had to endure at the sanatorium.

Snow began to fall again. The cold winter wind blew right through my coat, but I kept quiet about that. Under no circumstances did I want to go back to the sanatorium earlier than we had to. My grandma shivered, took us by our hands and led us inside the Café.

How very warm that little place felt. We could even take our coats off. It didn't look like a church though. People sat around tables, drinking, smoking, talking, and laughing. I had never seen that in our church. This place reminded me of our tavern, except in our tavern, only men folks visited for a while. This café had women visitors also.

My grandma ordered a cup of coffee for herself and a cookie for each of us. The friendly woman who took our order came back to our table with a can of coffee, two cups of hot, steaming milk, and a plate full of cookies. She smiled at my grandma and said, "Merry Christmas, there's no charge. Please stay as long as you'd like."

I liked that place. The radio played fine Christmas music, the cookies tasted great, and I was going home tomorrow.

The snow began to fall harder and my grandma said that we needed to leave. We finished all our cookies and the hot milk. Then we thanked the nice woman, bundled up and walked toward the door.

A tall man came to us and asked my grandma if he could take all of us somewhere. Grandma gladly accepted his offer. He sure had a fine car, with soft seats and a radio which also played Christmas music. I truly enjoyed my first ride in a car.

The snow came down even harder now. From my window, I saw big flakes passing by fast. I pretended that the beautiful doll I saw sitting in the store window, sat next to me while we drove home. Too soon for me, we found ourselves back at the sanatorium. Grandma thanked the man for giving us a ride.

Back inside, the nurse declared it time for my sister and me to wash up and go to sleep. Out of fear of not going home with my grandma, I desperately clung to her.

The nurse told me, "Your grandma will sleep in the room where the adults that work here sleep, since we have many empty beds. All the other visitors sleep there also tonight."

I didn't want to let loose of my grandma.

The nurse had to pry me from her and she said, "You can see your grandma in the morning."

When the nurse carried me away, I looked around at my grandma. She had tears in her eyes, which frightened me. Something was wrong.

When everyone had fallen asleep, I snuck downstairs to see if I could find my grandma in the bedroom with the other visitors. Slowly, I tried to open the big door but found it locked. Scared and angry, I walked back upstairs.

I took my two blankets, wrapped them around me and sat down by the big window, from where I could clearly see the front of our building as soon as daylight arrived. I wanted to make sure my grandma wouldn't leave without me. I desperately tried to stay awake, but sleep overcame me.

When I awoke, I heard noises downstairs. Hurriedly I ran down all those flights. The big door to the bedroom of the adults stood open now. All the visitors had left, even my grandma. I couldn't believe that she went home without me.

As fast as my legs could carry me, I ran to the railroad station. When I arrived, I saw only empty tracks. The train had left. Out of breath and ever so disappointed, I sat down on the tracks and cried.

I thought of walking home on those railroad tracks, but feared it too long a walk in this cold weather. I remembered it took us almost a whole day on the train to get here, and the train sure ran faster than I could. I needed to wait until the end of winter. With a heavy load of homesickness and tears running down my cheeks, I walked back to the sanatorium, the place I now lived and hated from the first day on.

Yes, I had to wash all those stairs again for leaving the building by myself.

My grandma could not have taken me home with her, but I was too young to understand that.

Then came a day when I woke up mad, really angry. I don't know exactly why, but I didn't care to stay in this institution any longer. I started a fight in the washroom, but nobody fought back, which did nothing to cool my anger.

After breakfast, they allowed us to play in our huge hall. All the different age groups, except the toddlers, came together there in the harsh winter. A big girl pushed me away from the bench I wanted to sit on. That did it! With so much anger stored up inside me, I hit her like a mad grizzly bear. She fought back, and so did I.

Before long, everyone in the room fought and screamed. The real small children threw their building blocks at us and laughed. Someone sat in a chair in front of the door so none of the staff could enter the play hall.

We ripped each other's hair out and bit each other on uncountable parts of our bodies. We landed on the floor and got stepped on or trampled on. When the smaller children ran out of building blocks, they threw books at us. I fell hard against a chair and it broke. We ripped each other's clothing to pieces and we screamed and screamed. We vented our anger and frustration on each other.

With a huge bang, our short, fat director broke a big window and climbed through it. He had a big stick with him, which he freely swung across his angry, purple face. He looked ready to mow all of our heads off with his big stick.

The fights slowly stopped. The person in the chair in front of the door moved and the rest of the staff streamed inside. Peace came over us fighting voyagers quickly. We looked at each other and started to laugh very loud, somehow with great relief! Apparently, the fight had done us all some good by allowing us to blow off some of our stored up frustrations and anger. However, our steaming mad director didn't see it that way.

He looked around at us and said, "One week of house arrest. No play time inside this room, and you will clean up all of this mess right now!"

In came Miss Rena, second in charge. Though skinny and old, she had a tremendous, powerful thundering voice. She could even see in our eyes when we lied to her. I often wondered if she had a slight touch of witchery. She was, however, a fair and wise woman. She divided us into groups to clean up the mess and we obeyed her.

The next day, we all looked interesting with deep blue and purple eyes, strange hairdos, swollen noses, and a few bandages on arms and fingers. Some of us had bite marks and swollen lips. We felt happy and laughed a lot at each other. By midmorning, we had the place back in order. Then came a nice, sunny afternoon, but we couldn't leave the building.

By the next afternoon, we grew restless. Here and there, arguments and small fights started. Miss Rena blew her whistle. She opened the old door and let us run outside to play. I heard her talking to the director. She told him that to avoid more trouble she stopped the house arrest and he agreed.

Happily, we ran around in the snow spending all our energy. Slowly, things got back to normal, thanks to a wise Miss Rena.

C8C8C8

On a warm fall day, after our group came back to the sanatorium from a long walk on the beach, I stopped, completely shocked. There, in front of our building, stood my grandma and Aunt Kate. I wiped my eyes once to see if they had played a trick on me. When I opened my eyes again, sure enough, they still stood in front of our building, waving at me. They were really here!

With happy tears in my eyes, I ran toward them as fast as I could. I jumped into my grandma's open arms and wrapped my arms around her neck, holding onto her for dear life. Aunt Kate picked up my little sister and whispered something in her ear.

Had that doctor said that I was healed? All spring and summer long, I held my hands over my ears each time he looked at my lungs. I couldn't bear to hear the deeply hurtful "no" any longer.

Then, with a huge smile on her face, my grandma said, "We've come to take you home."

A second or two passed before I realized that the day I had

hoped and prayed for, for such a long time, had finally arrived. With great excitement, I jumped up and down, screaming to the world, "I'm going home!"

The four of us walked into the office. My grandma and Aunt Kate talked to our director. They read some papers and signed them. Meanwhile a nurse brought down our belongings. She asked my grandma if we'd like to stay for our noon meal.

Before my grandma could even think of an answer, I blurted, "No way!" I feared that someone would change their mind about us leaving this place.

My grandma looked at me and smiled. She turned to the nurse and said, "No thank you."

The friendly nurse smiled and said, "I'll get something you can take with you."

Miss Rena came into the office. I feared the worst. Perhaps someone had made a mistake and we couldn't leave. Instead, she came over to me, hugged me gently and said goodbye. She wished my little sister well and gave her a hug too. By the time Miss Rena wished my grandma and Aunt Kate farewell, the nurse arrived with a sack of food for us.

I ran out of the building. No more cod liver oil! No more doctor who put his always ice-cold, hands on my chest! Most of all, no more homesickness. I was the happiest girl in the whole, wide world! I just wished I could take one of the fine, big bathtubs with me.

On the way to town my grandma told us, "Your mom is still very sick and she needs to stay in the sanatorium for a while."

I wondered if my mom felt homesick too. I decided to write her a nice letter and draw a pretty picture, as soon as we got home.

Then my grandma said that Mom wanted to let my little sister live with Aunt Kate and Uncle Werner. They had no children and would love to take care of her.

My little sister stopped walking, let loose of my grandma's hand, and looked into Aunt Kate's face. They smiled at each other.

My little sister then took Aunt Kate's hand and we walked on.

With a squeeze of her hand, my grandma said, "And you can live with me."

That made me very happy. I loved my grandma.

The train waited at the railroad station. So very glad to finally go home, I ran toward the passenger car and climbed on board laughing ever so loud. I would not miss this train.

Grandma waved me to come back out of the train, and that worried me. Was I going back to the sanatorium? Ever so hesitantly, I departed the railroad car and stood outside of it, hoping that I didn't have to go back to the institution.

Grandma called, "Come sit down with us, child and have a bite to eat. The train won't leave for another two hours."

With great relief, I sat on the bench next to my little sister and ate a great jelly sandwich my grandma handed to me. I kept a close eye on that train, though. I'd make sure to board that train at the first sign of its departure.

After we all finished eating, Grandma and Aunt Kate talked about old times. I took my sister's hand and slowly walked around the train with her. I felt strange. I never liked her a lot, but I had taken care of her at the institution. I protected her from the children who tried to beat her up. When someone stole her doll, I fought to get it back for her. That was worth washing all the stairs.

At times, we cried together. Someone told me she had saved my life when I walked out onto the ice to go home. Now we were being separated. I hoped my sister, Uschi, would have a nice home with my aunt and uncle.

I told her, "I'll write to you and visit you when I can."

She looked up at me and simply said, "Yes."

Soon, I saw the engineman enter the locomotive, a sure sign to get onto the train. I helped my little sister by holding her hand and pulling her up the stairs into the railroad car. Grandma and Aunt Kate climbed in behind us. We sat on facing benches. My little sister, Uschi, and Aunt Kate sat down on one bench, my grandma and I on the other. I stuck my head out the open window to watch the locomotive get ready to pull us home.

The engineman now started the big, black locomotive's engine. It stuttered at first and then slowly huffed and puffed. As it gained its powerful strength, the locomotive began to shake. Steam escaped from near the wheels of this giant machine and grey smoke streamed out of its chimney into the cloudy sky. One quick, short pull and a long squeal, and we moved forward. Now I knew that this so long, very wished for day of going home, was real. Relaxed, I sat back down and smiled. No more painful, never-ending homesickness for me. My Aunt Kate held my little sleeping sister in her lap, just as my mom did on occasions. I hoped she'd treat her kindly.

Several stops later, we arrived in the town of Oldeslohe, where Aunt Kate and my uncle lived. After short, tearful hugs from both of us, my aunt carried my little sister, my crying friend, from the railroad car. I waved goodbye to her, but she stayed fast asleep.

Through the window, I saw my Uncle Werner waiting to pick them up. I felt strange, as if I had lost something. I laid my tired head in my grandma's lap and happily drifted away to where small children go to play without a tear to shed.

When I woke, I looked at the purple, dark, grey sky. Lightning danced in the far distance and the wind whipped the trees around. Bits and pieces of branches and leaves flew around in the air and I worried that the wind would blow our train away. Grandma assured me that wouldn't happen.

After a short while, the heavy, dark clouds dipped lower. I felt I could have touched them if I had opened the window, but I feared the strong wind could hurt us.

Our train cut the clouds apart and ran right through them. What a show! I pretended to race to heaven with that beautiful doll I saw sitting in the store window in my arms, and I wondered what heaven might look like.

Soon our train had raced through all the low clouds and started to slow down. I came back from my ride to heaven with that beautiful doll, which I named Erika. From the window I saw our ocean to my left. That meant that we had almost come to the end of the railroad's run. My beautiful island lay just a ferry ride away and I felt so happy.

On the other side of the train, I saw a serious lightning display on the horizon. It looked as though the ocean was the stage of a wild, dramatic performance. The lightning strikes reflected from the ocean back up into the sky. What a beautiful, but scary play.

Our train came to a stop and the ferry operator came inside to greet us. Now that the huge, strong engine of the locomotive died, I heard waves pounding the shore. In the now closer, huge performance of the lightning storm, I had a first look at my not very distant island. My heart jumped faster at the longed for sight. I surely wore the biggest smile in the world.

The ferry operator told us he couldn't take the ferry out to sea in this big storm and offered us his strongly built shack for the night.

He said, "There's wood for the little stove and an old sofa to sleep on. I'll bring you something to eat."

Grandma gladly accepted his fine offer.

He then told us, "Hold onto each other very tightly, or the strong storm will blow you over." The ferryman took our few precious bundles and held onto them with his big, strong hands, as if they were bags full of gold.

Grandma held on to me as we slowly stepped from the train. The wind blew wildly at us. Sand and parts of vegetation hit me in the face. I closed my eyes and clung to grandma's hand for dear life.

I found it hard to breathe. My nose collected all sorts of objects and I sneezed a lot. The three of us were very glad when we reached the shack. After a few more deep sneezes and a lot of coughing, I started to breathe normally again. My grandma kept sneezing for a little longer.

Something soft touched my legs. Hurriedly I turned around and looked down. Two big, soft brown eyes looked back at me. Then the big, brown dog licked my knees with his long, rough tongue. When I bent down to pat him, he sat up and reached out his paw. I shook hands with him. He sure had very long, curly fur and was a gentle dog. I liked him a lot.

The ferryman lit the little stove, and it did its best to warm up the small shack. The smart dog lay down next to the stove for warmth. The ferryman told the dog to stay, when he left to fetch us some food. I was glad about that. Perhaps I could pat and talk to the dog for a while.

Full of excitement at the thought of going home, I walked over to the small window that overlooked the sea. The grand lightning display had drawn much closer now and lit up the whole sky as far as I could see. The wind howled past the small shack which I hoped wouldn't blow over.

The angry sea slammed her strong, tall waves mercilessly against the shore. She ripped away piece after piece of the sand dunes and took them out to sea with her. Thunder rolled in from many directions and sounded as though a dozen drums marched toward us. What an impressive sight. When lightning flashed in the sky, I could see my island clearly. I was so happy to be away from the big sanatorium.

When I glanced over toward the ferry landing, I saw no ferry. Had the outraged sea swallowed it? How would we get home? Just when I was about to ask my grandma how we'd get home, the ferry operator came inside the small shack bringing us each a fine sandwich, consisting of two slices of dark bread with a thick slice of blood sausage in the middle. He also brought us a can of hot tea, water and food for the dog.

He said, "It will be best to let the dog stay with you. If you need help, just let the dog out. He's trained to go home and bark at the door. I'll then come over and check on you." He wished us a good night and left.

My grandma moved a small wooden box closer to the sofa. She laid our food on it and poured the tea into two old metal cups she found in the corner of the little shack. We sat on the old sofa and began to eat. The brown dog came over, jumped on the sofa and sat down next to me. His wet, sniffing nose came close to my sandwich. I gave him a small part of it. He liked it a lot and came to sit a little closer to me. His soft brown eyes followed every move of my sandwich.

We didn't have to light the small candle the ferryman brought us. The constant lightning provided plenty of light, as though we had a lamp with an old, flickering light bulb.

Suddenly, hail began to fall, hitting the tin roof with the sound of a thousand tiny bells. The echoing thunder played the drums in this concert and the angry sea sang dramatically along with them. We had an exciting, wonderful concert with our dinner.

I felt so happy and safe with my grandma inside this little tin shack. Tonight, I wouldn't have to cry myself to sleep, because of homesickness. Tonight, even though the mighty storm raged outside, I'd go to sleep smiling, the first time in such a long time.

I drank the rest of the tea and gave the brown dog the last bite of my sandwich. I hadn't felt so happy in such a long time. Grandma lay on the small sofa, barely big enough for her if she lay sideways. I took the two blankets my grandma handed me, walked over to the little, hot stove, and cuddled up with the dog. I patted him and whispered good night into his ear.

He stared at me with his soft brown eyes and yawned. I figured he said good night to me in dog words. Just before I slipped into dreamland, I wondered if this was my sister's first night too without crying herself asleep. I hoped so.

Soon her little face faded away. I found myself on the train with the pretty doll from Niendorf. I don't know where we were going, but the train ran very fast and all of a sudden flew up into the sky.

Early the next morning I awoke to a silent world. I couldn't even hear the waves of the sea washing onto the shore. For just a split second, I thought that I had returned to the sanatorium and everything else had just been a dream. Then a wet, soft nose greeted me. At that moment, I knew that I lay in the small tin shack with my grandma and this gentle, brown dog.

I jumped up to look out the window at the landing, where we needed to board the ferry. With fear, I realized that no ferry waited for us. The brown dog stood up and my grandma awoke.

I said, "Grandma, I don't see the ferry at its landing."

"Well, go outside, climb on top of a sand dune and look for it," she said while yawning.

I did just that with the dog following me excitedly.

Way on the top of the closest, tallest sand dune, I looked around for the ferryboat. Sure enough, from around the corner of a sand dune below me came two plow horses dragging the small ferryboat behind them. The ferryman had cleverly hidden the ferry away in the sand dunes from the angry sea. From my vantage point, I watched them guide the ferryboat gently back into the sea.

Before long, the boat settled into place. Grandma, the brown dog and I walked down to the landing.

As soon as I stepped onto the ferry, I jumped up high and shouted out loud, "Hello, my beautiful island! I'm coming home!"

The sunrise painted my island pink, which made her look like she glowed for my arrival. Slowly the little boat made its way through the strong current of the deep sea to my island.

Gently, I patted the brown dog and whispered farewell. A happy tear or two ran down my face and collected in the brown dog's fur. He turned, looked at me and slowly licked my face. When the ferry landed, the dog walked over to his owner and watched us depart the small, old boat.

Hand in hand, my grandma and I walked home to our fishing village. Eleven months of never-ending homesickness, hurtful disappointments, washing many stairs and so many sad tears ended. I had finally come home.

I still wonder today how my lungs healed under those circumstances.

Maybe that darn cod liver oil had something to do with it.

No peppermint sticks, telephone, Xerox or stew in a can.

Chapter 31

The pleading eyes.

Occasionally we raised a pig, which our neighbors helped us feed. They saved all the parts of vegetation not meant for human consumption, perhaps spoiled or rotten food, and brought it to us for our pig. We also added fresh seaweed and the undesirable fish parts to its diet. We bought or traded for sacks of hull and mixed it into the pig's meal.

Excitement rose among the adults when fall came and the outside temperature dropped down to freezing. That meant slaughter day approached. Early one morning on such a cool fall day, the neighbors who had helped us raise our pig came over to our house to help slaughter it.

I stood in our yard watching. At least four strong men wrestled that poor pig to the ground. Then the men sat on that defenseless pig and held it down, while another man cut the desperately struggling pig's throat wide open. Two women then caught the blood in buckets, which now poured out of the wildly screaming pig's throat.

The scene totally shocked me. Crying and shivering in disbelief at the cruelty, I screamed as loud as I could, "Let the pig go! Let the pig go!"

No one paid attention to my pleading screams. I wanted to run and rescue the helpless animal, but I couldn't move. My feet felt glued to the ground.

In one desperate last, strong move to escape its murderers, the weakening pig threw a man from its body. My stomach roiled and I could no longer scream.

The pleading eyes of the still barely screaming and shivering pig now focused on me, as though asking me for help. Unable to do anything, I just watched the last bit of life and blood drain from this poor, defenseless animal. With one more short grunt, its eyes still focused on me, its feet barely moving as though running from its murderers, the pig's life ended.

Black dots danced before my eyes. I didn't feel myself hit the ground. When I woke, I saw the pig's body hanging upside down on a ladder which leaned against the wall of our house. Someone had already gutted the pig, and I saw the warmth of its body escaping into the cool, frosty morning air.

In anger and shame over the cruel way this pig died, I walked down to the soothing sea to touch her cool water and tell her my problems. At nine-years-old, I promised myself to rid the world of such cruelty as soon as I figured out how to do it.

When I reached the shore, I walked out into the sea on the long stone walk that led to the little lighthouse, where I took many dead creatures for rebirth. There I sat and asked God to please give the cruelly killed pig another chance to live. I didn't know if He could answer my prayer since I had no body to give to the sea. Then I asked God to please forgive us people for killing His animals in such cruel ways. I pleaded to Him to show me a better way and to do it very soon. I said the prayer very loud to make sure God could hear me over the splashing waves.

Then I leaned back onto a big boulder, watching the noisy seagulls feasting on the plentiful fish. Slowly, my cried out eyes looked up at the clouds. I wished I could sit on one of those clouds and see what the world looked like from way up there.

Tired and in turmoil, I closed my eyes. Soon I no longer heard the seagulls' cries. The splashing waves grew silent and gently stored away my anger and shame. A cloud reached down and took me away from the brutal event I had witnessed.

In my sleep, I slipped down onto one of the lower boulders and a big wave splashed all over me. Quickly, I grabbed onto a boulder so I wouldn't slip into the ice-cold sea. Freezing and sad, but no longer so awfully outraged, I left my friend, the calming, green sea.

I returned home in the early evening and the pig's body no longer hung on the ladder. I saw an older boy washing the axes and saw at the pump. The men who had helped to slaughter the defenseless pig, sat around on the pile of driftwood Grandma and I had gathered over the summer. They celebrated with a sip from Grandma's cellar and very big, green cigars.

My grandma grew the tobacco plants in her garden now, since the cancer came and took grandpa away. The grey smoke from their green cigars lingered around their heads on this calm afternoon. I liked the smell of it, but the smoke made me cough a lot.

Inside the house, the women worked hard. My grandma cooked her famous blood soup, which everyone would gorge themselves on tonight. I used to like the soup too, especially the soft dumplings she added to the sweet sour soup. When I saw the pot full of blood soup boiling on the stove, my mind went back to the morning when I saw the pig's throat so cruelly slit open, and decided I'd no longer eat the blood soup.

My Aunt Hilde made sausages, usually my mom's job, but she was still so faraway in a sanatorium. The other neighbors placed parts of the pig's meat into different containers, according to Grandma's commands.

They placed some pieces in the salt barrel, and set aside others to take to the smokehouse in the next village. All the neighbors who helped raise and slaughter our pig got generous portions to take home with them. Next year, someone else would raise a pig and my family would help them to feed it and kill it.

With great excitement, my grandma announced, "The blood soup is ready!"

She ladled it out of the big pot into many cups or soup plates, whichever each of the helpers had brought with them, making sure everyone had their fill of the once-a-year delicacy. With great delight and laughter, everyone ate the blood that ran from the cruelly murdered, screaming pig, just this morning.

I walked away just a short distance and watched in disbelief how my family and neighbors gorged themselves.

The hurting, pleading eyes of the pig that asked me for help still clearly stare at me now and then today.

I do enjoy a good sausage or pork chop though.

*No Wal-Mart, waffles, Frisbees or
tiny carrots in plastic bags.*

Chapter 32

No Way, Grandma!

Just before I turned ten, my grandma had set her mind on teaching me how to kill. I begged her not to make me do this. I didn't want to kill anything.

"Nonsense, it's time for you to learn," she insisted.

She walked inside the chicken cube and fetched the old white hen which no longer laid eggs. Then she walked over to the chopping block. Grandma called me to her side and insisted that I stand beside her. With a bad feeling, I slowly walked over to her.

She held the hen up by its legs, laid it on the chopping block, took my hand and showed me how to hold the chicken down on the chopping block. My grandma handed me the ax and showed me exactly where to chop the chicken's head off.

I had no intention to kill this poor, struggling animal. She flapped her wings in distress, fiercely moved her legs to get a hold of something to be able to run or fly away from the chopping block. She lifted her head and looked at me sideways with one red eye while she desperately screamed for help. All the other chickens hovered together with fear in the farthest corner of the pen. I felt so sorry for them, having to watch the killing of one of their flock.

Loudly my grandma hollered, "Now girl, kill that chicken!"

The white hen still screamed violently. Her tongue hung out of her beak now. I wanted to let go of the poor bird.

I heard my grandma's loud voice again. "Kill that chicken now, girl!"

I couldn't just let go of the hen. That would really upset my grandma. I needed to make it look like I honestly tried to kill that chicken. I took a good look at the chopping block where the hen's head hung down to the side of it now. She still screamed and her small heart raced wildly in her quivering body. I wanted to bring the ax down at the edge of the chopping block, missing the bird's head completely, and at the same time, quickly let the chicken loose.

Grandma's voice came at me again. "Kill that hen!"

This time she sounded mad.

With hope that my plan would work and a tear in my eye, I lifted the ax high. Then I swung the ax down and let the chicken go. The ax landed exactly where I wanted it to, at the edge of the chopping block. The frightened old hen flew from the block in a great hurry. She then ran and partially flew amazingly fast away in a hurry, minus just a few feathers, which slowly fell from the chopping block.

With relief I turned from my grandma and smiled. In my mind, I screamed, "Run, chicken, run!"

My grandma ran after that hen, but it knew what would happen if she caught it, so it ran much quicker than my grandma. It looked very funny seeing my grandma running after the white old hen, yelling at it, "Stand still darned!"

After a good while, my grandma came back to our place without the white chicken. Exhausted, she sat down on the garden bench.

Struggling for breath, she said harshly, "Go fetch me some water, Edith!"

When I handed her a cup of fresh, cool water, she gave me a disgusted look I shall never forget.

The next afternoon, while gathering mushrooms in the horse

pasture on the north side of our island, I saw our old, white hen. She had joined a flock of colorful runaway chickens. That made me very happy, but I kept my mouth shut.

My grandma never asked me to kill again!

No lemonade, generators, ketchup or
lifejackets on board our boats.

Chapter 33

The most beautiful, bright light.

We didn't have a gym at our school, but we had a ball field nearby, which had a sandbox on one side. In fair weather, we ran around the field and jumped into the sandbox to see who could run the fastest and jump the farthest. The lucky children wore regular leather shoes to school, even if they had holes in them or didn't quite fit, but I didn't.

At that time, I only had one pair of old rubber boots with worn down soles. I found it awkward to run and jump in my rubber boots. Mom always bought them a size or two too big so she wouldn't have to buy a new pair as often.

When I jumped in the sandbox, I usually slipped out of at least one of the boots and often fell face down into the sand. That of course, started the laughter which embarrassed me. I could actually run very fast, but not with my rubber boots on.

The teacher didn't let me take off my clumsy boots for our weekly physical education hour. We didn't have enough money to buy a pair of regular shoes, and no one wasted money on such nonsense as tennis shoes on our island. I really hated our weekly hour of gym. I dreamed up so many excuses to get out of gym class, or just walked away from school.

One summer, our teacher had a wonderful idea. He excitedly announced, "Gym will be at the beach, wear your swim outfits."

Our whole class jumped up and down and screamed with excitement. Now that sounded like fun, gym without rubber boots. I always had a wonderful time in our salty, cool sea. We learned how to swim in different ways, how to dive into the water in fancy styles and how to rescue drowning people.

On this particular sunny summer's day, in our gym hour on the beach, our teacher instructed us to swim far out to sea to jump off the observation tower, as we did so many times before. I loved to jump off the high tower and dive way down into the sea to see the many beautiful things that lived in her water.

That wooden tower, erected during the last war, had a little shed way at the top of the tower. Many years ago, a man sat in that shed to watch out for Russian ships that might come too close to our island. However, some years ago a strong storm had come through and blew off that little shed, leaving a nice platform from which we jumped into the sea.

Soon we arrived at the tower. Our teacher followed us in his rowboat and tied his boat to the tower. Then he loudly reminded us, "Don't jump into the sea until the person that jumped before you emerges among the green waves and swims to the side."

Excitedly, I climbed up the tower looking forward to the dive. Maybe, if I held my body perfectly straight, I could gain enough speed to stay at the bottom of that magic underwater world a little longer. The sea was deep here and so full of wonders. I loved to spend time at the sandy bottom.

Finally, my turn came to jump. After taking in as much air as my lungs could possibly hold, I jumped head first from the jumping tower, holding my body straight. Quickly, I dropped through the air, the wind rushing by my ears made the only sound I heard.

In no time, I plunged into the cold seawater. Down I dove, all the way to the sandy sea bottom of this magic world. I landed right next to a large patch of dark green seaweed, which gently swayed in the current. The sun's rays gave a bright, silvery shine to a huge school of tiny fish when they turned a certain way.

My arrival disturbed a huge, fat, grey sea eel. He looked me over and showed me his saw-toothed teeth. A small group of crabs walked out of the dark green seaweed patch. The huge sea eel lost interest in me right away and followed the crabs. In a few seconds, he inhaled and swallowed all of them. Something softly nibbled on my feet. With a closer look, I recognized it as a bunch of tiny flounders checking to see if I was edible.

I'd have loved to spend the whole day down there, but I used up all the air I had come down with and had to leave this sea paradise. Pushing myself hard off the sandy sea bottom, I regretfully left the beautiful world. The sun's rays shone more brightly as I struggled to reach the surface.

I realized now that I stayed too long on the bottom of the sea. My lungs ached for a breath of air. With a last, desperate, agonizing effort, I pushed myself upward. Finally, I saw the surface draw near. I pulled and pushed hard to reach the air I so desperately needed, until my outstretched arms felt air. At that moment, I knew I would not drown and anticipated my first breath of fresh air.

Someone had not paid attention to the teacher's warning and dove on top of me with great force, before I could take one so desperately needed sweet breath of air. That forced me back down to the sea bottom. I was in big trouble now. I had neither air nor strength left in me to make it out of this ocean alive.

Without panic, I started to breathe in seawater and looked around at this amazing world. The colors of the surrounding seawater and plants slowly changed into a warmer, lighter color, as if someone had turned on a light. The seawater felt warm like never before. I heard a soft sound in the distance of someone singing.

I knew I was drowning. I didn't hurt, neither did I struggle. I felt at peace. The light around me slowly grew brighter. I wondered who would help my grandma now to clean up her room if I drowned.

Many important events of my young life ran in front of me, like in a movie house. I saw our outhouse burning with me inside of it. I saw my mom's hurting, sad face, when they took her away to the sanatorium, and the nurse who came with the spoonful of cod liver oil.

I saw Albert when he hung in the tree. Then I saw myself walking hand in hand with Grandma on sinners' row, while our island witch smiled at me. Zissie with her only surviving kitten, Peter, flashed by in those quickly moving pictures. My little sister's face beneath the ice became blurry. I saw a few more scenes, but they were too blurry to identify now. Then the pictures abruptly stopped.

The warm, glowing light turned very bright and formed a wide, upward path on which I slowly floated, higher and higher. I felt at peace and without pain. The beautiful light drew me like a magnet. I enjoyed the sensation of floating upward in its warm, golden light. The soft singing sounded more clearly. From the distance, a faint hand reached out to me. I stretched both of my hands out to touch the faint hand. Soon an old, smiling face became visible. Could it be my grandpa, or was it God? I felt happy and ready to float to him.

Before I could reach those hands, everything grew dark and ever so icy cold. I lay on the beach feeling terrible. Someone pounded on me, water ran from my mouth, and I woke up coughing and shaking. At that moment, I realized that I was no longer in the warm seawater with the golden, bright light lifting me upwards. I never reached the hands stretched out to me at the end of the most beautiful light. For a brief moment, sadness overwhelmed me. I had come back to the land of the living.

I have seen many lights in this world since then, but none as beautiful.

No vacuum cleaner, pizza, or Long John Silver.

Chapter 34

The missing piece.

Somewhere around the age of ten, my grandma asked me to help her dig a big hole in our garden to plant a good sized cherry tree. Gladly I said, "Sure, grandma!" I loved to dig in the dirt. With our spades in our hands, we walked down to the end of our long garden. I felt very grown up by now and proud that Grandma trusted in me to help her.

On that cool, early fall day, we sang a song or two while we dug. Suddenly, my little spade refused to dig deeper into the soft earth, no matter how hard I pushed down on it. I figured I had hit a rock.

I said to my grandma, "Stop digging for a moment so I can get inside the hole to get the rock out."

With one quick jump, I landed inside our hole on top of the hard object. I brushed the earth from it to find a place to get a hold on the stone to lift it out. To my great surprise, the stone shone brilliantly.

Excited, my grandma stepped down into the hole with me. She ever so gently pulled and wiped the earth away from the object. Soon she pulled out a serving tray. Earth stuck to it, except in one place, where I had without knowing, removed the earth and the hard, lard like protective coating. My grandma climbed out of the hole. She laughed and danced around the hole with the plate held above her head.

All excited and with a big smile on her face grandma said, "We need to dig very carefully now. Most likely we'll find more buried treasure. Now go run and fetch our small hand shovels."

When I came back to the hole, I found my grandma lying down next to the hole, reaching inside of it and removing earth. I lay down next to her, handed her a small shovel, and gently both of us dug a little deeper.

Next, I uncovered a bowl and a dinner plate. Oh, how excited I was! Before long, we had discovered eight pieces of tableware. As we dug deeper to uncover more treasures, the earth turned into hard, bluish gray clay and it became impossible to dig any further. We took our findings to the water pump and cleaned them thoroughly.

All eight pieces, genuine, very old silver tableware, sparkled so nicely in the sunshine. Two had very pretty patterns on them, and looked as though someone had scratched them in with perhaps a sharp nail. We set all the clean pieces on Grandma's bed and admired them. I wished the original owners had left a note with the buried pieces, perhaps their name and why they had to bury their goods.

My grandma gave away seven pieces of the silver tableware to close family members. She kept the most beautiful piece, the serving tray with the flower pattern, for herself.

Many people found such treasures over the years. Around the late 1970s, someone founded a small museum on our island and asked people to donate some of the old treasures they had found to preserve them for the future. Everyone in our family proudly gave their piece of pure silver dinnerware to the museum. In all, our family handed over seven freshly polished pieces to the museum.

No one seemed to know the whereabouts of the eighth piece, the one grandma kept for herself. After every close family member thought back to when they had last seen that beautiful serving tray, standing all polished up on Grandma's small dresser, they decided that it had been years before Grandma's death.

Had my grandma given that silver tray to someone, or had she buried it so someday someone could find it and get very excited about finding it, just as the two of us were? Perhaps she buried the tray at sinners' row in the grave she cared so well for, the one she always left with a tear in her eyes and a smile on her face.

No vitamin pills, cotton swabs, Kool-Aid, or spaghetti.

Chapter 35

One more soul.

Early in the winter of 1953, whooping cough invaded our island, and my poor little body. The high fever made me awfully weak and I often didn't know where or who I was. Thankfully, after a hard and long time of coughing, trying to breathe and fighting the high fevers, everyone in our house survived. Two old men and six very young children in our fishing village died of the terrible disease.

The sea, still completely frozen over at this time of year, made the usual sea burial for the very young impossible. To bury the young ones in the ground, still possible at this time because some graves had been dug before the frost moved in, would take away their chance of rebirth.

Like every winter, people decided to wrap the small bodies up in white sheets and place them in the "Waiting Shed," a small wooden shed down by the harbor inside a small, quiet stand of pine trees. Away from houses and the silo, where people stored wheat and other important foods, the little bodies waited safely from rats and other varmints in the big metal box that stood inside the shed.

At times, some women sat by the Waiting Shed and silently cried. Another just stood there with an expressionless stare in her eyes, looking far out to sea. My Aunt Martha, who lost her two-month-old baby girl, stood by the shed almost every afternoon. She screamed and cursed God in fierce anger. She hit her fists on the side of the shed and screamed in desperation, "Wake up my child, wake up!"

The mother of the youngest infant walked into the shed daily and carried her stiff infant's body outside. She sat down in the snow, cradled it, and sang to it. She spoke softly to her dead baby and often kissed it.

She never left on her own. Her husband always came to take her home. He ever so gently took the bundle from her arms and placed it back into the metal box. Then he draped his arms around his bitterly crying wife and walked her home. His strength and gentle support of his wife totally amazed me. At that time, I dearly hoped to someday have a man like that to take care of me.

Eventually spring arrived. The thick ice shell weakened and slowly broke apart. The people gathered at the pier to help the fishermen push their boats down the ramp back into the sea. After a few days of work, they had the first three fishing boats seaworthy. On their first trip, they would take the six small souls to rest in their sea graves.

Women could only step onto a fishing boat during these events because people believed that if women boarded a fishing boat at any other time, great disaster would befall her crew. Fire could break out from out of nowhere. Unexpected storms could appear too quickly to make it back safely to harbor. Nets would tangle in the reefs and break. Fish would disappear, and very likely, men would fall overboard, drown, or be swallowed by a whale.

Such stories made me wonder where the women obtained their great power from to cause such great disasters.

I asked my mom and my grandma a few times, and they always answered, "You're too young, child. Don't bother yourself with such matters!"

Perhaps I would soon feel the mighty power of a woman growing inside of me. I had to smile at the thought and about what I'd be able to do. I could barely wait.

When I stepped onto the fishing boat, I took a good look around me to see who could stop the great destructive power of all the women. I saw no one but our village people, and I didn't believe any of them had such great power. And no one reached down from the heavens to put a spell on the women. This sure confused me at around the age of ten.

Three small fishing boats slowly left the harbor. Each carried two little bodies, wrapped in their white sheets, as their families and friends somberly stood around them. I stood beside my Aunt Martha on one of those boats. Pitifully, she clutched her frozen first born baby girl to her breast.

She walked around to everyone so they could touch the tiny body one last time to say goodbye. Though I couldn't feel her pain, I saw it in her red, cried out eyes. She came to me, lowered the dead baby gently to me.

My Aunt Martha whispered, "Her name is Elise. I named her after your grandma, who delivered her."

As I kissed the tiny body goodbye, a few of my tears fell onto her face to travel with her to her sea grave.

A young couple and their family that lost their first born in that terrible epidemic also stood at the rear of the boat. They lived a little outside of our village, not far from us though. That young mother was the one who took the stiff little body from the box every afternoon.

She stood looking up to the heavens while tears rolled down her face. She whispered over and over, "Why, Lord, why?"

Her husband took the little body of his boy from his wife's arms and started the goodbye walk around the boat. Tears streamed down his face too. I had never seen a man cry before that. I had thought that only children and women cried.

As we left the bay, the fishermen shut off their small motors and hoisted their sails. While they steered carefully around sheets of floating ice, the soft breeze filled our sails and we arrived at the sea graveyard. Four black buoys with big white crosses marked it.

Out of respect for the dead, no one ever entered this area except to give a body to the sea to be reborn.

The boats gathered in a circle, dropped anchor, and dropped sail. Eerily, the sea suddenly calmed, as though aware of this very sad occasion.

I had only been here one time before for a burial, and I didn't really remember much of that. I looked down into the clear water and saw green seaweed gently swaying at the bottom of the sea. A school of tiny fish swam in the water. The sun shining into the water made them sparkle like silver. Everything looked so peaceful down there.

Our preacher started to talk about something that confused me. He said, "These little souls will go to heaven to live with God."

I looked up at my grandma and pulled her hand to get her attention. She bent down to me and I whispered in her ear, "Grandma, I thought those little souls would be born again, just like all the dead animals that I gave back to the sea."

My grandma smiled. "Everyone on this island absolutely believes that all the young ones who died too early and have been put into the sea will definitely have another chance at life. The preacher only asked God to help them to go back to where everything begins."

What a smart grandma I had.

After our preacher ended his sermon, he asked everyone to join him in singing a funeral song, but that didn't work out very well. People cried more than they sang. After the second verse, even our preacher quit singing.

Then everyone stood. Since it was too early into the season to have real flowers, each of the people on board held a homemade paper flower, or a dried flower. Though crudely made from anything handy, a lot of love went into those paper flowers. Most people had painted their flowers, but some, too poor to afford paint, wrote the first letter of the color they meant for the flower to be on it.

A red flower, real or painted, expressed love for the dead person. A white flower recalled the nice, good times one had with the dead person. A yellow flower told the dead person what a bad, annoying or downright mean person he or she was.

I've actually seen a horse-drawn wagon with a coffin full of just yellow flowers. At each stop along its route to the cemetery, island people came to the wagon and threw yellow flowers onto his coffin. Even the wife of this dead man threw a bunch of yellow dandelions onto his coffin. She laughed and kicked her heels up as if she wanted to dance. She sure seemed glad to get rid of him.

Then the time came to let the little bodies go to be born again. The parents gave their still, wrapped bundles to the sea one at a time. Then people dropped their flowers into the water.

The tiny bodies floated for a brief moment, then slowly sank to the bottom of the deep, clear sea. The flowers fell apart quickly and sank as well. A huge piece of ice floated by when my Aunt Martha stepped forward to let go of her little girl. She stood up straight like a statue and handed her dead little girl to her husband. Her haggard, cried out face looked ever so faraway out to sea. She mumbled something to her husband as he slowly let the tiny body slide into the cold, salty sea.

As soon as the tiny baby began to sink, Aunt Martha gave out a tremendous painful scream and jumped into the ice-cold sea. She retrieved the sinking child, held the little body in her arms and began to surface. She struggled in the awfully cold water. A man climbed down on a rope to help her up. Another big piece of ice came floating by.

Aunt Martha came up under the big piece of ice and went right back down with her baby in her arms. A fine line of blood escaped from her head. Her husband jumped off the boat and tried to reach her. Other men lowered a small paddleboat overboard into the water to help in the rescue. Way down below, in the clear seawater, I saw my Aunt Martha lying on the bottom of the sea in a bed of dark green seaweed. She still held her baby in her arms.

Only the seaweeds gently moved.

Her husband went into shock in the freezing water. Someone reached him before he sank to join his young child and wife and pulled him out of the water. One more man needed rescuing. He had slipped off the ice into the killing, freezing seawater, but someone quickly pulled him out.

After everyone had come back on board, our preacher said another prayer for Aunt Martha's soul. "May she rest in peace."

The fishermen weighed anchor and set sail. With the wind, gently moving our sails now and the mournful cries of the many on board, we slowly drifted toward shore. I looked down to the sea bottom one more time. Aunt Martha still lay there, so peacefully, with her baby in her arms.

One more soul had left us. I can still see her lying there at the bottom of the sea in the gently swaying dark green seaweeds.

No box springs, store-bought mattresses,
Chinese food, or Halloween.

Chapter 36

Our business

My Uncle Fred and I looked forward to the huge storms in spring and summer, which turned the usually calm ocean into a raging cauldron. In its fury, it ripped out masses of seaweed and deposited it on our beaches. We gazed at the sky quite often and grew excited when dark clouds appeared and the wind started to howl. As soon as the first big storm of the year left our island and took all its anger to another place, the two of us went to work in our little business.

We took Uncle Fred's wooden handcart and borrowed the neighbor's two big, strong dogs to pull the wagon to the beach. My uncle and I sat in the wagon. He controlled the dogs so they wouldn't run too fast, and I held onto our pitchforks.

We stopped at our favorite spot where the seaweed that lends itself best for our job washed onto the beach. My uncle turned the two big dogs loose so they could have some fun. Right away, they ran into the sea, took a good swim, and played with the wave's white combs. We always had fun watching them for a moment or two.

After making sure we had found the right kind of seaweed for the job, we took our shoes and socks off and started our seasonal business. A pitchfork full at a time, we picked up the seaweed from the sandy beach, took it into the salty water and rinsed most of the sand from it. Then we dropped our wet harvest into our cart.

The water felt very cold on my legs, but I didn't worry about that. I looked forward to making some money in these hard times.

When we filled our cart, we took a break and played with the dogs while most of the seawater drained from the cart. Less water made for an easier ride home for the dogs and us.

We threw sticks as far as we could and waited for the dogs to bring them back. I wished so very much that I could have a dog all to myself, but my mom always said dogs needed a lot of food, which we couldn't afford.

Grandma agreed. She even said, "A dog can eat as much as a pig. We wouldn't eat the dog, but we could eat the pig and therefore, we'd waste no money."

As soon as our cart quit dripping, I called the dogs. They obeyed my command, but didn't like being strapped back into their harnesses to pull the cart. I walked next to the dogs, holding the guide leash to lead them home. My uncle pushed on the back end of the cart as much as he could to help the dogs.

Before we reached our village, a woman who walked on the footpath in the fields stopped us to place her order. As we passed our tiny store, the owner came out and placed his big order. In exchange, Uncle Fred got credit at the store for what he needed for his family in the harsh winter months. Some people paid cash for their purchases on our island, but most bartered.

When we arrived home, Grandma handed us a note with an order written on it. The order was from Mister Ed who lived on the east side of the island. He grew a lot of hops and barley and brewed beer.

A strange smell drifted from his place, not sweet like in Grandma's cellar. The two of them got along all right in business matters, but my grandma really did not like Mister Ed at all. She believed that he had killed his young wife by working her to death in his fields. When my grandma believed to know something, no one could change her mind.

With this last order, Uncle Fred and I knew we'd have to get at least another four carts full of seaweed. Our business boomed!

We took the first load of seaweed into our backyard. Uncle Fred hauled the long, shallow wooden box, which had chicken wire on the bottom of it, out of the lean-to. He placed it close to our pump. We took all the seaweed out of the cart and loaded it into the box. Next, I pumped water into a bucket and my uncle poured it over the seaweed to wash out the rest of the sand. Then he cut our harvest into small pieces, about a foot long or so.

In the meantime, I washed out the cart and gave the hard-working dogs some bread with pork grease on it, which they eagerly ate. After that, I took the dogs home to our neighbors and thanked them. I asked them if we could please borrow the dogs four more days.

Our neighbor said, "Yes gladly. The dogs love to get off their chains."

Over the next days, the seaweed dried in the sun and I turned it over twice a day. As soon as it had completely dried, Grandma came into our business. Over the winter, she had hand sewn many sacks from all sorts of strong material in different sizes. She handed us her bundle with a bright smile. Next came a very important part that had to be learned from an expert like my mom, our stuffer.

We could barter a good, thick, evenly-stuffed mattress for a grown goose, two laying hens, garden products, or whatever our family needed. My mom could stuff them perfectly.

At the end of our short seasonal business, my uncle paid me one shiny German mark. I was very proud of that money. Happily, I handed the money over to my mom. At that time, my mom could buy a ten-pound sack of flour for that mark, or a big bucket full of fish to feed us all week long.

What a fine business we had going.

No instant pudding, garden hoses or
patterns to sew or knit clothing by.

Chapter 37

A feathered king

My Aunt Annie had the meanest gander on our island, perhaps the meanest in the whole wide world. Even the big, strong dogs feared him. They had learned as young, playful pups how painful his needle sharp teeth were, especially when he sank them into their ears.

That gander sat mostly hidden away under a bush in his front yard near the dirt road. His long neck allowed him to stick his head clear through the bush to observe his territory without being seen. All feathered creatures were safe from his brutal attacks. I guess he figured they belonged to the same race. But every person or animal, even the milkman's horse, crossed over to the other side of the dirt road out of fear while passing Aunt Annie's house.

Only the unaware or forgetful young ones, like me, dared to walk right by the gander's side of the dirt road. As soon as the alert gander spotted me, he came out from underneath his bush with lightning speed. His fierce, loud, high pitched screams sent shivers through my body. His neck, down almost on the ground and his head held up, let me know that I was in big trouble. With his wings spread out wide, flapping fast, and whirling up the dust on the ground, he instantly attacked my naked legs with his needle-sharp teeth. I screamed in pain.

I tried my best to run away, but he wouldn't let me go. I

stumbled and fell down, head first, into the dirt. He jumped on top of me and sank his sharp teeth deeply into my tender flesh, right through my underpants.

I screamed, and kicked the gander, but he kept biting me until my aunt came to my rescue. One hit with her broom on the gander's neck and he climbed off me. He kept arguing with her while she helped me up from the dirt. Another swift hit with the broom and the gander went home.

Of course he complained loudly about his treatment all the way to his garden. He stopped now and then and turned around, as if to come back and finish his attack, but my aunt held her broom at the ready, which kept him at bay. Still complaining loudly, he waddled back beneath his bush.

My aunt yelled one more time at the gander. "You'll be Christmas dinner if you keep this up," and then she took me into her house.

She cleaned my bleeding wounds, dried my tears, and gave me a big piece of sweet bread, which swam in a plate of warm milk. I quickly forgot my pains.

About that time, we had a new, big cat. She had adopted us shortly before by bringing us a big, fat rat. That cat was the only animal I knew that had the right to walk through the gander's yard.

When they first met, they had a fierce fight in the gander's yard. The gander walked away from the fight with a big gash in his neck and minus one eye. That settled the right of way dispute. I don't think he ever came to like the cat, but he had great respect for her.

The gander had a fine mate. Whenever she sat on their eggs or when their brood hatched, the gander grew extremely protective. At those times, instead of sitting under his bush to wait for a victim to show up, he constantly walked around his territory in attack mode, screaming like a wild beast. Even my aunt had a hard time then to get him inside the stall, particularly if he got too carried away. Sometimes she had to grab him by the neck, put her arm around him and carry him inside the stall. What a disagreeable, loud outcry he made then.

But he could be gentle and loving to his mate. Whenever she sat on her eggs, the gander took short time outs from his vicious patrolling. He shook the dust from his feathers, smoothed them back in place and calmly entered the stall. Gently he walked over to his partner, rubbed his head softly against hers, and whispered sweet things into her ear. She then lifted her wings and stood up just a little. The gander bent down his neck. The goose allowed him to check on the eggs. He looked as though he quietly talked to the eggs. One more gentle rub on his mate's neck and he went back outside to patrol his yard.

As soon as the first gosling hatched, the gander went absolutely nuts. He flew up the stairs to Aunt Annie's front door, knocked at it with his beak and made a loud concert of different sounds until she came to the door. The time of day or night didn't matter to him. When my aunt came outside, he led her to the stall, practically flying all the way with great excitement. He looked around a few times though to make sure she followed him.

Inside the stall, he touched his mate gently with his wing and whispered something to her. She in return lifted her wing on the side where the first hatched gosling lay so my aunt could take a good look at it. The proud gander stood up tall and stretched his long neck high up into the air until my aunt patted him and told him how proud she was of him. From now on, the gander stood close to the stall door and guarded his precious family day and night. I wondered if he ever slept.

When the day arrived to take his mate and their brood out to the nearby pond, people gathered to see the show.

First, out of the stall came the proud, very protective gander. His posture and his high-pitched hissing showed his determination that he would kill whatever or whoever got in his way. With his first jump and his mighty wings spread out wide up into the air, he showed everyone his power. He even ran off the village dogs that had followed the people to see the sight. To give the gander plenty of room and perhaps out of fear, the people stepped back. Seeing his way safe for his family to go to the pond, he called them outside. His mate came out next and then all the cute little goslings followed in a fairly straight row, seeing the outside world for their first time. The very nervous gander flew around his family, showing off his mighty strength. Before he even arrived at the pond with his family, the other users of the pond heard his aggressive warnings and quickly climbed out to safety.

Soon the gander and his family entered the pond. The goslings, a little shy at first, jumped into the water after seeing their parents' example. All the other users of the pond waited patiently in the tall grass for the big gander to calm down, so they could go back inside the pond to enjoy the clear water with all the soft, green, eatable plants.

The gander swam around the pond with his big wings flapping, showing off his strength. He told everyone with his high-pitched screams that he was the king. After everyone showed him great respect by staying out of the pond, he calmed down. Slowly, one by one, the gander granted the waiting occupants of the pond the privilege of entering the sweet water again.

No electric blankets, refrigerators or erasers.

Chapter 38

Our luxury liner.

Our summer came and left us quickly. I went to school early every morning and worked in the fields every afternoon. My mom still lived in the sanatorium, faraway in the mountains.

My grandma and I had a great life together. If the fieldwork ended before twilight, I ran home to join her in her evening walk. We walked along the shore and gathered driftwood to feed grandma's iron stove the next day. On the way home from the beach, I picked all the dandelions I could find to hang up to dry beneath our eaves so we could have some fine teas.

We always stopped by the shallow, clear bay, where we caught a slow fish in our crab net for that night's dinner, or perhaps a bunch of green crabs, which grandma made into a delicious soup. Many times, we sat in the sand after we caught our meal and watched the sun slowly sink into her salty seabed. Grandma answered all my "why" questions and patiently explained things. Oh yes, I loved my grandma. I knew she was the smartest person in the world.

Winter knocked on our door early one night with a vicious hailstorm that brought an end to the fieldwork for me. Since Grandma and I had harvested and gathered all we needed for the long winter months, we had nothing left to do but have fun.

Happy and excited, I walked down to the bay, where I found

some of my friends sitting around, discussing what to do. After I joined them, I suggested all of us should go on a trip around the bay in our luxury liner, a small, discarded, leaky and very old wooden rowboat. Only the top row of wood was missing on the left side. We got our paddles from parts of a clapboard house which had fallen down in a storm and was never rebuilt. We had two old, rusty cans on board to bail out the seawater. We declared ourselves seaworthy and ready to go.

Slowly, we pushed our luxury liner off the tiny islet I named Fillalilla, into the shallow water. After all six of us took off our shoes and socks and left them on the isle, we stuffed our skirts into our underpants so they wouldn't get wet and climbed into our dreamboat. We imagined ourselves the meanest pirates in the world.

We pretended the handful of islets in the bay were important castles and we would conquer those castles and steal all the treasures we pretended existed. With loud, scary screams, we landed and overtook the first islet in no time at all. The imaginary people, the seagulls, flew away the moment they saw us. We killed all the huge, strong ghosts on that isle with our sharp sabers, actually large sticks we kept in our warship for protection. Someone hit me in the head with one of those sharp stick sabers and I fell down into wet sand. They declared me dead on the spot without even asking me. We were a tough bunch.

The next adventure led us to the islet where we would determine the brave leader of our group for this day. We screamed and charged onto the islet, waving our sharp sabers above our heads. Again, the inhabitants of this castle, which knew us as cruel barbarians of the worst kind, left the islet by air in a hurry. Now, we'd see who would be today's bravest.

This islet, just barely above seawater, had a shallow pond in the middle. The water in this pond smelled like sulfur combined with a rotten odor. The water had a pinkish color and the bottom of the pond was not stable. If you stepped into it, you'd slowly sink into the ground.

We gathered around the edge of this stinking body of water, a brave, screaming bunch. Who would be our leader? Together, we walked into the pond. Slowly, we sank into the stinking mess. Staying in the pond until one's knees stuck down into the mess was considered brave. Sinking any farther into it marked the person as definite leadership material.

I slowly sank. Mud covered my knees. I looked around me. Only one other girl remained, and she had sunk in deeper than I had. About that time, I thought I should give up and get out of the pond, not because it scared me, of course. I looked at the other girl, and noticed that she sank very fast.

I hurriedly got out of the pond and screamed for the others. I pointed to the sinking girl. We all got back into the pond to rescue our friend.

We grabbed her by the hands, stepped backward, and slowly with all the strength we had, pulled her out of the pond. What a mess we were. Our rescued buddy had sunk into the stinking pond all the way up to her buttocks, and we declared her the brave leader of the day.

After we cleaned our legs, and rinsed off our muddy skirts and underwear, we put them back on and had a good laugh. But we had all experienced a scary moment.

The next isle, the biggest one, had a fort. Many years ago, the isle had been above sea level and attached to the solid ground of our island. Pirates had built the fort, like so many other forts or castles, and named her Plambeck. Now, only the lookout tower remained above sea level. The ever-changing sea had swallowed up the rest a long time ago.

Here, on top of the lookout tower, we fought demons so strong they could only exist in a child's mind. Our imaginary spears flew high and our enemies died by the dozen and fell into the sea. Finally, after our brave leader declared the castle ours, the fight ended and after a lot of loud victory screams, we climbed down from the tower.

Hungry from all our war games, we got ready to go home, but where was our warship? We walked around the outer stone wall, which sat about two feet under water now, to find our boat. The wide ditch between the stone wall and the castle had been filled with seawater long ago when it was built to keep enemies from entering the castle.

We didn't see our paddleboat until I looked down into the water where we had landed. There she sat, our precious, seaworthy rowboat on the bottom of the bay. We had stayed on the lookout tower too long. The hole in her belly was just too big to leave her sitting in the water by herself for long.

A sadness settled over our little group. Our luxury liner had sunk. We didn't even have a rope to heave her back up. We had no choice but to walk through the cold water, perhaps swim for a while, and then walk home in our wet clothing, unless a miracle happened.

While the daylight slowly disappeared and we stared at our sunken boat, our fearless leader for the day said, "Let us pray for God to help us."

All of us killing pirates bowed our heads and folded our hands. Our leader looked to the heavens and said, "Hello, God, will you please do a little miracle and raise our sunken boat, so we don't have to swim back to our island in this ice cold water. We promise to be good for at least a week. Amen."

We all echoed her "Amen" and stared at our sunken boat while we gave God a little while to send us a small miracle.

When God didn't answer our prayers to lift our boat, and night crept onto our island, we disappointedly decided we had better get home by ourselves before the devil came out with the darkness and stole our souls. We all believed that he liked to pick up small children in the dark of night if they weren't at home.

We, no longer brave pirates, held hands and walked into the ice cold water. As fast as we could, we walked and swam through the deeper parts of the bay's very cold water to reach home before deep darkness engulfed our island.

Happy and relieved, we reached our island. Shivering something awful, we climbed out of the water, took our clothing off, wrung it out and put it back on. Then we brave pirates ran home as quickly as our legs could carry us to avoid getting snatched up by the devil.

No record player, marshmallows,
Velveeta cheese, or blueberries.

Chapter 39

My secret, dark corner.

Through my grandma's window, I watched the first, big, pretty snowflakes of this winter gently fall to earth. My excitement grew as I anticipated sledding down the dike. While I watched the grey world turn into a pretty white one, I heard the wheels of a horse-drawn wagon rumbling down our dirt road. I wondered who could possibly be coming to visit our village. Quickly, my grandma and I threw our coats on and walked outside.

The driver pulled the horses to a stop right in front of our house. Then he stepped down and said, "Erna is home."

Grandma smiled and walked to the back of the wagon with the driver. I just stood there, wondering what the driver meant.

The man lifted a woman out of the back of the wagon and I wondered who she was. In awe, my grandma whispered my mom's name and wiped tears from her face. This woman didn't look like my mom at all.

She had very pale skin, and dark circles surrounded her sad eyes. As thin as a reed, she couldn't even stand on her own. When the driver carried her close to me, she asked him with a very painful face to stop. She ever so gently laid her shaking hand on my head and whispered my name while tears ran down her face.

Shocked, I heard my mom's voice drift from this frail

creature. But this woman looked just like one of our neighbors the day she had died of stomach cancer. People said that she practically starved to death. When the driver carried the woman upstairs and laid her on the small couch in my mom's room, I knew it had to be my mom. Fright and panic took hold of me. I thought she too would soon die. Grandma covered my mom with her feather bedcover and thanked the driver as he left. When my grandma lit our small iron stove, I ran outside to fetch some fresh water to make hot tea for my mom. She shivered so badly, I hoped the hot tea would warm her.

When I entered our little room, my mom lay asleep and my nervous grandma whispered, "I'll come right back."

The little iron stove did its best to warm the room, and I placed the teakettle on the stove to heat the water. Then I took a close look at my mom. To my great relief she continued to breathe. I took our three metal cups and some spoons out of our dish box. Quietly, I left the room to get a handful of the dried dandelions for our tea, which hung under the eaves of our house.

I heard my grandma come back upstairs. She held a bottle in her hand, one of the bottles marked with an "X," which meant for medicinal purposes only. When the two of us entered our little room, we found my mom awake and coughing fiercely. Grandma gave her a big spoonful of the stuff from her brown bottle. Mom leaned up and swallowed it. That took care of her awful cough for now. I brewed some tea for us and Grandma added a little beet sugar to each cup to sweeten the tea.

We both sat by our small table to enjoy our hot drink. My mom sat up a bit by leaning against the wall and enjoyed her hot drink too.

Soon she began to talk. "I stayed at a very nice place among huge mountains in Bavaria. We had plenty of good food to eat. They kept the place warm and very clean. Friendly people took good care of us, but so many died of the tuberculosis. I found that place very scary." Then my mom took a deep breath. "I'm lucky to get out of there alive."

She took another deep breath, opened her jacket, rolled up her heavy undergown, and showed us her upper body. She pointed to the side of her chest that stuck out a little higher and told us that that side now lay still to heal.

Then she explained, "The doctors pushed big needles inside that part of my lung and filled it with air so it couldn't work. The other side of my lung has already healed enough to work, as long as I take it very easy, which means bed rest for now."

My mom spoke about the pain of those injections. Then she mentioned, "Our island doctor will come and administer those injections to me here. I hope that I'll heal enough to have a normal life someday. Perhaps even get a job. "

Tears streamed down her face, and Grandma and I joined in her sadness. Since I couldn't really see my mom's chest from where I sat, I stood up to get a look. What a shock! The whole front of her upper body was bruised and full of big needle marks. Some had healed over, others had not yet, and a few oozed.

I quickly slammed both hands over my mouth to hold back a loud, fearful scream. I clenched my teeth. My mom's chest looked so severely injured and skinny. Fear of her imminent death took hold of me, and I didn't know how to help her. I needed someone to comfort and hold me, but my grandma held Mom's hand to comfort her.

With both of my most important people in the world crying and my mom looking like she was dying, I felt my whole world falling apart. I turned and left our little room in turmoil.

As if in some kind of dream, I took my pillow off my bed and crawled underneath it into the dark, secret corner, where my invisible friend lived. I buried my face in my pillow and cried out for him. He came to me quickly, held me tight and made my gloomy evening bright. He told me that my mom would get well, wiped my tears away, and sang me gently to sleep.

No shoe polish, high school, tartar or cocktail sauce.

Chapter 40

What a Torment

Many eels gathered in our bay in the early winter to spend the coming hostile months in a little better environment than the open sea offered them. They came into our bay very fat and spent the winter on the bottom of the bay in a kind of hibernation. By spring, they had lost all their extra fat and that made them ever so delicious. Now the time had come to catch our share of the eels before they swam out to the deeper ocean again.

It was important to catch them alive. Two people needed to work on this task together. My grandma decided that I had to learn the trade. We took our crab nets, which had tight nettings on them, and a big bucket with a lid on it and walked down to our bay.

There we picked up two big stones. I placed one stone inside the bucket to hold it steady in the shallow seawater, and used the other to secure the lid on top of the bucket. Soon we had our socks and shoes off and slowly walked into the frigid water. We lifted our skirts and secured them in our underpants to keep them dry.

Just after the saltwater reached above my knees, we stopped. Grandma let some water run into the bucket and sat it down. Ever so slowly, we lowered our nets into the water. Patiently, we waited for the disturbed water to clear up again.

Grandma explained, "The male eel is skinny and can get a yard or so long. The female eel is about half that long, but she has much more meat on her, therefore, we want her for the smoking barrel. We either pickle or fry the long male eels. The very young eel we let loose so they can grow some more."

The sea cleared up quickly, and we saw our first eel about two steps away from us. We lowered our nets into the water. Ever so slowly, we stepped closer to the sleeping eel. When close enough, Grandma gently placed her net in front of the eel and I placed mine at its tail. With a nod of Grandma's head, we quickly slammed our nets together perfectly, just as we had practiced on land on the way down here.

The eel had no escape. Into the bucket he went. I quickly put the lid on top of the bucket and secured it with the other heavy stone.

What luck. Before we froze too much, we had filled our bucket and we walked home. On our way home, the seawater from the bucket slowly leaked out through a little hole Grandma had punched into the bucket long ago. Before we arrived home, all the water in the bucket had run out. Those eel could live for a long time out of the seawater, perhaps two days or so.

They were very slimy, great escape artists, and very smart. They understood that the lid of the bucket opened and sometimes got their strength together to lift it and escape.

At home, Grandma took a shovelful of the salt and dumped it into the bucket with the live eels. She did that so the eel would rub off all their slime in the salt. All hell broke loose in the bucket.

The poor eel tried to get away from the salt, which burned their eyes, their skin, and the inside of their mouths. The whole bucket rocked, and I heard their bodies slapping against the lid to escape this gruesome torture. Grandma just put another big stone on top of the bucket. Then she went inside and made herself a cup of coffee out of burned wheat. Real coffee beans didn't make it to our island very often.

I watched the eel racing around in the bucket wildly with the salt obviously causing them tremendous pain. I felt so guilty, because I helped to catch them. I wanted so much to let them go back into the sea so they could clean the salt off their bodies and stop the horrible pain. I thought about kicking the bucket over to let the poor eel escape.

At that moment, my grandma came outside. She saw the tears in my eyes, took me by my hand and led me inside. She said, "Girl, the eel don't feel a thing."

That was the first time in my young life that I didn't believe my grandma. What a sad and disappointing moment for me.

The year before, I saw a very strong eel, wild with pain, lifting the lid just slightly and slide out of the bucket, but nothing had prepared me for what I saw next. The moment I stepped back outside, the whole bucket fell over.

I screamed for my grandma and she came in a hurry. All our eel slid away quickly. What a strange, sad sight, to see the salt covered, hurting eel, most likely blind now, trying to escape from their great pain. They all slid into Grandma's front yard among her tulips.

My grandma shouted for help and neighbors came in a hurry. Everyone helped to catch the eels. I caught one but it slithered right out of my hands. Before long, darkness came and we gave up the search. We had caught twenty but five were still missing. Grandma put a little more coarse salt into the bucket and secured the lid with two huge stones.

What an ever so cruel way for the desperately fighting eel to spend their last night. Early the next morning, Grandma relieved the eel from their torture. She took the still barely fighting eel out of the bucket one by one. She slit their bellies open, ripped out their guts, rinsed them off under the pump, put a rod through the eyes of the females and hung them inside the smoking barrels. She cut the males' heads off and ripped their guts out. Then she cut them into small pieces and dropped them into her cook pot. They no longer struggled. Their pain had ended but what a terrible way to die.

Sadly, I walked into our outhouse to relieve myself. When I sat down on the freshly washed bench, something wet touched my naked buttocks. I jumped up and screamed like hell! Looking down at the fairly full bucket, I saw a huge eel sticking its head up, looking back at me.

Grandma opened the outhouse door to see what had caused me to scream so desperately and I pointed to the bucket. Surprised, Grandma reached inside the bucket and pulled the huge eel out. She rinsed him off underneath the pump, cut his head off, gutted him and cut him into small pieces. With a satisfied grin, she threw the pieces into her pot to fry or pickle with the rest.

That night I had terrible dreams. I dreamt that a huge eel tried to swallow me while I sat down in the outhouse. I couldn't move away from it. That frightened me so badly that my loud screams woke everyone in our house.

I didn't visit our outhouse for many days. I did my business behind the bushes out in the fields. When my mom noticed my strange behavior, she assured me with a calm voice that our new cat just brought the last eel home and ate it. What a great relief.

For the next days, my grandma had neighbors helping her catch the eel, prepare them, fry and pickle them.

She told my Uncle Fred, "Take the girl with you."

We had charge of hauling in sawdust from anyone who had some, to feed the smoking barrel. I felt much better doing this instead of catching the poor critters. Grandma herself handled the smoking barrels. A day or so later the fish men arrived in their truck. They bought all the smoked, pickled and fried eel we had, and a good supply of grandma's liquors. Before they left, all the adults sat down, passed a bottle around from grandma's cellar, and the fish men told stories, which everyone listened to in surprise, well into the deep night. They called those stories news.

How I long for a piece of such deliciously smoked eel today.

No Dairy Queen, raspberries or meatloaf.

Chapter 41

Never again!

By 1953, the year of my tenth birthday, my four best friends and I had grown pretty brave as a group, and we had the constant need to prove our bravery to each other.

One nice, calm Sunday afternoon, as we sat down by the harbor, eating our stolen carrots and trying to figure out what we could do next, one of my friends came up with the idea that we should paddle out to the forbidden sea burial grounds to have a look around. What a scary idea.

All my friends agreed, but I really didn't want to go there. But, if I refused, they'd have laughed at me and teased me. So, I took a deep breath and bravely said, "Yes, let's go!"

After our luxury liner sank on one of our earlier adventures, my uncle had raised it and nailed part of a wooden plank over the hole. We were very glad to have our fine boat back, and it didn't matter to us that it still leaked. In no time at all, we pushed our old rowboat into the bay, and I took my turn as navigator. Two of my friends paddled, and the others constantly scooped seawater out of the boat.

When we left our protected bay, I took a good look around the sky. I hoped to see dark clouds on the horizon so I could cancel this trip, but saw no sign of a storm brewing anywhere. Only happy little white clouds danced over a calm ocean.

Though scared, I declared in a bold voice, "It's safe to go on with our great adventure."

We all raised our right arms into the air and fearlessly screamed, "Yeah, here we go!"

I wondered if my friends had the same frightening feelings that I did, or if they really felt that brave.

We rowed for quite a while to reach the sea burial grounds. Too soon for me the black buoys with white crosses on them which clearly marked the sea burial ground, slowly swayed up and down in the ocean right next to us. I wanted to turn around. I had the feeling that others felt the same way, but I didn't dare voice my uneasiness. Everyone wore a somber expression as we slowly entered the forbidden grounds.

Our makeshift paddles rested inside our boat now. With our heads hanging over the side searching for something out of the ordinary, we slowly drifted inside the forbidden zone.

One of my friends said, "We'd better not touch the seawater. God could be mad at us for coming inside the burial grounds. Maybe He has sent the devil down below into the deep water to wait for us."

Another girl with a shaking voice said, "The moment we reach down into the water, the devil could snatch our hands, pull us down into the sea and take us to hell."

Hurriedly, we all agreed not to touch the water.

The calm sea now looked like a mirror. We could see the sandy bottom and the reefs filled with schools of tiny, silvery fish trying to escape the jaws of bigger fish. Behind boulders and inside many crevices of the reef, crabs of all sizes waited for dinner to float by. A huge sea eel came gliding by. With his pointed snout, he sucked out a fine meal of crabs from the crevices.

As we drifted into a deeper channel, we saw huge boulders in the water and deep green sea grass growing in the seabed. Suddenly, in the sea grass between two boulders, I saw two skulls and many bones scattered about.

Shivering with fear, I quickly pointed the location out to my friends. We all looked at the bones in dread. One of the skulls was very tiny and the other one fully grown. My mind raced back to my Aunt Martha at her tiny baby's sea funeral. I wondered if these skulls belonged to them. If so, how could the baby be reborn without its skull?

At that moment, our paddleboat hit a boulder. We capsized and went down into the sea, into the water we were not going to touch out of fear of the devil. I just knew my life would end right there and then.

As I drifted toward the seabed, I looked for the devil to come out from behind a boulder and grab me to take me to hell. I wished so awfully much that I had not come on this trip. When my feet touched the sea grass and I saw the skulls lying right next to me, panic set in. I needed to get out of this water before the devil noticed me.

With all my strength, I pushed up from the grassy bottom with fear spreading quickly through me. My hearth raced and my whole body shook. With a loud scream, I reached the surface relieved to have escaped the clutches of the devil. I took a few long breaths of the sweet air.

When I looked around, I saw all my friends clinging to our capsized boat. I saw tears rolling down some of their faces. Fear still raced through my body, but I also felt grateful to see all four of them alive. I silently thanked God for not sending the devil after us and for not sinking our rowboat.

Gently, we rocked our boat off the boulder and put her upright. She was damaged on the top right side, but that wouldn't keep us from climbing inside and paddling out of there. But where were our important rusted cans? We all looked around in dismay. Without the cans, we'd never make it out of this forbidden place. One look below and I saw one of our precious cans lying on a boulder, but I didn't see the other.

Happy to see at least one, I pointed it out to my friends. Everyone looked at me and begged me to dive down to fetch the rusty old can, our lifesaver. Not even thinking about the devil now,

I dove down and fetched the can. Coming up quickly, I saw a huge sea eel gliding toward me. Was it the devil in disguise? Before I could take a second look, my head bobbed above the surface.

We struggled to get back inside our boat. When all of us had settled in safely, we noticed that we had also lost our makeshift paddles. We searched the ocean around us, but they were nowhere in sight.

As the sun slowly sank in the west, the wind began to pick up. Dark clouds came up on the horizon and moved toward us. I told everyone except Angie who hurriedly ladled the water out of our boat, to hang over the side and use their hands for paddles.

Ever so slowly and in silence, we paddled our way out of the forbidden burial grounds. Once out of the frightening boundaries, we breathed a big sigh of relief and began to talk again. Darkness closed in, and in the distance, we saw the blinking entry light to our bay, showing us our way home. Short, bluish lightning zigzagged across the sky behind us, and I worried that we might not make it home safely.

Suddenly, a gust of wind changed course slightly to our advantage. With the help of the wind and holding the bigger parts of our clothes up for sails, we soon entered our bay. Exhausted, hungry, and shivering, we landed safely in our harbor. We walked home in our wet clothing, glad to be alive. Never did any of us suggest a visit to the forbidden sea burial grounds again.

No dentist, radar, or nail file.

Chapter 42

The king's horse that spoke to me.

By late summer, everyone had harvested all their fruits and vegetables. My mom still rested on her couch most of the time, and I did what little housework we had to do. Every morning before I went to school, I hauled wood and water upstairs and took the dirty water back downstairs

After school, I worked in the fields trying to find potatoes, or anything else edible that someone had left behind by mistake, to eat or to take to our little store to sell. With the little money I made and a lot of help from relatives and neighbors, we barely got by.

One night I heard my mom saying to my grandma, "The winter months will be very hard on Edith and me. Soon she'll no longer find a handful of eatables in the fields. She needs winter clothing and a lot more food to eat than we have." With her voice shaking, my mom asked my grandma, "Please mail this letter for me. I'm desperate and I need to ask our doctor for help."

I wondered if she had decided to send me away to live with one of my aunts and uncles like she did with my sister. I really didn't want to leave my home ever again. The long, terrible time I spent in the sanatorium remained very clear on my mind.

Many days later, my mom sent me to the ferryboat to see if her medicine arrived. I borrowed a neighbor's dog and walked to the ferry landing. The little dog and I sat down in the sand to await the ferry's arrival. I liked this gentle dog a lot, and we loved to run together. How I wished to have this dog for my own.

Soon, I heard the ferry coming. I stood up and could barely believe what I saw. A beautiful, tall black horse stood on the deck. Though smaller than our plow horses, it looked so elegant, just like the king's horses in my grandma's stories.

Was a king coming to our island? My excitement grew. But, where was the king? As I turned to run home and tell everyone about our visitor, the king, I realized that I had to check if Mom's medication had arrived.

I hurried down to the landing to meet the ferry that brought a beautiful horse. From around the ferryman's steering hut came a tall, young man dressed in a fine riding outfit and a hat. That had to be the king. Sure enough, he walked over to the beautiful horse and led it off the ferry. I stood in amazement. Though not quite as elegantly dressed as in my grandma's stories, he was nevertheless very handsome.

Perhaps he had come to take me away to his beautiful castle. Hurriedly, I wiped the sand from my dress to look presentable. The ferryman walked beside the king with a bag in his hands. When he saw me, he walked over to me with the king and the pretty black horse.

Flabbergasted, I couldn't even say hello. The ferryman introduced me to the king. The king reached down and shook my hand.

He said, "I'm the doctor from the health center. I've come to check on your mother and a few other people. Would you be so kind as to show me the way to your house?"

I managed to stutter, "Yes, of course."

The king mounted his beautiful, black horse and as I made ready to run ahead of him to show him the way, he asked me with a warm smile, "Would you like to ride in back of me on my horse?"

"Oh yes, I'd surely like that!" I answered in surprise.

The ferryman helped me onto the horse. He then handed the king my mom's medication, which he stuck in his saddlebag.

"All right, young lady. Hold on tight to me."

I did so with great pleasure.

As the king and I rode to our house on his beautiful, black horse, I felt like the luckiest girl in the whole wide world. The neighbor's dog ran ahead of us, barking with excitement. I wondered why a king worked in a health center. Since I couldn't figure out what a health center was, I quickly gave that thought up. I hoped the king came to take me with him to his big, beautiful castle and make me his queen, just like in my grandma's stories.

Too soon for me, we arrived at our village. The neighbor's dog, still leading the way, barked insistently, and people came out of their houses to see what was going on. They looked up to the king and me, smiled and waved. The villagers whispered and pointed at me. What a moment in my young life. I felt so important and rich, like in my mind a queen would feel.

When we reached our house, my exciting wishful trip ended. In front of our house, with all the village children watching, the king helped me down from his beautiful, black horse and I became a plain girl again.

Grandma stood in front of our house to meet the king, and all our neighbors approached. Everyone admired that shiny, black horse and all the children wanted to touch him. The king let them gently touch his horse. Then he tied it to a tree in front of our house.

He turned to me. "Would you please fetch a bucket of water for my horse?"

I nodded and gladly did so in a hurry.

When I set the bucket of water down in front of the king's horse, he took a good, long look at me with his fiery wild, dark eyes. I stepped back a little out of fear.

When the king went inside our house, I told all the children, "This is the king's horse."

"How do you know that? How can you tell?" they asked.

I looked the black horse straight into his wild eyes and asked, "Are you the horse of a king?"

The horse nodded his head up and down and whinnied loudly.

A wave of astonished mumbles came over the village children, making this another great moment in my young life. The king's beautiful horse talked to me. With a proud, satisfied smile, I walked inside our house.

Upstairs in our little room, my grandma and the king sat at the table next to my mom's bed. They stopped talking for a moment when I walked inside.

"Excuse me," I said to the king. "Are you really a king and will you take me with you to your big, beautiful castle? I need to know so I can get ready and pack my belongings."

Everyone smiled at me and laughed.

Slowly my grandma explained, "This man is not a king. He's a doctor here to help your mom and to check on her health."

Her answer disappointed me, but I wasn't too sad. I decided I really wanted to stay here with my family anyway.

The man checked my mom's chest with a strange, round thing at one end, which he moved around on my mom's lungs, and two little knobs on the other end, which he stuck into his ears. I wondered what my mom's lungs told him. Then he took some blood out of her arm with a big needle and looked around our little room and at me.

I suddenly feared that he'd stick that huge needle into my arm and ran out of the room in a great hurry.

My grandma came after me and shouted, "That nice man wants to ask you something, so get back up here!"

Reluctantly, I followed my grandma's orders.

When I slowly walked back into Mom's room, I stood by the door, just in case he decided to come toward me with that huge needle.

Then the man smiled and asked me, "Would you like to go on

a vacation this winter, faraway to Bavaria where the huge mountains reach up into the sky? A train will take you there, and you'll live with a lot of other children in a wonderful place."

I said, "No thank you, I need to stay here and take care of my mom."

At that time, the German welfare system often sent poor children and adults to very nice facilities to rest, recuperate and get away from their daily humongous health or financial problems. They hoped that with some weeks of care, good nutritious meals, doctors to help with their physical problems, medications, and advice on how to cope better in the situations they left behind, they'd grow strong again. Perhaps they'd learn in a relaxing, fun time, to handle the stress of life better at home. The government offered this completely free of charge to the poor.

Often, sending the children away from ill, poor, or suffering parents gave them a rest from the responsibility of feeding and managing their children for a while so they could recover themselves. I don't know if this help is still available to the poor people in Germany.

At any rate, after my answer, the health care man went silent. He took some papers and an envelope out of his saddlebag. I watched him over his shoulder writing Mom's name down and where we lived.

He handed my mom some money and told her, "You'll get the same amount sent to you here every month by mail until you can work again. When your doctor declares you healed, the money will stop."

Now tears ran down my mom's face, but she smiled. My mom looked at me with her wet, smiling face and said, "Please go on this nice vacation. You deserve to go and have a good time. Grandma will help me here."

I looked over at my grandma and she nodded at me.

I asked the health care man, "Is that place in the mountains a sanatorium?"

He smiled warmly and said, "No child, it's a big, warm house where lots of kids get together for a short while to have some fun. They have plenty of good food, a lot of toys, shoes and clothing. You won't have to bring anything. The government pays for everything."

One more look at my mom's wet nodding face and I said, "Yes, I'll go."

Grandma left the room and touched my head gently. "I'll be right back."

I had only agreed to go on this vacation to do my mom and my grandma a favor, though it scared me and I really rather would have stayed at home. However, the mention of plentiful food sounded great to me. A long time had passed since we had enough to eat. The health care center man wrote down some instructions and handed them to my mom.

Grandma came up with some plain tea. I wondered why she hadn't brought up some sweets from her cellar to celebrate as she usually did on happy occasions. After everyone drank their tea, Grandma gave the health care man directions to the other people he wanted to see. Those people would also welcome him and most likely invite him and his beautiful horse to spend the night. Outside, everyone still admired the shiny, black horse and we all bid the pair farewell. I never told anyone that he really wasn't a king's horse, and for me, he'd forever remain just that, a king's horse that spoke to me, a child's wishful imagination. Slowly, into the calm evening, the king rode away on his beautiful, black horse with the deep, shiny eyes.

No copy machine, Cheerios or Valentines.

Chapter 43

The celebration.

After the health care man rode away on the king's beautiful black horse, I turned to my friends and told them about my upcoming vacation to where the mountains reached into the sky.

Some of them pleaded, "Take me with you!"

Others laughed at me and said, "No one in our fishing village goes away on vacation. We're all poor people. Where do you think you're going to get the money from?"

I answered, "The government will pay for it."

Now all the children laughed even louder and walked away. I started to wonder who the government was and how he got so rich that he could pay for my vacation.

Seeing my Uncle Fred coming home made me forget about the government, and I ran toward him. He walked through our village every late afternoon, pulling his cart with smoked fish behind him trying to sell all the fish my grandma had smoked in her barrels since long before dawn.

When I reached him, he stopped and asked me, "Why are you in such a great hurry, girl?"

Quickly I told him all about the day's events.

He laughed. "Oh, my, we need to celebrate!"

Before we even reached home, I heard laughter in our house, a sound that always made me feel so good. My uncle handed me the four smoked mackerels he hadn't sold and asked me to take them inside. The mackerels looked so delicious I hoped that we could afford to eat them tonight.

Inside, I saw three women sitting together around my uncle's kitchen table having tea. A bottle with a reddish content stood on the table. This time they drank tea spiced with sweets from Grandma's cellar. Seeing my mom among them lounging in a chair, especially surprised me. This was the first time I saw her downstairs since she had come back from the sanatorium.

My Aunt Hilde asked me to fetch a bunch of onions that hung in the lean-to. When I came back inside, I saw my mom actually sitting up in a chair by the iron stove now. She added a big amount of pork grease to a huge frying pan. Now I knew that we'd celebrate and have plenty to eat tonight.

My aunt added the sliced, raw potatoes and the chopped onions to the hot grease in the black frying pan. The wet vegetables meeting the hot grease caused quite some spitting and splattering. I worried that my mom, sitting so close to the frying pan, could get hurt, but she sat and smiled, still looking ever so frail. With a flat wooden spoon in her hand, she slowly stirred the vegetables.

My aunt kept a watchful eye on my mom as she took part in her first activity since she had come home from that institution. I was so thankful to see her out of her bed.

Grandma almost constantly fed the little iron stove, and it grew nicely warm in the kitchen. We could even take our jackets off. Then my earlier wish came true as my uncle took a cutting board from the wall and divided the smoked mackerels into many different sized pieces.

Then he pushed the cutting board to the middle of the table, sat down and lit part of a green cigar. He liked to smoke. His young children climbed onto his lap and laughed at the smoke clouds he exhaled for them in different shapes and forms.

Grandma started to whistle a tune, and everyone began to sing.

We considered ourselves great singers and took singing seriously. We sang loud, not always in tune, but we had fun. I longingly gazed at all the fish pieces and the big pan, full to the brim, with potatoes and onions, and my mouth watered. I felt awfully hungry.

Before long, the whole kitchen had a wonderful smell from the frying pork grease. I hurried upstairs and fetched a plate and fork for my mom and myself.

Soon, we all sat down for our celebration dinner. The adults filled the chairs around the kitchen table, and we five children sat on the kitchen floor and used a bench as our table.

Grandma filled our plates with fried potatoes and a generous piece of smoked mackerel. We passed around a steaming teapot that smelled of peppermint tea. I stood up and filled all of us children's metal mugs half full, just as my mom had taught me long ago.

We lifted our metal cups up high while my grandma stood up and spoke. She placed her hands together, lifted her head up to look at the ceiling and said, "Thanks for sending the health care center man and for letting my daughter receive some money to support herself."

Then we all took a drink of the fine sweet tea. Again my grandma looked back up at the ceiling, and with one little tear rolling down her cheek she said solemnly, "Special thanks for letting my daughter get well again and letting my granddaughter, Edith, go on a vacation to Bavaria, where the mountains reach into the sky."

We all said thanks and took another drink. I hoped my grandma had finished thanking, because I heard my stomach growl. The food on my plate looked so great and there was so much of it.

Finally, Grandma started to sit down. In a hurry I grabbed my fork and heaped it full of potatoes. I had nearly shoved it into my mouth when my grandma changed her mind about sitting down. There I sat, my first bite in front of my mouth, so awfully hungry, and my grandma stood up with her cup held up high again.

Disappointed, I put my filled fork back on my plate. Grandma stood there, looking like she forgot something. Suddenly, she seemed to remember. She smiled and said, "Thanks, Lord and please watch over Grandpa!" Finally, she sat down all the way.

The exciting feast began. Before I had halfway finished eating my delicious and plentiful food, one of the children moved and the bench with all our food on it tipped over. What a disaster! All the plates with the great food and the mugs scattered all over the kitchen floor. Just as I felt the tears form in my eyes, my aunt and my grandma came to our rescue.

"Okay, children. Stand back."

We all backed away from the mess. Then they picked the food off the floor with their hands and placed it back on our plates. They righted the bench and quickly cleaned the floor with some rags. When the women had finished, they told us all to sit back down and finish eating.

I ate everything on my plate and wondered if I could have seconds, but knew better than to ask for it because everyone considered that bad manners, so I just sat in my place and waited. The two younger boys stood up and went outside to play while the three of us girls sat and waited in silence for more food.

Before long, my aunt looked over at us. She stood up, grabbed the frying pan and gave us each another heaping spoonful of fried potatoes. We thanked her and ate all of it. Everyone in our house had plenty to eat and drink that night.

All warm, well fed, and thankful, the adults sent the little children to bed and then settled in to play cards. I washed the dishes and saved all the mackerel bones and the few non-edible parts of the fish for Grandma's cat. That night, Grandma would let her sleep inside instead of making her go outside to hunt for her supper. One lucky mouse would live another night.

Soon, my Aunt Hilde carried my sleeping mom upstairs and laid her on her bed. When I opened the back door to empty out the dirty water from the bowl I had washed the dishes in, Grandma's cat came inside. She took one sniff and hurried into the kitchen. When I walked back inside, I gave the cat a plate full of fish bones, heads, fins and some skin. She quickly busied herself over her plate, just as I had done over mine.

After watching her for a moment, I joined the adults in a card game and Grandma poured a small amount of her great tasting strawberry liquor into my mug. There we sat, in the warm, smoke filled kitchen, our bellies full, happy, contented, and playing cards. Grandma cheated like hell, but we all knew it. The trick was to out cheat her, which I never fully learned.

Soon midnight came and our celebration ended. I walked upstairs, checked on my mom and went to bed. That night the beautiful, shiny, king's horse came to me. I jumped on top of him. He spread his huge, black wings wide and we flew away to a castle made of sugar and cocoa.

No flea collars, napkins, or mayonnaise.

Chapter 44

The great fear.

Slowly my mom recovered from the drastic effects of the tuberculosis. Before long, with someone's help, she could bundle up and very slowly walk outside to sit in the front yard of our house for a while. She enjoyed the different view and the fresh, cool winds, all clear signs of the coming winter. I often sat beside her shelling peas or beans, or doing some other chores that didn't need my close attention. Some days we worked on schoolwork together if I didn't have to write things down. During this time, my mom taught me the multiplication tables, how to spell a few new words, and she taught me their meanings.

I noticed that while we sat out there together, our neighbors shied away from us. They often crossed over to the other side of the road, lowered their heads, and quickly passed our house. Most people didn't want anything to do with my mom. Not even my friends were allowed to come to our house to play since my mom had come home from the sanatorium.

As we sat out there, Mom often raised her hand and loudly sent a greeting across the dirt road to someone who passed by our house. But no greeting ever came in return. No one ever came to visit her, and when two of her old friends walked by and didn't reply to her greetings, I saw tears in my mom's eyes. She looked so sad and I felt very bad for her.

I softly reached for her hand and asked, "What's the matter, Mom?"

With her voice shaking she said, "The people shy away from me and the other people who had TB, because they're afraid we can still infect them. They don't believe we're cured."

I felt so sorry for my mom. Our neighbors' reaction to her not only deeply hurt her, but left her very lonely. I talked to our neighbors and told them that my mom said she could no longer infect anyone, but still nobody stopped by to say hello or just acknowledge her greetings while walking by.

I asked my grandma and my Uncle Fred what I could do to make the people change their mind and they told me that people might listen to the island doctor, our witch, or our preacher, preferably all three together at the church. People usually had more respect for things said inside the church.

The next day, I sat down and wrote a letter to our island doctor and asked his help for my mom and other people on our island. I took my letter to our nurse to get the doctor's address. She wrote it down for me on an envelope, told me to put the letter inside of it and take it to our mailman. A week later, our mailman arrived in his little boat. I proudly handed him my letter and the pennies it cost to mail it.

One Sunday morning not long after I mailed my letter to our doctor, our special bell rang in our tall church tower shortly before the scheduled service. That signaled everyone to the church now, including the men. Something important either had happened or was about to happen.

Before long, our church had filled with people. When I entered, I saw our island witch sitting on a pillar by the huge pipe organ, her favorite place. People huddled together in fear. They whispered and wondered what was about to happen. Fear rippled through me as well. Perhaps I had done something so terribly wrong that everyone needed to know, even our island witch. In my mind, she was more important than God. She really could change things, whereas God, so far in my life, never did, even though I had asked Him many times.

A hush fell over the crowd when the preacher and our island doctor entered the church. Together they walked up the stairs to the pulpit, which stood quite a bit above from where we sat. When they reached the pulpit, our island witch played a few deep notes on the huge pipe organ to remind everyone of her presence as well.

Those dramatic, short notes, with their deep sounds, shook everyone. They grabbed me by my neck and put goose bumps all over my body. It was scary, very scary. In my imagination, those notes were the song people heard as they entered hell.

After the witch's short, scary introduction, the preacher's voice thundered.

"Something is wrong on our little island. I want you all to listen to what our island doctor has to say and listen well to his words."

I swallowed hard and hoped very much that I was not in trouble, such big trouble that the three very important people on our island had to get together in our church. My mind raced back over recent things that I had done which fell into the bad behavior area. Before I could figure anything out, the doctor started to speak.

I couldn't believe my ears at first. Our island doctor spoke about the letter I had written to him! I wasn't in trouble at all. What a relief.

In a slow, loud, commanding voice, he explained that all the people and children who had come home from the sanatoriums had come home healed and that they could no longer infect anyone else.

Then our preacher took over. With his fist held high, he said, "All of you better treat each other like brothers and sisters. Amen!"

He then slowly stepped back, while our island witch stepped forward. A hush spread through the people. Most of them bent their heads out of respect and to avoid looking directly into her face. Only those she blessed looked directly at her. There she stood, glancing over her flock. She lifted her right hand and pointed down at us.

With her loud voice echoing through our church, everyone clearly heard her command to treat the healed with dignity and without fear. Even those few who stood just outside the door heard her.

People nodded in agreement and some softly mumbled, "Yes, of course."

Then the preacher and the doctor walked down from the pulpit, one behind the other. I waited for our island witch to come walking down those stairs, but she just disappeared.

Soon a church bell announced the start of Sunday service with her happy sound. At that signal, all the men inside the church walked out to go across the dirt road to the town's tavern for their church service.

People whispered among each other. Our island doctor walked straight toward me and shook my hand. "Thank you for your letter, Edith. You have helped to right a great wrong."

I stared at him in disbelief.

"Would you like to come with me for a treat at the tavern?"

I smiled. "Yes, thank you."

Our island doctor held my hand as we walked from the church and across the dirt road. When we entered the small tavern, all the men stopped talking and stared at us.

The doctor announced, "This little girl bravely told me about the trouble on the island, and I'm very proud of her."

His words and attention quite embarrassed me, but it felt very good.

The doctor walked me up to the bar, picked me up and sat me on a tall chair. He ordered a beer for himself and hot milk and cookies for me.

As soon as we had our drinks, he lifted his glass, turned around to the men and said, "Let's drink to our brave little girl,

Edith."

Everyone lifted their glasses and toasted my way. I didn't know what to do, so I just sat and smiled.

As I slowly drank my hot milk and ate the delicious cookies, I looked around the room. I knew everyone very well. I recognized all the liquor bottles on the shelf. I had helped my grandma collect the fruits and berries to make those sweet, colored drinks. I knew that they tasted great. I didn't like the sharp, biting taste of the light brown liquor in one of the other bottles.

As I looked at everyone and everything around me, I thought this a strange place to worship. All the men talked at the same time, and this tavern didn't even have a pulpit. I wondered why the men didn't join the women in our beautiful, huge church to worship.

Then I realized that every man held a mug or glass with something to drink, and that answered my question. There was absolutely nothing to drink in our church. I decided to ask my grandma about this matter as soon as I saw her.

I felt uncomfortable inside the tavern and was glad when our church bells announced the end of our Sunday service. All the men left the tavern to escort their loved ones home. I thanked the doctor for the milk and cookies and ran home. By the time I reached home, word had passed already on to my mom of what had happened before today's church service. How fast news can travel, even without a single telephone on our island. She smiled at me and gave me a long hug. She thanked me and told me that I had made her very proud.

Then I heard my grandma coming upstairs. I opened the door for her. She carried a pot of fragrant, hot coffee made from burned wheat.

When we sat down by our table, I asked my grandma, "Why don't we serve drinks in our church like they do in the tavern so the men can worship with their families?"

Both my grandma and my mom laughed out loud. When they

finally stopped laughing my grandma said, "Men consider themselves strong and so they don't think they need God. They can take care of their own problems. But they think of women as weak and in need of help from God to get along in this world."

Then they both started to laugh again.

My mom said, "I've seen many weak men in my life."

Grandma nodded. "Yes, I know what you mean."

Now that completely confused me.

After that day in the church, it still took a while before all the people on our island came around and associated with the survivors of the tuberculosis, but eventually they did. Nevertheless, things got better, and I was very proud of myself for writing the letter to our island doctor.

No barbeque grill, charcoal,
cornstarch, or asparagus.

Chapter 45

The treasure hunt.

A month or so before my tenth birthday, on a day too cold to go for a swim, I decided to walk to the east side of our island, to a stand of very tall pine trees I loved to climb. But first, I decided to look for treasures in the dark forest.

After sticking my noon meal, a pork grease sandwich, into my pants pocket, I started on my way. I carefully and quietly walked around the stone mound graves, so as not to wake the grouchy old ghost. Then I sneezed, a sound that would wake the old ghost for sure.

I began to run when I heard him grumble. He threw stones at me. I ran faster. One stone hit my back hard. I stumbled, but steadied myself quickly and ran on. One big jump over the next ditch brought me out of his territory. Nobody ever saw that old ghost. He slept most of the time, but when awakened, he threw many stones at the intruders.

Glad to be out of the ghost's reach and only feeling slight pain from the stone bruise, I walked toward the tall pine trees. When I entered the great-smelling pine forest, I started to look for treasures. Right away, I found an arrowhead in the dugout dirt of someone's den. I turned it over in my hand and found it to be in great shape and the biggest one I had ever found. To see if I could find more treasures lying around, I stuck my head inside the den, but didn't see any. An upset porcupine, the occupant of this den, snorted at me. I retreated in a hurry.

After searching a while longer for treasures and not finding any, I decided to climb the tallest pine tree and look out at the mighty ocean. I picked a tree that had branches all the way down its trunk to the forest floor and stood at the edge of the steep coastline. In no time at all, I climbed to the highest branch that could still support me. What a sight!

On this clear day, I could see all the way to the far northern horizon. I saw a faint, grey line, the south coast of Denmark, and wondered what that land looked like. I hoped to travel there someday. Far to the east, I saw the faint line of an island in East Germany, which at this time belonged to Russia. Someday I wanted to travel there too.

On the open ocean, merchant ships glided northward with their white sails billowing in the wind. I thought what a wonderful thing it would be to sail on one of those ships. I wanted to see the whole world so badly. Many of the older boys on our island who left after basic education hired on to work on those ships. Perhaps I could dress up like a boy and someone could hire me on someday.

The ocean's dark blue water gently rushed onto the shore with just a whisper. A strange sound came with the whispering waves, though. I listened closer. There it was again. I heard the whining and faint barking of a dog, as though it needed help.

I looked down the steep coast. There, way below me, among the grey boulders in the seawater, stood a black dog on one of the taller rocks. The dog faced the open ocean and looked down into the water. I saw blood on the stone where he stood and one of his hind legs hung down in an odd way. That dog needed help.

Carefully, but in a hurry, I climbed down the tall pine tree. I looked again and could see the dog more clearly. He tried to get off the big stone at the side that faced out to sea. As loud as I could, I called down to the dog, hoping it would turn around toward me and slide off the lower part of the big rock by itself. The black dog stopped his crying briefly and looked toward me. Quickly he looked back down into the seawater and his barks and pleading cries grew more intense.

I looked down the very steep coast for a way to get down to the sea to help the dog off the rock, but saw no easy way. If I just had a rope, I could tie it to a tree to support myself and walk down the steep coast backwards.

The closest village was a long walk away, even if I had enough courage to walk through the ghost's territory. I decided against that. I took a deep breath and screamed for help. There came no answer except the dog's begging cries. He scratched on the stone desperately now, as if to get down into the shallow water, but I couldn't figure out why on the side that faced out to sea.

I screamed for help one more time. The deep patch of pine trees swallowed my voice and returned no answer.

From all the scratching on the grey boulder, the black dog started to bleed on his front paws now. That was it. I needed to get down this very steep coast to rescue the dog.

Slowly, I sat down on the edge of a little overhang. I made the first jump from that overhang to a small bush easily enough. Now came the real steep part. Without much to hold onto, I lay on my back and started to slide down. I braced myself on anything I could get a hold of with my feet or hands and landed down in the shallow water with a splash. Gladly I noticed that I made it down here with just a few scrapes and bruises.

When the black dog saw me coming toward him, he grew very excited. He scratched his bleeding front paws on the hard rock even faster, as though he wanted to rip the big rock apart. He still tried to get off it facing toward the ocean.

In a few steps, I reached the lower part of the big boulder where he stood. From there, I could reach him if he'd come to me. I gently called him. He wanted to come, but something held him back. I tried and tried again, but he wouldn't come. He just glanced at me and cried more desperately, scratching with his bloody paws on the hard boulder again. Carefully, I walked around the boulder in the cold, salty water to the side the black dog had tried to climb down.

When I reached that side, I stood shocked! In the shallow seawater lay a boy, a little smaller than myself. His head lay above the water, resting on a pile of fresh seaweed. The water around his head had a reddish color. I immediately feared the worst, but when I lifted him up a bit, I saw that he was still breathing. His head no longer bled, but it had a big gash on one side of it. I grabbed the boy under both his arms and started to pull him ashore.

The black dog barked fiercely for help now. After I leaned the boy gently against the boulder, I reached up to the lower side of it and called the dog. He now ran to me quickly and jumped into my open arms. I lowered him down into the sea where he hurriedly dashed through the shallow water to the boy. He licked his face over and over, as thought trying to awaken the boy, but the boy didn't wake up.

I tried to pick the boy up to carry him onto the shore, but he was too heavy. Slowly, so as not to injure him anymore, I dragged him onto land. The black dog followed us. I placed the boy in the sand with his injured head up on soft, dried seaweed. The black dog crawled up to him and began licking his face again. The dog whined with every lick across the boy's face, begging him to wake up.

I gently shook the boy and talked to him, but he didn't respond. His chest slowly moved up and down with every breath. The black dog crawled on top of him now, lay down on the boy and licked his own wounds. I hoped he could keep the boy warm. Night would come soon, and with it, the cold air. I took all my dirty clothing off, rinsed them out in the sea, wrung them out and put them back on with the hope they would dry before nightfall. I was too shy to undress the boy to do the same with his clothing.

With a helpless, scared feeling, I took a long look at the steep coastline. I figured I had a slim chance of climbing up the coast by myself, but definitely no chance with the unconscious boy. I could walk out of here along the seashore with him, but that was a long way and I didn't think I should drag him that far. Perhaps I would hurt him even more, or actually kill him.

Leaving him here in the sand all by himself, didn't seem right to me either. What if he woke up just partially, stumbled back into the seawater and drowned? In dismay, I watched the sun sink into the glowing ocean. I held the boy's hand and prayed for help.

Soon, the first lighthouse sent its blinking warning light out to the passing ships. The dog now slept peacefully atop the boy's chest. When the first cold night breeze sent shivers through me, I started to gather dry seaweed to cover us up to help us stay warm through the night.

Suddenly, I clearly heard a shot not far from us. The black dog awoke and started to bark wildly. I screamed for help as loudly as I could. Another shot rang out and a huge dog appeared at the edge of the tall pine trees. That dog started to bark back at us. I jumped up, waving and screaming for help.

Astonished, I watched as a man on his horse appeared in the twilight at the edge of the tall pine forest. He waved to let me know that he saw me. I quit screaming and told the black dog to be quiet too. The man on the horse must have given his dog the same command.

The rider shouted down to me. "I'll be right back with help!"

So glad and relieved, I sank to the sand, hugged the black dog, and cried for joy. He licked the salty tears from my face.

At that moment, I fell in love with the black dog and wished he could be mine. He was so brave, staying with the boy on the boulder, barking for help. He seemed still young, but awfully skinny. I petted him and told him repeatedly, "You're a brave dog."

Before long, I saw a few men step off their horses at the edge of the coast. In the moonlight, they swung ropes around the trees and then tied them to the horses. Two men came down on those ropes. In no time, they landed on the seashore.

They walked over to me, greeted me nicely, looked at the boy and shouted up to the other people. "Yes, it's Elmer's son."

A woman appeared on top of the steep coast. She ran to one of the men and placed her arms around him and cried out.

One young man lifted the boy from the ground, gently placed him over the other man's shoulder and tied him to his body. All of us walked over to the ropes, and the horses pulled the young man with the injured boy on his back straight up.

The man still down on the seashore with me said, "I'm going to get you up next."

I asked him, "What about the dog?"

He answered, "That dog is just a stray. He can find his own way up."

I was not about to leave that brave, hurting dog behind. "But that dog rescued the boy. I'll stay with him. I'll carry him out if I have to walk along the whole coast with him. He's very brave. I won't leave him here."

The man looked at me for a brief moment, and then he shouted up to the others, "Throw down a sack. The girl wants to take the dog up too!"

The sack tumbled down. I gently placed the dog into it, tied the ends together and lifted him up into my arms. Meanwhile the man tied himself to the rope and asked me to come and sit in his lap. When I sat in his lap, he tied part of a rope around his and my legs. Then he tied us together around the waist.

He said, "Hold on tight to the dog. If he starts to struggle, let go of him."

Frightened I'd lose the black dog I now loved so much, I held on for dear life. I gently talked to him, assuring him that all was well.

Slowly, the horse pulled us up the steep coast. The man pushed us away from the sharp stones and thorn bushes that we encountered on our way up the coast. The small dog in my arms didn't struggle. He lay quietly in my arms, though at times he shook with fear. It was a scary lift up the steep coast.

I breathed a deep sigh of relief when we arrived on the top. People helped to untie us. When I first stood, I found my knees quite wobbly, but I soon regained control. Slowly, I opened the sack to let the black dog out. He stood close to me, licking my legs as I told everyone that had gathered what had happened that afternoon.

A tall woman among them came to me. She thanked me, hugged me and said, "I'm the mother of the boy you rescued."

I really didn't know what to say, so I just smiled at her.

She asked, "Would you like to ride with me in the wagon to our village?"

I happily accepted her offer because then I didn't have to worry about that grumpy old ghost throwing stones at the dog and me. With a handful of people walking around his territory, he wouldn't dare get violent.

The black, brave dog limped beside me on his three legs. When we arrived at the horse-drawn wagon, I picked him up and asked if he could ride with me in the wagon since he had a hurt leg. The mother of the boy nodded and pointed for me to sit up front with her. In the back of the wagon, the boy's father held his son in his arms. I held the black dog in my lap, as we rode to their village.

After a short trip, without harassment from the grouchy old ghost, we arrived at their village, called Katharinenhof. We stopped in front of a large farm house with a reed roof and a stall in the back for animals.

People rushed outside and the mother told everyone what had happened. The unconscious boy's father carried him inside and everyone followed, leaving me sitting in the wagon by myself. As I wondered if I should follow them or just walk home, the mother came back outside and invited me in.

She looked at the black dog in my lap and said, "Yes, he can come too."

She led me inside a big room filled with people. The boy lay on a couch, covered up with blankets. His father held his head up while an older woman tried to feed him hot soup, but it just ran out of his mouth and down his chin.

Then a very old woman arrived, the healer of this village. Everyone stepped back so she could attend to the boy. The healer took a small handful of dried weeds from her purse. She wiped the boy's face with it, stuck the ends of it inside the boy's nose, and gently moved it back and forth. To my great surprise, the boy awoke. He sneezed so violently that I feared his head would fall off. Still sneezing, he sat up and looked around with a puzzled expression. His mom, the tall woman, hurried and hugged her boy, who cried out in pain. A relieved hush spread through the worried people in the room.

The healer came to me and thanked me for saving the boy's life. I pleaded with her to heal the black dog's leg.

She said, "Let's take a look at it."

She had me put the dog on the table. After a lot of looking and feeling the dog's leg, she told me that it was broken. My heart sank because I feared that my new friend whom I had come to love, would have to be put to sleep.

The healer sent a boy outside to fetch a stick. "Now it must be strong and straight." With her hands, she showed him how long it should be. Then the healer woman asked for old pieces of cloth to use as bandages. Her words made me very happy. She would fix the brave little dog's leg.

In no time at all, she had people hold the dog's leg in a certain way, used the stick the boy brought her as a splint, and wrapped the leg up with many pieces of cloth that had been ripped into bandages. The healer then tied the black dog's broken lower leg up to his upper leg so he couldn't walk on it. She told me to let the dog rest in a warm place until she came to check on him.

I was so very happy that my new friend could go home with

me. Then I remembered what Mom and Grandma had said a long time ago when I asked to have a dog all to myself. They always gave me the same answer. "We don't have enough food to feed a dog, we barely have enough to fill our bellies. A big dog can eat as much as a pig. At least we can eat the pig later."

Sadly, I walked outside to go home. There I found the father of the boy loading two heavy sacks onto the wagon we had come here with. He smiled and said, "I'm going to take you home."

He helped my dog and me up onto the wagon and sat us in front with him. He went back inside for two lanterns to hang on the wagon. When he came back outside, many people came out too.

They came close to the wagon, smiled, thanked me and said, "Stop by next time you come this way." While I held my dog in my lap, we slowly drove home. The bright stars lit our way. The lanterns hung on each side of the wagon so people could see us coming and get out of our way. The father of the boy talked very nicely to me the whole way home, yet I was afraid and sad that most likely I wouldn't be able to keep my new friend. I held back my tears, but suddenly, they started to roll down my face.

The boy's father saw my tears and asked, "Why are you crying?"

I took a few deep breaths and said, "I'm afraid my mom and grandma won't let me keep my new friend." I hugged the dog closer.

After a moment he said, "I'll ask them to let you keep the dog. If they say no, the dog can live with us and you can come every day to take him for a walk or play with him."

How nice of him. I believe that was the first time in my young life that I wished I had a father. I wiped the tears from my cheeks with my hand and thanked the nice man.

No matter how much I wished our house was a thousand miles away so I could keep holding my dog, it finally came into view. I hugged the black dog, kissed him and said, "You're so brave. I promise I'll come to see you every day if you can't stay with me."

My tears fell onto his fur. He gently licked my face and I felt as though he loved me too.

When the boy's father stopped the wagon, my grandma and my mom came outside to see who had arrived. He jumped off the wagon, took one of the huge sacks on his back and walked toward my mom and grandma. They knew each other and greeted each other nicely.

The man put down the heavy sack in front of Grandma and came back to the wagon to help me down. He then took the other sack of the wagon and together we walked the few steps toward my grandma and my mom. I held the brave, black dog in my arms, hoping they'd let me keep him. My heart raced with fear.

The boy's father put down the heavy sack, held my hand, and told my mom and my grandma all that had happened that evening. He ended by telling them that the black dog and I were heroes. He opened one sack and took a whole, big smoked ham out of it. He handed it to my grandma and asked if I could keep the black dog. He said, "We'd like you to have the ham and the flour in gratitude for Edith rescuing my son."

My grandma and mom stood in astonishment, their mouths open at what they just heard and what the man was offering them.

The boy's father asked one more time, "Can she keep the brave dog?"

Both said "yes" and nodded at the same moment.

They said yes!

A few seconds passed before I realized what they had said. I instantly became the happiest girl in the whole wide world! Now he was my black dog! My heart jumped with joy! Finally, after wishing for such a long time, I had my own dog. What great fun we'd have together.

With one more hug, a well meant thank you, the boy's father climbed up on his wagon. He gave the horses a light touch with the reins, and disappeared down the road.

I put my black dog down and gave Mom and Grandma a big

hug. I thanked both for letting me have the dog.

My mom said, "You need to find a place for your dog to sleep. He can't come inside the house at all, unless it gets bitterly cold. Then we allow all our animals inside to save them from freezing to death. You must also feed him and keep him clean."

Grandma added, "Teach him what he's allowed to do and what he's not allowed to do. Now, let's go check him for fleas."

Grandma walked inside our stall while my dog and I followed her. She lit a lantern and placed it on the old bench. She asked me to pick my dog up and put his head close to the lamp. I followed her orders and my dog sat on the bench, well behaved. My grandma moved her fingers back and forth through the black fur around his neck. In only a brief moment, she declared that my dog had fleas. She sent me inside to fetch the bag of powder which killed just about everything that bit us now and then. I hurriedly ran inside to get the powder for her.

My dog held very still while Grandma spread the powder all over him, until grandma's cat came to check out the latest excitement. With a single glance, the dog jumped off the bench in a great hurry and chased after that cat as if he were protecting us from the devil himself. He sure could move fast on only three legs. Then I remembered the healer woman had told me that my dog should rest until she came to take the bandages off. Now what?

Very quickly, my dog learned that cats have sharp claws, which can move at high speed into a dog's tender nose. Whining and bleeding, licking his hurting nose, he came back to us. I felt so sorry for him. I helped him back onto the bench so my grandma could finish powdering him.

I told my grandma what the healer had said. She checked his splint and his bandages and said, "Everything's still in place. He'll be fine." Then she hugged me and said, "He's a young male, fully grown, but, Edith, he's far too skinny. You're going to need to feed him a lot. He looks like a fine dog."

I carried my sweet little black dog into the lean-to that my grandpa had fixed up for himself to live in many years ago, when my grandma kicked him out of her bed. The roof didn't leak in here and with the wallboards nailed close together the cold wind couldn't howl through them. Grandpa's old bed, the one he had built by himself, still stood in here. I often spent a night in here, pretending to be away in some foreign land, with flowers made of sugar eggs and cocoa and I could eat as many of them as I liked. Sometimes I pretended to sail on one of those huge merchant ships going around the world. My, what I saw on those trips in my grandpa's bed.

Of course, I had plenty of food and many sweet treats on board of those huge ships. I'd tell my new friend, my black dog, all about those imaginary trips. Perhaps we could go together on such trips. After all, I had plenty of room to take him along.

I laid my sweet dog gently down onto my grandpa's bed, took the folded old blanket, shook it out outside and covered him with it. In the corner of this lean-to, I found a rusted old can which I rinsed out beneath the pump and filled with fresh water for him. I worried about food for him and about my grandma's cat who slept inside this place too. She had a nice straw nest on top of a shelf across this tiny room. I worried that the cat would hurt my dog.

At that moment, my mom called me to come and have dinner. I told my dog, "Please stay. I'll come right back with some food."

Ever so hungry, I hurried upstairs to our room. My mom had fixed me a plate of boiled cabbage and some fried potatoes with lots of pork grease. She had even put a small slice of the smoked ham the boy's father gave us on my plate. When I sat down to eat my special meal, I noticed that my mom had fixed a small plate of potatoes and grease for someone else. I wondered if it was for my black dog.

At that moment, I remembered what my grandma and the village healer had said about my dog needing a lot to eat. I asked my mom, "Can I please go and eat with my dog in the lean-to?"

She said, "Sure, and take this plate for him!"

Ever so happy, I took both plates and walked downstairs.

Before I could open the front door my grandma came out of her room with a bowl full of fish guts. She handed the bowl to me and said, "It's for your dog."

I thanked her and walked into the lean-to.

My dog still lay on grandpa's bed sleeping, but he woke up quickly when he smelled the food. He wagged his tail in anticipation. I sat down on the bed next to him and gave him grandma's bowl with the fish guts. He wolfed them down in seconds. Then I gave him the plate with the fried potatoes and extra pig grease on it. He ate that too in no time at all, but his nose still sniffed at something.

He looked at me, saw my plate, and came closer. He sat down in front of me and stared at my heaping plate of food. Though so hungry myself, his begging expression won me over. I gave him my plate of food. He quickly devoured that too, and then he came over to me and licked my hands as if to thank me.

I knew I couldn't have any more food tonight, but it did not matter. I was so extremely happy to have my new friend here with me that the hunger didn't bother me too much that night. I spread the old blanket out over the narrow bed, crawled underneath it, called my sweet, new friend next to me and kissed him on his nose. Then I covered both of us completely up with that old blanket, held him in my arms and gently stroked his body.

When I heard grandma's cat come inside, my dog shivered with fear. I held onto him tightly. The cat didn't attack the dog. She just sat next to our bed and complained that she did not like this arrangement. Soon she went on her night hunt and the tiny room grew quiet.

Though I have so many happy memories of my young life, perhaps that moment, laying in the old bed curled up with my new friend, was the happiest one. That night I named my dog Harras, after a brave Nordic King who had long, curly black hair too.

What treasure I had found that day.

No garlic, bingo or popcorn.

Chapter 46

My tenth birthday

On October 12, 1953, I turned ten years old. Early in the morning, the healer woman who set my dog's leg arrived at our house. My grandma welcomed her as one of her best friends. They had a lot to talk about before anyone asked me to bring my dog inside my grandma's room.

The healer woman slowly took my dog's bandages off. She felt the leg and declared that it had grown back together just fine. For the first time in a long time, my dog stood on all four legs again. He bent his head and looked at the healed leg. Then he happily jumped up and down.

"Is it all right if I take him for a walk?" I asked.

My grandma and the healer said I could so I dressed warmly and we went on our first long walk.

What a happy dog. He ran around in the soft snow, trying to catch his long tail. When he met all our village dogs, they sniffed him all over, and he didn't seem to mind. He just held still. I showed and told him about my aunt's mean gander and hoped he understood. As I looked more closely at his leg, it seemed to me that it had healed a bit crooked, but it sure held up. He listened well to me and stayed close by me, which made me feel great.

When we arrived at our beach, he sat down in the snow-covered sand and stared out to sea. I wondered if he thought about the injured boy whom we had rescued a month ago. The moment I sat next to him to comfort him, he jumped in my lap and thoroughly licked my face, just as he had done to the unconscious boy. I hugged him and told him how much I loved him. Then I got up and the two of us raced along the beach. Though I ran quickly, he ran much faster than I did. Tired, but so very happy to have my dog, Harras, all healed up, we walked home together.

Outside our house, I smelled something baking in someone's oven. After taking Harras into the lean-to and giving him some fresh water, I walked upstairs into our room. My mom had just taken a small yeast sheet cake out of our little iron oven, and it looked delicious. It had apple slices on it and beet sugar dribbled on top.

Baking something in the very small iron herd was not easy at those times. The oven had no controls to regulate the heat, and we had no instrument to stick inside to measure the temperature. You could only minimally regulate the heat by leaving the door open a little if the baking compartment got too hot, or by adding more fuel to increase the temperature.

After my mom set the cake down on the table, she hugged me and wished me happy birthday. She handed me a beautiful skirt that she had sewn by hand from the useable parts of one of her dresses.

"Oh, Mom, it's so very pretty. I like it very much." I gave her a big hug. I wore that skirt as part of my Sunday outfit for many years.

Mom invited Grandma and her friend, the healer woman, upstairs to celebrate my birthday. All four of us had a nice slice of apple cake and peppermint tea to drink. Oh, how delicious that cake tasted. Without letting anyone see me, I stuck a few crumbs of this very delicious cake in my pants pocket to give to Harras a little later.

As a special treat, my grandma invited me to spend the night with her.

She whispered in my ear, "You can bring Harras inside too, but don't tell your mother."

What a wonderful birthday surprise! I could barely wait for the evening to arrive.

Then I took the cake pieces to my dog. He liked them a lot and sniffed at my pocket for more. I told him, "Both of us are invited into Grandma's room tonight to celebrate my tenth birthday."

I don't think he knew what that meant. Instead of a happy smile about the invitation, he just looked at me with his shiny dark eyes, as though looking all the way through me.

During the day, it started to snow again. The big snowflakes fell almost straight down to earth. I took Harras outside and we ran and played in the falling snow. When the evening finally crawled upon our island, the two of us sat on our front step eagerly awaiting my grandma's call to come inside her room.

As the front door opened, my grandma's head appeared and she very quietly asked me to come inside the house.

I turned to Harras and warned him one more time. "You are not to run after Grandma's cat which will most likely lay curled up in her bed."

He looked at me and yawned. I took his yawn as his way of saying, "I won't bother the cat."

At this point in my life, I wasn't sure how much of our language dogs understood.

Quietly, we walked inside Grandma's cozy room. She smiled and gave me a long hug to wish me happy birthday. She bent down and patted my dog to welcome him. Then my grandma handed me the two most beautiful, shiny, pink ribbons for my braided hair that I had ever seen. I could barely believe it. I had adored those ribbons in our small store for months. Each time I had a chance to go inside the store I stared at them and dreamed of someday buying them.

My grandma took the old, grey, worn strings from the end of my braids and replaced them with the beautiful, shiny, pink ones. I felt wonderful. The two of us held hands and danced around her table. She sang a song to me in a foreign language. We laughed and danced around her table a few more times, then Grandma got out of breath.

She sat down and said, "This was your leaving-your-childhood song and dance like we celebrated when I turned ten. We've passed this on for generations from a faraway land called Norway."

My grandma seemed sad for just a brief moment. I wondered what she had on her mind. Perhaps she thought of our departed relatives from that faraway land, or maybe she thought of her young life. Each time I had asked her to tell me about her young life, she said, "In time, my child, in time."

Quickly, my grandma got her smile back. She stood up and decked the table with three plates. Two plates had a fork beside them, and the third one did not. I wondered if Grandma invited my mom also and she just forgot to place a fork at her plate.

I asked her, but my grandma said, "No child, I didn't invite your mother. This night is especially just for us. I set that plate for your friend, Harras. I figured he couldn't use a fork yet, or did you teach him that already?"

Her reply completely flabbergasted me. First, Grandma allowed my dog into her room, and then she placed a plate for him on her table. Was he going to eat with us inside her room on her table? I hoped my mom didn't come down. She didn't even allow Harras inside the house except for the brutally cold days in our harsh winters. This was surely a very special birthday evening.

My grandma sliced three pieces of black bread from her big, round loaf, spread pork grease on them, and placed one slice on each plate. Harras sniffed now in the direction of the table. I hoped that he behaved.

Next, Grandma opened her stove's baking door and took out three large baked flounders swimming in fragrant fat. She placed one on each plate, poured tea and a little cherry liqueur from her cellar into two cups. She even had a little cup with pine tree branches inside of it sitting on the table. How festive the table looked.

It reminded me that Christmas was not faraway and that I would spend it in the mountains that reached up into the heavens. I remembered something about mountains from the Bible and figured that God lived on top of the tallest mountain, among the clouds. I got all excited to visit Him up in His place and have a talk with Him.

Grandma asked my Harras to sit on the sofa, where she had placed an old rag. He obeyed, and right in front of him, on the table, he found a plate full of great smelling food, his food.

My grandma told Harras, "Wait, boy!"

His long tongue hung out of his mouth, and his tail wagged as fast as I had ever seen. His shiny, dark eyes stared at the plate full of food. His nose inhaled the good smells with a slight shiver and from his open mouth small drips of saliva escaped and landed at his plate.

When my grandma sat down she said, "Let's eat."

I couldn't believe it. As though Harras understood what my grandma said, he put his paws on the table and quickly slung down the flounder and the rest of his food on his plate. He then licked the surroundings of his mouth while he gazed onto our plates.

Grandma told him, "That's all for now, boy. Lay down."

After one more wishful look at our plates, he lay down and went to sleep.

Grandma and I laughed. What a very special birthday this was! I felt so great! Since her last tooth fell out some days ago, my grandma slowly chewed her food with her gums now. We ate our lavish meal, talked and laughed until we finished all the food on our plates. Soon the dark, cloudy night covered our island. Grandma lit a candle and let the little iron stove starve. The time had come to go to bed. We dressed in our nightclothes and snuggled together under Grandma's thick feather bedcover.

She prayed to God, "Please make the transition from childhood to becoming an adult easy for my grandchild, Edith, and watch over her closely so no harm will come to her."

Harras, still fast asleep on the old sofa, had either not yet detected Grandma's cat, which slept at the end of her bed tonight, or had learned to have great respect for her. I hoped it was the latter. Oh, how I loved to have my friend, my black dog, inside the house. I wished my mom would let him come inside too. He could sleep underneath my bed on his old blanket.

I felt so secure here in bed with my grandma. The wind howled outside now and I snuggled a little closer to her and asked her, "What were you doing at the age of ten?"

My grandma sat up a bit and took another drink from her mug. "Child, this is not a story. Let me tell you tonight, on your special birthday, what really happened to me."

"At the age of ten, we moved off our island and just before my mom died in childbirth, my parents sent me away from home to a small village not far from here to work on a farm. I worked hard in the fields at first to earn my keep. After a few years, I worked inside the main house doing all the work they gave me to do just for the food I ate and the roof of the stall over my head. It was the way things were done at that time.

"Before long, the farmer forced himself on me and said that if I said anything about this to anyone, he'd shoot me. He came to me night after night and hurt me terribly. Soon, the farmer's wife and I knew that I was pregnant. She asked me who had slept with me. I told her that nobody had slept with me, but that her husband had hurt me terribly in my straw bed night after night.

"Angry, the farmer's wife told me, 'Pack your bundle and get out of my place now!' She did give me a small amount of coins to support myself while I made my way home. When I arrived home, a different family lived in my parents' house. They told me that my father had moved on, but they asked me nicely to spend the night at their place and fed me well.

"The next morning I went to the cemetery to cry my heart out on my mom's grave. I asked her for help and to show me a way out of my trouble. I knew she couldn't answer me, but she was the only one left of my family in that village. At only fourteen years old, I had no idea about giving birth to the child inside of me. Oh, how desperately I needed my mom.

"Slowly, I cried all my tears out and a strange calmness came over me. I felt someone walking toward me. A slight touch on my shoulder and a friendly, 'Hello, can I help you,' made me shiver. When I looked up, I saw a smiling young man looking back at me. I broke down crying again and told him about my trouble.

"He said, 'I'm going to the island of Fehmarn to help my brother build a house and barn. Would you like to come along? Perhaps you can find a place to stay and work on the island.' I gladly said, yes. At that time, I firmly believed my mom heard my pleading cries up in the heavens and sent this young man to help me. I'm not so sure about that these days anymore.

"We started to walk together toward the ocean. A friendly old man with a rowboat took us across the grey ocean to the island. By late evening, we arrived at the first, very small village of Wulfen with only four small houses.

"People sat outside on the dirt road watching the sun setting into the vast ocean. They greeted us with friendly smiles and asked if we needed help. The young man beside me told them of our situation. An elderly woman stood up and offered me to stay with her for food and shelter. I gladly accepted her offer. The young man, Frantz, bade me farewell and asked, 'Can I come and visit you?' I gladly said yes and held back the tears.

"The elderly woman treated me well. She fed me well and let me sleep in a dry corner near her kitchen. I was almost fifteen when my baby girl was born with the help of the nice woman I lived with, but I had no way of supporting my baby.

"The woman I worked for said, 'My sister and husband have no children at all and perhaps they'd like to raise your girl as their own.' Gently she asked, 'Elise, are you willing to give up your baby?' Heartbroken, I agreed to let my baby girl go to them. A few weeks later I handed over my baby, I had named Annie, to a smiling elderly couple. They told me that I could come and see my precious Annie any time."

My grandma blew out the candle and lay back down. I hugged her and gave her a goodnight kiss on her wet cheek.

She hugged me back and said, "You will become a woman soon, my girl. Be careful around boys and men. Don't let them talk you into anything."

Slowly, I drifted away into the land where girls grew wings and had the ability to fly away when boys or men came around to do them harm.

What a wonderful birthday I had.

Edy and cat at the age of ten.

Still no sewing machine, soup in cans or evaporated milk.

Chapter 47

Where was God?

Mom and my grandma grew more excited every day about my vacation in the big mountains of Bavaria.

I asked my mom, "Are the mountains in Bavaria bigger than the mountain our island church stands on?"

She laughed out loud. "Our church stands only on a small hill. Those mountains in Bavaria reach all the way up into the clouds. Some of the mountains I saw were so high up in the sky that they always had snow on top of them."

Now I began to get excited as well. Perhaps I could walk up on one of those high mountains and check up on God. I wondered lately if something had happened to Him. I had asked Him so many times to heal my mom, but she was still not well. I always asked very politely, saying please and thank you. I also asked Him a few questions about boys and why they acted so stupid, but he hadn't answered those questions either. I gave God plenty of time, because I figured He was a busy man, but lately I began to wonder if He had died.

My grandma knitted a new hat for me to take with me. She called it a devil's hat. She had made it out of red and green yarn, and it fit nicely over my ears. My mom took my old, faded winter coat apart, turned it inside out, and sewed it back together. She sure could sew well. The coat looked pretty again and had no more faded spots. I proudly wore the fine coat and pretty hat.

Though excited about my trip, I had mixed feelings about this vacation. I still remembered the long, terrible time I had to spend in the sanatorium and the terrible homesickness. My mom and grandma repeatedly told me to expect a very nice place, nothing at all like the sanatorium. I hoped they were right.

Soon the day arrived for me to leave. After one long goodbye hug and kiss from my mom, I walked out the door, holding my grandma's hand. Just about all the children and a few adults from our village stood in front of our house. What a surprise!

They bid me farewell and wished me a wonderful time with hugs and handshakes. Some of the children still begged to go with me, even though I had explained many times that they couldn't come along. After all the goodbyes, my closest friends, my grandma and my dog, Harras, walked me to our little ferryboat. My mom was still too weak for this long walk.

They all sang happy songs and asked me to tell them all about the huge mountains when I came back. They made me promise to say hello to God if I saw Him, and to tell Him that they were good girls. I clung desperately to my grandma's hand, felt sad and scared to leave, remembering so clearly the awful time I spent in the sanatorium.

Soon we arrived at the ferry landing where the old ferryboat waited, tied to a sturdy pole.

I made my grandma promise one last time that she'd take very good care of my sweet dog and then I let go of her hand. When she hugged me, I wanted to cry, but I held back my tears. Quickly, I bent down, hugged my dog, and told him to mind my grandma. Hurriedly, I ran onto the ferry so no one would see my tears.

My friends cheered me on, jumped up and down and frantically waved goodbye to me. As the ferry slowly left our island, my sweet dog barked and tried to come after me, but my grandma picked him up and held him in her arms. Now my tears streamed down my face. I wanted to jump off the ferry and swim back home, but that would really disappoint my family. I held onto the slightly wet railing of the small boat to steady myself and watched my island disappear in the morning fog. I left my island for the second time in my young life.

Slowly I began to settle down, and the excitement to see the high mountains and most likely, God, returned to me. With my mittens, I wiped the last tears from my cold face. Before the ferry landed on the mainland, I heard the distinct noise of a train. Now that sound really excited me. I loved to ride on a train.

After the men tethered the ferry to a short post, I walked off through the glistening snow toward the train station. The huge locomotive came to a halt with a loud, unpleasant screech, and goose bumps danced all over my body.

A smiling lady came out of the first passenger car, which had a sign on it saying "Welfare Department." She greeted me, asked my name and helped me inside the warm passenger car. I took off my pretty coat and hung it on the hook near the window. I kept a close eye on it so no one would take it by mistake. It was the only coat I had. My mom had so proudly made it look new again. I sat right next to the window so I could see everything as we passed by. With a loud roar from the locomotive, we started to move forward. The big engine labored, and huffed, and puffed to get us going. She spit and hissed, and belched dark grey steam from her tall chimney high up into the sky. Soon the huge locomotive recovered and we moved swiftly along the tracks. I shared this car with three other children.

The smiling woman came and put a nametag on me and my pretty coat. I found that neat. Now no one would take my nice coat by mistake. The beautiful snow-covered landscape flew by me, never looking exactly the same. All the towns with so many buildings, cars and people interested me very much. In almost every town, another child boarded. By the afternoon, children of all ages completely filled our car.

The sun glowed with the fire of beautiful bedtime colors of

orange, red, crimson, and a dark shade of purple. She even made the snowy landscape turn into many bright colors. The sun itself finally faded to a deep shade of gold now, and it looked as though she boiled in the sky. Steam escaped from her and rose up all around her. What an awesome splendorous sight.

I stared out of the window in amazement. I wondered where the sun would sleep tonight, since there was no waterbed for her here to sink into. At the next stop, someone brought a huge can of water and cups inside so we could all have a drink. It started to get dark now and I had grown tired. With the light on inside the railroad car, I could no longer see the outside world running by. I leaned my head back and fell asleep.

Suddenly, a loud, squeaking noise woke me. I couldn't believe what I saw. Our train had driven inside a huge house with many lights inside of it and many glass windows all over the walls and on the ceiling. They left a big opening on each end of this huge house, and I saw other trains inside here too.

Many people walked around in this amazingly huge house, like ants on a warm summer's day. A very big sign said Luebeck. I knew where we were. I had learned about this town in school. It seemed far away from our island, and according to our teacher, was a big city. I couldn't figure out what we were doing inside this huge house.

A few older women came into our passenger car. They asked us to please take our belongings and step out of the train. I was so excited to see the huge mountains that I forgot my pretty coat in the train. Hurriedly, I ran back inside the train to retrieve it. Inside the passenger car, I ran straight into one of the older women. She almost fell over. I apologized to her and told her that I needed to get my pretty coat my mom had sewn for me.

The woman smiled and asked, "Is it one of these coats?" She showed me an armful of coats. Sure enough, the top coat belonged to me. Ever so happy to get it back, I thanked the woman many times.

Soon after, the women lined us up by twos and led us out of the huge railroad station's house. The sight of all the big buildings with so many lights stunned me. They even had lights hanging on poles, shining down onto the streets. I wondered who fed all the coins to the electric boxes.

I saw so many different cars, which I had never seen before. They all drove so fast. I got dizzy trying to count them. Wires hung down from poles all over the streets like a net strung over a baby's carriage. Herds of busy people scurried in all directions, as if some strange force drove them. I hoped they wouldn't run into each other.

What a completely different world this was from my island. I looked around to find the mountains, but the streetlights blinded my vision. I couldn't even see the stars clearly, as I could at home. These stars seemed so faraway and just faintly visible. The streets had no trees and the noise was almost overwhelming. A bad odor hung in the air, and the wind blew trash around the corner.

Cold and very hungry, I wondered why they had us stand here, just outside the railroad station, in this city that was such a sad sight.

I found the closest older woman and asked, "Why are we standing here in the cold wind, and how come I can't see the mountains?"

She bent down toward me and said, "We're waiting for a streetcar to come to take us to the youth hostel. There we'll have a fine meal and spend the night. The next morning you'll all go on a very long, fast train to Bavaria, where the tall mountains reach into the sky. They're much taller than you most likely can imagine. It is such a beautiful place to visit!" She gently touched my head.

What she told me made me very happy. I felt so glad that I didn't have to stay in this strange, sad town, where people didn't even stop to say hello to each other.

Then the streetcar pulled up. How I wished that my mom and my grandma could see this thing, a huge car that rode on tracks, like a train, in the middle of the street. A strange iron arm attached it to the net of wires, which hung above it. Bluish and white sparks constantly jumped out of the wires like the ones from our old electric box with the devil inside of it, which scared me to death.

Oh no, I thought I had killed the devil when I hit the electric box hard with my mom's broom until it fell apart. But here he sat of top of the wire net, spitting out even bigger sparks than at home. Now I felt so desperately scared again of being electrocuted.

With a slight ring of a bell this huge car abruptly stopped, but without the screeching and squeaking noise of the train. This streetcar frightened me. I thought the sparks could hurt me, or perhaps kill me. I told the elderly, nice woman my fears and asked her to let me stay and wait outside the railroad station until we had to board our next train. She smiled, held my hand, and said, "I'll protect you."

Fearfully, I stepped inside the streetcar, holding onto that kind woman's hand for dear life. Another ring of a bell and we moved forward. I forgot my fear and stared in amazement at the big houses.

How closely they huddled together, as if afraid to fall down if they had to stand by themselves. Some of those houses stood five stories high. Most of the windows glowed in the darkness. In fact, the whole street had lights on, and I wondered why.

I thought the people here must be very rich to be able to pay for all the power it takes to light all those lamps. At home, my grandma would deposit two ten-cent pieces into the electric box to light all three lamps in our house for one evening. I tried to count all the lights to figure out how much it cost to light this town for one night, but got lost before I got very far. There were just too many lamps to count.

I could still see no trees anywhere in the streets, and I didn't see any gardens, just a lot of people with somber faces going in different directions. Nobody stopped to talk or said hello. I couldn't even see the stars anymore. Too many lights blinded my view now.

Different cars drove all over the streets honking and almost pushing each other forward. What a crowded city. With all the bluish smoke from the cars, the air stank. I knew I wouldn't like to live here.

On the third stop, the women led us from the streetcar into the street. I looked to see where the locomotive of the streetcar was. To my astonishment I saw no locomotive pushing it. I knew from entering the streetcar that it had no locomotive pulling it either. How I wished my family at home could see the streetcar that moved without a locomotive. What a completely different world this was.

One more look down the busy, snow-covered street and we entered a tall house which had the name "Youth Hostel" painted on the yellow door in big, black letters. We entered a very big, well lit, warm room. Many small tables with chairs around them stood to the right of me. When I looked to the left side, I stared in amazement. There stood a long table with pots and dishes full of steaming food. Never in my young life had I seen so much food on one table, not even in the sanatorium. By now I had grown awfully hungry and hoped that I could have at least a little of this great smelling food.

The women asked us to form a single line, take a plate, and walk slowly along the long table to select whatever food we wanted.

"Please, children, take only as much as you think you can eat. You may come back for seconds if you wish."

Had I heard correctly? Take all the food we wanted and come back for seconds? I watched the children in front of me, so I knew to act appropriately at my turn. Sure enough, the children just pointed to different food items and the women behind the table placed that item on their plates. I could barely believe my eyes. One more step and I found myself at the bountiful table.

Though it smelled good, I passed by the big soup kettle with all the cups standing around it. I had eaten soup quite often lately at home. Though always good, it didn't still my hunger for long. The next bowl had a potato dish in it. I pointed to it.

The smiling woman said, "That's potato salad."

I politely thanked her. Then, on a big plate, I saw steaming hot sausages stacked up high. It had been so long since I had a sausage. I pointed to it, and with a smile from the serving woman, it appeared on my plate. I also pointed to the next bowl of warm food, even though I didn't know what it was.

The young serving woman said, "That's rice with vegetables, fried liver and eggs."

On the next plate I saw various small breads. I selected one I had never seen. It looked almost white. Next, I saw boiled cabbage with ham pieces. I had a helping of that too. By now, I held a full plate. More food filled this wonderful long table, but I decided to sit down and eat all of what I had on my plate first.

I found forks and spoons on the table and each cup had hot milk in it. The only familiar item on my plate was the sausage. I had never seen any of the other foods before. In a hurry, I began to eat, and everything tasted great. For the first time in a long time I filled my belly completely. The dining room grew quiet except for the sounds of flatware scraping metal plates.

I looked over to the plate with the sausages. Someone had filled it back up. I really didn't need any more food, but I bravely stood up, walked to the long table and pointed to the sausage plate. The woman smiled and gave me two.

Somehow I felt guilty for having all the food to eat I wished for. How great if only all the people in our house could come here and feast on this meal. I dearly hoped everyone at home had enough to eat tonight.

Then someone asked us to bring our dishes, cups and utensils to the kitchen. As I stood up to do just that, I noticed another group of children entering the room. The adults stayed busy refilling the pots and plates with food and placing utensils on the tables to feed this new group.

Our group followed a woman upstairs to a room with funny beds that stood on top of each other, like nothing I had ever seen. How clever though. A lot more children could sleep in this room that way.

I climbed up the little ladder and claimed a bed on the top for myself. Exhausted, I barely remembered to take off my pretty coat so I wouldn't get it all wrinkled up. I laid it beside me, crawled partially underneath the blankets and fell asleep before I even took my shoes off.

Early the next morning, before the sun chased away the night, women awakened us. The streetcar took us back to the train station through the bright streets. This time I saw only a handful of people and cars on the street, hurriedly going to somewhere.

Half asleep, I walked onto the train and sat down on a bench by a window. I leaned back and tried to stay awake for the ride to the huge mountains that reached into the sky. I didn't want to miss a thing. After the train left the lit railroad station, I could see that the dark night still had hold of the land. I closed my eyes and let the rhythm of the moving train rock me to sleep.

Suddenly, with squealing brakes the train stopped. I fell off the bench onto the hard floor and thought we had an accident. Quickly I stood up and looked out the window. Our train had stopped inside an even bigger house than in the last city.

Long trains filled that house, and a big sign that read "Hamburg" hung down from the ceiling.

One of the women clapped her hands for our attention and said, "Children, let's all please leave the train now and follow the woman with the small flag in her hand to another train." A woman held her flag high above her head so we could all see it.

I wondered why we had to leave one train and go right back inside another. None of this made any sense to me, but I followed the leader.

Everything went fine until I realized I had forgotten my pretty coat again. I turned around to go back to that train we had just left but fear overcame me when I saw that train moving away.

I screamed to stop the train and started to cry. I tried to run after that train, but the woman who escorted us held me back.

I looked up to her, still crying and screaming. "My coat! My coat is in that train!"

Then I realized that she held my pretty coat in her hand. What a relief. I thanked her very much. I didn't want to lose my coat again, so I decided to keep it on for the rest of the ride. My mom had worked so hard to make it look pretty again. I didn't want to disappoint her by returning home without it.

We walked up some stairs, all the way down a wide hallway and back down some stairs to our waiting train. The sleeping locomotive was a lot bigger than the one on the last train. A huge wagon full of coal sat behind it, followed by a long line of passenger cars. I counted sixteen before the train curved around and I could no longer see the end of it.

The moment we entered this train, I noticed a complete difference. This car had soft seats and little rooms where we sat. The rooms even had doors, and the big window actually opened. Very small tables folded up and down from the wall below the window and the walls by the door.

Quickly, I claimed a window seat. Someone brought jelly sandwiches, milk, and apples into our little room for a much appreciated breakfast. I felt so rich and important in that fancy train.

Then we felt a quick rumble and heard clear signs of noises of an awakening locomotive. Young boys in green uniforms came inside the train and gave every one of us a small flag. The flags had the colors of black, red and gold on them, the colors of Schleswig Holstein, my home state. The boys asked us to open the windows and wave the flags when we left the station. Now this sounded like fun.

I hurried and opened our window all the way. All eight of us in this small room crawled on top of each other and stuck our heads out. People packed the station, all standing around, as if waiting for something. Some carried banners with names on them. Others held small flags just like ours, and a few men with huge cameras stood not far from us. Behind a slightly elevated stand, a big flag hung on the wall. All the people seemed to look in that direction, and I wondered what they expected to see.

I stood inside the second passenger car behind the massive locomotive and now saw black smoke belch from its chimney. The whole locomotive vibrated, and hot, white steam escaped from beneath its wheels now and then. I worried how long that huge monster engine could hold its massive power back before it blew apart.

Another group of children entered the third passenger car down from ours. A handful of old men started to play music that echoed from the ceiling of the railroad's huge house, making for a loud and festive atmosphere. All eight of us hung out of the window, still piled up on top of each other. We waved our flags to the rhythm of the music as did the children in the other three passenger cars. What fun we had.

Abruptly, the music stopped. An elderly man stepped up on the elevated stand and waved to the crowd. The crowd, in return, waved back and whistled at him. Some shouted at the man, and I wondered what was going on. I couldn't understand what that man on the stand said because the people around him talked too loud. When the speaker stopped talking, many people applauded, but some screamed in anger. The music started again. With one loud, strong blow from the locomotive, our train crept forward.

The band played. Photographers with huge flash cameras took pictures of us and we waved and waved our flags in sheer excitement, though we had no idea why. Slowly, we left the huge house of the trains in Hamburg.

When our train finally gained full power, we moved unbelievably quickly through the land and small towns. At first, the speed of the train frightened me, but I soon found it exciting. I expected the train to fly off the tracks at any minute now and perhaps fly up into the clouds. I then could check up on God, to see if He was still alive.

That fast train didn't stop in every town, as the small train did, but rather rushed right through them. The fancy train even had a heater on the floor by the window, which kept the small room cozy. That amazed me! Oh, what I could tell my family when I returned home. In the early afternoon, I saw mountains on the far horizon but they disappointed me because they weren't even as big as the hill our church stood on.

Someone brought us delicious sandwiches with real meat between two slices of bread. They also brought us metal cups filled with milk. Sudden, I felt very tired. I looked around our little room and saw that most of the other children had their eyes closed and leaned back in their seats. I laid my head down on the little table and closed my eyes. What a big disappointment the tiny mountains were.

A very loud blow from the locomotive woke me instantly. I opened my eyes to find it dark. We didn't even have any lights on in our room. One louder blow and sunlight appeared instantly. I stood up immediately, disbelieving what my eyes told me. The mountains on either side of us reached to the sky. I couldn't even see the top of some of them, no matter how I bent and stretched my head on the window.

In excitement, I jumped up and down and screamed, "Mountains! Mountains!"

All the other children in our little room woke up and quickly came to the window. What astounded faces they had. I ran out of our room to have a look at the other side of our train. Sure enough, beautiful, huge mountains loomed there too. Then suddenly, our fast train slowed to a crawl.

I opened the window all the way and stuck my head out to see the top of the mountains. The ice-cold wind fiercely bit into my face. Mom was right. Some of those tall mountains reached right into the clouds. I desperately hoped that we were in Bavaria. I wanted to climb one of those huge mountains to check on God.

The train moved slowly over a high bridge. Way below me, a river ran through a snow-covered forest of pine trees. How beautiful. The tall mountains reached up high with pride surrounded by the thick forest. I wondered how many animals this forest sheltered. The glistening snow made everything look so beautiful, just like in my grandma's stories.

Leaving the tall bridge behind us, our train traveled very slowly, almost in a circle around a fat, squat mountain. I could see the last car of our train. Hurriedly, I counted twenty-three passenger cars, two luggage cars and one empty, open car.

To my surprise, I saw a huge locomotive on the end of our train, that also blew out big clouds of grey smoke, just like the locomotive that pulled us. I wondered how one locomotive could pull the train and then have another pushing it.

The icy wind stung my face more fiercely now. The moment I moved to re-enter the passenger compartment, an awfully loud blast came from the front locomotive. When I looked toward her, the sight shocked me! The front part of our train crawled inside a mountain. Very quickly, I pulled my head inside so the mountain wouldn't hurt me. Before I could close the window completely, we found ourselves in complete darkness inside the mountain, and it frightened me a great deal. Why did the train run inside of a mountain? Some children screamed, others laughed. I silently nursed my fear.

In no time at all, fingers of light made their way into our windows and we left the inside of the mountain. What a relief! Still shaking, I sat down.

Our escort came into our compartment, and with a big smile said, "Get ready to depart the train."

In a hurry, I went to the bathroom to relieve myself. To my surprise, this bathroom had a small sink with water that actually ran out of the faucet. I wished I could show this to my folks at home.

Our train stopped in a town called Bad Toelz in the southern part of Bavaria, right at the edge of the mighty Alps. All the children on the train walked outside with astounded faces, staring at the tall mountains. Some people helped us onto big horse drawn sleds. They had lots of bales of straw to sit on in the sleds and blankets to cover the children who didn't have coats.

I couldn't get over the many impressive mountains that surrounded us. Many rose up into the clouds. While I gazed in awe at the mountains, the horses started to move and I fell head first onto a straw bail. Everyone laughed at me. Embarrassed, I lifted myself out of the straw and sat down. With each step the horses took, a happy jingle sounded from the small bells that hung from collars around their necks.

Shortly after we left the town, some of the gray snow clouds moved away and the sun smiled down at us. She made the snow glisten and sparkle everywhere. With the clouds mostly gone now, the mountains showed their full heights. What a surprise to see how high and pretty they were. I could barely believe that such beauty existed. Straight ahead of us, I saw the tallest mountain with its top in a snow cloud. I decided that I'd climb that one to check up on God.

Closer and closer, we rode toward the tallest mountain and finally reached Bayravies, a village nestled in a beautiful snow-covered valley. A very tall, dense pine forest embraced the colorful houses of the village as though protecting them from harm. The horses slowed as we turned onto a narrow, snow covered road that led us right into the darkness of the tall pine forest. The trees stood so closely together that the sun barely filtered through their canopy. Somehow it felt warmer though, and so safe inside the deep forest. Snow barely covered the ground.

Just a short way inside the dense forest stood a huge three-story house with pretty flowers painted on the walls.

As the horses stopped, a woman said, "This is the Alpenheim, your beautiful home for the next six weeks."

Excited, I jumped off the big sled. The beauty of the place, the huge mountains, the beautiful, deep forest and the pretty painted house, all captivated me. And I could call this home for the next six weeks!

The tallest mountain, still straight ahead of me, rose into the clouds. God had to live there.

I smiled at the mountain and whispered, "I will come and see you, God!"

Feeling very good now, I walked inside the huge building and into a big, warm room with tables and benches. When all the children had come inside, an elderly woman speaking a strange dialect said something I really didn't understand. She smiled and waved her hand to welcome us. I smiled and waved back to her. Slowly, looking at me, the other children did the same.

Then a young woman took over. She spoke without the strange dialect. She asked us to look at the numbers on the long tables and go the table which had the number of our age on it. She also wanted the boys to go to the blue numbers and the girls to the pink ones.

Instant confusion took hold. Sisters and brothers had to let go of each other, and some young siblings absolutely refused to let go of the hand of the older one. Some older children tried to get rid of their younger siblings by slapping them. Most likely they had tired of having to care for them. I saw the pink ten and snuck out among the commotion of dividing us into groups. The brightly glowing evening sun had started to disappear slowly behind the tallest mountain. She painted the whole snow-covered valley and mountains in bright orange, deep reds and flaming gold colors. She sent her last crimson and purple beams way up into the heavens from above the top of the tallest mountain. As I watched her slowly sink into her rocky bed among the mountains, everything close around her looked like a pot of boiling gold. Filled with wonder, I watched the sky until the sun completely disappeared behind the tallest mountain, the one I would climb.

Happily, dreaming about climbing the mountain, I walked back inside hoping to get something to eat soon. I arrived just in time to hear, "Children ten and above are considered grown up enough to take care of themselves and can do as they please except for a few chores." Then the chores were handed out.

I had to help dress and undress the very small children in the mornings and evenings. Then the woman said while waving her finger at us, "You big girls, make sure you're on time for all meals and inside by dark."

That was all. This would be a great vacation.

Then amazingly, someone folded up a wall and revealed another long table with all sorts of food on it, just as I saw before in the town of Luebeck. We all ran for it. The adults behind the long table filled our plates and told us in their dialect the names of the different dishes. I didn't understand a word, but the food tasted great and they had a lot of it.

I kind of missed potatoes, since we often had them at home, but they had dumplings here, which I came to like a lot. I couldn't believe it at first, but they actually had sweet, hot cocoa here and they said, "You can have hot cocoa every day!"

What an amazing place! I could have all the food I could eat and live in a warm house. I had only a few chores to do and got hot, sweet cocoa every day.

After everyone had their fill of all the delicious food, they led us upstairs to our bedrooms. I even had my own bed, and the water toilets had doors on them. They had placed a nightgown and fresh underwear on each bed. Eight of us slept in one room and we grew into a close group very soon. Even our bedroom felt comfortably warm. I wondered where the big stove stood that heated all the rooms.

Finally, I took my pretty coat off and hung it proudly over the headboard of my bed. I dressed in my nightgown but didn't know what to do with the fresh underwear, so I watched the other girls. They placed the fresh underwear on their nightstands and so I imitated them. We all talked for a bit about our plans for the next day, then sleep crept into my body. I drifted off to the tall mountain I would climb.

Early the next morning before breakfast, the ladies asked us to go down to the cellar where we found what looked like a huge warehouse. Adults had stacks of clothing on long tables and they handed each of us one stack. Then a woman told us to go to the corner of the cellar and select a pair of boots. I soon found they were real leather boots with a soft lining inside. The third pair I tried on fit fine, and were so elegant. I wondered if I could keep them when I went back home.

They then led us into the next room filled with books and toys.

The woman in that room said, "You're welcome to play in this room any time during the day." She handed each of us a book and a deck of cards.

I thanked her very much.

Another woman led us back upstairs to our bedroom. On our way, she showed us the washroom and instructed us to meet her there with a fresh set of clothes. Excited, I spread my new stack of clothes out over my bed. I had two very thick pair of long pants, three pretty, colorful sweaters, gloves, socks and heavy, long underwear. I hardly believed all this belonged to me. I never owned so much clothing at the same time in my whole life. Excited, I jumped around the room.

Then I selected my outfit, folded the rest of the fine clothes, and placed them in my nightstand. When everyone had finished selecting their clothes for the day, we ran to the washroom.

In the big washroom, we had to strip off our clothes and the women checked us for lice and other possible things crawling around on our bodies. A woman then handed us soap, shampoo, a towel, and a comb. Then she walked us to a line of little stalls without doors. There she asked each of us to stand inside of one of those stalls. She explained that warm water would come down from the top of the wall and we could wash our whole body and our hair with plenty of soap and shampoo.

At the moment I looked up at the ceiling of the tiny stall, warm water came down on me like a summer shower. How wonderful it felt. This was the first shower inside a house I had ever had. I washed every last inch of my body, even between my toes, something that we seldom if ever did in the middle of winter at our house. I really liked this shower.

When I had dressed in my new clothes, the woman took me over to the row of small sinks. She handed me a very tiny brush and a tube. Not exactly remembering from my stay at the sanatorium or knowing what to do with this tiny brush, I looked around the room to see what my roommates were doing. Some had opened the tube and squeezed a small amount of its ingredients onto the tiny brush. Some children seemed lost, just like me.

To my surprise, others actually had the tiny brush inside their mouths and brushed their teeth. They spit out white foam now and then, and it didn't look good to me. I had never seen or heard of brushing one's teeth at home. I decided to try it out though. The paste didn't taste good at all. Therefore, that was the end of brushing my teeth for many years to come.

Next came time for breakfast. Hurriedly, I helped to dress a few young children as expected. Hunger drove me down to the dining room quickly. I desperately hoped that I didn't have to take a spoonful of cod liver oil with my meals, as I had to take in the sanatorium.

As I entered the dining room, the great smell of something delicious made me even hungrier. I looked around for my roommates and found them sitting at a table by a big window. They waved at me to come over, which I quickly did. In the middle of our table stood a pot with steaming milk soup that had sausage pieces and potatoes in it. A big plate with freshly cut, warm pieces of great smelling bread stood next to it. A jar of red marmalade and

258

real butter stood on the other side. A young woman walked around with a huge can full of hot cocoa for everyone to enjoy. I saw no nurse with her spoon and bottle full of cod liver oil. This place sure looked like heaven to me.

After I filled my bowl to the rim with the delicious looking milk soup and placed two big slices of warm bread on my plate, I sat down. The other children at our table passed down the real butter and the red marmalade to me. I spread plenty of both on my bread.

The young woman came over to our table and filled my metal cup full of great smelling hot cocoa. Here I sat at the table of plenty, able to eat as much as I desired, and all cleaned up in the middle of winter. I had new clothes on, and this big house was warm in every room. I worried if my sick mom could afford to light her little stove today to have at least a cup of hot tea. I wondered why some people had so much and others had just about nothing.

After breakfast, my roommates and I dressed warmly and took a walk through the pretty village. All the houses stood faraway from each other, like on our island, proud to stand up by themselves. Unlike ours, these houses built of wood, all had a second-story balcony, and all of them were painted in a light color with flowers and people on them in various colors. Such a pretty village. People waved at us and smiled. We waved and smiled back. On the way back up the mountain to our children's home, I found it much harder to walk up the mountain than down.

After a filling lunch of pork stew with dumplings, a jelly-filled donut, and plenty refills of hot cocoa, I announced that I wanted to take a long walk into the dark, dense forest. All my roommates followed me. The slight, cold breeze that greeted us outside bit into our faces. Some of the older boys playing ball in the snow, made lots of noise. When we walked passed them, they huddled together, stood still, looked at us and whispered something to each other. What strange creatures. Just a few more steps and we had left the biting wind behind us. Inside the dense, deep pine forest, the ice-cold wind could no longer touch us. The forest with its strong, very tall trees standing together so closely, protected us.

We soon found a narrow path lined with dark green moss and followed it. Only occasional small patches of snow lay here and there. The dense cover of the forest's canopy held most of the snow back at this point.

We stood still and listened to the complete silence. Even the occasional falling pinecone fell quietly onto the soft, deep moss. We could no longer hear the screaming of those silly boys at the children's home either. Though dark in here, our eyes soon adjusted and we could see very well.

I had a great idea. I asked my roommates, "Why don't we build a dream village with all our special things inside of it that we hope and dream of?"

Everyone looked at me in surprise.

I said, "We can build it out of moss, sticks, pine cones, pine needles and whatever we can find. Perhaps we can find great treasures inside the tall trash cans at the children's home."

Now my roommate's faces lit up. Everyone started to talk at once with great excitement. I decided that we should look for the right spot today and start building tomorrow. We needed a spot off the path so that the animals using the path wouldn't damage our dream village. Yet, it had to be far enough from the children's home so no one could destroy it.

After a short while, I found a perfect, secluded place with lots of green moss growing around. On our way back to the home, we collected many things we thought usable to build our dream village. At the children's home, we raided the tall trash cans. What riches we found!

We came upon scraps of colored paper to make fancy dresses for our stick people and empty cans that could serve as support for our castles. We found strings of all lengths and colors which we could use for various projects, like marking sidewalks or streets.

By the time we had finished raiding the tall trash cans, we had filled all our pockets with treasures.

That evening, while I helped the small children undress, I asked the young woman who seemed to be in charge of this part of the children's home if I could climb the tallest mountain.

She smiled and said, "We plan to take all the older children on a beautiful sleigh ride up on the tallest mountain on Christmas day."

My heart jumped high with joy! When I had undressed the little ones that needed help, I ran up to my bedroom, opened the window, looked at the tall mountain and whispered, "God, I'm coming to check up on you!"

For many days, we spent time in the deep, silent forest on our secret project, our dream village. We built many houses and a few big castles with windows and door openings in them. A barn with a herd of pine cone cows around it made quite a sight. The cows had white snow eyes and string tails. We marked our roads on each side with strings and we removed the moss from them. Many stick people dressed in fancy paper clothes walked around the village.

On one end of our village, we made a forest of pine twigs, and on the other end we constructed a large chicken cube enclosed by a fence made of sticks and strings. Inside the chicken cube grew grass made with pine needles sticking up out of the moss. We had forty orange-pit chickens running around in it. We used acorns, which we found underneath the huge oak tree at the yard of the children's home for dogs. We didn't tie them on leashes since we wanted them to be free. They did have a good assortment of colored tails of all sizes on them. Oh, how much fun we had.

Since Christmas Eve would arrive in a few days, we built a big church with a nativity scene. We made the three kings and Jesus from acorns and used a matchbox filled with pine needles for the crib where Jesus lay. For the gifts brought by the kings, we used colored chips from a broken butter dish we found inside a trash can. After lots of work, two small torn socks served as Mary and

Joseph. I sewed them a real face, cut a little of my hair off and sewed it onto Mary's head. Joseph had a fine hat made from orange peel. We decided to leave the roof of our church open, so we could look inside and see our beautiful nativity scene. In the early afternoon on Christmas Eve, we finally finished building our dream village.

As we proudly stood and silently admired our work, my mind drifted home to my island. On this Christmas Eve, I wondered if my mom and grandma would have a warm room and a filling meal. Would they have a fine drink from my grandma's cellar and tell old stories over again, the ones that grow longer and funnier each time they tell them?

Would they care for my dear friend, my dog Harras? I dearly hoped so. I looked at our small group of eight girls, all who had come here for a while to escape different sad circumstances. Their expressions showed me that they too might have gone home for a brief moment on this Christmas Eve afternoon.

Grandma's nightly candle came to my mind. Excited I said, "Hey, we need candles in every building and light them when it gets dark. Then we could ask for everyone to come and look at our dream village."

Their faces lit up, but we had no idea where we could get candles. We knew the tiny village store had candles, but none of us had a penny to our name. Solemnly we looked at each other, so I decided that we needed to go back to the children's home, explain what we wanted to do on this Christmas Eve and ask someone for candles. They all quickly agreed that we should go together, but that I should ask.

Home we walked, through this impressive, deep pine forest. I walked straight up the front steps and to the office of the always smiling old woman who managed this home. Everyone followed me. We found the door to her office open, like always.

I stuck my head inside and said, "Hello."

"Hello. Please come in," the woman said.

Everyone followed closely. I told her, "We built a wonderful dream village with a nativity scene and need some candles to light our buildings tonight. Then everyone can come out to our dream village after it gets dark and have a look at it."

She stood up with great excitement. "Would you show your village to me now?"

"Oh, sure," we answered.

The smiling woman put on her big coat and out we walked to our dream village. What she saw totally surprised her.

She clasped her hands together and said, "Oh yes, you absolutely need to light this pretty village this evening, and I'll make sure everyone can come to see it."

On our way back to the home she said, "We have many pieces of partially burnt candles left from the last time the electricity went out briefly. You can have them all."

Full of excitement, we walked back to the home to get the candles. The shadows grew longer. Darkness moved in slowly. At her office, she handed us a bunch of candles and three packages of matches.

"Now remember to be careful," she said."It will take about thirty minutes before all the children and escorts get dressed and ready to leave the building. I'll lead them to your beautiful dream village myself. By the time we have walked halfway toward your village, I'll whistle a Christmas song. That's your sign to light the candles." She handed us a lantern, shook my hand and smiled even more broadly than usual. Ever so excited, we ran out the door and toward the thick, dark forest.

A few steps inside the dense pine forest, darkness embraced us. I lit the lantern to light the way to our dream village. When we reached our moss village, we realized that we had enough pieces of candles to place two in every building and five inside our big church. With great anticipation, we waited for the start of a whistled Christmas song so we could start lighting our candles.

I quickly organized us so that everyone knew which part of

our village to light. Soon we heard our sign, a whistle, trying to make the musical tones of "Oh Christmas Tree." We carefully lit all the candles. What a surprise! I never imagined that our dream village would look so awesomely beautiful!

We stood and gazed at our lit village in wonder. The sight stunned me. Soon we heard the voices of the arriving children. I blew out our lantern and we stood together a few steps away from our dream village, which had come alive with the softly flickering candles.

One after another, the astounded children of all ages and the chaperons gathered in amazement around our glowing village. In complete silence, everyone admired our village with the Christmas nativity scene. Most likely, some of the children wandered off in their minds to a place far from here. I knew my mind drifted home to my family. A few children silently shed a tear or two and wiped them away with their mittens.

Slowly a small, very fragile looking child came close to our moss church and began to sing "Silent Night" in an unsteady voice. Everyone joined in, and when we sang the first verse the third time, the only one we seemed to know, we sang with happy voices, almost in tune with each other. A slight breeze barely moved the tall trees. Our candles flickered once and died. The chaperons lit their lanterns, and a wonderfully touching time ended.

Slowly, I followed the trail of children leaving the shelter of the deep pine forest, but I kept a picture of that beautiful little village with the candles softly flickering in my mind forever.

A bright moon greeted us on the edge of the forest, and we saw so many fresh animal tracks in the snow. I wondered if they too had looked at and admired our dream village. Perhaps they had listened or even joined us in our song. Then I remembered that we forgot to place animals in the church's nativity scene. I hoped the animals inside this forest wouldn't feel sad because we left them out of the Christmas scene.

As soon as I entered the front door of our home, I smelled

fried sausages. Oh how I liked them. I looked forward to a wonderful Christmas Eve meal. In a hurry, I took my coat off, hung it on the hook in the hallway and entered the dining room.

What a surprise! A tall Christmas tree stood in the middle of the room. Beautiful decorations hung on it and many white candles glowed brightly from its branches. I never saw such a big tree inside a house lit, and with so many candles. I knew it would have never fit in my mom's little room. I stood and admired it. The flickering candles brought me back to our dream village for just a brief moment.

All the chaperons and other people who worked in this home came inside the dining room with huge boxes. When they set the huge boxes down, I saw that they held many small, wrapped boxes.

The adults started to sing "Oh Christmas Tree." One of the young women signaled us with her hand to join in the singing. We surely did. Many of the children only knew the first verse, which included me, but the adults kept on singing and singing.

Despite the happiness that filled the room, my stomach begged for the fried sausages something fierce. When I thought that they had finally finished singing, they sang the first verse again and asked us to join in. I sang, but anxiously hoped that we didn't have to sing or listen to all those verses again.

Then, with a loud, Merry Christmas, they asked us to sit down in our regular places. Servers set out bowls full of potato salad, and trays filled with fried, sizzling sausages. The young women poured hot cocoa into our mugs. Then they set freshly baked, fine smelling apple cake and a pot with cream in front of us. What a heavenly meal. I hoped tonight's prayer wouldn't take long so I could still my growling stomach.

Then came the woman who always smiled to say the prayer. She always said the prayer in her heavy Bavarian dialect, even though she could speak the regular German language. I never understood a word of her prayers. I just hoped she didn't ask for all of us to go to hell.

When I thought she had finished praying, I grabbed a sausage, but she had just taken a deep breath and went on with her prayer. A little embarrassed, I laid the sausage back on the plate. Finally, she said, "Amen" and ended her prayer. We all began to eat.

I filled my plate full to the rim. The second sausage even hung over my plate on one side and dripped hot grease on the table. I hoped nobody saw my bad manners, but how wonderful this food tasted! While I shoveled down my food, I began to wonder why we needed to say a prayer before we ate. Why couldn't we say a prayer after we ate and change the words a little? That way I could get to the food much faster.

After people came and collected the dishes, the woman asked us to stay. The adults came around, smiled at each of us, and gave us a gift. I really didn't expect a gift. All the great food they fed us had to cost a lot of money already.

Carefully, I opened the wrapped gift. Inside the box I found a big chocolate bar, a storybook with pictures about Christmas, and a beautiful light blue pullover. The gifts totally surprised me and I didn't quite know what to say or do. So, I stood up and loudly said, "Thank you very much."

The other children, a few at a time, stood up and repeated the thank you. Their voices sounded like an echoing wave floating through the room. All the adults smiled at us and nodded their heads. Then they gently told us, "It's time to go to bed, children. We have a great day ahead of us tomorrow."

On my way up to the bedroom, I stopped and looked for a brief moment at the beautiful, lit Christmas tree. My mom's and my grandma's faint faces looked back at me, smiling. I whispered a Merry Christmas to them and then a good night.

In the bedroom I looked out the window again, whispering toward the tallest mountain, "Good night, God. I'll see you tomorrow."

As Christmas Eve ended, my excitement over Christmas Day grew. The next morning, I awoke long before the sun ever thought about rising from her bed. After I dressed, I walked in the dim hallways, thinking over what I'd say to God when I saw him up there in His house among the clouds. I had so many questions and suggestions how He could do a better job on earth. I decided that I may need to stay a day or so up there with Him to tell Him everything I wanted to.

Since I wouldn't have breakfast until ten, I decided to walk out to our dream village as soon as daylight arrived. Before long, the sun's tall beams painted the few snow clouds a pretty, soft pink. Outside, I breathed in the crisp morning air, and the snow crunched beneath my shoes with every step I took. Exhaling my warm breath into the cold air made short-lived clouds. In no time at all, I reached the big, dense pine forest where it always felt much warmer inside. I still occupied my mind with putting my questions and suggestions for God in the right order, when I heard a soft noise.

I stood completely still and listened. Yes, there it was again, a soft, faint breathing noise that seemed to come from our dream village. Then I heard a louder, snorting noise. As quietly as I could, I walked closer. A few steps closer and I saw something big moving around. A little frightened, but nosy enough to move closer, I hid behind the big tree trunks and crept forward to the big, still faint, shapes.

Daylight glowed a little brighter now, even inside the dense pine forest. With a few steps closer to our moss village, I clearly saw a herd of whitetail deer standing around our village, just looking at it. A few more steps closer, I sat down behind a huge tree trunk and took in the sight. All the deer stood looking at our dream village. Perhaps they had come to be in the nativity scene since I had forgotten to put animals inside our moss church.

Suddenly, they lifted their heads, looked toward me and heavily sniffed the air. Slowly, the herd stirred and walked away into the quiet pine forest. I stood up, walked to our dream village to check if the deer had destroyed it. To my surprise, I found our moss village in good condition. Only the acorn dogs had disappeared. I wondered if the deer ate them. I looked around for the long, colored strings the acorn dogs had as tails, but found none. I wondered if the deer had eaten them too.

Happy to have seen the herd of deer and that our moss village remained intact, I walked back to the children's home. What a wonderful day lay ahead, perhaps the best ever. I hoped to find God alive so I could talk to Him up there on the tall mountain, among His clouds.

Back at the home, the children busily got their day started. I helped the little ones to get dressed and sang a happy Christmas song to them. I was so happy this day had finally come.

They served us an outstanding breakfast of fried apple dumplings with crisp bacon slices on top. I had two helpings, and of course, a mug full of hot cocoa. While eating breakfast, I constantly looked out the window for the promised horse-drawn sleds to arrive that would take us up the tall mountain.

Then I saw them. Extremely excited, I jumped up from the table and screamed, "They're here! They're here!" Then I ran to the hall to get my coat, gloves and hat.

Hurriedly, I dressed on the way out the door. At breakfast, our chaperons had given us little pieces of paper marked with a number. We needed to go onto the sled, which matched our number. I ran to the sled with my number on it and arrived first.

A young, very handsome man who stood by the sled greeted me with a huge smile. "Since you're the first girl here, you can ride up front with me, if you'd like."

I nodded excitedly. "Oh, yes!"

He helped me up and handed me a blanket to wrap myself up in. It didn't take long before all three big sleds filled with laughing children. With a slight click of the driver's tongue, the horses began to move forward to our great adventure.

The horses wore a leather belt with small, silver bells around their necks too, just like the ones that picked us up at the train station. All the small bells jingled so lovely with every step they took. Steam rose from the horses' bodies and they blew little clouds into the cold, still morning air. Fresh snow had covered the land overnight in a beautiful white glistening coat. Someone started to sing a Christmas song and everyone joined in. We sang with happy, strong voices, not all that far out of tune.

When we reached the small village, the drivers stopped the horses. People came to us with smiling faces, wishing us a very Merry Christmas. They handed each sled of children a bag full of cookies and candy. We thanked them and sang the first verse of "Silent Night" for those gracious village people twice. We sang it from our heart, loud enough so the whole village could hear it.

A little way out of the small village, our sleds separated. I asked the young driver why, and he said, "Every sled will stop at a different farmhouse to get a hot drink and warm up for a short time. After the break, we'll meet again at this place and drive a good ways up the tallest mountain to the end of the road. There, whoever would like to can follow me and walk higher up onto the beautiful mountain. The other children who don't wish to walk up the mountain, can play in the snow or go inside the big, warm cabin and listen to a Christmas story."

Wondering if the fine horses had to stay out in the cold, I asked him, "Where will the horses rest when we walk up the mountain?"

He said, "We'll take them inside a stall on the end of the road where someone will give them warm water to drink and wheat to eat, so they'll have the strength to take us back home after we come back down off the mountain."

Knowing that someone would take care of the horses made me glad.

Proudly, I told the nice, good looking young man, "I'm going to walk all the way up the tallest mountain into God's cloud house to see if He's still alive. If I find Him, I'm going to ask Him many questions I have on my mind. Perhaps I'll give Him a little advice on how to run His earth better."

The young man looked at me, nodded his head and smiled.

I asked him, "Did you ever see God up there?"

He looked at me again, shook his head and said, "No, I never saw God up there."

His answer sorely disappointed me.

Soon we stopped in front of a huge farmhouse. The driver asked us to jump off the sled and go inside. An older man came with buckets of water for the horses. A woman brought heavy blankets, which she threw over the horses' backs to keep them warm. A young girl came out of the barn with a basket full of apples for the horses.

When she came close to me, I asked her, "Can I give the horses on this sled each an apple?"

She smiled. "Sure." Then she handed me two apples.

While I gave each horse their apple, I thanked them for the fine ride. They looked at me with their big, dark, shiny eyes as if they looked deep into my soul.

Bashfully, I entered the huge farmhouse. The big room, larger than our whole house on the island, amazed me. I even saw more rooms down the hall. Then I spotted a wide staircase that led up to the second story and realized that our little house could fit inside this huge place many times. My eyes slowly wandered around this beautiful room, staring at all the pretty furnishings, which I had never seen before.

In the corner, next to the wide staircase, stood the tallest Christmas tree I had ever seen, even taller than the one in the children's home. At the very top sat a large angel.

The angel's curly, blond hair hung far down on the sides of the tree. Her white, silvery, sparkling wings spread out wide, as if she was about to fly away. She had a realistic ceramic face and hands. Her blue glass eyes sparkled, and she wore a long, white satin dress with embroidered white lace. I stared at the beautiful angel. I had never seen anything that pretty on a tree before.

The dark green Christmas tree had many white candles on it and many pretty, colorful glass ornaments of different shapes. The other children silently stared in wonder at the tall, beautiful tree too. As was customary, the candles were not lit during the day. How I wished to see them lit at night for just a brief moment.

With a big bang, a wide door swung open to both sides. Three women walked through it side by side. One of them carried a big plateful of delicious smelling marble cake. Another woman had a can of steaming hot milk, and the last carried mugs and plates inside. One of the women who looked a lot like my grandma, told us to sit down on the chairs at the very long table and enjoy the food and the hot milk.

We managed to eat every crumb of the marble cake and empty the can of hot milk. We all thanked the kind people very much. Then we stopped at the outhouse, which they had three of inside the big barn close to the house. After that, we climbed back onto the sleds.

When I sat next to the young man on the driver's bench, I looked up at the tallest mountain. I excitedly whispered to myself, "Here I come, God!"

Heavy, dark grey snow clouds hung around the top of the mountain. We met the other sleds and started to climb up the mountain road. The horses worked hard, dragging the big sleds upward. Around the outside of the mountain we climbed, around and around, higher and higher. Though hard for the horses, they made it up the mountain to the end of the road. They breathed hard and sweated a lot, even on such a very cold day.

As soon as a man released them from the big sleds, they walked into the barn on their own and I could hear them sucking up water. I knew they must be glad to rest.

Full of excitement and energy, we all climbed or jumped off the sleds. A bit of chaos reigned until all the children decided what they wanted to do. All the children on the sled with me stood close to the young driver to walk up the mountain. A few more children joined our group and soon the chaos ended.

Our young man gave us one rule. "Follow me in a single line and do not stray off the path." He said it twice with a stern voice. Then he said, "Let's have some fun!"

Excitedly we started to walk up the tall mountain. The heavy cloud in which I believed God lived, floated not far above us. I began to grow a little nervous and a little scared, but still hoped desperately that God still lived so I could talk to Him. Perhaps some of the other children here also wondered why He had never fulfilled their many tearful prayers.

Around the next bend in the trail, I reached up and touched my first cloud. It wasn't solid, as I had expected, but rather more like fog. I started to look around for God, or a house where he could live. Two more sharp turns in the path and the grey clouds completely embraced us. This had to be where God lived! I strained my eyes to find a sign of Him. I even called Him by His name. My call echoed repeatedly around the high mountains, but no sign or answer came from Him.

In desperation, I stepped off the snowy walking path, knelt in the snow, folded my hands and very politely prayed for God to come and see me. I listened for an answer in the silence of this white land, but none came. Only the cold, lonely wind slightly blew his whining song along the naked, rough boulders.

I called to Him again. "I have so much I need to ask you, please come to me!" I wanted to tell Him about all the terrible, cruel things going on in His world and ask Him to change them, but only the sad, lonely wind whispered back at me.

With my tears frozen to my cheeks, I stood up from the snow-covered ground and with a last flicker of hope to see God, I looked heavenward. A lone, cold snowflake fell in my face. I stood close to a huge frozen boulder, forlorn and deeply disappointed, I believed God had died. My tears ran freely, even though I didn't know Him and never met Him. No wonder none of my pleading prayers had been answered.

Then the snow started to fall more heavily. I wondered where they had buried God. I decided to ask our preacher when I got back home. He should know, since he had that big book which told him what had happened and will happen. Perhaps God knew He was dying and sent the big book, the Bible, to us from his mountain so we'd learn how to take care of ourselves.

The snow came down heavier and heavier and I had lost sight of the group I came up here with. I could no longer hear them. I couldn't even see the trail. The snow had covered their footprints. At that moment, I grew very frightened of being unable to find my way down off the tall mountain. I figured I'd better turn around and walk down on the path we came up on. Slowly, with one hand holding onto the boulders as best as I could and the other hand in front of my face, to keep the heavy falling snow out of my eyes, I stumbled along. At a particularly steep part, I slipped and fell into the snow. When I desperately tried to stand back up, I slid further down and hit my head on something hard.

I drifted off to a faintly noticeable warm place. Someone bent down to me, softly held my hand and helped me up out of the snow. As I stood there, somewhat dizzy, I wondered who helped me get back on my feet. I looked around, but saw no one. I decided to call for help, but the wind swallowed my desperate call.

Scared and unsure if I walked on the right path, I started to walk down the mountain. Strangely, I noticed that the wind twirled around me quite a bit and lifted just enough fresh snow off the ground so I could make out part of a footprint in front of me. In a short while, I realized that I followed a trail off the mountain.

Happiness shot through me. I felt safe now, as if a warm hand held my hand and guided me off the mountain, but I didn't see anyone. Before long, I heard the voices of children and could make out part of the cabin where we had started from. The wind quit twirling around me, and the partial soft imprints in the snow in front of me had disappeared as did the warm feeling of someone's hand. I didn't know why, but I turned around and softly whispered at the wind, "Thank you so very much."

When I reached the cabin, I found everyone busily climbing back onto the sleds. In a hurry, worried that they might leave me behind, I ran to the sled with my number on it and climbed up to sit next to the driver.

He turned to me and said, "Hello. "How did you like the hike?"

I answered, "It was great." I knew that wasn't quite the truth, but I didn't feel like telling him what had really happened to me.

The driver gave the horses just a tap with the reins and we began our trip back home.

The snow continued to fall heavily, and I could barely see the horses on our sled. As soon as we rounded the first bend in the road, the wind started to howl. The big snowflakes flew sideways at us. The horses wanted to run faster, but the driver held them back hard as we descended the steep mountain.

The temperature dropped and the children at the back of the sled lay down to avoid the ice-cold wind blowing into their faces. I wrapped my blanket a little tighter around my body, hoping to reach the home soon.

As we came off the mountain, the powerful storm pounded us. I had no idea where we were. I only saw snow flying sideways into my face. The horses' many neighs sounded like complaints about the wild snowstorm, but they faithfully plodded forward.

Finally we stopped. The driver asked us, "Step off the sled and hold tightly onto the side of the wagon until I come to you." He held both of my hands and helped me down.

Still holding onto each other, we walked over to the waiting children. He had us form a single line and told us, "Hold on tightly to each other's hands so we don't lose anyone in this blizzard!"

He led the children, and I found myself last in the line of frightened, freezing children.

We walked through knee-deep snow, and the howling wind tore at my pretty coat. I hoped it wouldn't rip it apart. I didn't want to disappoint my mom by coming home with a torn coat after she had worked such long time sewing it for me.

A violent gust hit me from behind and I fell over, head first, into the snow. The soft snow cushioned my fall. I wasn't t hurt at all, but I had lost the hand to hold onto to guide me to the children's home.

After I stood up, I leaned into the strong, angry wind, hoping it wouldn't knock me over again. My eyes searched all around for the children's home, but I only saw white snow speeding down from the heavens. For just a brief second, a sound, as if someone called me, flew by my ears. Then the howling wind took over again.

My face started to burn from the lashing wind. Shivering wildly from the cold, deep fear overcame me that this raging blizzard would bury me here. I needed shelter quickly.

Recollecting that I had not gone far from the sled before the wind had blown me over, I turned to what I thought was the direction of the sled. Carefully, I started to walk through the deep snow. I hoped to reach the horses. Surely, someone would come quickly to lead them into a barn.

I started to pray to God for help, but then I remembered that He had died. Slowly, step by step through the deep snow, fighting the strong wind, I walked, hoping I walked in the right direction to reach the horses.

A split second break of the heavily falling snow let me see a faint part of the outline of the sled. What a happy moment! Just as the wild, threatening blizzard started to show me that it had even more strength, I reached the sled. As I climbed onto the driver's bench, the horses nervously neighed and turned their heads toward me. I knew how to lead a team, but where to? I waited a brief moment for someone to come and guide the horses to shelter, but no one came.

The horses snorted wildly now, and I recognized in them an unwillingness to stay out here in this raging blizzard any longer. I took the reins in my hands and gave the nervous horses a very gentle touch to get going. With all my heart, I hoped they knew the way. My grandma had often told me that animals were very smart in finding their way home by smelling. I hoped that included horses. They sure had big noses.

Usually huge plow horses like these, remained calm and never ran, but under these circumstances, the storm frightened them and they started to run. It took all my strength to hold those strong, very nervous plow horses back, even though I lifted the brake on the sled up high.

Before I could think of what to do, the horses burst through the barn doors and I fell off the driver's seat onto the wooden planks of the sled. Scared to death but unhurt, I just briefly wondered if I was still alive. The horses stopped immediately inside the barn and someone closed the slightly damaged doors.

I gathered what little strength I had left and shakily stepped off the sled. My legs wobbled, and I fell to the barn floor next to a bale of straw. I heard voices and realized that I had not come to the barn at the children's home, but inside a much bigger one.

People came running from inside the huge barn and from the hallway that connected the house and the barn. As they came closer, I recognized the young man who had driven our sled. He came to me, picked me off the floor and embraced me with a huge smile.

With a shaky voice he said, "Oh, how I worried about you. I looked and called your name outside in the snow, but couldn't find you in the wild blizzard. When I ran to take the horses inside the barn, I found them just busting through the barn door."

The other children from the same sled came inside the barn as well. Everyone came over to me, smiled and hugged me. Then they walked in different directions. Each small group had an adult with them. The boys in our group helped the young driver to dry the wet horses. They were obviously having fun! A girl fed the chickens, and another girl tried to milk a cow. That girl had to be new at this chore. The cow complained a lot.

A few pigs had a big disagreement about something. A big black and white cat walked by me with a fat rat in her mouth. She surely caught a fine meal tonight. While pigeons settled down for the night in the loft, a white duck pulled on my boot strings. I slowly warmed up and stopped shaking.

What a big, comfortable barn that sheltered so many animals. Even a couple of huge dogs stood in a stall next to me. They looked well cared for and loved. That reminded me of my dog, Harras. I hoped Grandma took good care of him and that he had a warm place to sleep. I missed him an awful lot.

When the laughter and talk inside the barn stopped for a brief moment, I heard the wind still howling bitterly outside. The lantern near the big barn door flickered once and died. The boys finished drying off the big plow horses, led them into their stalls, and gave them a huge amount of hay. With the horses in their stalls, I now wondered about getting back to the children's home. I surely didn't want to have to walk the long way home through the raging blizzard.

I looked around at this barn with all its soft straw bales, and thought it a nice place to spend the night. I needed to gather the children together and ask the owners very politely if we could stay in the barn overnight.

At that moment, the old woman, who looked a lot like my grandma, came into the barn. She waved her hand at us to come and gather at her side.

She waited until we all stood by her side, and then she said, "The dangerous blizzard is still much alive outside. The horses cannot pull a sled through the storm to take you to your children's home. All of you have to stay here tonight."

We all thanked her very much with a big smile.

I walked over to the large stack of straw bales and claimed my space for the night. Some children did the same while others walked around looking at all the animals. Though tired and awfully hungry, I knew my hunger would have to wait. At least I could give my exhausted body the rest it needed on the soft straw. I lay back and instantly went to sleep.

Someone softly called my name and gently shook me. When I opened my eyes, I saw the young driver kneeling next to me.

With a smile, he said, "All the children will sleep inside the cozy house. Come, follow me."

Quickly, I brushed the straw out of my hair and off my pretty coat and followed him inside the huge house.

There I joined the rest of our group on a house tour. First, we walked through a room separated from the living area, called the kitchen, a very big room, bigger than the first floor of our entire house on the island. In there I saw not one, but two of the biggest stoves I had ever seen in my life.

Delicious smelling food bubbled in pots on top of those stoves. Then I saw an oven inside a wall, a sight by itself, and four big loaves of bread baked inside of it, all at the same time. My stomach growled loudly, which embarrassed me. Though so hungry, I couldn't expect these nice people to feed me too.

In the corner of the kitchen stood a large metal sink at the same level as the table, and I saw a pump standing right next to it. A young girl pumped water into the sink—water right inside the kitchen that didn't come out of the wall. What a brilliant idea! I couldn't wait to tell my mom and my grandma about this.

The old woman gently directed the three young women around the kitchen. One of the young women took a tall stack of plates out of a cupboard and took them into the room where we had cake and hot milk on our way to the tallest mountain. According to the tall stack of plates, they surely had a large family.

Next, we walked up the wide staircase that led to a long hallway with many doors that opened into bedrooms. The woman opened doors and told us who of her family slept in which room. Each room had nice furnishings. They even had curtains on the windows and big closets in two of the rooms.

I didn't think that the closets would even fit through our front door, and definitely not inside my mom's room. At the end of the hall we came to four small, unoccupied rooms. Inside each room we saw a bed, a chair, and a small table with a porcelain bowl and pitcher on it. Underneath the beds stood fine looking chamber pots with lids attached to them, not just an old pail, as we had at home.

The friendly woman assigned two children to each bed and handed them each a towel. She showed them the water in the pitchers and the soap right next to the bowls. Then the woman handed the rest of us a pillow and a blanket. She told us that we could sleep on the sofas downstairs in the parlor and in the living room. We could wash up in the kitchen sink and that we'd find soap and towels down there.

On the way downstairs I wondered about a parlor. I thought perhaps it was a slang word for barn. Suddenly, everyone stopped walking and whispered "Ooh!" and "Aah!" I looked down and what a sight I saw. All the candles on the huge, beautiful Christmas tree glowed! I missed the next step and tumbled down the remaining steps, knocking down a few of the children. What a commotion. Out of embarrassment, I started to cry.

The noise had brought the three young women out of the kitchen to us in a hurry. They asked if we had hurt ourselves and then helped us up with warm smiles. No one was hurt badly. I was sure though, a few scratches and some bruises would show up later. All of our little group gathered around the prettiest Christmas tree in our world and stared at it in admiration. Oh, how I wished my mom and my grandma could see this wonderful tree. I missed them so much, but I didn't suffer from the awful feeling of homesickness that I had at the sanatorium.

The ringing of a little silver bell made me turn. There, on the even longer table, sat the smiling old woman ringing the bell again. She waved her hand for us to come close. The long table was set for a lot of people with fancy, shiny silverware and fine china plates with silver roses painted on them.

I had only seen such pretty plates inside a store. At home and other places, I had only eaten from metal plates. Someone had also added many extra chairs since this morning. The old woman waved us on to sit down at the table.

I hesitated. I couldn't believe that these people would feed all of us. The other children stood back too, hesitating to sit down at this fine table.

The friendly old woman stood up, pulled some chairs back and gave us the hand signal to sit down. Every one of the children looked at me, wanting to know what to do.

Quietly I said, "Let's sit down at the table, but let's not eat too much food so these nice people have enough to eat for their family."

With heads nodding in agreement, everyone sat down at this fancy table.

A real old man and four middle-aged couples dressed in fancy clothes, came and sat down at the table. Looking straight ahead, I noticed a big hole in the wall with pieces of wood inside it. I had never seen anything like that. Perhaps they used it as a place to dry their wood for the kitchen stoves.

When most of the chairs had filled with people and children, the old, happy looking woman opened a huge book, which looked like our preacher's bible, and began to read. She read in her Bavarian dialect and I didn't understand a word she said. I just waited patiently for her to say Amen.

The handsome, young sled driver came inside the room with some paper in his hand. He stuffed the paper beneath the big pieces of wood inside the hole in the wall. I looked back at the old woman, reading her big book. Just as I nearly nodded off to sleep, on the fine decked table, something drew my attention back to the handsome driver. A fire raged inside the hole of the wall!

Loudly I screamed, "Fire, fire!" and ran outside in a hurry, right into the raging blizzard. Many of the other children screamed and followed me outside. I felt so sad and scared for the people inside of the burning house and hoped they'd run outside before the house burned down with them inside of it.

Here they came, but only to the door. The young driver ran over to me, grabbed me and said, "The house isn't burning!"

He waved and screamed for everyone to come back inside. With everyone back inside the house, the old woman explained to us, "The hole in the wall is a fireplace."

She said, "The fire will stay inside the hole and you don't have to fear that the house will burn down. Please sit back down at the table."

Embarrassed for all the commotion I caused, I silently did as she asked. When the room quieted, I looked at the old woman and politely asked, "Please forgive me."

She smiled at me, nodded her head and started to read again.

From where I sat, I could see the fireplace clearly. The big red and orange flames danced wildly in the hole. I didn't care what the woman had said, it still looked scary to me. What if this hot monster crawled out of its hole and licked us with his long, red, burning tongues? I made sure to keep an eye on the scary monster in the wall. The smallest movement out of its hole would send me out the door.

When the fine old woman closed her big book, someone said loudly, "Thank you God for letting all of us be safe in this room tonight."

Then everyone said Amen. I guessed they still thought God lived up on that mountain.

The three young women brought freshly baked slices of bread spread with butter and honey to the table. On their next trip from of the kitchen, they each carried a big bowl of something which smelled wonderful. All of the people at the table passed their soup plates around, and the young women ladled a big amount into each.

My stomach growled loudly again and I hoped no one heard it. Someone passed a soup plate to me filled with pea soup, which I liked very much. The friendly old woman began to eat, our sign that we could begin to eat also.

We greatly appreciated the pea soup and the bread. Then someone asked if we wanted seconds, but we politely answered, "No thank you," even though most likely all of us children could have eaten another helping.

Then we had another surprise. The three young women came with more food. They served each of us a plateful of steaming hot stew and filled our mugs with sweet buttermilk.

Astounded and with anticipation, we looked at each other and the old woman. She smiled and nodded her head for us to start eating. Eagerly we began. This food had such a wonderful flavor, and there was so much of it. I ate the whole plateful. When I looked around the table, I noticed that all the children had eaten their food and were licking their plates clean. Gently, but a little worried I might break the fancy plate in front of me, I picked it up and licked it clean.

The young driver fed the fire monster a few big pieces of wood that the monster must not have liked. He spat out many sparks at the young man and made a lot of hissing sounds. His big, red tongues eventually died down, and he puffed dark, grey smoke up the hole in the wall.

I could barely believe it when the young women came around and served dessert, baked apples with butter and real white sugar, just like my grandma and my mom made at home on special occasions. These people had treated us so nicely. I figured they had to be awful rich to eat so well, have such a huge house and barn and still have enough to give so much to us. At the moment, I made up my young mind that I would be rich someday. Suddenly, the fire monster began to like his new food and ate at it with his huge, red tongues. His flaming, restless tongues reached high up into the wall again. Strong now, he roared to show off his ability to eat whatever stood in his way. I desperately hoped that he didn't escape from his hole in the wall.

The elderly woman noticed my fearful expression and walked over to me. She placed her shaking hand on my head, bent down and whispered in my ear, "The fire will not harm you, my child!" Then she sat back down at the long, festive table.

A middle-aged man and woman who sat at the edge of the table next to the old woman, asked two of the boys, brothers, to come and sit in the parlor with them. The boys obediently followed the couple. I watched so that later I could have a look to see what a parlor looked like.

The old woman asked us girls to please carefully take the dishes into the kitchen and then gather around the Christmas tree. We followed her request and managed to accomplish her wish without breaking even one piece of the fine china.

Soon all of us gathered around the glorious, Christmas tree. We sang Christmas songs together with the adults of this beautiful, big house. Our language was not the same, but somehow the songs we sang sounded great.

At the last flicker of the candles I gathered my courage and stepped up a few steps on the stairs and announced, "I'm going to sing the Christmas song which I always sing solo in our church's Christmas plays."

I looked at the lovely angel on top of the prettiest Christmas tree I had ever seen, and began to sing the song, *"Es ist ein Rose entsprungen."*

Translated, the song talks about a red rose that sprung up out of the snow in the dark night when Christ was born. I don't know if the song has made it to this country, or its English title.

I sang all the verses exactly the right way, pretending I sang them at home with my grandma, sitting inside our old, amazingly beautiful church.

When I finished my song, all the lit candles on the Christmas tree had burned out and electric lights lit up the big house. I stood in complete silence for a moment. As I looked around at the gathered faces, I saw a tear or two rolling down some children's faces and the old woman's face. I knew the reasons for the children's tears, but not the reasons for the old woman's tears. I wondered why she cried. Perhaps the memories of a long gone loved one had entered her mind and her heart.

Then came bedtime. I claimed a sofa for my bed, from where I could keep an eye on the fire monster in the wall. Happy, I cuddled beneath my blanket on the comfortable sofa in that cozy room. I felt so thankful with my stomach full of delicious food and safe inside this fine house. I took one more look at the fire monster. He had eaten all his food. His long, red hot tongues had starved. However, his soul continued to glow among the grey ashes, pleading for more food. The young man placed a screen in front of the hole in the wall to lock the starving monster's soul inside. I felt safe enough to go to sleep.

Some noise inside the big kitchen woke me early the next morning. I looked first at the hole in the wall to check on the fire monster. He now lay dead. Even his glowing soul had disappeared. Looking out the window, I noticed the destructive blizzard had moved on to bother someone else.

The sun, barely out of her bed, tried with all her strength, to warm the earth. One of the young women came to wake us and told us that we'd leave soon to go back to the children's home.

Quickly, I walked to the room called the parlor to see what it looked like. Through the open door, I saw that the children who had slept on the sofas had just begun crawling out from beneath their blankets. The room had three short couches, six upholstered chairs and a few small tables standing around, which had crocheted doilies on them.

Big, landscape pictures hung on the walls, and pretty figurines stood around on the small tables. Long, dark, green velvet curtains hung on the windows. Golden colored, plaited ropes, with golden bells at the end of the ropes, held them back from the windows. I stared at the beautiful, decorated windows in awe. What a difference from my mom's plain curtains made from useless pillow covers. Right close to the glass of the windows hung white lace curtains. I stood in the fanciest room I had ever seen in my life. I was stunned.

Since I, and most likely the other children also had slept in our street clothes, we were ready to leave in no time at all. The young women handed every one of us a hefty ham sandwich. The thick slice of ham hung out on all sides between the two slices of warm, black bread. I took a big bite out of it immediately and found it totally delicious.

When I walked outside, I saw how much it had snowed. The snow reached almost to the horse's belly, but someone had shoveled it away so we could enter the sled easily. We all waved goodbye and thanked the friendly, gracious people one more time. After I took my second, giant bite out of my delicious ham sandwich, I noticed that we missed the brothers who walked to the parlor last night with a middle-aged couple.

Quickly, I told the driver, "We forgot the two boys."

He shook his head. "The boys are orphans and the couple you saw them going into the parlor with will adopt both of them. The couple own the beautiful big house you slept in last night. If after a year, the boys still like it there and the couple is pleased with them, the boys will have a new mom and dad."

Momentary jealousy rippled through me. I'd have loved to stay in that pretty, big house with all the food to eat and the amazing Christmas tree. I'd never have to drag buckets of water upstairs and the dirty water back downstairs. Perhaps I could have my own bed in a room all to myself and never have to go to the outhouse outside in the bitter cold winters.

Then I thought of my mom, my grandma, and my dog, and quickly changed my mind about living with these rich people. I could never just leave my family; it would break my heart. Then I came up with the perfect solution. We could all live in this big, nice house together, but I saw no way for that to happen. For the first time in my life, I realized that our family was poor, very poor, though I really didn't feel like it. At that time, it didn't bother me, but it surely did some years later, when it changed my life completely.

After another fun sleigh ride, we arrived at the children's home. After a few more weeks of fun, warm showers and all the excellent food, I could eat, the time came for me to pack my bundle for home.

I took one last trip to our beautiful dream moss city, with my group of friends. There we said our farewells to each other and the wonderful, easy times of plenty, we had enjoyed for a while. In silence, our thoughts faraway from this worry-free place, we slowly walked back to the children's home that greeted us once more with its warmth.

That last night, I dressed warmly and quietly walked outside into the almost star clear night. Thin, grey clouds shrouded only the tallest mountain top. They moved around the top of the mountain, as though dancing to a slow song. After I sat beneath an isolated, snow-covered pine tree, I looked up at the tallest mountain. I wanted to give God another chance to let me know if He was still alive before I had to leave these tall mountains.

I prayed, "Please give me a sign!"

Patiently, I waited until I started to shiver. Very disappointed and sad, I stood up. With frozen, bitter tears on my cheek, I lifted my hand and bid the tallest mountain farewell.

The next morning, sleds waited in front of the children's home for those of us who had to go home. Proudly, I carried my bundle of new clothing, playing cards, storybooks and the cookies I had saved up for my mom and my grandma, onto one of the sled. They had even let me take the real leather boots home. How gracious of them.

When the horses began to move, everyone left behind at the home came outside and waved goodbye. All of us on the sleds waved and shouted goodbye back. Slowly, with a heavy heart and silent tears, I watched the tallest mountain with its top in the clouds, where I was sure God had lived, becoming smaller in the distance. I wondered why He died.

We rode the long sleigh ride to the train station in silence. The horses no longer had their bells on their harnesses and none of us smiled. Perhaps all of the other children wondered what awaited them at home too. I wondered if Mom would still be sick. Would there be a warm room with enough food to eat? Were Grandma and my sweet dog still alive?

The train we boarded with our escort left the station in no time at all. With a sad feeling, I stared out of the window, watching the beautiful mountains slowly vanish in the distance from the glistening, snowy landscape. In the evening, our train stopped inside the huge train station of Luebeck again. The spark spitting streetcar came to take us to the same youth hostel in which I had spent the night on the way to the Bavaria. My fear of her remained strong, but she didn't electrocute me.

We found another rich table set for our evening meal. I stuffed my pockets full of fruit and chocolates for my mom and my grandma. I rolled up a thick slice of ham for my sweet dog whom I missed so much, and stuffed it in my pants pocket before I walked upstairs.

Sitting on my upper bunk, I stashed all my goodies in my bundle, took off my pretty coat and crawled under the blankets. My mind wandered off to my family, their faces looked so clear in my happy dream. We held hands and walked through the huge, pretty farmhouse. So many things about the house astounded them, especially the fire monster in the wall and the pump in the kitchen.

A loud noise woke me, and when I looked around, I saw all the children already packed and ready to leave the youth hostel. I hurried out of my bed, took my coat and my bundle, and ran downstairs after them.

In the big dining room, mugs with steaming hot milk and honey sandwiches awaited us. I felt so hungry again and ate very much. The hot milk felt good in my stomach. Divided into groups, we entered the spark spitting streetcar again, which took us back to the train station.

An older woman took our group all the way to the last stairs and down to the same kind of slower train we had come here with six weeks ago. She made sure all of us boarded the passenger car, which had the sign "Welfare" on it. Inside the car, she studied a list and then counted us.

"Good," she said, smiled and sat down.

The big locomotive shook with power, ready to run down the tracks. One loud blow from the engine and we left the amazing big house of the trains. As we slowly picked up speed down the tracks, we left the lights of the city behind us. Happy now and so very excited to see my family and my dog again, I leaned close to the window and watched the sun rise over a flat, snow-covered land. She tried her best to show her pink beams among the clouds, but the grey, heavy snow clouds took over the sky. We stopped in every town along the way to let children leave our railroad car and see them greet their smiling relatives. At nearly every stop, a snowman stood waiting to greet us. They sure looked nice, but my, were they different from each other!

I loved to travel by train. I found it so exciting to see new towns, different people and completely new scenery. I thought that perhaps I could work on a train someday when I got older. I wondered though, why I saw only men working on the trains.

At the next stop, our escort and four children left the train, and that left me all by myself in this passenger car now. But before she left, our escort had told me that I needed to get off the train at the next stop, and that the conductor would make sure that I did.

This was great! I stood up and pretended to be the driver of the train. I steered my train through some rough mountains, around curves and over bridges. We sped along like lightning. Too late, I noticed that the real driver of the train put on the brakes while I still stood. I landed on my butt on the hard floor of the train and slid down the aisle a ways. A little sore and worried that I had torn my pretty coat, I stood up. A quick look at the back of my coat assured me that I had not damaged it.

I fetched my bundle, and as I made ready to step off the train, the conductor came inside to check on me. I waved at him, smiled and stepped off the train into the deep, cold snow. He waved back at me through the passenger car's window as the train slowly left.

Snow fell softly now. Not too far distant, I saw my home, my island. When I looked toward the landing, I saw no ferryboat, only ice and snow. The ocean had frozen over as far as I could see, and that provided the only way home. However, this narrow pass of just a few miles had dangerously swift water and may not have frozen over completely in the middle. I had to walk very carefully.

Slowly I walked down to the ferry landing and stepped onto the frozen ocean. The soft snow had not completely covered some fresh dog sled tracks. Since I saw so many dog tracks of different sizes in front of the sled tracks, I figured they must have pulled a very heavy load, and if the snow stopped and let me follow the tracks, I could find a safe way over to my island, or return to the mainland, if the tracks turned around.

Before I crossed about a third of the frozen ocean, snow had covered all the tracks. I tried to sweep it away in front of me with my hands to find the tracks, but with no success. It started to snow harder now. I could barely make out my island.

Gradually, I walked straight forward, keeping an eye on my feet to make sure I continued straight ahead. I listened intently for the slightest sound of water lapping onto the ice shell or rushing by in the distance. A seagull's cry would also warn me of open water close by. So far, this white, frozen world remained mostly quiet and the ice shell sturdy.

Scared to death, I slowly pushed forward. Suddenly, from straight ahead of me, my ears picked up a strange, faraway sound. I stopped walking to listen better. I knew it wasn't a seagull, or the ocean leaping onto the ice shell. Neither was it the rushing water of the open sea. The unidentified sound drew closer, and I didn't know what to make of it. I stood still, frightened of what it might be. I wanted to ask God for help, but saw no sense in it, since He died.

The cold snow fell even harder now, and I could barely see my outstretched hand. Then I recognized the approaching noise: the hard breathing of running dogs. I screamed for help as loud as I could. The sled rushed by me, but a voice commanded the dogs to halt. I desperately hoped that person would come back for me. To my great relief, I heard the heavy breathing of the dogs again. In no time at all, the sled stopped right beside me. I recognized the dogs right away. They belonged to our neighbors in our village. When the man on the sled pulled his scarf off his face, I recognized him also as my Uncle Fred!

Happy and so relieved, I stepped over to him and gave him a long hug.

He said, "I'm very sorry to be so late to pick you up from the train. The sled fell over on its way and the dogs got tangled up with each other."

I asked my uncle, "Are you hurt?"

He smiled and shook his head. After I sat down next to him and wrapped a blanket around me, my uncle gave the dogs a short whistle. Eagerly they took off running toward our village in the heavy falling snow.

Without running into something in the blinding snowstorm, we arrived home. While my uncle took the big dogs back to our neighbors, I anxiously ran inside our house. My grandma opened her door to her room and out ran Harras. Excited, so glad to see me, he jumped up on me, knocked me over and gave me a thorough welcome licking over every inch of my face, with his tail wagging awfully fast. My grandma rescued me from the floor. So awfully glad to see her again, I fell into her arms and hugged her.

Then, my mom stuck her head out of Grandma's room. I hurried to her, embraced her, and told her how much I missed her. Out of the corner of my eye, I saw my dog picking up my bundle, which had landed on the floor as well. I saw him trying to open it, most likely wanting to reach the thick piece of ham I brought home for him. I took my bundle from him, and inside my grandma's room, I opened it and gave my dog the thick piece of ham.

Both my grandma and my mom looked at me, bewildered. Then I proudly gave them both the cookies, fruit and candies I saved up for them. I felt so proud to give something to my most-loved people in the world. Both looked a little confused until I told them where I had received the seldom heard of and likely never seen treats.

All excited, I showed my mom and my grandma my new clothing, books, playing cards and my real leather boots. Both of them looked astounded. When I showed them the little brush and toothpaste, that really confused them.

My grandma asked, "What in the heck do you do with such a little brush?"

After I told them that the people in Bavaria brushed their teeth with the brush and paste, they both began to laugh out loud.

After Uncle Fred and Aunt Hilde came into my grandma's room to welcome me home, my grandma brewed tea and brought up a bottle of plum liquor to sweeten the tea. Way into the night, I told them about my wonderful vacation in Bavaria.

When I came to the part of how I had found out that God was dead, my mom said, "I knew that."

My uncle nodded his head to agree with my mom. Aunt Hilde's mouth opened astonished, but she didn't say a word. My grandma had a questioning look on her face, but she didn't say a word either. She just passed around the bottle of plum liquor. When I told them about the fire monster inside the wall of the farmer's house, they questioned my honesty.

Within the next days, all my friends, neighbors and anybody who asked or had time to listen, heard about my vacation in the rich land of Bavaria and that God had died. Perhaps a few heard the story twice. Most were not surprised to hear of God's death, but they sure looked surprised about all the food and clothing available on the mainland, the inside plumbing and the fine furnishings, but I don't think anyone believed that there could be a fire inside a wall of a house without the whole house burning down.

The next Sunday morning, when our big, heavy preacher slowly pulled himself up the squeaking steps to reach his pulpit, he looked straight at me with a stern face. When he reached his pulpit and got a hold of his breath, he lifted his big bible up high and slammed it down hard on the edge of his pulpit. A big cloud of dust ever so slowly and gently snowed down onto the first two rows of churchgoers in their Sunday dresses.

With an almost purple, angry face, he raged down at us that we had plenty of sinners among us who believed God was dead. Both fists up high in the air, looking straight at me, with foam escaping from his mouth, our preacher declared that God lived!

His words totally shocked and embarrassed me. The floor of our church ever so slightly trembled beneath my feet, but it didn't open to swallow me, to take me where my ancestors lay. Ever so slowly, as if someone held my hand to lead me, I stood up and walked down the aisle toward the exit of our church. On the way out, I saw our island witch sitting on a pillar next to our church's huge organ looking down at me.

No store bought clothing, antibiotics,
pretty linens, or candy bars.

Chapter 48

The mean rooster.

My grandma's chicken flock had grown quiet large. She had all hens, except for one, huge, mean rooster. He scared both me and Harras. Once, when I fed the chickens, Harras followed me inside the chicken pen. While I tossed the chickens some fresh greens, the rooster instantly attacked my dog. He flew on top of him and pecked his head bloody.

I screamed and kicked the rooster hard, but he wouldn't let up. Luckily, Grandma came around the corner and hurried inside. She grabbed the wild darn rooster by its neck and threw him all the way to the end of their big enclosure. He complained loudly, flapped his wings in disagreement and stared at Grandma.

My dog hurried out of the pen, whining and licking the blood from his face. I ran after him to care for him. Ever since then, Harras stayed faraway from the chicken pen. I wished I could do the same, but every time I had to feed the chickens and complained about being too scared to go inside the chicken cube, my mom or grandma always just answered, "Girl, that's nonsense!"

I asked my grandma why she kept that darn rooster. I always saw him get on top of the lady chickens, and while holding onto their combs with his beak, he flapped his wings like crazy. After the darn rooster got off the ladies, he scratched in the dirt like crazy, making it fly all over the chicken pen and the lady chickens. Then he crowed wildly and ran around among the ladies as if totally nuts.

His behavior frightened them, and they ran from one corner of the pen to the other. Besides that, he didn't even lay any eggs.

My grandma smiled at me and said, "That darn rooster takes good care of his ladies."

I wasn't so sure what my grandma meant by that, but I wondered why the lady chickens didn't get organized and fight the rooster off their backs.

I didn't mind gathering seashells, seaweeds, dandelions, and earthworms for the chickens, or hauling down hull from the mill. But then when I turned ten, my mom and grandma declared that I was old enough to feed the chickens by myself every morning before I went to school and in the evening before bedtime. The idea of feeding them by myself frightened me a great deal. That darn rooster had attacked my grandma's legs a few times, but she always gave him a swift kick and then he quit bothering her, but I wasn't so sure I could kick that darn rooster the right way.

We kept the supplies to feed the chickens inside a small shed which stood inside the large chicken pen. That meant that I had to actually go all the way inside the chicken pen instead of just opening the door and throwing feed inside as I did until now. I just knew that darn rooster would attack me.

All that day, I thought of how I could go inside the pen without getting attacked by that darn rooster. In the evening, I came to the conclusion that if I threw just a handful of greens at the rooster and quickly ran into the shed, that should keep me safe. Coming back out of the shed with the chicken feed would be no trouble. That rooster loved to eat.

A scary dream of having my eyes pecked out by the rooster awoke me early the next morning. While the adults in our house left to work in the fields, I slid out of bed and got dressed to go to school, but first I had to feed the chickens, and the thought absolutely scared me to death.

In our backyard, I picked a handful of fresh dandelions and walked toward the chicken cube. Shaking with fear, I opened the wire door to the pen and hesitantly stepped inside. The darn rooster stood up from his favorite place beneath the big pear tree, gave me an evil eye, stretched out his wings in attack mode and charged toward me.

Quickly, I threw the dandelions at him, then ran toward the shed where we stored the chicken feed. Before I reached the shed, that darn rooster had latched onto my naked left leg. His sharp claws dug into my skin below my knee. With amazing speed, he jammed his beak viciously into my flesh slightly below my kneecap. In extreme pain, I yelled out loud for help. Then I remembered that everyone had left the house early. I had to help myself.

I picked up my right leg as I saw my grandma had done, and kicked the rooster with all the strength I had. That made me lose my balance and I fell onto the ground. The rooster, still on my leg, pecked at my knee. In terrible pain and with blood running down my leg, my fear grew.

I grabbed that rooster's neck just below his head with both of my hands. Out of desperation, I squeezed his neck hard until he pulled his sharp claws out of my leg. His wings hung still beside him now and he held one eye almost closed. I eased up on my grip around his neck, but still felt too scared to let him go. I thought he'd attack me again after what I had done to him.

Holding onto the limp rooster with one hand, I managed to get out of the dirt and take him inside the storage shed. There I placed him on a bale of hay, loosened my grip and hurriedly stepped back in case he decided to attack me. He just lay there, his head down in the hay, his wings hanging limply beside his body. Panic rushed through my mind as I thought that maybe I had killed him.

Carefully, I stepped closer to see if he was still alive. I touched his neck and felt a heartbeat, which relieved me. I gently stroked him, begging him to forgive me. "Please stay alive," I pleaded.

He opened his beak, took a long breath and closed his eyes completely. I checked his heart and heard it still beating. I wanted to stay with him, but I had to get to school on time, otherwise my mom would get very upset with me and dish out a stiff punishment. I had no time to wash out my wound. Ever in such a big hurry, I ran toward school. In the schoolyard, I fell down into the dirt, but I made it in time for the start of school. During the first intermission, I rinsed my leg off beneath the pump in our schoolyard. All the blood and dirt came off, except right in the spot where the darn rooster had picked pretty deeply into my flesh. A scab had already formed over the wound and I could see little stones beneath the scab, which I was scared to dig out.

All during the rest of the day, I couldn't pay attention to my teacher. I could only think about that stupid rooster. I intensely hoped that he still lived. What could I tell my grandma, that I murdered her rooster, who she claimed took such great care of her hens? Finally, school ended and I ran home, as if the devil were after me.

Out of breath, I stood by the chicken pen looking for the rooster. Fear overcame me when I didn't see him strutting among the lady chickens. Slowly I opened the wire door to the pen and walked inside. Then I saw him, still lying in the same place I had left him.

My heart raced with fear. I walked over to the rooster. He didn't move a muscle. My fear grew. Surely he was dead. Guilt ridden, I sat down beside the rooster and gently stroked his many colored feathers and started to cry.

Then I noticed that his body still felt warm and he took shallow breaths. Touching his little belly, I felt a very slow heartbeat.

With such great hope that the rooster would live, I whispered to him, "Please stand up."

He lifted his head just barely off the ground and opened his eyes. I tried to help him stand, but he fell right back down.

Then I noticed that all the rooster's ladies had gathered at the open shed door looking at us. Surely they blamed me that their rooster was dying. They had witnessed what I had done to him in the morning. Maybe they'd all get together and peck me to death. I felt as though I certainly deserved it.

In the middle of my guilty thoughts, my grandma walked into the shed. So glad to see her, I stretched out my arms but what could I tell her, to keep her from getting angry with me? She silently helped me up off the ground and wiped the tears from my face.

She then hugged me gently and said, "Don't cry over the old dying rooster, child." She picked the rooster up by his neck and together we walked out of the chicken pen.

I wanted to tell my grandma what actually happened to the rooster but feared the punishment and her disappointment in me, so I kept quiet.

My grandma took the rooster to the chopping block. She took the ax and with her next downward move, the darn rooster's head fell to the ground. She brought his body to the pump and flung it over a stone to let the blood run out of it. Sorrowfully, I stared at the limp body of the rooster, watching his life run out of him. I closed my eyes and wished the day never happened, but it didn't go away.

My grandma shook me and asked, "What happened to your knee?"

Not looking into her face, I quietly said, "I fell down in the schoolyard." Though actually not a lie, it wasn't the whole truth either.

I walked upstairs and fetched the requested small sack which hung beneath our roof inside the attic. Together, Grandma and I sat down on our old bench in our backyard and began to pluck the rooster's feathers. She handed me the large wing feathers and I ripped the colorful feathers off the hard middle core with ease. All the feathers went into the same sack to be washed and air dried later on. Then we used them to stuff our fine featherbed covers and pillows. I had an awful time sitting next to my grandma and not telling her the whole truth.

When we finished, I took my towel, whistled for my dog, and we ran down to the ocean. We swam out far and fast until I had no more strength. Harras kept up with me. Extremely exhausted, I turned around and ever so slowly floated and swam back to the beach. By the time we reached the beach, the glowing sun was leaving our part of the world in her most colorful display of rays of gold, purple and many shades of red and orange. The two of us sat down in the sand and watched the stunning drama.

When the sun doused her last rays in her watery bed, I gently hugged my dog and told him about my troubled day. He patiently waited until I finished talking and crying before he dried my face with his tongue. The hard, long swim and confiding in my dog gave me peace from the turmoil of the day. Refreshed and hungry I walked home hoping we'd both have something to eat.

Before I even entered our house, I smelled something delicious cooking. I saw Uncle Fred's door open, and everyone gathered around his table. To my surprise, my grandma stood by my uncle's iron stove and fried chicken, a feast for only special occasions. Usually we had chicken soup with lots of vegetables and plenty of water in it to last a few days. I wondered about the special occasion. As I walked into the kitchen, my grandma smiled at me and winked. I looked into the frying pan and among the pieces of meat, I saw the legs of a chicken with its feet and huge claws still attached. At that moment, I realized the remains of that darn rooster lay in that frying pan. Oh no, I couldn't eat that rooster, not after I had killed him.

Grandma started to fill the plates. With a great smile and another wink of her eye, she handed me a plate filled with delicious fried potatoes swimming in pork grease and a fried chicken leg with the rooster's sharp claws still on it. I wondered if

Grandma really knew what happened.

Looking at my plate of such delicious looking and fine smelling food, hunger overcame my guilty feelings. I figured that rooster might have recovered if my grandma hadn't killed him. Then I took a big bite out of the leg that had hurt me so badly in the morning, and it tasted delicious. Biting into the rooster's leg made me feel as though I were getting a little even for all the pain and the frustration he had caused me that day. After I ate all my food and sucked every morsel of meat off that chicken's leg, I handed it to my dog. To this day, I carry around a little souvenir from that darn rooster, the little stones beneath my skin on my left kneecap.

No bathtub, watermelons, hamsters or hot dogs.

Chapter 49

The big fight.

Life passed peacefully on our island. No child dared to tease my sister or me. They all knew me as a strong fighter. However, a new boy in our school totally disrupted our peace.

He stood a head taller than I and looked very strong. I wondered if I should beat him up right away to establish that my sister and I were off limits for teasing, or wait until he started to bother either one of us.

I kept an eye on him the first day of school. He stood together with a few of the big boys and showed off his strength by grabbing the smaller boys, picking them up and holding them up high in the air until they started to scream. That made me mad, and I no longer deliberated whether I should attack him, but rather how and when. The next school day, at the first intermission, the new boy walked over to me with a grin on his face. A few of the boys followed him.

He stopped walking in front of me and said, "The boys told me that you were in charge in this school."

I looked him straight in his face and said, "Yes I am!"

With a hateful look in his face, he screamed at me, "There's no way a puny, stupid girl of a redheaded woman can be in charge of anything!" He spit at the ground and hit me hard in my stomach.

In great pain that I didn't allow him to see, his fist came at me again. This time I quickly stepped aside and he fell flat onto the schoolyard. With his nose bleeding, he slowly stood up with a wild look on his face. All the children had gathered around us now and laughed out loud at him.

He couldn't let the fight end in such embarrassment in front of all the children. With a killer's hardened, bloody face and both fists up, he came at me again. I couldn't let him put an end to the peaceful life that I had fought to establish over the years. What kind of life would we have then? Before he hit me again, I quickly kicked him with all the power I had, right between his legs.

He bent over and screamed like hell. I took my fist and hit him right into his face. That hit made him fall back down onto the schoolyard. Everyone in the schoolyard cheered me on. My blood boiled. I jumped down on him and hit him hard, straight in his face.

At the third hit, he grabbed my neck and squeezed it hard. Now I really got angry. I bent down and pretended to give up the fight. When he let loose of my neck, I jammed my teeth into his earlobe.

He screamed like a pig being slaughtered. I tasted the blood that ran out of his ear.

All the kids in the schoolyard screamed, "Edith, you won!"

I let him go, but before he covered his ear with his hand, I saw that I had almost bitten off his earlobe. A big part of it just dangled there. The children in the schoolyard got quiet, a sure sign the teacher approached. Quickly I hurried off the still screaming boy.

As fast as his old legs could carry him and constantly blowing his loud whistle, our old teacher came nearer. When he reached us, he gave me a mean look, picked the bitterly crying boy out of the dirt and looked at his ear. Immediately, he took the boy by his hand and walked toward the tiny one-room clapboard hospital to the nurse to help the injured boy.

As he walked away, he yelled at us over his shoulder, "Take a long recess!"

I had no idea what my teacher would do to me when he came

back. He had been angry at me for a long time now, because I now and then picked a good fight. Since I hadn't started this fight, I hoped he wouldn't be too hard on me. His long willow stick hurt an awful lot when he hit it down hard on the palm of my hand, and my hand swelled up quite a lot. If my mom saw my swollen hand, she'd know that I had behaved badly at school and would punish me again. I never thought being punished twice for the same thing was quite fair.

We had the longest recess ever, except for the time I took the old teacher's alarm clock, which awakened him after a little recess nap, all the way across the cemetery where he couldn't hear the alarm going off. I'd have just shut it off, but didn't know how.

Here came my teacher, stomping and breathing heavily, his face purple with anger. He came straight to me. All the other children gathered around quickly. With an angry voice, he demanded to know who started the fight, while looking directly at me.

At the same time I shook my head all the other children said loudly, "The new boy started the fight."

I smiled with relief. My teacher gave me an evil look though, pointed his shaking finger at me and said, "You stay after school lets out!"

Oh, no. I had smiled too early.

Angry and scared, I stayed in our classroom after all the other children left. My teacher came to me with his whipping stick in his hand. He told me to hold out my left hand. I did as he asked: closed my eyes; and bit my lips together so I wouldn't scream out in pain. He then hit the palm of my hand hard. The pain shot up my arm. I wanted so badly to reach out and hit him back, but I didn't.

He then told me, "You sit in the classroom for one hour and think about that poor boy's ear." He sat his clock in front of me and left.

After he left the room, I cried out in pain and sat down on my bench. I couldn't believe he punished me for a fight I hadn't started. I stood up and walked over to the window. I saw my teacher start on his way home. As soon as he was out of sight, I left the classroom and walked home too.

Somehow, my teacher found out that I left the classroom before the hour had ended. And the next day, as school ended, he said to me, "You'll stay here an hour after school today since you left early yesterday. This time I'll lock the door." On his way out he said, "Someone will come and let you out in an hour."

I heard him lock the door, then I checked it. Sure enough, he had locked me inside the classroom. What a terrible situation.

Looking outside the window, I didn't see my teacher leave the school today. I thought that perhaps he decided to take a different route home. Then I noticed the sturdy, wide rainspout connected to our schoolhouse with big clamps. It ran down right past our window and by our two seated outhouse. The clamps stuck out just far enough from the wall to hold part of my feet. My hands could hold onto the pipe. I only needed to climb down on it about ten feet or so. Then I could jump onto the outhouse. From there I could easily jump to the ground.

All right, I said to myself, let's get out of here. I climbed out of the window and down the rainspout without any problems. With one jump I landed on the roof of the outhouse. Once more I had fooled that old teacher. One more jump down off the outhouse and I landed in the dirt. Freedom!

When I started to get up out of the dirt, I noticed two huge shoes in front of me. Slowly I looked up to see who stood inside those shoes. In complete shock, I looked into my teacher's face. His purple, outraged face scared me tremendously. I wondered if teachers had the right to kill children.

He grabbed my hand, lifted me up and said, "I'll take you home and let your mother decide what to do with you. You're a wild child, girl!"

I had a hard time keeping up with his long, fast steps, and with each step I grew more angry. I had only protected myself in a fight.

Admittedly, I shouldn't have bitten the boy's ear so hard, but how else could I have stopped the fight before he really hurt me?

Still angry and foaming at the mouth, my teacher walked me home. My mom and my grandma stood in front of our house, looking toward the teacher and me. Right in front of them, my teacher abruptly let go of my arm.

As he opened his big mouth to speak, my mom said, "We know what happened. Should she have let the boy kill her?"

The teacher closed his mouth and stared at my mom. Stunned, he turned and stomped away. Loudly he screamed, "I will have no more fights in my schoolyard. You keep this wild child under control."

My mom asked me what the boy had said to me before the fight started. I told her the truth, but left the insulting part about my redheaded mom out so as not to hurt her feelings. I didn't think that counted as lying. My mom told me to go upstairs and that she'd come along soon.

Slowly, and fearful of what my punishment would be this time, I walked up the stairs and into our little room. There I sat awaiting my penalty. Pretty soon, I heard my mom coming up the stairs. I braced myself for my sentence. My mom came inside our room with a slight smile on her face. What a relief!

She sat down next to me and reached out to hold my hand. My mom looked straight into my eyes and said, "When will the girl come out of this tomboy?" She then stroked my hair. "You had the right to fight back." Then with a big sigh she said, "But please girl, fight somewhere else than in the schoolyard."

I just sat there trying to grasp what she had said to me. As far as I understood, there was no punishment. I waited just another moment to make sure. Mom took her knitting and walked downstairs. I was off the hook.

I took my pencil and a piece of my fine school paper out of my backpack and drew a pretty picture of seabirds in flight. In clean handwriting, I asked our island witch, "Please take away our old teacher, Herr von Osten!" I signed my name to it, folded the paper neatly and drew a crying flower on the outside of the note. When no one was looking, I stuck my note beneath our island witch's door.

I did this for the next seven days, the last days of my third grade school year. After a one-week Easter break, I started fourth grade, even though my teacher, out of bitterness, had barely promoted me. I honestly hated school again, or better said, I hated my old teacher. Every day that I faithfully stuck my nice notes beneath our island witch's door, I noticed that many notes rested beneath her door. Some looked like my notes, with pretty pictures on them. I desperately hoped she'd find the time to take care of my request.

No ballpoint pens, sweet potatoes, or pepper.

Chapter 50

A thousand thank-yous to our island witch!

Easter vacation passed too quickly and I had to go back to school. I hated to think about going back there. I had gotten into more than the normal amount of fights at school in the last year, and that got my teacher angry at me, so he stopped giving me upgraded work to keep the school days interesting. As a result, I was bored, angry, and daydreamed the school hours away. Gently, I tried to reason with my mom while she made one of her skirts smaller so I could wear it to school. I tried to tell her that I'd be much better off quitting school. I offered to go to work in the fields all day long because I knew we desperately needed the money. Plus, I figured I'd be happier outside all day than sitting all those long hours on the school bench, dozing the day away. Sternly, but with a smile, my mom said, "You're going back to school!"

Eleven days had passed since I stuck my first pleading note underneath our island witch's door, and a day ago, I saw my teacher sitting in his front yard, napping in the warm sun. In my last daring attempt to have our island witch fulfill my request to take away my old teacher, I told my grandma about my trouble and asked her what I should do. I could always depend on her for good advice.

She put on her thinking face, and after a few moments, my grandma said, "This is a hard request you've made of the witch.

Let me get you a fine bottle of my sweets from my cellar to place in front of the witch's door with your request."

That evening I drew the best picture I ever made in my young life and wrote my last request in my best handwriting. When our sun retrieved her last orange beams into the seawater, I walked to our island witch's tiny house. By the time I reached her house, darkness had fallen, and a candle flickered in her window as it always did, day or night, to indicate she was home.

Very glad I had found her home, I slowly crawled beneath her window and carefully placed the bottle of fine liquor beside her open door along with the note. I heard her talking to what sounded like a young man, but I didn't recognize his voice. Then he formally addressed her as Great Aunt Ola in their happy conversation. I wondered what a great aunt was.

Ever so quietly, I left her front yard and walked home with the silvery half moon smiling at me. On the way I thought hard about what to do next if our island witch denied my request, when my dog ran to me. He found a short, thick stick and laid it down by my feet. He looked at me with an expression that I couldn't refuse. Quickly I picked up and threw the stick for him, which he retrieved many times, until we arrived home. He surely let me forget about my trouble for a little while.

Way too soon, the first day of fourth grade arrived. In an angry, gloomy mood, I walked to school. I sat in my regular seat, in the last row, closest to the door, just in case the opportunity arose for me to sneak quickly out of this hated room. I lay my head down on the bench and daydreamed of running away from home.

When the king and his beautiful black horse with its eyes agleam came to take me away, the door to our classroom opened. In came a handsome young man, playing a harmonica while dancing toward the podium. For a brief moment, I thought I was dreaming. All the children stood up and looked at the young man in awe. No one said a word. Only the happy song of the harmonica filled the room. The young man quit playing when he reached the podium.

Bewildered, we stared at him while he put his harmonica into his shirt pocket.

He smiled and said, "Hello, I'm your new teacher. Is anyone ready for a parade?"

We continued to stare silently. I pinched myself and shook my head hard to get out of this dream but nothing changed. This was real, ever so welcome, but so hard to believe.

Once more, the good looking young man asked, with a louder voice this time, "Is anyone ready for a parade?"

Out of our bedazzlement by now, every one of us jumped up and down and screamed, "Yes! Yes!"

Happy confusion followed. Children excitedly hugged each other and laughed with relief, and many of us shed happy tears. When our new teacher asked us to form a single line and follow him, I realized that I had heard his happy voice before, but didn't know where. As we followed our new teacher out of the classroom, I whispered many thanks to our island witch. All of a sudden, I remembered where I heard the new teacher's voice before. I had heard it at our island witch's house, on the night I took my last wish to her with the bottle of sweets from grandma's cellar.

Our new teacher played songs on his harmonica, which all of us knew. We sang to them and hopped all the way through the village. Some adults on their way to or from somewhere stood still for a moment and looked at us in amazement. Others stared at us in disbelief and shook their heads. Our preacher came out of his house to see why we made so much noise. He had a somber face. We all waved at him, but he didn't wave back.

On our way back to our schoolhouse, we stopped in the middle of the village at the aging old oak tree. It took six of us ten-year-olds with outstretched arms to encircle its huge trunk. Beneath the tree stood a pump, a trough and a bench. Many animals had stilled their thirst in this trough. Not long ago it had served as a deathbed for a drunken soul. He had fallen off the bench, which made a fine bed for the ones who could not find their way home after the tavern closed, and drowned in the trough. During the day hours, people exchanged gossip and added to it on this bench.

We all took a cool drink from the pump's sweet water, then our new teacher asked us to sit on the ground. He said, "We're going to play a math game." Then he explained how it worked.

Our teacher sang the question, "Six times six is?"

The small children sang the question again. The big children, which included me, sang the answer, thirty six. We definitely didn't all arrive at the same answer all the time, but my, we had such fun. I wondered what all the standing adults thought about our fun school activities.

Then our happy parade hopped and sang to the new teacher's songs, down to the cemetery, which embraced our mighty old church. There, he asked us to read the gravestones. The small children had to identify just the letters on them. When we came to the very old part of the cemetery that had gravestones with letters of the alphabet written in a very different way, I proudly showed off and translated every last headstone's engraving. My grandmother had taught me this language years ago.

Before I even realized how much time had passed, our new teacher said, "Today we had math, music, gym and reading. School is over. For your homework, you must ask the old people in your family where they came from and what their lives were like when they grew up. In tomorrow's history class, we'll all walk to the old, dilapidated castle on the beach and tell our stories to the wind. There I'll tell you where I came from."

Disappointed that school had ended for the day, I slowly walked back to our schoolroom to pick up my backpack. All the older girls had gathered in a corner giggling, smiling and whispering. Their behavior told me that they too liked the handsome young teacher.

On my way home, I daydreamed about our new teacher and walked straight into a big tree. My nose started to bleed and I didn't have a handkerchief. Someone behind me handed me his. Oh, no, it was our new teacher! He must have seen me walking into that big tree, a thought that really embarrassed me.

After I quickly thanked him for his handkerchief and promised to return it clean, I walked home. When I passed the old teacher's house, I saw him working in his garden. I wished I knew how our island witch got us a new teacher without killing the old one. At home, I wrote a thousand thank-yous on a fine piece of school paper, drew a smiling flower on the other side of the paper and put the note underneath our witch's door. Many notes already lay there. Most of them started with a thank you.

Our new teacher's energy and capability to teach sure made my life and the other children's lives great. Every evening, I eagerly awaited the next school day. Whenever possible we had school outside. We learned so much about our surroundings, even how to tell the birds apart from each other and learn their names.

We learned which plants we could eat and which would make us sick. We learned about the creatures that lived in the ocean, and that math was really easy to learn. We went to the ponds on our island and looked through the new teacher's big magnifying glass to see what lived there. I saw things I had never seen before and that seemed like a miracle to me. Never again did I even think about dozing the days away in school. Anxiously and accurately, I did all my homework. This year, for the first time since I started school, I hoped my report card would knock my mom's socks off.

No ice tea, cinnamon or electric irons.

Chapter 51

A rare meeting.

On a Friday afternoon when I sat on our stairs doing my homework for our new teacher, our only man of the law walked into our house. He told my grandma with a worried voice, "I want all islanders to come to a very important meeting this Sunday. Spread my order to all the people and tell them to bring their school age children."

My grandma agreed and hurriedly walked outside to tell the neighbors. Our lawman didn't usually call for a meeting. He mostly took care of matters by himself in his own way.

Grandma liked him and often said, "He's a plain man, but a fair man. I did hear some people whisper different though."

Amazingly, without even one telephone on our island, his word got around our island very quickly, and that Sunday morning, an hour before the service, people filled the benches of our church, just two days after the announcement of the meeting.

Our only man of the law, our new teacher and our preacher walked up the pulpit. A short, astounded whisper fell over the people, and then it grew silent.

After a slight clearing of his throat, our only man of the law said, "Good morning."

A low mumble of good mornings echoed back through our church. He then asked all the school-aged children to come up front and gather beneath the pulpit, facing the people on their benches. As I walked up to the pulpit, I wondered if I had done something so terribly wrong that I needed to be punished in front of all these people. I could see the same thought reflected in the faces of the other children as well. Quietly, all of us children stood beneath the pulpit. I looked up to our humongous pipe organ. There she sat, our island witch, in her usual place, on a pillar at the side of the pipe organ. I had wondered lately if a witch belonged inside of a church. But then, our preacher had reminded us in every Sunday service that the devil sat among us. If he could sit inside the church, why not our witch?

Then, our lawman began to speak. "I've had a lot of complaints about how our new teacher is teaching your children. Many of you have said he lets the children run around the island wild, singing and laughing instead of sitting in the classroom. Some of you even mentioned that no good could come of having fun while learning. A handful of you believe the magnifying glass is the devil's work and puts foolish ideas in your children's heads. Then, a few of you actually believe that this young teacher is too handsome to teach the older girls because they get distracted by him."

He then took a big breath. "All of you know three of my children go to school now. For the first time, since the new teacher came to us, they can't wait to go to school every morning. They've learned more in his short time here than they have in the whole last school year.

"Now, I don't want to be the one who decides if the new schoolteacher stays or goes. Let's have the children vote." He looked down at us and asked, "Children, if you like your teacher, please raise your hand."

Every one of us raised both of our hands high up into the air.

Our man of the law raised his hand, pointed at the teacher and loudly declared, "The new teacher will stay! Whoever complains to me about him again has to buy me a drink of the finest brandy in the tavern." He quickly nodded and left the pulpit.

The happy screams of the children echoed loudly through our church. Quite a few of us waved and smiled up at our island witch. Out of sheer happiness that our new teacher could stay, I began to sing our multiplication song. I did the teacher's part and all the children eagerly sang the answers. We sure were a happy bunch.

A few thundering notes from our huge pipe organ reminded us that church service would start soon. I lifted my hand once more to thank our island witch, but she had already left. Only her black scarf hung down from the pillar she sat on. All the men inside the church left to go across the road to have their church service in the tavern. I climbed up the narrow, dark stairs on the inside of the huge pipe organ to fetch the witch's scarf and take it to her.

Then I noticed something strange. The old woman who played the pipe organ and the boys that worked the heavy handle to produce wind for the pipe organ weren't here. I couldn't see anyone, but I felt someone's presence. Goose bumps crawled up and down my spine. Fear rippled through me, but something held me there. I stood still, frozen to the pipe organ's wooden floor in the small, dark inner room. I didn't even move my eyes. My ears strained to pick up the slightest sound, but silence reigned.

Suddenly, I felt the air around me move ever so slightly. My fear grew. I reached for the black shawl. Someone held my hand tightly, but gently, in midair. Quickly, I turned. Through the gloom, I recognized our island witch holding my hand. I shivered with fear and hoped against hope that she didn't think that I intended to steal her scarf.

Quickly I looked away, because I had learned never to look into her face, unless she blessed me.

She held my hand a little tighter and said, "Child, don't be scared. You're a different child. Someday I'll tell you whose child you are. Go straight to where you need to go, but look back with pleasant thoughts. From now on, you can look into my face whenever we meet because today, I bless you."

Our island witch released my hand and disappeared. A long, black string dangled from my hand. Still shaking badly, I walked down the narrow stairs. As soon as I reached the church floor, the woman organ player and her boys made ready to go upstairs. She asked me, "Are you sick? Do you need help?"

I gently said, "No, no thank you."

Slowly, like in a dream, I walked over to the bench where my grandma sat. Relieved, I sat down next to her, clutching the long, black string. When my grandma saw the string in my hand, she smiled and her eyes gleamed. Church service started before I could ask her why she smiled.

On our way home that Sunday after church, my grandma said, "Remember, child, now you're a blessed child of the island witch."

Since the word "blessed" meant something good to me, I felt happy. At the age of ten, I never thought to ask what the witch's blessing really meant.

No hand lotions or pearls.
Women didn't shave their legs and underarms.

Chapter 52

The amazing garden.

When our island witch blessed me and handed me a thread from her big, black shawl, my life changed. I could now look into her face and walk into her house at any time.

The first time Ola asked me to come inside her house, fear settled over me again. I thought that she planned to punish me because I had two stolen carrots hidden in my skirt pocket. All the bad and cruel stories the old ones whispered among themselves ran through my mind. What if she changed me into a killing monster, or just let the devil have me? Some people even whispered that the devil and she were related.

Slowly, shaking with fear, I walked behind her into her one room house. Though dark inside, the candle on the windowsill shone with enough light for me to see where Ola headed. She opened the back door and walked out into a lovely garden. I followed her out and saw the beautiful spot for the first time.

A tall stone fence surrounded her small backyard, preventing anyone from looking in at her garden, even me. I routinely climbed tall trees and walls but I never climbed her wall out of fear of her harsh punishments.

Though fall, her trees and flowers still bloomed in deep,

magnificent colors, which strangely sparkled with each light touch of the wind. I stood in awe, staring at all those strange, colorful flowers, which I had never seen before in my life.

A child's laugh made me look toward a small patch of green grass. There, Ola and two girls I knew well sat together. They waved me on to come over to them, which I did, and sat down with them. In the middle of the small, green patch of grass stood a bowl of water, and a big, black raven drank out of it. The golden sun smiled down on this garden. When I had received my invitation to come into the house, the clouds hung low in the sky and I worried that it would rain again soon. How quickly the clouds disappeared.

Then Ola smiled. "We're going to play a game. On one side of each piece of paper you see numbers and on the other side words. Let's see if you can remember the numbers for each word and perhaps form a sentence with those numbers."

When I realized that Ola had not planned to punish me, I relaxed and had fun. After I left the house, I noticed low and heavy clouds in the sky again, and it began to sprinkle.

At our next meeting inside her beautiful garden, our island witch asked me, "Edith, please tell me what you did all week that was important to you."

I quit looking at the thirsty big raven and shyly, still with some fear, faced Ola. Her now green eyes looked straight through me, and when I began to tell her the things of significance to me in the last week, I felt warmth coming into my body from her deep eyes.

All my fear of her disappeared. As I told her of my important moments she asked, "Did you wear a pink sweater? Was the sea rough? Did your dog sit beside you?" and so on.

I answered every one of her questions in the affirmative. It was as though Ola saw my important times through my eyes, as if she had been there with me.

Before long, she taught me how to read in people's faces what they had not said by their expressions and body language. We often sat on the old graveyard's stonewall, hidden away inside a bush, watching people walking by, trying to determine if they were happy or not. Then she gently started to teach me how to control my mind while asleep; how to realize that I was dreaming; and how to get out of a bad dream. She also taught me how to get into a dream or to continue a special dream. She gave me the knowledge of how to fly; how to breathe under water in my dreams; and how to disappear from sight if needed. She always reminded me to take care not to stray from her teachings and to keep all her lessons to myself.

I spent some of the greatest times in my young life in her fantastic garden, but my grandma worried a lot about me during that time.

She told me often, "Be careful not to slip into the devil's hands."

I listened to what she had to say, but wasn't sure what she meant at the time. I had fun and loved the time I spent with our island witch and the other girls inside her beautiful garden. I often wondered though why that big, black raven always drank so much water.

During our long, harsh winters, while we remained homebound for weeks at a time, I often practiced talking to Ola and the other girls with numbers, in silence of course. She strictly forbade us to let anyone hear us using the number language. At times, I felt like someone answered me in that language. Perhaps it was just wishful thinking.

Later that year, I escaped from a horrible dream in which I saw the numbers that said, "Farewell my friend," encircled by water. That dream frightened me so much that I couldn't get back to sleep. The following morning, on the way to school, I found out that the youngest girl in our small group at the witch's house was missing.

Hurriedly, I ran toward Ola's house. Many people had already gathered around her place. Ola stood on her threshold with a somber face, holding her hand up for everyone to quiet down.

When the crowd quieted, she slowly dropped her arm and bitterly said, "Little Angie got raped and brutally killed last night by her insane brother."

Outraged, people wanted to kill the boy. Ola lifted her arm up again to calm the people. When fire escaped from her fingers into the foggy morning, silence immediately took hold.

With her arm still held up, she looked at the girl's parents and spoke. "You'll find Angie in a shallow grave behind your wheat field. You'll find your insane son hanging in the willow tree near the coast. I gave his violent soul to the devil last night." While the gathered people began to scream and cry, Ola walked back into her little house.

My legs began to shake and I sat down on the ground near Ola's fence. Bewildered, I recalled the numbers I saw in my scary dream over and over. Yes, the message was clear, it read, "Farewell my friend."

I started to shake and cry.

Someone gently touched my shoulder. I looked up and into Ola's worried face. She extended her hands to me. I held onto them, stood up, and together we walked through her house and into the gorgeous garden. There, while the black raven drank plenty of water again, I told Ola about my secret number message.

She smiled. "That's wonderful, my child."

Confused, I asked, "Why didn't I know the message came from Angie, and why was water all around the numbers?"

She held my hands and looked at me with her deep eyes. Smiling slightly she answered, "You're just making the first, wobbly, unsure steps into witchery. Time, a lot of time, will tell if perhaps you have the capability to join me in my rank and someday replace me on this earth."

No corn chips, diamond wedding bands or tumbleweeds.

Chapter 53

My report card.

School continued as a wonderful thing for me. Our new teacher made learning easy and fun, besides that, he was young and very good looking. Some of us older girls fell hopelessly in love with him. We often fought over who would carry his leather briefcase home for him because that girl could walk beside him and talk to him.

I learned so very much about my surroundings, all the life on our island and inside the sea that I couldn't even see without his big looking glass. One day, though, when he told us that our earth was round and just floating in the air, all of us started to laugh. We thought he joked with us. The old, small world map still hung on the wall and we saw a flat world. But then, he showed us pretty colored pictures of our earth in his big book and read it to us. This new knowledge absolutely amazed me.

In early fall, at the end of a school day, our new teacher handed us our first report cards.

Excitedly, I opened the folded page right away. "Yes!" I screamed, and jumped up into the air. "I did it! I have all As!" Then I settled down, a bit embarrassed at my outburst. Our teacher just laughed.

I ran home in a hurry to show my report card to my mom and my grandma. Out of breath and stumbling on the way up our stairs,

I proudly handed my mom my report card. She sat down on her small couch and studied it with a somber face.

She looked so serious, that for a moment, I thought she had read her death sentence. Then she looked up at me with a tear rolling down her cheek. "Is this report card real?"

Very proudly, I smiled and said, "Yes!"

My mom stood up and gave me a long, warm hug. "I'm very proud of you. With these fine grades you can do anything you'd like in this world."

With a sure voice, I said, "I'm going to be a veterinarian so I can help all the sick and injured animals on our island."

Mom stood still, stared at me and reached for her handkerchief. After blowing her nose and wiping a tear from her face, she smiled at me and nodded. I saw sadness in my mom's eyes and the happiness in her smile had faded.

At that time, I didn't know why bitterness had tinged her smile and sadness filled her eyes, but I'd find out many years later.

No dental floss, crayons or candles on a birthday cake.

Chapter 54

Terrible treatment.

Every once in while, when my mom saw me scratching my backside a lot, she declared a deworming day.

First thing in the morning, she took a good-sized herring from the salt barrel, rinsed it off and placed it on a plate on our table right in front of me. Then she cut that fish into small pieces and told me to eat it. I knew it tasted horrible because she had administered this treatment before. Again, I tried to talk my way out of this torture, but she remained firm.

She stared at me with an angry face, sat down next to me and shouted, "Swallow those pieces now!"

With tears running down my face, I picked up the first piece. The salt on the fish's skin sparkled a little in the sunlight. I tried to put that horrible tasting piece into my pants' pocket, but my mom stared at me with a face that told me a good whipping would follow. Under protest from my stomach, I swallowed down the first piece of salted fish. My mouth burned from the salt and my stomach refused to accept what I had just swallowed and I started to vomit.

"Swallow!" She held a cup of water to my mouth. I took a big drink and sent the salty stuff back down. When I refused to open my mouth to swallow anymore, my mom squeezed my mouth open and stuffed the pieces inside.

What a horrible procedure. I cried and screamed. Mom slapped my face a few times, and eventually I swallowed the last piece of that terrible fish and ran out of the house.

Amazingly, even though my stomach hurt a lot, I didn't vomit. By late afternoon, I had to use the outhouse. After all the salty stuff left my body, I looked into the can to see if I could see any worms. Sure enough, a few long, white worms floated lifelessly in the can. One was more than a foot long. Disgusted and weak from the terrible treatment, I left the outhouse.

My grandma stood by her chicken enclosure, telling her flock, "I need sixteen eggs by morning. Get busy girls!"

Still a little shaky, I walked over to her. She turned, looked at me and opened her arms wide. Gladly, I fell into her arms and she hugged me tightly. After I dried my tears in my sleeves, I asked her how worms get into my body.

She shook her head and said, "Child, we don't know that, but we do know they can kill us."

No champagne, baby food in jars or jellybeans.

Chapter 55

My sister's return.

By early fall in 1953 my mom continued to get well, though very slowly. She looked a lot better and she smiled again. We even took walks together to the beach and collected driftwood to feed our little iron stove. Though against doctor's orders, she found herself a part-time job in the only small, one-room café in our village, at the harbor, not far from our house. the café opened for only two hours every evening, in the warm season. A few visitors that came by boat and perhaps an occasional hungry islander now and then patronized the café.

This little place didn't have a menu card, but it actually had two tables in the room. The owner's wife cooked, and my mom served the food, washed the dishes, and all sorts of other jobs. Every evening when the café opened, one could have fine tasting bean soup, and fried fish with fried or mashed potatoes.

My mom proudly brought home a little money and occasionally a plate of leftovers which the guests had left. I really enjoyed the delicious food she brought home. Some days she even brought home enough food for both my grandma and me to enjoy.

Every Monday during the warm season, the owner's wife cooked her big pot of bean soup for the week with lots of pig feet in it. She let the soup cook all day long, and when it finished, she fished out all the bones, stripped them, and placed the meat back inside the big pot. That evening my mom brought home all the naked bones for my dog. He was in heaven on those days.

He lay next to his pile of bones and guarded them fiercely while he gnawed on them. When he had eaten his fill, he buried the rest of the bones in my grandma's garden. Over the next days, Harras dug the bones back out of the earth and enjoyed them.

One evening when my mom came home from work, she said happily, "Since I feel better now and am making a little money, I've decide to write my brother and his wife to send your sister, Uschi, home."

I didn't like the sound of that, but no one asked me. I just hoped I didn't have to let her tag along with me again. Life had been so nice without her. I could do what I liked and go where I pleased.

Two days later, the mailman arrived in our harbor. My mom gave me her letter and enough change for the postage and said, "Take this to the mailman now."

On the way to the harbor, I thought about just dropping the letter in the ocean. That way, I wouldn't have to take care of my sister again. I could even buy some sweets for the stamp money.

The moment I arrived at the harbor I started to rethink things. If my mom found out that I threw the letter into the ocean, she'd give me the biggest whipping I ever had. Slowly, I walked over to the mail boat and with a sad feeling, handed the mailman my letter and the postage. On the way home, I prayed for God to send a storm, capsize the little boat and send all the letters to the bottom of the sea.

However, the ocean stayed calm, and two weeks later when our mail boat arrived, the mailman handed me a letter for my mom. In a gloomy mood because of what I figured was inside, I walked home. When I handed my mom her letter and she realized it had come from her brother, she smiled and anxiously opened the letter. She smiled even more and a happy tear escaped from her eyes. She loudly announced, "My girl is coming home!"

Then my mom hurried past me and ran downstairs. Grandma heard the commotion and met her at the stairs. I stood at our top stair and watched my mom eagerly reading the letter to my grandma. My uncle's letter told about the day and time of my little sister's arrival by train at the ferryboat landing across the ocean from our island.

The two of them hugged each other intensely, sniffled quietly, and laughed. Then my aunt and uncle walked out of their kitchen, and when my mom told them the news, they too acted so happy and excited.

They all walked into my uncle's kitchen and my grandma turned to me and said, "Girl, go fetch one of the brown bottles from my cellar."

When I walked down the steps to the cellar, I realized that I was the only one sad and mad about my sister's return. I fetched one of the old bottles, walked upstairs and handed it to my grandma. Then I quickly walked outside so no one could see my angry tears. Out there, I whistled for Harras and we ran down to the beach to our secret place, among the huge boulders, where I told him my problems. He crawled up in my lap and licked my face.

A week later or so, my mom, my dog and I walked down to the ferry landing to pick up my little sister. My mom seemed so happy at the prospect of having her daughter home soon. I dragged along reluctantly and only because my mom told me that I had to come along.

Down the path a ways I bravely asked my mom, "Do I have to take Uschi along with me all the time again?"

Mom abruptly stopped, looked at me and said, "Of course you do, she's your little sister!"

Oh, how those words hurt me and made me hate my sister. Shortly we arrived at the ferry landing and saw the old ferry had already crossed half of the extremely fast currents of the ocean between the mainland of Germany and our island.

I reached for my mom's hand out of fear that she loved my sister much more than me, but she didn't take my hand into hers. She jumped up and down in excitement and waved at the crossing ferry. Soon the ferry landed and the old engineer held my sister's hand and a big bundle over his shoulder and came walking off the boat.

Mom ran toward them, bent down, and embraced my little sister for quite a while. Jealousy turned me green and I wanted to scream but I bit my teeth together and kept quiet. My sister had grown much bigger than I remembered, and what fancy clothes she wore. She cried a little and remained quiet on our way home, but my mom talked up a storm, even though my sister did not answer any of her questions. I had to carry her big, heavy bundle on my back. I wondered what she had inside it.

At home, my grandma greeted my sister with a big, warm hug and carried her inside her room. She took off my sister's new, fine coat and asked her to sit in the chair she pulled back for her. Proudly, my grandma announced that she cooked a noon meal for all of us. It smelled so good, and I was very hungry after all the walking. Hurriedly, I sat down in my usual chair and waited for a plate of something good to eat to come my way.

With a big, satisfied smile my grandma said, "I've cooked a stew with fish, cabbage and potatoes," and she placed a filled plate in front of all of us.

My sister looked at the food on her plate, pushed the plate away and said, "I don't like it."

My grandma's face showed her hurt feelings. I felt so sorry for my grandma and got mad at my sister. Most likely, our grandma had used up days of supplies to cook this meal for us, and my sister didn't even show a little appreciation.

Grandma took my sister's food and put it back into the pot on the stove. I couldn't believe that my sister then had the bad manners to ask for something else to eat. Mom almost choked on her food when she heard my sister's request for different food.

Grandma just shook her head at my little sister in disbelief.

After our meal, my mom took us both upstairs. When we walked up the stairs, my sister asked, "Where's my room? Where's my bed? Where's my closet?"

Mom gently explained, "You don't have your own room here, or you own bed. We don't have a closet. You may use the box underneath your shared bed to put your belongings in."

As soon as we reached the top of our stairs, my mom showed my sister the bed under the eaves of the house, where we both slept.

My sister, Uschi, began to cry. "That's not even a room. I had my own room with pretty furniture, a lot of toys, a real closet full of nice dresses and a radio. I want to go back to my uncle and aunt!"

Mom picked her up and sat her on our bed. My sister started to scream and kick my mom. Silently, with tears running down her face, my mom walked inside her little room.

Now I really got angry at my sister. She had hurt the two people I loved most in this world. I wanted to beat her up. When she looked at me with her tear-reddened eyes and asked me to help her to get back to our uncle's house, I decided that might be a better idea than beating her up.

I walked downstairs and took my dog for a long walk down to the steep coast, where the waves came in tall and strong this time of year. Harras and I climbed on top of a tall boulder, my boulder, and sat and listened to the tall waves rushing onto the shore. I thought about how to get my sister back to my aunt and uncle's place.

After many false starts at trying to work out a way to get her back to them which really wouldn't work, I came up with a great idea. During this time of year, mackerel season, the fishermen caught many of those fish and sold them to the men with the fish truck. Those men in their pickup truck came to our harbor every second day lately and I figured they could take my sister with them. I decided to ask them that very night, then I could have my mom, my grandma, and our bed to myself again. What a brilliant idea.

On my way back home, I stopped at the harbor. My heart jumped with joy when I saw the truck parked near the pier where the fishing boats would soon dock. A handful of men stood around the truck, smoking, drinking beer and laughing, while waiting for the boats to come back home with their rich catches.

Finally, I gathered all my courage and walked up to the men. Nicely, I asked them if they drove all the way to the city of Oldeslohe, the city my sister needed to reach.

The man nearest me answered, "Yes, we do."

Politely, I asked if he could take my sister with him to that town. I said, "She's small and won't take up much room." I also told him why she wanted to go back there.

The tall man said, "Sure. Just let your mom bring her here in about two hours."

I thanked the tall man and walked away very disappointed. I knew my mom wouldn't bring my sister here to the truck, to send her back to my relatives in Oldeslohe. Now what? Sitting behind the harbormaster's house, I watched the fishing boats moor and unload their bountiful catch from the sea. They loaded the mackerel into low, wooden boxes and weighed them on a big scale. Then one of the men pulled down the tailgate of the truck and they loaded many wooden boxes onto the pickup truck. Next, they threw a big, black tarp over the boxes. When I saw that there was enough room for my little sister to sit in between the rows of filled boxes, a great idea raced through my mind. Then all the men exchanged money, poured a drink into their mugs, raised the mugs high and thanked the sea for the rich catch.

They exchanged a few more words while they finished drinking and then they separated. The driver started the pickup. With a lot of blue grey smoke rising from the truck and some arguments from the engine, the truck slowly left our harbor.

I jumped up into the air and screamed, "Yes, it will work!"

Ever so happy at the thought of getting rid of my sister, I ran home to tell her that she could go back to Oldeslohe! She smiled at me, gave me a hug and whispered thanks into my ear.

She started to pack her fine belongings.

I told her, "You need to keep your leaving a secret, so don't say anything or mom will notice that something is going on. If she finds out what I'm planning, you'll have to stay here for sure. Only pack a small bundle so it will fit on the truck."

She agreed and put most of her fine belongings back into our carton beneath our bed. Then she took a few dried peas from our sack on the wall, stuck them up her nose, lay down, and smiled. A while later she tried to get those peas out of her nose, but they had swollen from the moisture and would no longer come out.

In panic, she screamed for mom. Our mother tried her best to get those peas out of her nose but couldn't. Hearing all the screaming, our grandma came upstairs to my sister's rescue. She simply sucked the peas out of my sister's nose. I stood amazed and anticipated that someone would give my sister a good whipping, but they didn't punish her.

The next afternoon I stood outside our house, waiting and hoping for the fish buyer's pickup truck to come. After a short while, I heard the noisy motor long before I actually saw the vehicle. Excitedly, I walked upstairs and whispered to my sister that her ride had arrived. She smiled and followed me out of our house happily. I held her hand, carried her small bundle and quickly we walked down to the pier.

There I hid behind the harbormaster's house and told my sister to sit down low, so no one would see us. The fishing boats had already moored and the men had begun to load the filled cases onto the truck. When the money exchange started, I took my sister's hand and quickly walked over to the pickup. I helped her up onto the truck and gave her the note with our relative's address on it. I told her to hold onto the wooden boxes so she wouldn't fall off, since the men had left the truck's tailgate down. I also told her to stay underneath the tarp.

As if nothing was going on, but with my heart beating ever so fast, I walked back to the harbormaster's house, staying out of sight, waiting for the truck to leave with my sister on board.

Before long, the two men finished their business and entered their truck. After a few tries, the truck finally started. With a stinking blue-grey cloud hanging in the air, the pickup truck slowly left the pier. I saw my sister sitting among the loaded cases of fish. Oh, how it pleased me to see her go.

I jumped high with joy and somersaulted down our dirt road. Life was great again. I had my grandma and my mom to myself again, and didn't have to take my little sister along with me all the time.

When I opened the door to mom's room, I knew I was in more than huge trouble. My sister lay on the couch. She cried bitterly and her hands and knees bled. Her small bundle, with part of her pretty belongings, lay beside her on the floor.

My mom tended to her wounds, stopped for a moment, and angrily turned to me. "Stay here, I'll get to you next!"

I knew what that meant.

Sure enough, I got a whipping, which on a scale from one to ten I'd call a ten plus. I thought it very unfair since my sister actually wanted to leave.

That night in our bed my little sister said, "I fell off the pickup truck, around the first curve, because I couldn't hold onto the boxes of fish. A neighbor picked me up off the dirt road and brought me home. I'm sorry mom whipped you so hard!"

I hated my sister at that moment, but I didn't tell her that. She still stank like fish, even though my mom washed her and changed her clothes.

No Listerine, Q-Tips or sweet suckers!

Chapter 56

How I hated those words!

Since my attempt to get rid of my sister failed, I snuck out of our house the next day, stepping only onto the stairs that didn't squeak, so I could go play with my friends without having to take her along.

As soon as I opened our front door, my mom shouted at me from her room. "Take your sister along!"There they were again, the words I hated so badly.

I had had such a nice time without her while she lived with my aunt and uncle faraway. I liked to spend time with my friends without dragging along my sister, the blabbermouth. My friends and I did things we didn't need our moms to know.

Among many other things, we stole carrots and apples out of gardens to feed to the newborn, cute horses and to still our hunger. We also watched the young lovers roll around and moan in the fresh spring grass. We outwitted the grumpy old ghost and crawled into the mound graves to see what treasures they held. Moms didn't need to know these things.

My little sister couldn't even jump over a ditch without falling into it, or dive way down into the old castles that the sea had claimed to check on the new inhabitants, the fish and the crabs.

Many times, my friends and I ran away and hid so my sister couldn't follow us. Often I beat her up if she followed me. Of course, my sister told my mom what I did to her and Mom punished me. Slowly my anger turned into big hate. I started to hit my sister any time my mom wasn't around and of course, she told on me. This terrible situation went on for quite some time. I wonder if my mom actually knew that she made me hate my sister.

Finally, one day when my mom got ready to punish me again for hitting my sister, I disobeyed all the rules and screamed at her, "My sister isn't my responsibility! She's your child and you should take care of her!"

Having said that and frightened of a huge punishment, I ran out of the house. I called my dog and together we raced toward the beach. I cried out of fear, anger, and confusion. Together we sped away until I could go no farther. Then I sat down on a tall sand dune and looked out to sea.

My dog tried to catch seagulls which sat on small stones in the shallow parts of the ocean. They waited for some small fish to swim by so they could pick them out of the water and swallow them. He seemed to have a lot of fun, but had no chance to catch the quick and very alert birds.

Slowly, I breathed easier and in a way felt glad that I had spoken my mind. I felt much relieved, but worried what to do next. I wished I hadn't screamed at Mom in such anger. She'd likely be very angry with me for a long time and most likely would think of some huge punishment. I never wanted to hurt her feelings, but I was sure I had. I loved my mom most of the time.

The sun started to crawl into her watery bed and the first cold night wind made me shiver. Though cold and hungry, I wasn't ready to face my mom. Suddenly, when the lighthouse on the northern side of our island began to flash its warning lights to the sailors, I knew what to do. I'd walk to Miss Mali, the operator of the lighthouse, and the palm reader and fortuneteller of our island. Perhaps she could read my hand and tell me what to do.

Miss Mali and my grandma were very close friends and we visited her often. Some people shied away from her out of fear.

They thought she knew everything on this island. Most came only to see her when they needed her advice. She didn't charge for her readings, but people always brought something to thank her.

One whistle and my dog and I started on our way. Walking through the soft sand, I realized that I had nothing to give to her for the reading of my palm. Then I realized that I could offer to do a chore for her. Now I felt better.

Miss Mali saw me coming and stretched out her arms to welcome me. She hugged me gently with a warm smile. Her huge, white, curly coated dog greeted my dog excitedly. While the dogs tumbled and played along the edge of the beach, we sat down in the sand.

She put her arm around me, looked into my cried out face and asked me, "What's the matter, child?"

With a shaking voice, I told her all about my problem of having to take my little sister along with me all the time and that I screamed at my mom. Then I took a deep breath and asked her if she could please read my palm and tell me what I should do next and what my life would hold for me.

She smiled at me and gently reached for my right hand. After a hard study of my lifelines on my palm, she began to talk. Slowly she said, "There will be a great disappointment in your life a few years from now when you finish school. Your life will not be easy, but you're strong enough to make your life a mostly happy one. You will marry and travel faraway over the big ocean to a different land.

"There I see other men in your life and two children. You have a long lifeline, which is good. As for right now, you must spend the night with me because a storm is brewing up over the ocean. Tomorrow you'll take a note from me to your mom and your life will change."

Before she let go of my hand she said, "I see you've been blessed by our island witch."

Greatly relieved, I wanted to ask her how she could see that, but a loud thunder rolled over our island.

In a hurry, we ran to the tree where her fishing rod stood. Quickly she reeled her line in. What a surprise! A big, fat flounder flopped around on the hook. Both of us laughed loudly and smiled at each other. Oh yes, I liked this woman. Our dogs ran toward us to investigate the commotion. They looked exhausted from all the rough play, but they sure looked happy, funny, and full of sand and a little seaweed.

A sudden strong wind woke up the smooth sea. The white-capped waves hurried onto the shore. The dark, almost purple clouds flew toward us, cutting off the sun's rays to our island. One amazingly beautiful, wide lightning bolt which started out in one thick, bluish line down toward earth, split in midair into six bolts. Those six, almost pink lightning bolts, now hit the ocean at the same time with all their force. The seawater raged high into the air while I stared in awe.

When the next lightning bolt struck down near us and the sand blew sideways at us, we ran toward the lighthouse. She carried the fat, flapping flounder and I carried her fishing rod. Our dogs passed us by in a hurry while running for safety, as if playing an exciting new game. Sand and seawater trailed behind them with every quick leap. With the next loud, rolling thunder, it seemed our small island trembled with fear of splitting apart.

The mighty ocean roared now, smashing its tall waves with outrage onto the shore. As the first hail pummeled us, we reached the lighthouse. Our dogs, already there, huddled as close to the door as they could.

With the next loud and violent peal of thunder, we all ran inside the lighthouse at the same time. The dogs shook themselves to get rid of the remaining sand and water. We held on to each other to keep from sliding around on the wet floor, but before we could stop running, both of us fell onto the floor. Laughing loudly, we helped each other up. We didn't get hurt, but the fat flounder had disappeared in the dark hallway.

The dogs began to bark and chased something around the hallway. Hurriedly, Miss Mali fetched a lantern and lit the area so we could find our dinner before the dogs did.

We finally found it, flapping on the wet floor toward the living room, with two hungry, fighting dogs chasing it. The big flounder fled to safety, sliding beneath the couch. The dogs, though too big to crawl beneath her couch, desperately tried, while snapping at each other.

Miss Mali took two pieces of bread and coaxed the dogs into the stairway, which led up to the top of the lighthouse. She threw the two pieces of bread onto the stairs. The dogs ran quickly after them and she closed the door. Amidst the raging thunderstorm, with the hail crashing down, we tried to get our dinner out from underneath her couch.

There wasn't enough space for me to crawl beneath it, so I stretched my arm out, but still couldn't reach the flounder. Miss Mali tried to reach it with her broom, but it still had enough life in it to move over just enough to avoid capture. I felt a little sad and wondered if the flounder knew that we intended to kill it and eat it. We decided to move the couch over a little so I could reach it. That finally worked.

When I handed Miss Mali the barely living flounder, I saw how it desperately struggled to stay alive. The fish opened its mouth wide to breathe in seawater, and foam came out of its gills. I wanted to take the poor, dying flounder back to the ocean so it could live, but it didn't belong to me to do with as I pleased.

Quickly, Miss Mali reached for a knife in her cabinet, held the flounder over a big bowl and cut its head off. Then she ripped the flounder's intestines out. The flounder's headless body faintly moved one more time and then it lay still in the bowl beside its intestines and head. I sadly stared in the bowl where death had just taken place, while the light in the lighthouse tower slowly blinked to warn the sailors of a quick death on the dangerous reefs in the mighty ocean, on this side of our island.

While Miss Mali prepared the flounder for our evening meal, I climbed to the top of the light tower, four stories up. The dogs followed me with great enthusiasm. Breathlessly, I reached the top. The small cube, which enclosed the important, huge warning light, had walls of glass around it.

In awe, I watched the vicious thunderstorm display its raw power around our little island. I dearly hoped the intense storm wouldn't break our island and let the ocean swallow it.

In the wide beam of the light tower's warning light, I saw a big merchant ship dancing up and down among the wild waves of the angry ocean, with its sails torn. The strong wind ripped at the dangling pieces. I saw not a single light on the ship, and worried for the safety of the crew. In the next few seconds it took the warning light to shine back at the merchant ship, a huge bolt of lightning went down in that direction and scared me tremendously.

When the warning light blinked toward the merchant ship again, the sight that greeted me shocked me. The big ship lay on its side in the wild ocean, and flames ate at it. I screamed for Miss Mali to come up. With another blink of the strong, bright light shining in the direction of the merchant ship, I saw just a huge, high flame.

When Miss Mali reached the top of the lighthouse, I hurriedly told her what I had seen. When the warning light blinked in the direction of the sinking merchant ship again, the ship was no longer in sight. The wild ocean had swallowed the merchant ship. Frightened, I tightly grasped her hand and hoped to see the ship upright in the next turn of the warning light, but to my grave dismay, I only saw the violent ocean.

Still clinging to her hand and deeply hurting by what I witnessed, I followed her down the stairs of the lighthouse. At that time, we had no lifeboat on our island, or any way to contact a place that had a lifeboat that could go out to sea in this vicious storm. I thought about all the sailors that most likely faced death. At this vulnerable moment in my young life, I decided against hiring on, or taking a ride on a boat or ship.

By the time we reached the living room, the severe thunderstorm had lost most of its brutal power. The dogs sat next to me by the small stove, watching the flounder fry in a deep frying pan. I'm sure they hoped the flounder would jump out of the pan so they could devour it.

In silence, Miss Mali divided the fish guts, fins and the head of the flounder into two small bowls and gave one bowl to each dog. They quickly ate their entire share and looked around for more. She then brought two overflowing plates to the little table. The fried flounder pieces smelled delicious as well as the bread soaked in the hot grease.

Slowly, we ate our delicious meal. I couldn't finish all the good food on my plate and asked if I could save it for the morning meal. She said I could, then wrapped my plate in a kitchen towel so the flies couldn't eat the leftovers or lay their eggs in it, and sat it on the counter.

Since I had no gift to bring her for reading my palm, I asked if I could wash the dishes for her. She smiled and nodded as if she had other things on her mind. Perhaps she thought of the sunken ship as I did. As I washed the few dishes and looked around, I saw Miss Mali staring into the flickering light of the oil lamp. I wondered, since she could foretell the future, if she saw what happened to the sailors on the sinking merchant ship. When I dried the last fork, she opened the door and whispered outside to the leaving thunderstorm, "They're all dead now!"

The storm answered her with one last crackling lightning bolt, and an eerie silence followed.

With a warm good-night hug, she handed me a blanket. I asked her if I could sleep up in the tiny cube of the warning light.

She said, "Yes my child, of course you can," and handed me the lantern.

With my dog in tow, I walked up all the stairs again. I stood near the warning light's strong, bright beam and watched its blinks out onto the ocean, shining onto the very small parts of the huge reefs that stuck out of the water. I hoped to see some sailors walking onto them, or onto the shore, but the ocean showed no mercy.

Disappointed, I lay down on the wooden floor next to my dog and covered both of us up with the blanket. By the slow clicking of the light tower's warning light, I drifted away into the relieving sweet dreams of castles, chocolate and dogs that can fly.

Early in the morning, my dog woke me by licking my face, as if I needed a good washing. I took one more look outside. A wondrous sunrise painted the sky and the ocean in pure gold. Pink, lacy clouds hung between the mighty, golden beams of the sun, and the completely calm ocean mirrored back the spectacular sunrise. I wondered how at times this big ocean can be so amazingly beautiful and at other times, a merciless, outraged killer.

Our preacher tried to teach me in Sunday school that God was still alive and in charge of everything. I found it hard to believe how cruel God could be. On one hand, He's supposed to forgive all our sins lovingly, no matter what they may be, and on the other hand, He sends violent storms, and helpless people die. None of it made sense to me at that age. With my head full of thoughts about God, I walked down the stairs of the light tower into the living room. Miss Mali greeted me with a smile and a warm hello.

Her small iron stove's cook top glowed fiery red, and the leftovers from last night warmed in the deep frying pan. The whole, small room smelled so great, and I was very hungry. While the dogs went outside to catch seabirds without any success, Miss Mali and I ate our delicious leftovers. My sadness and fear grew with every minute. I didn't look forward to going home to face my mom.

After Miss Mali gave the dogs the grease and the leftover bread out of the frying pan, she came to me, handed me a closed letter and wished me a good walk home. I thanked her, and unwillingly left for home. On the way, I hoped the good parts she read from my palm came true, especially the immediate one, facing my mom at home.

Slowly I walked home, clinging tightly to the letter, which Miss Mali said would change my life. At the bay, before reaching our village, I sat down in the warm sand. My eyes wandered out to sea and I thought about all the sailors on the merchant ship that lost their lives. Somehow, I gained strength from that moment and walked straight home to face my mom.

When I walked into our house, I heard my grandma and my mom talking in my mom's room upstairs. Very glad to catch them both together, I walked upstairs. I knew that Grandma would protect me from too severe a punishment. Bravely, I walked upstairs and entered my mom's room.

Quickly, I handed her the letter. Mom sat down and opened it. She read it in silence and handed the letter to my grandma. I stood there, scared, and wondered what would happen to me. Then my mom stood up from her chair and came over to me. She didn't look angry as I expected. Instead, she looked sad and a tear slowly ran down her cheek.

Gently she hugged me and said, "I'm sorry. I didn't realize that you saw your sister as a burden. From now on you never have to take her along with you again."

Her words stunned me, but made me oh so happy and greatly relieved that she wouldn't punish me.

Miss Mali was right. Nice times lay ahead of me. I still wonder today what she wrote in that letter to my mom. And yes, a great disappointment followed toward the end of my schooling; and I did go faraway over a big ocean to a different part of this world, America. Yes, I had different men in my life, but I had only one child.

No chili, French toast or shredded cheese.

Chapter 57

Did they dance at Sinners' Row?

In spring, our new teacher suddenly grew ill. That meant school closed for a while, and since it was too early to go to work in the fields, I had time to have fun. I gathered my friends together and suggested, "Let's take a trip to the mound graves on the east side of our island. It will be a great adventure to trick the old, grumpy ghost who still faithfully watches over the old graves. We can crawl inside of one of the graves and see what treasures we can find."

Right away, two of my friends refused and walked off. The other two, more daring, excitedly agreed to go along.

I decided that everyone should bring a candle and matches so we could see inside the completely dark graves and of course some food, since we'd be gone all day and night, and it was too early in the season to steal vegetables from the fields.

In no time at all, I had a grease sandwich and a quite dried out apple in one of my pants pockets, part of a candle, matches, and my grandpa's old pocketknife in the other pocket. I grabbed my heavy jacket on the way down the stairs.

The moment I opened the front door, I loudly announced, "I'll come back tomorrow."

My mom and grandma shouted back, "Have fun and don't get in trouble!"

A loud whistle brought my dog out of his dream with an excited jump. Quickly, he came to my side. Both of my friends came from their houses and we walked on to our big adventure.

Harras ran circles around us in excitement. Even with his slight limp, he could run like lightning, especially when he chased rabbits. He just never figured out how to completely turn around in midair and run off in a different direction like the rabbits did. He didn't get to eat rabbit very often.

Singing silly songs and working up our courage, we joked about what the old ghost could do to us, and we happily walked on our way. Suddenly, a faint sound of thunder rolled over our island. I looked at the sky, and when I saw dark clouds rushing our way, I knew we needed to find shelter.

Soon, the storm clouds overcame the sun. We sought out the only nearby building, the old windmill across the dirt road from the new cemetery, which by now was hundreds of years old. The real old cemetery, around our amazingly beautiful church, had long ago filled up. No one remembered who the buried souls where anymore, or where they came from.

At this time of the year the old windmill sat at rest. At harvest time, everyone could hear her busy squeaking, rumbling noise all over our island. Just as the rain started to pour down on us, we ran inside the old, rat-infested building. With all the noise we made, we woke up my dog's dinner of many fat rats. He busied himself catching his meal while the three of us looked for a dry place to wait out the storm. In one corner of the old windmill, where all the flour sacks sat stacked up, the roof didn't leak, so we made ourselves comfortable there.

The storm, though not strong or heavy, dragged on. We shared our food and told scary stories all afternoon until the big, old, church clock rang nine times.

The storm with its rain lingered. Finally, we decided to spend the night at the old mill instead of going on to the mound graves. We arranged flour sacks on the dry floor and lay down on them to go to sleep. My sweet Harras, whose belly stuck out with his filling meal, lay down beside me. I covered us with my jacket. Quickly I sank into dreamland, where the clouds lifted me up and let me ride on them into a land where the river ran softly with pure chocolate.

Before I could drink from the chocolate river, an outraged, violent bark and growl awoke me out of my sweet dream. My dog stared out of a good-size hole in the wood siding of the windmill. The fur on his neck stood up straight, and he let us know in the most extreme way, of nearby danger.

Immediately, all three of us woke, ran to my dog, and looked out of holes in the siding of the windmill. The rain had stopped and our church's clock rang in midnight. We looked toward the cemetery, where my dog seemed to have spotted the danger. Between his barking and growling, we heard voices, but none of us could hear what they said. I tried my best to calm Harras so we could understand the voices and hear where they came from. But he wouldn't quiet down.

As a last resort, I gently tied his mouth closed with my sock so he could no longer bark. We listened into the quiet night with the half moon hiding behind a big cloud. I clearly heard two different voices coming from the direction of the cemetery.

I barely made out their laughing and singing. I saw that they embraced each other while walking through the graveyard. When the half moon crawled out from behind a big cloud to light the earth, I clearly saw two shadows dancing in the cemetery. Too quickly, the half moon hid behind the next cloud and I couldn't recognize the shadows.

I wondered if the old people of our island were right. They often whispered among themselves about the devil and our island witch dancing on Sinners' Row when the moon showed half of his face. The old people also whispered that if anyone disturbed them in their dance, they'd reap a terrible punishment, perhaps immediate damnation.

What a chance this was. I could see if the old people's

whispers were true. Though fear took hold of me, I shook it off and the temptation to go over to the cemetery to check this out won. I talked my friends into going with me, which helped to calm my fears.

After I tied my dog to a big, wooden post inside the old windmill, the three of us quietly left the old building. Silently, I bent over and walked in the shadows of the tall bushes, and my friends followed me. We crossed over the small dirt road and carefully crept along inside the ditch with the tall hedge hiding us. Since the entrance gate to the cemetery squeaked when opened, we crawled inside beneath it.

Ever so slowly, without a word, I led my friends among the headstones and bushes of the graves close enough to see the faint figures of the dancing couple more clearly. When I lifted my head just a little above a headstone to look, I definitely saw two figures dancing toward the end of our cemetery. I recognized the voice of our island witch, but not the other voice, so I figured it had to be the devil. Suddenly, the two faint figures stopped dancing and looked our way. We knew right away that we were in more than huge trouble. Scared to death, we lay down in the dirt on someone's grave, hiding among the evergreen bushes. Shaking with fear, I desperately hoped we wouldn't be discovered.

After a short while, I got a little braver and carefully lifted myself high enough to see if they still danced in Sinners' Row. The bright, half-moon shone on the earth, as though helping me to see clearly, in this scary night.

I saw the dancing pair actually dancing on the graves in Sinners' Row, and I clearly saw our island witch's smiling face. Our old people had told the truth. Our island witch did dance with the devil at Sinners' Row. Oh my, now what?

Scared to death, I sat back down in the wet dirt of the grave. Shivering with fear and in a shaky voice, I softly whispered into my friends' ears what I saw. A deep fear shook them as well. We needed to get out of the cemetery now, as discreetly as we had arrived, otherwise our lives could end in a terrible death.

By mostly crawling low among the graves and biting my teeth together so their loud clatter wouldn't give us away, I led the three of us close to the front gate of the cemetery. One quick, short run and we'd be out of here.

Just at the moment I signaled my friends to stand up and run toward the gate, my dog ran toward us, happily barking without the sock over his mouth and with part of the rope dangling down his neck. So glad to find us, he jumped up and down on us.

In wild panic, the three of us ran as fast as we could to the gate. A loud, vicious laugh came from Sinners' Row, and a powerful lightning bolt hit down close to us. While I ran for my life, my heart pumped wildly.

We all made it safely back to the old windmill. We collapsed on the rough wooden entrance, scared and panting for air. My chest hurt with every breath I took. I believe that was the fastest I ever ran in my entire life.

Suddenly, the heavy, old door of the mill, which had not been closed in years, closed with a loud bang. At that moment, I clearly heard our island witch's loud, shrill laugh. Deep fear crawled through me, and I wondered if we were locked inside this old windmill.

I once saw two big men try to close the broken door and fail. Ever since then, it had remained open. Who had closed it, and how would we get out of here? Huddled together and silently shivering with fear, none of us had the courage to get up and check if the heavy door had completely closed.

We held on to each other for a long time in silence. I finally lit my candle and walked slowly to the heavy, old, wooden door. My friends followed me. In dismay, I discovered that the door had indeed closed all the way and locked us inside.

All our pushing and kicking never even shook the heavy door.

I screamed, "We're trapped!"

Another bold laugh came from the top of the old windmill. We recognized the witch's laugh and knew she was punishing us. We sat, bewildered, not knowing what to do next.

Suddenly, the half-moon came out from behind a cloud and shone its light through all the holes in the wood siding and the roof of the old windmill. That was it! We needed to find a hole big enough to crawl through to the outside. Excited at the prospect of escape, we searched all the walls for a hole big enough.

One of my friends shouted in excitement, "Your dog found a place to get out! He's drinking water out there from a puddle."

I looked out through a missing piece of the wood and sure enough, there sat Harras lapping up water from a big puddle. I needed to find out how he got there. Perhaps we could get out the same way. When I called him to come to me, all three of us watched him enter the mill.

Quickly, we all ran to the hole where he had entered. In big disappointment, we realized the hole was way too small for us to crawl through. We kicked the adjoining wooden boards hard but they didn't budge. We looked up to see them attached to huge diagonal beams with very big nails. In a last, daring attempt to escape, I took my lit candle and climbed up the steep, old ladders to see if we could get out through the roof.

With every frightening step I took onto the flimsy ladders, they squeaked and bent a little to one side or to the other. By the time I finally reached the top floor of the windmill, clouds had hidden the half-moon. My little candle had burned out on the way up, and I could see absolutely nothing in this pitch-dark night. I waited for the moon to come back out from behind the clouds so I could look for a way out through the roof.

After just a brief moment, another storm had drifted over us. Rain began to fall, and the water poured down at me through the leaky roof. One of my brave friends came partially up the ladders with a lit candle to guide me down. The old church's clock in the tall bell tower rang twice.

Ever so carefully, I started to back down the now wet ladders.

345

The old windmill moaned and groaned with the wind and the rain. Halfway down the first ladder, my brave friend's candle died. Darkness surrounded us. I clung to my ladder, shaking and scared. I took each downward step carefully so I wouldn't slip and slide to my death. The encouraging words from my friends below me slowly got louder. I hoped to reach them still alive.

When I finally reached my friends, joy overcame me and I swore to myself never to climb these dangerous ladders again. All of us, soaked to the bones by now, looked desperately for a dry place. We lit our last candle and walked back to the place where the empty flour sacks sat stacked and the roof didn't leak.

We took off all our wet clothes, hung them over a wooden rail and wrapped ourselves up with some dry flour sacks. The three of us sat on the ground and huddled close to watch our last candle slowly burn down. The lightning storm still hit down hard on us and pounded the old mill with hail. For a brief moment, we looked at ourselves wearing flour sacks, and realizing how hilarious we looked in those outfits, we laughed loudly. Then we quickly comprehended the seriousness of our situation.

We had no idea what our island witch and the devil would do to us. Would they poke out our eyes, or perhaps bury us alive at Sinners' Row? One of my friends said she heard from the old ones that if you went against the rules, you'd die a slow, cruel death, hanging upside down from a tree. The other friend said she heard sinners like us would have all their limbs cut off and have to watch while the pigs ate them. Our situation grew worse with each passing minute. We held on to each other tightly, promising to talk no longer until daylight.

The church's big clock rang four times. Too scared to sleep, we silently watched our last candle burn down. Suddenly, from all around us, rats crawled toward us. Their tiny, dark eyes glistened in the candlelight. Their noses moved as if they sniffed to see if we were edible

I had heard people talking many times that rats often attacked small children in their beds and ate their flesh. Was this our punishment from our island witch and the devil? Being eaten by rats?

Scared out of our minds, we grabbed loose pieces of wood to defend ourselves. The moment we stood up to protect ourselves, Harras came flying down from the flour sacks and caught the closest rat. He ate it in front of the rat's clan. They stared at my dog with their little bodies shaking in disbelief. When my dog swallowed the last part of their relative and readied himself for his next kill, all the rats scattered.

In the last flicker of our candlelight, I saw Harras licking the rat's blood from his nose. The church tower's clock rang five times. One more roll of thunder, and the storm moved off our island to plague someone else. Before long, the sun would bring light to this pitch-dark world, and with it, hopefully a solution to get us out of here.

Exhausted, we sat down on the dirt floor, promising each other to stay awake. I don't remember falling asleep, but I clearly remember waking up on a wet, muddy floor. The dim light of the early morning, shining through the holes in the windmill's siding, let me see that all three of us lay in a puddle of mud.

Disgusted, I screamed, "Wake up!"

In a hurry, we tried to stand up to get out of the mud, but it wasn't that easy. We kept on sliding and falling back down into the slippery mud. Finally, we managed to stand up beside the large puddle, holding onto the railing where our clothes used to hang. I could not believe what we looked like. We had mud all over our bodies, even in our hair. One of my friends kept spitting mud out of her mouth. In the turmoil of getting out of the mud, we had somehow managed to pull down our clothes and yes, all of it lay in the mud.

In dismay, we started to laugh out very loud, holding back a few tears. That woke my dog. He came down from his bed on the flour sacks, yawning and stretching his body to greet the morning.

He was the only one without mud on his body. He sure picked the right place to sleep. What a smart dog I owned.

After we wiped the mud from our bodies and wrapped dry flour sacks around us, the sun started to rise from her watery bed. I decided that all of us should find a hole in the old windmill's siding on the side of the dirt road and wait there until someone passed by. At that moment, all of us should scream for help at once. That surely should get us out of here.

The church's clock rang six times, while we sat by the holes of the old windmill, with our heads stuck outside, eagerly awaiting someone to come our way. The mud on my body started to crack and fall off in places. I was very hungry, and everyone complained of thirst while we watched my dog lap up fresh water from the puddle just outside the mill.

When I glanced over to the cemetery where our trouble had started the night before, I wondered what would happen to us when the night took hold of our island again. Would the witch, or perhaps the devil, or both of them come back and finish their punishment?

Overcome with terrible fear and guilt, I whispered in my newly-learned, secret number language, into the slowly passing wind, "I'm so sorry, Ola, for sneaking into the cemetery to watch you dance on Sinners' Row." I hoped our island witch could hear me. I'd have said it louder, but I didn't want my friends to know my new secret language and how scared I really was.

All of a sudden, someone came walking down the dirt road toward us. Help had arrived in the form of a man. He had flowers in his hand, most likely to bring to a loved one in the cemetery. As he came closer, I recognized him by his severe limp. Grandma called him the town drunk and her best customer. She always treated him nicely and often invited him inside for a meal since his wife had died.

At my signal, when the man had come close enough, all three of us screamed for help as loudly as we could. Our screams echoed

348

on in the old windmill. The old man stopped walking immediately, looked toward the cemetery, dropped his flowers and ran as fast as his crippled legs could take him back toward the village. What a deep disappointment.

Time went on without anyone coming into view on the dirt road we watched so intensely. Slowly, very hungry, filthy and ever so thirsty, our belief in spotting someone on the dirt road grew very gloomy. The sun had long risen with a promise for a beautiful day, and here we sat, locked inside the old windmill, most likely starving to death or worse. Both of my friends began to cry. I worked very hard to hold back my own tears. When the church's bell had finished ringing in midday, a very loud noise shook the old windmill. Something had slammed hard against its wood sidings. Scared that our time to die had come, we huddled together and braced ourselves for an extremely painful death, which we deserved, since we had disobeyed our island witch's rules.

I could no longer hold back my tears. There we sat, in complete defeat, shivering with fear and crying out loud. I felt so very guilty about talking my friends into going inside the cemetery to spy on the devil and our island witch. Clinging together, we loudly begged the devil and our island witch for forgiveness.

Somehow, between crying and begging for forgiveness I glanced up and just happened to look toward the old windmill's heavy, wooden door. The door stood open! The sun shone right through the opening. Bewildered, I stood up and stared at the open door. I touched my crying friends' shoulders and pointed. Instantly they stopped crying.

In a mighty hurry, we grabbed our muddy clothes, wrapped the flour sacks a little tighter to our bodies and hurried out of the old windmill. My dog, reluctant to leave this place of very fast food, finally followed us after another whistle. I took one more quick glance back at the old windmill and noticed some long, black strings hanging on the heavy old wooden door, our island witch's signature.

We needed to get out of these flour sacks and somewhat cleaned up before we could show ourselves in public. The nearest pond was in the cemetery, but we didn't dare enter that place again out of fear. So, we walked through the fields, behind tall bushes, making sure no one saw us, to the next pond. There we took our flour sacks off, and with our clothes in our hands, we walked into the icy cold water of the pond. When a handful of ducks and a few geese saw us entering the pond they quickly cleared out. Even all the frogs climbed out of the pond, sat still at the pond's edge and stared at us.

Inside the deep pond, we washed most of the mud from our bodies and our clothes while the feathered flock watched us and softly talked to each other. I wondered what they whispered to each other. With most of the heavy mud washed off us and out of our clothing, we dressed in our wet clothes and ran home, shivering all the way, but ever so relieved to get out of the old windmill.

The mound gravesites, guarded by the grumpy old ghost, had to wait for another day. We had satisfied our need for excitement for the next few days.

At home, I quietly entered my grandma's room without knocking on her door first. I wanted to avoid my mom's sure punishment. Grandma stared at me in disbelief with her mouth wide open.

I whispered to my grandma, "Please help me and don't tell Mom."

She nodded, took me outside, stripped off my clothes, and washed me beneath the pump. "You're lucky. Your mom won't be home from work for a while." She wrapped me up in a towel and said, "Now go upstairs and get dressed."

After I dressed in my other set of clothing, I hurried downstairs to wash the mud from my wet clothes before my mom came home.

By the time I got downstairs, my grandma had already washed

my clothes under the pump and had hung them on the clothesline. I thanked her very much.

Then she took my hand and led me into her room. In silence she brewed some tea, sat down on the old, red sofa next to me, put her big arm around me and said, "Now child, tell me exactly what happened to you!"

In detail, I told my grandma what happened while my dog lay close to her warm stove, moving his feet in his dream. I was sure he ran after another fat rat in the windmill.

When I finished talking, my grandma smiled and cuddled me into her arms. For many days afterward, my two brave friends and I, with my grandma in charge, washed all the flour sacks in the pond, let them dry in the wind and placed them back where they belonged. I don't believe my mom ever found out about this adventure. If she did, she didn't mention it.

Thank you, grandma!

Cଊଊଊ

Early the next day I walked to our island witch's house feeling very guilty. The closer I came to her house, the slower I walked, debating if I really should apologize to her. I knew I needed to because I wasn't supposed to be in the cemetery at midnight, disturbing her, but the thought of possible punishment scared me to death.

The stories the old ones told among themselves sounded awfully gruesome, especially when they sat around a cooking fire and had a few drinks. I still shivered with fear when I thought of the story which I heard one night where our witch set a man on fire in the middle of the road and let him burn to death.

When I asked my grandma if this really happened, she said, "It might have happened long ago."

My heart sank when I realized that I stood in front of Ola's house and she stood outside in her small front garden. I couldn't just walk past her. With great fear, I slowly put one foot in front of the other and walked toward her.

I offered my shaking hand to greet her, looked her straight into her face and said, "Please forgive me Ola, I did wrong last night, watching you in the cemetery. I will never do that again."

She took my small hand in her rough, old hand, smiled at me and said, "I silently invited you to come inside the cemetery because I wanted to see if you had the will to follow my invitation anywhere, even inside the graveyard at such a strange hour, which you did. I stayed with you through the night, even though you didn't see me, to see if in scary situations, you'd break our secret communications, but you didn't. You did well, my girl. You surely are a different child. Now run along and have fun!"

No Vicks Vapor Rub, balloons or electric heaters.

Chapter 58

What a filthy job!

Every early spring our village people came together to collect the valued seagull eggs. Only the big children joined the adults in that chore because of the danger involved. Now at ten years old and declared just about grown up, I would join our village people this year.

We had to protect ourselves from the angry attacks of the seagulls. Their sharp beaks, pecking at our heads with quite some speed, could hurt tremendously. In some instances, they had damaged people's eyes or pecked them out completely. Also important, we had to go in a large group, so the thousands of seagulls didn't just concentrate and storm down on one person to protect their eggs. As their secondary defense, they used a constant shower of flying poop.

For many years, I watched the gathering. All of us small children had laughed until we hurt at the way the villagers dressed and protected their heads. Now I had to join the adults and outfit myself for the seagull egg gathering.

My Uncle Fred built a wire cage for my head protection and filled it with grass, leaving spaces for me to see and breathe. My grandma wrapped me up in her seagull egg-collecting blanket and tied it to my body. She didn't have to go with our family any longer since I took her place. That old, genuine blanket stank just as our island did on natural fertilizing day. Wearing it gave me a sick feeling and I almost threw up. After I recovered, Grandma handed me her collecting basket, wished me good luck and on our way our family went to meet with the rest of the people of our village down at the silo by the pier.

What a hilarious sight we made! When we met the rest of our people, I couldn't help but giggle. My mom tried her best to keep me quiet, but I couldn't hold back from giggling at this strange parade. Some people wore buckets on their heads with holes cut out of them to see and breathe through. Others wore chamber pots on their heads, with cloth hanging down in front of their faces. A few people had wrapped their heads up with sacks, and pieces of it dangled down over their faces. Wire cages with many different fillings seemed to most popular for the younger generation. Some men wore helmets from the war and nothing over their faces.

The poop protection looked just as funny. Most of the villagers wrapped up in heavily-pooped-on, raggedy blankets, or pieces of unidentifiable clothing, which showed years of use on this special trip. A few people had constructed something similar to today's umbrella for their poop protection and tied them to their backs. One old fisherman wore only fishing net around his head and nothing else. He left his body completely naked, and his private parts dangled down between his legs. That was the first time I saw a man completely naked. I was so glad not to have those ugly pieces hanging between my legs. All the women looked at him, put their hands in front of their mouths and giggled.

Soon we walked the short way to the seabirds' breeding isle. The smaller children left behind, laughed out in sheer fun at our funny looking group, just as I had for years before I turned ten. A lot of old poop fell off my blanket with each step I took.

As soon as we came close to the seabirds' breeding islet, which sat only about a foot above the bay water, a thousand or so nesting seabirds took flight. Their immensely loud, shrill screams sounded like a violent concert in minutes.

At the edge of the bay, we took off our footwear and slowly waded toward the seagulls' islet. When I looked up into the sky, I saw the seagulls folding back their wings to gain speed while diving toward us. One after another, they slammed my head protection to protect their next generation.

Poop plopped down on me as I never imagined. I held on tightly to my basket and tried not to step on the coarse, sharp sea grasses which grew on the islet and in the water surrounding the islet. Their new shoots, barely visible, cut into skin like a sharp knife.

The seagulls' nests, built close together on this sandy islet, almost touched each other. The seagulls had built them on the sand with sea grasses and kelp, and lined them with soft down feathers from their own bodies. They laid their small eggs, usually two or three per nest, on top of the soft feathers.

As we gathered the eggs, we followed one simple rule: leave one egg in each nest, and put one in an empty nest, which most likely got robbed by some other creature. This helped ensure next season's plentiful gathering.

Faithfully, I picked up and placed the fragile seagull eggs in my basket, while the seagulls attacked me from above and the sharp sea grasses cut into my feet. I felt pain in my arms from the seagulls' attacks, even though I wore my grandma's heavy blanket over them.

My ice-cold feet hurt and bled. This sure was no fun. No wonder my grandma happily stayed home. At that moment, I made the mistake of looking up at the seagulls again, which everyone had told me not to do. Quickly, I learned why not to look up. Seagull poop landed in one of my eyes, and besides stinging, I could no longer see out of that eye. My fingers couldn't reach through the fine wire mesh on my head protection to wipe the poop out of my eye. I was miserable and very glad when the egg gathering ended.

Careful not to drop my basket full of seagull eggs, I waded

back through the shallow seawater to the sandy beach of our bay. My mom and I sat down in the sand and took our protections off, while the seagulls returned to their nests with loud mourning cries. I felt sad and guilty for stealing their eggs and therefore killing their unborn chicks.

Gladly, I took off the stinking blanket and my head cage. Blood dripped from my wounds and I did just like everyone else; I walked back into the cold saltwater and washed the poop out of my eye and the blood off my arms and feet. Yes, it hurt a lot, but I no longer cried out.

After I cleaned myself and waited for my feet to stop bleeding so I could slip into my socks and rubber boots, I looked at the now quiet seagull islet with guilt. My eyes drifted over to the old fisherman who had washed the seagull poop from his body and still naked, walked out of the bay water. I wondered if all men had those ugly parts hanging between their legs and why.

On our way home, proudly carrying my basket full of seagull eggs, I asked my mom about those strange parts hanging between that old man's legs.

She said, "You're too young, my child, to worry about that."

I guessed my mom really did not know either.

Grandma was happy to see all the eggs I collected and said, "I'm very proud of you and glad you took my place on seagull egg collection day."

The adult women in our house boiled and pickled many of the small eggs for future use. For the next days, my mom made delicious meals out of the seagull eggs; scrambled egg sandwiches and potato pancakes I enjoyed the most, besides my grandma's pan full of fried potatoes with seagull eggs stirred in. Those eggs had a fishy taste to them, but my, we gladly and thankfully lived on the fat side for a while.

No chocolate cakes, salsa or mousetraps
and we didn't know what germs were.

Chapter 59

Still today, this dream is part of my life, my escape.

At the beginning of this dream I saw myself walking down grey cobblestone stairs. Though scared, Ola taught me well to recognize when I was dreaming and how to get out of a dream when it got too scary. I could now wake myself out of my dreams, fly away, become invisible in an instant, or go back into a dream when I so desired. For many dreams to come I always started out on the same stair step that I had left in the dream before, which someone had marked with a scratch. I was never sure why I went so far down all those stairs, but something immensely strong had drawn me there.

A few more dreams later, walls enclose the stairs and I know I'm going down the stairs of an old castle. I see grey, old walls and small, empty cubicles, but feel there used to be life here. Motionless, I listen for voices but complete silence surrounds me.

Slowly, in the next few dreams, I leave the castle to go farther down. In each succeeding dream, it grows darker. I'm not sure where the very dim light comes from that guides me down. I now realize the walls around me are dirt, and the cobblestone stairs have become slippery. Frightened, I'm thinking about leaving this dream, but something keeps me going slowly down the now moss covered stairs. I support myself from sliding down those wet stairs by pressing my hands against the cold, earthen wall.

A few more dreams later, I feel that I'm now walking down earthen stairs in complete darkness. I touch a cold, dirt wall to guide me down the stairs. I feel like I'm about to reach the end of the stairs and wonder what will be there. I still realize that I'm in a dream and can end this dream whenever I want. Suddenly, I feel a slight vibration in the wall. I feel as though something very important lay just ahead of me. I put my ear closely to the earthen wall and to my surprise, find that it's wet.

Soon I hear a very faint rustling sound of perhaps metal chains, and a soft whisper. In the next few dreams and without visual marks now, I feel I still come back exactly to where I left the dream the night before.

Slowly, over many dreams to come, the voices grow clearer and the rustling sound now changes to a rattle of metal chains. Quickly the stairs end and the goose bumps on my neck grow more intense with every careful step. The rattle of the chains gets louder, and the whispering voices cry out. The earthen walls begin to shake and crumble. I feel as though there's a room on my left, and all this bitterness lives there, but I slowly pass by this room, and in the next dream, silence surrounds me again.

I feel at peace now, not scared any longer, and I surely follow the dirt path to wherever it leads me. Soon I sit down and ever so slowly slide downwards in the dark. My hands feel the cold dirt becoming warmer with every little slide forward. I'm not sure how many nights I slide down the earth, in the dark, hoping to reach my destination.

I faintly hear water rushing by below me. To my right, way below me, a soft, warm light appears. I can make out that I'm definitely underground, and the place turns very warm. Some slight vapor rises around me. I stand in a narrow corridor, about to enter a cave, but I cannot tell yet how large it is. I'm very attracted to the soft, warm light. While I climb down toward the light, the sound of the rushing water grows louder. In my next dream, I climb down into the cave. I find it very warm and hard to breathe. I can walk toward the soft light now. The ground here is fairly straight, but ever so slightly vibrates. The soft, warm light grows very bright as I walk closer to it. The rushing water roars by me now, but I cannot see it yet.

A few dreams later, I reach what seems the end of this huge, strange cave. I stand on a tall cliff. Below me, a dark, roaring river speeds by. I feel like the mad, boiling river will kill any living thing it touches.

Big boulders hang over the wild, dangerous river. Human skeletons dangle from those cliffs, chained to strong, rusted metal chains. A grey, cloud-like figure, like the old grumpy ghost on our island, keeps watch over them. He slowly drifts back and forth over the skeletons and rattles their metal chains. The ghost sees me and drifts close to me. At this moment, I debate whether to get out of this dream, but something tells me that I'll be all right, because it's just a dream.

The ghost comes closer and touches me with fire hot hands and bitterly laughs, but I don't let myself feel any pain. At that moment, to my right, the soft, warm light becomes a tremendous, golden sunrise. The sun's rays touch me gently, and the ghost hurriedly shies away from the bright light. He drifts back to his stone overhang and angrily rattles a rusted, metal chain of one of the skeletons. I feel safe, turn and thank the sun.

The golden sun now shines inside a beautiful, huge grotto. There is life. Trees, flowers and grasses grow inside it. Birds and colorful butterflies fly happily around inside the grotto. I hear soft music and someone singing.

The dark, wild river changed at the grotto's opening. The water runs calmly and clearly inside the grotto. So many colorful fish swim and play there. An orange tree on the edge of the river bears many ripe, delicious looking fruit. A cool breeze invites me to come into the huge, extremely pretty grotto. I stand on the tall cliff in awe, wondering how to get into the amazing grotto I so intensely want to reach. That night I awoke sweating and gasping for air.

For a few nights, I didn't enter this dream again. During the day hours, I wondered how I could reach the peaceful, pretty grotto. From where I stand in my dream, on the tall cliff, I can see only one way into the beautiful grotto. I need to jump off the tall cliff and dive into the dark, raging river. Then I would need to swim against its mighty current into a long natural underground tunnel, which led into the grotto. Severe fear came over me each time I thought of how far I had to swim without breathing.

Something inside of me said, "You know it's just a dream. Go ahead and jump. You can always escape if things go wrong."

The next dark night, I stand on the tall cliff again and the beautiful grotto grows even lovelier. Now a big apple tree is added, with red apples hanging down on every limb. An empty swing hangs from the apple tree, gently swaying in the soft wind. A few shreds of black cloth dangle from the swing, which I assumed came from Ola's shawl. Frogs sunbath at the edge of the clear, calm river. My dead grandpa walks through the scene, waves at me, smiles and floats away into the puffy white clouds.

Disappointed and angry I scream aloud, "I can't breathe under water. I need help!"

Tears run down my cheeks. From my left, where the skeletons are hanging down from the ceiling, a soft whisper reaches my ear: "Everything is possible way down here!"

A chain rattles, and a skeleton with chains attached to it, falls into the wild, dark river. Now the grey, cloud like ghost drifts over to me again.

Bewildered but bold, I stretch my hands up high and jump, head first, off the tall cliff into the scary, dark river. No sound of air rushes by me as I fly through the air. I'm not hurt when I dive down deep into the completely black, bottomless river. When I stretch out to swim toward the grotto, the darkness leaves the wild river. Bright sunlight inside the long, tunnel draws me toward the grotto. The water is warm and filled with pretty, colorful creatures, unknown to me.

Frantically, I realize that I've run out of air. Anxiously, I think about leaving this dream, but then I remember I'm just dreaming and anything is possible down here. I open my mouth and take a deep breath. Amazingly, I realize my lungs are satisfied and I relax to breathe normally underwater now. Studying all the strange creatures in this warm, clear river, a strange feeling of swimming toward home overcomes me.

When I arrive at the grotto, a hand reaches down to me and helps me out of the lovely river. I don't see anyone attached to the hand. Oh, what an extremely amazing place I've found. Warm air and singing birds greet me. I lie down in the soft green grasses, feeling faraway from danger and somehow very loved. The pretty grotto shelters me and lets me adore her deep beauty. I hear her heart softly beating.

I could never stay very long inside the wonderful grotto, but I can still go back to my amazing grotto today. Now the dream always begins with me jumping into the dark raging river. I no longer fear jumping into the river though, because I know that I can breathe underwater now in my dreams.

No meat thermometer, snow cones or rattlesnakes.

Chapter 60

Please send down one small eye!

One early summer afternoon, my mom sent me to collect driftwood on our beach so she could cook a hot meal for us. While I slowly walked along the shore looking for wood, I noticed many seagulls picking on something small and furry lying in the wet sand on the edge of the ocean. I felt sad for the little animal and ran toward it.

I scared the seagulls away from picking at it by throwing driftwood up into the air and screaming at them. When I knelt beside the small creature, I realized that it was a very young, grey squirrel and the seagulls had picked on this little creature quite a bit.

Blood seeped from various places of its small body, and the seagulls had pecked out one of its eyes. When I lifted the little squirrel up, I noticed that it was still alive, and its little heart raced. Gently, I wrapped the tiny body in my shawl, placed it in my basket and ran home.

Near tears, for fear the little squirrel would die, I arrived home completely out of breath. The moment I opened our front door, I called for help and stumbled up the stairs. My mom came down a few steps and took hold of me to keep me from falling. In our room, I handed her the tiny squirrel. She carefully unwrapped the small body, full of sand, dried blood and seagull poop. Though its heart continued to beat, the baby squirrel didn't move.

My mom turned to me and said, "Go fetch the little bowl we use to wash up in and fill it half way up with warm water."

Hurriedly, I mixed the hot water from the teakettle with some cold water from our bucket and set the bowl on the table. Mom cleaned the little squirrel's body in the warm water while I held its tiny head. Then I wrapped the clean little squirrel up in a soft towel and held it close to my body to warm it.

I prayed to God, just in case he still lived, which our preacher tried to convince me of, to please let the tiny squirrel live and send down a small new eye for it. I made sure to say that it didn't matter what color He made the eye.

Before long, the tiny squirrel moved ever so gently. Excitedly, I looked at the small creature. Its head wobbled, and it looked at me through its one eye. Slowly, I unwrapped the tiny creature and held it in my hands. Mom came over to have a look at it also.

Both of its front legs moved just fine, but only one of its back legs moved. The other one, badly damaged, just hung beside its body.

My mom said, "We need to cut his damaged leg off if we want to keep him alive. Otherwise, the injured leg can get infected and that most likely means death for the little fellow."

I stared at my mom and shivered with fear for the pain the tiny animal would have to endure.

Then she said, "Look, the leg is just attached by a small amount of skin anymore, and he'll probably feel very little pain. The worst has already been done."

My mom fetched her scissors and rinsed them off in hot water. I laid the tiny squirrel on its side and held it tightly so mom could cut off her bad hind leg. I quickly prayed the squirrel wouldn't feel too much pain.

As Mom cut the little leg off, its body shook for an instant and she squealed briefly. Then the squirrel desperately tried to escape my grasp. I held it tightly against my warm body and ever so gently stroked its fur. The squirrel calmed quickly, closed its eye and went to sleep.

I placed the little creature down on Mom's sofa and searched for something to fix a nest for it. Mom's old cook pot, which had a hole in it, seemed best. I lined it with soft straw and old rags, and the little squirrel didn't even wake up when I gently place it inside its new nest.

Mom looked at the sleeping animal sadly. "This little squirrel is a girl." She looked at the sleeping animal with a grave face. "This tiny animal still needs to nurse from its mom. She can't eat any other food yet. She's way too young."

Now I worried a lot. What were we going to do? I told my mom the tiny squirrel could have all my milk until it could eat other food.

She smiled and said, "That's not the right kind of milk, girl. Let's consult Grandma." Feeling hopeful now, I carried my tiny animal in its nest, the old pot, down the stairs to my grandma's room. She always knew what to do. My grandma looked at the tiny, helpless squirrel and smiled.

"What does she need to eat, Grandma?"

She said, "This little baby needs milk from its mother. So where did you find her?"

When I told her the story, Grandma shook her head and sat down. "There's no way to know then which nest it fell from, and it doesn't make any sense to put her into just any nest. Squirrels only take care of their own young ones."

Again, I worried for the little animal's survival and grew very sad. Grandma sat in her chair and began to think very seriously. Suddenly, a big, broad smile came over her face.

My grandma stood up and said, "The neighbor's old cat gave birth yesterday to one dead kitten. She's full of milk. Let's walk over and see if the old cat lets the squirrel nurse!"

Encouraged, I picked up the old pot and followed my mom and grandma across the dirt road to our neighbor's house.

Grandma explained why we had come and the neighbor led us in her backyard and inside a small lean-to. There, on a bed of straw, lay her old cat, all swollen up with milk. She desperately tried to clean herself from the milk that dripped from her nipples.

My grandma walked over to the old cat and stroked here gently, all the while talking to her in a soothing way. Then my grandma took the little squirrel, unwrapped it, showed it to the old cat, let her sniff it and placed it on one of her swollen teats. The little squirrel immediately suckled on the cat's teat, as though starving. The old cat looked at the tiny squirrel, lay back, and relaxed.

The adults smiled and laughed a little. Grandma suggested that we leave the tiny squirrel with the cat until it got big enough to eat solid food. I felt relieved that the cat accepted the tiny squirrel, but I still worried that the cat might kill the helpless animal. I asked to stay with them in the lean-to for the night. All three adults granted permission.

Soon the hungry little baby squirrel had eaten her fill and lay down next to the old cat and fell asleep. I worried when the cat sat up and sniffed the sleeping squirrel. Quickly, I stepped next to them, ready to rescue my little foundling. I didn't need to worry. The old cat just gave the little one a thorough cleaning. She concentrated especially on cleaning out the injured eye socket. I felt so happy and relieved.

Mom brought my pillow, blanket and a pig lard sandwich over to me and wished me good night. I shared my big sandwich with the gracious cat. I made myself comfortable on the dirt floor, and after I watched the old cat nurse the tiny grey squirrel again, I thanked her and rolled over to go to sleep. Perhaps tonight God would send down the little new eye I had asked Him for.

When I woke early the next morning, I found the old cat nursing my little foundling again. The small squirrel looked a lot more alive now, which made me very happy, but I felt a bit disappointed that God had not sent a new eye overnight for the squirrel. I gently touched the old cat and my little baby squirrel and told them, "I'll come back after school lets out." Over the next weeks, I spent a great deal of time in the neighbor's lean-to, watching my little squirrel grow up in a hurry. I named her Marla. Soon she had tiny white teeth and ran around the lean-to like lightning. One morning, when I woke, the old cat lay motionless next to the chattering squirrel. I touched her and felt for a heartbeat, but her poor little heart lay still. What a fine deed she had done at the end of her life.

My friend Marla and I moved back home into the lean-to. I built her a fine cage from leftover wire and wood in which she needed to spend the times I left home. Grandma's huge, yellow cat couldn't understand why I locked away such a delicious meal every time I left.

By now, Marla ate seeds of any variety, bread and acorns. She even nibbled on grasses, and she drank water out of a bowl or the pond. Every day after school and fieldwork, I took her for a long walk to gather her food and let her run around. While I walked through our village, she sat on my shoulder, holding on tightly, chattering away in excitement. She didn't mind my friends, or Harras, to come along on our walks, but she did fear the village dogs.

When even a single dog came into sight, she dug her claws into my shoulder to hold on, while chattering faster and louder like a mad mom. As soon as we walked outside our village and left the dogs behind, she jumped off my shoulder. Wildly, she ran up and down trees, enjoying life. The loss of her one hind leg and eye didn't seem to bother her. She grew more independent with each passing day, and I felt happy and sad at the same time. I knew I'd have to set her free soon.

Sure enough, a day or so later my mom and my grandma said, "It's time to let the squirrel free, girl."

Sadly, I agreed to let her free the next morning, a Sunday, when I didn't have to go to school or do fieldwork. I had more time to take my friend back to the faraway tall stand of oaks where I had found her. I knew there lived some fine looking grey squirrels in the tall trees and hoped that my friend Marla could fit into the group of her own kind easily and have a fine life! That last night together, in Grandma's lean-to, I begged God one more time, "Please send down a little eye for her so she can see well like the other squirrels in the forest."

Sunday morning came and my squirrel still had only one eye. I was awfully disappointed and angry with God. I told Him so too, and gave Him one more minute to send down one little eye for my squirrel. I closed my eyes and slowly counted to sixty. Hopeful, I opened my eyes and looked at my friend, but she still had only one eye.

Our preacher told us often, "God made this great world in six days." Now, why couldn't He make a little eye for my gray squirrel and send it down? I surely had asked Him nicely and often and gave Him plenty time to make one little eye. Our preacher had to be wrong.

Sadly, I dressed, walked inside our house and upstairs to our room. I sliced off enough bread to fix pork grease sandwiches for my sister and myself for our breakfast and a slice each for my dog and my squirrel. I hoped my mom wouldn't notice the extra two slices of bread I took when she came home from work. Since my sister still slept, I left her sandwich on the table, stuffed the rest into my skirt pocket and walked down the stairs to the lean-to. There I fetched my friend Marla and my dog to walk to the tall stand of oak trees to set her free.

My heart felt heavy, and my eyes filled with tears. Harras held his nose close to the ground, following an important trail. He had long learned not to bother my fast, furry friend with the knife sharp claws. My friend, the bushy-tailed, big grey squirrel, jumped and ran around, enjoying herself to the fullest. Even though I told her last night that I'd need to set her free today, I wondered if she understood that we would part today.

When we approached the tall stand of oak trees, where I had never taken her before, she jumped back onto my shoulder in fear. Ever so slowly, I walked into the small forest where birds and squirrels talked to each other. Harras had faithfully followed his important trail in a different direction, so the two of us entered the small oak forest by ourselves. Marla clung to my shoulder and listened to the many sounds of the forest.

Her sharp claws dug painfully into my skin, but I needed to let her hold onto me for this scary and confusing moment. When she let out a soft squeak, the whole forest fell silent as though trying to figure out the strange noise. I felt as if every eye in the forest watched us. Soon the birds began to sing again and the grey squirrels came down from their trees to have a closer look at us.

I sat beneath one of the larger oak trees to introduce my beautiful grey squirrel to the rest of them. I counted eight fine bushy-tailed, grey squirrels staring at us from the bottom of their trees. They started to communicate with Marla. Though excited, I could see her lack of confidence.

Suddenly, she jumped off me and ran up the big oak tree a little, chattering away. Then she came back down and jumped back onto my shoulder, chattering constantly. After she calmed down a bit, I took my sandwich and one extra slice of bread from my pocket. I broke the extra slice into very small pieces and handed Marla one small piece at a time. She eagerly ate the pieces, holding them neatly in her front paws, standing on her only hind leg.

The other grey squirrels looked at her and talked among each other. Soon one of them jumped off a tree and walked a little closer toward us. This big male, more of a silver gray than the rest of them, came fairly close to us. He stood up on his hind legs and looked at us. His wiggling, searching nose must have told him that we meant no harm.

Slowly, he walked closer, constantly testing the air. His closeness didn't upset my pretty squirrel. She kept looking at him while eating her bread. Just a few feet away from us, he timidly stood up on his hind legs, still testing the air. Very slowly, I broke off a little piece of my sandwich, stretched out my hand and leaned toward him.

Shyly but bravely, he crept forward to reach my hand. His dark, shiny eyes kept a hold on my eyes, ready to flee in a spilt second, if necessary. His bushy, almost completely silver tail curled up over his head and moved rapidly. His whole, beautiful body quivered with extreme alertness. One more shaking step and he reached my hand. So as not to scare him, I sat motionless and only took shallow breaths. Looking at me intensely now, the silver gray squirrel stretched out and grabbed the small piece of my bread with his right front paw. I expected him to run away quickly to eat the bread in safety, but he didn't. Still very alert, he stepped back and walked around my legs over to my left side where Marla sat.

Very surprised, I saw the big silver grey squirrel sit in front of her and eat his morsel of bread. He stepped close to her and nervously reached for a piece of bread from the small pile in front of her. She let him take it. After they shared all her bread, they began to sniff each other and chatter away.

To my complete surprise, all the other squirrels lined up just below my feet, staring at me, or perhaps my sandwich. I tore my sandwich in small pieces, bent over and placed them at my feet. Before I even leaned back up onto the huge oak tree's trunk, the squirrels took every last morsel of my breakfast sandwich. What a show! I wanted to laugh out loud, but didn't want to scare all the lovely creatures away, so I held my hand over my mouth and laughed quietly.

Suddenly, the beautiful silver grey male sensed danger and gave out a loud high-pitched squeal. In no time, all the squirrels had scurried high up into their trees, except for the big male. He hung upside down a few feet up in the big oak tree I sat under, trying to convince my friend Marla to follow him. She just looked at me and jumped onto my shoulder.

Perhaps the whole gang of village dogs was on their way here to harm the squirrels. Hurriedly, I climbed up the old oak tree with Marla still on my shoulder. After I reached a safe height, I sat down on a sturdy limb and waited for the danger to arrive.

Here came my dog, all by himself, slowly strolling into the forest, sniffing around the mighty oak trees. When he heard my laughter, he looked up and wagged his tail in excitement to have found me. The big male squirrel, still close by, talked to Marla. When I decided to climb back down the old huge tree, she jumped off my shoulder and followed the big male all the way up to the top of that huge tree. I saw that she had much more fun climbing a tree with him than with me. He climbed so much faster than I could ever dream. Perhaps this was our parting moment.

With a sad, heavy heart, I climbed down the old tree and sat in the soft, green grass below it, trying to hold my tears back. While letting Harras eat his slice of bread, I listened to the two squirrels' chatter and watched them run up and down the very tall oak tree in a wild frenzy. Oh, how much fun they had.

When I stood to leave, I looked up the oak tree and told my friend a tearful goodbye. Marla came down the trunk of the old tree and jumped onto my shoulder, ready to go home with me. The silver grey male hung on the bottom of the tree trunk calling her. I gently took Marla off my shoulder, placed her back on the tree trunk near the big male and told her that she had to stay. I touched her soft fur and promised that I'd visit her often. She chattered something back at me while I walked away. I imagined she said farewell. One look behind me told me that she had not followed me. She hung next to the big silver grey male on the strong tree trunk, and watched me.

In deep sadness, I left the stand of oaks and walked to the beach. There I undressed down to my underpants and jumped into the salty sea. Harras followed me, and together we swam far out into the ocean. The seawater swallowed my tears and its coolness calmed me. Exhausted, I turned around and let the strong, short waves carry me back onto shore. Harras shook himself dry while I dressed, and we walked home as the golden, setting sun began to declare the end of daylight.

I went back to visit with my friend, Marla, many times and always took a slice or two of bread with me, depending on how much I could slice off our weekly loaf without Mom noticing. I often found Marla in the same tree where I had left her. She sometimes chattered away with the silver grey male, other times she played with the rest of the clan. She always looked so glad to see me and came over eagerly to greet me.

I used to climb up the tree with her a little ways and she filled me in on all the latest squirrel gossip while eating the bread I brought. I told her all about my life, while Harras kept his nose to the ground, following one more of his important trails. Each farewell got a little easier since I knew that she was doing well. That fall I noticed a large, strong nest in a hole of a big, dead limb of the old oak tree. I wondered if Marla had built it.

Soon winter took charge of our island. The cold snows piled up high and I couldn't go to see my friend any longer. I worried if she had stored away enough food in her nest for the winter. This year, after only five months of hard winter, the sun had her strength back to lick away the snow slowly. As soon as I received my mom's permission to go outside for a long walk, I took my noon meal, two large carrots and stuck them in my pocket. Then in a great hurry, I strapped on my snowshoes, bundled up and left the house. Ever so excited, I went on my way to the small forest to check on my friend, Marla.

I wondered if she'd still remember me or if she were even still alive. Had God finally sent down a small new eye for her? I tried to run in my snowshoes but fell down into the deep snow a few times. That made me slow down and walk the rest of the way.

Still full of excitement, but somewhat scared, I took off my snowshoes and entered the small forest. Complete silence surrounded me. Not even the occasional falling oak leaves made a sound when landing on the snow. I only heard the slight crunch of the snow beneath my feet. The songbirds hadn't returned yet, but I didn't see or hear the squirrels. I knew they over wintered here, but I didn't know if they stayed active, or hibernated.

Complete silence reigned when I arrived at the tallest oak tree where I had let my friend free. I feared that she and all the pretty squirrels had died in the bitter cold winter. Scared, I climbed up the tall oak tree to look inside the deep nest in the hole of the big, dead limb.

What a happy surprise greeted me. There, inside the deep nest, in complete harmony and all cuddled together, lay three sleeping squirrels. When I said hello, they woke up and looked at me startled. The silver grey male, my friend Marla (still without a new eye) and one other fine looking grey squirrel stretched and yawned,

How wonderful it felt to see my friend alive and safe in the company of others of her kind. Marla recognized me and came over to me, still trying to wake up. She greeted me gently, while sniffing the air. When I took the bread from my pocket, she grew very alert.

Proudly, I handed her the two slices of dark bread. She took them to her nest, and all three of them nibbled until they finished it. Then they cuddled up together again and went back to sleep. Ever so happy, I climbed down the tall, snow-covered oak and hurried home on that bitter cold afternoon.

I thanked God that I had found Marla still alive and safe, but told Him that I was very disappointed because He had not sent a new eye for her yet! All the power He had to create this world, so our preacher said, and He wouldn't even send a small new eye to my grey squirrel.

Before long, many pretty flowers covered our island. The birds returned and sang their hearts out. The squirrels busily repaired and built nests, except for the silver grey, who mostly slept in the sun in the soft, green grass.

On my next visit, Marla was glad to see me, but she spent her time gathering small sticks, dried grasses and feathers the seabirds had lost. She worked to repair her nest in the dead limb of the tall oak tree. As I looked closer at her, I thought her belly had grown quite a bit. At the thought that she might be pregnant, I got very excited. With the spring, fieldwork began again and I could only see Marla on Sundays. The first Sunday it rained hard all day long and Mom forbade me to go outside in the bad weather. The next Sunday, I had to stay home for my sister's birthday. I thought Mom might bake a sweet, round bread, slice it and spread honey on it. Or, she might bake a sheet cake with apples and beet sugar on top. Both tasted delicious and were rare feasts at our house, but I just had to see my friend Marla. I snuck out of our house, hoping my mom would save some of the special baked birthday goody for me.

All excited, I mostly ran to the small oak forest to see my friend. I had a piece of black bread, saved from the two pieces from my breakfast that morning, tucked away in my pocket. Completely out of breath, I reached the fresh smelling forest. Slowly, so as not to disturb the busy inhabitants of the forest, I walked over to the tallest oak tree that held Marla's nest.

I called her by her name. She stuck her head out and excitedly chattered away while looking down at me, but she didn't come down to greet me. Carefully, I climbed up the old oak. She stuck her head out of her nest now and then to watch me get closer to her. She chattered up a storm and got more excited the closer I came to her nest.

When I almost reached the dead branch, Marla came out of her nest. Slim again, she jumped back and forth from her nest to me. I never saw her so excited. One more step toward the dead branch and I sat next to Marla's nest. Now she came to me and sat in my lap. I gently stroked her soft fur and handed her a small piece of the black bread. She eagerly took the bread, but couldn't sit still in my lap to eat it, as she usually did. She kept on jumping back to look into her nest. I wondered if she had given birth.

When she jumped back into my lap and stood on her hind leg, I could see her enlarged nipples on her belly. What a great surprise! Marla had given birth! I wanted to look inside her nest but wondered if she'd feel comfortable enough with me to let me take a close look at her brood.

I broke off another piece of the bread and handed it to her. She took it and jumped over to her nest. She looked inside and then at me, chattering away, as though inviting me to have a look inside her home. Holding onto an upper limb of the oak tree to support myself, I bent over enough to look inside her home. Marla didn't seem to mind. She sat at the edge and ate her bread while still excitedly chattering away. One small step forward onto the dead limb and I could see inside Marla's home.

A most beautiful surprise lay inside her nest. I saw four tiny, naked baby squirrels moving their little feet. So surprised and amazed, I let loose of the branch above me and almost fell off the tall old oak tree. Barely holding onto the dead limb of Marla's nest with my hands, I looked down to the ground and got awfully scared. I had climbed too high up to jump and expect to live. By swinging my legs back and forth, I somehow managed to get back onto the limb and held on for dear life.

After a short rest, calming down from the scary ordeal of nearly falling to my death, I took another look inside Marla's nest. She had built the nest out of sticks, kind of woven together. Then she had lined it with leaves, dried grasses and feathers. On top of that, she had placed a layer of her own fur.

I was very impressed with the construction of the nest and its location. The bitter cold, northern winds couldn't reach it inside the hollow part of this old oak tree's dead limb. Marla finished her last morsel of the black bread and went inside to nurse her babies. They each found a nipple and suckled away, while Marla looked at me. I think she smiled. I know I did.

I could have watched her forever, but it grew colder by the minute. The wind had come to life, and hunger plagued me.

Slowly, I climbed down from the slightly shaking tree while the promise of an evening storm filled the air. Reaching the floor of the small forest safely, I looked up to Marla's nest to bid her farewell. She didn't come outside to see me leave. She stayed inside her well built nest to feed and keep her little ones warm.

Even though the icy wind of the oncoming storm bit clear through my clothes, I walked home in the darkening evening with a warm feeling. I knew Marla fared well, even though God never sent her the small eye I had asked Him for so many times!

When I got home, I found no birthday goody saved for me. As punishment for not attending my sister's birthday celebration, I had to go to bed without an evening meal. My stomach growled a lot, but that didn't bother me too much. I drifted away in a glow, proud of myself for rescuing Marla. Soon I drifted into dreamland, where loaded tables with plenty of food, chocolate bars, and sweet eggs invited me. A month or so later, while visiting Marla, I realized that three of her young ones looked exactly like her. One big, bushy-tailed, dominating young male looked just like the silver gray male that slept in a sunny spot on a limb of the old, tall oak tree.

Marla did fine without one of her hind legs and only one eye for many years. One early spring day, I no longer found her in the small oak forest. I believed that she went to squirrel heaven and there God finally gave her a new eye and even a new leg.

No sunglasses, bacon, or chili.

Chapter 61

Swimming to Russia.

On Saturdays, our school ended at noon. Without fieldwork available on this particular day, my three best friends and I walked home together. We excitedly debated what we could do after we finished our chores at home.

Two big boys, the Norsen brothers, stepped in front of us and said, "Hey girls, we're going to swim over to Russia. If you're not too chicken you could come along."

I looked them straight into their grinning faces and told them, "No one can swim all the way to the land of Russia and back."

The bigger boy said, "Well, just into their territory in the ocean, where the buoys mark the border."

I looked at the bigger boy, Robert, who had beautiful baby blue eyes and a handsome smile, and agreed to swim to Russia with him. I liked him a lot, but this was the first time he had paid any attention to me, and I felt quiet smitten at the age of twelve.

My three close friends agreed quickly to go along too.

Since the closest buoy floated a few miles out to sea, I told the boys, "We better start out swimming at the forbidden place, where the strong current can help us out to sea. Since the current will be too strong to swim back the same way, we can turn to our left at the nearest border buoy and swim back to our island that way, just like I see the very small fishing boats do."

We all agreed to meet in two hours at the south side, near the smallest opening of the ocean between the mainland and our island.

Actually, it wasn't Russia we could faintly see on very clear days and were about to swim toward, but rather East Germany, ruled by the Russians. I'm not sure why we called it Russia, perhaps because their border patrol ships had the Russian flag flying on all their warships and the ships had Russian soldiers on board. They patrolled the border heavily, especially at night. Since there was almost no way to escape by land, people tried to flee from East Germany to our part of the world on boats or anything that floated. Some said that many had drowned trying to escape. Many dead bodies or parts of bodies wound up in our fishermen's nets, or drifted onto shore.

When those desperate people made it over the sea border marked by big buoys, they reached freedom. Our island people took them in, cared for them and helped them to reach family members in our country. We heard from those who had crossed over the border how cruelly they punished people who got caught trying to escape. Often, the authorities executed those people in public, or sent them to Siberia to live their lives out in the hard labor camps in the frozen wilderness.

If the people in East Germany managed to flee in a boat, the Russians came into our harbor to retrieve their property because everything in their country belonged to the country, not to individuals. Those young Russian men weren't mean people. They just followed orders. Many times our village people hosted fine parties for those Russian soldiers.

The time drew near for me to leave to go to our meeting point, but my mom still had many chores for me to do. When she stepped into our outhouse, I quickly sneaked away and hurried to our meeting point by the beach, a point sternly forbidden by parents to enter the ocean.

The two brothers and my three close girlfriends waited for me.

Quickly, I stripped to my underwear. Since I turned ten my mom often told me, "Girl, you have to leave your undershirt on now, so the boys won't see you're soon to develop breasts."

I put a stone on top of my clothing I had just taken off, so it wouldn't blow away while I was gone, and excitedly followed my friends and that handsome baby blue-eyed-boy, Robert, to the edge of the ocean.

We clearly saw the nearest border buoy, pointed in that direction and in utmost excitement entered the ocean. So much for all the warnings from our parents. I found the water shockingly cold and the current much stronger than I had imagined. We moved along quickly, without having to use much of our strength. We actually lay on our backs often and just let the current take us out to sea. What fun we had. We laughed ourselves silly and waved at the happy, little white clouds above us.

All of a sudden, in great dismay, I saw the closest border buoy way to the left of us. We had drifted into Russian territory. Anxiously, I pointed this out to our group and we quickly turned left to swim back, past the border buoy and on to our island. Robert, probably our strongest swimmer and for sure the best looking boy on our island, took our lead now to get us back.

Very soon, we found out that swimming against this strong current was sheer hard labor. All the fun had evaporated. When we realized that we had not moved forward at all, but just held our place, we got very scared. We saw no boat or ship to help us, and we had come too far from our island for anyone to hear us, even if we all screamed together as loud as we could. The ocean would just swallow our screams and properly laugh at us fools. Though very good swimmers, the strong current took all our strength. We had no more energy left to swim against her. Scared to death by now, we floated and paddled in the great ocean's cold water to stay alive

As we drifted out farther into the Russian territory, the ocean grew rougher. I felt death creeping closer. I found it hard to keep above the pounding waves. I wanted to end the fight and slip down into my sea grave to follow the bright, warm golden light upward, as I had experienced before. Somehow, though, I didn't want to leave my friends alone out here. On top of a big wave now, I looked around for help and happily discovered another huge border buoy. I pointed and screamed to my friends to head for that buoy. At that precise moment, I noticed someone missing from our group, but with a tall wave quickly crashing over me, I couldn't see who.

All of a sudden, the strong current ceased, and without much strength left but with a strong will to survive, we reached the big border buoy. Defeated and in dread we hung onto the iron ladder on one side of the buoy. Bewildered, shaking in the cold sea and breathing hard, we looked at each other. Though not dead yet, I'm sure that thought went through everyone's mind.

At that moment, I realized we missed Robert, the strongest swimmer in our group. I hoped he'd join us soon, or make it back to our island safely. The big buoy swayed hard in the rough sea.

I pointed to the top part of the buoy with a rail-enclosed walkway. "We need to climb up there," I said.

The iron ladder, overgrown on the first few steps with sea algae, made climbing slippery. Holding onto each other and the ladder, we finally made it up to the enclosed walkway. There we sat, holding onto the railing of the heavily swaying buoy for dear life. I looked out over the ocean for Robert. I called his name loudly each time I had a little strength to do so, but heard no answer.

The golden sun painted a beautiful picture of many colors on the sky before she sank into her watery bed. Soon the red light of the big buoys began to blink. The ocean calmed a bit, and it grew very cold. We hovered together in our wet underclothes on the side of the swaying buoy where the wind could not reach us.

I stood watch first, while some of my friends shivered and cried. Others clung to each other and let sleep overcome them.

Exhausted, I stood on the walkway holding onto the railing. I saw neither Robert nor a boat. I could barely see our island from here. The strong current had taken us far out to sea. I begged God to help us, but He didn't answer.

Soon the stars and the bright moon shone in all their glory. The deep ocean transformed into a silvery, shimmering field through my tears. Dizziness overcame me. I needed to sit down. Someone stood up to take over my watch. My stomach ached and my dry, cracked lips started to bleed; all this water around us, but nothing to drink. Carefully, I sat. Holding my head on my knees, I fell asleep and slipped off the big buoy.

Hitting the cold ocean water didn't wake me immediately. For just a moment, I thought I still dreamed. I heard my friends above me, screaming for me to come back up. Then reality set in. While swimming around the buoy to the ladder, I realized that all of us had better stay awake, so we wouldn't slide off the buoy and kill ourselves.

On my way up the slippery ladder, I wondered what had happened to Robert. I hoped that he had made it safely back to our island. Maybe he had the strength to tell someone what we had done and that we were in trouble, since we hadn't returned. I really didn't think he'd tell on us though.

First, he didn't really know if we had run into trouble; and second, children at that time didn't tell grownups the forbidden things they did out of fear of punishment. Parents often allowed children to stay away from home for a night, or perhaps a few days, but we had to be in school and on time. Therefore, no one would miss us until Monday morning, two days from now. Add to that that they wouldn't know where to look for us, and we had real trouble. No one would think to look for us here. Oh, Robert, please tell someone.

To keep awake and look out for help, I suggested we walk around and around the walkway and sing, or tell stories. We lifted our arms up high and pretended to be seagulls on a faraway warm island with chocolate trees and a pond filled with hot soup. When we ran out of ideas for our imaginary island, we changed into angels on a rescue mission.

We walked and walked around the buoy until all of a sudden I spotted a faint light in the distance. It moved slowly across the water from one buoy to the next and way out into the ocean. A Russian border patrol ship!

We stood still in awe, silently staring intensely out to sea at the faraway ship. The waves, rolling toward shore, made hurried, rushing sounds. The soft wind whispering by me hurt my cracked skin, but I quietly stared out to sea at the faraway ship.

When we saw that the Russian ship cruised toward us, we went wild. I believe we screamed louder than we ever had in our young lives. We jumped up and down and waved our hands, even though most likely they neither could hear nor see us. After what seemed a long time, the welcome stream of light from the searchlight shone on us. It didn't just swing by, but held steady on us. They saw us! Yes, they would rescue us! Crying out of happiness and still screaming like crazy, we danced around the buoy, waving our hands in the air.

Soon we heard the motor of the big warship close by and they turned the huge searchlight down. We could clearly see the ship now, and its big guns on deck, as men dropped anchors into the sea. Then they heaved a small powerboat with an outboard motor attached to it down into the water. Two men on board started the motor and with big guns over their shoulders, guided the small boat our way.

On the deck of the big warship, men removed canvasses from the big guns. I hoped they wouldn't shoot us. We all got very scared again. We wondered if they didn't kill us, where they would take us and what would happen to us? I had heard so many gruesome stories from refugees that made it to our island.

I whispered to my friends, "If the Russian ship takes us on board and sails away from the border buoys toward Russia, we jump overboard and swim home."

All of my friends agreed.

The little boat arrived at the buoy when the early morning wind announced its arrival with a harsh blow. I shivered so hard that my teeth bit into my tongue and warm blood ran down my chin. But in the excitement of the rescue, I barely felt the pain.

With fear and gratitude, I watched one soldier climbing up the ladder while the other tied the little boat to the buoy. Quickly I looked around the ocean for other help, but found none. We had no choice but to submit to these Russian soldiers. Automatically we raised our arms high up into the air to make sure the soldiers knew we surrendered.

There we stood on the swaying buoy, in our wet underwear. When the waves hit the buoy, they sprayed bitter cold seawater all over us. Freezing and scared to death, we wondered what would happen to us. So tired, worn out and in pain, I looked down into the dark blue water and seriously considered jumping off the buoy into the deep; to never return; to let go and float upward to the soft, warm, yellow light I had experienced before; to grab the hand that reached out for me to see where it would take me.

The Russian soldier must have read my mind. He grabbed my arm and smiled at me. He looked around the side of the buoy, as if expecting someone else to hide there, and asked us in Russian to climb down and get inside the small boat.

When he realized that we didn't understand him, he started to laugh loudly and shouted something down to his comrade. His comrade, in return, started to laugh also. I pointed toward our island and told him that we lived there.

He asked me in his broken German dialect, "What the hell are you children doing out here in the middle of the wild ocean without a boat?"

With a very shaky voice and still scared to death, I told him how we had come here and why. He laughed again and pointed toward the little boat. I climbed down the slick iron ladder of the buoy and safely sat down in the little boat. All my friends followed unsure, but unhurt. On the ride to the big Russian warship, I told the soldier, who spoke some German, that we missed Robert, who had swum here with us.

With their guns beside them now, the soldier who spoke some German shouted something to his comrade, and the little boat started to roar and race across the sea toward the big Russian ship. When we reached the big ship, both soldiers yelled something up to their comrades on the mighty ship.

Instantly, they turned the big searchlight on again. The German-speaking soldier explained that they searched for Robert. That made me glad, but I wished with all my heart that Robert had long ago reached our island. The huge searchlight scanned the dark, restless ocean repeatedly.

Slowly, completely out of energy, and with lots of help from the Russian soldiers, we climbed up on a long rope ladder onto the large warship. The men on board had re-covered the big guns with canvases, which made me feel a little more at ease.

Some of the young soldiers handed us each a blanket and showed us where to sit on the mid-deck of the ship. I had never stepped onto such a huge ship. I had only seen them from a distance. The engine vibrated the whole ship and it almost felt like a fast heartbeat. Ever so gladly, I sat and huddled up in the thick blanket handed to me. One young soldier brought us hot tea in big metal mugs, which I really appreciated.

Soon they turned the huge searchlight off. The engines began to howl violently and now shook the mighty ship. They brought up the anchors and with a loud ringing of a bell, the Russian warship moved forward. I thought it amazing how fast that ship sliced through the seawater. It created many high, white-combed waves beside it. I felt excited about seeing this but still feared what might happen to us.

All the young Russian soldiers ran around except for one. He stood watching us with his gun over his shoulder. He smiled each time I looked at him. Finishing my hot drink, I leaned back and let my tired, aching body relax. Looking around at our group, I noticed that most of them had fallen asleep. I wondered how I could quietly awaken them so the soldier that was watching over us wouldn't notice me doing so, in case we needed to jump off this warship should it change course and go on to Russia. So far, we sailed along the border toward our island. I could clearly see the blinking red lights of the border buoys. I found it awfully hard to stay awake, especially since all of my friends lay around me asleep now. In the eastern horizon, the first faint line of grey appeared to announce the beginning of a brand new day. I wondered if we'd find it a day of turmoil, hurt and sorrows, or a day of homecoming. I wished for the thousandth time that I had never gone on this adventure.

Through very tired and blurry eyes, I saw the German-speaking soldier inside a hut, which had glass windows and a very tall antenna on top of it. He spoke with an officer who wore a fine looking uniform with many medals on his chest and to the radio operator. Our harbormaster had a radio like this inside his house, but a lot smaller. He had told me that the German army gave it to him during the Second World War so he could let them know if the Russians came onto our island. I grew dizzy, leaned back onto a big box and closed my eyes just for a moment. I must have slept for quite a while because when the German-speaking soldier shook me hard to wake me, the sun shone high in the sky. He happily said, "You girls are going home to Mama. Your harbormaster granted us entrance into your harbor."

Though still tired and exhausted, I jumped up, hugged the young soldier, thanked him, and left a few happy tears on his uniform. He said something in his mother language I did not understand, but what a great smile he had when he said it.

Hurriedly, I woke everyone and told them the wonderful news. We hugged each other, laughed and shed a few happy tears. Amid our welcome relief, the big engines of the mighty warship slowed down. I looked out toward the ocean and realized that we had just passed our island's blinking light tower and ever so slowly moved along the marked channel in the bay toward our harbor. I saw many people standing around and realized that my very angry mom most likely stood among them.

I didn't know what creative punishment she had in mind for me. I just knew it would be severe. As far as I could think back, this adventure, on a scale of one to ten, ranked well above a ten.

The big ship crawled closer to our harbor where nearly everyone on the island waited. All the small fishing boats had anchored in the bay to let this mighty Russian warship into the harbor.

Then I saw her. My mom stood close to the mooring, tall and somber, next to my sweet grandma, who seemed to enjoy the excitement. Next to them stood our only man of the law, with his two guns dangling beside him and his hands near them. I think that was the first and only time I saw him carrying two guns.

The ship's engines stopped racing. The crew threw lines down onto the dock and our village men tied the Russian ship to the big, wooden tree trunks, which had been tied together and anchored, deep into the harbor. In no time at all, the men of the island had secured the mighty Russian warship.

The ship's heartbeat slowed way down and then abruptly stopped. All the Russian soldiers came up on the deck of the big ship, waved and smiled at our village people. The island people in return waved back at them and invited them to come onto our island. The commander, in his fine looking uniform, saluted our people and gave some commands to his soldiers, which I didn't understand. Quickly, the crew let down a long, iron walk with rails to hold onto. While the commander walked down the walk, stretching out his chest with all his medals on it, I waved at my mom. She looked at me with a grim face and did not wave back. My sweet grandma smiled and waved back at me excitedly. At least I wasn't in trouble with her.

When the soldiers on board of the warship took off their guns and laid them down on the ship's deck, our only man of the law took both of his guns off his hips and laid them on the ground. The Russian commander waited at the end of the ship's gangway for our lawman to arrive. When the two of them stood together, the commander offered his hand to our only man of the law. They both shook a long, robust welcome with their hands and embraced each other like comrades. After that, the Russian commander stepped onto the earth of our island.

A hush fell over the mumbling crowd as the commander called the young translator off the ship. When he stood beside his commander he translated to the island people, "I come in peace. I brought your children home."

The commander waved at us and crewmen escorted us, still wrapped up in warm blankets, down the narrow gangway.

When I passed by the commander, I stopped and said, "Thank you so very much for rescuing us."

The smiling young Russian soldier translated it to his commander, who then picked me up and gave me a kiss on my cheek. He gently let me back down and I ran to my mom.

She picked me up and held me tight for a brief moment without saying a word. I did see a tear rolling down her face. Had I scared her so badly? Grandma almost smothered me. Ever so glad to see me, she asked me a hundred questions all at once. Looking back toward the mighty warship, I saw the commander and our only man of the law walking toward our small harbor restaurant and tavern which served my grandma's fine liquor and beer brewed across our island. Some Russian soldiers and island people followed them.

I looked around for Robert, but I couldn't see him. I spotted his parents with Robert's brother, Karl, who swam with us, but not Robert. Perhaps his parents had punished him and not allowed him to come to the harbor. With an awkward feeling, I walked home between my silent mom and my chattering grandma. I waited for my mom's announcement of my punishment, but my mom remained silent. Would I actually get away without at least a good whipping? At home, my family stayed busy, while I sat on the stairs, tired and hungry, awaiting my sentence. Grandma hurriedly walked down to her cellar. My mom put on her only fine dress, the one she wore at weddings, funerals and all other celebrations, brushed her hair and ran downstairs to help my grandma carry up a big, wooden box with many bottles.

Gently, they loaded it onto Uncle Fred's wagon. He took all the smoked fish out of the smoking ton and loaded them onto the wagon. His wife, Aunt Hilde, added her freshly baked bread to it. Grandma told my sister to fetch all the big onions from the garden and load them onto the wagon.

Before they all left together, my mom sternly told me, "You stay inside our house!"

There I sat, all alone, on the stairs of our house, so exhausted, hungry and worried about my punishment. Even my loyal dog went with my family to celebrate at the harbor with the Russian soldiers. Our clock showed noon and I crawled into bed.

Hunger woke me, and to my surprise, it had grown dark outside. Quietly, so as not to wake my sister, I climbed out of our bed and walked into our room to get something to eat and drink. The quarter moon's light, shining through our window, let me see enough so that I did not have to light a candle. I hoped my mom lay in a deep sleep.

Stepping over the creaking boards so as not to wake her, I reached our table where Mom kept the bread beneath a kitchen towel to keep the flies off it. What a surprise! I found a thick slice of bread spread with plenty of pig lard, and a mug full of water. A note said, "Enjoy your dinner, Edith. I will talk to you later. Mom."

I glanced over to the couch, but Mom wasn't there. I looked at our little wind-up alarm clock that stood on the windowsill next to the couch, and saw that it was ten o'clock. Most likely, she stayed at the harbor, working and celebrating.

When I opened the window in our room, I heard a lot of singing, laughing and harmonicas playing. I folded my sandwich over, ate it in a hurry and drank some water. Then I dressed warmly, and even though Mom told me to stay inside, I left. I wanted to see the celebration. I wanted to find Mom, to watch her and sit somewhere in hiding to enjoy the celebration. When she left for home, I planned to quickly run home and get into bed. What a great idea.

I ran through the fields to the harbor so no one noticed me. There I found a great hiding place among the stacks of empty wooden fish boxes. From here, I could see in all directions. What a celebration! The commander of the Russian warship lay in a wheelbarrow right next to the wooden stack of fish boxes, where I had chosen to hide. He grasped a nearly empty bottle of vodka in his hand and a half eaten smoked eel lay across his chest. I clearly saw the grease leaking out of the eel onto his fine uniform as he snored quite loudly.

Some of our island people played their harmonicas, makeshift drums, washboards and trumpet-like instruments, to which the Russian soldiers sang and danced in a strange, but neat way. They held onto each other and almost danced in a circle. Around and around, they went, dancing and singing very loudly.

Grandma played cards with a handful of older soldiers. The Russian soldiers shook their heads in disbelief while my grandma smiled. With all the different ways my grandma knew how to cheat, the Russian soldiers stood no chance of winning. My Uncle Fred sat next to his empty wagon, drinking beer and discussing some great, important matter with the Russian soldiers. He waved his arms to describe things and drew pictures in the dirt to communicate with them since he didn't speak their language. His wife, my Aunt Hilde, entertained some young soldiers with her wild, suggestive dancing.

My mom and some other women inside the small kitchen of

the tavern fried fish by the dozens while children of my age sold the fried fish to the people. They likely earned some change tonight. I could have been among them, having fun, if my mom had not told me to stay home. I envied those children and grew angry at my mom.

I didn't count the people, but surely just about every soul able to walk or get onto a wagon had gathered here tonight, celebrating and making a little money. Even the man from the far northeast side of our island who brewed beer had come with a few barrels of his labor.

The island dogs ate well tonight on all the discarded fish bones and the parts of the fish the people didn't eat, or a not carefully watched plate. Harras just stole a half-eaten, fried fish from a Russian soldier, who put his plate on the ground to go dancing. He came running with his catch toward me. Hurriedly, he squeezed between the empty fish boxes to eat his stolen fish in peace. He didn't notice me until I whispered his name. Then he turned, looked at me, wagged his tail and came to me, while licking the fish grease off his snout. He gave me one lick to greet me and ran right back to the celebration. At least he couldn't tell my mom about my being here.

The Russian soldiers' dances grew very wild after another bottle of my grandma's brew passed through the crowd. All of a sudden, one soldier danced too close to the water, slipped and fell into the harbor. The whole dancing line, still holding on to each other, followed him into the harbor. It looked so funny, I couldn't help from laughing out loud. That woke the Russian commander. He sat up, had a long drink from his vodka bottle, and with the help of two of his soldiers stood up. He said something in his language to his comrades, and all three laughed heartily. When the two soldiers left to play some cards with my grandma, the commander turned around, opened his pants and relieved himself on our fish boxes for a long time. When the puddle he made reached my feet, I decided to get out from between the fish boxes.

One look toward the small kitchen told me that the cooking had ended. My mom could come home any time now, or perhaps she'd stay and celebrate. I found it best to get myself home before I got in even deeper trouble.

As I started to walk home the same way, I heard some giggling behind a bush. Slowly, I lay on the ground and crawled closer to the bush where the giggling came from. To my surprise, I found the nice young soldier who spoke our language, kissing and talking to one of the older girls of our village. In a strange way, I wished I were the girl with him. Quietly, I left them and walked home. I reached home before any of my family did and crawled back into bed with my sister, thankful for not getting caught disobeying my mom's order.

Very early the next morning, the sun's first rays woke me. Figuring Mom's order for me to stay home had expired with the new day, I dressed and ran down to the harbor. The mighty Russian warship still sat secured to the dock. While its engine purred away, soldiers busily prepared to leave. Many people from our island either stayed to see the mighty warship leave, or had gotten up early for the occasion.

Our harbor was too small for the warship to turn around. Slowly, with the engine still just purring, the mighty vessel moved in reverse out of our harbor. Everyone on ship and on land waved goodbye. Watching the big ship back out in our channel move through the bay to the open ocean made me kind of sad, though I didn't know why. Perhaps I didn't want to see the young, German-speaking soldier leave. He had paid such attention to me.

Someone tapped me lightly on my shoulder. Looking back, I fearfully recognized my mom.

She said, "Didn't I tell you to stay home?"

I answered, "Yes, Mom, but that was for yesterday."

She didn't say a word, but her harsh look told me that I shouldn't have said what I did. Together, in silence, we walked home. At home, my mom told me to sit down and listen. I got very worried because I knew she'd dish out my punishment.

Sure enough, my mom said, "For the stupid thing you did, going swimming out that far into the Russian zone and for starting out in the strong, dangerous current, which I strongly forbade you to do, you shall empty the outhouse bucket for the whole next year. You'll do it each time it gets half full, so you can carry it. Grandma will tell you where to dig the hole to empty the can. Now go and get your clothes from the beach."

I couldn't believe what my mom had just said. Empty the outhouse bucket for a whole year and dig the hole to empty the bucket into also? My mom surely could dream up some awful punishments. Something seemed strange though because my mom didn't hit me. Angry over my punishment, I walked down the stairs and into my grandma's room.

After I told her how badly Mom punished me, my grandma said, "Well, child, you deserve it. This was the most dangerous thing I ever heard of you doing. By the way, Robert is still missing. Who came up with this idea?"

I told my grandma the truth. She stood up and embraced me. "I'm so glad that you're still alive. I'll help you with emptying the outhouse bucket."

I thanked my grandma and held on to her for a brief moment. Leaving her room, I quickly wiped the tears from my eyes. Outside, my dog greeted me happily and together we walked to the beach. My thoughts turned to Robert. I desperately hoped that he had come home alive.

Soon we reached the beach. For some reason though, with every step closer to the spot where we had jumped so happily into the ocean, I feared more that Robert had drowned. I walked and looked around the beach to see if his body had washed onto the shore, but the white, empty beach didn't cradle his body in her lap. His missing clothes gave me hope though. Perhaps my handsome, baby-blue-eyed boy had arrived home.

I sat in the sand and tried to remember the last moment I saw him. It was way out to sea, after we realized that the strong current dragged us far off course. I folded my hands, looked up to the heavens and said a long prayer to God to let Robert be alive and safe. Just in case God hadn't listened the first time, I said my prayer a second time a little louder. When I looked back down to earth, my dog sat in front of me with my clothes in his mouth. Together, in dread of what news awaited me, we walked home.

When I reached our village, I saw Robert's brother sitting on the dike all alone, looking out toward the ocean.

I stopped beside him and he said, "No, Robert hasn't come home yet." Then he asked, "Do you think he's dead?"

Shaking my head, I said, "I hope very much that your brother is alive." Then I walked away in a hurry to clear my throat and hide my tears.

Monday came, and Robert didn't come to school. His brother told me by silently shaking his head, that Robert hadn't returned yet. Somehow, at that moment, I believed Robert had died. Still though, I kept on praying to God to spare Robert's life. The day a fisherman caught a body in his net, I stopped praying. No one could identify the body any longer. Since we missed no one else on our island, the authorities declared it to be Robert's body.

My heart sank low. My world turned profoundly gloomy. Little silver stars danced in my eyes. The handsome baby-blue-eyed boy I had liked so much left this world. I wondered why the ocean didn't keep him so he could be born again. I guessed he was too old. My grandma had explained to me some years ago that only the young, innocent ones were born again when buried at sea.

Slowly, as in a dream, I walked to the ocean, stood on top of a big boulder and with tears streaming down my face, furiously screamed at God for not sparing Robert's life. I felt a little better afterward, but it didn't take away my guilt. That evening, I walked to the small chapel inside our cemetery, where after the initial day at home, people laid out the dead ones. They placed them on a stone table in the small, dark chamber until they dug their grave.

Since Robert's family sat inside the chapel and I really didn't want them to see me, I climbed up the tall weeping willow tree near the chapel and waited for them to leave. From up there, I could see two old men digging a grave, probably Robert's. Before long, his family left the chapel. With sad and eerie feelings, I climbed down the tall tree and walked through the doorless opening, into the dark chapel. People believed that a door on the chapel's entry interfered with the dead's soul helpers to come and go as they wished.

On the small altar burned a tall, white candle that gently flickered in the draft I caused when I slowly walked passed it. Four wooden benches stood before the altar. The chapel had no windows because people believed it dangerous to let light interfere with the traveling soul of the dead. To my right, stood a tiny stone chamber with a narrow opening. Inside there, on the stone table, lay Robert's remains. I felt an urgent need to go inside the dark, small chamber to say farewell to my once handsome, baby-blue-eyed boy.

In dismay, I stood at the opening of the chamber for the dead and saw a black cloth hanging over something on the stone table. I wanted to take the candle off the altar and go inside the dark chamber to tell Robert how sorry I felt for suggesting that we start our adventure at the forbidden, dangerous point of the ocean, but the rules forbade taking light into the death chamber. The leaving soul of the dead could get blinded and never find its way to where it needed to go. I debated about what to do. Without the candle, I was too scared to enter the dark chamber, but I didn't want to interfere with Robert's soul's traveling plans.

Daringly, I took the candle from the small altar, and sheltering it from the draft with my hand, I carried it to the entrance of the death chamber. There I sat on the cold cobblestone floor, holding the candle just a little inside the dark chamber. I figured since souls go up to heaven and the top part of the chamber remained dark, I couldn't blind his soul. With deep feelings, I whispered my apology and farewell to the handsome, baby-blue-eyed boy, whom

I would never see again. The black cloth over Robert's body moved slightly. The big candle flickered and died. Afraid of being in grave danger with the spirits of the dead world, I hurried out of the old stone chapel and ran all the way home.

The next day, around noon, our teacher told us to line up by pairs. After we followed his orders he said, "We're going to walk absolutely quietly to the cemetery and stay for Robert's funeral. There, each of you can walk by his open grave and bid him farewell. Whoever cannot keep completely quiet, will do the extra pages of math I wrote on the blackboard. After the funeral ends you may all leave."

Those extra pages of homework got our attention. Onward to the cemetery we marched, totally quiet and in a straight line.

In my heavy heart, I kept seeing Robert's face the way he stood in front of us girls with his big smile, asking us, "If you girls aren't too chicken, you can come with us to swim to Russia."

If only I just had said, "No way, Robert!"

The teasing from the other children and the fights to win my status back would have been less hurtful than Robert's death. I had a hard time holding my tears back while walking to our cemetery with a heavy heart and deep, guilty feelings. I didn't let myself cry and show my weakness in front of all my schoolmates.

Before long, we reached the rusty, squeaking gate of the cemetery. Now in a single file, we followed our teacher to Robert's gravesite. There we stood in a half circle around his grave, embracing his family and many other adults.

Our church choir director started to sing the usual song which started every funeral service. We all followed in singing the song we knew so well. I don't remember the title of it, but it had to do with forgiving our sins and letting this poor soul into heaven. At the same moment, four somber looking men carried Robert's body toward the gravesite in a shallow, wooden box. Most people at that time were still buried wrapped up inside a blanket or sheet.

My sad mind escaped and wandered off to the days I walked

through our cemetery and read all the headstones. I noticed that a lot more women than men were buried here. The great, wild ocean had swallowed many of the men of our island. I wondered if the ocean swallowed them because she was mad that they killed and took so much of her great wealth from her.

The singing ended abruptly and the men set the coffin on the ground. Our preacher said many nice words and then the men slowly lowered Robert, inside his shallow box, into his grave. At that moment, a lot of weeping started among the adult women, and I had a very hard time not to do the same in front of my peers.

Looking away from the cemetery up into the sunny sky, I wondered where I would go if I died right now. Too old and surely not innocent, I no longer qualified for a sea grave. With and without my mom, I stole many vegetables from the fields of the farmers when we had nothing else to eat, and I had done my share of lying by now.

Before I could figure out where I would go when I died, someone pushed me and said, "Go on!"

Our line of children slowly moved by Robert's open grave to bid him farewell. Every child picked up a handful of dirt and gently threw it into Robert's grave. Some said goodbye aloud, others just quietly looked down into his grave.

Soon, my turn came. I knelt, picked up the dirt, and let it slowly fall onto Robert's coffin. It made a soft, dull sound when it hit the wood of his coffin. With my tears falling down into his grave, I gently whispered goodbye and threw him a kiss. Then I quickly ran down the dirt walkway between the rows of graves and hid behind a tombstone so nobody would see my tears.

Next the adults came to say their farewells. One by one they walked by his open grave, spending time to say something, dropping flowers into his grave, praying, and crying. Robert's parents stayed to the last to bid their farewell. Holding hands, they stood there, staring into the open grave. His mom trembled and cried. She dropped a bunch of flowers into her son's grave, knelt, folded her hands, and angrily howled out to God. Her mother took her hand, lifted her up and took her out of the cemetery. Robert's father and a few other men took their shovels and closed Robert's grave.

In a strange daze, I walked home, called my dog, and the two of us ran to our favorite spot by the ocean. There we climbed on top of our big boulder and watched the stars light up the dark, cold night. I wished we could fly away with the wind to another place where death could not find us. I lay next to my dog and stared at the twinkling stars through my tear-filled eyes. Soon, sleep took my pain away and brought me to my wonderful dream place where I found refuge for so many times in my life.

And yes, I emptied that darn, stinking outhouse bucket for the next whole year.

No Cool Whip, microwave oven, or bicycle.

Chapter 62

A day of plenty.

My mom gave me twenty Pfennigs, worth about eight pennies today, handed me our bucket, and sent my sister and me to the harbor to buy some fish. Usually, the fishermen gave us half a bucket of assorted fish, which Mom used to make us some fine meals for the whole week. This time they filled our bucket all the way. My sister and I had a hard time carrying the full bucket back home.

When my mom saw all the fish we brought home, she smiled with surprise. The fisherman had filled our bucket all the way because many of the fish had broken apart. Mom didn't mind that. She still smiled while rinsing and sorting out the fish beneath our outside pump. She put all the pieces of flesh, heads, bones and fins inside the big soup pot. She gave some of the whole fish to my grandma to smoke and sell the next day. The big cod, about two feet long, went into another big pot to be boiled for heavenly meals. Mom boiled it in salt water together with a handful of potatoes. Then she made gravy out of that water, flour, and chopped greens from our garden.

When the fish and potatoes finished cooking, she placed our portions on our plates and poured the mustard tasting gravy all over our meal. On the next day, my mom took all the leftover meat from the big, boiled cod and tore it into small pieces. She added salt, flour and an egg. Then she took half of the mixture and formed three round, thick patties and fried them in hot pig grease. I could barely wait to sink my teeth into one of those thick patties. The next day she added vegetables and shredded potatoes to the mixture. Then she fried it in grease on her little iron stove. What a heavenly smell that created. What a wonderful cook my mom was, when she had food to cook for us.

Both my mom and grandma loved to eat the egg sacks of the female fish and the males' sacks. They carefully cut those parts out of the fish and put them in a special pan to smoke for a while with the rest of the fish inside my grandma's smoking tons. The next day, both of them savored their smoked dish with great excitement. They ate it ever so slowly and in small bites, with a nip now and then from a small glass of Grandma's best home brew. Soon both of them laughed and carried on about the old times. When I finally did get to taste a morsel of this special dish, which was seldom, I also liked it a lot.

Mom also pickled some pieces of the fish like she did with small parts of the pig meat on slaughter day, but I don't remember how she did it.

Flat fish, like flounders, didn't smoke or boil well. Mom fried them instead for a fine meal. Today though, Mom made fish soup for dinner. She carried the big soup pot to a stack of crudely arranged stones in our backyard and set it down. My grandma came with a bundle of wood, and soon the flames licked the big soup pot. We walked through our large garden to fetch an armful of vegetables to add to the fish soup.

When the big soup pot started to boil, our whole yard smelled great. Meanwhile, my grandma washed and cut the vegetables into small pieces and added them to the steaming pot. I grew hungrier by the minute, and so did a few other people in our house. My uncle and aunt, their children, my sister, my dog and our cat came to sit beside the boiling pot, waiting to eat some of the great smelling fish soup.

After a while of listening to Grandma's stories from a long time back, which were always very interesting, my mom took one more look inside the big pot and declared the soup ready. Carefully, she fished out all the bones, heads, fins and skin. Then she slit the fish heads open, cut out the fish's brain and eyes, and returned them to the steaming soup pot.

Mom divided the parts not good for human consumption between my dog and our cat, who hurriedly gorged them down. Meanwhile, my grandma handed me a bowl with ingredients inside of it for dumplings and told me to knead it well. My mom sent my sister upstairs to our room to fetch our bowls and spoons, while my aunt walked inside to her kitchen to gather her family's utensils.

Grandma told another story while keeping a watchful eye on me as I kneaded the dough for the dumplings. One more look at the dough and my grandma said, "Good job girl, the dough is ready."

Then she showed me how to rip just the right amount off the dough with my fingers and place it into the boiling soup pot without burning my fingers. I felt proud to contribute in making my grandma's dumplings, our family's favorite.

Soon, all the dumplings swam on top of the soup. Now came our time to enjoy this delicacy. On this special day, everyone would have plenty of food. I could clearly see the soup pot held enough for seconds. How well I remember those special days of plenty.

No hamburgers, tacos, or life insurance.

Chapter 63

Buried alive.

One fine, early Sunday summer day I decided to visit my friends, the grey foxes, again. They lived inside one of the mound graves on the edge of the grumpy old ghost's territory on the north side of our island. I stuffed a short candle, matches, and my noon meal, the usual pork grease sandwich, in one of my pants pockets. Ever so quietly, I walked down the stairs and into our backyard where my grandma's smoke tons busily smoked fish she'd sell in the late afternoon.

Carefully, so as not to alert anyone in our house, I opened the metal door of the ton that didn't squeak so much and stole a good-sized herring. Gently, so as not to tear it apart, I stuffed it into my other pocket.

I left our yard quickly before someone in our house saw me and had chores for me to do. Happily, I went on my way to see the foxes, without my dog. He had to stay home because the fox family didn't like him at all.

Before I left my village, my three close friends caught up with me and asked, "Where are you going?"

I answered, "I'm going to see my friends, the foxes."

Quickly they asked, "Can we come along?"

I said, "Sure, come on!"

Talking up a storm, most of the time all at once, we happily walked to the site of the mound graves.

All of us knew we had to stay absolutely quiet now so as not to wake the grumpy old ghost, or he'd batter us with a shower of stones. Completely silent, we crawled into his territory and reached the mound grave where the fox pair lived. Ever so careful not to awaken the old ghost, we gently rolled the boulder aside, which allowed us to enter the grave. One after the other, we crawled down deep into the dark, age old grave.

Safely inside, I lit my candle, told my friends to keep quiet and looked around the low chamber for the foxes. What a surprise. There in the farthest corner, lay the female grey fox, with her bushy tail up in the air. She alertly looked in our direction, while busily tending to four tiny, barely moving young ones. She greeted me with a whispered whine, but didn't come to me, as she usually did. Her nose sniffed at the aroma of my herring, but she wouldn't leave her litter. My friends watched in awe and stared at the fox and her tiny newborns.

My grandma told me that people had built these graves many centuries ago. Those island people somehow dug out deep holes in the ground and gathered many stones to make pillars which supported the boulders that formed the roofs of these chambers. Then they filled the small openings between the boulders with pebbles. After that, they shoveled dirt over the mound to protect the dead from grave robbers and evil spirits.

In this particular mound grave, eight small, dark brown human skeletons lay scattered about. They had adult-sized heads, but their bodies seemed a lot smaller than today's adults. Some animals had gnawed on some of those skeletons extensively. Colorful small stones lay near the skeleton's heads, and crudely made stone spears, without handles, stuck out of their eye sockets. In the middle of the low chamber we saw two skeletons lying atop each other, face to face. A tiny baby's skeleton that looked ready to fall apart, lay beside them.

A black substance, similar to ashes, lay all over the ground of the chamber, and the air smelled strangely sweet. I found it quite eerie here, but what a perfect, safe place for my friends, the grey foxes, to live.

While inside this grave, I remembered my grandma telling me a while back, that all together, this area had eighteen such graves which the grumpy, old, mean ghost guarded. Many of those aged graves had long ago caved in, and the ever restless and changing sea had swallowed them up.

Many years later after I left, our island grew into a famous summer vacation spot and someone opened a museum. Some of the dark brown bones, especially the intact skulls and other items found in the remaining graves, were displayed in that museum.

I wanted to give the new mama fox the partially smoked herring, but I didn't know if she felt comfortable enough for me to crawl real close to her. At that moment, the beautiful grey male, with his thick fur, crouched into their home. Immediately, he came over to me and greeted me with a warm, thorough licking over every inch of my face. Then he took a closer look and gave a slight snarl to my friends.

I told them, "Sit still and don't be afraid."

He walked toward them and sniffed them all over.

When he had finished investigating my friends, he came back to me. His nose told him that I brought a fine smelling gift. He lay in front of me and looked into my eyes. Slowly, I pulled the big, slightly smoked herring out of my pocket and handed it to the fox. I told him to share it with his mate. With a short, happy squeal, he accepted the gift and crouched over to his mate.

Inside that part of the old grave, where she decided to deliver her litter, the ceiling was high enough for the fox to stand up straight, but he crouched lowly toward her as if to beg for acceptance to come nearer. The female fox lifted her head and wagged her bushy tail in excitement to see her partner. He wagged his tail also, stood up and walked to her. With one short, high-pitched squeal, he placed the big herring in front of her and lay down. She gave him a lick on his snout, looked at her young litter nestled onto her teats, and in leisure, ate the big herring while her mate proudly looked on.

How happy and exciting it was to witness this. I quietly mentioned to my friends that we should leave since my candle had almost burned out. As we turned to leave the very old grave, a loud, cruel laugh came from above, and the big entrance stone slammed into place. My small candle flickered once, burned down, and darkness surrounded us, except for the faint sliver of light which came into the very small opening of the foxes' entryway.

I recognized the deep, dark laugh as belonging to the grumpy old ghost. Even though we had taken such care to enter his territory and crawled into this grave, he had either heard or seen us. We all got scared to death. We were buried alive!

I heard sniffles, but couldn't see in the dark who cried. How could we move the big stone, which kept us inside this grave, from the inside? We couldn't even see it. I knew of no other way out except through the foxes' exit, just a small hole between two huge boulders, barely big enough for the foxes to squeeze through.

Then I remembered the entrance that I had always used just right of the foxes' entrance. I crawled in that direction with my friends following me. Two of them cried now, scared to death down here in this old, musty grave. The male fox watched us in our dismay.

When we reached the outside wall, I explained to my friends, "We have to be careful not to push hard on any boulders until we find the one that's our exit, or the whole grave could possibly cave in on top of us."

Gently, we pushed on the boulders along the wall near the entrance, in hopes of finding our exit. I looked for just the tiniest sliver of light shining through anywhere, to find the boulder we needed to push to get out of here, but no light shone through at all.

I had run out of ideas of how to get out of this grave alive. Shivering in fear, I wondered how long it would take to die in here, and I too started to cry, but silently. The beautiful, grey male fox came over to me. He gently licked my face, whined shortly and crouched toward his exit.

He looked at me, as if to say, "Follow me."

I guessed he didn't know that we couldn't squeeze through his small exit. When the male fox reached the outside, he stuck his head back inside, looked at us and howled shortly. Then he disappeared.

Our situation looked very gloomy. Since we dare not tell anyone that we came to this forbidden place, no one would look for us here. With a slight glimmer, I hoped the old ghost would show mercy and let us out after a while.

After we lay in the dark grave for what seemed forever, afraid we'd die here, I silently, but with all my strength and in desperation, told our island witch in our private number language what had happened and begged for her help. We talked to each other in our language when apart, but so far, I hadn't yet mastered that skill. I hoped she could sense me in this dreadful time. I lay down and let my silent tears roll onto the cold dirt.

Suddenly in the darkness, numbers entered my eyes, saying, "Help is on its way."

My completely burnt down candle lit itself again. As I stared at it in awe, the female fox left her young litter, came over to me and looked strangely long into my eyes as though she read something in them. Suddenly, her partner called for her from the outside. One look at her tiny offspring and she left through the small opening to meet him.

I thought it awfully strange to see her leave the young ones unprotected. Astounded, I wondered what was happening. At that almost quiet moment, among just an occasional sniffle, I heard a strange sound. The others heard it also and their sniffles stopped. There, it came again, that scratching sound from outside on the wall of this age-old grave. Then I heard a loud howl from the male fox.

I crawled toward his howl, and the scratching noise grew louder. I held my ear against the stones I passed to hear the scratching more clearly. Then I heard it loud and clear.

"Yes!" I screamed.

The grey foxes answered me with loud howls. Was this just wishful thinking, or had the grey foxes been wise enough to notice our terrible situation and knew exactly how to rescue us? Or had our island witch heard or felt my silent begging to rescue us? Had she whispered inside the beautiful grey foxes' minds and told them what to do?

We lay almost on top of each other when we started to push on the boulder. Sure enough, the boulder moved! Light and fresh air flooded the grave and blew out our ghostly candle, which seemed to burn on air. A few more pushes and all of us, so happy and relieved, exited the old grave. The beautiful grey foxes sat with proud smiles and watched us crawl out of the grave.

We all walked over to them, thanked them, and gently stroked their heads. Every one of us promised to bring them a good-sized fish soon. The proud grey foxes whined softly, licked my hand and crawled back into their home.

We hurriedly rolled the boulder back into its place and ran from the ghost's territory. He spotted us and hurled stones down on us. We all stumbled a lot, but kept on running, scared he'd kill us. Almost out of his territory, I looked around to get a glimpse of the grumpy old ghost, but only saw a dark, fast moving, shimmering, cloudy form of sort of a crude human figure drifting over the mound graves. Together, we ran home, so very happy to have escaped what could have been our own grave.

At home, I found Grandma sitting on the little bench in our front yard shelling dried beans. She waved at me to come to her, which I did.

She asked, "Child, were you in trouble?"

I hugged her.

She said, "I felt strange all afternoon, like you needed help."

I kissed my grandma on her cheek and smiled. Relieved at my safety, I sat down next to my grandma and helped her shell the beans for next week's soup without her asking me to do so.

She didn't ask where I had been, and I didn't tell her. I tried to hide my bruises from all the stones the old mean ghost threw at my body, but my mom noticed the ones on my head and arms the next morning. She gave me a stern look, shook her head and walked off.

When my grandma saw my bruises, she nodded her head and said, "Yes, my child, for some reason I felt that you visited the old mound graves."

I stood amazed at getting away without any punishment.

Early the next morning, I took the thank you note I had written, gathered a big bunch of blooming dandelions, and tied them together with a long grass leaf. Ever so happy to still walk among the living, I ran up the road to our island witch's small house. After my gentle knock, she opened the door. A little afraid, I looked into her old face and handed her the yellow flowers and my thank you note.

Then I asked Ola , "Is there anything I can do for you?"

She looked long and deep into my soul, touched my chin, smiled and said, "Child, you are a different child!" Slowly, she walked back into her small house and closed the squeaking, old, woodworm infested door.

On my way home, I wondered what our island witch meant, by saying, "You are a different child."

No animal shelter, grapes or electric mixer.

Chapter 64

When it rained fish.

When the deep, harsh winters had a hold of our part of the country, we had something special to watch.

In our part of the Baltic Sea, the tides of the ocean come and go with little notice. The sea level rises and falls at a rate of a few inches and not at a regular schedule. At strange intervals, though, the tides may rise or fall anywhere between two or three feet, very noticeable in our harbor. The decks of the fishing boats rose way above the edge of the dock with the high tide, or fell way below it at the low tide. Both made unloading fish more complicated.

Way into our harsh winters, the huge part of the ocean where I lived froze over completely with a tremendously thick ice shell. At those times, when a high tide came and had nowhere to go, the rising sea level, with its great power, searched for a way to release all its salty water. Tremendous pressure built up beneath the ice shell and eventually, with a very loud explosion, the thick ice shell gave away under the forceful pressure of the seawater.

After the first loud cracks in the frozen sea, we bundled up in all the clothes we owned, took a blanket with us, put on our snowshoes, and walked over the frozen bay to the open ocean. Mom always carried a bucket with her.

By now, all the seagulls that had not yet starved to death, had gathered by the beach, screaming excitedly and looking hopefully out to sea. Our village dogs and a handful of hungry people also joined us. My mom stood on the frozen ocean with my dog next to her. My sister and I huddled down in the snow-covered dunes, beneath our blanket, so we could watch the excitement.

Before long, the ice shell began to moan and groan loudly as though giving birth to a huge child. The seagulls instantly took flight, and the hungry people and village dogs moved toward the moaning ice shell. Next, I heard a loud cracking sound.

Then, with a release of extreme pressure, the ocean water broke through the thick ice shell with a loud explosion. Saltwater spouted way into the sky, perhaps two or three stories high. What a sight! And with the water, all sorts of fish flew into the air. The seagulls arrived first at the table of plenty. They caught the smaller fish and the small pieces of the ripped apart fish in midair and hastily swallowed them. The bigger fish fell down and slid on the ice in the cascading seawater.

The strong pressure of the explosion ripped most of them apart. The hungry people and village dogs didn't mind though, and hurriedly harvested whatever they could reach before the fish froze to the ice shell. People took great care not to go too close to the still high spouting eruption. If caught in the cascading seawater, or perhaps in the next explosion on their way back to the shore, death would come instantly.

When the people of our island had their buckets full of fish, and the village dogs had filled their hungry bellies, they all quickly returned to shore. The icy seawater coming down from such explosions, froze almost instantly when it hit the thick ice shell.

Over the next months, those violent outbursts created an awesomely, beautiful mountain landscape on the frozen ocean. I can still see those amazing scenes in my memory.

No calculators, zippers or raisins.

Chapter 65

The other side of the world.

During one early summer, my mom didn't work in the fields. She often lay on her couch, held her belly with both hands and cried a lot. I wondered if she had a baby inside her, but at that time and place, children didn't ask such rude questions. I'm sure she would have responded with a harsh hit across my face.

The food portions Mom handed out to us got awfully small and hunger constantly nagged at us. Lately, we had soup every day, with very little swimming in it.

One late morning, when my mom came back from our small, clapboard hospital, she announced with a bittersweet face, "Both of you will go to live in a children's home for some months to come."

While she turned her face away from us she said, "You will go to different homes."

Right away, I thought of all the food they had in the beautiful children's home in Bavaria where I had spent a wonderful time.

Excited, I asked my mom, "Am I going back to the home in Bavaria?"

Then, with a shaking voice, my mom said, "No, you're going to a home on a very small island in the North Sea, which is called Amrum." She told my sister, "You're going to a home in the Black Forest.

After a brief moment of silence, my mom blew her nose hard into her handkerchief. When she turned around to face us, her eyes, the color of the sea, looked red and swollen, and pain filled her face.

First thing the next morning, my mom packed our bundles. After saying farewell to all our family members and my sweet dog, Mom walked us to the ferryboat. She held my hand tightly, as if something terrible was wrong.

I looked up to my mom and into her reddened eyes and asked, "Why do we need to leave? And do you really want us back?"

My mom bent down, hugged me, and with a shaking voice said, "Yes, I want you back."

Though the rough sea tossed us about a bit, I found the ferry ride fun. My sister and I held on tight with one hand to the metal railing on the ferry. With our other hands, we waved goodbye to our mom until she disappeared on the horizon. I didn't feel afraid to leave our island again, but I felt strangely sad and worried about my mom.

A smiling old woman met us on the mainland by the waiting train. She asked us our names and pinned tags on us, which told of our destination.

I politely asked her if I could go with my sister to the Black Forest, but she said, "No girl, that's not possible!"

Disappointed, I took my sister's hand, walked inside the train and found us a seat by the window.

Two small towns later, we arrived in Heiligenhafen, located on the East Sea. Someone escorted my little sister off the train and handed her over to a tall man. He took her onto the waiting train, which stood on the track next to our train. She turned toward me and waved.

I waved back at her and yelled out of the open window, "I'll see you again after a while!"

My sister didn't answer me. Perhaps she didn't hear me.

About a dozen children of all ages walked into our

compartment. Soon, the big, black locomotive rumbled, and with a loud roar from the engine, we moved forward.

The slow train took me from our island in the East Sea across the northern part of Germany to the North Sea. The exciting train ride took almost all day. The landscape stayed pretty much the same, lush green with tall trees swaying in the by now gently blowing wind. Healthy looking vegetables grew in so many fields. The cows, horses and sheep stood still and looked at us in bewilderment as we moved past them.

I found the villages and towns we stopped at so exciting. I marveled at the differently dressed people, cars, motorcycles and fancy buggies at the train stations waiting to greet, or bring people to the train. Some of those people laughed happily, welcoming their visitors, others sniffled saying their farewells. I wondered where they all traveled to.

At noon, when the train stopped in a small village, a tall old man brought a big box into our passenger car. He handed each of us a fine sandwich, which consisted of two slices of grey bread with a thick piece of boiled kidney and cooked red, sweet cabbage in the middle of it. He also brought buttermilk for every one of us. Ever so awfully hungry, I surely welcomed this delicious sandwich.

Soon after, he passed a metal mug around the compartment and I enjoyed a long, cool drink of buttermilk. It felt so great to eat that entire sandwich by myself. This was the first time in many months that I actually had a filling meal.

To my surprise, our travel guide announced that we could step off the train and run around for a while.

She said, "At the first whistle of the locomotive all of you need to hurry back onto the train."

How exciting! Quickly, I jumped outside. I ran around the train, which had two passenger cars, one mail and baggage car and one huge, black, vibrating locomotive. Almost all of the other children followed me, happy to move around for a change. We shouted and laughed while running around the train, a bunch of children, forgetting for a moment that we had to leave home for most likely one sad reason or another.

By the fourth time around the train, I felt completely exhausted and wondered why I couldn't run as fast and as long as I used to. Breathing extremely fast, I lay down in the tall, green grass next to the train tracks to catch my breath. I noticed two girls lying down beside me. Everyone else had given up running around the train earlier. While catching my breath, I looked up into the slowly moving white clouds and wondered about my mom and my little sister. I hoped my sweet grandma took good care of my dog. I loved him so much.

A loud, but faraway blow of a train quickly pulled me out of my daydream. Hurriedly, I stood up to walk back to my assigned car, when I saw another train coming into the station. It looked just about like the one I came here with.

Huge towers of almost black smoke spouted out of its short, completely black chimney. The locomotive shook with great force when the engineer put the brakes on to stop this huge, dangerous looking machine. With violent squeals, the train slowly rolled into the station and came to a stop right next to the train I had arrived on.

The next loud blow came from my locomotive. In a great hurry, I ran back to my assigned passenger car. After I sat down in my window seat and looked around the car, I noticed that many new children had joined our group. Some happily chattered away, while others sat silently staring out the windows. One very young child cried for her mom. Soon, the train started to move.

Our chaperon stood up and explained, "We'll stop on the coast of the North Sea very soon. From there we'll ride in horse-drawn wagons over the North Sea to the island of Amrum."

I laughed out very loud and many children joined me. Coming from an island, I knew better than to ride a horse-drawn wagon through the sea.

When all the laughter stopped, I stood up and loudly told our chaperon that we needed a boat. She just smiled at me and sat down. I began to wonder if she wanted to kill all of us and the horses too. Was that possible? I quickly decided to jump off the train and run away, as soon as I saw the North Sea.

In just a short while, our train slowed. I frantically looked out the window to see if we had reached the North Sea, but I couldn't see any ocean at all around me. Abruptly the train stopped in a small village and our chaperone asked us to depart our passenger car. Stepping off the train, I saw eight wagons with two horses on each of them, standing on an endless field of wet sand. Far away in this field of sand, I could faintly see a sort of round mass of land. Where was the North Sea's water? A sea had to have water.

As most of us stood in bewilderment, our escort told us with a smile that all the water in this sea goes away twice a day for some hours and then comes back to stay for a while. I never heard of anything like that. I just couldn't believe that all the water left and wondered why. Our smiling escort asked us to walk down to the wagons and climb into them.

Hesitating to follow her request, I asked, "Do you know when the ocean's water comes back?"

She answered, "No, I don't know, but the men inside the wagons do."

Then I asked, "Are we going to be tied down inside the wagons?"

She looked at me and laughed. "No child, you won't get tied down in those wagons!"

At that moment, I decided to follow our group down to the wagons that stood in the field of sand. I figured that if the water of the North Sea came back while we rode in the wagons, I'd jump off the wagon and swim back to this village.

Still frightened of this idea of riding across the North Sea, I climbed into the first wagon I reached. Slowly the horses pulled us across the bottom of the sea where I saw small puddles and channels of seawater left behind, in which many sea creatures had gathered. I guessed they missed the departure of the seawater. I hoped to walk among these puddles and small channels some day and take a close look at all those different creatures. What fun that would be. Slowly, we neared the island of Amrum. The tall, almost round sand pile in the middle of the field of sand, called the North Sea, sure looked strange to me. I couldn't wait to tell my grandma and my mom about this. I wasn't sure if they'd believe such a strange thing.

When we arrived at the island, the horses pulled us all the way up onto it on sort of a dirt road where a bunch of friendly adults greeted us. While we walked to the children's home, I saw the drivers free the big, strong horses from the wagons and walk them into a big stall. I wondered if they would spend the night there. The sign on the children's home read Seagull. That name made me feel good because when my human life ended, I planned to ask God to let me come back to earth as a seagull. I wanted to fly and see the whole world. They had built the three-story children's home out of wood. How strange!

I saw no fences to keep us locked inside, which made me happy. Lots of children of all ages ran around and played while older children worked at chores around the house and garden.

An escort showed everyone in our group, according to age, to a large sleeping room. My room, where I would sleep and store my precious few belongings, had thirty single bunk beds. A woman led me to a bed on the bottom.

I put my few belongings, one other dress and underwear, socks and a sweet note from my mom and grandma in the box next to my bed. Then awfully hungry again, I wondered if they planned to feed us before bedtime.

Slowly, I walked over to the window to watch the sun leave this part of the earth. She didn't have a watery bed to slip into here. She just sank into the field of sand. Suddenly, lights blazed to light up the huge house, and a loud bell rang. Children in my sleeping

414

hall stormed out of the door, so I followed them.

We wound up in a very large room with long tables and many chairs beside them, and it smelled so great in here. There at the rear of this room sat a table with food and plates. My eyes widened in disbelief. I stared at all the food, wondering how they had so much here when we had barely enough to keep us alive.

Adults stood behind the tables, ready to fill our plates. Since I found myself toward the back of the line, I desperately hoped I'd find something left for me to eat.

Finally, the slow food line moved, and my turn came to grab a plate. The first woman asked me if I wanted fish stew. Politely I answered yes and smiled at her. The next woman handed me two big slices of dark bread. Then someone handed me a small bowl filled with steaming mashed potatoes and gravy. The next two bowls looked empty, but the woman smiled at me. At the end of the tables, a real old woman handed me a strange thing, a long and yellow thing she called a banana. I couldn't remember if I had ever seen such a strange thing, but took it and thanked her.

By the time I sat down to eat, most of the children had already finished eating and made their way outside. I ate all my great tasting food and drank the warm milk, which mom could no longer buy for us anymore on Sundays. What a heavenly feast. Oh, yes, I liked this place of plenty.

Then I looked up to see what the few other children, still remaining in the eating hall, did with the long, yellow strange thing the old woman gave me. Either they had eaten it already, or it still lay on the table next to them. I waited for a moment hoping to see someone doing something with this yellow thing called a banana.

Tired of waiting, and coming to the conclusion that since these people served it to us, we could eat it. I took a bite of it. My goodness, the outside of this banana thing was tough to chew and didn't taste good. Some of the remaining children looked at me and laughed. Then, one of the children stood up, took her banana, peeled the tough outside off it and ate the rest of it. I waved at her to thank her, peeled my banana and ate it. Delicious! I hoped to get one every day. Perhaps I could take one home for my mom and grandma to enjoy.

I slept well that night with a full stomach, wondering if everyone in our house at my island had enough food. Early the next morning, after a plentiful breakfast of hot cereal with sweet molasses, a woman called us newcomers into a room and assigned chores. Since I could identify all the young vegetable plants the woman held in her hand, she assigned me to the fieldwork group. I needed to report to the supervisor right after breakfast and work in the gardens, or fields, until noon. The rest of the day I could do as I pleased, since they considered me grown up at the age of over ten.

On the first free afternoon, I walked down to the beach to take a long swim. Well, I found no ocean, just the mighty sand field with its shallow puddles and narrow streams of seawater. Then I decided to walk out on this sand field to explore the creatures in the remaining seawater. Many small fish chose to stay behind, but I also saw large flounders burrowed in the sand. Dozens of strange small grey things, which had many long legs and no fins walked and swam around in the shallow ponds. Some creatures, also with many legs and as big as my foot, crawled around on the bottom of the puddles. I sat down on a rock, dangled my bare feet in the seawater and wondered where the entire ocean's water went and why.

Before long, I concluded that some faraway ocean must have lost all its water and borrowed this ocean's water for a while. The people there could catch the fish which the huge ocean took with her back and forth. That way they had something to eat. Who had such great power, though, to move a mighty ocean back and forth? I needed to watch very closely to see who actually moved the vast ocean! My, what I could tell my people at home.

After hours of exploring this strange sand field, I climbed up on top of the tallest sand dune, waiting to see who had the enormous strength to move the entire ocean's water. The endless seagulls screamed and gorged themselves on the poor, trapped fish in the small puddles and streams.

Suddenly, among the seagulls' shrill cries, I heard a strange sound, like the rushing of an oncoming, gentle wind. Sure enough, soon I felt a breeze. To my great surprise, I saw the ocean coming back, not with a huge, tall wave as I had imagined, but rather just running as if someone had opened a gate, slowly filling the complete sand field with water.

I desperately looked all around me to see who moved the ocean's water back, but saw no one, not even up in the heavens. Perhaps many invisible ghosts had this hard task. After a long time of watching and disappointed not to see who moved the vast ocean, I climbed down the tall sand dune to take a swim.

The refreshing water reached my knees now, but it looked muddy and not clear like our part of the ocean, and it tasted much saltier. I could feel the power of the returning ocean and found it hard to swim against the current. After a while, I gave up and walked back to the children's home.

I barely made it in time for dinner. I honestly didn't hear the dinner bell ringing. One of the women who worked in the home scolded me, but she didn't send me to bed hungry. I wound up with a big bowl of great tasting pea soup, some bread, and one of those strange looking, round balls, which smelled great. After I finished my soup and bread, I looked around to see what to do with this orange colored round thing. To my dismay, everyone had left the eating hall. I gently squeezed the orange ball, and my, it smelled wonderful. One of the old women, who so happily handed us generous amounts of food, came walking by and stopped.

"Do you know what this round fruit is?" she asked.

I shook my head.

She then sat down on the bench next to me. "We call this an orange, and it tastes very delicious." She reached for it, and I handed it to her. The old woman then slowly peeled the skin off the fruit, pulled it apart into small pieces, and handed it back to me.

One bite of the orange segment and I remembered that I had eaten this heavenly fruit in one of those children's homes before. I smiled, offered her a piece and thanked the nice old woman for her help. She just smiled and walked away without taking the piece of the orange I offered her. Right then, I made up my mind to save up some of these strange fruits and take them home for my family to enjoy.

Soon, by watching the vast ocean's rhythm, I figured out what time of day the ocean would come back to this strange field of sand and when it would leave again. I went for long, satisfying swims, but the longing inside of me to go and float out with this huge ocean, to see where it had the need to go to, grew stronger every day.

During one especially beautiful sunset, while sitting on top of a large sand dune, with the motionless sea reflecting the flaming red and orange colors of the setting sun, I decided to let the mighty ocean take me with her, out to wherever she had to go and bring me back to this place. At that evening's meal, I stuck a sandwich and an orange in my skirt pocket, walked upstairs to grab my towel and left the children's home. Surely, nobody would miss me with so many children there and only one old woman on night duty.

So excited by my soon to start adventure, I ran down to the small landing dock where someone had tied a big, inflated inner tube to a pole many days ago. I rationalized that it wasn't stealing if I only borrowed it for the night. At home, on my island, people borrowed all sorts of things from each other, but to my knowledge, they asked first. In this case, I figured that if I asked someone from the home to borrow this inner tube, the answer would most likely be no. To get back on God's good side to make up for what I figured at least partially wrong, I'd make sure to say an extra prayer at next Sunday's service.

Slowly, the billions upon billions of stars began to sparkle brightly in the clear sky. Before long, a slight restless rush came over the motionless ocean and the gentle moves of the waves washed away the reflecting sky with all its beautiful, brightly shining stars. This was my signal. The enormous ocean began leaving for a place I would soon discover. So very happy and filled with enthusiasm, I walked down to the small landing and untied the inner tube from the pier.

Then I took off my shoes and dress, hid them among the many boulders by the seashore, wrapped my food inside my towel and lay down on my back inside the middle of the inner tube on the attached sailcloth. Ever so slowly, using my hands as paddles at first, I floated out into the unknown. Soon, the now very restless, grey ocean hurried to leave this part of the world, taking me along with it. I looked up at the silvery sparkling stars and could barely wait to arrive at the other side of the world, or so I thought.

In a great hurry with tall, but gently rolling waves, the ocean rushed toward its destination with me in tow. I desperately clung onto my sandwich, so the seawater wouldn't drench it or take it from me. A big meteor shower put on an exciting show right above me. I tried to count the falling stars, but there were just too many.

I closed my eyes and made a wish. I wished very hard that I would see the other side of the world soon. After a while, I could no longer see the island of Amrum. Slowly the smiling, silvery stars blurred. I closed my eyes for just a moment to imagine what the other side of the world would look like.

From a faraway land the soft wind whispered a lullaby gently across my face. The tall, gentle waves, with their age-old urge to go onward, cradled me safely in their lap. From somewhere, my grandma smiled at me as I drifted away to where dreams rule.

With great pain in both of my hands and a loud scream, I awoke. Abruptly, I sat up and quickly jerked my hands out of the water. With another loud scream and in great panic, I realized I had two big crabs on each hand, nibbling away on my fingers. I tried to shake them off but they held on tight. I reached down to shake them into the seawater, but saw no water to speak of, just a very small puddle here and there. I hit my hands, with the crabs dangling from my fingers, hard against a boulder.

I heard a slight cracking sound, and two of the crabs fell onto the sand. Their cracked shells oozed a light green liquid. The other two let loose of my fingers quickly and fell onto the sand unhurt. The two broken crabs lay upside down in the wet sand with their legs desperately moving up into the air, as if to run away from their pain. Feeling guilty, I wanted to get out of the inner tube, take a stone, hit them hard and relieve them of their pain.

A quick, close look around me, in the still very faint, early morning light, told me in a hurry not to get out of the inner tube. Thousands of different size crabs scurried around in the shallow puddles and on the wet sand. They sure looked different from the small whitish ones we had on our island. These had a bluish grey color, and some of them grew quite big, much bigger than both of my hands held together. Those on the wet sand blew very small bubbles out of their mouths and fought to get into the shallow puddles of seawater.

Some of the crabs tried to climb into my inner tube, which scared me. In a hurry, I picked up a small stone from the puddle I sat in and hit the uninvited crabs gently on their shells. They waved their big, sharp fighting claws at me, as if to attack. A second, more intense hit on their shell made them understand that I did not welcome them in my inner tube. The crabs let go of the rope which hung overboard and fell back into the puddle.

Somehow, after a short while, the crabs suddenly stopped bothering me. They ran around in excitement and raised their two front claws. I thought that those crabs had decided to attack me. Shaking with fear and crying out for help, I waited for their painful attack with my eyes completely closed. When nothing happened, I opened my eyes and quit screaming.

The crabs stood still as though waiting for something.

At that peaceful moment, I realized that I had not come to the other side of the world. Instead, the mighty ocean had stranded me here among these huge boulders, inside the crab's territory, and it had gone on to the other side of the world without me. Sad, angry and scared of how I could get out of all these huge boulders, I looked up into the gloomy grey sky and folded my hands to ask for help.

Then I realized that the huge ocean had to come back this way and surely lift me out of these huge boulders. Now assured, I quit bothering God for help.

Eating the well-soaked, salty sandwich I had brought with me and watching the excited crabs running around in frenzy now, I heard a faint, familiar rushing noise. In no time at all, the water in the shallow ponds began to rise. The powerful ocean began to return. I don't know who got more excited, the thousands of anxious crabs or me.

Before I finished my wet sandwich, the returning ocean lifted me up far enough out of the huge boulders and I floated out of them. In a great hurry, the powerful current took me with her. It was fun to float on top of the water, watching the seagulls screaming and diving into the grey ocean to fetch their breakfast.

Low, heavy clouds hung in the sky. In the east, a small stripe of yellow on the horizon slowly crawled out of the ocean. The sun tried its best to light up the morning, but the heavy storm clouds wouldn't let her.

Soon, a heavy wind took hold of this part of the world. Small waves started to form on the ocean and gave me quite a scare. Before long, the small waves grew into very big ones, and the wind started to howl. Up high and way down, the tall white-capped waves took me. Scared to death and screaming, I held on tight to the inner tube so the angry sea wouldn't swallow me.

Way on top of the next tall wave I looked around in desperation, hoping to see the island I started this adventure out from, but the heavy, low clouds opened their gates and rain poured on me. I couldn't see anything but grey all around me. In total desperation, I cried out for help to my grandma, our island witch and God.

421

Suddenly, on a powerful wave, the strong ocean spit the inner tube with me inside of it onto the seashore. In a great hurry, I jumped up, grabbed the inner tube and ran up to the sand dunes for safety from the fury of the wild ocean.

Looking around the beach I landed on in the heavy rain, I checked for any familiar landmarks. I saw the small pier where I had found the inner tube. Happy and so thankful, I realized that I had come back to Amrum. I knew I'd see the children's home right behind me on top of the island.

Still shaking with fear, I sat down in the wet sand and let the cold rain pour over me. Slowly, I stopped crying. The severe fear of being swallowed by the rough ocean left me, and my body quit shaking. Silently and with great relief, I gave thanks to the three persons I begged to help me. I guessed that maybe God was still alive.

Quickly the storm moved on to another part of this world, and the sun shone her light down on this small island now. Standing on my wobbly legs, I walked toward the small pier from where I had borrowed the inner tube. Somewhere there, secured by a stone, I should find my dress and shoes. After tying the inner tube back up to the pier, I looked for my belongings but couldn't find them. The great storm must have taken them. My mom would be very mad at me for losing my shoes and my dress.

Completely soaked and cold, I walked and stumbled through the sand dunes in my wet underwear back to the children's home, absolutely too tired and exhausted to feel the sharp sand grasses cutting into my feet. When I reached the children's home and tried to wipe the sand from my feet on the doormat, I saw blood slowly dripping from my wounds, but I felt too exhausted to worry about it.

I found the children's home in its usual morning turmoil of who got to use the few toilets and sinks first. No one noticed me dragging my wet, bleeding body up to the room where I slept with many other children. There, I took off my wet underclothes and crawled into my bed. Slipping away quickly into the land of dreams, I promised the familiar, soothing, but faint faces of my faraway family, which floated into my dreams, to never go to see the other side of this world on an inner tube again.

C3C3C3

She never came back.

One morning, while still in the same children's home, one of the women told me to go with a group of children to the garden to harvest potatoes. We found a few men already at the field digging up the potato plants when our small group arrived. Someone handed us buckets and told us to gather all the potatoes from the ground into them, then empty the filled buckets into the big horse-drawn wagon, which stood on the end of the field. Having done this many times before at home, it sounded like an easy task on this beautiful, sunny day.

Immediately, we started to gather row after row of potatoes of all sizes while we sang and chattered away. Suddenly, as I grabbed for some potatoes without looking down at them, I felt something warm and wet in my hand. A quick look caused a jolt of fear to surged through me.

I held a full grown mouse in my hand, which had been stabbed through her belly with a pitchfork, which the men had used to get the potatoes out of the ground. Her still body lay in my hand, and her blood seeped slowly between my fingers. I touched her tiny heart with my finger to feel for a heartbeat, but felt nothing.

Overcome with sadness, I glanced at the ground. There on the sandy ground lay her litter, six small bloody bodies. Our entire little group had gathered around me by now to see the tragedy. Bewildered, we stared at the bloody bodies of the mice. Tears spilled from my eyes. I knelt and started to dig a grave for the mice in the soft, sandy earth. The kids in this little group knelt too, and soon, with our bare hands, we had dug a fine hole in the soft ground.

With tears running down my cheeks, I gently placed the small bodies close to their mother in their sandy grave. When I picked up the last bloody body to place it next to its dead mother, it moved and softly squeaked. Completely surprised at finding it alive among this pile of dead, bloody mice, I cradled the tiny mouse in both of my hands and looked it over closely.

Though it had blood all over its body, it had no holes on its body. It had lost one hind leg, but that injury didn't bleed at the moment. The little fellow shivered and ever so softly squeaked for help. Its tiny whiskers barely moved while it opened its mouth to squeak again. I know it must have been very scared and most likely in pain.

When one of the men came over to see why our group had stopped collecting potatoes, I quickly placed the tiny mouse in my skirt pocket. Hurriedly, so the man wouldn't discover the dead mice and perhaps do something cruel to them, we covered them with the soft earth and went on with our chores.

I told our small group, "I'll keep the little creature, raise it and set it free when it's grown up enough to care for its own self. Please don't tell anyone about this!"

Everyone promised not to tell. Most of them asked to help with caring for the tiny orphan creature, except for Rosa, who mostly had the job of cleaning the bathrooms. She had a disgusted look on her face and didn't even help to bury the poor, bloody, dead mice. Though she was somewhat bigger, I wasn't scared of her.

I looked her straight in the eye and said, "Rosa, if you squeal on me, I'll beat you up!"

She just smiled at me.

Finally, the noon hour arrived and our workday came to an end. In a great hurry, I ran back to the children's home, holding the small mouse gently in my hands. Upstairs, I took one of my socks off and let the little mouse crawl inside of it. Then I tied a loose knot in the end of the sock and placed it beneath my bed.

Downstairs, I met some of the children I worked with that morning in the potato field. I asked them to help me look through the big trash container for a tall metal can or a small wooden box, or anything we could use to house the small mouse. Eagerly they agreed to help, and together we walked over to the trash container and removed the heavy lid.

I quickly spotted the ideal home for the mouse, a tin can about a foot tall and wide, but I couldn't reach it. I needed to climb inside the stinking trash container. With the help of my friends lifting me up, I climbed in. It stank almost as bad as our outhouse at home. Wading through the stinking mess, I finally reached the tin can.

In a great hurry, I picked it up, and with more help from my friends, I got out of that container. After dumping the rotten, maggot infested waste out of the tin can, we closely inspected it and found it a perfect house for my mouse.

In our bathroom, I washed the tall tin can out and dried it completely with my towel. Then, I thoroughly cleaned the garbage off my legs while my friends shredded up toilet paper to place at the bottom of the can to make a soft nest for the little mouse.

We all felt good about saving this mouse's life. Other children who came to use the bathroom stared at us in strange ways, most likely wondering why we acted so happy. Next came an important part.

I needed to wash the dried blood off the little mouse in privacy, so I patiently waited for the bell to ring, which announced our mealtimes. When all the children had gone downstairs to the dining hall, I'd have the needed privacy. I couldn't let anyone else find out about the mouse.

On our first day here, the director of this place, also called Little God, had told us the rules of this, his home. He warned us with his loud, rough voice, among other things, to bring no animals inside his home. He never smiled at us and I heard whispers that he hit children.

Finally, the bell rang loud and clear. Everyone except my friends and I ran downstairs to the dining hall. Quickly, I ran to my bedroom and retrieved the little mouse from beneath my bed. In the bathroom, with my friends guarding the door from the outside so no one could enter, I gave my mouse a bath in the sink.

All the dried blood came off easily with a little soap. I rinsed her off well and dried her little, shaking body. I don't think she liked her bath because she squeaked bitterly all the way through it. Then, ever so gently, I put her into her new home, the tin can.

Receiving a clear signal from my friends, I left the bathroom to hide my Mousy beneath my bed. All of my helper friends took a good look at my clean, three-legged Mousy and smiled. For the first time in my young life, I felt like a mother protecting her child.

With my Mousy safe, my friends and I quickly ran downstairs to the dining hall. I saved part of my bread, cheese, and anything else I thought she might like to eat and put it inside my pockets. After a few days, I figured out what my Mousy liked to eat best and I brought her just that, but plenty of it.

She liked the grass seeds I gathered for her from the fields and ditches the best. Soon my Mousy grew a sleek, light gray coat and tried her best to get out of the tall tin can. At that time, I let her out of her can at night when everyone slept so she could run around underneath my bedcover for a while. She had no trouble getting around on her three legs.

She quickly grew into a big mouse, and I took her down to the beach with me to let her run in the sand for a while to get some exercise. After a few days of running in the sand, I sadly realized that I needed to set my Mousy free. She no longer wanted to go back into her tin can.

The next free afternoon, I walked back to the potato field to see if enough grasses grew around the ditch for her to live on. Sure enough, the ditch and in some places the potato field had plenty of ripe grass seeds growing all around them. Assured, I walked back to the children's home.

Somewhat sad, but knowing that I needed to set her free, I walked upstairs to the bedroom and sat down on my bed. I picked up the tall tin can from underneath my bed and whispered to my Mousy that I'd set her free early the next morning, a Sunday morning. Then, a little sad, I placed her back beneath my bed and lay down on my bed for a little while before the evening meal to daydream how happy my Mousy would feel the next morning. Suddenly, a loud, angry voice brought me back to reality.

The tall, heavy man, Little god, stood in front of me. His face glowed red as he yelled at me. "Hand over your mouse!"

Shocked stiff, I just stared at him in disbelief.

He hit me hard in my face, but I refused to hand my Mousy over to him.

He screamed at me once more and hit me hard again, this time on the side of my head.

In a blur, I saw him reaching beneath my bed, pulling out the tin can. With all my strength I screamed for help, kicked the mean man and begged him to let my Mousy live!

With tears streaming from my eyes I yelled, "I'll set her free right now! Please give her to me!"

The outraged man took my sweet Mousy from the tin can, put her on the floor, and stepped hard on her with his big foot.

With one last loud squeak, my dear mouse's blood and guts squirted from beneath the shoe of the fat, ugly, man.

Taking his big foot off my mouse's squashed body he screamed, "Clean up the mess!"

Barely grasping what just happened, outraged hate for this man brewed inside of me. In a daze, I sat up and stared at the remains. Some of my friends, who had gathered at the door, came to me and sat beside me on my bed. They held my hands and cried with me.

Slowly, I knelt in front of my mouse's totally flattened, bloody body and folded my hands. I closed my eyes and asked God for a small miracle, "Please put my Mousy back together."

After quite some moments when no miracle happened, I stood up very disappointed and asked God to at least send down some lightning and kill this evil man.

One of my friends handed me a small box. "For Mousy's funeral. I stole it from the office."

All four of my friends and I carefully scraped my friend's remains off the cold floor and gently placed every piece inside the small box.

So far away from home and having only each other, we stuck together in such a trying moment to comfort each other. With the last tear rolling down my face and my Mousy inside the fine box, I looked at my friends, and with terrible, bitter hate, I screamed, "I need to know who squealed on me!"

They all shook their heads. No one knew. But they said, "We'll find out."

I whispered, "Also, let's think how we could punish the manager of this children's home for killing my Mousy."

That night after the home grew quiet, I snuck downstairs and climbed out the bathroom window with the box of my mouse's remains. I wanted to give her a sea burial so the still young and innocent mouse could be born again. Perhaps my Mousy could go out with the tide and live on the other side of this world.

On my short way through the sand dunes, down to the mighty ocean, I gathered a few grass seeds and flowers and placed them inside her box. Sitting in the wet sand close to the sea, I wondered if the other side of the world had a better place for my Mousy to live.

Slowly, the gentle waves lapping against my feet announced the departure of the huge ocean from this part of the world. While singing a verse of a funeral song, I sadly placed my so loved Mousy into the now restless, big ocean. The retrieving water took my Mousy with it. Soon I could no longer see the pretty little box that held her remains.

I waited for a long time for a thunderstorm to arrive and

lightning to strike the house where the manager of this home lived, but the sky stayed clear with thousands of twinkling stars looking down at me. The bright, almost full moon came out from behind the only small, almost pink cloud in the sky and smiled at the world. Slowly, I drifted away with my Mousy to a different place.

The hungry, screaming seagulls woke me in the grey, gloomy morning. Deeply disappointed in God for not sending a thunderstorm to kill the most vicious, ugliest man I knew right then, I slowly walked back to the children's home, still raging with awful hate.

The Seagull children's home remained quiet and dark, so I climbed back inside through the downstairs bathroom window. The moment I reached my bed, the wake up bell rang and the morning turmoil began. Surprised, I saw two of my best friends, still in their nightgowns, hurrying toward me with smiles on their faces.

When they reached me and no one else remained in the room, they proudly announced, "It was Rosa, the girl who usually cleans the bathrooms that squealed on you!"

"Are you sure?" I asked.

"Absolutely," they assured me.

Right after breakfast, during chore assignment, four of my best friends and I hid behind the big, stinking trash container to avoid work. Today I planned to get even with Rosa for squealing on me.

When all the older children left for their assigned morning jobs, all of us walked away from the trash container toward the upstairs bathroom, as if we had to work there this morning. We hoped to find Rosa there. My heart jumped high when I saw her walking inside the bathroom. Soon, I'd get my revenge.

When Rosa walked into the bathroom, I gave two of my friends the silent signal we had agreed to use. They stood guard to let no one inside the bathroom until I came back out. One of them stood watch at the end of the hall. My strongest friend stood guard at the bathroom door in case I needed help. All agreed with a nod of their head to scream if someone came our way.

Silently, shaking with feverish anger, I walked into the bathroom. When I whispered, "Rosa," she turned around and looked at me in surprise.

"Rosa, did you tell anyone about my Mousy?"

She looked at me, smiled and said, "Yes, we...."

Before she could finish her sentence, one quick, angry hit with my right fist into her face sent her to the floor.

Astounded, she looked up at me and screamed, "Those filthy mice don't belong inside this home! I wanted you to take it outside!"

Then, with pretended calm, I ever so slowly told her in a gory way what happened to my Mousy. With her mouth wide open, she stared at me in disbelief. Before she could get up off the dirty floor or scream for help, I let my anger loose and kicked her hard in her face. "That's for killing my Mousy!"

Blood ran from her nose, and she was obviously in pain.

Pointing my fist at her, still so angry, I said, "If you scream or tell anyone that I hit you, I'll find you and bust your head wide open so your brains can leak out of it, like my mouse's brains did!"

With that, I walked out of the bathroom, leaving Rosa lying on the floor with blood running out of her nose. Feeling much better now, my friends and I walked down to the beach and took a long swim in the cold, but calm ocean.

Rosa didn't squeal on me again. She told the nurse that she fell down on the wet bathroom floor and they sent her to the nearest hospital to have her broken nose fixed. She never came back to the home named Seagull in the humongous field of sand.

C3C3C3

Sweet revenge.

For many weeks, my best friends and I in the Seagull home

thought of what we could do to get even for what that cruel director of the home did to my Mousy. We watched him almost constantly to see what he really liked or cherished. We peeked through the keyhole at his office door and watched him working inside of it.

Behind his big desk stood a cabinet with pictures of his family and his cute dog. Below it, he had a drawer with many files inside it. Every morning, he opened the door of the cabinet and pulled out the drawer. He took some papers out of the different colored files, wrote something inside of them, and stuck them back into the files. He smiled a lot while he worked on those papers. Actually, it was the only time I ever saw him smile. He must have liked those files with all the sheets of written words in them. That was it! We just had to figure out what to do to those papers to hurt him good and not get caught.

Two weeks later, our nurse told us to go outside and wait in the yard for the director of the Seagull to announce who would go home. What an exciting moment! There we stood in the yard, on a cold, foggy, drizzly morning. We didn't mind the cold weather though, since we all hoped to go home soon.

Silently I said, "Oh, please let me go home this time!" I'm sure every other child in the yard uttered the same silent prayer.

Finally he came, the man I hated so much, our director. There he stood on the covered porch with papers in his hand, deciding our future. One great cough and he began to read names from his list. The children whose names he called jumped up in great excitement and ran inside to pack their belongings.

He called all the names of my closest friends. Through the windows of the home, I saw them laughing, embracing each other, and dancing with joy, while I remained standing in the cold drizzle, losing hope. I didn't even feel the rain begin to pour down on me. When only about two dozen children stood in the yard, my hope to go home sank deep, and I wondered if perhaps my mom didn't want me anymore.

From deep down inside of me, tears crept into my eyes. I just had to go home with this big group. I stood in the cold rain, so scared to be left here, trying to figure out how I could sneak out of this place without being noticed, when he called my name.

Stunned, I stood in awe.

Then the director announced, "You're leaving on a boat in the early morning. I won't be here to tell you good-bye, because I need to leave with my family this evening."

Finally, I grasped the good news and ran inside the home. Screaming, laughing and jumping up and down on our beds with my friends, I celebrated the good news. Then I noticed tear-filled faces in our bedroom. For a short moment, I felt sorry for those children who had to stay here.

On our last night inside this home, our plan to get revenge for the cruel way the director killed my Mousy was just steps away. My best friends and I had carefully planned and thought our steps through for many weeks. We would use this night for sweet revenge.

Just before midnight, everyone inside the home had finally fallen asleep, except for my friends and me. With our pillowcases over our shoulders, we slowly and ever so quietly snuck down the stairs, avoiding stepping on the squeaking boards. Since the last six steps of the stairs squeaked especially loud, we slid down the wooden handrail.

As we sneaked by the night watchperson's room, we heard her loud snore, assuring us that she, too, slept. Full of excitement, we walked down the hall to our director's office.

I reached underneath the doormat and retrieved the key to his office. One big grin at each other and with a happy handshake from my friends, I opened the door to the office of the meanest man I knew. Oh, how he had hurt me by killing my sweet, innocent Mousy, right in front of me, even though I begged him to let me set her free. Quietly, I opened the door and we entered the room of the little god's place with silent laughter and smiling eyes, to seek our revenge.

Gently, I opened the cabinet door and slid out the drawer with his important files. While I took out all the files, my friends took out all the written on pages and stuffed them in our pillowcases. Then we drew a smiling mouse on all the empty files and put them back into the drawer. After closing the cabinet door, we opened the small window in the office, climbed out of it with our filled pillowcases and walked toward the beach. A distance away, sure that no one could hear us any longer, we sat down in the sand dunes and laughed until we cried.

Then we walked to the beach and gave all the pages to the mighty, retreating ocean as we shouted, "Here you go, you mean little god! This is for killing Mousy!"

Oh, how much fun and relief it gave us. The quickly retreating ocean took every last piece of paper with her. When we no longer could see the floating papers, we danced around in the wet sand like crazy, with the full moon smiling down at us. Oh, sweet revenge!

On the night of our sweet revenge, I dreamed that the big ocean brought back all the papers we gave to her. While our mean director stood on the beach with an angry face, fire flared from his eyes and he raised his fists high to the heavens. His wild, unnatural scream sent shivers of great fear through my body.

When I finally escaped from the horrible dream, I realized one of my friends was shaking me hard.

She said, "Get up. It's time to have breakfast and go home!"

I jumped out of bed and hurriedly dressed. Downstairs in the dining hall, I told my best friends about my horrible dream. Their faces grew somber, and worry crept through all of us. I decided to quickly climb up the tall sand dune near the seagull's home and have a look at the beach.

Completely out of breath, and with my lungs hurting, I reached the top of the dune. In the early morning light, even though the fog still lay close to the ground, I could clearly see the beach, and I didn't see a single page floating in the sea!

With great relief, I sat down in the cool sand and slid down the tall dune. With a few cuts from the sharp sand grasses in my thighs and sand all over me, I landed at the bottom. My close friends stood there, still with worried faces, and helped me up out of the sand. With a great, excited smile, I told them that the sea did not return the written on pages we gave to her last night. We hugged each other, held hands tightly and laughed our worries away. A happy tear or two rolled down some faces.

A bell rang and the nurse ordered, "All of you that are going home, line up now!"

In a great hurry, I ran inside the home and grabbed my bundle. Down to the small pier we walked, waving goodbye to the crying children who had to stay here. I sat down close to the open end of the barge-like boat, where I could see out toward the island we had just left.

I clung to my precious bag with all the strange fruits inside of it, which I had saved to surprise my family with. Ever so slowly, the island of Amrum, with the Seagull children's home on it, disappeared on the horizon in the wet morning fog among the great waters of the wide, grey ocean.

I wished I could have seen the cruel director's face,when he opened his file cabinet. Perhaps he looked just like in my horrible dream. A very satisfied smile came up from deep inside of me. How very sweet revenge felt. When I lay back to rest a while and closed my eyes, I saw my Mousy smiling and dancing on the other side of this world inside a huge castle made out of all the written pages we gave to the sea. And she lived in a house filled with the seeds she loved so much.

No maple syrup, ravioli, or broccoli.

Chapter 66

Home again.

The train ride home disappointed me because a blanket of heavy grey fog hung over the land and I couldn't even see the signs of the train stations we stopped at. My closest friends and I sat together. Excited to go home, we talked about the mean director of the Seagull children's home and what he looked like when he found out that all his written papers had disappeared and only a smiling mouse looked at him from the folders. We had fun and laughed until we hurt.

Soon, the train stopped again and the escort asked my friends to depart. What a sad moment. We hugged each other and promised to write and stay dear friends forever. When they walked off the train, I opened the window, waved and shouted goodbye, until the thick fog swallowed them. I could still hear them when the train started to move. Afraid of never seeing them again, I closed the window and sat down. The steady rhythm of the moving train rocked me gently to sleep. The little god's outraged face came to me, and I laughed at him and told him, "You shouldn't have killed my dear, innocent friend, Mousy!"

Before I knew it, someone shook me and called my name. My escort said, "Edith, you get off the train at the next stop." She then asked me, "Are you able to walk onto the little ferry by yourself?"

Proudly, I answered, "Yes, ma'am."

In a short moment, the brakes of the train began to squeak loudly. I took my bundle and walked toward the exit door. When the grey locomotive stopped, I hopped down the few stairs, waved goodbye to the escort, and walked toward the ferry landing.

I found the little ferryboat waiting for me, and soon we chugged out to sea. The heavy fog still embraced everything, and I began to wonder if the old engineer could find the landing on my island, but he did. When the little ferry landed on my island, my sweet dog ran toward me with all the speed his four legs could manage. I bent down to greet him, and he licked my face repeatedly between short, soft whining sounds. Oh, how glad I felt to see him.

Then my smiling grandma came on board the ferry. She hugged me and said, "It's wonderful to have you back, girl!"

On our walk home, I told my grandma all about the tides of the great, grey ocean and the strange fruits I had inside my bundle. She listened with a somewhat strange smile on her face. My dog ran ahead to our village and excitedly barked loud and long. When we arrived, most of the inhabitants stood outside of their small houses, or huts, to greet us with a smile and a friendly wave. So glad to finally be home, I happily smiled and waved back.

Inside our house, everyone had gathered in my uncle's kitchen, the biggest room in our small house, to welcome me home. After lots of hugs and kisses, I opened my bundle and proudly handed everyone one of the strange fruits I had saved for them. Then I showed them how to peel the bananas and the oranges. They sure seemed surprised and liked the sweet taste of the strange fruits very much.

Then I told them all about the enormous, grey ocean which completely left to the other side of the world at a regular rhythm. They rewarded me with astounded expressions, some in complete disbelief.

Everyone was surprised about the size of the big crabs, which I saw so many of in the North Sea. I told them the sad story about my Mousy, but I left the sweet revenge of it out. I also found it wiser not to tell my family about my trip on the inner tube, trying to see the other side of the world, riding on the restless waves of the gigantic ocean.

For days afterward, I stayed busy telling everyone what I had seen and all about my time on the island of Amrum, in the grey, mighty North Sea. I only shared the adventures I hid from my family with my most trusted friends, and surprised and amused them.

No nail clippers, rat poison or Olive Garden restaurants.

Chapter 67

My mom's cried out eyes.

After a few days at home, when I finally settled down and had told my exciting adventures on the North Sea to everyone at least twice, I noticed that my mom looked and acted differently. She didn't go on walks with me to collect driftwood for our little iron stove, or pick greens for the chickens.

Mom had barely listened to all I told her about my time away. She wasn't her happy self and had red, cried out eyes most of the time. I wondered if she had tuberculosis again. Lying in my bed that night, scared about the possibility of my mom getting sick again, I decided, though it went against the common upbringing, I would ask her in the morning what bothered her. The next day I awoke early, before the sun rose completely. Quietly, I dressed myself underneath my bedcover, then went into my mom's room to get a drink of water out of our big bucket. To my great surprise, I found my mom sitting by the small window in her room, staring out into the still dark, grey world. She had her dress on and her couch had not been made up into a bed. She shivered inside the cold, small room. Mom had not even lit the little stove yet. When she turned her face toward me, I saw a tear rolling down her cheek. She quickly wiped that tear away with a soaking wet handkerchief.

I stood frozen with fear. I had only seen my mom cry once, so long ago, when she had open tuberculosis and they sent her faraway to a sanatorium. Slowly, I walked over to her and gently held her big, trembling hand. Bravely, I asked, "What's the matter, Mom?"

She held onto my small hand tightly, wiped her tears from her face with her other hand and asked me to sit on her lap. She helped me up, and carefully, so as not to hurt her, I sat down on her slightly shaking lap. While she still stared out into the cold, slowly awakening grey day, my mom put her arms around me and with a shaking voice began to speak.

"I sent your sister and you away to children's homes for some time because I was pregnant and unable to make money in the fields to feed the two of you. I gave birth to a healthy baby boy. He has curly blond hair and deep green eyes, just like our ocean. I spent two stressful days of hard labor to bring him into this world. I nursed him and loved him for a few days, but I knew I had to give him away. I can't even provide adequately for the two of you."

After a moment of trying to quit crying, my mom said, "I gave him to a childless, elderly, married couple from Denmark. They own a small grocery store and can provide him with whatever he needs in the future. They gave me their address and lovingly told me to come and visit any time." With many tears rolling down my mom's face she cried out, "It broke my heart to let my sweet little baby boy go!"

By now, tears streamed down my face as well. We embraced each other and let the tears flow.

After we had shed all our tears, my mom made me promise never to mention my little brother's birth again. I promised her. Gently, I slipped off her lap and walked over to our iron stove. In a daze, I stuffed dried grasses and small wood chips into the hungry mouth of the little stove and lit it. Right away, the small, red flames licked away the soft fuel. Quickly I added larger pieces of wood to its hungry mouth.

When the top of our little stove began to turn fiery red, the water in our teapot, which always stood on the stove, began to boil.

Immediately, I reached for our mugs, put a pinch of dried dandelion flowers inside them and added the boiling water. While my mom still silently stared out the small window into the arriving morning, I sliced us each a small piece of dark bread from the dwindling loaf and carefully placed our tea and bread on the windowsill. My mom smiled at me and thanked me. Just as the first shy pink and yellow rays of the sun emerged from the almost black sea, we silently took in our breakfast.

My thoughts went back to the story my grandma told me on my tenth birthday, when she allowed me to spend the night with her in her cozy bed. How bad she felt, when she had to give away her firstborn child. As far as I knew, I was my mom's firstborn. Looking into my mom's tired, worn face, I wondered how I could help her to be a happy mom again. I felt awfully helpless, and tears crept up to my eyes again. Unsure of what to do next, I reached over with both arms and ever so gently hugged my mom.

She stood up and grabbed our coats and our basket in which we collected driftwood. So relieved that she came on a walk with me, I held back my tears and shoved them back deep inside of me. After we dressed warmly, my mom and I walked down the stairs hand in hand and out of the front door into the crisp, promising morning. We walked past the empty harbor and along the bottom of the strong earthen dike. We collected lots of wood in the shallow shore water. On our way back home, Mom broke off a few small willow branches of the huge bushes that grew on the dike to place in water inside our little room.

Within a few days, they'd think spring had come inside our warm little room and bring forth lovely, silver-grey flowers and soft green leaves, which look so lovely and make our room so festive. During the mostly silent walk, my mom's teary eyes dried out.

That dark, cloudy night, my mom, grandma and many of our village people and I walked up the dirt road in complete silence toward our island witch's small house for the ceremony of promise and forgiveness. That night, my mom would find forgiveness for giving away her baby boy, and people had to swear not to talk about him again. If someone, even if absent from this ceremony, mentioned him again, our island witch would know it and use her power to punish that person.

Since I had come to this ceremony a few times before and Ola blessed me, it no longer frightened me. This time, I wouldn't close my eyes completely, like told, when the ceremony began. I wanted to see what our island witch did. Only the softly blowing wind had the courage to whisper past us on this strictly silent walk.

In front of the witch's house, everyone stood still and stared toward her door. My mom walked toward the front of the silent crowd. Soon Ola came outside with a big, lit candle in her hand. I hid way in the back among the people from our village. When everyone closed their eyes and looked to the ground, I closed my eyes just enough to still see what would happen.

The small flame of the candle flickered gently in the wind, and my mom raised both of her hands in the dark night. Our witch raised her candle way up into the air and let go of it. She lifted and spread her arms out wide and mumbled something. The lit candle just hung there way above her head for a moment, and then it slowly moved upward by itself and glowed brightly. The dark clouds moved away from the candle's bright light in a great hurry, as if afraid of it. The amazingly bright candle lit up a circle around us almost like daylight.

Then our witch bent over and spit smoke out of her mouth with great ugly noises. When she stood up straight again, she crossed her arms over her chest and screamed, "You will forgive!"

Everyone, including me, gently whispered, "Yes."

At that precise moment, the gathered people opened their eyes and the bright, now flickering flame of the big candle shot up, way into the air and died. A hush came over the people. The dark clouds that surrounded us on the way here had disappeared, and the moon lit our way home. The ceremony fascinated me, and I wondered, excitedly, but with some fear, if Ola really would teach me all this someday.

My mom held my hand on our way home, smiled and said, "I am forgiven. No one shall blame me now or talk about my son. If they do, our witch will punish them fiercely."

I kept my promise of not telling about my brother, until today, seven years after my mom's death and some fifty-four years after my little brother's birth. Over the years, I wondered from whom I kept this secret. Surely, everyone on our island knew that my mom gave birth to a baby boy and that she gave him away to a couple in Denmark.

The people on my island had great respect for our witch and kept their secrets, especially if they had sworn to do so at night in sight of our island witch. My little sister, Uschi, too young yet to come to this ceremony, and my two brothers not yet born, don't know of their brother with the blond hair and dark, green eyes, for whom my mom cried so painfully.

I wonder if such a promise to a witch has a time limit.

CRCRCR

In 1996, on my last visit to see my mom in Germany for her 75th birthday, I bravely asked her where my little brother lived in Denmark. In somewhat of a daze, overcome by Parkinson's disease and all the medications she had to take, she mentioned a few towns in Denmark, but shook her head at each name. Her eyes wandered faraway into the past with each name she mentioned, and she grew sad. Slowly, with a strange smile on her face, she slipped away into her long afternoon nap.

Perhaps I could find a note among my mom's important papers and pictures inside the shoebox she held so dear and looked through often. Quietly and with great hope, I searched through the shoebox and through the whole room inside the fine nursing home she now lived in, but I found no such note. My mom had made an ending to that part of her life.

Before I left my island to return to America, I looked through the church register book for my brother's birth entry, but found none. Seven months later, my mom closed her eyes forever, never to cry again.

The grown up man with curly, blond hair and dark green eyes like the sea will never know his birth mother.

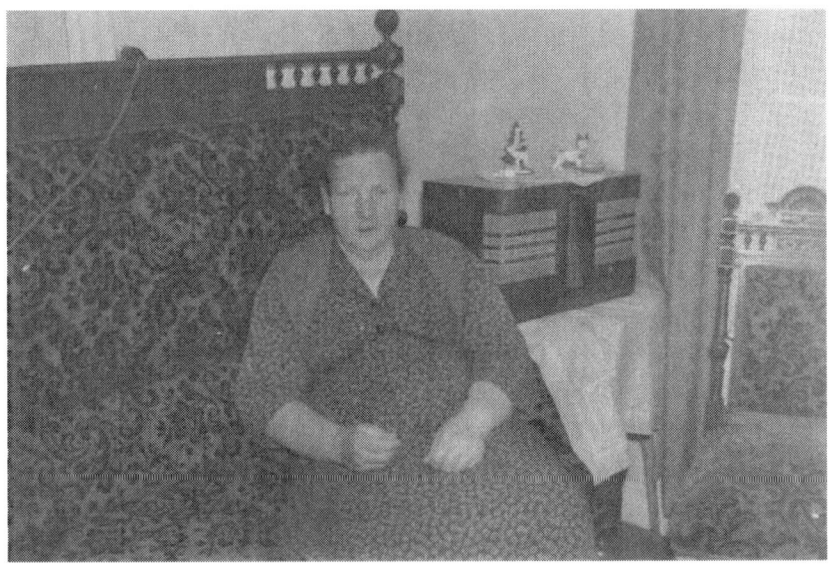

Oma (Grandma)
Died February 11, 1961

No Maxi pads, soap on a rope,
Teflon cookware or French-fries.

Chapter 68

Ola's warm, reassuring hand.

One early, beautiful spring day, to everyone's surprise, my grandma went to bed at noon and stayed there all day. I checked on her in the evening but found her still asleep. She didn't look good at all. Her face looked very white, and her eyes had big, dark circles around them. She drooled heavily and briefly stopped breathing now and then.

Afraid she was dying, I took both of my small hands, grabbed her by the shoulders, lifted her as much as I could and tried hard to shake her awake, but my sweet grandma didn't wake up. Scared, but gently, I let loose of her and she fell back onto her pillow. Her head rolled back to one side, and she lay motionless with her eyes closed and her mouth wide open now. I had never seen her like this and felt terribly afraid.

As loud as I could, I screamed for help. My mom, Uncle Fred and his wife, Aunt Hilde, answered my call and ran into my grandma's room. For a seemingly long time they fussed over my grandma. They held her up and tried to have her drink some tea, which just ran out of her mouth and down her chest.

They talked and screamed very loudly at her, to awaken her, but she didn't wake up. Then my mom even slapped my grandma's face. I could no longer watch what my family did to my grandma. I

444

ran out of the room, sat down outside of our house on the front door steps and cried. I folded my hands and desperately begged God to let my grandma wake up.

Before long, my mom came outside and sat down next to me. She wrapped her arms around me and said, "Your grandma may wake up tomorrow or the next day, or perhaps she might never wake up." Then my mom gently stroked my head and without another word, walked back into our house.

I shook with fear, unable to believe that my grandma could lay in her bed forever. Who would do all her work and hold our family together in hard times, or hold my hand and tell me everything will be fine, and wipe the tears from my face?

She woke up so very early every morning, tending to her smoke tons, working in her garden, and stirring, or mixing her fine liquors in her cellar. While the sun slowly rose, she walked out to our front yard to greet the gathered neighbors.

My grandma was the early, daily, oral newspaper of our island. While she kept her hands busy knitting on her newest project, she told what happened in our village the night before. She whispered the names of the people who saw each other under the dark cover of the night and who would expect a child soon.

She knew who had cheated on their partner or who stole from the ready to harvest fields. Oh yes, my grandma knew everything. Sometimes the neighbors shook their heads in disbelief and opened their mouths wide, ever so astounded by what my grandma told them. Other times people just nodded and laughed out loud in agreement before they walked back to their houses.

From there, the news my grandma told the neighbors traveled all over our island and back to us. Mostly everyone added their own touch to the story. If a girl walked hand in hand with a man in the dark of the night out of our village, she had given birth to three children, out of wedlock, by the time the news came back to our part of the island. Sometimes it took only days for the news to come back to us. It scared me to think that a woman could have so many children in such a little time. Oh, grandma, you have to wake up!

The cold wind brought me back to reality and I walked into my grandma's room. Still asleep, she didn't move when I called out for her. Slowly, I knelt down next to her bed and begged God again to let her wake up. I waited a long time for God to wake her up, but He didn't. Very disappointed, I gently slipped into Grandma's bed.

Underneath her feather bedcover, I hugged her and cuddled up tightly next to her. With tears running down my face, I whispered some fine stories to her, all the great ones she had told me over the years, and I pleaded with her to wake up. Grandma didn't wake up. Disappointed and awfully scared, I cried myself to sleep, letting my salty tears run down onto my dear grandma's cool body.

In the still dark early morning, voices inside the room awoke me. I opened my eyes to see the room full of our village people. Our midwife, the healing woman and our nurse stood closest to my grandma's bed. Mom asked me to get out of bed, which I quickly did.

Someone asked, "When is the doctor due to visit our island?"

The nurse answered, "In about three weeks."

I stood on the end of my grandma's bed, holding onto the footboard with shaking hands, watching the nurse and healing woman holding her head up. They moved a small bottle of smelling salt in front of her nose, but she didn't wake up.

The midwife and her husband grabbed my grandma and shook her hard. It scared me and I wondered why her head didn't fall off. She just fell back into her bed and kept on sleeping. Even the fine brandy that they poured into her mouth didn't awaken her, it just ran out of her mouth onto her pillow. When everyone had run out of ideas and prayers trying to wake her, they slowly walked outside my grandma's room with very somber faces.

My mom came to me, took my hand and we walked outside our house to the dirt road. Just about our whole village had gathered there by now. At first, I heard just a whisper that someone should tell our island witch, and then the voices swelled. Soon everyone agreed to contact our island witch, but they didn't know who should visit her and ask her for help.

People looked at me and said, "She's the only blessed one in our village and therefore, doesn't need to wait for our island witch's twilight visiting hours. Let her go!"

My mom agreed right away, and I of course wanted to go and get help for my grandma. Then most of the village people walked slowly back to their homes with grim, worried faces.

By this time, at age eleven, the island witch no longer frightened me. We had had many visits and had taken many fun walks together. And by now, I could read and study in her dusty, aged books. The pages actually stayed blank, until I completely cleared my mind and concentrated hard on them. Then the letters and numbers appeared and taught me a little more each day about witchery. I saw it as a fun game.

Mom took me by my hand and we walked upstairs to our little room in a hurry. There she poured a small amount of water in our washbowl and told me to wash my hands and face with the soap she handed me. Quickly, I reminded her that she made me wash both of my hands in the morning already.

My mom looked at me sternly. "Wash up and wear your Sunday dress. You're going to visit our island witch with honors."

I hurriedly washed myself, dressed in my tight, outgrown Sunday dress and walked downstairs. There my aunt handed me a bunch of pretty flowers from our garden and a bottle of Grandma's finest liquor from her cellar. After my mom told me to behave politely and calmly ask our island witch for her help, I started on my way.

Walking up our dirt road in my Sunday dress on a weekday stirred up quite some attention among the smaller children. They didn't know why I had dressed like that or where I headed. They stopped their important games and stared at me in disbelief. Before they could laugh at me, the adults who stood nearby, called them to their sides and whispered something to the small children, which made them stand still and quietly look at me.

In a single person parade, I walked up our dirt road, stared at by our silent village people standing on the side of the road with hope in their hearts and tears in their eyes. With scrubbed clean hands, I held onto the pretty flowers and the bottle of my grandma's finest brew from her cellar, while I walked up to our witch's small house.

For just a brief moment in front of her house, I collected my thoughts of how to ask her for help. Then I walked toward her front door, with desperate hope in my heart that Ola could awaken my grandma. I squeezed the pretty flowers in one hand awfully hard! Droplets of their moisture dripped down my hand. When I raised my hand to knock on our island witch's door, she opened it and asked me to come inside.

She guided me over to a small sofa and invited me to sit. Her big, loosely-woven, black shawl hung over the side of the old sofa. The curtain on the only window in the room remained shut to keep the daylight out. On a round table stood a tall, white candle with a slightly flickering reddish flame, which softly lit the whole room.

When Ola sat down next to me, I handed her the gifts I brought. The pretty, by now somewhat droopy, flowers perked up the moment she touched them.

As I opened my mouth to ask her to help my grandma, she touched my face with her rough, cold hand, looked deeply into my eyes and said somberly, "Yes, my child, you now have the strength and knowledge to follow my orders. Your grandma's spirit has left her body, but it's confused and doesn't know where to go. Someone in the other world made a mistake. I see it has to be you, the first stillborn twin of your grandma, to bring her spirit back into her soul."

I didn't understand the meaning of Ola's words, but wasn't about to question her. At that moment, I felt warmth entering my body from our island witch's assuring, glistening eyes and her warm hand on my shoulder.

After a moment, Ola smiled and held both my hands. "You need to find a completely white chicken, kill it and pull out all its feathers. Then you need to place all the feathers on and around your grandma inside her bed. Be careful to gather all the feathers. Don't miss a single one. This will show her spirit how to come back to her.

"Do this before midnight tonight. Then light a candle beside your grandma's bed. Look at the ceiling of her room, where her spirit hovers. Concentrate hard with all your strength on breathing in the confused spirit. Do it deeply, and then breathe it out into your grandma's mouth. If the candle near her bed dies, you used the power which I gave you for this night wisely, and your grandma will awaken. Remember now, you're a different child, your grandma's child. Her spirit will listen to you. The whole village may help you, but at midnight when you give your grandma her spirit back, you must be alone with her. Now, go on home my child."

I stood up from the small sofa and turned to thank her, but she and her black shawl had disappeared. The reddish flame of the tall, white candle flickered once more and died, sending light grey smoke to the ceiling of the small, dark room.

I found my way out of the room by the small shaft of light that crept beneath the front door. When I opened the door, the bright light of the noon sun blinded me for a brief moment. When I could see again, I found my mom and many of our village people waiting for me. In excitement the wanted to hear what our island witch had told me, and so I told them exactly what Ola had said to do.

My mom took charge. She told everyone to go home and look for a pure white chicken among their flocks. In a great hurry, we ran home and checked Grandma's chickens. Most of them had brown, or reddish-brown feathers, but we found four white ones. With Uncle Fred's help, we gathered the white chickens, held them up by their legs to check for a pure, white plumage.

When they furiously flapped their wings to get out of our grip, we sadly discovered that all four had very light gray tips under their wing feathers. We loosened our grips on the outraged chickens and they flew to the ground and ran as far away from us as they could, inside their huge enclosure.

On our way out of our yard to go check on our neighbors' chickens, I got very scared and asked my mom, "What if we don't find a pure white chicken?"

"My mom and Uncle Fred both answered, "There has to be a pure white chicken on this island."

At that moment, two people came walking toward us, each of them with a chicken under their arms. Happily they announced, "These chickens are pure white, but they're roosters!"

While the adults discussed if we could use a rooster since he actually was a chicken, but not called so, an older woman from our village came to us with a pure white hen.

As she handed the chicken over to me, she smiled and said, "For your grandma, child. We desperately need her to wake up."

Everyone agreed to use the hen to follow our witch's orders in detail. My Uncle Fred fetched a chicken from Grandma's flock and gave it to the woman in exchange for her pure white one.

She said, "It's not necessary," but my uncle and my mom insisted on it.

A widow for years, she lived in a small shack by the bay, trying to raise her six children. The mighty sea, in one of its wild furies, had taken her husband some years ago.

As the sun sank and night crawled over our island, my mom chopped the chicken's head off on the chopping block. I felt sad to see the life running out of the pure, white, innocent chicken. One last hopeless move of the headless chicken's feet to escape her killer, and her life ended. Mom dunked her body into the water she had heated outside over a wood fire, to make the chicken's skin softer, so we could pluck her feathers out more easily.

By now, night had settled, and heavy, dark clouds hung low. Lightning played a pretty game on the horizon in the east. Inside our house, in Uncle Fred's kitchen, my mom and I plucked every last feather from that chicken. Many of our neighbors stopped by that night. Some offered their help, others brought food and sat with my sleeping grandma for a while.

The adults thought it best if I, by myself, would cover my sweet grandma with all the white feathers. Slowly, I walked toward her room with two lightly filled pillowcases of all the white feathers, but I carried a very heavy burden in my heart. What if I failed to catch my grandma's spirit to give it back to her? Would she then die? I loved her so much, perhaps I could go to heaven with her. Surely she knew the way. She knew everything.

When I entered my grandma's room, the visiting neighbors respectfully stepped out into the hallway. The little windup clock on the night table read 11 p.m. The small, dim electric light bulb which hung from the ceiling, lit my grandma's sleeping face. She looked ghostly to me with her very white face and deep wrinkles. I wondered how far away her spirit lingered and hoped with all my heart that I'd do everything right to bring it back.

My mind raced back to the important visit with our island witch. She said to cover my grandma completely with all the white feathers before midnight. Then light a white candle, look up to the ceiling, breathe in grandma's spirit and exhale it into her mouth exactly at midnight.

Frightened, and with tears in my eyes but careful not to wet the white feathers, I covered my grandma's face, except her mouth, and all of her body with the white feathers. Seeing her lying there, breathing the white feathers in and out of her nose, made me giggle a bit. Then the seriousness of this night quickly took me back to reality and I got scared again of failing this important task.

Thunder started to roll in over our island and rain poured down, playing a heavy, serious concert on Grandma's window. I desperately hoped that I could reach my grandma's spirit in this wild storm. While I waited for midnight to arrive and hoped the glass windows could hold up to the rain's big, violent drops pounding on them, my mind raced back to our island witch. Silently and so awfully scared, I begged her for help in our number language.

Before I had finished my plea, I felt a warm, reassuring hand on my shoulder and a soft voice, Ola's voice, saying, "Your grandma's spirit still lingers inside the room."

I looked around but saw neither Ola nor my grandma's spirit.

One more look at the small clock showed me that the time had come to light the white candle and prepare to give my grandma back her spirit, which I hoped would make her wake up. After lighting the white candle and turning off the electric light, I closed my eyes and in desperation, asked our island witch once more, "Please help me." When I opened my eyes, I felt very warm, suddenly sure of myself, and ready for midnight to arrive.

Patiently, I sat very still on the edge of Grandma's bed. I watched a slightly grey cloud forming over her bed, which seemed to gather its strength from the smoke of the candle. When the old clock showed that midnight neared, I calmly climbed off her bed and stood next to it.

The howling storm with its crackling silver lightning lit up the room through the closed curtains with ghostly scenes, while the rumbling thunder vibrated the house with each hit. For the first time in my young life, I had no fear of the horrible storm. I did worry that the violent storm might scare away Grandma's spirit though. Right away, without seeing her, Ola assured me that the spirit still hovered over my grandma's body.

With a soft knock on the door, my mom reminded me that midnight would arrive in twenty seconds. The people in our house counted down the seconds loud enough for me to hear them clearly. At the number fifty, I lifted my head up high over my grandma and took a deep breath like the ones I took when I dove down into the cold, but beautiful, deep ocean. Then I bent down

452

over Grandma to reach her mouth. At exactly midnight, I closed my eyes, and with all the force I could manage, I blew all the air into her mouth.

At that moment, with my eyes still closed, I felt Ola's warm, reassuring hand on my shoulder again. Perhaps it had been there all along.

Exhausted, I sat up, gasping for air and staring at my grandma. She continued to sleep. Afraid that I had done something wrong, I quickly glanced over to the candle. The candle slightly flickered once and died, the sign our island witch told me to watch for, which meant that I had done everything right and Grandma's spirit had found its way back into her body.

At that frightening moment, the door opened and my mom turned on the light. Suddenly, my big grandma lifted herself up to a sitting position, coughing, spitting feathers out of her mouth, and yelling like crazy. At that moment, she made me absolutely the happiest girl in the whole, wide world!

I jumped into her bed and hugged her tightly. As though someone flipped a switch, the raging storm stopped. All of our village neighbors filled the room and showed their relief that my grandma woke up. Everyone but my grandma laughed at the sight of the two of us in her bed with all the white feathers floating and flying around us.

Grandma sneezed over and over again, which really made the white feathers fly up high. Out of excitement to have her back awake, I jumped up and down on her bed, trying to catch the white, flying feathers without great success.

Mom ended my excitement when she yelled, "Get off the bed now!"

All our neighbors who had come, now walked past Grandma's bed, while she continued to sneeze. They touched her, smiled, and welcomed her back. Some had tears in their eyes, even though they smiled. I guessed they shed happy tears like I did. Soon all the neighbors left for home.

When my grandma quit sneezing she yelled, "What kind of a joke is this? Who put all the feathers in my bed? Did my pillow break? Why am I so awfully hungry?"

My mom sat down beside my grandma and explained in detail what happened to her. My grandma sat still, listened with a very astounded face and a few white feathers still dancing around her. When my mom finished talking, Grandma asked me to come to her. She held me for a long time in her big, shaking arms and thanked me. Something wet, perhaps grandma's tears, slowly ran down my neck.

When my Uncle Fred entered the room with a whole jar of pickled eel and a huge slice of bread, my grandma abruptly let loose of me. She motioned him to set the food on her bed. While the little clock's handle turned toward the number one, my grandma and I ate delicious eel and bread in her bed.

I noticed that my grandma was very hungry and not very careful how she put the food into her mouth. A lot of pickle juice ran down her face and wound up in her bed, but it didn't matter. She woke up! She invited me to sleep with her inside her bed that night and my mom said I could.

After my grandma finally finished eating and everyone of my family had left the room, my mom took the empty jar of pickled eel, turned off the dim electric lamp and said good-night.

While my grandma licked the pickle juice and perhaps a morsel or two of the eel from her fingers, we snuggled beneath her bedcover.

After a genuine big hug and kiss, she said, "Let me tell you a very special story."

I fell asleep in my grandma's big arms before she even started that special story, but not before I saw our island witch's smiling face, felt her warm touch, and thanked her a thousand times in our secret number language.

Very early the next morning, before the daylight lit up my grandma's room, she woke me and said, "Let's celebrate life, girl!

Let this day be a great holiday for our whole village!"

She slid out of bed and dressed while humming a happy song. Then she lit the candle near her bed and started to light the small iron stove. Still awfully tired from last night's excitement, I turned over in my grandma's big bed and went back to sleep.

Barely drifting back into sleep, Grandma's loud singing and the clattering of her pans on the stove woke me. Still very tired, I decided to get out of bed because something smelled awfully good. My grandma busied herself frying dumplings with onions in a huge pan full of pork grease.

As she cut up apples to add to the pan, I reached her and said, "Good morning."

She turned to me, picked me up and swung me around the room twice. She then started to sing and dance a polka with me in her arms around her table.

With all this commotion, the rest of our family woke up and slowly gathered in the room. Grandma continued to sing and laugh while finishing cooking the most festive meal I ever remember having for breakfast in my young years. Compared to today's standards, Grandma's dumplings with onions and apples and fried in lots of pork grease would be a Thanksgiving meal with all the trimmings.

The adults gave each other questioning looks about Grandma's odd behavior but kept quiet. All of us children sat on our grandma's bed now, excitedly waiting for the moment when she would put the big pan with the great feast on the table.

Finally, the great moment arrived. Grandma took the big pan full of delicious smelling food off the stove and set it down on a flat brick in the middle of her table. All six of us hungry children jumped up in a hurry to get close. There it sat, the great feast, still bubbling and smelling wonderful. A meal fit for a king.

My Uncle Fred came into the room, carrying two chairs. We had just enough room around the table for the four adults to sit down on the chairs. All of us children squeezed between the adults, standing up, waiting for someone to hand us a spoon to dig into the big pan full of fine looking food.

Excitement grew when my grandma handed out spoons, but we had to wait for her to finish speaking to nature, our island witch, and sometimes to God. My, was I hungry. I didn't get much to eat of the pickled eel last night because my grandma ate so much so fast to make up for all the time she had slept and didn't eat.

Finally, my grandma sat down, closed her eyes and softly spoke to nature, thanking her for letting food grow on our island to enable us to live here. Next, she said a big thank you to our island witch for giving me the power to retrieve her spirit and blow it back into her body so she could wake up. My stomach growled loudly. I had set my gaze on the exact spot that I'd dig my spoon into the delicious, big meal.

Grandma sat silently for a short moment and I waited for her to say something to God, but for some reason she didn't talk to Him today. Instead, to my surprise, she said, "Let's eat!"

In a hurry, I landed my spoon in the big pot and fished out a dumpling with apple pieces, onions and lots of pork grease. When I put the spoon near my lips, I realized that the food was still way too hot to eat, so I blew on it until it cooled enough to eat. I must have blown too hard on my food because the dumpling slid off my spoon and onto the table. I tried to grab it, but it slid onto the floor.

While everyone laughed at me, I quickly bent down and retrieved my dumpling from the floor. I didn't bother to place it back onto the spoon, but I hurriedly stuck it into my mouth. Oh, how delicious! Greedily, I reached for another spoonful of food from the huge pot. We ate, and laughed, and talked, so completely happy to have Grandma back awake.

We ate many one-pot meals like that, especially when we didn't have enough dishes, or room to set them on the table.

After we managed to eat all the great food, I felt tired and walked over to my grandma's bed to take a nap.

I heard her say, "Let her nap. She didn't get much sleep last night."

Before I closed my eyes and slipped back into the wonderful land of dreams, I saw my grandma take her big gun out of the drawer. She held it up high into the air and looked into the barrel. Then she put some bullets in it and walked outside with the rest of our family following her.

I awoke that afternoon to a quiet house, but I heard a lot of singing and talking outside.

As I slipped out of bed, Mom came into the room and said, "Come outside and join the party."

On the way out she said, "Grandma shot two wild ducks and we're about to take them out of her smoking ton."

That woke me up completely. Another grand feast on the same day! How lucky we were!

Outside on the dirt road, many, perhaps all of the people from our village had gathered. Some men sat together on wooden boxes, smoking green cigars and gutting out fish. Others played familiar songs on their harmonicas, which many women sang or hummed to while heating up the pork grease in their pans over small wood fires.

The older girls helped their mothers prepare their family meal by cutting up potatoes, cabbage and onions. The older boys stood aside a ways and kept looking at the girls, smiling and giggling like a bunch of nuts. The very young children sat together on the dirt floor by Grandma's green, bushy hedge, while an old woman told them stories. The rest of the village children and various dogs ran around laughing, jumping, and being yelled at once in a while for coming too close to the fires.

Grandma sat in the middle of all our neighbors in her favorite chair and waved me over to her. I ran over to her and jumped onto her lap.

She hugged and squeezed me a lot. "Thank you, my child."

When she finally let loose of me, I saw the adults passing

around many of her fine bottles of different liquors. My Aunt Hilde was dancing, like always, free and just a little wild. The men watched her intensely with longing eyes. I hoped very much to be able to dance so well and freely in my later life.

Actually I did, many years later. I won the Disco Dancing competition in St. Louis and was named Disco Queen for that year. My, how great I felt. I believe I danced just like my Aunt Hilde, moving my body ever so freely and with joy.

Soon, the women had all sorts of foods frying in those heavy black pots in the hot, spitting greases. The wonderful smell permeated the air and made me hungry again. When every family gave my grandma the thumbs up sign, she shot her big gun three times into the air. That got rid of all the village dogs for a while and the rowdy children settled down on the dirt road next to their parents' fires.

My Uncle Fred came out of our backyard with a big plate, full of pieces of the smoked ducks. My mom fished the fried potatoes out of the hot grease, placed them into a bowl and handed everyone in our family a spoon, except for my Aunt Hilde who kept on dancing.

When everyone had sat on the ground, huddled around their fires with spoons in their hands, ready to eat, my grandma lifted the bottle of her finest from her cellar and took a big drink. Then she bowed her head to talk to someone in prayer as she often did before eating. I watched everyone else bow their heads out of respect for her, and I did the same.

Patiently, everyone waited for my grandma to speak, but she didn't say a word. I got worried, turned a little and looked at her. My grandma had closed her eyes and began to snore very loudly. People looked up, smiled and giggled.

Mom took over, stood up, held her spoon high, and said, "Let's eat!"

In a hurry, I jumped off Grandma's lap and sat down on the ground with my family to enjoy that outstanding, plentiful meal. I grabbed a big piece of the smoked duck and loaded up my spoon many times with those great tasting fried potatoes.

How great it felt to eat all I could. Before long, our very harsh winter would arrive and we'd find food scarce again, so scarce that my mom often said she wasn't hungry, but longingly looked at the little food she had to serve my sister and me.

Someone stood up and said, "We need to take some food to our island witch to thank her for giving Edith the great power to wake up her grandma."

A united grumble of agreement traveled like a wave among our village people, except for my Aunt Hilde, who continued to dance and could care less about anything else now. Of course my grandma didn't care at this moment either, as she snored away.

My mom stood up and said, "I'll get a basket and pass it around." When she came back with the handmade willow branch basket, Mom picked up a few big pieces of our smoked duck and placed them inside it. She then passed the basket along to our village neighbors.

When the very powerful sun slowly sank in the west with all its glory, painting the sky in amazing warm, striking colors of gold, orange, purple and some light green, everyone stood up and stared at the horizon in amazement. Even my Aunt Hilde quit dancing and stood still to watch the magic show of the setting sun. Soon the golden sun looked like a ball of fire, with flames of deep red and gold boiling up from its inner body.

Inch by inch the sun sank into the blood colored water of the huge, tame ocean. Then she retrieved her powerful, tall rays of gold from the sky and crawled into her waterbed. Dark, purple clouds took over the sky. Some village people bowed their heads in silence. Others lifted their hands, with pleading hope in their eyes, for the sun to return in the morning.

Shortly after this touching moment, people stirred their fires, the music and singing started again and yes, my Aunt Hilde started to dance again to the delight of most of the village men. I noticed though that many men, even just taking a quick glance at her, received a quick kick from their wives and I wondered why.

My mom volunteered four young, strong men to carry my still sleeping grandma inside her room and put her into her bed. Mom carried her plate of fried potatoes and smoked duck, which she hadn't touched yet, inside our house. While the men carried my grandma inside our house, she awoke. With a loud, strong voice, she started to sing a song in a strange language, while she swung her homemade bottle of her finest liquor high up into the air. The four strong men had a hard time carrying such a big, heavy woman, but they finally made it inside. Our village people smiled with relief of having my grandma back among the waking and waved at her with their hands held up high.

By the time my mom came back outside, darkness had settled over our island. People sang and danced, or just lay dreaming by the fires. The willow basket made its way around and came back to us completely filled with lots of different foods. Our village neighbors gathered closely around us and decided that I should take the filled basket to our island witch. Glad to do so, I looked at them and agreed. I figured this might be a good time to thank our island witch for giving me the power to wake up my sweet grandma.

My mom took the loaded basket, added a bottle of sweet liquor to it, handed it to me and said, "Go on your way, girl. Make sure you speak politely to our island witch. We all owe her that."

On my way I walked, leaving the celebrating village neighbors and the warm, inviting fires behind me. Dark clouds hid most of the moon and the stars, but a little light from the stars shone down to let me see my way to our island witch's little house. Though not afraid of the dark, creepy thoughts started to run through my mind. People claimed that Ola had such great power, and I heard many whisper of how she punished people who didn't follow her orders, or just plain didn't believe in her abilities. They claimed that some of her punishments included children born without much of a brain, or perhaps they turned into mad monsters, like the boy who burned down the barn with his sister inside of it. She could make cows go dry and horses drop dead instantly. They said she could send lightning down to burn the crops, or have the rain drown them.

She could calm the furious sea and talk away deadly diseases. She could keep the mad ghosts inside our church's huge attic so they wouldn't come out and kill innocent islanders. She knew what everyone was about to do, or did. She freely talked to the moon and yes, she danced with the devil on Sinners' Row.

I'll never forget that totally scary night when I saw her there. In actuality, she kept order on our island, more so than our only man of the law did, or our preacher. A very kind witch with great power, she often helped us out in many terrible, life threatening situations. I had great respect for her, liked our lessons together, and by now came to have an easy, loving relationship with her. But the thought of possibly becoming an important powerful person like her frightened me.

A moment before I reached her house, it started to rain. In a great hurry, I ran toward her front door so all the good food wouldn't get wet. When I passed her window to knock on her door, I saw her standing in her house and the front door swung open by itself. Ola waved me inside her house. I wiped my feet on her outside rug and entered her house.

When I handed her the filled basket, she smiled at me. I told her, "All our village people and I are ever so grateful to have my grandma back awake."

She placed her hand on my head for just a brief moment, without saying a word. I felt something powerful leaving my body, but I felt no fear.

Then Ola thanked me for the filled basket. She handed me a lit candle and said, "Take this candle to light your way home and protect you from the rain."

When I walked out of her door, she whispered, "You did well, my child."

Amazingly, the little candle did indeed protect me from the rain and stayed lit all the way home. When I stepped inside our house, the little candle softly flickered and died. In the dark hallway of our house, I opened my hand to see if I had enough of the candle left to save and light it again at another time, but I saw absolutely nothing in my hand. Completely dry and amazed at what had just taken place, I shivered in the darkness.

Very tired, stepping over the stairs that squeaked so as not to awaken anyone, I walked up the dark stairs to go to bed. Before I reached the top of the stairs, I felt someone near, perhaps my mom waited up for me. I softly called her, but heard no answer. Carefully, I walked up onto the next stair and looked up, hoping to see my mom.

There on the last stair, in a slight shimmer of faint, yellow light stood our island witch. The sight frightened me at first and I hesitated to go toward her. When she gently waved for me to come to her, I walked up the last few steps. Exhausted and so confused of what happened that night, I reached for her.

She picked me up and carried me to my bed where my little sister already lay sleeping.

She put me down gently, covered me, and said, "You are a different child, girl, but not the devil's child, like the preacher told you. You are your grandma's child, the first-born twin that never had a chance to take one breath on this earth. They buried you in the mighty sea to have another chance at life, and here you are. You have your grandma's soul, child. Sleep with ease,"

The shimmer of light around our smiling island witch disappeared and I could no longer see her. The deep darkness took away my tired body and soul into a restful dream, where things were much simpler than in life.

No Jell-O puddings, vegetable oil, or fly screens.

Chapter 69

The devil's fingers.

On one unusually warm spring day, disaster lurked nearby, and no one on our island knew it. Most of our village people worked out in a nearby field planting cabbage seedlings into the black dirt. They laughed and talked as they finally got to plant the seedlings which they had painstakingly raised on their windowsills. This big field of cabbage could nourish many hungry souls through the next bitter winter, which would come too soon again and hold us in its powerful grip for many months.

Suddenly, everyone except the smaller children, grew quiet. People stood still and stared with solemn faces up into the sky, pointing their fingers upward for others to see what came toward us.

Dark, purplish clouds filled most of the eastern sky. One of the biggest, darkest clouds moved quickly toward us. Astounded, I watched two huge fingers reaching down out of that humongous, black cloud, touching the ocean. The big, usually grey-green ocean darkened like the cloud, and waves churned violently. It looked like the powerful, creepy fingers of the huge cloud had a great fight with our ocean.

The scary, moving dark fingers grabbed the ocean and sucked it up high. Then in its madness, and roaring with anger, it let loose of the water. The ocean fell back down, foaming and twisting in great anger, creating huge waves. Lots of violent, silvery lightning helped the mean, fearless cloud to see where it traveled. Frightened, I stood rooted to the ground.

When the seabirds in our bay took off in flight to escape the killer storm, my grandma screamed, "The devil's fingers are reaching down to kill us!"

The devil's fingers? If these were only his fingers, he must be awfully huge, perhaps as big as the whole sky. Now fear took over and I wet my pants.

"Run fast to the grain silo," Grandma's order came!

Men picked up their small children. Women hurriedly grabbed the cabbage seedlings still in their baskets and quickly ripped out some they had already planted on their way to the strong building.

In a great turmoil, all of our village dogs and our people ran for their lives. With the bold, growing storm behind us, we headed into our almost empty grain silo. The nearest building, built with big boulders, it stood two stories high and everyone considered it the strongest building on our island, besides our huge church. The men and women closed the heavy, tall wooden doors and stacked heavy equipment behind them, hoping the wild storm wouldn't rip them open.

I wanted to watch the roaring storm. Unnoticed in the dark, I sneaked up the wooden steps to near the second story of the empty silo to look out of the window. One of the frequent storms had long ago ripped out the glass from the frame. With one big jump up, I grabbed onto the iron bars of the window. Eagerly, I pulled myself up and sat down on the stone windowsill to watch the devil's fingers fighting with our sea.

Looking down from there to the silo's door to see if it remained closed, I noticed a small, white dog scratching on the wooden door of the silo, begging for entrance. Between the loud thunderclaps rolling over the ocean, I could hear the poor, small dog barking and whining desperately to get inside the silo to be with all his comrades.

I knew the adults wouldn't open the big wooden door to let him inside, and I felt so sorry for the little dog that I decided to rescue it. Hoping the storm would wait a moment to reach us, I squeezed through the window bars and climbed out onto the iron outside stairs, which led all the way up to the top of the silo and down to the ground.

I sat down on the closest stair and held onto the railing, so the wind wouldn't blow me off and throw me down to the ground. At the next short break between the loud crashes of the thunderstorm, I threw my small shovel down at the little dog to get its attention.

It worked! The little dog looked up. I whistled as loud as I could and waved for him to come upstairs. Somehow, among the wild noises of the mad storm, the little dog understood me. He hopped up the stairs, pushed back by the dangerous wind often, but he determined to make it up those stairs. As he reached the last stair, I let loose from the railing with one hand and grabbed him by the long hair on his neck.

Quickly, I stuck him inside my way too big, loose pants, with his head sticking out of my waistband. The small dog breathed very fast, but he looked at me with a happy smile. While he stayed inside my pants, I carefully slid on my buttocks over to the window I needed to climb back inside of, to safety.

Unhurt, we made it back into the silo. With great relief, I pulled the small, shaking dog out of my pants and gave him a hug. He licked my face thoroughly and repeatedly, while the storm grew louder with each deep, rolling thunder. At the next big close lightning strike, I placed the little white dog on the stairs and told him to go on down. He looked at me once more with his dark brown eyes and smiled. Then he waddled down the stairs.

One big jump up and I sat on the wide, stone windowsill again, looking out to sea. In the pitch dark, the rain mixed with hail and poured down heavily from the heavens. In the bright lightning, I saw the devil's fingers still fighting with our ocean. I wondered why his fingers sucked up the water out of the sea and then spit it back down a short while later. Perhaps our salty ocean didn't taste good to him.

What an exciting show! Almost pink lightning slammed down into our ocean simultaneously now. The whole sky lit up as though on fire. Each time the lightning hit our ocean, she sent great bursts of her water into the sky and killed the fiery lightning strike.

Amidst all the amazing commotion, I saw one of the devil's fingers creeping closer toward our bay. Just a moment later, I heard a strange, deep roar and felt as if something were sucking away the air. Before I could see what happened, a strong force of water hit me and knocked me completely off my lookout windowsill.

I landed hard on the wooden steps and slid down a few before I could grab hold of the wall of the old silo and steady myself. Shocked at what had just happened to me, I couldn't scream for help.

As quickly as the strong wall of water hit the silo and came inside of it, it disappeared. I sat on the dark stairs, wet and shaking with fear, wondering if our island witch was mad at us and had sent the devil after us. Downstairs, our village people scrambled around in the dark, calling out in fear for their loved ones.

Part of the big, old, heavy wooden door, which slightly broke when the water came into our silo, squeaked loudly under the force of the leaving water. I just sat on the old wooden step, holding on as tight as I could. I heard my mom calling me, but I felt too stunned to answer. The words wouldn't come out of my mouth.

I don't remember how long it took before I loosened my bleeding hands from the old stair, and realized that the roaring fingers of the devil had left. Rain and hail continued to pelt the old silo, but it felt as though the devil took the dangerous thunderstorm with him, dancing his wild, angry dance over the north side of our island.

Slowly, the rain and hail stopped. The deep, dark clouds

moved away and a touch of daylight came into the broken old door and the window. I saw my mom and shouted to her. A few men opened the heavy door and cautiously looked around at the sky and our pier, while all our wet village dogs ran out of the silo in excitement.

In a moment, the men decided we could safely leave the silo. Hesitantly, I stood up on my wobbling knees and followed our village people out. All our soaking wet people stepped outside and stood in complete silence. When I finally walked around the quiet group to see what they stared at, I couldn't believe what I saw.

The storm had ripped apart all our small fishing boats. Pieces of the wood lay strewn all around, as far as I could see. The devil's fingers tore off the tops of many trees and deposited them on roofs of our houses and in the vegetable gardens and fields that we so dssperately needed for our survival.

Clotheslines with unidentifiable shreds of clothing hung in bushes and twisted around chimneys. The important outhouses had mostly disappeared. Fish lay scattered all over the ground. A few lived through the ordeal, but most got torn apart. Instinctively, the women excitedly gathered their aprons up and quickly started to collect the bounty of the sea before the dogs ate every morsel. Every piece would make a fine meal. The filled soup pots would cook tonight, and nobody needed to go to sleep hungry.

On our slow walk home, I saw that the glass windows in every house had disappeared. Many strange items from people's houses lay in the dirt road. Grandma, my mom, and neighbors checked inside of every one of our older neighbors' houses to see if they had survived. By the time we arrived at our house, we could not account for two people. I hoped they rode out the angry devil's attack in a safe place.

When we arrived home, I heard my sweet dog barking up a storm in our backyard. In a hurry, I opened the gate to see why he barked. There he stood on top of our crapper. The storm had taken the walls and roof of our outhouse away. Well, at least the important part remained. I liked the idea of a fresh-air outhouse.

Our lean-to somehow managed to survive, though caved in and lying on the ground with a couple of tree branches on top of it. The two small windows on the south side of our house where my aunt and uncle lived, had lost their glass.

Our newly-planted gardens looked horrible. The storm had ripped out bushes, broken fruit trees, and had blown away most of the vegetable plants. To my grandma's delight the carrots, turnips, onions and beets remained in the ground with all their leaves ripped off.

Grandma said, "They'll grow new leaves and will recover." Our big chicken enclosure with the nesting shed had little damage. The shed just lost its roof. We found all of our chickens inside it, though very disturbed. They huddled together in one corner of the shed, on top of each other, and complained loudly. We found all the eggs in their nests broken, but were very glad the chickens survived. The new, young rooster had a hurt neck, but after taking a close look at him my mom declared, "He'll live."

So he did for many years to come, taking care of all his ladies, but he could never lift his head up straight again. It always hung to his left. The ladies didn't seem to mind it though.

After this short, quick inventory of our place, we went to look for the two missing older people. Our village people formed four groups to search for the missing ones and spread out in different directions. My family and some neighbors of ours walked toward the field where we planted the cabbage seedlings earlier.

The storm had ripped all the precious seedlings out of the ground and had blown them away. The adults stared at the empty field with grim faces.

Mom asked, "How will we make it through this winter?" She held my sister's and my hand tightly and just stood there in silence, while tears filled her eyes.

A loud, high-pitched scream caused everyone to turn toward the end of the empty field where a body lay in the dirt. Quickly everyone forgot about the slim winter we would have without enough cabbage and ran toward the body.

Next to the small, shallow ditch lay our old neighbor, Miss Emma. Her loose, white hair blew in the wind. Her terrified eyes looked up to the heavens. Her face showed great pain, but she didn't move. A pitchfork stuck deep in her belly and she lay in her own blood. Some slightly foaming, white matter still seeped from her belly.

I stood frozen to the ground in disbelief. A few feet away from her lay the old bedridden man, Mister Singer. I wondered how he got so faraway from his shack. A tree limb had smashed his face in completely. How could God have let this happen? Was the devil stronger than God, or did a loving, forgiving, gentle God even exist? At that moment, I didn't think so.

My grandma held Miss Emma's head up, closed her eyes and said, "She's dead."

My head started to spin. My stomach sent the food I had eaten long ago back up and I fell down to the ground. Silvery stars danced in front of me for a brief moment and then deep darkness took me away from this cruel scene.

I awoke inside Miss Emma's small room, lying in her bed. Still somewhat dizzy, I sat up to see what was going on. Miss Emma lay naked on her little table with her legs dangling off one end.

Grandma, my mom and some village women washed her body with a lot of soap. After they dried her body, they clothed her in her other dress, the one worn to church on Sundays and for all the important engagements. I wondered where dead people went and why you had to wash them and dress them in their good set of clothes. How could she climb out of her grave to go anywhere?

Soon the group of women decided the nighttime watches. Some village people believed there had to be two women, or girls, on watch all night long to protect the dead from the evil spirits until the sun rose. They needed to sit or stand next to the dead person and hold their hand. Others believed in taking the dead to the age-old, open chapel at the cemetery and letting the good and bad spirits fight it out and help the dead into their next life. At eleven, I decided I would never die. The thought of all those spirits was just too scary.

Tradition absolutely forbade men to enter the room where a dead person was laid out. They had the responsibility of digging the grave, finding a wagon and horse, and getting the body to the cemetery. They also had to build a simple coffin, or wrap the body in a blanket, before they let it down into its grave.

With a stern face, my grandma looked at me and announced, "Girl, it's time for you to learn how to sit with the dead. I'll teach you tonight."

Everyone agreed that we should take the first shift. Frightened, I really didn't want to learn how to sit with the dead, but since as a child I couldn't disagree with an adult, I kept quiet. To my great dismay, I walked out of the room, whistled for my dog and together we walked down to the sea to our secret place, where I worked out many problems in my young life.

After both of us climbed up to our tall, secret boulder, I sat down and Harras cuddled up in my lap. After a moment of stroking my faithful friend and watching the soothing, white combed waves rolling onto the shore, I told my dog in anger that I refused to watch over the dead tonight. Always honest with him, I told him that the thought of all those spirits frightened me. He licked my face in understanding. Feeling much better now, I took off all my clothes, and together we dove into the bitter cold water of our salty sea to take a refreshing swim.

By the time the sun sank low into the grey ocean and the sitting of the dead should begin, my dog and I floated lazily back to shore on the gentle waves of the mighty sea. Somehow, I remember that we both wore huge smiles. We found a nice, soft place beneath the tall, old pine trees to bed down for the night.

Soon the stars came out and lit the dark sky. Their twinkle

made me smile and hope none of my family would get angry at me for not wanting to watch over the dead. With my warm friend in my arms, I flew away to the magic land of dreams where they had no dead people to watch over.

The foghorn on the nearby lighthouse, with its deep warning sound, woke me. The dark still surrounded me. The tree limbs hung down low, heavy from the fog settling down on them. Little droplets of water dripped down onto me. I felt wet, cold, and very hungry. I scratched my friend's fur and told him that we should go home.

He stretched his body and shook the water from his fur. Together we ran home in the heavy, drizzling fog with the eerie sound of the foghorn following us. I often wondered if that deep, eerie sound came from someone who wanted to get out of his grave. The old ones on our island often whispered that at times, people were buried alive because they had fallen into a deep sleep and no one could detect even the slightest heartbeat. I wondered how I'd get out of my grave if that ever happened to me.

Before I could figure out that problem, I had come close enough to our house to see many people standing around with lit lanterns in their hands. They huddled close together in the drizzling fog for warmth. Slowly I walked closer to see what had happened.

I saw a healing woman from the north village of our island standing among our village people, talking and crying bitterly. I heard her say, "The devil's fingers reached down and completely took away two villages. Dead people and animals lay strewn all over the land. Even bodies, or parts of them, lay in the dirt, still wearing shreds of sailor outfits. Nobody knows where they came from!"

Our village people in complete dismay, held onto each other, trying to hide their fears and tears.

My grandma raised her hand and commanded everyone's attention. She slowly but loudly declared, "We need to go to the northern villages and see what we need to do!"

After everyone agreed, my grandma said, "Please go home and gather all the tools you have, food and sweet water. Bring matches, pots to cook in, plates, mugs and blankets to sleep under and warm clothing. John and Klaus, bring your horses and wagons. Since we can't bury the dead ones at night, because the devil's helper will grab their souls, we'll bury both of our beloved, old neighbors at sunrise and then move on to the northern villages."

Everyone knew the wisdom of her words and walked back to their own place, except my grandma. She grabbed my arm, and with an angry face, walked me over to Miss Emma, our dead neighbor. There she smiled at the two older girls and told them to go home. My grandma pointed to a chair for me to sit in. I sat down in a hurry so as not to make her angrier. There I sat, next to Miss Emma's body still lying on her short table, with her legs hanging down on one end.

The slightly-flickering white candle near her head made ghostly shadows dance across her face. Grandma took my hand and placed it on top of Miss Emma's folded hands, then she told me to pray for the entrance of Miss Emma's soul into heaven. She handed me her bible, showed me which pages to read silently and sat down next to me.

Miss Emma's hands felt so cold. Blood no longer moved through them. This whole thing scared me to death. I didn't even know where heaven was or the true nature of a soul. Since at this moment I didn't believe in God and His heaven, I silently asked our island witch repeatedly to please send Miss Emma to the right place so my grandma wouldn't punish me for messing up the sitting over the dead.

A slight, faint light appeared, just barely hanging over Miss Emma's dead body for a brief moment. I took that as an answer from our island witch that she'd take Miss Emma's soul to its right place. I thanked her many times and grew at ease. I pretended to read the pages in the bible my grandma told me to while holding

Miss Emma's cold, stiff hands. I felt awfully tired, but every time I dozed off, my grandma gave me a slight kick with her elbow to prevent me from falling asleep.

Finally, the first strong rays of the sun crept up from the grey, sleepy ocean and started to suck away the heavy fog. Grandma took my hand off Miss Emma's dead, folded hands, patted my head and told me with a smile to go home. In sort of a daze, I walked the few steps home, planning never to die out of fear of where the spirits might take me.

In the meantime, I found our village people very busy in front of our house. The two wagons with two horses tied in front of each of them, which my grandma had asked for, stood waiting. People had loaded all sorts of tools, cooking utensils, food and bundles onto the wagons. They had carried the old, bedridden people into the village's big barn and laid them on the hay and straw, which the owner had stored there for the winter. Two women, one of them my Aunt Hilde, and two girls my age, walked into the barn to take care of them while the rest of us made ready to leave soon.

Aunt Hilde carried a basket with bottles from my grandma's cellar. The old and sick always wanted her to take care of them, no matter if we had to work on the north side of our island and didn't come home for days, or if we celebrated a wedding for a few days away from our village. Perhaps she sang and danced for them all night. She sure had a talent for that, or perhaps she shared some of the liquor with them.

By the time the sun smiled over our island, our caravan was ready to leave our village. The very small children, not yet able to walk the two hours to the north side of our island, sat on top of the tools and supplies in one wagon. The two crazy, dangerous twin girls seldom seen outside their shack, sat tied down on top of the other wagon next to the driver. They screamed, scratched and kicked each other as though trying to kill each other. I felt sad for both of them.

Grandma always said their birth resulted from our island

witch's revenge. Their father had done our witch wrong. In the deep, ice-cold winter, before their birth, she had asked him to bring some wood to her house and he refused. During the next fall, after the birth of the mentally ill children, he left his shack one night. Someone found him days later in a cabbage field without his hands. Some people believed the foxes had chewed his hands off, but others strongly shook their heads in disbelief. They whispered of the witch's revenge.

Our preacher had sent his older son to the north part of our island the night before. He had some emotional problems, but no one considered him dangerous. He had a habit of walking toward his destination for a short while, then would abruptly turn around and walk back and end up close to where he had started out. He often took days to reach his destination on our small island. All of our island dogs absolutely avoided getting near him. When they saw him, they ran in the other direction. Yes, my grandma knew. She blamed the preacher that his son had been born this way because he didn't believe in our witch's power. Mom heartily agreed with her.

The bodies of Miss Emma and the old, bedridden man, lay on top of all sorts of supplies on the second wagon. The old man had worked at the pier for many years helping unloading the fish before his arthritis-stricken body could no longer slide the filled, wooden boxes over to the scale. People still respected him though and often brought a fish or two to his shack.

With my grandma in front of this caravan and our village dogs around us ready to run, we began to move. I pleadingly asked my mom to stay home today because I was so awful tired and hungry.

Mom turned to me and said sharply, "If you had obeyed your grandma last night and had taken the first watch of the dead with her, you'd have eaten your evening meal and had a fine night of sleep. Now, walk on and don't complain."

Before long, we reached our village cemetery. Without a long ceremony, the villagers laid Miss Emma and the old crippled man,

474

wrapped up in sheets, side by side into the same grave. We didn't sing at this funeral. While our preacher said a prayer to his God to take the dead ones in His arms and into the heavens, a few strong men with their shovels hurriedly closed the grave. The usual fine meeting after a funeral, where everyone got together, brought food, drinks and talked about the old days and ways, didn't happen this time. We had to move on to the north side of our island to help our neighbors.

Somehow, I glanced over to the centuries-old, sorry looking chapel for the dead. There, in the gaping entrance, stood our island witch. Her presence reassured me. Silently, with my eyes closed, I asked her one more time to show these two souls where they needed to go. If their souls came back to haunt us, my grandma would be awfully mad at me for doing wrong at the sitting by the dead. When I opened my eyes and looked at the chapel's entrance again, our island witch had disappeared. One small, black string lazily dangled from one of the old stones of the chapel's entry.

My grandma's voice brought me back to the moment. "Let's move on now!"

Slowly, mostly in silence, we moved away from the cemetery. I could barely keep pace with our caravan. I felt awfully tired and weak. Each time I stumbled, my mom's quick jerk on my arm brought me back awake enough so I wouldn't fall onto the dirt road. How I hated to have to walk.

Muffled screams of the women in our group, soon interrupted our silent trip and served to wake me from my fatigue. We had arrived at the first, tiny settlement past our village. The women screamed at what they saw, or rather what they didn't see.

The devil's fingers had taken the farmer's entire house, his stalls, and the six shacks of his workers. We couldn't find a single human or animal, alive or dead. Something had ripped away every treetop and whisked them away. And no vegetation remained in the fields. The devil's long, crooked fingers had ripped everything out and taken it away.

Only two things remained to remind us that people had once lived here: the stone oven where people baked their bread, and the old, iron pump over the dugout well. I stood there bewildered and scared, wondering why this had happened. After our preacher said a short prayer, our sorrowful group moved silently on its way to the northern end of our small island. I read the fear in the faces of the adults. Some men crunched their fists together in anger and sent them up to the heavens.

Suddenly, the small children on the second wagon began to giggle and pointed to the back of our small caravan. Everyone stopped and turned back to see a heavily pregnant, domestic sow trying to catch up with our caravan. Angry, she squealed up a storm.

For a brief moment, all the sad, scared faces of the adults wore smiles. When the angry sow reached our group, she stopped and squealed even louder. Someone fetched a bucket of water from the wagon and she drank nearly all of it. I could see her unborn piglets moving inside of her belly and milk slowly dripping from her swollen teats.

Our midwife took a good look at the sow and said, "She'll give birth tonight. We'd better take her with us. Her offspring might help us live through the winter."

The strong, young men of our village gathered around the pregnant sow, and under the supervision of our only man of the law who also raised pigs, laid many blankets beside her and pushed the exhausted sow onto those blankets. With their great strength, the young men lifted the sow up and into the wagon where the small children sat.

The older girls giggled and uttered sighs of astonishment about the strength of those fine looking young men. They in return smiled at the girls. The small children laughed and tried to touch the sow, but when she moved a little, they quickly retrieved their hands. The tired sow eventually closed her eyes and went to sleep. I wondered how she survived and where she came from.

As we slowly moved north, we saw no change in the destruction. Even some of the big trees had been ripped from the ground, or just cut off a few feet above the ground and blown away. We found no animals in the fields and no people. I wondered if the devil had taken them with him also.

I found the quiet so very eerie, and looked up to the heavens with many questions in my heart. But before I could find an answer in the happy white clouds above me, our caravan stopped. We had arrived at the northern part of our island. I could see the steep coast from here and the calm ocean behind it.

To our left and to our right a little ways, used to stand two small settlements. In one lived the fishermen with their families, and in the other, a farmer family with all his workers. In the middle, between these small villages, they had built a tiny clapboard chapel in which to share a simple Sunday prayer.

A small graveyard with huge oak trees had surrounded the chapel. Now, we stood there in fear, staring at the destroyed surroundings. We knew we stood at the small cemetery because the graves had heavy boulders for headstones which the storm had not taken. The very tall oak trees, ripped from the ground, and dead themselves now, covered the graves.

We found not a shred of the clapboard chapel anywhere. I felt thankful the devil had not ripped the dead ones from their graves and taken them with him, but I felt steaming mad at both God and the devil for this disaster. Shaken with fear, I held on tightly to my mom's big hand.

Amidst the extreme silence of our dismayed village people, we suddenly heard a soft, faint sound of a crying baby. I quit breathing and held my hand to my ear. In just a second, I heard the cry again as did many adults. Mom held my hand tightly while we walked in the direction of the crying baby. With the next cry, I discovered in shock that the cry came from below where we stood, from a grave, covered by two huge, fallen oak trees.

Fear ran through me like lightning. Had someone buried the

baby alive, like the old ones whispered happened now and then by mistake? Everyone stood glued to the spot in fear, looking down between the huge, fallen oak trees, waiting for another cry. After an intense moment of listening, we heard a frightened, weak call from a woman deep below us.

"Help, please help us!"

The sound of her voice coming from below us, completely freaked me out. Had someone buried a mother and child while still alive? I let go of my mom's hand. My shaking knees gave away and I sat in the dirt.

The adults answered the voice. "We've come to help you!"

A big, relieved cry came from a woman inside the deep grave. Quickly, all our village people, under the instruction of our sawmill owner, grabbed hold of one of the huge uprooted oak trees and with their combined strength, moved it off a little to the side of the grave. The woman's pleading voice grew much louder. People walked close to the grave and looked down into it between the tree limbs. I wondered when they would get their shovels to dig out the buried ones. Relieved smiles came over their faces. Two of the young, handsome men of our village climbed down into the grave. Still with struggling knees, I stood up and walked closer to get a better look. I felt very ashamed of my wet and muddy underpants, but I didn't even notice that I had urinated in them until this moment.

When I looked down into the grave, the sight happily surprised me. Someone had dug out the grave, but didn't cover up the people inside it. They must have sought refuge there during the terrible storm.

Slowly, I saw a year-old crying baby passed up out of the grave. My mom took it in her arms, gently talked to it, and soothed its fear. Then, the men helped two little boys with tear-reddend eyes and dirty faces out of the grave. Someone took their hands and walked them away from this sight.

One of the young men from our village called from inside the grave for a ladder. Quickly, the men brought a ladder from the supply wagon and carefully let it down into the grave. With much encouragement from the people below, a very pregnant woman slowly crawled up the ladder and out of the grave. When she stepped off the ladder onto the ground, she held her belly with both hands, and her painful face brought our midwife to her side in a hurry.

Next, out climbed a haggard old woman, smiling and waving her fist at the heavens. Repeatedly she said, "You darn, mean devil. I told you I wasn't going with you!"

When she stepped off the ladder onto the ground of the cemetery, she took a big stone and hurled it up high into the sky with a very loud, angry scream. At that moment, seeing the power she had to hurl the stone so far up into the sky that it didn't return to earth, I wondered if perhaps she was related to our island witch. I hoped she killed the devil with that stone.

Next out of the grave crawled two grim men. They sat on the ground and silently buried their faces in their laps. After that, the men freed a rooster with four hens from the grave. They all kind of flew and ran with loud complaints, as fast as they could, away from the cemetery. I wondered if they would ever return.

After a silent moment, one of our young village men came out of the grave with a shivering dog in his arms. When he sat her down on the ground, I noticed her swollen teats. She looked inside the grave and barked awfully loud. Within a moment, the dog's fierce bark turned into a whine. Our other young village man appeared above ground with his shirt in one hand full of little, squeaking puppies.

One of the older men stood up and said, "As we started to close our father's grave, the devil's fingers reached down in anger. The first touch of his fingers picked us up and threw us inside the grave on top of our dead father, with the chickens and the dog following right behind us. We heard the other people at the graveside screaming with fear. Then the mad, howling storm uprooted the huge trees, and with an earthshaking noise, they fell on top of us.

"It felt horrible to be imprisoned in the dark grave, but it surely saved us from the wild, killing fingers of the devil. We sat our dead father up in one corner of the grave so we'd have room to sit down, even though his old bones creaked in disagreement. In silence, we shivered with fear and tried to cuddle the little ones asleep while we waited out the devil's curse.

"After the raging storm moved out to sea, we tried our hardest all night long, to lift the trees enough to get out of the grave, but we couldn't budge them. We stood on top of each other, so our village people might hear our screams of help outside the grave, but no one answered.

"Ever so exhausted, we huddled down in the small grave to gain our strength back so we could try to get out in the morning. That horrible night, inside the small, dark grave, the dog gave birth with just a whine now and then. I held the small, wet bodies in my hand and begged God repeatedly to get us out of the grave until I eventually dozed off.

"Then I felt my wife's nails digging painfully into my hand as she whispered in my ear, 'I'm in labor.' I panicked and in desperation screamed for help again and again, as loudly as I could. We hoped someone would hear us and help us out, but nothing worked until you came. We're all very thankful and deeply in debt to you!"

Then he took the puppies and walked away with the mama dog following him, toward the wagon where his wife lay, about to give birth. He laid the tiny puppies gently on the ground and the mama dog carefully carried them away one by one into the stripped fields. I watched her scratching out a shallow place in the dirt. She then laid all her six pups inside it, settled down next to them and let them nurse. Our village dogs, even though they watched her closely, had the manners to keep their distance from her and her newborn pups.

A few painful, earthshaking screams from the wagon, where the pregnant woman lay, caused everyone to stand still and look toward the wagon. The women's motionless, somber faces reminded me of faces at a funeral. To everyone's great relief, a very small, soft cry came from the wagon next. Bright, warm smiles filled the somber faces of the small crowd now, and everyone walked slowly toward the wagon to see the newborn baby.

The shaking father proudly held his newborn up high for everyone to see. "It's a girl! We'll name her Elise after the great woman who organized and led the caravan here."

My grandma's eyes twinkled and she smiled proudly when she heard they named the newborn girl after her.

All the women admired the newborn baby and told the parents how pretty she was. I didn't see her as pretty at all. She had a red, wrinkled face with many tiny pimples, and no hair at all. And, she kept her eyes squeezed shut while she screamed. She clenched both of her small fists tightly, and she moved them as though ready to fight.

Politely, I told the smiling parents, just as all the other women did, "You have a beautiful baby."

Before the women had finished admiring the newborn, the men had emptied the supply wagon and formed groups to search the grounds for survivors. Grandma told an older girl to take care of the very young ones and all the other children to go and collect lots of firewood. She reminded them, "Without the wood we'll have no food to eat tonight."

With happy laughter, they ran to gather firewood, glad to help.

The women decided among themselves where to lay down the bedding and what to cook for the evening meal.

I heard my mom say, "We're having a measly meal tonight with the few supplies we brought." Then she looked at a few older boys who stood around admiring the big trees that lay on the graves and called them over to her.

She said, "Go and find some sticks and dig anything edible out of the ground that the devil has left behind."

They didn't smile when they left to do their chore, but they nodded and walked away toward the stripped fields.

While an old man from our village left to untie the horses and take them to find some food, my grandma studied the empty grounds around the cemetery of the two very small twin villages.

I walked over to her and asked, "What are you looking for?"

My grandma said, "I'm looking for the exact route the devil took the people and their belongings on."

I didn't really know what she meant, but I stared at the ground, looking for a trail, as she did.

Suddenly my grandma abruptly stopped, pointed at the dirt and said, "There, you see? That's the way he took the people, their belongings and animals, right into the mighty ocean."

I couldn't see what my grandma saw, but I agreed with her because my grandma was never wrong. Slowly, holding onto some boulders, now and then slipping in the wet dirt, we climbed down the steep coast to the sandy shore. All the way down, my grandma reassured me that the devil had taken his bounty this way. When we reached the soft, white shore, she took her hands and felt the salty seawater.

With her eyes closed she said, "The devil no longer controls the sea. We need to wait here, because some of the things he took, the sea will most likely bring back to this sandy shore." Then she asked me, "Go back to the camp and tell the others to come down by dark."

After climbing back up the steep coast, I swiftly walked over to where we made camp to deliver my grandma's important news. Before I reached the camp, I saw some of our village men carrying two people over their shoulders. I hoped they were still alive.

All the women busily cooked over their small fires which they had set up next to the cemetery. They had placed the bedding all around the wagons, and someone had built a makeshift pen underneath one wagon to temporarily house the sow and her expected piglets.

As two strong men extended the grave of the dead old man quite a bit, fear crept up inside of me. Slowly I walked closer to the graveyard. There, on the ground next to the gravediggers, laid dead bodies. I stopped walking and stared at all the dead bodies in disbelief. I counted eleven bodies of different sizes. I had never seen so many dead people together. Small, silvery stars started to dance before me and I felt sick to my stomach again.

A harsh embrace from my mom chased away the stars in front of me. She held my hand, walked me over to the warming fires and tried to cheer me up. She pointed to a group of people who warmed themselves over a close fire.

She said, "Our men rescued those people from a root cellar at the farmer's house in the twin village. The devil's fingers ripped away the farmer's fine house, knocked over the tall stone chimney and dropped it down over the root cellar's door." With a proud smile my mom said, "Our men freed the door from the huge stones and helped the people out. They even brought enough stones here to temporarily set up an oven to bake bread in."

Though thankful for their rescue, the image of all the dead people kept dancing around in my mind.

As I told my mom of Grandma's important news, a group of our older village boys came toward us. They dragged an injured cow and a very upset, bleeding horse along with them. One of the boys carried a screaming piglet in his arms. Two limping dogs followed the group into our camp.

Right away, everyone walked over to them to see what they could do to help those animals. At that moment, I felt just too exhausted to get up. I lay down by the warming fire and watched the wet wood spitting out many colorful, hot sparks. In my dream, the fiery sparks turned into the devil's reddish hot fingers and they reached down to grab me.

My own loud scream woke me and Mom ran toward me. She

shook me and asked, "What's the matter?"

After I told her about my horrible dream, she held me for a moment and said, "I'll never let the devil kill you." She soothed my fear and stilled my tears, like so many times before.

Once the people had taken care of the injured animals, they gathered around the fires and shared what little food they had. My mom's hot soup tasted great, but it had too little solid food floating in it to fill my stomach. I desperately hoped that we'd have more to eat in the morning.

When my mom told everyone about my grandma's prediction, most adults grabbed their bedding and walked toward the beach to join my grandma. My mom told me, "Stay with the young children for the evening." Then she took the rest of the thin soup, poured it into my grandma's cup, grabbed her blanket and joined the group of people that walked toward the beach.

I wanted to go with them but knew I had to obey my mom's orders without complaining, or making a face to show my displeasure. After walking around the small camp's bed site and realizing that all the young children had fallen asleep, I crawled beneath my blanket next to my little sister and quickly fell asleep with my stomach still growling for more food.

My dream took me to a big soup pot filled to the brim with steaming pea soup and heavily loaded with big chunks of potatoes, vegetables and real big pieces of meat. Next to it, stood a huge plate full of sliced bread and a smiling man, who dished out the soup into very large mugs. Hungrily, I ate the especially great tasting soup and bread. Every time I took the last bite of the thick slice of dark bread and the last spoonful of the delicious, filling pea soup, the plate of bread and the big mug of soup refilled itself. This sure felt like heaven.

In the first, still very dim, grey light of the early misty morning, someone stumbled onto me and I awoke. For a brief moment, I thought the devil had come back to fetch me. When the child who had fallen on me stood back up, I realized that our small camp had awakened and was preparing for something.

Men and women carried all sorts of tools, blankets, pots and wooden poles. In great excitement, they walked hurriedly toward the beach. One quick look around me told me that most of the little children remained asleep. The midwife tended to the slightly moaning, heavily pregnant sow. Unsure of myself, but hopeful, I walked over to her to ask her if she could watch the young, sleeping children so I could go down to the beach to see what caused all the excitement. Before I reached her, she turned her head toward me and waved for me to come to her in a hurry. With a few quick steps, I stood at her side.

The sow squealed fiercely, and the midwife held the first pink, tiny piglet in her hands. She told me to hold the tiny newborn, which I did. It just lay there in my hands, limp and not breathing, though blood ran through the umbilical court into its tiny, warm body.

The midwife said, "We have to hurry to take the piglets off the umbilical cord. The sow is giving birth too fast to chew through the cords to free the tiny piglets!"

In a great hurry, she wiped the first piglet's face free of debris, laid it down on the ground, held the umbilical court in two places, and asked me to cut it right in the middle while the next piglet was born. I followed all her orders quickly, and we had twelve pink, and one black screaming piglet on our hands.

The midwife looked up at me, smiled and said, "We did it. We saved all those piglets!"

At that moment, while the sow slowly got up to take a good, long sniff at her small, screaming piglets, one more very tiny piglet fell out of her, about half the size of the others.

The midwife wiped its face, and I cut its cord. I saw its tiny heart beating for a moment, but then it quit. The last, smallest, pink and black piglet didn't breathe. Our midwife gently massaged the tiny, lifeless body and breathed into its mouth, but she couldn't revive it. She handed me the lifeless body and told me to take it to the dog, which had just given birth to a litter. She said, "It'll make a good meal for the nursing dog."

Overwhelmed by the birth of all the piglets, I just sat there, holding the tiny piglet and stared at the lifeless body in disbelief. I didn't feel sad, or happy, at the moment. I didn't feel or think at all. In a bit of a daze, I wondered why the tiny piglet had been born if it never even had a chance to live.

As ordered by our midwife, I took the soft, tiny body to the nursing dog. With a soft whisper of farewell and a tear rolling from my eyes, I handed the soft body to the dog and quickly ran away to avoid watching the dog eat the little piglet that never had a chance to live.

I ran toward the sea to sit beside one of the huge boulders to have a good cry, but before I reached the coast, someone shouted at me. "Look out there! Elise is right, the sea is returning something!"

A few hurried steps and I stood on the edge of the steep coastline. In the dim, early light of the still dense fog, I stared out to sea in uttermost disbelief. The ocean, covered with all sorts of debris, slowly floated its load back toward the beach. The moving fog looked as though it danced on top of and around the floating planks, parts of houses and ever so many pieces of broken wood and torn clothing. It made an eerie, silent sight.

Not one of the people near me said a word. Then, someone grabbed my hand and helped me down the steep coast. Arriving safely at the beach, I ran into my grandma's waiting arms. She lifted me up and hugged me gently. We sat down next to each other in the cold sand, holding hands and watching the entangled debris slowly move closer toward us.

Soon, the welcomed sun rose. She sent down her hot rays that began to lick away the dense fog. With the disappearing fog, we stood up to better see what floated toward the beach. In awe, my grandma and I stared out to sea. Debris floated on the surface for as far as we could see to both sides and in front of us.

People gathered around us and asked her what to do. I heard seagulls screaming from faraway. I pulled on my grandma's hand to get her attention to tell her about the seagulls. When she stopped talking and looked down at me, I excitedly told her to listen. Sure enough, we heard the cries of the seagulls again. This time, everyone around us heard their harsh screams. People looked out to the ocean and smiled when they saw a big flock of our seabirds in a great feeding frenzy amidst the huge floating island of debris.

When the wind awoke and started to move the wide ocean's body, the waves brought the strange island of debris closer to us. What a horrible scene. Parts of human and animal bodies lay on some of the wood or floated among it. To the delight of the many returning species of seabirds, plenty of dead or injured fish floated among the debris.

On top of a partial wooden roof clung a dozen or so very upset chickens. Down below the roof, a cat hung onto the wood for dear life. Ducks of all sort crowded onto a humongous mast of a sailing ship. A horse's head lay in a wooden box, its dark eyes staring up to the heavens. A few rats gnawed at the bodiless head.

Grandma let go of my hand, told me to stay on the beach, and waded into the cold seawater with all the rest of our island people. Slowly, like in a bad dream, I climbed up the steep coast a little and sat down near a small bush. From there, I watched our island people rescue the live animals and pull out as much wood as they could to feed the fires, or perhaps build a shack or barn.

Though I sat watching my family and neighbors struggling in the sea, the horrible scene didn't seem real to me. I felt, as if I watched a terrible story unfold from a thousand miles away. I didn't cry. I just held on to the small bush next to me for dear life and dug my feet into the soft sand.

My faithful dog, who jumped into my lap and licked my face with all the exciting energy of a young dog, brought me back to reality. I lost my grip on the small bush, and both of us slid down to the beach. When I stood up, I saw all the adults pointing out to sea. A few men started to wade out through the debris to a broken lifeboat. I saw four sailors in their torn, blue uniforms, hanging on to a partial lifeboat and waving frantically.

Not far from them floated a part of the front of a ship. It had the name *Lore* painted on it in blue. I knew this ship as a merchant marine training ship. I had seen it many times sailing proudly past our island with all its white sails standing out above the dark, blue grey ocean. Some young boys of our island, just out of basic school at the age of fourteen or so, had hired on for their sailor's education on that ship.

They had to work hard during the daytime and often through the night without pay. They just worked so awfully hard for one year on the school ship to earn their merchant marine certificates. With that certification, they could hope to hire onto one of those huge vessels that sailed so faraway, even to the other side of the world. Though this great disaster scared me deeply, I still wished I were a boy and able to go and hire on to one of those great ships to see the rest of the world.

In no time at all, some of our men reached the broken lifeboat, pulled it onto the beach, and the sailors climbed out onto solid ground. Exhausted, but ever so happy, they embraced the men and women on the beach and thanked them for their rescue. Then they just fell down onto the soft sand and cried.

I wanted to go to the young boys and ease their pain, but was too shy to do so. If they had been girls or women, I'd have walked over and tried to comfort them, perhaps just hold their hand and listen to them, as my grandma did to so many people who came over to our house, crying, sick or sad about something.

When I looked back to the broken lifeboat, I saw our men untie two bodies from the wooden crates behind the broken lifeboat and carry them over to the pile of human remains. I don't know why, but somehow that shook me deeply, and I ran down to my grandma to help in the rescue. She stood amidst the debris, up to her knees in the cold sea, sorting out the different incoming species of fowl.

She gave the injured ones with a chance to live to some women to carry on to our island and set free. Grandma took the badly injured ones and deposited them into a sack which she called soup pot. When she saw me standing next to her, she handed me a basket and filled it with dead birds. Then she told me, "Go and feed the surviving dogs, cats and the pig."

A woman with an empty sack relieved our neighbor who had a sack full of soup pot birds. She smiled at me and said, "Let's go together."

She didn't have much movement or protest coming from her sack, but blood slowly oozed from it. I felt so awfully sorry for those dying birds and wondered why the fingers of the devil hurt, killed and destroyed so much. Where was God?

After the two of us climbed up the steep coast, I took one more look down at the sad, shocking sight of the calm sea and beach with all the debris floating toward our island. In terrible shock, I spotted the small steeple from the twin settlement's chapel floating far out at sea. There, at the very top, two small children clung desperately to the wood. One brave woman held onto one side of the steeple and kicked her feet hard to steer the small, broken tower toward our island.

I screamed down to the busy rescuers and pointed out to sea toward the floating wooden steeple. Quickly, a few men waded, and then swam to the steeple. They tied a rope to it and with heavy strokes pulled it toward land.

Thankfully, the woman and the children reached our beach. My eyes swept over the huge island of debris one more time, before I decided to walk to our campsite. What a horrible disaster our poor island had endured.

The woman with the sack full of soup pot birds had left, and I walked along in deep thought, with my basket full of dead birds, to our camp in a strange and frightened mood. Tears of relief from this gruesome day did not come yet.

Without paying attention, I handed out the dead birds to the hungry dogs. Then, I sat down on the ground next to my mom. She stayed busy gutting out the headless birds a man handed her. Other women dipped the different birds in a kettle of steaming water, plucked out all the feathers and threw the birds into the soup pot. The damp, little grey cat had followed me and now ate her fill of the discarded insides of the birds. She then walked over to me, and together, we snuggled up under my blanket next to the roaring fire with the huge, boiling soup pot on it.

I gently stroked the shivering cat and closed my eyes. Quickly, she grew into a huge, but friendly lion. I hopped on top of her and with strong, fast leaps, she took me away from this horrible disaster. Soon, she spread her wings, and we laughed and flew among the gentle, smiling clouds.

My mom's hard shake ended my escape dream, and I awoke to a very dark night. Heavy clouds hung in the sky, hiding the stars and the moon. Mom handed me a big mug with some great smelling soup. That got my attention in a hurry.

Quickly, I sat up, took the steaming mug with a smile, and thanked her. How great it tasted with all the meat and dumplings in it. With my second spoonful, I noticed with delight that it had plenty of carrots, potatoes and onions in it too. The boys must have found those in the nearby fields which the devil had stripped of all the top growth.

Slowly, the little grey cat crawled out from beneath my blanket. Though now completely dry, she still shivered. After I let her lick up several spoonfuls of my warm soup, she quit shivering and crawled back underneath my blanket. I was awfully glad to have her near me and hoped we could take her home with us.

With all the fires going around our camp, I could see people building shacks from the gathered wood. A few men dug a very long grave in the small cemetery. Someone had fixed the broken steeple of the small chapel and placed it where the chapel had once stood.

I wondered if God had sent this steeple back to beg for forgiveness, or if the devil had sent it back with a big laugh. I wished for someone I could talk to, but all the adults kept busy digging, building, preparing for bed, or talking to each other. Sadly, I picked up the stray grey cat and my blanket and walked toward our sleeping area. Finally, covered up with my blanket and telling the grey cat all my feelings, tears of relief ran down my cheeks. She licked my face, and before long, I had cried myself to sleep.

For many more days, the scene at the beach remained the same. We rescued what drifted in alive. We buried the dead. We built shacks or fixed up partially surviving structures. We built a large chicken enclosure and the hens began to lay eggs. The pig got fat on all the dead fish, and her piglets gave us quite a time. They figured out a different way to get out of their makeshift pen every moment, then they ran around screaming for their mom. Those little piglets sure kept the young boys busy trying to catch them.

I worked hard, like everyone else. Some days I carried wood from the beach up to our camp all day long. When my mom saw how tired this all made me, she told me to help with the cooking and baking. That was a great relief, but I wished we could go home soon.

Finally, one early morning, the huge island of debris shrank to merely a few planks and wooden boxes of canned goods. By midday, our calm, grey ocean had subsided to a mirror of water again, all clean and precious to look at. I stood on top of the steep coast staring down in disbelief. I saw absolutely nothing to fish out of the water anymore.

That day my grandma declared, "It's time for a holiday!"

I believe the children's happy screams sounded louder than the excited barks of our surviving island dogs.

Somehow, someone formed groups, and most of the children, except for the very young, hurried away from our camp, followed by running dogs. Even the hammering and pounding of building the shacks stopped. Solemnly, the adults walked over to the long grave, which they had only partially covered to keep the smell of rotting flesh away from our camp and to make it easy to add any more bodies if they needed to. Not ready mentally to celebrate yet, I respectfully followed the adults.

Our preacher stood at the graveside with his small, worn out bible in his hand. His clean, black robe swayed softly in the wind. After everyone gathered, I noticed that the preacher wore the only clean and intact piece of cloth in this group. How sad and dirty we looked. I know my family didn't bring a second set of clothes on this trip, and I'm sure no one else did either. We considered ourselves lucky to have two sets of clothing to our name besides our Sunday dress. We brought our coat and one pair of rubber boots with us. Many people weren't so lucky, but my mom, a great seamstress, sewed all our clothes from hand-me-downs or scraps, by hand.

After a few words from the preacher about hell and heaven, the men started to close the long grave. The rescued sailor boys began to sing "Ave Maria," but didn't know the words after the first line. I took my grandma's hand and began to sing. She joined in right away, and so did many people. Those who didn't know the words hummed along, and it turned into a very special, almost festive burial.

With the long grave completely covered, a very old man with a white beard pushed a wooden cross into the soft, black dirt. He had deeply carved the number 48 into it in big, bold letters. He removed his cap and stood silently with his shaking, crippled hands folded and his head bowed. His lips moved, but no words came out of his mouth. When he slowly limped away from the huge grave, the rest of the weary people went back to finish the repairs on the farmer's house and the extension of the pig's enclosure.

On our last evening there, we sat together and relaxed by a

roaring fire, glad to go home the next morning. The men smoked green cigars and told wild stories about their times at sea. They always included pretty mermaids, half fish and half human, combing their long hair and singing enticing songs in their stories.

I had asked my grandma long ago about those mermaids, and she simply said, "A ship full of lonely men, a keg full of strong rum, and soon the mermaids and other fine illusions rose from their drunken minds."

I didn't know what the word illusion meant, but from the sailors' stories, I figured it must mean a fine dance, where they held the pretty mermaids close to their bodies and asked them to spend the night with them.

The freshly caught fish cooked in the fire on long metal sticks, dripping fat into the burning wood, making the fire angrily spit out red hot sparks in all directions.

My mom asked the sailor boys, "Please tell us all once more, before we part, what happened that night when the devil's fingers reached down from the heavens to grab your school ship."

The tallest of the boys stood up and began to speak. "Some of us saw the storm coming over your island and we alerted our captain. He immediately ordered us to lower all sails, turn the ship to head into the storm, and lower all four anchors. Everyone on board ran to their stations to quickly follow the captain's orders. The sea grew rough, and the storm came upon us in a great hurry. I had climbed only half-way up on the main mast to lower the sails when I saw the devil's fingers reaching down.

"The whole sky, a dark purple color now, surrounded us, and lightning crashed down all around us. Our ship rocked sideways and screeched as though it would fall apart any second. The men and boys on board screamed desperately, while huge walls of twisting water washed them overboard. Repeatedly the waves hammered our broken ship, ripping it apart with every pounding wave.

"Then the devil's enormous finger reached straight down

toward our ship, bombarding us with all sorts of debris, but I couldn't make out what it consisted of in the dark. The storm ripped the sails to shreds, and parts of torn ropes flew around me, while I clung to the mast for dear life. One long rope wrapped itself around me and actually tied me to the mast. I could only hear the awful, roaring noise of the angry devil's finger. When the lightning lit up the sky, I saw the high walls of seawater crashing down mercilessly on our helpless ship. I knew then that my life would end at any second. My family's faces danced through my mind while the rough sea tried to capsize our ship.

"All of a sudden, the devil's fingers lifted our broken school ship out of the ocean and turned it around several times in midair. Then, as though it didn't want our ship, it let go of her. She crashed down into the wild ocean and broke apart with loud, wailing noises. The mast I clung to broke apart as well, but the rope held me tightly to the mast. With its great power, the devil threw me with the partial mast down way below sea level. In my mind, I thanked my mom for raising me and kissed my sweet little sister goodbye.

"With my last air escaping from my lungs, I prepared to die. I closed my eyes and said a prayer for God to watch over my family. At that moment my stump of the wooden mast hit the bottom of the grey ocean with great force. In a split second, we surged upward. I don't remember reaching the surface or taking my first, struggling breath. I only remember that my schoolmates shook me and slapped me enough to come to myself. Then, they untied me from the rodent polluted mast and helped me into their broken lifeboat. There we floated slowly amidst a huge island of all sorts of debris, acres of pieces of wood, dead fish, birds, and many dead bodies. We had no idea where the sea would take us, but we were ever so glad to escape death. I held my bleeding, injured feet in the saltwater for a while to clean out the wounds.

"One of us stayed awake all the time in hopes of spotting land. We ate some of the raw, dead fish to still our hunger, but the thirst bothered us most. All the salty water around us seemed to smile at us as our throats grew drier and drier. Then finally, on the third day we saw land, your island. We took our broken boards that served as paddles and steered our part of a lifeboat with great hope toward you."

Tears ran down his cheeks when he thanked all of us for their rescue and our hospitality. Gently, he sat down next to the other sailor boys, who held their heads low so as not to show their tears.

Someone played a harmonica while others started to sing to the familiar tune of Lorelei, the beautiful mermaid who lures sailors onto the rocks with her enchanting songs. Their ships would crash onto the high, dangerous rocks, and of course, all of them would die.

Grandma had told me years ago that Lorelei was also one of the enchanting mermaids. I had often sat out on the last part of our stone walk that led into the deep ocean and looked for those mermaids, but sadly, I never saw even one. I figured that perhaps they didn't show up because I wasn't a man. Since the mermaids were all females, I decided to become one.

When I asked my grandma how to become a mermaid, she abruptly told me, "Girl, get that idea out of your mind right now!"

Well, so much for that dream.

One of our neighbors took the cooked herrings off the iron rods and placed them on the wooden stump which we used as a table. With a great smile she said, "We have enough fish so everyone can have a whole one, even the children."

My mom stood up, walked over to the makeshift table with a plate, and fetched us each a big herring. They weighed so much that she had to hold the plate with two hands. I could barely wait to take my first bite.

The farmer from one of the twin settlements came around with a big bucket full of milk. He ladled some of the fresh milk into everyone's cup and thanked them for all their help. His wife handed each of us a huge piece of freshly baked bread. She too, smiled and thanked every last one of us for our help. Then someone's grandma walked by and placed an apple on each of our plates. This seemed just too good to be true. I had a whole plate full of such wonderful food and even fresh, steaming milk with all the cream floating on top of it. I couldn't remember ever having such a luxury to drink. Mom bought us the cheap milk, the one with all the cream taken out of it, whenever she could afford to spend a few pennies. We didn't even know, at that time, of the health benefits of fat-free milk.

Anxious to start eating the feast in front of me, I started to look around for my grandma or someone else to stand up and say the usual things before all of us could start eating. I didn't see my grandma anywhere, and nobody stood up to say some words so we could start eating. All the people just sat on the ground, silently staring into the dark night. I could wait no longer. My stomach growled painfully for food, Slowly, I moved my right hand closer to my plate. When I almost reached the huge piece of great smelling bread, my mom slapped my hand hard. Quickly, I retrieved it so she wouldn't hit me again.

Shortly after that, my grandma came walking out of the dark woods with the cross from the long grave in her hand. She held the cross up to the heavens, with the number 48 facing up so God could see it, and cursed out loud. After a brief moment, as though waiting for an answer from above, my angry grandma spit in the still hot fire and said, "Let's eat!" She wore an angrier expression than I had ever seen in all my life.

Everyone ate very well that night, for the first time in a long time. Even the dogs and cats gorged on plenty of fish guts, bones and an occasional crumb that fell to the ground from the small children's plates. Hurriedly, I emptied my plate of delicious food and drank all the sweet, creamy milk. Then I picked up my blanket and walked away from our campsite. My black dog and the grey cat, which I had come to love, followed me down toward the steep coast.

I sat in a soft bed of sand, on the edge of the coast, behind a boulder. My sweet animals crawled under my blanket and lay right next to me. While I slowly stroked them, they went to sleep. I heard only their soft, shallow breathing on that calm night.

The seabirds had long gone to sleep and I lay far enough away from our camp not to hear the singing or talking of the people. The sea slumbered, motionless in her bed. The bright stars from above reflected in it, as though it were a mirror. What a peaceful night. I closed my eyes, leaned back onto the tall boulder and wondered who was in charge of this world. Before I could answer my deep question, I drifted away and disappeared, dancing with my animals, among the shining stars.

Droplets of the early morning fog, falling from the grey clouds, woke me. One good stretch, and both of my animals woke up. They crawled off my body and stuck their heads out of the blanket to have a look at the new day. Before they could decide to crawl back under, I stood up, shook out my damp blanket and folded it up.

After a few yawns and stretches, my friends followed me to the seashore. A few splashes of cold saltwater in my face and I felt ready to face the new day and return home. One last look out to sea, where the killing fingers of the devil did their twisting, fatal dance and viciously shattered to shred so many lives, and I walked back to our campsite with a heavy, bewildered mind.

At our campsite, people packed and loaded their belongings onto the wagons. Grandma stood next to one wagon, loading up the very small children and babies. She settled them down in between people's belongings so that they'd have a comfortable ride home.

I didn't see my mom, so I thought this a perfect time to plead with my grandma to take my new friend, the grey cat, along in the wagon. I knew my mom would most likely say, "No way! Who's going to feed that animal?" I didn't think that my new friend would follow us home, walking beside us, since cats like to stay where they're at.

With a sweet smile, I asked my grandma, "Please, let my cat ride on the wagon home with us."

Grandma looked at me with a serious face and I feared the worst in her silence. Then to my delight, my grandma said, "Hurry up and get the cat, before your mother sees what we're doing."

Quickly I ran over to the bush where I left my blanket with the grey cat sitting on top of it, hoping to see her there. Sure enough, I found her all curled up, sleeping on my blanket. I wrapped my fine cat up in the thin blanket, so my mom wouldn't discover her in case she saw us walking back to the wagon. Gently, I handed my grandma the little cat and she placed her and my blanket inside a wire cage in which a few chickens had arrived here earlier and had since been eaten. Jumping with joy that my lovely cat had a safe ride home with us, I hurried up and helped loading up the rest of our meager belongings.

A few more goodbyes, a short command to the horses to move, and we started on our way home. About half-way home, we stopped to give the old horses a break. Mom handed me a thick slice of dark bread and a mug full of water for my noon meal.

Watching my mom carefully, I slowly walked over to the wagon which had my cat on it, climbed up and walked to her cage. She gave me a bewildered look. I guess she had never been in a small cage. I sat down next to her and offered her a big chunk of my bread. She ate it but wasn't interested in the water I offered her.

Very quietly I whispered to her, "I love you and I'll let you out at home."

When my grandma stood up from her stool, everyone took that as the signal to move on. The few people who had stayed behind welcomed us home. When the unloading began in front of our house, my grandma winked at me and said, "I need your help, girl!"

In a hurry, I followed my grandma to the wagon with my cat

on it. She told me to climb up and take my grey cat out of the cage, to wrap her up in the blanket and walk behind her. Grandma had her stool and her blankets in her arms and I followed her order to walk behind her.

We snuck my lovely grey cat into my grandma's room without my mom noticing. After I unwrapped my confused cat to let her free, Grandma and I smiled and hugged each other. On our next trip into our house, my mom opened the door to my grandma's room to take in some of the dishes. She saw my grey cat and looked at my grandma with a questioning face.

Fearful that I would lose my new friend, I held my breath. My grandma and I exchanged glances.

Then my grandma said, "Oh, that cat must have followed us all the way here. Looks like a good mouser."

My mom didn't say a word, and my heart jumped with joy.

C3C3C3

After many years, the people erected a tall, black, skinny stone monument just past the twin settlements. It looked like a finger and had the number 48 deeply engraved in it with very large numbers.

On my last visit to my island, in 1996, I walked along the beach to see the long grave and the tall monument one more time. The wild ocean had claimed many meters of the beach, and the tall, black monument stood now a ways out in the ocean, the perfect place. With its black finger boldly pointing up into the sky, it stood to remind me of the frailty of us humans. The grave, though closer to the water's edge now, remained. On the right side of it sat a grey stone with the word *Lore* engraved in it. On the left side stood a weathered, dark wooden cross with seventeen names of the dead twin village people painted on it in fresh, white paint. Bushes of wild pink roses bloomed profusely on the long grave.

I guessed the old wooden cross with the number 48 carved into it for the nameless sailors which my grandma held up to the heavens in raging anger, must have long rotted away, like her body deep below the earth, buried not far from here also so long ago.

No chocolate bars, Windex or chicken fried steaks.

Chapter 70

What was I thinking?

One day while I walked with a group of my friends through the old graveyard that encircled our church, I opened my big mouth and shocked my friends when I suggested, "Come on, let's walk all the way up the tall bell tower!" The adults had told us time and time again, "Don't climb up the old bell tower!"

Everyone knew that mean ghosts lived in the attic of our church and could get inside the tower any time. Sometimes during Sunday service, we heard them laughing, pounding, or angrily throwing stones down the wooden stairs of the tower. People on our island often talked about the bad and mischievous things those ghosts did.

Two men who repaired the roof of the old church from the outside screamed loudly for help one afternoon while some of the ghosts laughed in joy, and no one ever saw those two men again, or found their bodies. One Sunday morning, people discovered the brave man who always repaired the big clock in the bell tower hanging from the ropes of the bells.

Sometimes, the ghosts played with all six bells in the church's tower at the same time. Only our island witch had the power to stop them. She didn't even have to walk over to our church to make them quit. She just raised her hand and pointed toward the church. Immediately, the angry ghosts stopped their bad behavior.

She amazed us all with her power. Some time back, I had asked my grandma why those ghosts lived in the attic of our big old church. She told me that those were the souls of the pirate Stoertebaecker and his faithful followers.

I remember Grandma giggling as she said, "Can you imagine what a show it was, seeing twenty-eight heads rolling down the church's aisle! God definitely didn't want those mean, murdering souls in His fine heaven. The devil was scared to death of the brutal group and refused to let them inside his hell. Therefore, their angry souls got stuck in the attic of our church."

Quickly remembering what my grandma had told me, I wondered why I opened my big mouth and suggested that we climb up the bell tower. Once I thought about it, I grew frightened.

My friends looked at me amazed and said, "You're the bravest one, so you go on and climb up the bell tower while we wait right here. When you reach the top of the tower, wave at us, and we'll tell everyone that you're the bravest!"

What could I do? If I changed my mind about climbing up the tower, they'd all laugh at me and call me names. I wished for the earth to open up and swallow me, but that didn't happen.

Ever so slowly, with my knees shaking and my teeth chattering, I walked over to the huge, old wooden door of the bell tower. I prayed over and over, "Please let the door be locked."

When I reached the ancient door, I realized it didn't even have a lock. My heart sank as my last hope of getting out of this situation gracefully disappeared. Desperately I looked back at my friends, but they didn't call me back. Instead, they started to giggle and pointed their fingers at me. I just couldn't quit now and become the laughingstock of all the schoolchildren.

Hesitatingly and awfully scared, I slowly opened the heavy door. The hinges squeaked and moaned loudly, as though protesting the movement. I wondered if the ghosts were giving me a sign not to enter the tall bell tower. With one last look at my now surprised friends, I stepped inside the tower. The old door closed by itself with a loud bang, which echoed forever in the tower. Even if the ghosts were asleep, that loud noise surely woke them.

Out of great fear, I stood still waiting for the ghosts to come and kill me. Slowly, my eyes adjusted to the dim light which entered through the open top of the building. I stood in a big room with many thick ropes hanging from all the bells. Dust played in the dim rays of the sun that reached this floor, and the musty air smelled of death. One fat rat walked by me and I wondered what that rat lived on. Perhaps she feasted at the dead bodies in the graveyard. I hoped and prayed that someone would come inside the tower to pull one of the ropes, to inform our island people what was happening that moment. That would have provided the perfect excuse for me to run outside, but no one came.

More than scared to death, with my heart racing, I walked over to the wooden steps to climb up the tower. The steps had neither a handrail nor a wall to hold onto, and they stood far apart from each other. Scared, I crawled up those steps, one at a time, holding onto the step in front of me for support. When one of the thick ropes moved, kind of twitching back and forth, I sat still in the eerie silence. For a moment, it reminded me of Albert's hanging. That even scared me more. What if the ghosts hanged me?

As I slowly climbed up higher, the sunlight grew brighter. At about the third story, I could see pretty well, and fresh air replaced the musty, old smell. The steady, loud ticking of the big old clock seemed like the bell tower's heartbeat. Somehow, it made me feel a little better.

I could see all the spider webs in front of me now and all the deep foot and handprints I left in the heavy dust on the stairs. Looking down to the bottom of the tower made me a little dizzy and scared again, and I wondered if I'd make it back down alive. Our island witch's faded face appeared in front of me and she smiled at me. Somehow, that suddenly gave me the courage to climb up higher without fear.

At about the fifth story level, I reached the door that opened into the attic above our church, where the restless, angry ghosts lived. I found the door open and the attic very quiet. Carefully, I climbed farther up the stairs, hoping to reach the open top of the tower soon. The last flight of stairs was still wet from an early morning shower, but I carefully made my way up and didn't slip once.

My heart filled with great joy, I walked over to the right side of the open dome where I knew my friends could see me. Carefully, I stepped to the edge, held on to the rail and proudly yelled down to my friends. "Hey guys, I made it!"

The very surprised bunch stared up at me and waved for me to come down. Relieved, I walked over to the wet stairs, sat down on the first step and tried to figure out how I could get all the way down without falling and killing myself.

My voice, from shouting down to my friends, still echoed around inside the mighty stone tower. When I made my first attempt to reach the step below me, I started to slip. The door to the attic of our church, where the ghosts lived, shut with a very loud bang, and a thin, yellowish cloud crawled out from beneath the closed door.

I heard voices, but couldn't understand what they said. The yellowish cloud drifted toward me. I had no more strength to hold onto to the wet step I barely sat on. My bloody hands gave away and I tumbled down the stairs. Darkness surrounded me. I couldn't see anything, but I felt like someone held me and we gently drifted downward.

Suddenly, I smelled the musty air again. Then I heard the aged door open, complaining again with loud squeaking and rumbling noises. The moment I was gently set onto the ground, I awoke all the way. My friends screamed like crazy and ran away.

After sitting on the ground next to the closed bell tower's door for a few minutes trying to figure out what just happened, I stood up and walked home in a bit of a daze. The only person I could tell about what happened to me and without punishing me was my loving grandma. Ever so gently, so my mom would not hear me in her room upstairs, I knocked on my grandma's door and whispered that I really needed to see her.

She opened the door, took my hand and led me inside her room. There she took a close look at me and said, "Child, what happened to you? You look like the Holy Ghost had a hold of you."

Slowly, I told my grandma exactly what happened, she stared out of her window for a short while as though waiting for something. I thought that she might wait for an answer from God. I looked out her window as well and watched for words to appear in the sky, but didn't see any.

Soon my wise grandma turned and looked at me. She held my small hands lovingly in her big, warm ones, smiled at me and said, "Yes child, we've known that some of the rejected souls of the beheaded pirates try to buy their way out of the church's attic by doing good deeds. Someone stopped two disasters at church for our family long ago and now someone saved your life.

"The first happened when the earth shook and the statue of a saint fell right beside me instead on top of me, which would have killed me. At that moment, I saw a slight grey cloud pushing the falling statue slightly away from where I sat. The other time was when my daughter, Martha, gave birth too soon, so unexpectedly, outside the church in the graveyard. The small child didn't breathe, no matter what we did to make it take the first breath of life. After we laid the dead child in its mother's arms, a light surrounded us and suddenly lifted the dead baby way above the mother. Then, with its first whining cry, the child slowly floated down into its mother's arms. She's your cousin Elle.

"The pirate's names have been passed on for many generations, and two of them carried our family name. Perhaps they're trying to buy their way out of the attic to move on to wherever pirates' souls go. Their headless bodies surely rotted away long ago with the rest of the brutal gang in the big old grave by the sea, which the sea itself claimed slowly over the years."

From that day on, for a long time, when I walked by our church, I stopped, looked at the old church's attic and whispered a thank you. For a few days, my peers acted as though they were afraid of me. They watched me closely from a distance and told everyone how brave I was to climb up that tower and that a ghost carried me back down. They looked upon me with fear and admiration, which I greatly enjoyed. Before long, my friends lost their fear of me and we spent time together again, running around on our little island and enjoying our wild freedom.

From that day on, I mostly tried to think things over before I opened my big mouth, but it didn't always work.

No ambulance, lemons, ultrasound or Pampers.

Chapter 71

The tears that really matter.

On a fine summer's day, after my mom and I collected driftwood, we sat down in the tall grass by the bay to take a break. The fishing boats chugged into our harbor with their daily catch on board. At least a thousand seagulls followed the boats, cried out loudly, and fought over the fish guts which the fishermen threw overboard.

My mind drifted up to the small white clouds that slowly moved away, and I wondered where they traveled to. Just about as I imagined sitting on one of those clouds and traveling away with it to wonderful places, my mom gently shook me and brought me back to earth.

I thought we needed to go home and tried to stand up, when my mom said, "Sit still, I have to tell you something very important." With a somber face, my mom looked at me, held my hand and said, "I'm going to have a baby."

Excitement washed over me, but I didn't know what to say. She didn't look happy, but she didn't cry.

I embraced my mom and asked her, "Do you have to give this baby away too?"

With a big sigh of relief my mom answered, "We can keep this child. Its father lives here on our island and will support me to raise this child."

Excitedly I wondered if my mom would marry him and give me a new father. Two days passed before I got enough courage to ask her if she would marry.

With a bitter smile, my mom said, "No, my child, I'm not going to get married. The father of this child is married already and he has two young girls."

Very disappointed at not getting a new father, I sat on my bed and wondered why my mom got pregnant by a married man. At just a little over twelve, I began to think about such confusing matters, but I couldn't ask. At that time, no one ever discussed what happened between a woman and a man. No one ever educated children about sex. Everyone kept it a deep, dark secret.

Soon my days and nights filled with dreams of babies. I helped my mom sew very small clothes and diapers by hand for the little one. We even sewed a little pillow and blanket out of torn sheets and placed them inside the wicker cloth basket for the baby's bed. I knew I felt much more excitement about the arrival of the new baby than my mom, but at least she didn't cry.

Sometime in the middle of the night of September 27, 1956, my mom woke me and whispered, "Edith, it's time to go to the hospital. The baby wants to be born."

Oh, what excitement! I dressed the fastest I had ever dressed in my life. Hand in hand, we climbed down our stairs. We walked to the small clapboard hospital, the place women now chose to deliver their children, instead of at home.

Mom leaned onto me heavily at times, crunching up her face in pain and holding onto her belly. Suddenly, she gripped my hand hard with both of hers and sat down on the stone stairs of a house. Water leaked from her, and I could see she was in great pain. Blood dripped from her mouth, and that really frightened me. I thought she might die. Mom pointed toward the hospital, and I ran as fast as I could toward it to get help. When my feet began to hurt, I realized I had forgotten to put my shoes on.

Screaming loudly for help while I ran, the two men that sat on a bench outside of the small hospital came running toward me. They stopped and asked me, "What's the matter?"

As fast as I could I told them, "My mom's baby is coming!" and pointed toward her.

The men saw her sitting on the stone steps, holding her belly. Both of them ran over to her, lifted her up and gently carried her inside the hospital. There they laid her on a narrow bed and hurried out of the room. Mom's face showed her pain, but she didn't scream.

I saw four narrow beds inside the one-room hospital. Women who held babies to their breasts occupied two of the beds. The woman in the bed next to my mom looked ready to give birth and screamed as if she were dying.

Our midwife greeted my mom and touched her belly. She said, "Erna, it will take a while before you give birth." Then she noticed me and said, "Girl, you need to go and wait outside."

I looked at my mom. She nodded her head and tried to smile, but the pains wouldn't let her.

The nurse told me, "I'll let you know as soon as your mom gives birth."

Slowly, in somewhat of a daze and awfully scared, I walked outside. The two strong men who carried my mom to this hospital still sat outside on the stone steps, smoking big cigars. I thanked them both for helping my mom and walked over to the tall mulberry tree. For a brief moment, I sat down in the grass beneath the huge tree, but then I decided to climb the tree so I could see inside the hospital through the open window.

About a third of the way up, I found a nice, strong limb to sit on. From there I could see the inside of the well lit hospital room. The woman in the bed next to my mom still screamed like a deadly injured animal. My mom's face looked so full of pain. She opened her mouth as though trying to scream, but no sound came out. She grabbed her belly and twisted back and forth in her narrow bed. Right there and then, I decided to never give birth. I'd just buy a child, or two, as the people from Denmark did when they heard that someone on our island wanted to let someone adopt their child.

Finally, a very tiny, dark bluish baby slipped out of the screaming woman. I had never seen a baby of that color and wondered how that happened. After one quick look at her newborn, the mother's head fell to one side and she closed her eyes. The midwife laid the tiny baby into a small, wooden box and closed the lid of the box. She then walked outside, handed one of the men the box, said something I couldn't understand and walked back inside. Both men stood there for a while, speechless, staring at the box with the dead baby inside of it. Then they walked away with their heads shaking in disbelief.

Quiet now inside our clapboard hospital, two newborn babies lay inside a woven willow basket, sleeping away. The midwife lay down on an empty cot, while the young nurse cleaned up the woman who had just had the dead baby. My mom still tossed and turned in her bed, and I hoped she wouldn't fall out of it. Though obviously in a lot of pain, she still didn't scream. Again, I swore to myself that I'd never give birth to a child, and I wondered why these women, including my mom, go through all the pain to have a baby when you could buy one.

I grew very tired and decided to climb out of the mulberry tree before I fell out of it. I wanted to stay close to my mom, thinking it might help her through the hard time she had. Tired, I lay down in the grass beneath the tree, trying desperately to stay awake. Dark clouds rushed by the moon and the leaves rustled in the trees. Though a chilly night, soon I no longer felt the cold. Someone held me tight in his arms in my warm dream.

The cold, early morning rain awoke me. I jumped up off the ground and ran over to our small hospital to check on my mom. The young, friendly nurse greeted me and asked me to come inside the room. Smiling, she led me to my mom's bed where she lay sleeping, the pain in her face gone. I looked over to the basket with the two babies inside of it.

To my great surprise, I saw three sleeping babies inside of it now.

My mom woke and reached out for my hand. She smiled, while a single tear ran down her cheek. She said, "You have a brother. I named him Willie."

I didn't know what to do, or say, so I just bent down and hugged my mom. She wrapped her strong arms around me and with a shaking voice whispered in my ear, "We are fine."

First, one gentle cry came from the wicker basket. A few short moments later, I heard three demanding screams. The moment I wanted to walk over to the babies' basket, the young nurse came, walked to the basket and picked up one of the screaming newborns. She came over to us and handed the baby to my mom.

Mom took him in her arms, uncovered his head and said, "Willie, have a look at your big sister Edith."

There he lay, my little brother. He looked straight at me with his big, dark, blue-green eyes. Short, tight, blond curls covered his little head. He lifted one small arm out of the blanket that wrapped him, opened his tiny mouth, and let out a fierce scream.

His tiny fist shook up and down, as though ready to fight. When my mom laid him onto her breast, he immediately quit screaming and began to suckle. Strange feelings crept up from deep inside of me, feelings I never felt before. I wanted to protect him, make sure he had enough to eat. I wanted to hold him close to me. I felt extremely excited and somewhat confused.

After every woman in the small room had finished nursing their newborns, the smiling nurse changed the babies' diapers and gently placed them back into the wicker basket. Then she walked to the door and let the waiting visitors inside. Every woman in that room had a few visitors who brought sandwiches and baked goods for their loved ones to eat, except for my mom. She just had me. Pretty flowers stood beside each of their beds on the rusty nightstands, except for my mom's.

Just a while later, when the nurse entered the small room again, she told us, "Visiting hours are over."

I gave my mom another hug and said, "I'll come back soon."

She closed her eyes and smiled.

On the way out of the hospital, the young nurse asked me, "Would you please take the time to wash the bucket full of diapers, I'm awfully tired, taking care of so many babies and women. I'd surely welcome a short nap before the next feeding of the newborns."

I said, "Yes, I'd be glad to help."

She then told me, "The pails with the dirty diapers and blankets are outside behind the hospital, next to the hand pump."

Quickly I walked to the back of the building to get the wash done. I had many diapers to wash and began to worry when I'd have time to run home and fetch some food for my mom. At that time, the small hospital didn't feed the patients. They relied on family or friends to bring them food.

When I had just about finished washing and rinsing all those diapers, I heard my grandma's voice nearby. Quickly I ran around the front of the small building to greet her and tell her about the birth of my brother. Before I could say a word, my sweet grandma sat down her basket, opened her arms and congratulated me on the birth of my brother with a great hug.

She asked me, "What are you doing behind the building?"

When I told her that I had washed the newborns' diapers, my grandma turned to our neighbor, who had come along with her, and suggested that she help me. Then my grandma walked inside the hospital and took charge. I heard her sending the tired nurse home to get some sleep and volunteering two other visiting women to clean the place up.

While our neighbor and I finished washing the soiled cloths and hanging them on the clothesline to dry, we saw and heard people carrying buckets of soapy water inside. They scrubbed floors, emptied bedpans, swatted at flies, and someone threw a mouse through the open door, which one of our island hounds caught in midair. The moment I caught the scent of brewing coffee out of burned wheat, I knew they had finished their chores and I walked inside the hospital.

Grandma handed me mugs full of great smelling coffee and parts of smoked eels to take to the patients. Then she sliced a loaf of bread into eight pieces and told me to take it to the women. All of them happily accepted the fine food, except for the woman who gave birth to the dead baby. She completely refused nourishment. Grandma handed me her portions and I sat on my mom's bed and ate all of it. Was I ever glad to finally get something to eat and even gladder that my mom had plenty of food now.

After my mom and the other mothers fed their babies again, they went to sleep. One more look at my pretty little brother and I walked over to the grassy field to take a short nap in the warm sunshine. When I lay down, I realized that my mom may feel bad. She was the only one without flowers on her nightstand.

I knew it was customary for the men to bring flowers to their wives, mothers, or any other sick female, either at home or in the hospital. Since my mom didn't have a man to bring her flowers, and I was sure she felt bad about not having any, I decided to bend the rules just a little.

My short nap turned into a long one. I awoke when the sun made ready to crawl into the ocean with all the splendor of a colorful display. The sky and part of the ocean blazed with a fire of deep red, purple, and many different shades of golden colors. The sun painted all the happy little clouds around her pink, and many variations of red and gold. Some clouds farther away from her had a light green color. I always wondered how most sunsets turned out so very pretty.

Then I remembered all the diapers and baby clothes I had hung up on the clothes line. In a great hurry, I gathered them and took them inside to the young nurse. From the entrance of the room, I saw my mom sitting up in her bed, eating a hefty sandwich. She smiled at me and waved me on to come to her. I walked over to her and sat beside her on the narrow bed.

She asked me, "What do you think about your little brother?"

I smiled and happily told her, "I like him a lot, and he's so pretty!"

I felt so much more inside of me than just liking my new baby brother, but I didn't understand those new, tender feelings yet.

My mom must have known that I experienced my first motherly feelings in my life. She looked deep into my eyes and smiled ever so warmly. When my mom had finished eating, the nurse brought my baby brother over.

Mom told her, "Hand him to my daughter."

The nurse showed me how to hold him safely, and I sat for the longest time holding my precious little brother in my arms. A strange, warm feeling overcame me. I began to shake, and goose bumps ran down my back while I held this new, precious life in my arms. Oh, yes, I swore to myself to protect him, care for him and love him.

From deep inside of me, tears started to brim in my eyes, not sad or happy tears, but much more important ones. They came from my heart and really mattered. Gently, I kissed my baby brother on his cheek. He opened his big, blue-green eyes and let out a hungry scream. Carefully, I handed him over to my mom and left the one-room clapboard hospital quickly before my mom saw the tears from my heart running from my eyes.

Because we had a sick uncle living with us for a while, and my aunt and uncle had a new baby in the spring, and my mother expected a new baby in the fall, my grandma decided earlier on that we needed to plant just vegetables that spring, to feed everyone. No flowers at all. I had no money to buy flowers for my mom, but I decided she'd have the prettiest bouquet by morning. On my way home, I looked around to see which gardens had the prettiest flowers.

That night, under the protection of our cloudy sky and with a little prayer to God to forgive my sin, I silently stole only one of the prettiest gladioli out of each garden. Perhaps people wouldn't notice only one missing. By the time I reached the small hospital, I had eight beautiful, tall flowers in my arms. The church clock rang three times when I looked inside the small hospital room. Everyone was asleep, even the friendly nurse.

Quietly, I filled the rusted can I had brought with me, with fresh water from the outside pump. Then I snuck inside the little room and carefully, not to awake anyone, placed the flowers inside the old can and set them on top of my mom's nightstand. Proudly, because my mom now had the prettiest bouquet, I walked outside.

The next morning when I arrived at school, our teacher walked over to me and said, "You can take the day off to spend it with your mom at the hospital."

What a nice surprise! Ever so excited, I ran out of our schoolhouse and to our hospital. My mom sat up in her bed and smiled when she saw me coming. She thanked me for the beautiful flowers. I hoped she wouldn't ask where I stole them from. She knew very well that I had no money to buy such luxury. Mom didn't ask though. She just smiled warmly at me, hugged me and thanked me. Quickly, she took her hand and wiped something wet from her cheek.

That day, the friendly, young nurse showed me how to wash all three babies, change their diapers and powder their behinds. She also showed me how to bandage their navels and how to wrap the babies up completely in small blankets. I watched my mom nurse my brother many times. She contently smiled at him. When he had enough to drink, I held him and walked around the small room, whispering promises to him. With a tear slowly emerging from deep inside my heart again, I kissed his little cheek, told him that I loved him and that I'd take good care of him. On my way out of the building, that heavy tear slowly ran down my face.

A week or so later, my mom and I walked out of the tiny hospital's room. I proudly carried my little brother all the way home. My mom went back to work in the fields right away to make some money before the harsh winter came and ended her income. Being the oldest in our little family, I now had to take care of my brand new brother and my smaller sister. My sister, a year-and- a-half younger than I, pretty much took care of herself by now. In the early mornings, my mom woke me before she left for work. After I quickly dressed, I went outside by our pump, washed my little brother's diapers and hung them up on our clothesline. Back inside, I changed and cleaned him and prepared two bottles of milk for him. I held him in my arms and fed him one of his bottles. He always ate well and smiled so sweetly at me at feeding time. I saved the other bottle for his next feeding at school. Then I boiled a large carrot or some other vegetable for him, mashed it well, and placed it in a jar to take with us to school.

Next, I shook my sister and made sure she got out of bed. While she dressed, I fixed a pork grease sandwich with salt sprinkled on it for her and me to eat on our way to school. After I wrapped my brother up, all three of us went downstairs. I laid him in his stroller, and off to school we went. I still sat in the last row of our classroom and had my brother right next to me. He usually slept through the first few hours of school. If he started to cry, I had to push him out into the hallway where I changed him, fed him, and rocked him in his stroller until he fell back asleep. Then we both went back into the classroom. He was a real good baby and ever so pretty, with his big, blue-green eyes and his tight, blond curly hair.

At recess, all the other girls always asked me, "Can I help take care of him?"

"Can I hold him?"

I always proudly said, "No, thank you!"

They looked inside his stroller and smiled at him. If he was awake, he smiled back at them.

School let out at noon in the warm season. My grandma, having her chores away from home done, came to take my little brother home with her. My younger sister and I climbed onto a horse-drawn wagon, which took us out to work in the fields. The fieldwork season never lasted long, and we had to earn as much money as possible, so hunger wouldn't plague us during the long, bitter cold winters.

Work ended at about six in the evening. The farmers paid us and my sister and I walked home together with my mom, unless we worked faraway from our village. On those occasions, the farmer took us close to our village in his horse-drawn wagon. I liked that a lot because I loved to sit in the wagon and see the fields pass by us. My loose hair waved in the breeze, and I often pretended to fly ever so far away from here, to a land of plenty.

At home in our little room, all three of us put our hard earned money into our tall can. If my mom came home with us from work, fun time began. My sister and I ran down to the nearby bay. There we met our friends, played games and tried out to see who could swim the fastest across the bay. Hunger eventually drove us home. If my mom stayed at the farmer's house to do some extra work to earn some money, perhaps prepare meat or vegetables, I'd pick up my sweet brother from my grandma. After I changed his diapers and fed him, I'd take him in my arms and walk outside to the garden with him. There I showed him and told him the names of flowers, birds and whatever came in sight. He smiled and blabbered back at me.

Oh yes, I loved my little brother, and I had a lot of fun taking care of him. Deep inside of me, strange feelings grew that I couldn't understand at the age of thirteen. When he went to sleep in my arms, I took him inside and laid him in his basket. Quickly, I sliced up some potatoes, added pork grease and fried up my sister's and my evening meal. I always left some for my mom in case she wanted something to eat when she arrived home.

During that next winter, while the three of us knitted and sewed outfits for my brother, he looked up at me from his warm blanket, smiled, waved his little fist up into the air and called me,

"Ma." All three of us laughed. There it came again, one of those tears that really mattered, crept up from way down in my heart. I quickly turned my head so no one could see it running down my cheek.

No vanilla, incubators, or fire department.

Chapter 72

A damaged soul.

No school on Sundays and for most of the time, no fieldwork except when it was critical to harvest something before the weather turned bad.

My mom didn't force me to go to church, but I liked to sing in the choir, and we opened every Sunday service with a song. After we sang the opening song, I usually left the church now with most of the other children to have some fun, or go on an adventure, perhaps discover something new. I had lost interest in Sunday service because I had heard all the stories the preacher read to us already twice. I wondered when he would get a new book to read to us.

On this particular Sunday, just as we got ready to sing the opening song, a man came into our church and screamed, "Fire! There's a fire on the north side and it's coming closer to our only barley field!"

I had never seen so many women leaving our church so fast. They almost trampled on top of each other. The man who alerted us must have alarmed all our island men in the tavern first because when I ran out of our church, I saw them already running toward the field.

They had shovels, axes and other equipment over their shoulders to stop the fire and rescue the crop, which was ready to harvest. Without the barley, we'd have no beer to drink on our island, and we'd have nothing to thicken our already too thin soups with. What a sight they made. All the kids in the choir ran ahead of the women and small children, trying to get to the fire first. Our pack of island dogs ran around among us, barking like crazy, not knowing where to run and most likely not knowing why. Our silver, fire emergency bell on our tall church tower rang loud and clear over all the commotion around us. They rang it to make sure that the people who didn't attend Sunday service knew to come and help put out the fire.

We had left the village in no time at all. Now I clearly saw a very tall fire burning not far from us. The men, sweating and breathing hard with their firefighting tools, started to run faster now and passed our choir group. Their faces glowed red with exhaustion and pain, but they ran on, while we children stood still, desperately taking in a few deep breaths.

In a matter of a few more minutes, the men reached the fire. At the same time, a horse-drawn wagon from our village arrived with sickles and other farm equipment to harvest the barley quickly, before the fire could destroy it. I found it amazing how quickly everyone went to work. All the men dug a wide, shallow trench, cut the bushes, and sawed down a small tree to keep the fire from moving into the barley field. The women cut down the barley with their sickles on the side of the field closest to the fire. Birds took off in flight. Rabbits left in a great hurry, and I saw quite a few field mice disappear into their burrows.

Our tavern keeper commanded all the children of school age to quickly gather the cut barley and throw it inside the empty wagon. We followed his order quickly. The horses grew nervous as the roaring fire came closer, but the owners held them securely in place.

For a brief moment, when the wild fire came close to the trench, everyone held their breath, stood still and watched as the tall, red flames whispered and spit sparks into the air. They sucked up the air and fuel from the nearby dry stubble field, embraced each other and danced a wild dance of destruction.

I felt the warmth from the fire now and smelled the burning vegetation. The horses got very upset, and some small children started to cry. In a great hurry, someone loaded those children onto the wagon and the driver moved them away from the still raging fire. By now, I was very scared. I kept looking for the first person to start running away from the fire, and I promised myself to follow right behind them. Very quickly, the hot, rolling wall of fire reached the freshly dug trench. Having no more fuel to feed its dancing flames, the flames slowly died down. The red hot coals of the once raging fire madly hissed and spit for a while. Then the coals slowly lost their power and turned black. Soon the proud fire died. The last, dark smoke slowly rose from the hot, burned earth straight up to the heavens.

Thank goodness, the people killed the fire. Everyone began to relax and stopped harvesting the barley. Our choir director waved us on to come over to her.

After all of us gathered around her, she said, "Let's sing the hymn we practiced to sing in our church this morning."

So happy that the fire was out, we began singing our hymn loudly and mostly in tune.

Before we even sang the first verse, I saw Bern, a half-grown boy with a troubled soul, standing on the edge of the burned out field laughing and jumping up and down like a mad person. His father ran toward him. For some unknown reason, it frightened me. Quickly, I ran out of our singing group, yelled and pointed in their direction. Our man of the law and a few other people turned to where I pointed. Then a handful of them dropped their tools and ran across the burned out stubble field, trying to reach the father and son.

Our choir quit singing. Everyone stared at our running men and past them at the father and son. The father reached the still laughing and jumping boy. When he grabbed his son by his arm, the son quit laughing and jumping. The father said something to his son I couldn't understand. The son nodded his head and laughed out loud.

The moment he jumped back up in excitement with his hands swung up high, the father hit him hard with his fist.

Bern fell to the ground.

The father hit his son once more. He reached up to hit his son again, but the running men reached him and held him back from hitting his child again. A lot of swearing and yelling followed, while Bern lay motionless on the ground. Most of our island people hurried up and walked closer to get a better look.

I ran over to the wrestling men. Three men held down the completely outraged father, and two sat on the ground next to Bern. One of them held his small hand, and the other man tried to stop the blood from gushing out of a huge gash on the boy's head. He pressed his bloodstained, rolled-up shirt against the bleeding wound, but the blood didn't stop. The healing woman from our village hurried close to help. She took one close look at the large gash and sadly shook her head.

Bern's body twitched a little, and with his last breath, his blood stopped running from his head. It just barely seeped out. He lay there, completely still, with his broken head on top of a big, bloodstained stone.

I stood in shock and disbelief. Bern was dead.

Someone whispered, "All the blood ran out of the boy. Did his father kill him?"

When someone told the raging father that his boy was dead, he grew instantly subdued and walked over to his dead child.

He knelt beside him, picked him up a little, held him in his arms and cried. After he stood back up he quietly said, "Yes, my boy started the fire," and walked away.

No one said a word. Even our pack of village dogs sat in silence with respect. Amidst the quiet, I heard a faint bird call. When I looked up to the heavens to see what kind of birds made the slight noise, I saw a pair of storks taking up in flight from the roof of Bern's home. They flew south for the winter to a warm land. When they flew over us, I silently asked them, "Please take Bern's damaged soul up to the heavens!"

No library, jalapeños or school bus.

Chapter 73

The nice gift.

Just shortly before our harsh winters froze our large carp pond over completely, we harvested the carp, a delicacy at Christmas dinner for the rich people who lived faraway from our island.

The owner built the sweet water pond just a few feet above sea level, and dug it out very deep in the middle. However, in most places it was only two or three feet deep. On the side of our bay, it had a short, shallow dam with a round metal opening covered tightly by a heavy piece of wood. At harvest time, a few strong men pulled the heavy wood up and quickly let down a metal net to keep the fish in the pond and let the sweet water run slowly out into the bay. The thin, weak ice layer broke, fell into the still, warmer water, and melted. We'd begin harvesting Christmas dinner for the rich the next day.

We left our warm house early in the morning all bundled up and wearing our rubber boots. We each carried a bucket on this day and hoped to make a little money. Fieldwork had long ended, and so did our income. Perhaps we'd even bring home some morsels of the fancy fish for ourselves to enjoy.

When we arrived at the pond, only a few inches of water remained except in the middle. All the willing and hungry people of our island had already gathered, ready to go to work. A fresh water tank stood on top of a sturdy wagon that had four plow horses ready to pull the wagon at the given command.

The owner of this pond looked pleased and said to the crowd, "Same rules; same pay."

Just about everyone mumbled, "All right."

All the women and children waded into the pond with their buckets in their hands. The men stood on the edge of the pond and waited to carry our filled buckets to the water tank. Most of the really huge carp had gathered in the middle of the pond, but someone told me to leave them so they could breed for next year's crop. Some carp lay in the wet mud on the edge of the big pond. We had to work quickly and pick those up first before they buried themselves deeper into the mud and died. We could actually catch those easier than the ones in the remaining water because they didn't struggle so hard to get away from us.

Soon my grandma had filled her bucket and she waved her hand. A man brought her an empty bucket and carried hers to the big tank. There he counted the carp and wrote the amount down on a piece of paper. Quickly, an older boy climbed up the short ladder and gently dumped the fish into the warmer, fresh water. I felt absolutely sure that the stranded fish felt much better in the warmer water than in this very cold mud. Before long, I, too, filled my bucket with muddy carp. Barely moving, they desperately gasped for water.

I whispered to them, "Soon you'll swim in warm water and will breathe easily again."

Proudly, I raised my hand and a man took them to the tank.

After we had collected all the stranded fish, we waded toward the middle of the pond to catch the more lively ones, not an easy task since they wriggled and slithered right out of my hands. However, I managed to fill my bucket twice.

Then I saw a huge carp as long as my bucket, and decided to catch it.

When my mom saw me headed in that direction, she said, "Edith, leave that one alone."

But I didn't listen. I grabbed it by its back and squeezed my hands around its body hard. That huge carp turned its head, looked at me, turned sideways and jumped at me. Afraid it might bite me, I quickly let go of the huge carp, fell backwards and wound up sitting in the icy cold water. I looked at my bleeding hands while everyone laughed at me. I felt so embarrassed and wished that I had listened to my mom.

Wet and freezing now, I gathered one more bucket full of carp. Then the owner of this large pond declared the harvest over, even though we saw a few fish left in the shallow water. The huge carp I tried to catch swam among them. I felt as though he looked right at me and laughed his head off at foolish me.

Excited at earning some money, I walked over to the owner of the pond with my family to get paid. I caught twenty carp and got paid two pennies for each one. I clung proudly to the forty pennies in my hand. If my mom didn't need all my money this time, I could buy Christmas presents for her and my grandma, perhaps some sewing needles and twine, which they always needed. I felt happy and proud of myself.

The freshwater wagon left with the four plow horses pulling hard on it. The wagon, with the tank on top of it, headed for the owner's barn. To keep the water from freezing, he'd build a small fire underneath it until the carp buyers arrived. For the next six weeks, the owner would feed them milled grain to improve their taste.

Before we left to go home, the women divided the small pile of dead and damaged parts of the carps among themselves. Grandma and my mom took their share and we walked home. At home, I hurriedly cleaned myself and changed into dry clothes. While my mom gutted out the few slightly injured, dead fish and hung them over the outside clothesline to freeze for later use, I washed out my muddy clothes beneath the pump in our backyard and hung them over the wooden fence to dry. The damaged parts, such as the heads, fins, egg sacks of the females, the sperm sacks of the males, and some organs, wound up in the steaming soup pot on my uncle's big stove.

My mom asked me, "Bring the barley over here, girl, and the pail of prepared vegetables."

When I brought them to her, she added both to the soup, and I sat down on the floor near the stove, to get warm and inhale the fine aroma of the boiling soup. In a few hours, we'd have enough delicious soup to eat for everyone in our house. We might even have seconds today.

Mom let me keep half my pennies. Ever so anxiously, I ran to our small store to buy Christmas presents for the first time in my young life. At the store, I stared at the box with sewing goods and tried to figure out what I could afford to buy with my twenty pennies. Soon I figured out that I could buy one big pack of sewing needles and two spools of twine. I told the woman of the store what I wanted and handed her my pennies.

She smiled and asked me, "Are these Christmas presents?"

With a proud smile I answered, "Yes, they're for my mom and my grandma."

She handed me two small, clean pieces of real white paper and told me, "You can wrap your presents in these."

I thanked her and happily ran home, skipping and singing.

At home I opened the package of sewing needles and divided those equally: five of different sizes for Mom and the other five for my grandma. Then I wrapped the small gifts up in the clean, white paper and hid them inside my grandma's closet, beneath my dead grandpa's old shoes, so nobody would find them. What fine gifts I had for my two favorite people on this earth. What a wonderful Christmas lay ahead! I faithfully checked on my hidden presents every morning and smiled at them proudly.

No potato dishes out of boxes, plastic bags, or traffic light.

Chapter 74

How proud I was!

One early, bitter cold morning my mom woke me and said, "Today is the first day of December."

That announcement sure woke me in a hurry. Christmas, my favorite holiday, would soon be here.

My mom said, "We need to get some pine branches to decorate our table for tomorrow, the fourth Sunday before Christmas Eve, and therefore the first Sunday of Advent."

Excited, I waited for my mom to walk back into her room and then I hurriedly dressed beneath the warm bedcovers.

At midday, when the sun finally warmed the air a bit, my mom and I bundled up with all the outer clothing we owned. Holding hands, fearless of the biting wind and in anticipation of the holiday season to begin, we walked out into the icy, beautiful world of deep, glistening snow. The brutal bite of the northern wind didn't feel good at all in my covered face and through my long pants, but I felt warm in my heart. Christmas was coming, the happiest holiday of the year.

Hand in hand, we walked across the frozen bay, singing our first Christmas song for this year. Soon we reached a fine stand of short-needled pine trees near the wide, tall sandbank which divided the ocean from the bay. It sure felt great to walk inside the thick forest. The harsh wind could not reach us inside and bite through our clothing. For a brief moment, we leaned against the trunk of a huge, old tree to catch our breath. Then, with wide smiles on our faces and in our hearts, we walked on through the silent, old forest toward the younger stand of trees.

The first young tree we saw looked perfect. I brushed the snow from its branches near the earth, and my mom carefully sawed three of the bottom branches off with her precious bread knife, the only tool she had left for such a job. She had bartered all of her other tools for food long ago.

I didn't feel bad about taking those branches from the beautiful young tree because I knew it could live on and grow into a very tall tree. Mom let me carry the three branches home. Joyful, we walked back home over the frozen bay to our small village. The north wind only bit us in the back now, and that made the walk home easier. We sang more Christmas songs as we walked through the festive looking, snowed-in village. Some of our village people looked out of their closed windows and waved at us with a smile. Nobody dared to open their windows and join in our singing, knowing the ice-cold northern wind would quickly suck the warmth from their houses.

At home, my mom told me, "Take two branches of the pine tree inside our lean-to. They'll serve as our Christmas tree later on."

Quickly, I followed her orders and then took the other branch into our fairly warm room. After we took off all our outer clothing, both of us walked over to our little iron stove and rubbed our freezing hands over its rising heat, until they felt warm again. Mom filled the teakettle with water to brew some tea and prepare our simple evening meal of semolina soup, while I carefully cut the small branches off the big pine branch. I hoped she had sugar to add to the bland, watery soup.

When I had finished my chore, I stacked all the small, pretty pine branches up in the middle of our wooden table so my mom could make the Advent wreath.

With a smile, she said, "Go ahead child, and fix the Advent wreath!"

Her request that I perform such an important task, astounded and honored me. Proudly, I took each small pine branch and laid it on top of another in a small circle in the middle of our old table, just as I watched my mom do for so many years. I noticed that she looked away from her stove every once in a while to check on me, and each time she wore a smile.

Before long, I had stacked my wreath, and Mom had finished cooking our evening meal. She came over to me, put her arm around me, looked at my wreath, smiled and said, "Now, that's a perfect wreath!" She bent down and took our little box with the precious and important decorations, out from beneath the couch she slept on. What an exciting moment!

Carefully, Mom removed the dusty cardboard cover and placed it on the wooden floor. One side of the box contained the decorations for the Advent wreath, which also served to decorate the Christmas tree. The other side contained a few sheets of paper, which my mom called important papers. She took the precious decorations out of the box and handed them to me. Full of pride, I carefully placed the handful of various short, colorful strings of knitting yarn and the pretty, dried flower leaves on our wreath. Then my mom handed me four slightly used slim, white candles. With a shaking hand, I placed them on our table, in the middle of our Advent wreath.

Mom hugged me and said, "Now that's the prettiest wreath we've ever had!" Her eyes let go of a lonely tear. Quickly, she turned to the door, wiped her eyes and her nose and opened the door of our little room.

With a strange voice, she called my sister and my grandma to come upstairs for some hot soup. Within a few moments, both came up the stairs while my mom placed four mugs of steaming tea and four mugs of hot soup on our table. When they entered our little room, both stared at our pretty Advent wreath with smiles on their faces.

After we sat at our little table, my mom said, "Edith made this wreath all by herself for the first time. Let's celebrate the first Sunday of Advent just a few hours early and light a candle."

Mom lit the tallest of the four used candles and turned off the bare electric overhead light bulb. Silently, we stood around the table, holding hands, watching the candle magically flicker around the room. My mind wandered to Ola, and I wished her good night. I felt her warm smile taking over my body and the numbers of thank you entered my mind clearly. Usually people said a prayer at this moment, but my mom didn't pray. Neither did she like anyone to pray inside her room.

She still felt absolutely sure that our preacher took food away that people sent to the poor and that God let him get away with it. She often said, "Look how fat he and his family grew in these lean years!" She was right about that. All of them must have lived on the rich side. They had huge bodies.

I liked these silent moments of holding hands much more than some strange prayer of thanking Him for many things I never saw Him do or give to us. I felt closer to our island witch. I could see what she did. She helped and guarded us, told us what to do, and forgave us when we went wrong.

After that brief, touching moment, my mom turned the dim electric lamp back on, blew out the candle to save it for the Second Sunday of Advent, at which time we'd light two candles. We sat down and enjoyed our hot dandelion tea and soup. Yes, Mom had added a little beet sugar to our semolina soup, and it tasted great. Oh, how proud I felt for my mom's trust in me to lay out the important Advent wreath—my very first one.

No vacuum cleaner, sweet cereal in a box, or chewing gum.

Chapter 75

The sugar cookie.

A few days after the first Advent, exactly every year on the 6th of December, Saint Nickolaus came to us children. He always came at night. No matter how late I stayed awake, peeking out of the window to get a look at him, I never saw him.

On this night of nights, I had to make absolutely sure to clean both of my rubber boots of all dirt. Then, just as the world began to get dark, all of us children had to make a big decision. If we knew for sure that we had behaved well all year long, we set our right boot outside of our front door. If we weren't so sure, or knew we didn't behave all that well, we needed to place our left shoe or boot outside with a written note of apology inside and a promise to do better in the coming year.

If we didn't please Saint Nickolaus with our behavior, or set the wrong boot outside, or if we hadn't written the note of apology well enough, he'd stick a thin, freshly-cut switch in our boot. The parents then kept the stick to punish the unruly children with during the coming year. Whoever found pieces of dark coal in their boot had to work hard by doing extra chores to make up for bad behavior. However, good children found dried plums, a sweet sandwich, or perhaps even a sugar cookie in their boot or shoe.

Saint Nickolaus was a tough guy to please. Year after year, I politely set out my left boot with a well meant, written promise to be good for the whole next year. I always received a half sandwich with sweet marmalade, never a sugar cookie, like my sister had in her boot. That sweet sandwich tasted great though, since we didn't have marmalade often. The year I tied my sister to the tree and tried to burn her, I found a big switch and two pieces of coal in my well cleaned boot. What a disappointment!

I began to wonder how that old guy could see at night if the boots were clean, and how did he know who they belonged to? We had seven children in our house now, and we lined the boots up by size: the big one first, my boot, and so on, down to the baby's bootee. I had to come up with something to fool the old guy this year. I wanted a sugar cookie awfully bad, and this year I made up my mind to get one.

Bravely, for the first time in my young life, I took my right boot and cleaned just the top of it fairly well. After everyone had lined up their boots at the front door, I took my boot, moved my sister's rubber boot to the front into my place, and placed my boot in her place. Then, I stuck it a little deeper into the snow so Saint Nickolaus couldn't see the dirt on it, or that it was indeed the biggest boot. The lineup looked perfect to me. I figured that should fool the old guy. Then I went to bed smiling, ever so excited about my great idea. After I closed my eyes, sugar cookies began to appear in front of me. Soon, I danced among thousands of them.

Long before daybreak, something woke me. I quietly got out of bed and walked down the stairs to get my sugar cookie out of my boot. I lifted the door handle just a little, so it wouldn't squeak.

The snow-covered stair chilled my bare feet. Quickly, I reached down and fetched my boot, stepped back inside our house, and anxiously stuck my hand inside of my boot for my sugar cookie. Oh no! No sugar cookie in my boot! Instead, I found a piece of coal and a written note. Sad and angry, I opened our front door and stepped out again to read the note in the bright moonlight. It said, "Ha, ha, ha!" and was signed Saint Nickolaus.

I couldn't believe it. The old Saint knew what I had done.

Outraged and angry at getting caught, I reached into my sister's boot. Sure enough, she received a sugar cookie again. I took the cookie out of her rubber boot, stepped inside the house, closed the front door and sat down on the stairs.

I looked at that cookie for a moment and then ate it without feeling bad about it at all. Then bitter feelings crawled up inside of me. Slowly, I walked up the stairs, wishing I hadn't eaten that cookie. I crawled back into the warm bed next to my sleeping sister.

I couldn't go back to sleep. I felt angry and ashamed of myself for eating my sister's cookie. Soon, the usual morning noises of starting the stoves, and opening and shutting the doors, woke the other children, and every one of them ran to the front door to fetch their boot, or shoe, except for the baby. Aunt Hilde carried her to the door. I stood back behind the excited children, feeling very bad. After all of them had their shoe inside, I took my boot inside without any excitement because I already knew what I'd find. I watched my sister reach into her boot. I knew she'd feel so disappointed not to find a sugar cookie in her rubber boot. Since I didn't like my sister very much at that time, I suddenly felt good for a brief moment, waiting to see her disappointed face. Bewildered, I watched my little sister take two sugar cookies out of her boot. What a huge smile she had on her face.

How could that have happened? I turned my boot upside down just in case the saint had returned to put something inside of it after my first investigation. Sure enough, I found another note. It said, "This is the last time you set out your boot for Saint Nickolaus!" The signature read, "Mom!"

How could my mom have known what I did? Did that old saint tell her what I did?

Seeing only the piece of coal and a note in my hand, my little sister walked over to me and offered me one of her sugar cookies.

Deeply ashamed by now, I said, "No thank you," and enviously watched her eat both of those cookies.

No electric Christmas lights, no Christmas stockings, no gingerbread houses or poinsettias.
No turkey dinner, eggnog, nuts to crack open or plastic Christmas trees.
No green bean casserole, fruitcake, pies or ice cream for dessert.
No pretty wrapping paper, shiny bows or store-bought decorations.
We didn't write letters to Santa, and no one asked what we'd like to have for Christmas.
But, we had three days of Christmas and enjoyed them greatly!

Chapter 76

Christmas 1952, I was barely 10 years old.

Christmas Eve arrived, the most important day of the three holidays for the children of our village. We received gifts and most likely got to eat a great meal. At that time of my young life, I questioned the source of some gifts.

I knew that my grandma made her gifts and brought them to us. Some children said, "Santa Claus brings the gifts." Others said, "Kris Cringle brings them." Still others mentioned that the Christ Child Himself brought the gifts. The older children laughed at us for believing such nonsense. They said, "Only people lay gifts beneath the Christmas tree."

I gave that a lot of thought and decided that it really didn't matter who gave me a present, but I'd keep my eyes open this year to find out.

All day long, I wished for the sun to hurry and set so the festivities of Christmas Eve could begin. Repeatedly, I practiced the poem everyone expected me to recite tonight in front of our Christmas tree. My sister and I practiced our secret song we had to sing in front of our tree a few more times.

We practiced in the outhouse. With the lid on the crapper closed tightly, it didn't stink so badly inside there. We didn't think anyone would hear us in there and discover our secret song. Both of us had enough room to sit down together and sing our hearts out. Oh, how excited we were, when we finally learned all the words of the first two verses of this Christmas surprise hymn, "Silently Falls the Snow."

Glad to get out of the outhouse, I walked down to the frozen bay. There I met some of my friends who also excitedly waited for the sun to set. We had a good snowball fight and talked about what gifts we might get, if any. Impatiently, I stared over the frozen bay, waiting for the day to end. After I looked up at the sky again, for what seemed like the millionth time, the sun finally moved down toward her place in the sky where she left our part of the world. She even set the frozen ocean on fire this afternoon with her bright crimson colors.

A short moment later, she spilled all her hot, golden fiery colors over the ice, which looked as though the ice should melt, but it did not. Then her face slowly disappeared into the frozen ocean. With her last strength, the sun retrieved all her golden and red rays, leaving only a small, faint, reddish sliver on the horizon for a brief moment. Then she disappeared.

That was it. Soon night would move over our island and Christmas Eve could begin. I ran home as fast as I could. When I arrived there, my mom had just walked out of the lean-to holding the two branches of the pretty pine tree we brought home a few weeks ago. They looked as fresh as the day my mom had cut them off the little tree by the ocean.

Full of excitement, I followed her into the house.

Upstairs, before she opened the door to her room, she said, "Wait here until I call you!"

I sat on our bed next to my sister, waiting for whomever brings gifts to arrive. I listened for the front door to open, but it didn't. I looked out of our window into the dark night but couldn't see anyone. We didn't have a fireplace for someone to come inside our house, which I had heard about in some stories from faraway lands.

Then I had a great idea. The only other way, besides the door, into our house was through the windows. I quietly walked over to the door to Mom's room and looked through the slit in the door where part of the wood had split off long ago.

Afraid of discovery, but too nosy to step back from the door, I looked inside the room and saw my mom and our closed window. The two branches making up our Christmas tree stood in our extra mug in the middle of our table, decorated with the white paper snowflakes we made long ago. All the colored strings from the Advent wreath hung on them along with a few strings of shiny, silvery tinsel. How pretty our little tree looked.

Then my mom took two short candles and placed one on each side of our tree. A quick glance over to our window assured me that it remained closed. Shivering with excitement to see who would arrive and perhaps bring us a gift, I kept my eye at the hole in the door.

Astounded, I saw my mom setting the customary two small Christmas plates, filled with apples, dried plums and a big piece of candy on top of it, down next to our tree. My grandma made that delicious candy every Christmas for all the people in our house. My mouth started to yearn for it. If we got another gift someone should bring it now. I kept my eye on the closed window and my ears at our squeaking front door. This Christmas, I'd find out who brought the gifts and then tell everyone.

To my uttermost surprise, my mom laid a gift next to each

plate. I recognized that she had spent many hours knitting our gifts. After that, she sat down on one of our old chairs, faced the Christmas tree and put her hands over her face. For just a brief moment, it looked to me as though she would cry, but abruptly, she shook her head, stood up, took the matches, and lit both of the short candles. This was it! The festivities would begin!

Very quickly, I stepped back from the door. So, the older children knew. People brought the gifts. All the nice stories around Christmas of who brought gifts to the good children were just make believe. What about the baby Jesus? Did someone make Him up too? I felt a little sad, like I had lost something.

Before I could think any further, my mom opened the door to our little room and shouted, "Merry Christmas!" She had a great smile on her face, but sadness in her eyes.

In awe, I entered our little room. How festive it looked with the little Christmas tree and the lit candles on our small table. My mom sat down on her couch and looked to me to start our Christmas ritual.

Slowly, looking at the gifts, wondering which one she made for me, I recited my poem without too much stuttering. Then, my sister took her turn. She did very well. I only had to help her out once, by whispering the next few words so she could go on with her poem.

Our mom smiled at us and told us that we did very well. Then my sister and I sang the two verses of our surprise hymn.

I thought my mom would cry, but she stood up after we finished singing, hugged us and said, "Thanks for the song, it was beautiful!"

Next, before she gave us our presents, we readied ourselves for our festive Christmas Eve dinner. Mom busied herself by our little stove while the two of us sat down at the table admiring our pretty tree. My mind flew to Ola, and I wondered if she shared Christmas evening with anyone tonight. Looking over to the customary Christmas plate, I decided to save the fine candy for Ola and take it to her tomorrow.

Something sure smelled good!

Tonight, the rich, faraway people enjoyed the carp we had harvested. People who had either raised a goose or bought one, would eat it tonight. Some people even ate duck. I had heard my grandma saying that the goose and the duck tasted most delicious and wondered if we'd have one of those tonight.

Before I could go on wondering about anything else, my mom came over and placed three plates on our table. My sister's and my plate held a big helping of potato salad and part of a steaming, fried sausage, as long as my finger. What a great surprise!

After our mom poured some hot tea in our mugs and sat down, we began to eat this fine meal. I cut the great smelling sausage into small pieces, so I could enjoy it longer. While cutting the sausage grease escaped from it and I mixed it together with the potato salad. My, how delicious it tasted.

Mom's plate had no sausage, and only a small helping of potato salad.

When I looked at her, she said, "I'm not very hungry tonight," and smiled.

For some reason I didn't believe that. I took my fork, loaded it with small pieces of my sausage, and without a word, placed it on her plate. Mom smiled and turned her face away from us. After a moment, she turned back and slowly ate the sausage. After all of us finished every last morsel, I cleared the table and placed the dishes in our bowl to wash them later.

Now came the exciting part of Christmas. After the two of us sang our song again that we had practiced for so long in our outhouse, my mom stood up. She hugged both of us, wished us a Merry Christmas and handed us each our Christmas plate and our gift.

Gently, I unfolded my gift. I found a beautiful sweater made of many colored yarns. A small ball of yarn tucked inside the sweater fell out and rolled over the floor.

Mom caught it, handed it to me and said, "With this, you can knit your doll a fine hat to cover her cracked head."

Quickly I threw my arms around my mom and thanked her for the fine gifts. She took a strange, deep breath and hugged me. My sister received a similar sweater and a scarf for her doll. The short candles burnt down, sucked up the last drop of wax, flickered a few times, and died.

I turned on the dim electric lamp and walked over to our wooden stand which held the small bowl we washed everything in, even ourselves. Just as I poured the hot water into the old, rusty bowl, I heard the stairs in our house squeaking. I hurriedly opened the door to see Grandma with gifts in her hand and a pot that steamed and smelled like coffee. Oh, how my mom liked the coffee, even though it smelled like the kind made out of burned wheat.

Smiling ever so happily, my grandma came inside our little room and sat down on the first chair she reached, trying to catch her breath. Grandma was a big woman by now and had some kind of heart problem that prevented her from walking, or climbing stairs with ease.

After a brief moment of catching her breath, she handed my mom the coffeepot and said, "Merry Christmas!" Then she handed each of us our present.

I could barely believe it, but Grandma had knitted both of us a pair of very long stockings. She made them just about as long as my legs, and in my favorite color, blue. How snuggly warm they'd keep my legs. I never had such long stockings, only the ones that came up almost to my knees. I wondered how they'd stay up. Then I saw two thick strings attached to the top of each stocking, to tie them to my legs. How clever! While my mom and grandma drank coffee and talked about tomorrow, the first Christmas day's activities, I washed and dried our few dishes. Suddenly, I realized that I had forgotten to give them both my first store bought gifts. Anxiously, I ran out of the room and retrieved my precious gifts from beneath my dead grandpa's shoes. Full of excitement and gleaming with pride, I walked back into our little room and handed both of my favorite people their gifts.

I'll never forget the surprised looks on their faces. Both of them smiled and felt the clean white paper. I guessed that since my family never wasted money to wrap a gift, they might not know that it really concealed a gift. How wrong I was. Both opened their gifts at the same time, looked at me in surprise and with twinkling eyes.

My grandma said to my mother, "She's growing up fine."

Those words sure made me feel proud. Soon my grandma pulled a bottle of strawberry liquor from her apron pocket. She poured some of it into their mugs of hot coffee. Then she let my sister and me have a short drink of that sweet liquor right out of the bottle. How smooth it tasted, and how it warmed my stomach. We sang a few more Christmas songs together before my mom declared bedtime.

Together, my sister and I snuggled up beneath our thick, feather bedcover. Putting our icy cold feet near the almost hot bricks, my mom had laid in our bed, felt awfully good. I looked through the partially frozen window and silently wished our island witch a good night. A warm feeling came over me when I saw her faint, happy face on the slightly frozen glass of the window.

Thousands of large snowflakes tumbled down from the sky. What a pretty sight! I closed my eyes and soon danced among the million flakes, wearing my beautiful new sweater and the warm, long stockings. What a wonderful Christmas Eve we had and what a lucky child I was this year to receive three gifts.

CʒCʒCʒ

The next morning, on the first Christmas day, I woke up early. I wasn't sure if the great smell of baking bread woke me, or the movements under our bedcover by my feet, which scared me.

Were there rats in our bed? Perhaps they had already eaten my feet off.

I picked up my pillow in a hurry and slammed it down on whatever crawled around my feet. Before I even picked it up for the second hit, a short, quick whine came from beneath our bedcovers. That sure didn't sound like rats, but like a dog's cry!

At that moment, my little sister woke up. She must have felt the movement in our bed as well. When I saw her getting ready to scream, I put my hand over her mouth to stop her.

I whispered, "We're fine. If you scream, I'll hit you hard!"

She nodded her head.

There it came, crouching up between us and whining softly. I didn't think it could be my dog, but when I lifted the bedcover a bit, I saw Harras. He crouched up to me, stuck his head out from beneath our covers and greeted me with a soft lick across my face.

Oh boy, my mom had barely agreed that he could sleep beneath our bed in the harsh winter months, and here he sat in our bed. If she found out, my sweet dog would have to sleep in the cold lean-to again. I'd be in real trouble and that on the first Christmas day.

Hastily, I grabbed him and placed him down on the floor on his old, castaway blanket. What a relief that my mom hadn't seen him in our bed. Quickly I took my sister's and my clothes off our bedpost and climbed back under the warm feather cover. We warmed up our ice-cold day clothes for a moment and then, careful not to let the bitter cold air come into our bed, we dressed. This changing clothes just didn't make sense to me. Why not just sleep in our day clothes?

No matter how often or how nicely I tried to explain this to Mom, she didn't like that idea. She didn't even know that we dressed beneath our covers. I hoped she'd never find out.

When I saw the light on in my mom's room, I slipped out of bed to see what she was doing. A wonderful smell escaped from her room. Though still dark, the moonlight let me see enough to know that my dog looked at the stairs and me. I knew that look. He needed to go outside.

I held onto the handrail and walked down the stairs to the front door. I saw a light in Grandma's room, and it smelled great down there too. All that good smell made me very hungry even though I had a big Christmas Eve meal the night before.

When I opened the front door, extremely cold air bit into my naked face. My dog took one sniff at the awfully cold air and refused to go out into the bitter cold world. I had to pick him up and carry him outside to do his business.

Our two front steps barely had any snow on them, but past that, the snow came way up to my belly. In the clear sky, many thousands of stars lit the dark world. I looked for the bright star of Bethlehem, which in my young mind, should shine the night of Christ's birthday, but I couldn't find it. After one more ice-cold gust in my face, I gave up the search for the bright star. Very quickly, I stepped up the stairs over my dog's puddle, opened the door, and both of us quickly walked back inside, where the harsh wind could no longer bite at us.

While walking upstairs I wondered how many people would come to visit today. Family members customarily gathered at their parents' place or the home of the oldest living child. Some of my grandma's children lived on this island. They'd visit for sure, unless they got snowed in.

With a happy good morning greeting, I walked into my mom's already warm room. She had just placed a freshly baked, steaming bread on our table. Anticipating the great taste in a short while, I sat down next to the bread, inhaling its wonderful smell.

Mom poured hot peppermint tea into our mugs and fetched her bread knife. With a twinkle in her eyes and a smile on her face, she wished us a happy day and sliced up the complete round loaf of bread. She didn't bake the usual dark bread though. This loaf had a grey color and pieces of dried plums inside of it. Usually she only sliced the ration for each meal off the loaf and wrapped the rest of the bread up in a towel so the flies couldn't eat it. I wondered if this meant we could eat as much as we wanted to.

Ever so proudly, my mom passed the wooden board with the great smelling, steaming bread to me and said, "This morning you can eat all you want. Have a great Christmas!"

What a wonderful surprise! I took three pieces and spread a little precious honey on each of them. Slowly I ate all three delicious pieces of the holiday bread. We even had beet sugar for our tea. What a wonderful Christmas morning we had.

Slowly, daylight lit up our island and we had to go outside and shovel snow. In no time at all, with everyone out shoveling, except for the baby, we had cleared a narrow walk to each side of our neighbors. Then we spread cold ashes on it to make the path not so slippery. Looking south, all of the shoveled paths looked funny, like a snake had slithered down to the bay.

Finished shoveling, I walked inside our house, took my sweet, homemade candy off my Christmas plate and stuck it inside my coat pocket. I whistled for my dog to follow me. He looked at me with a questioning face, but obeyed. The snow on each side of the long, shoveled path stood higher than I, and the stinging wind couldn't reach me. My dog followed me willingly now and we ran up the path to our island witch's little house. He marked the path frequently.

Soon, we reached the small house. Grey smoke, with little sparks of red cinder rose from her tall chimney toward the blue sky. When I arrived at her house, I took off my messy rubber boots and knocked on her door. Ola opened the door and asked me nicely to come inside. I told my dog to stay outside, but she invited him in with a graceful move of her skinny, old hand. He quickly ran past me and jumped inside her warm house.

Once inside, I took my candy out of my pocket, reached up to Ola, gave her a tight hug, wished her a Merry Christmas and proudly handed her my candy.

She smiled at me, touched my head and answered, "Thank you

my child!"

At that moment, I felt more for her than just liking or admiring her, but I didn't know what to call it. With somewhat of a strange, but very happy feeling, I left her house.

On our way home, Harras ran tight circles around me. He seemed very excited about something. After a short walk on the shoveled path, my hands began to freeze and I stuck them in my coat pocket. I felt something in both of my pockets. How strange, because when I left our house, I only had the Christmas candy for Ola in one pocket.

Abruptly, I stopped and so did my dog. He sat up and stared at my pockets. A little confused, but excited, I grabbed the things inside my pockets and pulled them out. What a surprise! I had three hard Christmas candies, just like the ones my grandma made, in one hand and one good-size bone in the other hand!

For a moment, I stood in astonishment wondering where those treats came from. Then I smiled and silently thanked Ola in our secret way of talking to each other. Oh, how nice of her. Quickly, I sat down in the snow bank, handed my begging dog the fine bone and ever so slowly ate one of the sweet candies. Harras tried his best to eat the big bone, but he merely chewed off a small part. He then carried his fine gift home to hide it for a while until he got hungry for it again, and I did the same with my candy.

Back at home, after hiding my candy, I rubbed my stiff, freezing hands near our little oven until they warmed. Meanwhile, my dog desperately tried to find a place to hide his precious gift in the attic. Then I started to knit the hat for my doll.

By the time I began the second row, the front door opened and happy voices questioned, "Is anyone home?"

"Yes," I screamed and ran downstairs to greet the first visitors.

Two of my aunts with their husbands and children walked here from the next village to bring Christmas greetings to us. We didn't exchange gifts, but everyone brought something to eat with them. Before the friendly greetings had ended, more relatives arrived with their children. Now our house brimmed full of people, all laughing, hugging, and talking at the same time, except for the children.

My bored cousins and nephews gathered around me and said, "Let's do something!"

I took my coat, warm cap and my gloves off the stair railing and said, "Follow me!"

Outside, I declared that we should build a big snow bungalow in our large backyard. They responded with a loud "Yeah!" and happy laughter. I stopped at the lean-to and handed out all the tools we needed and a ready, willing bunch of us walked down our garden. My Uncle Fred had shown me some time back how to build a bungalow out of blocks of heavy snow. After I told everyone how to cut and stack the snow bricks, our whole group of about a dozen children or so got to work. Uncle Fred came outside a few times to see if we needed help, or perhaps guidance, but we were doing fine, at least we thought so. Halfway through building our snow fort, Grandma and Aunt Hilde came outside and brought us some hot tea.

They told us, "Let us know when you finish your snow fort so we can bring you some food to enjoy inside of it."

Anxiously we kept on building. We had so much fun. While we cut and stacked snow blocks, one of us started to make up a funny story and the next child added to it and so on down the line. We laughed, joked and had a very great time. Occasionally, someone slipped and fell in the snow, and the rest of us would all lie beside him and make snow angels.

In the early afternoon, when the sun sank into her frozen bed, we placed the last few critical snow blocks on top of our building to close the opening in our roof. We held our breath for a moment, hoping our building wouldn't collapse. The blocks hung motionless in their place. We all shouted, "Hooray, hooray!"

To celebrate our masterpiece, we had a good old fashioned, rowdy snowball fight in the next neighbor's yard. Soon, some adults with stacks of food and a lantern interrupted us. They set the lit lantern inside our bungalow and asked us to come to get some food. Hungry by now, I looked forward to eating something. The snowball fight stopped immediately, and everyone ran inside our snow bungalow.

The adults had brought warm sandwiches and more hot tea. The sandwiches consisted of two slices of dark bread with a thick slice of fried pork meat, and fried apple pieces in the middle of the bread. Still breathing heavily from our rowdy snowball fight, we sat down in our snow building and enjoyed our big, delicious sandwiches.

When we had just about finished eating, my Aunt Lenie came inside and gave all of us a sweet, brown cookie. What a surprise! Right behind her, Harras walked into our snow house. He looked at us, sniffed around for fallen crumbs, walked to the middle of our dear snow building and pooped on the floor. Outraged, all of us jumped up from the frozen ground at once. Someone must have touched the roof blocks, which made the roof collapse, and the snow bricks fell down on us.

What a disaster! Everyone screamed. The lantern fell over and darkness surrounded us. Falling snow blocks had knocked down some of the kids. I stumbled over someone and fell on top of him. Harras barked up a storm outside and I lost the last bite of my sweet, dark cookie.

I tried to stand up and walk outside, but something knocked me down again. When my eyes adjusted to the darkness, I saw the opening of our snow building. I crawled along the icy floor and reached the outside safely. Most of the children had already escaped, when suddenly, more of the snow bricks fell down.

We started to laugh until we noticed that little Harry was missing. A mass of upset relatives heard our screams and came running outside. When they reached us, I walked inside our damaged snow bungalow to look for Harry, but couldn't find him. Panic raced up in me.

I called his name, but got no answer. Then I saw the pile of snow moving. Out crawled Harry. He still had his cookie in his hand. What a relief. Now all my relatives laughed out loud for a short while. Then they gathered their children, hugged each other and bid us farewell.

They walked into the cold, dark night holding onto each other, talking and still laughing. After a few more hand waves, they disappeared from our sight. The sleepy wind blew a few snowflakes from the roof of our house into my face. Even though all my relatives were long out of sight, I lifted my hand and waved goodbye once more. What a wonderful fun filled day we had all enjoyed.

My mom pulled on my arm and said, "It's bedtime, child."

I followed her upstairs, undressed and quickly slipped on my nightclothes. The air felt almost as cold underneath the roof of our house as it did outside. Quietly, I slid into our bed next to my sleeping sister. How great it felt to put my ice-cold feet near the hot brick. My warm breath rose straight up in the cold air to the brick shingles of our roof. My eyes grew heavy, and the small icicles hanging down from the shingles began to change into big birds that lifted me up and took me near the warm sun.

That had been a magical day for me, but later on, at the age of twelve, I had to sit inside the house with all my relatives and listen to them talk all day long. I found it terribly boring in the beginning because I wanted to go outside and play. Then, slowly, I began to enjoy the meetings.

Suddenly, I found it interesting to hear about everyone else, especially about the births of their babies. Eventually, it amazed me what the real old folks saw in their lives, how they lived, and the stories they passed on from their long gone relatives. Oh, how I yearn today to go to one of those exciting meetings one more time.

C3C3C3

Almost all of our village people celebrated the second Christmas day together in Uncle Max's barn, the biggest building in our village.

About midmorning, the men of our village started to get busy in and around that barn. They cleaned the animal stalls, moved large bales of straw to the middle of the building and arranged them around the stone enclosed fire ring for people to sit on.

Someone opened the wooden roof window so the smoke could find its way out of the building. One man let down the crude metal hooks that were attached to chains from the ceiling, so people could hang their pots to cook fish or meat in them. The boys brought in lots of wood and many buckets of water for everyone's use and emergency needs, in case the fire got out of hand. With all the chores done, the men lit the fire to get the barn at least a little warm.

Uncle Max took the old wooden sled and tied one of his plow horses to it. Together with his sons, he traveled to the north side of our island to pick up some freshly brewed beer. On the way back, he'd pick up my grandma with her loaded basket of all sorts of bottles, filled with fine liquor from her cellar.

All the grownups in our house kept busy preparing things for our special second Christmas day celebration. My grandma boiled a huge cod all morning long. He hung inside the lean-to, frozen stiff for a few months. Now and then, she poked it with a fork and cursed at it. Mom wrapped up my grandma's liquor bottles with towels and pieces of our cloth, humming away. Aunt Hilde cut up many onions. Tears rolled down her cheeks, but she happily moved her feet around to my mom's tune, as though dancing. Uncle Fred, her husband, dusted off his fiddle and promised his misbehaved boys to lock them up inside our outhouse for the night. They immediately stopped fighting.

My little sister sat forlorn on the cement floor near my mom, digging in her nose and eating what she dug out of it. I stood by to help my grandma who waited for that huge cod to finish cooking.

Impatient for the festivities of the second Christmas day to start, I sat down on Grandma's old, red sofa, which had seen many better times, and drifted away, daydreaming about the great time, we had on this day a year ago.

My grandma's deep voice brought me back to reality. She said, "This big sucker is finally done." She stuck the big fork through its head and took the huge cod out of the pot.

Then my grandma slammed that cod on her table. Water spat all over the place, but Grandma laughed. Eagerly, I jumped off the sofa to help her. She handed me a big ceramic bowl, which only had a few pieces of its rim missing. Grandma had placed torn pieces of bread, dried parsley, salt and ten eggs in it.

Grandma looked at me and said, "Well girl?"

Quickly, I answered, "I remember, Grandma!"

Then I took all the eggs out of the bowl, cracked them carefully and let their contents leak into the bowl. With both of my hands, I started to knead and mix the ingredients together, while my grandma threw pieces of the huge, cooked cod's flesh into the bowl.

I found it hard to keep up with Grandma. She worked very fast. Aunt Hilde came over and dumped the finely cut onions into the bowl and started to mix and knead on the other side of the huge bowl. Together we kept up with Grandma, and in no time at all, we had all the ingredients mixed to my grandma's liking.

Now came the fun part. We made many round patties out of the whole bowlful of ingredients. We must have made five or six patties for each of us. I thought it too much food for each person to eat, so I asked my grandma, "Why so many patties?"

She answered, "To give to the people who have nothing to eat tonight."

Somehow, I felt ashamed of thinking that we'd have them all to ourselves.

Grandma took her big, flat iron pot, the one with the handle on it, out from underneath her sofa, blew the dust out of it, put two huge ladles of pork grease into it and added all the fish patties on top of it. She looked around the kitchen and asked, "Are we ready?"

The answers came loud and clear. "Yes, let's go and celebrate!"

Everyone bundled up and excitedly talked about what fun we'd have on that night. When I walked outside to call our animals, I heard Uncle Max's horse sled coming down our road. Quickly, I called the animals. Our cat came out of our lean-to, swallowing the rest of a small mouse. My dog came running toward me in a great hurry, ready to eat or play. I picked up our cat and walked into the stall. My dog followed me happily. Quickly, I told them both to behave and not to bother the chickens which wintered in the inside stall.

After I quickly closed the stall door, I ran inside the hallway and shouted, "Grandma he's coming!"

In less than a minute, we had all gathered outside. Excitement showed in everyone's face. Uncle Max pulled back on the horse's reins, and it stopped right beside us. He jumped off the old, wooden sled to help us. Ever so gently, he and my grandma took the basket full of her precious liquor and set it onto the sled. Then he helped my grandma up the sled. He waved for me to come and ride on the sled too. Happily, I climbed up and sat down next to the wooden beer barrel.

Grandma handed me the pot with all the patties inside of it and told me, "Hold onto it tightly, child!" She held onto her basket.

Uncle Fred had to ride on the sled too, because of his wooden leg. The rest of my family had to walk, except for the baby. Aunt Hilde left him at home in his crib, a customary thing to do. Gently, the old plow horse pulled the sled to the barn. The warm air coming out of its big nostrils sent grey clouds way up into the cold air. Far above us, a lone seagull circled the frozen world searching for something to eat. In a couple of minutes, we arrived at Uncle Max's barn.

Everyone greeted my grandma with great respect and a sweet smile. They offered their help to unload the wagon. After we had unloaded everything, Uncle Max gave the big horse a bucket full of water to drink. Then he went on another ride to pick up the old folks who couldn't walk to the barn any longer.

Surprisingly, it felt very comfortable inside the barn this year. The wind barely moved at all today, instead of blowing through the holes and slits of the wooden siding with all its force. I helped my grandma unwrap her bottles and set up shop on one side of the barn. People, mostly the men, came to her to barter for her fine spirits. They made deals, but never wrote anything down. I wondered how my grandma could remember who owed her how many, or what kind of fish that she'd smoke and sell, or barter later on. Or who owed her how much feed for her chickens, fruits or sawdust for her smoking ton, perhaps a sack of potatoes, a rubber shoe for the water pump, or a certain time of labor.

I noticed that the son of the beer brewer, who had set up shop across from us, had no business yet.

When my grandma closed shop before she sold all her bottles, I asked her, "What about the rest of the bottles and how can you remember what all those people bartered for with you and what they owe you?"

My grandma sat down next to me on the straw bale, held my hand and whispered into my ear. "The rest of my fine liquor I'll give to the old folks who have nothing to barter. You see, my child, in a way, the younger people that bartered for my fine spirits this afternoon, have paid for a nice drink for the poor, old people. They just don't know it, and so we won't tell them."

I promised not to tell.

After a few breaths, my grandma got real close to my ear again and whispered, "Most of our village people are very honest. I don't have to remember what and how much each individual owes me. You see, those people know! Their neighbors, who stood next to them, also know. I remember exactly what the few dishonest people owe me."

Amazed, I realized what a smart grandma I had.

Soon, the sled arrived with the old folks on it. Many of the village men went outside to carry them inside the barn and set them down on the straw bales next to each other near the fire. They had brought pillows, blankets, their cups and plates.

After all five of them seemed comfortable and began talking to each other, my grandma told me, "On this second Christmas night, I'd like you to keep these five old people happy."

She gave me one of her liquor bottles, showed me how much to pour into each of their cups, and said, "Smile, child, and go on."

The moment the old folks saw me walking toward them, they smiled. I reached out my hand, greeted them with great respect and a bright smile. They stopped talking among themselves and welcomed me with a friendly handshake. I poured them each the amount into their mugs that grandma told me.

They lifted their mugs toward me, and with big, toothless smiles they said, "Merry Christmas, girl!"

I wondered why none of them had any teeth in their mouths. At least my grandma had one and a half teeth left. I didn't know if I should stay there with the old folks or if I could walk around and have some fun. I looked at my grandma for an answer. She waved me to come to her. When I reached her, she explained how often to take drinks to the old ones and when to take them food.

Relieved not to have to stay near them all the time, I walked down the inside of the barn to see all the animals. The old plow horses stood in a stall, which no longer had a door on it. I walked close to them, stroked their heads and wished them a fine night. They lifted their large heads, looked at me for a moment with their mysterious, dark eyes, then they bent back down to chew away on some fine smelling hay.

The milk cow, stuck her head out of an opening in her pen and watched the festival with great interest. The light from the fire reflected in her big, brown eyes. She sure had long eyelashes. I gently stroked her face, and she stuck out her long, rough tongue to touch my hand.

A flock of noisy, upset chickens came running into this end of the barn to escape from all the loud people. Two sheep rested in the corner watching the fire, and Uncle Max had tied his big dogs up next to the sheep. They didn't like being tied up and complained about it to me with low whining noises. I told them that they wouldn't stay tied up for very long, but I don't think they believed me because they both kept on whining. Then I caught a whiff of a great smell and went to find out what it was. Some of our village women sat on straw bales, talking and laughing. Others tended to the food they had so dearly saved up for this special occasion. Many pots of various sizes hung over the burning fire. Some of them sizzled and the fine smell of pork grease filled the barn. Steam escaped from others, hiding their precious meal inside of them.

Five long eels hung down from one hook. Grease started to leak out of them into the big fire, making it blaze wildly and send sparks flying. One older boy with a bucket full of water, kept a keen eye on those sparks. He was ready to pour water on them, when needed.

Most of the men stood by themselves, away from the fire at this moment, smoking green cigars and having somber conversations. None of them laughed like the women and children did. Perhaps another passing of my grandma's fine liquor might ease their minds.

All the cooking filled the barn with a great smell, making me very hungry again. Mom tended to the flat pot with all the patties. Grandma had the big water bucket boiling and ladled out hot water into the children's and adults' cups they had brought with them to brew tea.

Some children played skip the stone while others played hide-and-seek. A few older girls watched the boys about their age who tended the fire. They giggled and whispered and giggled some more. How silly they acted. My grandma waved me to her.

She asked me, "Did you see anyone of the Willard family?"

I shook my head and said, "No, Grandma."

She then waved my Aunt Hilde over and told her, "Tend to the hot water."

She gave me a liquor bottle and told me to refill the old peoples' cups. Then, she slipped on her coat, put on her cap, and left the barn. In a great hurry, I refilled the smiling old folks' cups. Then I fetched my coat and ran after my grandma.

The Willard family lived in a stone house not far from us. The cruel ocean took Mister Willard's life about a year ago. He left behind eleven children and his pregnant wife. His widow supported her family with her ability to sew well by hand, and she and all her children worked hard in the fields during the warm season. However, despite all that, it wasn't enough income to get them through the long, harsh winters. Anyone who had a little extra food, even if only soup bones, gave it to them, but most families didn't have enough for themselves in the winter.

Mrs. Willard's baby, a tiny, red haired girl, died shortly after birth. Her mother gave her back to the sea to give her another chance to live. I dearly hoped she'd be born again to a rich family, one of those that ate carp for Christmas. Surely, there she'd have enough food to live for a long time.

I caught up with my grandma in front of the Willard's house. We knocked at their door.

A weak voice said, "Come on in."

We walked into the ice-cold, two-room house. Mrs. Willard sat on an old chair next to a small, cold oven with a blanket wrapped around herself and shivered fiercely. A empty pot sat on the stove, and I saw no food on the old table or shelf. Her red eyes filled with tears.

All eleven children were fully dressed, most likely with all the clothes they owned. They huddled together under some blankets in the only three beds that stood in the room. All of them looked at us with big, sad, hungry eyes. I felt so bad and ashamed that we had so much to eat tonight and a warm featherbed to sleep in, while these people, our neighbors, had just about nothing. Grandma opened her mouth, but no words came out of it. That was the first time I saw my grandma speechless.

In a moment, she put her arms around the shaking Mrs. Willard. "Right now I'd like all of you children get out of bed, wrap up in your blankets and hurry down to the Christmas celebration!"

Our neighbor shook her head and said in an unsteady voice, "We can't go. We have no food to bring. We ate our last bread on Christmas Eve."

My big grandma picked up the skinny neighbor from her chair and said, "I insist!"

That tone in her voice gave no one a choice other than to follow her orders.

All the hungry children jumped out of their beds, wrapped their blankets around themselves and ran out of their house in a great hurry, as though it were on fire. Both of us helped Mrs. Willard along. She could barely walk. I wondered when she last ate. At that moment, I decided to let her eat my patty tonight. Surely, Mom would have some bread for me in the morning. She usually did. Then I remembered that we made enough fish patties for all of us.

Soon we reached Uncle Max's barn and saw Mrs. Willard's children sitting together on a straw bale, close to the warming fire. They clutched their hands around the cups of hot tea which someone had handed them. Their eyes focused on all the hanging pots over the fire. We took their mom over to sit with her children near the warming fire.

I took my cup, added tea and hot water and placed it in her trembling hands. She thanked me with a tired smile.

Before long, women carefully took pots off the large, iron hooks and called the children to come and eat. Aunt Hilde sliced our long, dark bread all the way to its end. Grandma's big flat pot stood on the ground now with all those patties inside of it. They swam in the hot, bubbling lard. What a delicious smell came rising out of that pot.

My grandma told me to take two of our plates and place six slices of bread on each plate, which I did right away. Mom fished enough patties out of the hot lard to put one on each piece of bread.

Then my grandma said to me, "Come on girl. Carry one of those plates, and I'll carry the other."

Together we took the plates over to the straw bale, where the Willard family sat. When the children saw us coming, all of them stood up and stared at us with hope in their faces.

We handed each of them a warm fish patty, and they all hurriedly slung their food down. Mrs. Willard's tears dropped onto her patty, while she thanked us. I felt so great to give them some food. The rest of our village neighbors watched us and knew what to do. One elderly woman walked over to the needy family with her soup pot and ladled hot soup into their cups. Someone brought over whole, boiled potatoes. The old man, who cooked the eel over the fire, brought over a plate full of eel pieces. Just about every family in our village brought something to eat over to the Willard family. What a great village I lived in.

Then I heard my grandma's call, loud and clear. Quickly, I walked over to her. She handed me a plate with ten fish patties on it and the liquor bottle. I knew what I needed to do and walked over to the old folks. They thanked me for the food and refills of their drinks.

One of the old men told me, "My, you're a pretty girl," and the others agreed with him.

All the compliments embarrassed me, but I liked the flattery. I walked away from the old folks with a bright smile on my face.

When I sat down on the straw bale with my family, my mom handed every one of us a plate with two patties, and I ate both of mine. The still hot lard trickled out of the patty and soaked into the dark bread. What a delicious dinner we had.

Soon the meal ended, and Uncle Fred started to play his fiddle. Other men joined in with their harmonicas, and one woman played a long flute. We sang Christmas songs at first. After a while, the music changed to dance music.

The beer seller boy got busy and Aunt Hilde started to dance by herself. She was always the first one to dance and often the last one to quit. Her husband, Uncle Fred, could no longer dance with her, since he had long ago lost his right leg. She just stretched out her arms and pretended to hold onto him. By now, all the men mixed with the women and they, too, began to smile and laugh.

Uncle Max's oldest boy came toward the large fire ring leading one of the old plow horses. He asked if anyone wanted to ride on the big horse. Just about all of us smaller children screamed "Yeah!" and ran over to him. I reached him first. He lifted me up and sat me down real close to the horse's head. Then he lifted four more children up onto the big horse and sat them down behind me. Around and around the fire ring we rode. I lifted my arms, spread them out to my sides, and pretended that the old plow horse became a wild, black stallion with wings. I closed my eyes and left my island with him. We flew up high to the stars, along the mighty Milky Way. I felt his hot breath and smelled his sweat.

Too soon, this wonderful ride ended and I had to get off my wild, flying stallion. I petted the grey horse's neck and thanked him for the fine ride. He turned his head and looked at me with his huge, mysterious eyes. He had the same deep, dark, shiny eyes as the wild horses had in my feverish dream when I had smallpox.

All of us smaller children played hide-and-seek in that great barn way into the night. For a while, I couldn't find my sister. She hid behind an empty trough and fell asleep. At my next turn to find everyone, I found a couple of older children necking among the hay bales.

They got angry with me and wanted to hit me, but I told them, "I'll scream out loud so your parents can hear me and come to see you together in this hay." They quickly changed their mind.

The adults of our village had a short meeting between their dancing and frolicking. Then, all of them walked over to Mrs. Willard. Whatever they said to her, made her cry again, but she nodded her head in agreement. My grandma sat down next to her, poured a drink from her sweet liquor bottle into Mrs. Willard's mug, and put her arms around her. She buried her wet face on my grandma's big chest. Her whole body kept on shaking.

After a few more games, most of us smaller children sat down, exhausted.

My mom waved Uncle Fred to come to her and she told my fiddle playing uncle, "It's time to tell the kids a good night story."

This was a very special moment.

Only on rare occasions, but for sure on every second Christmas night, someone told us a good night story. Uncle Fred always told great stories, ranking second only to my grandma's. He waved his hand in the air, and we followed him into a stall filled with hay and blankets. How wonderful to lie down close together, in the soft, sweet-smelling hay, covered up with our blankets. The music started again, and so did the laughing and singing.

Though dark in this end of the barn, I could see the fire pit and part of the festivities from here. Aunt Hilde danced wilder and lifted her long skirt to show her ankles. I wondered how her husband felt since he couldn't dance with her anymore. Some of the older boys stared at her and grinned.

My uncle cleared his throat and began to tell his Christmas night story. Some people told the boring story about the baby Jesus' birth, which all of us knew already, but not Uncle Fred. His stories included scary ghosts, fire spitting dragons, blood-sucking monster spiders, and of course, the mighty devil himself—all in the barn where Jesus was born.

He made sure to talk quieter and quieter, as the story went on, until everyone had fallen asleep. None of us ever heard the endings of his stories and pleaded with him the next morning to tell the story again so we all could hear the ending. But he always answered, "Oh no, I can only tell these stories on the second Christmas night!"

Some time before the morning came over our island, the adults woke us. Mothers wrapped their children up in blankets. Fathers picked up the smallest of their children and everyone left the still warm barn, except for my Aunt Hilde who continued to dance.

My grandma and Uncle Fred sat in the sled, which took the old folks to their homes, too. Grandma held her basket full of empty bottles in one hand and her big, flat pot in the other. Her head hung down on her chest and she slept.

Mom held on tightly to my sister's hand and mine as we slowly walked to our house. Some neighbors sang all the way to their homes. Quite a few stumbled and fell into the snow. The three of us only fell down once. We found it hard to get Mom back up in the standing position because she kept on sliding back down when we pulled her up. Eventually, with the help of a neighbor, we lifted her up.

When we entered our house, Grandma's loud snore assured us that she had arrived home safely. Mom made it upstairs all right while holding onto the railing and with the two of us pushing on her buttocks. She waved us good night as she walked into her room. Quickly, my sister and I took off our blankets and our coats and jumped into our bed. We didn't change into our nightgowns. We figured Mom wouldn't check on us since she was too tired from celebrating all night long.

C3C3C3

For some reason unknown to me at the age of about ten, the next day was very strange. The adults in our house slept way into the day. After they finally got out of bed, they walked around very slowly, often holding their heads and constantly telling us, with a hurting look in their faces, to stay quiet.

That late afternoon, when my grandma felt better, I asked her why Mrs. Willard cried in the barn when the adults of our village talked to her.

She said, "Our neighbor cried out of relief. You see, she has no means to feed herself and her eleven children. All of them will starve to death unless we help them through this winter. Our village people talked her situation over and offered to help. Ten of our families will each take in one of her children through the winter. Mrs. Willard and her smallest son will stay here with me in my room. I know we'll be more crowded in this house and our food supply stretched way past its limit, but we have to help each other out. We do like my mom told me so long ago, 'Just add more water to the soup!'"

I looked up to my grandma with pride, hugged her and whispered in her ear, "You're the best person in the whole, wide world."

My grandma looked at her small windup clock and said, "People will come and get the Willard children soon. I need to go over to her house and help. Please come with me and bring little Emil back to my room and tell him some stories."

We put our coats on, walked down the snow covered path and knocked on Mrs. Willard's door. She opened the door with dry eyes, but she looked sad. All the children stood together with their blankets and a few pieces of clothing in their hands, waiting for someone to pick them up.

Though none of them cried, I wondered how they felt deep inside their hearts. She told her children, "You're lucky to go to someone's home, and I expect you to behave."

She promised them that they'd all come back together in spring, when the fieldwork started.

Her children nodded and said, "Yes, Mama."

I called little Emil, and he came to me. Hand in hand, we walked back to our house. I pulled one of Grandma's chairs close to the window, sat down in it and lifted Emil up into my lap.

Through the ice-free top of the window, I watched the Willard children leave one by one with an adult, while I told Emil sweet stories. He sat still in my lap and listened in awe.

Soon, my grandma and Mrs. Willard walked toward our house, carrying blankets and clothing. Emil smiled to see his mama again. He jumped off my lap and clung to her. She picked him up and walked close to Grandma's oven to warm her shaking body. Emil slept with Grandma inside her bed, and Mrs. Willard slept on Grandma's narrow old sofa.

Two days later, Mrs. Willard unexpectedly died in the dark, cold winter night. My grandma told me that she died of a broken heart. I wondered how hearts could break. All her children stayed with the people that chose them to stay for the winter until they could take care of themselves.

Little Emil often asked to see his mama.

Grandma always told him, "Your mama will come soon to take you with her."

The following spring, little Emil went to live with a childless couple in Denmark. He was almost four-years-old by then and happy "his" mama had come to pick him up. A lone tear slowly ran down my grandma's cheek, and her body trembled when he waved goodbye to her with a bright smile on his little face.

No curry, showers, or Oscar Meyer wieners.

Chapter 77

Happy New Year!

During the day of New Year's Eve, our preacher tried to visit as many people in the small town and nearby villages as the weather allowed. He spent just a short while to shake hands with the men and perhaps look at a newborn baby. The village people who could afford it, offered him a warm drink, perhaps a small sandwich, or a homegrown cigar.

Early that day, my mom walked downstairs and into my grandma's room and sharply asked my grandma, "What are you going to offer that no-good preacher this year?"

After a brief moment of silence, my grandma answered, "I've saved up just enough real coffee beans to brew him a fine cup of coffee."

As happened every year I can remember, my mom got angry with my grandma. She called the preacher a thief and a few other words I usually didn't hear in our house.

Then Mom slammed grandma's door and steamed upstairs, shouting, "I'll never talk to you again!"Grandma then shouted back at her. "Erna, this is none of your darn business!"

I always felt bad about my mom's behavior and went into my grandma's room, hugged her and told her, "My mom really isn't mad at you," to make her feel better.

Usually, Grandma just said, "That's all right, my girl. She'll change her mind by morning."

But this time, Grandma stopped slicing cabbage and looked directly at me. Then she said, "You see, you have a fine mother, but somehow she believes that I give away my precious few, real coffee beans to our preacher. She thinks that I believe that cup of real coffee gets me an extra prayer from the preacher so I'll go to heaven. You're big enough now to learn how I do business, so please stay and watch."

Soon, my grandma finished slicing the cabbage. She pushed a little metal pot closer to the middle of her stove. Soon, it began to boil and filled the whole room with the delicious aroma of real coffee. Grandma took an old sack and tightly wrapped up four bottles of the finest from her cellar.

She then said, "He'll bring four empty ones and will pay with real money."

Before long, a loud knock sounded on our wooden front door and in walked our huge, heavy preacher. With his deep voice he shouted out, "Happy New Year!"

I thought our small house shook a little.

My uncle came out of his part of our house and shook hands heftily with our preacher. He handed the preacher a home rolled, green cigar. Meanwhile my grandma poured the real coffee into her finest, small cup and set in onto her table. She then asked the preacher to come inside, which he did with a great smile on his fat face. She pointed toward the old, red sofa for him to sit down on.

The moment he sat down on the aged, woodworm infested sofa, it squeaked, moaned and bent down a lot in the middle onto the metal can which stood below it for support. I worried the sofa would break under the preacher's heavy weight, but though it complained on and off, it held together.

The preacher slurped my grandma's coffee down in a hurry and stood up. He handed her the sack with the empty bottles, reached inside his pants pocket and placed a huge amount of small coins on Grandma's table. I wondered if they had come from the

Sunday collection plate, money which was supposed to go to a land where the lepers lived.

With his right forefinger, our preacher split the change apart to count it quickly. After he assured himself that he had counted out the correct amount, he turned to my grandma, grabbed the sack she handed him and said, "Elise, you're the best!"

In the hallway, he looked up the stairs and shouted, "Come to church, Erna!"

My mom answered him, "The day the devil grabs your conniving soul and takes you to hell, I'll come to church again!"

Our preacher stomped out the door without an answer. He stashed the old sack with Grandma's liquor bottles on his sled and walked beside the horse to the next house.

My grandma sat down on the sofa and asked me to count all the change, which I happily did.

Then she said, "Now, take away the money that I usually sell these bottles for and see how much is left."

Surprised, I found out that we had enough money left to buy one more of my grandma's bottles.

She smiled at me and said, "You see my child, he paid for the small cup of coffee and for me to stay quiet about what he bought here."

Grandma took the coffee grounds out of the preacher's cup and poured them back into her little coffeepot. In no time at all, the pot boiled and she poured herself a fine cup of coffee. Then she grinned and said, "That's what you call good business. Now we have a secret together. You can't even tell your mom. I don't want to lose one of my few cash paying customers."

Seeing all the real small coins on the table made me ask my grandma, "Are they the coins out of the Sunday collection plate?"

She answered, "Most likely child. Where else would one find so many small coins!"

By early afternoon, darkness had chased the day away, and all the children in our house gathered in my grandma's room with our treasure boxes, or bags, and our metal mugs in our hands. Uncle Fred brought in the small branches from a hedge, or tree, he had cut in the fall and stored inside the lean-to. He handed each of us a fine branch.

With great eagerness, we opened our treasure boxes and began to decorate our branches with small pieces of wool too short to use for anything else. We used parts of shoestrings and shells that had a hole in them, so we could tie them on the branches. We hung bird feathers, pieces of paper and even fish bones onto the branches. We used everything we saved from the years before and what we found while combing through our island waste dump. The small dump seldom contained useable items in those times, but we faithfully checked it out anytime we walked passed it.

While the apples baked inside Grandma's stove, she asked us to tell about our best and our worst day of the whole last year while we decorated our dried branches. After we had decorated them, we carefully stood them up against the wall in our little hallway. Then we sat down on Grandma's old, red sofa.

The pan with the baked apples stood on the table now and my grandma carefully placed one of the apples in each of our metal cups. Oh, how great they smelled. All of us smiled when she sprinkled brown sugar on top of them. While the steaming hot apples stood in front of us, my grandma took her turn to tell about her best and worst day of the last year.

I always hoped she'd hurry up so we could eat those delicious apples, but my grandma took her time. While she talked, I watched the brown sugar slowly melt into the hollowed out core of the green apple. When she finished talking, she handed each of us a spoon and we began to enjoy the delicious baked apples.

That night we all slept in my grandma's room underneath her bed. We didn't even have to take off our street clothes or our shoes. Grandma was much more practical about such things than my mom.

Like sardines in a can, we crawled close together underneath her bed and covered up with our feather covers. Two good sips of strawberry liquor for each of us, and Grandma began to tell one of her many, wonderful stories. I don't remember hearing the end of some of her stories, or seeing the little windup clock slip her tiny fingers into the next year.

By the first light of the New Year, all the children in our village dressed warmly, tied on their snowshoes, and grabbed their decorated branches. We met in front of our house to start our parade. There we stuck our pretty branches in the snow and began to welcome the New Year with as much noise as we could possibly make.

Some of us had cook pot lids and slapped them together, as hard as we could, while screaming, "Happy New Year!" Others whistled loudly, and the lucky ones who owned a cowbell or a horn, brought them to our parade. What a sight we made.

One after the other we marched down to the bay, stopping at intervals, making as much noise as we could and waving our pretty, decorated branches in the air. All the village dogs joined us in our parade and greatly helped to wake up every one of our village people.

By the time we reached the bay and turned around, all the many bells of our centuries-old church rang in the New Year. I'll never forget that fine tuned concert. On the way to church many children and adults joined in on our parade. The closer we walked to the church, the louder the wonderful bell concert sounded. By the time we climbed the few stone steps up into the graveyard which surrounded the huge, old church, the mighty bell concert stopped.

When I walked into the church through the massive, stone bell tower, its walls still vibrated from the bell concert. I always touched the wall with both of my hands and put my ear on the huge stones. I lingered a moment to listen to the sound of the vibrating stones and wished I knew what they felt or wanted to tell me.

Inside our amazingly beautiful church, our two story high, old organ greeted us with forceful, dramatic notes. Everything came to a hush. Even the few brave dogs that followed us inside our church hurriedly hid underneath the benches and remained respectfully quiet throughout the sermon. My dog lay beneath my feet and slept, all the while his tail slowly moved back and forth. I wondered what he saw in his dreams. A slight kick from my grandma now and then kept me awake through the sermon.

No bouillon cubes, Oreo cookies or hearing aids.

Chapter 78

A wedding in our fishing village.

Most people married in early fall after they had finished all the fieldwork. First, the engagement of the young lovers took place when the young man called on his girl at her home. A small ceremony took place where the groom knelt and asked the father of the girl for her hand in marriage. If the father took his girl's hand, placed it in the young man's hand and said, "You have my blessing," the two of them could get engaged.

The young man then placed a ring on the girl's left hand and kissed her in front of everyone. The father of the young woman asked his new son-in-law-to-be to step outside. There they smoked a homemade cigar and had a long talk about how the young man intended to take care of his daughter. The women inside the house congratulated the young woman, and laughed and cried all at the same time. From then on, the engaged couple could spend days and nights together in either of their family's house.

The engagement would supposedly last a year, but an unplanned child often interrupted that year. In that case, the couple got married quickly and quietly by our only man of the law inside his house. Our preacher refused to marry women who looked pregnant. During the year-long engagement, the entire village prepared for the big day. In that year, the extended family of the bride raised a pig for the festivities, and all the females in the village started to sew and knit to fill the bride's hope chest with basic needs which included two sheets, two pillows, a few towels and a heavy bedcover. In addition, they made a few rags to wash and clean up with and placed a pot or two in the hope chest. Perhaps someone had some dishes to spare from a loved one who had passed on. They even sewed a few baby outfits and added them to the hope chest with lots of rags to use as diapers. Surely, a baby would arrive before long.

The groom's family grew many extra vegetables for the big festivities. They made room, found a room, or built a shack for the newlyweds to live in and sparsely furnished it. They built a bed and acquired an oven to cook on. Those included the necessities to start out a newly married life. Tools and help to build the rest for the room came later on after the wedding. People always helped each other.

Oh, how excited and busy our whole village got with the prospect of such a grand festivity. Grandma organized who should sew or knit what items and asked our village people to look for worn out knitted clothing to unravel to make baby outfits. She also asked for supplies to brew some extra liquor in her cellar for the bridal feast. Since my mom, Uncle Fred and I were the experts in making mattresses on our island, we built one for every young couple.

Old woman Navers took our village wedding dress out of her closet and started to alter it for the bride. The long dress, made of white cloth, had very small seashells attached to it in circular patterns, like small rings. Long ago, many able hands had crocheted the train of the dress from very thin, white twine. With many different flowers crocheted into it, it surely looked like a beautiful work of art. The women attached it to the bride's head on her wedding day with an adjustable metal ring, which they hid with many seasonal flowers.

Finally, the week of the wedding arrived. The bride's family had slaughtered the pig a while back, cut it into many fine pieces, and took those to the salt barrels. Fine sausages and ham hung in the smoke house for quite some time and were ready to eat. Every family received some pieces of the butchered pig, to prepare their special dish. Our whole village busied themselves preparing fine foods in their houses to take to our big barn, where most of the festivities in our village took place.

The very important clear wedding soup, was cooked in the biggest pot of our village at the bride's house. The soup contained water, many bones from the pig, salt and many stalks of leek. For days it slowly simmered, mostly outside over an open fire. Though the father of the bride cooked the soup, his wife oversaw the whole operation.

Other men stopped by, smelled the soup and talked a while. The cook eventually took all the bones and the leeks out of the pot and took the pot to the barn. There he kept the soup warm over a low fire until served as the first course on the day of the wedding party. It had a very fine flavor to it, but I couldn't see why all the adults got so excited about the wedding soup; it had nothing swimming inside of it to fill me up.

The day before the young lovers said, "I do," the festivities began at the young woman's house. In the early afternoon, the men of the village brought by all sorts of equipment for the party, while the young pair remained out of sight. After a good sip from my grandma's cellar by all participants, someone escorted the couple outside, and the oldest person in our village with a clear mind, gave a speech, which went sort of this way: "My dear children, marriage is a very serious step in your lives. You'll have many obstacles to overcome, which some of them you will experience this afternoon. Let me lead you to that tree stump and let you practice how well you need to work together to have a warm, fulfilled relationship."

He handed them a two-handed saw and asked them to decide together how they could saw that old, dried out tree stump apart. While everyone watched, the two of them walked around the tree stump, looked at it, argued a little about where to start, but soon the saw dust flew and they began to sweat. Occasionally, they rested a moment, stood together, held hands and kicked that old stump. The children cheered them on, while most of the women gathered inside the house to gossip and have a laugh. It took quite some time before the couple sawed that old stump apart and slowly sank down next to it. They embraced each other, and the children clapped their hands, while jumping up and running toward them. When they reached the young lovers, they laughed and threw sawdust all over them.

Then the exhausted lovers had to build a tower out of all sorts of different shaped stones by just stacking them on top of one another. They usually failed in their first few attempts. A few men walked closer to them and gave advice on how to place the stones, so the tower would hold up. When they placed the last stone on top of the tower, the bystander's big applause roared over our village.

For the next step, all the women came back outside. Darkness slowly came to our island and all the children went home to collect their junk and the pot lids. A very long, narrow tree trunk, which soaked in the sea for many days, lay on the ground, and the lovers had to walk on top of it barefooted, holding and supporting each other. Whenever they fell, or slipped off, they had to start all over again.

Some let the girl walk in front and held her to keep her from sliding off. Others picked the girl up and tried to carry her over the slippery trunk. For some reason, unknown to me, the challenge made the women giggle a lot. This young man, after trying a few different ways to walk on the slippery trunk, took a sturdy stick to support himself, let his future wife hang onto his neck and walked across without slipping off even once.

After all this, the people gave the lovers some privacy, but they knew the celebrations of the night before their wedding had not yet ended, the night we called "Polterabend" in our German language. We really have no exact translation for it in English.

Then, someone built a fire in the back yard and people sat around it. They had another drink from Grandma's fine brews while the mother of the bride brought out some great smelling bread for everyone to enjoy. While we children came back quietly with our pot lids and junk, my grandma kept her eyes on the open window of the young lovers' room, to time their surprise just right.

As soon as they blew their candle out, my grandma waved to us children to follow her to the front of the house. Excited, we followed her and the minute she gave us her sign, we clapped the pot lids together with all the strength we had and screamed louder than we ever imagined we could, "Congratulations!"

The almost wedded couple came to the window and waved at us. Then we took all the broken parts of cans, jars, glass and things no longer usable that we had found in our small junk yard, or saved up for this occasion, and threw them in front of the door. After that, we clapped our lids together again, danced around the front door and made all the noise we possibly could. Before long, we felt so tired from all the screaming and dancing and settled down among the adults.

After the people set a few wind-up alarm clocks below the open window of the lovers' room to ring at various times, the adults had one more short drink. Then our village people slowly walked to their own homes.

Early the next morning, long before dawn, the young lovers woke, but to a different alarm clock, the bride's mother. They had to get out of bed, and together, clean up all the rubbish from the front door. It was a bad omen to let people or the new day, see such a mess in front of one's house.

In the morning, all of us children went out in the fields to gather flowers of every kind we could find, and took them to my uncle's barn. The adults weaved the prettiest flowers together in a wreath to fit over the bride's head, like a crown. They used the rest to decorate the big, old plow horse and the two-wheeled cart with. They placed two chairs in the back of the cart and tied them together. Just before noon that day, my uncle hitched his horse to the cart. Mom hurried us home to dress in our Sunday outfits, while someone taught the young groom how to lead the old horse.

Quickly, I slipped my worn out outfit off, dressed in my fine Sunday clothes and ran back to my uncle's barn, leaving my mom's warning of, "Don't get your dress dirty!" behind.

The three musicians of our island stood in front of the pretty cart, discussing what songs to play. People smiled with excitement and I wondered what marriage was all about. The only thing I had at our house to compare it with was my uncle and aunt. My aunt yelled a lot at my uncle and he seemed so sad so often. I quickly let go of that thought when the music started and the cart started to roll toward the bride's house with most of our village people following behind it.

At the bride's house, the young groom stopped the horse and elegantly walked toward the front door with a beautiful bouquet of white tulips in his hand. The door opened and there she stood, the bride, in her stunning wedding dress. I held my breath for a moment while he handed her the flowers, kissed her gently on the lips and offered his hand to walk her out of the door. She briefly hesitated and quickly turned toward her mom, as if to say her farewells. Then she took his hand, and both walked slowly over to the waiting wedding cart. Some of the gathered women wiped tears from their faces, while others had bitter smiles on their faces. At thirteen, I had no way to make any sense out of this, but it scared me a bit.

Arriving at the pretty decorated cart, the groom lifted his bride up into his arms and climbed onto the cart with her. There they sat down together on the two chairs. The bride's grandma came walking over to the cart with a very long rope garland made of fresh flowers. With the help of a few small children, she placed the rope around the young lovers' necks and folded it over in their laps. She looked at them with her old, wise eyes that had seen so much, raised her arms and waved her skinny, shaking hand at them. She looked sad and bitter. For a brief moment, I closed my eyes and thanked Ola for teaching me to see all these feelings.

The music started and my uncle led the old horse toward our beautiful, huge church. More people joined the wedding parade on the way. The bride laid her head on her soon-to-be-husband's shoulder and whispered something into his ear. At that moment, the old plow horse stopped and even after a lot of coaxing and yelling, refused to go on. Soon the bells in the tower of our big church began to call the wedding in. The groom stood up from his chair, picked up his lovely bride, jumped off the cart and carried her toward our church.

People laughed, applauded and followed the young couple inside. The groom and the bride walked inside the small chapel, while everyone else sat down on the old, wooden benches inside our big church. By the first note of the huge pipe organ echoing through the church, everyone stood up.

Here came two young flower girls in their Sunday dresses, walking very slowly out of the chapel, dropping one flower at a time onto the grey cobblestone floor. Following them came the nervous bride and groom. The bride tried to smile, but it didn't look like a happy smile. Two small boys, all dressed up, carried her long train up the aisle to the altar of our church, where the couple knelt in front of our preacher. The young children, under eight-years-old in the wedding party and from inside the church, gathered around them and sat down on the floor.

The organ quit playing and people sat down. The preacher put one hand on top of each of the young couple's heads, blessed them, raised his hands up to the heavens and said, "Rise up, children!" Then he held their right hands together and asked them the question that would completely change their lives. Both answered, "Yes, I will."

The groom took the slender engagement ring off the bride's left hand and placed it on a finger on her right hand. He lifted her veil and sealed their marriage with a kiss. The huge pipe organ began to play while the newlyweds walked down the aisle to leave our church. Both now wore happy smiles.

The old plow horse had made it to the church, and the groom lifted his bride into the cart. The three musicians started to play and the parade toward the groom's place began. In front of his parents' home, he picked his young wife up and out of the cart. He placed the beautiful, long flower garland over the entry door of the house and then carried his young wife into the house. Inside a private room, the young man took off her wedding dress and spent the afternoon there with her.

Everyone else left to go home, changed back into their regular clothes and got busy for the big party. My grandma took a long nap and the rest of the adults gathered the cooked foods and drinks and carried them down to the barn. Mom put me in charge of taking enough tableware to the barn for our whole family.

The moment I stepped into the barn with my basket full of dishes and utensils, I felt a real fun evening coming up. The big pot with the important wedding soup stood to the side over a small fire in the fire ring. The whole barn smelled of fine food, and I grew hungrier by the second. I knew though that tonight I'd get plenty to eat and ignored my stomach's complaints. After I sat my basket down on a straw bale, I walked over to some friends of mine. Together, we decided to investigate why the big boys just sneaked out of the barn.

We followed far enough behind so they didn't see us. When they stopped at the newlyweds' house, we hid in the bushes just behind the house to watch. Slowly, the boys crawled toward the window of the private room of the newly married couple. Beneath their window, they carefully stood up to look inside of it.

While all of them peered into the open window, the groom pulled the curtain aside and the ingredients of a chamber pot flew out of the window, right on top of the nosy boys. They screamed and ran away in a great hurry. We girls almost laughed our heads off. By the time we arrived back at the barn, the sun began to sink and the wedding party was about to start.

The pot, full of the precious wedding soup, stood next to a table now, which had lots of bread and different pots of steaming ingredients on it. Grandma also stood there dishing out the spirits from her cellar to the old ones who could no longer move about.

All of a sudden, a hush fell over our village people. I looked toward the big barn door and there they stood, the newlyweds! The band, which consisted of five old men now, began to play the wedding march. I had heard this march many times by now and wondered why it never sounded exactly the same.

Everyone stood up, except those who no longer could, and watched them walk toward their specially decorated table, which had the very pretty flower rope from their house attached to its sides. After the young couple sat down, the adult women started to fill the stacked up plates with plenty of fine smelling food, and my aunt filled the mugs with the clear wedding soup.

My grandma carried two plates and two mugs to the newlyweds, took a bottle from her cellar out of her apron and placed it in front of the groom. She then said loud enough for everyone to hear, "May the two of you be able to hold hands until your last day on this earth."

Everyone in the barn answered, "Yah, yah!"

I sat near the loaded food table and watched all the filled plates passed to the old ones and then to the men. My stomach grumbled and my mouth could barely wait until someone handed me a plate. Finally, my turn came and I happily accepted the food. I found a real piece of meat on my plate and many vegetables. Many days had passed since we had meat to eat at our house. Quickly, I picked the meat up and took a huge bite out of it. My mom's stern look and her slightly shaking head made me put the rest of the meat back down on my plate and I ate it the polite way, with my flatware.

While I drank the special soup, I watched the men's plates getting filled again, and I waited for someone to offer us children more food. Patiently, I waited for the sign to come to the long table, while more and more food disappeared from it. Soon, only one big bratwurst and a few pieces of bread remained, and my mom gave it to the young couple. Though disappointed, I didn't think about it long.

Someone brought in a small, white cake and placed it on the table in front of the young lovers. They both stood up and together cut a piece out of the fine looking cake. Then the groom took that piece of cake and held it in front of his wife's mouth.

The bride took a bite out of the cake and ate it. Now she took the rest of that piece and fed it to her man. All our village people applauded. The musicians started to play a waltz, and my Aunt Hilde, ready to dance, had to wait. Only the newlyweds got to dance this time. They held each other close and slowly danced their first dance as a married couple together on the dirt floor of the barn. She had her Sunday dress on now and smiled a lot.

Both sets of parents joined in the next dance. They changed partners during the dance, so all the men danced with all three women. Throughout the long dance, someone had a hard time holding Aunt Hilde back from joining them. Finally, everyone could join in the next dances, and yes, my aunt was the first one to stir the dust up from the dirt floor.

My grandma had shown me how to dance, but the boys my age didn't ask me to dance. They just stood together in a corner, looked at us girls and giggled a lot. What a strange race they were. My close friends came walking over to me, also disappointed that the boys had not asked them to dance.

Then I said, "Let's forget those stupid boys and dance with each other."

By the next dance, the four of us had fun dancing with each other. While we waited at the edge of the dance floor for the musician to start playing again, my grandma marched over to the corner where the boys still giggled and pointed at us. Their faces grew serious when she reached them. We stood close enough to hear what my grandma told them.

With a stern, low voice she said, "If all of you aren't on the dance floor and dancing with a girl when the music starts, I'll tell your parents where you stole the green cigars from." She then pointed her finger at them and said, "You'll dance every dance until midnight."

A bunch of frightened boys looked at us and around the barn because stealing received a severe punishment on our island. The music started and here came the boys, looking like they walked to their own hanging. The four older boys asked my friends and me to dance, and the slightly younger ones went to fetch their sisters to dance with them.

That was the first time in my young life I danced with a boy. Hans and I stumbled across the dirt floor at first, but got the hang of it soon and started to have fun after a while. When he held me close at the last dance, I felt awkward. He stirred up a different feeling inside of me, which I had never felt before.

At midnight, the wedding party ended. The newlyweds left the barn first, and then anyone not asleep, followed. Hans left with his parents, and I crawled up a haystack and went to sleep. In my dream, someone fitted our village wedding dress on me and I woke up screaming.

No instant coffee or tea, sweet lollipops or tangerines, and we had no idea what cholesterol was.

Chapter 79

Thou shalt not steal!

As an almost constantly hungry child, I figured that commandment didn't include food.

One Sunday afternoon, my two friends and I walked by our preacher's house. All the windows in the house stood wide open and we could hear people laughing and talking. Carefully, we walked closer and peeked inside of his living room window. They celebrated our preacher's birthday, and we could see a handful of people sitting around his big, fancy, decorated table, enjoying a great smelling meal. I didn't recognize anyone. None of our island folks sat by his table, and I wondered why he never invited some of us.

Then we sneaked around to his kitchen window to have a look inside. I couldn't believe my eyes. A young person cut a three-layer chocolate cake into small pieces. This cake even had whipped chocolate cream on top and on all sides of it. In between the top and bottom layers, I saw a reddish fruit filling, and the middle layer looked as though it had whipped butter cream in it. The only time I had ever seen such an extravagant cake, was at the little bakery store around Christmas last year. How my mouth watered for a bite of that cake.

When the young woman finished cutting the cake, she placed

each slice on fine, real porcelain plates. Then she placed most of those plates on a big tray and carried them inside the large living room. She had left four plates with delicious looking cake on the table. We stared at each other and nodded.

The top part of the back door to the kitchen stood open. We only had to reach over the bottom part of the divided door, lift the small metal hook that held the door in place and open it.

Slowly and silently, we sneaked over to the back door. The moment I reached inside to unhook the door, the woman came back into the kitchen. Quickly, I pulled my hand back. Standing next to the door, just barely able to see inside without getting noticed, I saw the woman place the big, empty tray on the table. Then she picked up a big, fancy silver coffee can. When she walked back into the living room to pour coffee for the guests, I nodded my head to my friends to tell them to get ready.

After I unhooked the bottom part of the door, it swung wide open with ease and without a noise. We crept into the kitchen. My heart pounded with fear. Fast and so excited, all three of us grabbed a slice of cake and, in a great hurry left the preacher's large kitchen.

We ran up to the old cemetery and hid behind the big headstones of the very old graves. We giggled and enjoyed eating that heavenly piece of cake. I had never in my life tasted something so absolutely sweet and soft. The cake just melted in my mouth. Oh, how I longed to eat this fine food every day.

A woman's scream came from the preacher's kitchen. I worried just a little about getting caught, but then I didn't think anyone would look for us among these old graves with all the weeds and overgrown bushes. I grinned with delight in the safety of the thick brush and enjoyed licking all the cake crumbs and frosting off my hands.

Before long, we crawled out from beneath the old gravesite, jumped off the wall which enclosed the cemetery, and walked toward the village pond.

All of a sudden, someone behind us shouted, "Stand still!"

Fear raced through my body like lightning. I knew that voice. One quick glance justified my feelings. Our only man of the law stood behind us with an angry face.

He called us by our names and said, "You girls stole some of the preacher's cake!"

I wondered how he knew.

When none of us answered him, he shouted, "The chocolate cake crumbs and frosting are hanging around your mouths."

I hoped the earth would open up and swallow me, but that didn't happen. Our lawman marched us through the village, loudly calling us thieves so that everyone who walked by could hear it. How embarrassing.

He marched us up the stone stairs and into the old house in the middle of the village where he lived. He told us, "You are going to jail."

I knew by now that our island had no jail and started to feel a little better, thinking that he just wanted to scare us for a while and then let us go home.

He told us to sit down on the floor in the room he called his office. Then he sent his son out to fetch our parents. At that moment, a great fear ran through my body again. I knew a harsh whipping awaited me. I looked at my friends and saw the fear in their eyes also. It seemed to take forever for our parents to arrive.

When I heard my mom's voice, my behind started to feel pain already. Our only man of the law walked out of the room, closed the door and greeted our parents. I could hear that he told them what we did and that we needed a harsh punishment. To my great dismay, I heard all the mothers agree with him. I feared that this strong man could beat us to death. Why did I have to steal that piece of cake? In our number language, I silently asked Ola, our island witch, for help to save all three of us.

Then I heard our lawman say loud and clear, "A week in jail, hard work, and only bread and water to eat will teach them a lesson."

All the mothers agreed with him again. They walked outside and I could no longer hear their voices.

While we still sat on the floor, I asked my friends if they knew if we had a jail. Both shook their heads. I thought it strange that our lawman talked about a jail that none of us knew about.

Quite a while later, the door opened and our lawman stormed into the room shouting. "Get up and walk to church."

Oh no! Would our fat preacher give us a whipping? He looked like such an angry man up on his pulpit when he spoke down to us sinners, surely he'd whip us to death. I started to shake with fear. Our lawman led us into our huge church. I looked for our preacher with his long willow switch in his hand, which he slammed on his pulpit on occasion to keep his congregation awake through his long speeches, but I didn't see him.

Then our lawman's voice echoed through the church. "Get inside the chapel and stay there!"

We immediately obeyed.

He walked out of the church, and the big, old door slammed shut with a bang. We sat down on the wooden bench inside the small chapel and waited for our preacher to walk in and let us have our punishment, but he never came. I began to wonder what our lawman intended for us. Our chapel didn't serve as a jail.

I watched the sun through the beautiful stained-glass windows slowly sink in the west. The three of us started to talk about getting out of the chapel but let that idea fall apart quickly, thinking of what our parents would do to us.

Soon it grew dark. We looked for a light switch but didn't find one. The ghosts inside the church's attic sounded restless, which scared us. We huddled together behind the small altar in the chapel, hoping they wouldn't discover us. We prayed for help to God, and I started to ask Ola silently for help again in our secret language. I couldn't understand why she didn't answer me. Was she mad at me for stealing? The ghosts got louder and very unruly.

We held onto each other, shaking with fear, wishing desperately we had not stolen the pieces of cake.

Suddenly, the attic quieted and the candles on the small altar lit up. I carefully peeked out from behind the altar to see who came into the room, but couldn't see anyone. We waited and listened for sounds, but it remained very quiet. Then I saw Ola's answer in my mind: "I am here, my child."

That made me feel a lot better, and I felt braver.

I whispered to my friends, "We're going to be all right," and I let go from clinging to them and stood up.

They too calmed down, let loose from each other and stood up too. Carefully we looked around the little chapel, to see who lit the candles, but the room remained empty. Ever so relieved we walked away from behind the small altar to sit down on the first bench.

The big bells in the church's tall tower rang in the midnight loudly. Still hungry, tired, and scared to death, I lay down on the wooden bench to go to sleep. At that moment, I noticed a light in the main church. I told my friends about that light, and together we talked each other into stepping out of the chapel to investigate.

One step out of the chapel and I stared in awe at a table with a fat, white candle on it and three plates, heaped with food. At one end of the table stood Ola, our island witch, waving us over to the table. Bewildered, my friends and I stepped over to her.

Ola said, "Sit down and eat, girls. Don't worry about your lives. I'll stay near you." Then she slowly walked down the wide aisle of our huge, dark church and disappeared. I didn't hear the heavy old woodworm-infested door open, or close.

We ate all the fine food off the plates and drank the tea she brought us. We wondered what to do with the dishes and the table. When none of us came up with a bright idea, we decided to depend on Ola to take care of them.

I started to blow out the candle, but the flame didn't even flicker. All three of us blew hard at the burning candle, but again it wouldn't move. In the dim light of the burning candle, we walked back into the small chapel. To my surprise, when I laid down on one of the wooden benches, I discovered a warm blanket. Both of my friends had blankets to cover up with also. With the faint glow of the mysterious candle watching over us, I thanked our island witch once more for all her help and drifted away quickly to a place with ample, delicious three-layer chocolate cakes to eat.

Early the next morning, before daylight, our preacher woke us with his loud voice.

He screamed at us, "Get up! On your knees and bend over, you sinners!"

He set his lantern on the first bench and hit his willow switch against the wall with great force. The switch made a wild, high-pitched sound when it hit the wall and scared me. I could already feel the pain on my behind. The three of us started to shake and glanced at each other with painful faces.

The preacher came closer. He lifted his switch and hit it down hard next to me on the bench. Just when I got ready to close my eyes to prepare for his punishment, I saw the preacher's switch fly through the air and out the open door of the small chapel. Greatly amazed and with his mouth wide open the preacher stared at the disappearing switch. Ola's warning voice came out of the dark church. Slowly, she walked closer toward us. I could hear her footsteps echoing off the cobblestone floor.

Soon she appeared in the dim light of the preacher's lantern. She looked at our preacher with an angry face and said, "Is this a good morning to abuse a few small children?"

Perhaps it was the surprise of our island witch's appearance that made the preacher slip and fall hard onto the floor. Or had Ola punished him? I saw blood running from his nose, and a tooth rolled away from him. He moved his mouth as though screaming, but no sound came out.

Slowly, our heavy preacher managed to pull himself up by holding onto the rough boulders on the wall of the small chapel. While holding his bleeding nose with his left hand, he lifted his right hand and pointed his finger at us in great anger. The motion of his face clearly showed him screaming at us, but only small droplets of blood ran from his mouth. Our preacher had lost his voice! We heard him stomp out of the church in a hurry.

Slowly, Ola walked into the chapel all the way and said, "According to the rules of life on this island, you children did wrong. The simple minded, angry preacher, your scared parents, and the not-so-innocent man of law decided your punishment. The three of you will clean this huge church all week long. I will keep the furious preacher speechless and in great pain, until your punishment ends, so he'll occupy himself with something other than beating you."

So greatly relieved, all three of us walked over to Ola and thanked her with a hug for rescuing us from the wild preacher. With a smile on her face and a nod of her head, our island witch disappeared at an instant.

For the next seven days, all three of us washed, dusted and swept our huge church, a tiring and boring job. Every night, when the bell in the church tower rang in midnight, we waited for our island witch to come inside our church to bring us something to eat, but she never did again. The fat, white candle appeared every night on the altar and lit up softly until the sun greeted the morning, then it disappeared for the day.

The preacher's wife brought us a slice of bread and a can full of water three times a day. She told us which parts of the church to clean and checked our work. Our preacher never came inside our church to beat us, or for the Sunday service. The ghosts in the church's attic didn't harm us either. Ola kept them mostly quiet.

Finally, our last day of punishment had come. Even though we still had not dusted off the immense pipe organ, the preacher's wife released us. How wonderful to get out of the musty old church and take a fresh breath of air. Slowly, with a heavy heart, I walked home. I took a route along a ditch, among some fields, to avoid the stares of adults and teasing of other children. All the way home I feared what punishment awaited me there. Surely, my mom had thought of something fierce.

Sure enough, my mom greeted me with a stern face. "I'm very ashamed of you. You will not have any free time in the evening after the fieldwork. You'll go directly to our pier and help gut and unload the fish for the rest of the fishing season. The men will expect you."

The summer had just started. I couldn't believe how dearly I paid for that piece of chocolate cake. I took the Seventh Commandment very seriously from then on.

No nachos, salad dressings in a bottle or house shoes,
but our little store all of a sudden had small rolls of
brownish paper on a shelf.

When I asked my mom about the purpose of those rolls, she said, "For the outhouse."

After I took a closer look at those rolls of paper, I asked, "But they don't have any words written on them like on the small pieces of newspaper inside our outhouse. Mom, what do you do with these paper rolls?"

My mom harshly pulled me over to her side and told me to be quiet. A few people in the store stood grinning as we left. I never saw such rolls inside our outhouse.

Chapter 80

Farewell my friend, farewell!

One cool spring morning, a few of my friends and I decided to check on the two female cows out in their pasture to see if they had given birth yet. My dog trotted happily along beside us until he saw a little newborn calf standing on shaky legs beside its mom. He started to bark and ran toward the fenced field. Frightened that he'd hurt the little calf, I started to scream at him to come back, but he didn't listen.

All of us started to run toward him, screaming, "No, no, no!"

By the time, we reached the fence, my dog had crawled

beneath the barbed wire and ran toward the little calf. Afraid of what he might do, I climbed over the fence to save the calf from my dog. As I got ready to run after my dog, I heard a deep, long warning moo, and saw the big bull stomping his feet on the ground. His head hung low and he breathed heavily. I could see the warm air steaming from his nostrils into the cool air, ready to protect his ladies and young ones.

Suddenly, this huge bull started to run toward my dog. Realizing the danger, my dog ran toward me. All of my friends screamed in panic for me to get out of the field. Quickly, without caution, I climbed back up the wire fence. One jump and I landed safely on the ground, but not without tearing my skirt and ripping the skin apart on my leg.

Lying on the ground, I saw that the huge bull caught up with my dog and rolled him over with his long horns. So worried that the bull would kill my dog, I stood up quickly, waved my hands, jumped up and down and yelled at the big bull. All my friends joined in, which made the bull look up at us. Before he bent his head back down to kill my dog, Harras got up and ran away from the angry bull. We lifted up the bottom row of the barbed wire fence so he could quickly get out of the pasture.

When the huge bull started to run toward us, we ran away from the field, trying to save ourselves. I was very happy to see that Harras kept up with us. When we realized the bull would not break through the fence, we sat down to catch our breath. My dog crawled into my lap, breathing fast and his body shook even faster. A squeak came out of his throat with every breath he took. He looked completely exhausted. A little blood oozed from his tail and one of his ears, but I noticed that my precious dog otherwise seemed all right.

After quite a while of laughing, resting and glad to be alive, we decided to go on to the tall stand of mixed trees near the beach to challenge each other. We had simple rules: whoever climbed up closest to the top of a tree won the game.

When I climbed about a third of the way up my selected tree, a strangely mad looking grey squirrel came out of its nest and stumbled toward me with foam dripping from its mouth. I had never seen such strange behavior in an animal. Somehow, I remembered the warning told to me a few times: never get close to such an animal, but I couldn't remember why.

The mad squirrel stumbled closer toward me and frightened me. I desperately tried to get out of the tree, but the squirrel moved faster and clawed my hand. Then it lost its balance, fell off the tree, and landed on the ground next to my sleeping dog. Harras jumped up surprised at having a snack land right before him. Then he put his nose close to the squirrel to check for edibility.

At that moment, the sick squirrel stood up and bit my dog in his ear. Harras squealed and shook the squirrel off him. By the time the mad squirrel tried to bite my dog again, I landed on the ground, and without thinking about it, stepped on the sick animal's head and killed him. Quickly, I took my dog into the salty sea and thoroughly washed his ear and the scratches on my hand. The scratches on my hand were minor. The sick squirrel never broke through all the layers of my skin, but it bit right through Harras's ear. Somehow, I feared for his life.

When one of my friends said, "That squirrel has rabies," I remembered the terrible consequence that lay ahead for rabid animals and humans. With deep fear inside for my dear friend's life, I made all my friends swear not to mention the rabid squirrel at all. Out of fear for my good right-cross, they all quickly agreed.

Scared and sad, all of us walked home together. When we passed by the cow pasture, I watched my dog closely so he wouldn't get in trouble again. Harras sort of crept along with his head down low, tail between his legs, right beside me where the bull couldn't see him. He cautiously eyed over to him now and then. At home, I asked my grandma how people could tell when an animal had rabies. She described in detail how animals and humans get the terrible, deadly disease and how they reacted to it.

She told me the early and later symptoms in detail.

Since we had Easter vacation from school for quite a while, I told my mom, "I'm going to walk around our island and take my dog with me."

She answered, "Go ahead child, but make sure you come back when school starts." She handed me four thick slices of bread and one apple, which I stuck into my important traveling sack. My sack contained one fishhook, a long string, matches, part of a small candle and Grandpa's old pocketknife, which I proudly accepted so long ago.

With a heavy heart, I left our house and whistled for my dog. He quickly came running, and excitedly jumped up on me ready to go to have some good times. He happily ran down the path toward the sea, where we always started out on our long walks. Slowly, I followed him, scared and worried that both of us could get sick with the deadly rabies disease. I wasn't ready to die yet. I still wanted to see the rest of the world and have fun with my dog, but at least we'd be together if rabies ended our lives. Slowly, trying not to cry, I walked along the white beach, throwing sticks as faraway as I could for Harras to catch. He had lots of fun and my heart grew lighter.

We walked toward Seagull Cove where I climbed up on a boulder to watch a big sail ship travel past our island, while Harras had all the seagulls upset, trying to catch one of them. Soon the big ship got very small, and after a moment, disappeared. Harras lay in the wet sand near the sea, trying to catch his breath. The seagulls, now at ease, looked down into the salty water for dinner to swim by.

Soon, I became hungry and climbed off the boulder. I fetched a strong stick, tied my string to it and the fishhook with a small sliver of bread on its end. Before long, a fine size fish hung on my line.

I gathered some sticks and driftwood, lit the fire and placed the fish on top of it. Before the twilight gave away to the dark night, we shared the cooked fish and a slice of Mom's dark bread. Oh, how I loved my dog. That night we spent snuggled up together in the sand dunes beneath my warm jacket. The ocean softly whispered its lullaby, and the stars came out to watch over us. Before I could tell my dog all the names of the stars that I knew, we had both fallen asleep.

Some days we walked inland to get some fresh water to drink and spent the night in someone's barn. People seemed glad to see us coming. They knew my dog would fill his belly with a few of their pests. Often I caught enough fish to trade them for a fine sandwich and some buttermilk. I always shared my food and the buttermilk with my dog. Oh, how he loved buttermilk. At night, I cuddled up to him and desperately hoped that neither of us would get sick with the rabies.

The last evening before we had to walk home, because Easter break was over, we spent with the farmer whose son the two of us rescued. They invited both of us inside their home and let me sit at the table with them at dinnertime. Harras sat underneath my chair and behaved very well. I was very proud of him.

The farmer's wife handed me a plate loaded with potatoes, gravy, cabbage and a fine piece of meat. Oh, how great it tasted, and I quickly ate it all. The grandmother of the house fixed my dog a huge bowl full of leftovers, which he slung down in a hurry. His appetite constantly amazed me.

She handed me a few biscuits and said, "Both of you may sleep in the sweet hay in the barn."

I thanked everyone and walked out of the house. Tired and full of great food, we crawled on top of a haystack and went to sleep instantly.

The next morning, after the rooster woke us, the two of us climbed off the fine smelling hay and quenched our thirst at the outside pump. I hated to see our walk around our island end, but I had to return home. Thankful and so happy that neither of us had gotten sick, I walked down to the shore and turned toward home, singing some happy song.

Suddenly, I didn't see Harras anywhere. I called him and looked up and down the shore for him, but I couldn't see him. In a hurry, I ran back to where we started out and found him sitting near a boulder by the sea. So happy to have found him, I walked closer to him and stroked his head. He rose up and licked my hand.

When I called him to come along with me, he stood up, but stumbled and slowly lay back down. Shocked, I feared that this might be the first reactions of rabies, like my grandma described to me. My heart broke. In outrage, I screamed and cried out to the heavens.

Exhausted and so sorrowful, I sat down in the sand and let my hurting cries flow out. Harras came over to me, crawled into my lap and gently licked away the tears from my face. I couldn't believe that our friendship would end so soon. In the grey, windy day, I slowly walked toward our fishing village with great pain in my heart, no more tears left to cry and my friend in my arms.

Grandma stood in front of our house, talking to one of our neighbors. When she saw me walking toward them, she stopped talking and looked at us. I gently put my dog down and he tried to run toward my grandma, but he stumbled, fell down and just lay on the dusty ground.

Grandma's friendly look changed to an instant, shocking stare. With her arms wide open, she walked toward me.

When we met, my grandma took me into her arms and held me tightly. "I'm awfully sorry that your buddy caught that terrible disease."

I clung to her for a moment, shaking with fear and anger. Then I picked up my friend, held him gently in my arms again. Together, in silence, we walked the few steps to our backyard.

There my grandma asked me, "Has Harras bitten you or anyone else?"

I told her that he had not.

She breathed in with great relief, and said, "Your dog needs to stay inside the lean-to, until we see what will happen."

I asked my grandma, "Is there a medication he can take to get well?"

She shook her head and said, "No, child." Then she said, "We should end his life before he starts to suffer."

I nodded my head, and as though walking through a bad dream, I put my sweet dog into the lean-to.

Grandma had a steaming mug of good smelling fish soup and a thick slice of bread waiting for me on her table. I crumbled the slice of bread into my mug of soup and, without a word, left the room.

I took my evening meal and a can of fresh water to my best friend. He enthusiastically lapped down the soup, while I gathered some of the torn sheets from the shelf and made him a comfortable bed. With tears in my heart, I gently hugged him, told him how much I loved him, and wished him good night.

He snuggled down inside the bed I made for him, licked me across my face, yawned once, closed his eyes and went to sleep. In a very sorrowful state of mind, I left my friend, walked into our house and upstairs to my bed. Still dressed, I crawled into my bed and closed my cried out eyes. Sleep quickly relieved my painful fears.

A single, loud gunshot frightened me awake. While I jumped out of bed, I heard my mom and my grandma coming inside the house. By the time they closed the front door, I started to walk down the stairs.

I heard them whispering, "She's going to hurt in the morning."

Fear ran through my body. Did they talk about me? Did I have the rabies also?

Shocked, I asked, "Grandma, did you shoot your gun?"

After a brief moment of silence my mom said, "Girl, we had to shoot your dog before he gave the deadly disease to you or anyone else. Your fine friend didn't know what happened to him and he's on his way to heaven. We wrapped him up in the old sheets, and you can bury him in the garden in the morning."

I stood on the cold stairs, chattering with fear and hating what I had just heard. When my grandma opened the door to her room, I saw her holding her gun in her hand.

At that frightening moment, I knew that my mother had spoken the gruesome truth. In shock, I walked to the lean-to. The open door let the moonlight into the room, and I could clearly see my motionless dog lying on the ground with the top half of his body wrapped up in bloody sheets. At that moment in my young life, I felt the love for my two most important people in the whole world ripped from my heart.

With intense grief, I knelt on the dirt floor next to my best friend. I felt for a heartbeat, but his heart lay still. Gently, I unwrapped the upper part of his body to see his face once more and kiss him farewell. In great distress, I discovered the shot blew his head apart. Blood still seeped from it. My own grandma shot my friend in his head. He had no face to kiss farewell. In raging anger, I screamed and pounded my fists on the dirt floor. After a long, painful while, the anger left my body and only deep hurt stayed behind.

I knew my buddy had lived too long for me to bury him at sea to give him another chance at life. Therefore, I gently wrapped him back up, picked his still warm body up, and walked toward our new cemetery. The bright moon lit my way. I looked up to the thousands of stars for help, but they just hung there in the massive sky and sparkled. Harras felt heavy, but I often sat down a short while to rest. I cradled him in my lap and told him with streaming tears how wonderful he'd find heaven. Each time I picked him back up, he seemed much lighter and I walked on to our cemetery where I found Ola waiting for me by the open gate.

I asked her, "Please Ola, make my buddy alive again."

Sadly, she shook her head and answered, "Sorry my child, but I can't bring life back into your buddy."

She placed her hand on my shoulder and together, in silence, we walked into the old, small chapel. From there we borrowed two spades and walked over to my grandpa's grave. I gently laid my dear friend's cold, bloody body down onto the earth. Then Ola and I dug out a deep grave for my dead friend right on top of Grandpa's grave. With tears rolling down my face and a broken heart, I laid my best friend's body inside the dark grave.

Then I knelt down, folded my hands and asked my grandpa, "Please take care of my sweet buddy up there in the heavens. He always was a very good dog."

A bright star fell from the sky, and I took that as an answer from my grandpa that he'd take very good care of my sweet dog.

I looked around for Ola, but she had disappeared. My rubber boots, which I had forgotten to put on when I left home, stood next to me. With dawn about to break, I closed my buddy's grave. Then I stole a handful of pretty flowers from other graves and placed them on my sweet friend's grave. After I sang him the usual funeral song about asking forgiveness for the dead one's sins, I put my boots on and walked home in a daze with a very bitter, sad feeling inside of me.

Perhaps someday –
    In the soothing arms of time –
    The fury of our pain and our flowing tears –
    Will die off to a soft whisper!

Perhaps with the last tear shed –
    Our pain will finally cease altogether –
    And then perhaps sweet memory will rise –
    Through the stillness of our resting soul!

Perhaps it will reach deep and wide –
    To touch and hold with pride the sweet memories –
    Of a thousand painful nights –
    In an awesome warming light!

No grapes, hairspray or electric can opener.

Chapter 81

Doomsday?

I'll never forget that day in the early fall of 1957. The first, fresh snow had covered our island in a beautiful white, glistening blanket. On that early evening, while feeding our chickens, our high-pitched emergency church bell rang fast and loud. At the same time, our warning horn at the silo near the bay, began to send awfully loud, deep sounds over our small island. Both warnings at the same time only meant something terrible either is going on or had happened.

Immediately, I dropped the chicken feed from my hand, closed the door to the chicken cube, and ran toward our front door. My mom, my grandma, and the rest of my family had hurried out already and stood talking to each other, all at the same time.

My mom handed me my coat and said, "Come on, girl!"

Over all the noise of the warnings, I heard my grandma shouting, "We're absolutely in grave danger unless the ghosts inside our church's attic are playing with the church bells again."

Surely, our island witch would have stopped the ghosts by now, and they couldn't leave the church attic to sound the warning horn at the silo.

Our entire small village moved toward our island church where we held all important meetings. I don't think I had ever seen my grandma move so fast.

There she ran, leading her family and neighbors, hands raised high, steam coming from her mouth as she yelled, "Oh, Lord, what's happening?"

To me, my grandma looked like the engine of this bewildered, scared train of people.

Just before we reached the church, my grandma quit moving. Her hands no longer reached up to the heavens and she stood quietly. We all stopped and waited around those who had already gathered in silence. I couldn't see what everyone stared at because the adults stood in my way, but I saw my mom's and some of our neighbor's faces frozen in fear. I knew we stood in the front of our island witch's house. On the old roof of her small house sat a flock of big, black ravens. They too, sat absolutely quiet and motionless and stared down at the snow-covered ground.

When the church bell and the horn on our silo stopped their warning, a whispered hush of disbelief and fear went over the gathered people. My mom let go of my hand and placed both of her hands over her mouth, as if to silence her scream. I pushed and scrambled my way through the crowd to see why everyone stood in such fear. With a little push here and a kick there, I reached the front of the crowd.

To my left, stood all the important people of our island: our man of the law, the tavern keeper, and our preacher. With grim faces, they stared into the witch's very small front yard. One more step forward and I clearly saw over the short, darkened, picket fence into her front yard. I didn't want to believe what I saw, but there, in the cold snow of her yard, lay Ola, sprawled out with her face in the snow. Shock and fear crept up within me. Was our island witch dead?

Our only man of the law said, "Someone needs to go, turn her over and check if she's still alive."

My grandma whispered loud enough for the silent crowd to hear, "Only the blessed children can touch a witch that may be still alive."

With nodding heads and some mumbling, the people agreed. My grandma called the blessed children's names and told us to come forward. Slowly, the two other blessed children and I walked over to my grandma.

She instructed us how to turn our witch over and where to feel for a pulse and listen for her heartbeat. Scared to death, with shaking bodies, the three of us walked over to our island witch. Gently, just as my grandma told us, we turned her tall, skinny body over.

I brushed the snow from her face and found her mouth and her red eyes wide open, staring up to the heavens. Snow stuck in her huge teeth. Like my grandma told me, I knelt down, gently lowered my head to her heart and listened for her heartbeat, but her cold, still body lay silent.

After a long, sorrowful moment and leaving a few warm tears on her chest, I lifted my head, looked toward our island people and shook my head, to confirm the lack of a heartbeat.

Too shaky to stand, I sat next to her in the cold snow. The sun's last, bold, red ray tinted everything around us pink, even our witch's long, straight hair, which gently swayed in the soft evening wind. I wondered if witches had their own special heavens to go to, or if they just went to the ordinary ones.

I took her black shawl off her shoulders and covered up her tired, old face as I saw so many adults do to dead people. I wasn't sure why people didn't want the dead ones to see us any longer or where they got buried. Perhaps it was too sad for them.

Since we all figured Ola for dead, anyone could touch her now. Our midwife came over and touched her neck to feel for a sign of life. After a short moment, she, too, looked at our island people and shook her head. Loud and clear, our man of the law declared our island witch possibly dead.

Sad and frightened, I stood up from the snowy ground and walked over to my grandma, who stood real close to the low, dark fence of our witch's small front yard. She took me in her arms, wiped my tears away and comforted my bewildered soul.

The people whispered and mumbled among themselves about what to do with a dead witch. Should they lay out our island witch in her home, or in the small, old chapel at the cemetery? Where should they bury her?

Someone said, "On Sinners' Row."

The gathered crowd spoke up against that idea, and so did I. She had helped us an awfully lot through the years, kept order on our island, and even rescued many of us when epidemics struck our island.

Someone asked our preacher, "What does your big Bible say we should do with a dead witch?"

"It doesn't say anything," he replied.

One old fisherman from our village slowly made his way through the crowd. When he stood in front of the witch's yard, he held onto her low fence and waved his cane, an almost straight tree limb, up into the nearly dark night. Immediately, out of respect for the oldest, clear minded person on our island, the small crowd went silent, except for one disrespectful dog. One swift kick from someone and the dog quit howling.

With his cracked, weak voice and his old crippled body barely able to hold him up, the old man softly said, "Old witches just disappear. They don't get buried. A day or so before they leave this world, they present the island with a new witch to take her place. Since Ola has not announced who will take her place, she may not be dead yet. The young girls she has chosen to watch and educate in witchery are still too faraway from taking her place."

By now, the shaky old man had run out of breath and strength. His knees gave way and he slowly slipped to the ground. Two young, strong men ran over to him and caught him before he fell. They lifted him up and carried him away.

My grandma took over and announced, "If we lay Ola out for her burial and she's not really dead yet, she could get very angry at us and do some awful mean things to us. She might even end our lives. So, let's let her lie here in her yard until morning. When the sun rises we'll meet here again to see if she's alive or not, and then we'll decide what to do next."

In the dark, moonless night, people of our island walked to their homes in great fear. I stood for a while in front of the small yard, looking down at our island witch. She still lay motionless. Her long, white hair slightly waved in the soft wind. The faraway stars sent down enough light to make the white snow around her sparkle with silvery flakes. When I looked up to her house, her large, white candle in the only window in her house, lit up and softly flickered behind the clear glass. I wondered for a moment who had lit her candle.

Freezing, hungry and in turmoil, ready to walk home, I glanced one more time at our island witch in the cold snow. It startled me to see that all the big, black ravens had flown down from the rooftop of her house and sat on her body now. They sat in silence without moving a single feather.

The big ravens just stared at our witch's covered face as though they planned to watch over her for the night. I thought it would make Ola feel good to see the black ravens, who most likely were her friends since they always roosted around her house.

I slowly walked into the front yard and took her black shawl off her face. It made me feel good. All the ravens looked at me as though they thanked me for letting them see their friend's face. For a brief moment, the lit candle in the window grew very bright, and then it flickered and died. In a hurry, I ran home through the glistening snow, wondering if Mom saved me something to eat, and if I'd find Ola awake in the morning.

When I walked up our stairs at home, I smelled potatoes frying. My stomach hoped some would be left for me. Quickly, I entered our little room. Sure enough, my mom had saved a small plate full of potatoes for me. I ate the delicious feast in a hurry. Then I looked over to the stove to see if any more remained in the frying pan, but found none. Mom's sad eyes reminded me not to ask for more food.

That night, lying next to my sister in our bed, I prayed hard to God and all the statues of the saints that stood around in our big church to awaken Ola. I even prayed to the mysterious black raven, who always sat in the grass of her yard and drank water, to breathe life into our island witch. Sometime among all the praying, I fell asleep.

Very early the next morning, long before the sun rose, my mom shook me awake and told me to get dressed quickly. My grandma shouted from downstairs to hurry up. I wondered why we had to hurry. Perhaps our island witch woke up. As we walked out of our front door, into a grey, slightly cold morning, my grandma mumbled something about the sea being gone.

Other neighbors joined us and they too asked in great fear, "Is the sea really gone?"

Some people came up from our harbor and answered the feared question, "Yes, the entire ocean left!"

Some said the devil took the sea away and will end our lives. Others blamed our witch for leaving us unprotected. I never saw so many adults talking at the same time in such a frightening rage.

A few more steps and we stood at our harbor. In disbelief, I stared out at the sea. The massive ocean had disappeared except for a puddle here and there. And not a single seabird remained. All the small fishing boats lay on their sides.

The tides happen regularly on the other side of Germany, in the North Sea, as I saw when I spent some time there in a children's home, but not here by us in the East Sea. Our sea level only fluctuates a few inches now and then.

Bewildered and awfully afraid, people stood together in small groups, mostly silent now, looking out to sea.

Then they started to whisper that perhaps the devil had gotten angry at us and sucked out the entire ocean.

Others said, "God is angry at us. He took away our ocean to let us starve to death!"

A very old woman spoke up and declared that our dead witch had taken the life-giving ocean from us because we had sinned so often."

With her cracked voice and her cane waving up high into the air she said, "Our witch can look through walls and the dark nights. She can see the shameful things we do."

Silent now, people hung their heads in shame. Soon someone loudly declared that doomsday had arrived.

When I asked my grandma what that word meant, she said, "It means the end of the world, but perhaps just the end of our island."

I got scared to death. I didn't want to die. I didn't want to think about where I'd go. No one I asked seemed to have a clear idea of what happened when a person died. I knew I was too old by now to get buried at sea and have another chance at life.

When my grandma heard me crying, she bent down, hugged me and said, "Just in case doomsday doesn't arrive today, let's go and gather some fish from the puddles the sea left us."

Just about all the women and children walked out into the sandy, empty bay, held up their aprons as if to form a bucket, and by the moon's light, gathered all sorts of fish and crabs from the puddles. It felt strange to walk on the bottom of the sandy sea without the water there.

I found it hard to catch the slippery fish with my hands. I had more luck catching the crabs. After we had filled my mom's and my grandma's aprons full of flapping fish, we walked out of the bay.

Mom told me, "Stay out of the bay in case we get lucky and the seawater returns to us."

I answered, "Sure, mom."

Our village men stood together speechless, looking down the pier at their stranded fishing boats.

Suddenly, one of the men pointed out to sea. Excited and in a hurry, they all walked into our empty bay. I looked in the direction they still pointed, and to my great surprise, I saw a huge, grey fish lying on the sandy bottom of the waterless ocean. In a hurry, I followed the men, disregarding my mom's order.

When we crossed the bay, I saw the huge creature much clearer as it moved around in a shallow channel of seawater. I had had never seen such a strange creature. It surely didn't look like a fish to me. The men stopped at the edge of our bay, debating among themselves what to call this creature.

Soon they agreed that the huge creature was a whale and that it didn't belong here, surely a very bad omen. They also concluded that doomsday had arrived.

I stayed behind when our fishermen walked back through our bay toward our small harbor, and stared amazed at the huge creature. It moved its huge, grey body from side to side.

Not seeing my mom or grandma around, I slowly walked out into the empty ocean to get closer to the whale. My heart pounded with excitement and soon I got close enough to see that the grey creature had a huge tail.

Its big mouth astounded me and I wondered why it had such small eyes. The poor thing had found itself stranded in the small, shallow channel of seawater. Sadly, it tried repeatedly to swim away, but it didn't have enough water to do so.

I felt awfully sorry for the strange, huge creature. Another step and I softly touched the grey, skin of the amazing big whale. It felt wet, cold and a little slimy. At that moment it turned its head and looked at me sadly with both of its small eyes. Just as I asked the sad creature what I could do to help it, our silo's warning horn went off again.

I thought that perhaps the seawater returned and ran as fast as my legs could carry me toward our bay and across it. Completely out of breath, I reached our harbor and found no one in sight. Then I remembered that all of our island people had agreed to meet by the witch's house at sunrise.

One more faraway look at the grey whale I felt so sorry for

604

and I took off running toward our island witch's house. I hoped that the seawater came back soon to rescue the strange, sad creature. I also hoped and seriously prayed while I ran to see Ola alive and well again.

When I reached our witch's house, many bewildered people stood around and stared. I pushed my way up front to look into her yard. Our island witch no longer lay on the ground. Even the impression of her body in the snow had disappeared, though no new snow had fallen since last night. My heart jumped with joy. Ola, my friend, was still alive.

A woman next to me asked out loud, "Did someone perhaps take her body inside her house to lay her out?"

My eyes searched around the still mostly silent crowd for my mom, or my grandma. When I spotted them standing together, holding hands and looking awfully grave, fear crept up inside of me. Was our island witch dead? What about doomsday? When would it begin, and how?

Slowly, I squeezed my way over toward my family. As soon as I reached them, I grabbed my mom's hand and shook it to get her attention.

When she looked down at me, I asked her, "Where is Ola?"

With wet, sad eyes, my mom told me, "Ola has disappeared. The men of our island searched for her but didn't find her."

Our man of the law spoke first. He asked us to come inside the church. Slowly all the islanders followed him across the road and into our huge church. Even my mom, who still harbored anger at the preacher, walked into our church. Somehow, she still swore that our preacher kept relief packages meant for the poor people, for himself.

Just before I stepped inside our church, I looked up to the top of our tall church tower. Way up there, on the grey roof, sat a flock of big, black ravens, looking silently down at us. The biggest one of them had a black, long string from our witch's shawl in its beak. The string fluttered lightly upward in the soft breeze. I wondered if the mysterious, dark ravens had carried our witch up to her heaven. Then it quickly crossed my mind that they perhaps had eaten every part of her, but I thought that too cruel and disregarded the idea.

I was very surprised to see all the men of our island sitting down inside our church among the women. This had to be a very important meeting.

With everyone seated, our man of the law climbed up to the pulpit and asked, "What should we do?"

A large woman from our village stood. "We're doomed. Our witch, the most important person on our island, died before she taught someone her secrets of witchery to take her place. The young girls she blessed and from which she eventually would choose to teach all her secrets to, didn't have enough education to take her place. You all know we can't just elect a new witch among us, as if we do a preacher and our man of the law. A witch is born a special child and has to have special education, whereas a preacher just needs to read and speak up loud. Our man of the law only needs to have a quick, strong fist, a horse and a gun. He doesn't even have to know how to shoot that gun." Then she screamed, "No, folks, we are doomed!" and she sat down.

Turmoil began to brew. Most people screamed loudly to the heavens. Some just cried and others folded their hands and said nothing. A fight started in the front rows among a few men. A handful of boys walked closer and cheered them on. Mom stood, and looked at the unruly crowd in awe.

My grandma said, "I'll meet doomsday in my cellar." She stood up and walked down the aisle toward the big, old, worm infested wooden door that led outside. I wanted to see the sad whale one more time before doomsday started.

When I stood up to walk outside of our big, pretty church, our preacher's thundering voice from the pulpit had everyone's attention, including mine. The scared and angry people settled down and looked up to the pulpit, hoping that our preacher relieved them of their fear.

Then, as usual, he shouted, "God is near and so is the devil. Beg for forgiveness!"

I ran out of our church.

In a great hurry, I reached our house, walked over to our neighbor's house and freed the two big, friendly dogs from their chains so they could have a fun run before facing doomsday. Perhaps together, the three of us wouldn't be so afraid to die.

A few minutes later, we reached our strangely silent harbor. I felt uneasy, though not very scared now. The dogs stared at the drained bay with their ears straight up in attention. They even hesitated to follow me into the bay. At my second whistle for them to follow, they came along. At the first puddle, both eagerly tried to catch and eat all the fish inside of it. Half-way through our bay, I clearly saw that the huge creature the men called a whale still lived and slowly rocked back and forth, as if trying to swim away.

In a few moments, I stood by its side, but the dogs kept their distance, standing in the wet sand, growling fiercely, heavily sniffing the air, while their long tails hung down between their legs. They weren't sure at all about this creature. The sad, grey whale had somehow moved a lot of sand around its body away, and seawater from the small channel gathered around its huge body. The seawater came almost half way up to the huge creature now.

Then came something that totally surprised me. The whale stuck its head in the water and sucked up gallons of it. Then, all of sudden, a huge fountain of water came out of a hole on its neck and fell down all over its body. I don't know how it happened, but I found myself sitting in the wet sand, next to the whale. I got up and looked around for the dogs and saw my usually brave companions speeding through the waterless bottom of the ocean, heading straight for our island. Sand and water flew up high around them in great masses.

One more amazingly tall outburst of water from the creature, and the grey whale stopped all its desperate moves and lay completely still. I worried that it would die. The poor whale lay with its head out of the water and turned toward the wide, empty ocean, as though listening to something.

I turned and looked out to the strangely empty ocean and saw only sand and puddles of seawater here and there. After a moment, though, I heard a very faint sound from faraway. Ever so slowly it seemed to come closer. Another moment and I recognized the sound from my stay at the mighty North Sea. The ocean was coming back! Ever so happy for the huge whale and all of our island people, I jumped up and down in the wet sand and screamed, "Yes! Yes! Yes!"

Then I realized that I'd better hurry and get to higher ground. I took off my rubber boots and ran as fast as I ever did in my young life, out of the ocean's bottom, across the bay and onto our island. There, I collapsed next to our silo and let my hurting lungs catch air. My brave companions came slowly crouching around the corner of the silo. They licked my face and crawled up into my lap. I gently stroked them and told them, "Everything's all right and I love you."

The deep sound of the incoming ocean water grew louder and wilder than in the North Sea. I began to wonder if perhaps this started the beginning of doomsday and the wild water would swallow our small island. Afraid I'd drown in the wild wave, I knew I needed to get up higher and very quickly. Our church stood in the middle of our island, the highest point, but I didn't have enough time to get there. Then I saw a huge wall of foaming seawater rushing into the bay with awesome power.

A few feet away stood the huge, heavy wooden entrance door to our silo. With all the strength of my young body, I tried to push the heavy door open, but it refused to budge. One quick look out into our ocean told me that unless I sought shelter, the high, thundering wall of water would swallow me. As quickly as I could, I called the dogs and ran up the metal stairs outside the silo. Every now and then, one of the dogs slipped. I quickly grabbed him by his neck and pulled him up. On the last flight of stairs, three broken steps dangerously dangled in the air, but to our luck, we didn't have to try to climb them.

The wooden opening to our right that let fresh air into the silo leaned open. I knew it stood right next to the inside staircase. I grabbed the dogs, managed to push both through the small opening into the silo, and quickly crawled through it myself. Though heavily shaken with fear, I felt very glad to finally have reached the safety of the strong building.

While I looked out of the small opening, I folded my hands and seriously asked God and our island witch to cancel doomsday. I even promised to go to church every Sunday and never lie or steal again.

The huge wall of rolling water with its white, wildly foaming crest just rolled right over our tall sandbank which protected our harbor from the ocean. The narrow ship channel, where the whale lay, filled up with water quickly. To my surprise, the tall wave of foaming water broke apart and slowed to a crawl while it moved into our bay. By the time it reached our harbor, it had lost its fury but still rolled in with destructive strength.

The wave ripped the small fishing boats apart and smashed the big, old wooden door and outside stairs of the silo into many pieces. The water only came up to the first floor of the silo though, which made me happy. The water pounded on the few old shacks near the bay, which people called their homes, and pushed them over, as though made of paper. Scared and crying, I held on tightly to my neighbor's dogs and hoped the powerful wave wouldn't cave the silo in.

Then suddenly, the strong wave lost all of its power. Slowly, all the seawater retreated from the land back into its own territory, the bay and farther out into the wide ocean, and it took with it many planks from the destroyed shacks and fish it had carried with it.

Some of the rats in the silo which had climbed up the stairs for safety now served as the dogs' meals. When the dogs killed them, they squealed in pain. I felt so sorry for the rats, but as my grandma always said, the dogs had to eat too. Before long, all the seawater retreated from our land leaving behind strange containers of different sizes, parts of fish and lots of broken wood. Too scared of doomsday's next move, I waited in the silo and watched the horizon, when I suddenly heard a familiar sound. Our seagulls!

With loud, shrill screams, they returned home to our island. Ever so excited, I stood up and waved them on. I wondered if their arrival was a good omen. Out of the opening in the tall silo, I watched the screaming seagulls land and fight over all the pieces of death fish the ocean had left behind.

The dogs ran down the inside stairs of the silo and out through the shattered old heavy door. Both of them chased the seagulls away from a few big morsels they decided to eat themselves.

Unsure of what would come next, I looked back out to sea, but the sea, as far as I could see, looked calm. A spout of water came out of the ocean now and then. I hoped it came from the whale and I wished it would find its way home. Still looking out to sea, I started to daydream. The huge whale took me with him to a beautiful place in a warm part of the mighty sea where colorful flowers grew on the bottom of the sea. When we swam through a swaying forest of seaweed, a close sound quickly ended my escape from the silo.

Our people came back. Everyone stood astounded and felt so tremendously happy for the return of the sea. They hugged, danced, and laughed together. When I spotted my mom among the happy crowd, I felt sure enough that doomsday had ended and climbed down the stairs of the old silo with wobbly legs.

Our village people salvaged what they could use for the many repairs they needed to make. They decided among themselves who the now homeless would live with until they could rebuild their shacks. Then, everyone happily decided to celebrate life. As usual, the celebration would take place on the dirt road in front of our house.

As my mom and I walked home, holding hands, glad to be alive, I asked her, "Is doomsday over?"

She answered, "We're safe for now, child."

At home, my mom tried to get my grandma, a very important person during celebrations, out of her cellar. Our island people needed to barter with her for some of the finest liquor she brewed. My mom's first two knocks on Grandma's cellar's door were only answered with a calm, loud snore.

The third time my mom really knocked hard on her door, the snoring stopped and my grandma said with a strangely calm, slurring voice, "Get lost, doomsday!"

One more hard knock on her cellar's door and she answered, "I have a loaded shotgun and know how to pull the trigger to kill you, doomsday!" Then she started to snore again.

Our neighbors gathered with their food and firewood in front of our house, expecting my grandma to come outside to barter for her goods from the cellar, but my grandma, fighting doomsday in her cellar, was not about to come outside. My mom finally quietly sneaked into the cellar and brought bottles of Grandma's brew up, and she knew the art of bartering. The celebration of our life began.

The women cooked, gossiped, and laughed until the four young men came back from their second, thorough search for our island witch.

They shook their heads and one young man said, "There's no sign of our witch, neither dead, nor alive."

The people's faces turned somber again. After a while of whispering and mumbling among each other, one old man waved his hand in the air and spoke with a loud voice. "Let's make this night a happy wake for our nice island witch and thank her for bringing back our ocean's water."

After a very short moment of silence, everyone agreed to the idea and the celebration went on.

My plate full of fried fish tasted great, and so did the drink of strawberry liquor from Grandma's cellar. Tired and exhausted from the day's events, I walked into our house and inside my grandma's room. When I saw her empty bed, I took her feather bedcover and her long pillow and quietly walked down the dark stairs to the cellar, even though she had forbidden me to enter the cellar without her permission. I figured it an acceptable lie to say that she called me to cover her up, because it turned quite cold in that cellar.

Happily, I reached my grandma without waking her. A short, fat white candle burned next to her and made her face look ghostly in its flickering shadows. First, I placed the bedding on the earth floor, then I picked up the old, rusted gun and placed it in the farthest corner of the cellar so my grandma wouldn't shoot me, confusing me with doomsday. Then I gently lifted her head and pushed part of her long pillow beneath it. Carefully, I lay down next to her on the long pillow and covered both of us up with her warm bedcover. By my grandma's steady snore, I drifted away, wondering about Ola, and if the giant whale had found its way home. Then in my early dream, our fine witch sat on top of the huge whale, guiding it to its home.

For many days, all sorts of debris from the ocean washed up on our island. We welcomed the edible or useable items, but not all the trash. We buried many bodies, or parts of them, in a large grave in our new cemetery. Many souls out there must have experienced hell on earth. Some days after Ola disappeared, the fearful people of our island decided that nobody should ever enter her house or garden again. I felt very sad about that because I wanted to see the beautiful garden again and watch the huge, thirsty raven drink a lot of water.

On the next cloudy Sunday morning when most people had gone to church or to the tavern, I decided to look at the pretty garden even though our people had forbidden it. I waited on the dirt path behind her house until the church service started. When the big bells of our church quit ringing, I carefully climbed up the tall, rough stone wall which surrounded Ola's garden. Though frightened of what could happen to me, I was too nosy to quit. The moment my hands reached the top of the wall, I pulled myself all the way up. Bewildered, I stared into the small yard to see only tall weeds. What had happened to all the flowers and the blooming trees? Where had the sun gone that always smiled down on the garden? And where did the raven go?

A few black feathers lay motionless on the ground where the huge raven used to stand and drink water out of a fine bowl. Speechless, I stared into the unkempt yard. All the beautiful trees and flowers couldn't have died and been replaced with these tall weeds in just a few days.

The sky grew even darker and it began to rain. Very disappointed, I climbed down off the wall and stood in the rain wondering about the transformation. Perhaps our island witch took her beautiful garden with her as she took away the mighty ocean for a while. I checked her yard many more times in hopes that the amazing garden would return just like the ocean, but it never did.

Some nights, at half-moon, we heard loud, chilling screams coming from the cemetery in the middle of the night. Two days after our witch's death the oldest weed filled grave in our cemetery suddenly had abundant, beautiful flowers growing in its dark earth. No living soul on our island remembered who was buried there, not even my grandma.

People stopped there, stood silent for a moment with their heads bowed, and then went on their way with a small, bittersweet smile. Perhaps they left a tear or two on the grave. People whispered that the devil buried our island witch in that old grave, planted all those pretty flowers on it and that the sounds we heard came from his screams of pain and anger over his loss.

Every Christmas, a single white candle stood on her grave. Burning day and night, it made the snow around it shine and sparkle in its bright light. Even a strong snowstorm couldn't blow out its flame. The white candle just barely flickered.

Then one day, I asked my grandma, "Is our island witch really buried in that grave?"

She smiled at me and said, "It's good to believe so."

Each time the two of us walked to our cemetery to weed and take flowers to our family graves, we stopped at her grave. Grandma always closed her eyes and looked down on her grave for a moment. I silently begged Ola to come back to us because I missed her very much, but she never did and no one ever found her body. She was the last witch on our island.

So far, the ocean's water in the mighty East Sea never completely left again. The last time I visited the cemetery, I stopped at the still prettiest, oldest gave, knelt down and said in our secret language, "Hello, Ola. I sure miss you a lot."

One of those tears that really matter came crawling up from where it was born, in my heart.

No bingo games, speed limits, candy apples, or figs.

Chapter 82

The frightening snowstorm.

One early morning, in the middle of our deep, harsh winter, when I stepped out of our house to use the outhouse, a warming south wind caressed my face. What a fine surprise. At midday, the top layer of about three feet of snow on our ground began to melt. The adults in our house began to worry, especially my grandma.

She said, "This is a very bad omen," and asked everyone in our house to stay close by.

Before long, a few worried neighbors gathered in front of our house and looked up at the sunny sky with frightened faces. I looked up too, but couldn't see any danger in the blue sky.

Someone screamed, "The sun has fallen. It's coming nearer to earth and will burn all of us!"

An old woman shouted, "We no longer have our witch to tell us what to do, or protect us from evil!"

Now, I grew frightened too.

Someone cried out, "It's the devil's work!"

Another woman looked up to the heavens with her hands folded and demanded God to help us.

My mother said to her, "Emma, there is no God!"

That started loud arguments among the worried women of our neighbors. The men stood together at a distance, in silence, watching the sun with somber faces. The screaming and arguing about the existence of God got louder, and soon the women started to fight. I couldn't believe it.

My mom always told me, "Don't fight, girl. Leave the fighting to the boys." And here she was hitting away at our neighbors and they hit back.

The women ripped on each other's hair, spit at each other, kicked and screamed words at one another I had never heard before in my life.

I couldn't stand it any longer. Something inside of me shouted, "Let's fight!"

The moment I joined in the fight, all the other children, except the very young ones, joined in as well. I kicked and hit my mom's enemies as hard as I could. Suddenly, a very loud shot stopped everything immediately. There, at the entrance of our yard, stood my grandma with her big, smoking shotgun in her hand. On the other side of our road stood all the neighborhood men, laughing like crazy. Before anyone said a word, a deep, still faraway thunder got everyone's attention.

Instantly the arguments about God stopped. People looked toward the old ones for an explanation.

They shook their heads and whispered, "We've never heard of such a strange thing: thunder in the middle of our harsh winters."

Neither could they remember such a warm day in the middle of winter. After another growl of thunder, we could see a line of deep purple, almost black clouds emerging on the horizon in the north, creeping slowly toward us.

My grandma declared, "My arthritis knees have warned me for days about a huge snowstorm that will likely bury us."

She loudly advised everyone to hurry to their homes and prepare for such a disaster. One more quick look at the darkening northern sky and we saw a silvery, strong lightning bolt hitting down onto the frozen ocean. That loud display made all our village people rush to their homes.

The women of our house ran into our garden, where we kept

our hardy vegetables in an earthen mound. They removed the snow from the small earth mound's tightly-packed straw door and my mom crawled inside. With my grandma's instruction, she retrieved cabbages, onions, carrots and leeks for all three households. After mom crawled back out of the earthen mound, the women quickly closed the mound and hurried inside our house with the precious vegetables.

Meanwhile, Uncle Fred poured hot water into our hand pump over our deep well. He then wrapped straw around it and set it on fire to thaw the ice inside the parts of the pump that stood above ground. I watched him and hoped the pump thawed out so we could take the needed water inside the house.

The thunder rumbled louder and the dark, scary clouds moved closer. After the straw burned out, my uncle tried moving the pump's handle and it moved.

Excitedly, he screamed, "Come and get the water!"

Quickly, Mom, Grandma, and Aunt Hilde came outside, filling pots and buckets full of the valuable, fresh water.

All the children in our house, with the exception of the baby, brought in wood, cow chips, and dried peat pieces into the hallway. Someone broke the frozen fish off the clothesline and took them inside. Mom carried chicken feed from the lean-to inside our house and called the chickens into their inside stall. They freely came inside, and my mom closed their small door to the outside so they couldn't go out again.

Our cat, already inside, curled up close to my grandma's iron stove. She watched a fat mouse try to find a place to hide from being eaten. What a cruel cat. I felt awfully sorry for the mouse, but my grandma reminded me that that was nature, and that people, too, killed all sorts of animals for food.

After all the adults used the outhouse, they ordered us children to use it. As I came out of that important place, the dark clouds had reached us and it began to snow heavily. The thunder rolled angrily over our island. All of us quickly walked toward our house, stopping at the lean-to to pick up our old buckets with their dented lids, in case we couldn't reach the outhouse for some days to come.

Safely inside our little warm room, my mom put the teakettle on the stove. Something hot to drink sounded great to me. I dragged a chair close to the window and watched the storm through the partially thawed windowpane.

The snowstorm howled madly through our big trees, breaking off the small, frozen branches and taking them with it in its path. Huge bolts of silvery lightning crashed down onto our island without mercy. The horrifying, loud thunder didn't even take a split second break between its deep, angry rolling attacks. Each time the thunder smashed down on us, our house ever so slightly vibrated.

The next wide lightning bolt passing by our window lit up the whole neighborhood. The air inside our house started to smell very strange. Frightened, my mom called me away from the window. She told me to sit down and have some hot tea. Reluctant to leave my front row seat to watch this wild, fiery show, I sat down at the table.

My mom lit the little candle on our table and poured the tea. Then she put just a pinch of beet sugar in our mugs and sat down. At precisely that moment, lightning hit our house.

Our house shook as I had never felt it before. The table, with our precious sweet tea on it, jumped briefly upwards and spilled some of the tea on the table. The air was taken from my lungs. The little candle fell over and died. I felt as though something big fell onto our floor. My chair moved slightly sideways, but I managed to hold on to it. My sister screamed. The air smelled awful. With the next lightning strike, which lit up our room completely, I saw my mom scrambling off the floor and reaching for my little sister.

From downstairs, my grandma screamed, "We've been hit! We've been hit! Look for fire!"

Then she and my aunt came upstairs with needed buckets of water, to put out the fire. After close inspections, while the horrendous thunderstorm carried on hitting down on us, we all breathed a sigh of relief to find our house not burning. I will never forget how the adults hugged each other and wept with joy. My mom told us to take our teacups and go downstairs. When I saw all the sweet tea that spilled on the table, I bent my head down and sucked it off the table. Mom took her tiny cloth bag with all her important belongings inside of it, all of our bedcovers, and my sister downstairs. Having sucked up all the delicious tea from our table and too scared to stay upstairs with the dreadful storm still pounding down on us, I quickly grabbed my sister's and my nice, homemade dolls and ran downstairs.

In the very small hallway, the household cat plus one mouse and we eleven inhabitants, settled down on the floor. Grandma's door and my uncle and aunt's door remained open to let their warm air come into the hallway.

Mom wrapped both my sister and me up in our bedcovers and held us tightly in her arms. Though awfully tired, the bright, frightening lightning and the terrifying thunder kept me awake. With each wild, crash of thunder, I held on a little tighter to my mom.

As I drifted off to sleep, my grandma asked, "Did you hear that?"

Everyone answered, "No, what did you hear?"

Grandma said, "Hush, and listen."

Among the strong storm's fury, I heard a very soft knock on our door and so did almost everyone else now. What could it be? Was it perhaps a neighbor seeking help, or a broken tree limb knocking on our door? My grandma stood up and slowly walked the few steps to our front door. Uncle Fred stood right behind her to protect her. Ever so slowly, my grandma opened the front door just a little to glance outside with one eye.

Grandma said with great surprise, "What do we have here!" She opened the door a little wider, which let the bitter cold wind blow snow inside of our hallway.

Before anyone could complain and ask grandma to close the door, in walked a full-grown, bewildered, and outraged goose, flapping its wings and shaking its body to get rid of the snow. With its head held down in an attack mode and its beak slightly open, the goose made it clear to leave her along. Watchfully, it walked past us, making a hissing sound, then it waddled inside my grandma's room and made itself comfortable beneath her warm stove. Grandma smiled and licked her lips.

After a good laugh, we went back to holding on to each other, enduring the frightening thunderstorm. The huge lightning bolts and the awful, loud thunder sounded constantly.

My little sister screamed out, "When is it going to hit us, so we can get out of here?"

For just a brief moment, some of us laughed. Then Mom explained to my sister, "We don't want to get hit by the lightning."

My sister started to cry, and that made a few more children in our scared group cry.

Grandma stood up again, lit a candle and walked down into her cellar. She came back up with a bottle of her strawberry liquor and a cup in her hand. She poured some of the red liquor into her cup and said, "Let the children each drink a little of it."

Oh, how sweet it tasted and how warm it ran down my throat. Soon, the crying in our hallway stopped, but the storm still hammered us. I couldn't keep my eyes open. I leaned against my mom and escaped this scary world. I fell asleep amidst the raging storm.

I awoke in our bed, still fully dressed, with my sister next to me. In the darkness, I realized that the terrifying storm had moved on. I could barely hear the thunder anymore. What a great relief. Happily, I slipped out of bed, put my rubber boots on and walked down the dark stairs to go to the outhouse.

When I reached the hallway, I looked up to the small window in our front door and found it covered with snow. Slowly, I tried to push the door open, but it only moved slightly and lots of snow fell inside our hall. Quickly, I closed the door and walked upstairs. I knew where our bucket stood and relieved myself.

Not knowing the time, I started to crawl back into bed, when I noticed the dim light beneath my mom's door. Perhaps she awoke when I walked down the creaking stairs. Quietly, so as not to disturb my sister, Mom opened her door and asked me to come inside her room. She pointed toward our frozen window and brought the candle over to it. In just a few minutes, the warm flame of the white candle thawed a small part of the glass so we could see through it.

The storm had snowed us in. The snow came all the way up to our windowsill The clear sky now let the bright stars light the world. Our village looked like a beautiful sugar coated dreamland. I smiled in amazement.

Quickly, both of us breathed onto the frozen window to melt more ice. Before long, we could see all the way down to our harbor. The huge layer of snow covered up the fishing boats and all the small huts. Though beautiful, it looked ghostly. I hoped all the people in those small buildings didn't suffocate under all that snow.

A great commotion inside my grandma's room got our attention, and Mom and I hurried downstairs to investigate. There stood my sweet grandma with her broom in her hand, trying to get the big goose off her cat. The goose had the cat's ear in its beak and bit down on it.

Blood dripped out of the cat's ear and she screamed in pain. She tried to reach the goose with her paws to defend herself, but couldn't. Mom reached down, grabbed the big goose by its neck and squeezed a little. Quickly, the goose let go of the cat's ear and quit flopping its powerful wings. Then my mom picked up the goose, and with her other hand eased off on the grip around its neck.

Grandma said, "Take the goose into the stall and put it inside the big cage next to the chickens."

Completely snowed in now, we could only reach the inside stall through my uncle and aunt's kitchen. When my mom opened their door, with the complaining goose under her arm, a shivering, grey mouse took advantage of the confusing moment. She escaped from the cat's view, crossed our hallway quickly and slipped away hurriedly beneath Grandma's cellar door. Glad that she had escaped to safety for now, I hoped she wouldn't fall into one of my grandma's fruit pots that she slowly and carefully turned into some of her fine spirits.

With all those noises, everyone in our house woke up. My mom now had to clear the chimney, so we could fire up all three small stoves. The adults came up to the second story of our house to help my mom. She dressed warmly, wrapped the thick rope around her waist and opened the window.

My uncle leaned out of the window and threw the rest of the rope around our chimney. He caught the end of the falling rope and held on to it tightly. Mom strapped on her snowshoes, took her rake and stepped out of the window onto our roof. The snow on top of our roof held up, and she took the few steps to our chimney in no time at all. When she started to rake the snow off the chimney, partial bricks tumbled down with it.

Grandma said, "That's a bad sign!"

When I saw my grandma's worried face, I began to worry too.

A few more tumbling stones with the next raking and Mom freed our chimney of the tall snowcap. She slowly walked all the way around and inspected the damage. Then she stepped down backwards toward what we called our chimney window, with my uncle's help. He guided her down safely, holding onto the strong rope.

Back inside, Mom reported the damage of the lightning hit on our chimney in detail. The top two double rows of brick had fallen off and a fist wide crack ran down the side of the chimney into our house.

She said, "The crack only seems to run down on the outside of the chimney to the roof."

Those words eased some of the worried expressions in my grandma and uncle's face.

Both of them inspected all sides of the chimney, from inside the house, all the way downstairs and found no cracks. Only then did they decide to start a fire in my grandma's oven, with buckets of our precious water standing nearby.

Grandma layered dry grass, small sticks and a few bigger sticks in the mouth of her iron oven. Then, with a worried face, she struck the match and gently laid it close to the dry grass. The little flame on the match eagerly licked at the dry grass. Grandma quickly closed the oven door and watched the wall of the chimney, where the smoke traveled upward.

After a moment she said, "Great, no leaks here!"

Mom, who watched the chimney upstairs, shouted down from our room, "No leaks here."

Now, all of us waited for Uncle Fred's report as he watched the top of our chimney, from our window. A loud, "Yes, here it comes," made everyone inside our cold house very happy.

Excitedly, the adults fed lots of wood into the stoves. I sat by the frozen window and blew my warm air against the pretty ice flowers, until a small spot on the window melted again. In wonder, I gazed over our snowed-in village. Still dark, the bright stars made the pure, white snow sparkle in places.

I wondered if all the rabbits and other creatures found warmth in their underground housings. Grandma's teakettle whistled for her. Mom set our pot of leftover fish soup, which froze overnight, onto our iron stove. The big pot held enough rations for all of us to have warm meals for a few more days.

Downstairs, my aunt and uncle's baby cried. Grandma's cat jumped into my lap and started to lick my face. I held her head close to the window so we could breathe against it together. Soon, both of us had enough ice cleared from the windowpane to watch the wings of morning ever so softly appear out of the frozen ocean.

First, the sun sent up a shy touch of soft pink, then another, as if to gently feel out the right place to rise. Then somewhat surer, tall, yellow beams appeared at the horizon to clear a safe way for her majesty, the sun, to travel. A few moments later, I saw her slowly crawling out of her frozen ocean bed with hot, golden vapor flowing and steaming around her, to protect her inner fragile core of life. She turned the whole sky on fire now, with bold colors of bright red, orange and golden yellow. She even painted the frozen ocean and our snowed in island in her amazing colors. What a miraculous sight.

My mom's words of, "Warm soup," brought me away from our windowsill. We had no bread this morning, but I had a mug full of tasty, filling fish soup.

After I cleaned our mugs, I reached beneath my sister's and my bed and pulled out my snowshoes. As I tied them on, my mom came out of her room and said, "No, you cannot go outside now. It's just too bitter cold. Later, when the sun shines brighter, you may go."

What a disappointment.

To me it seemed like forever for the sun to rise high and warm the frigid air a little.

Finally, my mom said, "You can go outside for a while."

Hurriedly, I dressed, tied on my large snowshoes, and stepped out of our chimney window onto the snow. What fun to walk on top of the high snow. I could reach the top branches of some of the trees and stand on top of our outhouse. A few neighbor children came over and we started snowshoe races. Though not easy to race in those big, wooden snowshoes, we had such fun. We fell and sank down into the snow, but we managed to help each other up all the time. Then we divided into two teams and had an exciting and wonderful snowball fight.

Before long, I heard my mom's unwelcomed words. "Come inside to warm up."

The next day, my grandma decided we needed to find a way to

get to our most important places such as our water pump, our outhouse and our earth mound for food. First, we all shoveled a tall, short tunnel along the wall of the house to our pump. We sliced the tunnel out of the huge bank of snow and stomped the snow down, which did not work out well. We needed a way to get rid of the snow from inside the tunnel.

When we finally reached our pump, my uncle told all of us to get inside. He asked his wife to bring an armful of straw and the matches. I couldn't believe it for a moment, but he actually set fire to the straw inside our tunnel. As soon as the flames started, they licked away the surrounding snow in no time at all.

Suddenly, the snow roof over the pump caved in, burying my uncle beneath it. The tall flames died instantly. The adults went out into the tunnel and rescued my uncle. Thankfully, Uncle Fred didn't get hurt, and everyone began to laugh.

The still melting snow around the area of the pump soon started to turn to ice and formed a small ice cave with an open roof. The iced over sides soon grew strong enough to hold a ladder leaned up against them. My family then dug a narrow tunnel toward our outhouse, put the snow into buckets, climbed up the ladder and handed me the filled buckets. I walked across the tall top of the snow wearing my snowshoes, and dumped the buckets full of snow away from our immediate backyard and our earth mound. Ever so proudly we finally reached our outhouse.

Three more days of digging out snow, a little at a time, and we had a small tunnel that someone could crawl through to get to our earth mound for supplies. Safe now, the adults decided to celebrate.

Back at the house, my grandma took out her big pot from beneath her bed and set it on her hot stove. Then she took a bunch of fat cuttings from a pig's skin and the immediate layer beneath it out of the salt barrel and added it to her pot. The fat started to fry and spit. Oh my, how great it smelled. I knew my grandma cooked her much loved potato soup. She made it so rich, that if we only ate one helping at noon, it could nourish us all day long. In great anticipation, I tasted the creamy soup already in my mind.

The rest of our family brought cut up vegetables, especially potatoes and onions, to add to the big pot. We all gathered inside my grandma's small, warm room and she opened a bottle of her fine spirits. While the soup bubbled and the adults enjoyed their warming drink of my grandma's liquor, she began to reminisce about her past. She started to tell all of us about the long gone hard times. All of us listened in complete silence, even my aunt and uncle's small baby.

C3C3C3

To everyone's surprise, it didn't snow again that winter. We children built all sorts of tunnels beneath the snow, and one room, in which we could stand up straight and play. We found that room and the snow tunnels much warmer than the air on top of the high snow. When our sun started to melt all the snow, we walked around in mud and water for a long time.

When my grandma noticed that the goose was a lady goose and no one claimed her, she didn't place her into the soup pot. Grandma found her a visiting partner and started the goose business again to make life easier for all of us.

No wheelchairs, store-bought toys or insect spray.

Chapter 83

Disaster at sea.

When we finished all the spring planting, and had no school for two more days, the beautiful, early summer morning begged for big fun. Four of my friends and I decided to walk along the beach to Old Stone Cove and go swimming completely naked. We felt quite big now and noticed that our breasts had begun to grow. We started to look at the boys in a different way than as completely stupid human beings.

Each of us had a fine grease sandwich in our pocket, and we stole a handful of fresh, young carrots from a field along the way to the beach. I borrowed Grandma's crab net, brought my fine old pocketknife, and Lora always had matches to light our fires. Ellie stole five potatoes from her parents, and the twins, Carla and Amie, brought their brother's fine fishhooks and poles. What fun we would have.

Giggling and talking about what boys are good for and not finding an answer for that, we soon reached Old Stone Cove, a secluded place on the north side of our island. There the big ships had to sail closest to our island to avoid wrecking on the underwater reefs. We sat down on a big boulder, ate our fine sandwiches, shook the earth off the fresh carrots, and shared them equally.

After we finished eating, we walked inland to a small

cemetery, which had a pond. At the edge of the pond, we lay down in the soft grass, formed our hands into a shallow bowl and slowly lowered them into the pond to quench our thirst with the cool water. On the way back to the beach, we gathered wood for our evening fire.

As soon as we reached the beach, the twins picked up their fishing poles and ran down to the water to try to catch some fish for our supper. Lora combed the mighty ocean for ships to come near, so we could all show off our naked bodies. Ellie prepared a hole in the sand, stacked wood in it and laid the potatoes on top of it. Lora and I looked for some crabs to add to our meal but couldn't find any.

We then wandered around the beach looking for treasures. We found fine seashells and to our great surprise, many brownish stones, which a woman in our village called amber. She could polish the soft stones until they sparkled and we could see through them. Those stones always had something inside of them, like a leaf, or a tiny animal. She'd surely give us a few pennies each for this handful. I could see my mom's smile already when I handed her the money.

Soon our conversations drifted back to those strange creatures, boys. When we tried to figure out why the grown boys took the girls for walks and then disappeared into the bushes with them, the twins screamed, "Look at this!" They each had a fine size, wiggling herring on their hooks. We'd all fill our stomachs tonight. We ran over to the twins and quickly built a small enclosure out of stones in the water, where the fish could live and stay fresh until the time came to put them on a stick and cook them over the fire.

All of a sudden, Lora, still combing the vast ocean, screamed, "Ship in sight!"

All of us stood up and stared out to sea. Sure enough, a ship came sailing our way. Excitement tickled our young bodies while we watched the ship come closer, hoping it wouldn't turn away and take the northern route around our island. Soon, the big ship, a

Russian border patrol ship, came right toward us. We also knew from our rescue before, when we tried to swim to Russia, that it had many sailors on board.

The big ship kept sailing toward us, and we realized that it took the southern route, among the enormous reefs. All of us jumped up and down in great excitement and screamed, "Yes, she's coming our way!"

Quickly, we took all our clothes off and ran into the still ice-cold ocean. Giggling and laughing, we swam among the reefs until we reached the one with a flat top barely underwater. There we stopped and sat down on it. Eagerly we waited for the ship to come its closest. Slowly the big ship managed to sail through the deep channel, guided by red buoys on either side. Soon it came the closest it could without running onto the reefs.

Full of excitement, we loudly counted to three, jumped up all at the same time and showed those sailors our wiggling buttocks. Then we waved our hands up into the air and yelled as loud as we could, "Hi, boys!"

A little embarrassed, we quickly jumped off the reef, back into the salty ocean. Oh, what excitement! A long blow from the ship's horn assured us that the sailors saw us. We swam back to shore out of our minds, laughing, inhaling the salty water by mistake, spitting it back out and screaming, "We did it!" I scratched my leg pretty badly on one of those reefs, but couldn't quit laughing. I don't think that all of us ever laughed that much together again.

The moment we reached the shore, we stood up and showed those sailors our front side. Then we quickly ran for our clothes. I held my shirt in front of me and looked at the ship once more, still laughing.

At that precise moment, the huge Russian border patrol ship blew up like two mighty suns crashing together. Burning pieces of debris sailed through the air from the great inferno. I stood in shocked silence, staring at the disaster. Another big explosion and it looked like the fire ran over the ocean to all sides of the hellish scene. Then, with a very deep, moaning sound, the great inferno abruptly sank into the red, burning ocean. The angry, hurting ocean spit up a great wave with white combs at the top and killed the fire. We could no longer see the huge war ship, which protected the Russian border between East Germany and us.

We looked at each other in silence, shivering with fear. We heard the faint voices of people coming toward us. Quickly, we grabbed our clothes and ran into the tall bushes, just a short way up the steep coast. There we hurriedly dressed and watched a strange, big wave rage toward shore. By the time it reached our shore, it had lost its violence and it barely ran all the way to the steep coast. But, it buried our potatoes in the sand, took away our precious stones and deposited the fishing poles into a nearby bush. On its way out to sea, it left the beach filled with all sorts of dead fish.

Slowly, my mind began to function again, and I wondered if it was our fault that the big ship blew up.

With a shaking voice, I asked my friends, "Do you think the ship blew up because of what we did?"

All of them looked down and barely mumbled, "I think so."

Lora said, "The man who steered the ship most likely watched us and ran onto a reef."

I agreed with her and so did the rest of our frightened group. How guilty we felt.

Ellie looked at me and asked, "Will they hang us, for killing all the soldiers like they hung Albert?"

I cleared my throat. "Most likely."

By now, we felt much too scared to cry. We shivered with the fear of those facing a hanging.

Then I thought our situation over and realized that nobody knew where we went or what we did, and no one saw us all day long. That was the answer to our problem. Quickly, and in a somewhat lighter mood, I shared my thoughts with my friends, which relieved them a bit. Perhaps now no one would discover what we had done, and hang us. We knelt and swore to each other not to tell a soul of what we did, or witnessed.

I said, "If anyone asks where we spent the day, we all have to tell the same lie. We can say we spent the day fishing on the west side of our island and didn't hear a thing."

Ellie broke in. "No that won't work. Surely everyone on our island heard that loud explosion."

I realized that she was right. We agreed upon that we heard the explosion while we fished on the west side of our island.

Carla, the taller twin, said, "We have to get the fishing poles back to take home with us, otherwise, my brother will kill us." She quietly crawled down to the bush where the sea had dragged the poles and retrieved them without notice.

Then I realized that I left Grandma's crab net down at the beach and started to look for it. After a short moment, I saw it in the sand near an evergreen bush not far from us. Quietly, I crawled over to the bush and slowly reached for the net. Ever so carefully to avoid discovery, I pulled the net into the bush and joined my friends, to everyone's great relief. The beach grew crowded now. People gathered up the dead fish, talked, and pointed out to sea. Guilt ridden, we sat beneath the bushes until nightfall. Then, after everyone left, we crept out from our hiding place and cautiously walked down to the beach. Beneath a heavy cloud cover, we walked home with a very sick feeling in our stomachs. I saw myself hanging on a tree for murdering all those sailors, and wondered if dying hurt.

Though our church's clock rang eleven times, we still saw light in some of the houses at our village. We wondered why everyone had not already gone to bed. Were they waiting for us to come home and hang us? That thought scared us, and we talked each other into spending the night in our silo and leaving our island before dawn the next morning, in our makeshift luxury liner, to avoid hanging.

The silo stood mostly empty this time of year except for an extended family of rats. The big, heavy door hung open and we silently walked inside. Without a word, we felt our way over to the stack of empty sacks, crawled up it and lay down. After a few silent tears rolled down my face, exhaustion took me away into a completely dark land without any dreams.

Early the next morning I awoke to the talk of a few men at the silo's door.

One of them said, "What happened yesterday? I heard an explosion out at sea."

Our harbormaster answered, "Yes, a Russian border patrol ship ran over one of the mines from the war and blew up. It's the third mine the big minesweeper didn't find."

Oh, what a great relief. We had not caused the disaster at all. No one would hang us. With my hand over their mouths, I awoke my friends and whispered the welcome news into their ears. Though still dark and I couldn't see their faces, I felt everyone's smile, and a long trapped tear rolled freely down my cheek.

After the men left, we swore once more to each other never to tell that we swam on that part of our island, just in case the harbormaster had made a mistake. Then we walked home holding hands, finally breathing easier.

No bowling alley, tuna in a can, coffee filters or dates to eat.

Chapter 84

The bitter shock.

In the spring of 1957 at the age of barely fourteen, my last school year began. I felt very excited to fulfill my long dream. I wanted to go to veterinary college and eventually open my own clinic on our island to help all the suffering animals.

All the years since we had our exciting young teacher, my report card showed almost all straight A's. I clearly remembered the day my mom saw my first straight A report card and proudly said, "With these grades you can do whatever you'd like." I often talked my future over with my great teacher. He always encouraged me to go ahead and fulfill my dream. I liked him so much. Each time I brought up the subject to my mom or my grandma they quietly smiled but never said a word. I just figured they shared my excitement.

Spring and summer passed, while I worked hard at my schoolwork. I took on any work in the fields to provide some means for my family to live through the winter. Perhaps when I left our island I could work, besides going to school, and send some money home. I wondered how I could send money to another place, but figured in those higher schools surely someone knew how to do that.

Soon fall arrived, and my teacher handed two of us students with dreams in our heads, papers to fill out and have signed by a parent. Wolfgang's parents owned the little dairy on our island, and he had dreams of studying medicine. We talked a lot together about our dreams and hoped to go to the same school. We even figured that both of us could open our clinic together on our island. My heart pounded with great excitement while I anxiously wrote in the answers for the questions on the printed sheets of paper. Then I asked my teacher to look them over, which he did.

He handed the papers back to me with a great smile and said, "You filled them out perfectly." When he saw how excited Wolfgang and I acted, he laughed and said, "Go on home and have your parents fill out the last line and get it signed by them."

Both Wolfgang and I ran out of the schoolroom. We jumped up and down, and then we ran in different directions to get our papers signed.

I don't remember ever having run home that quickly and being so excited. I felt like I flew home, and arrived absolutely out of breath. When I opened the front door, I almost knocked my grandma down.

She looked at me with astounded eyes and said, "Sit down girl, and catch your breath!" She then called my mom to come down.

Mom came running down and asked me in a panic, "What happened?"

Ever so full of excitement, I waved the papers in the air and handed them to my mom. Still short on air I quickly asked her to fill out the last line and sign the papers.

Quietly, my mom sat down next to me on the stairs and read every word on the fine, white papers out loud. She started to read the last line very slowly, and her face took on a worried look when it asked in which big city I had people I could live with. Mom slowly went upstairs. She waved me to come with her. My somber mom sat down at our table and read the whole page again, in silence this time. Something seemed wrong. My mom looked worried.

I got very scared and wondered if she would let me go to a higher school. Gently, with a slightly shaking hand, I handed my mom a pencil and sat down next to her. She signed the papers, marked none to the question in which city I had people to live with, took a deep breath and looked straight into my face. To my relief, I didn't see anger in her face.

Then my mom took my hand and said, "You may not realize it, but we are poor people. All of us had big dreams once, but that's what poor people get, just their dreams." She handed me the papers, got up from the chair, took her old handkerchief out of her apron and walked over to our window.

I stared at the floor and worried about what all this meant. She couldn't be worried about my grades. I had all A's.

Amidst my confusing thoughts I heard my mom quietly say, "Go on back to school now, girl!"

Slowly, I stood up and walked downstairs. I stopped at my grandma's door to ask her why my mom acted so strangely, but my knocks went unanswered. In deep thought, I walked back to school. The closer I came to our school, the better I felt. I'd ask my teacher if I had good enough grades for a higher school to accept me. When I reached our school, it was morning intermission. Our teacher sat on the old tree stump, playing his harmonica. Some younger children danced around him, laughing happily. The older boys stood behind the outhouse, smoking a cigar and coughing up a storm. The rest of the children sat together talking and giggling.

I didn't feel like talking to anyone, so I sat down on the front stone step and waited for the intermission to end. As soon as I sat down, our teacher waved at me and walked toward me. I stood up and handed him my papers.

He smiled at me, when he saw my mom's signature, then asked, "Why do you look so sad?"

I told him what happened at home and that I worried about my grades.

He put his arm around me and said, "Girl, your grades are way above average. You have a great chance to get accepted into a higher school."

How great he made me feel! With a happy heart, I gave him a spontaneous hug and ran over to Wolfgang.

I asked him if he had someone to live with in a big city while he went to school there. He shook his head. Together, we wondered if we'd actually get to go to school somewhere after we finished this school year on our island.

A short, silent moment passed, and then Wolfgang said, "If I'm not accepted at another school, I'll hire on to one of those huge merchant ships and sail around the world."

For a short moment I wished I were a boy again so I could go along with him, just in case I wouldn't get accepted into a higher school either.

Inside our classroom, our teacher told the two of us to write down our dreams and what we'd like to do for the rest of our lives. I wrote my dream in detail and made sure I spelled everything correctly. He then attached each of our stories and our report card to the filled-out and signed papers.

He then put all of the papers inside a big envelope and announced to the whole classroom, "All of us will walk to our ferryboat tomorrow and send Edith's and Wolfgang's dream off to the big city of Berlin."

Everyone stood up, looked at the two of us sitting in the last row, clapped their hands, and shouted, "Yeah!"

Though a little embarrassed, I sure felt good inside.

The next morning, after all the children arrived at school, we placed our schoolbags inside our schoolroom and happily started on the trail to the ferryboat. The morning felt crisp, but the sun soon warmed our bodies.

We sang songs, did our spelling, and practiced multiplication tables. Within an hour, we arrived at the ferry landing. The little ferry labored hard against the strong current. Dark, grey smoke quickly belched from her chimney and rose up into the sunny sky.

Her old engine bellowed in distress, she laid deep in the sea and swung from one side to the other.

Quietly, I prayed, "Please don't break down today. Our important letters need to catch the train."

Before long, I saw why she had such a hard time. Big barrels and all sorts of boxes loaded the little ferry down. At that moment, I no longer worried that she'd break down. With a last big noise of the distressed engine, she came into the landing.

We all clapped our hands and shouted to the ferry, "Hello Lola." We all knew her name. The ferryman had painted it onto her right side planks in big purple letters.

As soon as the ferry landed, all the children offered their help to unload the boat, and the ferryman gladly accepted. In no time at all, we had the boat unloaded and everything stacked up in piles, according to the direction of the ferryman.

After that, our teacher handed the man the big envelope with our important papers. He told him with a smile the importance of those papers.

The old ferry operator looked at Wolfgang and me with a huge smile, which revealed his few brown front teeth. "Since all of you helped me unload the goods, I invite you for a free ride across the ocean."

We all looked at our teacher and screamed, "Please, please, please, Teacher!"

With a broad smile, he agreed. Then he asked the ferryman, "Do we have to swim back?"

With a straight face, the man said, "Yes."

We all looked at him in disbelief, because this part of the ocean had a very strong current, and everyone strictly forbade us to enter the water here.

He started to laugh loudly, which made his big belly shake up and down. Then, with a sweet voice, he said, "Of course I'll bring you back."

He calmly explained to us what not to do and where to stand.

In an orderly fashion, we boarded the ferry.

When we slowly began to move away from shore our teacher announced, "Today's homework is for everyone to write down what they see and how it feels to leave our island."

Oh my, that brought sensitive feelings up from deep inside, from the first sad times when I had to leave my island. Yes, I'd write about those feelings.

I looked around at my classmates. Most of them had never left the island. The smaller ones stood still and stared at our slowly diminishing island. One little first grade boy started to suck his thumb and held on tight to his older sister. The older boys all looked at the moving parts of the engine and asked the nice ferryman many questions. He smiled and patiently answered every one of them, while he puffed away on his pipe. The strong current shook the little ferry and made one girl sick. Our teacher picked her up, held her head, and let her spit up over the side of the boat into the ocean.

When we came close to the ferry landing on the other side of the ocean, a loud blow from an arriving train got everyone's immediate attention. After the ferryboat landed, the operator asked us if we had ever seen the inside of a train.

Most of the children shook their heads.

Then he said, "Well, let's go and see if the conductor will give you a tour."

All excited, the children followed him to the train. Our teacher gave Wolfgang and me the big envelope with the important papers. He handed us money for the postage and told us to take it to the conductor of the train.

So young and so full of hope, the two of us ran over to the train and handed the big envelope and the money to the conductor.

He looked at the address and said, "My, these papers will travel faraway to a huge town. They must be very important."

Both of us smiled and answered, "Yes, very important."

He put our envelope inside a big leather pouch and told us,

"I'll guard this letter and take it to the nearest post office."

For a second, I closed my eyes and silently begged God to let the letter arrive safely in Berlin.

Most of the children just coming out of the passenger car, now ran up to the huge, black locomotive. Out of respect or fear, they stood a distance away from the black, vibrating monster and stared at it in disbelief. Great masses of dirty, grey smoke escaped from its narrow chimney and rose up quickly into the blue sky.

A blow from the conductor's whistle told me that the train needed to leave. The engineman signaled his readiness to leave with a very loud blow from the huge locomotive. That loud noise and the massive amount of steam escaping from beneath the huge engine onto the group of children scared some of them a great deal. They screamed and ran down toward the ferry landing. The ferry operator, our teacher, and a few older children laughed and slowly walked after them.

With strange, fearful feelings, I reached down and gently held onto Wolfgang's warm hand. Together we watched the train with our future on it, roaring away into the vast distance. Somehow, from deep inside of me, a lone tear crawled up and escaped my eye. I quickly let go of Wolfgang's hand and wiped that tear from my face so he wouldn't notice it. In silence, we walked back to the little ferryboat.

We had a fine ferry ride back to our island. By the time we reached our schoolhouse, our teacher declared school over for the day. He loudly reminded us of our homework assignment.

Before I left the classroom, I walked over to him and asked, "When can I expect an answer from Berlin?"

He smiled and answered, "Most likely in February."

Hopeful and somewhat in a daze, I walked home daydreaming of my great future. Now and then, my mom's words of "All the poor folks get are their dreams," kept creeping back into my mind. February seemed years away.

Our mail came twice a week now, weather permitting of

course, and the man delivered the mail to our small store in the next village, Burg, which had grown a lot over the years and called itself a town now. I found it easy to stop there on my way to school, so I started to check on a letter for me in the middle of January. Soon, I didn't have to ask the owner anymore if I had any mail. The moment I opened the door of her store, she looked at me and just shook her head.

Finally, February arrived and I really grew anxious. Each time I brought up the subject of my future schooling to my family members, they looked at me and said, "You need to wait for an answer, child."

I couldn't understand why no one seemed excited about my plans for such a great future. The end of February came, but my letter didn't. My sadness grew. Perhaps my mom was right; that the poor people only get to dream about things they want.

Then one fine, sunny day in the early part on March when school had let out, the owner of the little store stood outside with a letter in her hand and waved at me. My heart jumped in anticipation. Could this be the letter I had dreamed of, hoped for, and prayed for?

Quickly, I ran over to her.

She smiled when she handed me the letter. "It's from Berlin." Then she handed me another letter and asked me, "Please take this one to Wolfgang."

For a brief moment, I stood stunned. His letter had come from Berlin too. Could this mean our dreams would come true or would the letters tell us otherwise? I dropped my school pack and ran with all the speed my young body could muster, north, toward Wolfgang's village.

Before long, I found him walking on the small path through the snow-covered fields. I called his name repeatedly, holding the letters up into the air, while I ran toward him. He finally heard me, stopped walking, turned around, dropped his school bundle and ran toward me. We ran into each other's arms and promptly fell down into the snow. After a moment of laughter, I handed him his letter. He smiled and his green eyes sparkled with excitement. We sat up in the deep snow, looked at each other and with great hope in our hearts, slowly opened our letters.

There, on a fine piece of absolutely white paper, it said in printed black letters:

"Dear Miss Edith,

We welcome you with honors to study for two years in our higher school. If you can keep up your excellent grades, you may enter our five year veterinarian program at our university, here in Berlin."

The letter went on, but I felt too overwhelmed to read it right then. I lay back down in the snow and screamed "Yes!" up to the blue sky at least a dozen times. I looked at Wolfgang. He slowly lay back down too, lifted his letter to the sky, and together we screamed and laughed for a long time. Then we stood up, hugged each other and ran in opposite directions toward our homes.

While I ran home, my heart pounded, and happy tears froze to my cheeks. I waved the letter in the air and yelled with pride at everyone I saw, "I'm going to Berlin!"

People stopped, smiled and waved back at me.

Absolutely exhausted, I walked into our house and screamed, "I'm going to school in Berlin!"

Mom rushed downstairs. Grandma's door and my aunt and uncle's door opened. All of my family members talked at the same time and congratulated me. I handed my mom the letter and sat down on our stairs. While everyone quieted down, she slowly began to read the letter. After the first great part of the letter, she took a deep breath and read on.

"The schooling and all the materials you need for your lessons are free of course.

We found you a family that you can live with. They will feed you twice a day and you can sleep on their couch in their cellar. The cost for that will be twenty-five Marks each quarter of the year."

Then, the letter went on, telling me when and where to check in and what to bring. It even told me which train to take, how much the ride would cost and how much money to bring for incidentals. I didn't know what the word *incidentals* meant, but I felt too happy to worry about that now.

A short moment of silence and my mom said with a shaky voice, "Sorry child, we don't have that kind of money. We don't even have enough for the train ride. We have nothing to sell to get enough money together for your education." Then she handed me my letter back, touched my head gently and said, "I'm so awfully sorry, Edith."

Shock jolted through me. Grasping for a last chance to fulfill my dream, I said, "I could get a night job in the city to feed myself. Perhaps I could sleep on a church bench."

My mom shook her head. "No child, it won't work out."

I looked for help to the rest of my family, but they just looked back at me with sad, shaking faces. There I sat on the stairs of our house, feeling like my world just ended. A few black spots danced before my open eyes.

As though talking from faraway, I heard my mom say, "If anyone needs a good education it's your brother Willie. He'll need to support a family some day. Your husband will most likely support you. If you were a boy, I'd let you go and hire on to one of those big merchant ships you always watch sailing by our island, but you're not a boy. I'll try my best to find you a job on our island where you can sleep and eat. Perhaps if they're willing to pay you for your work, we can save up some money together for your brother's education." Then my mother walked slowly up the stairs, crying, with her head held down and her shoulders shaking.

In stunned disbelief, I realized that my dreams, my future lay smashed into a million pieces. I remained sitting on the stairs while the rest of my family walked back into their rooms. Soon the black spots before my eyes disappeared. I clutched the letter to my heart and left the house.

As if in a dream, I walked out over our frozen bay to the tall stand of pine trees. The usual cold winter wind could not reach me inside the small forest. There I sat under one of those huge trees near the end of the stand, and stared out over the frozen ocean. My mind wandered faraway to the town of Berlin, which I had never seen. I imagined what the city and my school looked like. I saw myself going to the Berliner University, holding hands with Wolfgang. The day both of us came back to our island to open our clinic danced in my head for a while. With a thankful look in their eyes, groups of different animals thanked me for stilling their pains.

The evening stars twinkled in the sky and the wind died. Night descended upon the earth in absolute silence. The soft, low moon illuminated the tall, strange icebergs the ocean had formed over the brutal winter, in a silvery, ghostly light.

Somehow, I didn't feel alone. I looked around, but saw no one, only the long shadows of the faraway icebergs. With great pain in my heart, I stood and walked down to the snowy beach. There I stepped onto the thick ice sheet of the mighty ocean.

Gradually, with my letter clutched to my heart, I walked out toward the sparkling, strange formations of the icebergs. The moon had risen high and shone brightly by the time I reached them. I felt as though they watched me. All of a sudden, a star fell from the sky with its long tail of light trailing behind. At that moment, I decided that the falling star had come as an omen from above. I had to say farewell to my fine future right there.

I took my letter of acceptance out of its envelope and gently kissed it goodbye. Then I raised my hand up into the still air to throw my letter up and let it fly away. Surprisingly, a gust of wind blew past me, took my letter out of my hand and lifted it way up into the sky.

The night grew still again, but the pages of my letter flew high, way past the icebergs now. As I stood watching my desired future fly away, tears from deep inside me, the ones that really matter, welled up from my heart and rolled silently from my eyes. In a daze, forlorn and bitter, I walked home.

The next day, a Sunday, I met Wolfgang in our church. He sang in our choir also. He smiled when he saw me walking over to him.

All excited, he asked me, "Are you going on to school?"

I shook my head. "No. Are you going?"

With a bright smile and happy eyes, he answered, "Yes, I can go."

I didn't want him to see my tears, so I turned around and snuck out of the church. When I walked by our long gone island witch's house, I stopped for a moment and sadly wished she were still alive so I could talk to her. A white, lit candle softly flickered in the window, as it always did, even though she had long disappeared. One big, black raven sat silently on the steeple, staring down at me. For a second, I thought the curtain in her window slightly moved, but then I disregarded that since no one dared to live inside her house.

When I entered our house, my grandma called me into her room. She hugged me gently and asked me to sit down with her on her sofa. She tried her best to tell me that my life had not ended, and that so many good times still lay ahead of me, even without a higher education.

Grandma stood up when her teakettle called for her. She brewed us some peppermint tea and poured it into our mugs. Then she added some fine, sweet red liquor to the tea. It tasted wonderful and warmed my whole body. Soon, my grandma, while telling me about her childhood, served us both a plate with fried eggs on top of a thick slice of bread. Oh, how hunger plagued me. After we ate the delicious meal and had another cup of sweet tea, I laid my head down on my grandma's old sofa and went to sleep.

The next day in school, I told my teacher that my dreams for a higher education were over and why.

He felt very sorry for me and said, "You can skip school for the next two weeks. I'll still give you a perfect A report card. Just show up on the last day of school for the last hour."

I nodded and walked out of the classroom. At home, I walked upstairs, sat by the window and just stared out of it. I wandered far, faraway, where I wanted to be, in the city of Berlin.

My mom entered the room and called out my name, which abruptly brought me back to reality.

She said, "This is your lucky day, girl, I found you a job. The butcher in the village to our west will kindly let you live and work in his house. Think how much you can eat there. You'll start the day after your confirmation, which always falls on the same day school lets out for Easter break.

"They'll feed you and you can share a bed with their small daughter. If you work very hard, they might pay you a little, which I hope you'll bring home to me. If they don't pay you, I'll save at least a little by not having to feed you. Your little sister is big enough now to take care of your brother Willie."

I heard the words my mom spoke and understood their meaning, but somehow I couldn't believe what she said. I wanted to rescue and heal animals, not help the butcher kill them and feast on them.

Spring moved in early this year and with it its welcomed, warm winds. The thick ice sheet on the ocean began to crack and formed small islands, which the strong current of the mighty sea took away. I always liked to watch this yearly event, especially this year. I'd pick a fast floating ice island and dream that it took me faraway to some pretty, imaginary land which of course, had lots of food. This year, my ice island took me to Berlin and let me see the higher school I came close to attending. Oh, how big and pretty it looked in my mind.

For the next weeks, I wandered around the island looking for a job and always got the same answer: "No sorry, not until summer, when the fieldwork starts." Longingly, I often sat down by the ferry landing and looked across the ocean to the mainland of Germany.

On one of those foggy days down by the landing, I saw our island witch. She smiled at me and waved for me to come to her while she slowly drifted away amongst the fog over the smooth water toward the mainland. To see her so clearly surprised me greatly.

When I told my grandma about that event, she looked at me astounded and said, "Well, child, our island witch blessed you a while back. Surely she entered your heart and mind, before she disappeared. Most likely, she sensed your deep hurt and came to help you."

That night, all snuggled up in my bed next to my sister, a warm, soft glow appeared on the naked shingles above our bed. A faint, warm hand reached down and gently touched my face. Calmness came over me, chased my bitterness and hurt away. While I looked up at the soft, disappearing glow, I whispered with a smile inside of my heart, "Thank you, Ola!"

Gladness filled me to feel her so close in my time of bitter confusion.

No charcoal, discotheque or graduation ceremony.

Chapter 85

My last day of school.

The evening before my last day of school and my confirmation, my mom cut my long hair.

We had talked about it and I pleaded with her not to cut my hair, but my mom sternly said, "My daughter has to look like a grown up woman now, not like a wild child any longer. What would people say if I let you run around looking like this?"

After cutting my hair, she wet it, rolled it up tight in many small wooden curlers and told me, "You have to sleep with the curlers in your hair through the night."

Angry about the whole process, I had a hard time falling asleep with all those hard curlers on my head. I didn't like any of this at all. The next morning, Mom, took out all the darn curlers and gently combed my hair. She handed me the small part of a mirror she treasured and commented, "See how pretty you look!"

Oh, how I hated my short, curly hair!

Faithfully, as my great teacher requested, I walked into my classroom one hour before spring break. With a strange feeling of fear, I sat down in my old seat in the last bench and the closest seat to the door, where I sat for all eight years.

Our teacher smiled at me and welcomed me. Then he asked the three of us, for whom it was the last day of school, to come forward and sit next to him. After we took our seats, the other children in the room stood up and sang a happy farewell song for us. A young boy came up to us and handed each of us a fine sheet of paper with best wishes for our future written on it and signed by everyone in the schoolroom.

Our teacher then handed out report cards to every child and announced the end of school. Some of the children jumped up in delight and ran out of the room. Others walked out in silence. I stood for a moment wondering what my life would hold for me without the happy hours I spent inside this room and after seeing my dreams of going on to the higher school in Berlin destroyed.

A gentle hug from my teacher and good wishes for my future told me that the time had come to leave my schoolroom forever. When I shook my teacher's hand and thanked him for all his help, I saw his sad eyes looking back at me. Quickly, I left the room so he wouldn't see my tears.

As if in a trance, I left the schoolyard, walked slowly through the old cemetery and inside the small chapel which adjoined our big, old church. Wolfgang and the other girl from his village had already arrived. I quietly sat down next to them on the small bench.

I had always liked this little chapel. It felt like a happier place than the huge church. The sun shone through its colorful, stained glass windows almost all day long, and as far as we knew, nobody was buried beneath the ground of this little chapel. Some say it was the first building of our giant church that our people had completed so many centuries ago.

A huge boulder in the inside south corner of the chapel always felt wet to the touch. At times, droplets of water actually slowly trickled from the boulder onto the earthen floor. Our people called that boulder Forget Me Not.

Grandma said, "Those droplets are the tears of the young children who died too early in their lives."

Women came and knelt before the huge boulder in silence. Some brought flowers and laid them near the wet ground. Others brought small candles, stuck them into the mud beneath the boulder, and lit them.

Three completely black outfits hung over the bench next to us. Three black Bibles sat on the bench. A small bunch of pure white lilies of the valley flowers, tied together with a black ribbon, lay on top of the Bibles. These beautiful flowers blossomed all over our island this time of the year.

One of the church bells began to call people to come to the church, and our preacher walked into the chapel. He looked at us shortly, opened his big Bible, told us to kneel down and ask God for forgiveness. I couldn't think of anything I needed to ask forgiveness for at the moment, so I asked Him seriously for taking care of all my family members, especially my sweet little brother Willie, who I'd miss a whole lot. Then our preacher told us again about the seriousness of confirmation, but I really didn't pay attention to him.

The bell quit ringing and the preacher's daughter began to play the big pipe organ. Our preacher told us to pick up the clothes which hung beside the Bible and dress in the borrowed black clothes. He told us two girls to step behind the small altar to get dressed. He took Wolfgang out of the chapel to get dressed in the short hall. My borrowed dress fit nicely, but I had to squeeze my feet into the shoes. I picked up my Bible with the beautiful flowers on top of it and walked clumsily over to our preacher. I hoped I wouldn't stumble and fall onto the cobblestone floor of our church in front of everyone.

Soon, all dressed, the three of us stood in front of our preacher ready to get confirmed. He walked out of the little chapel in front of us with his big Bible in his hands. The organ stopped playing, and all the island people who had gathered, stood.

Down the long, wide aisle, we walked in a single line, the preacher in front, then us two girls and Wolfgang at the end. People nodded at us and smiled. All dressed in black and walking down the aisle single file made me think of funerals. I started to shiver, wondering about my future. When we reached the wide bench just below the spectacular ivory altar, the preacher pointed for us to sit. This wide bench had no back to lean onto, and was used to place the coffins on for those who wanted a church ceremony before they buried their loved ones.

We sat down, facing the congregation. Someone played the huge pipe organ and the church choir sang without me. I'd never sing with them again. I was too old now. My feet hurt badly in the small shoes and I couldn't quit shaking. I was miserable.

With the last tones of the pipe organ and the voices of the choir echoing through our church, I lifted my head and looked at the pillar above the organ, where our island witch used to sit on important occasions. I saw a few black threads from her shawl swaying slightly back and forth on the pillar, and a very faint light above the pillar. I didn't see her, but I felt her presence, and that made me extremely happy. I quit shaking and slipped my heels slightly out of my shoes, which with great relief, ended my pains.

While our preacher thundered down his sermon to us sinners from his pulpit, I searched over the congregation for my grandma. When I found her sitting about half way down the church, she raised her hand slightly and smiled at me. Quickly, I looked up at the tall pillar to tell my grandma who was here. Grandma got my message, turned around and looked up at the pillar. She looked back at me and nodded. I knew then that she saw the threads of our island witch's shawl too.

I focused on the tall pillar through the completely boring ceremony. My mind wandered back in time to the day our island witch disappeared. I had often felt her closeness, saw some signs of her, but never saw her in person. Still though, she brought great comfort to me, especially when I had no one else to turn to. Somehow, at that young age, and the time and the place I grew up in, I figured that witches never really leave when they die, they just become invisible.

The mighty sound of our pipe organ ripped me from my thoughts. The confirmation ceremony had ended. Our preacher handed us each a certificate, shook our hands and blessed our souls. The congregation shouted, "Hallelujah," and started to leave the church. I looked up at the tall pillar once more where Ola often sat. The black strings of her shawl had disappeared. Only a faint light remained for another brief moment.

My grandma and the rest of my family in our house, except my mom, waited for me at the church's exit. All of them happily congratulated me, but I felt very sad.

When Grandma hugged me, I asked her, "Did you see the signs of Ola on the tall pillar?"

She said, "Yes, child, I did." She smiled and a happy tear left her eye.

Together, we walked home in the slowly darkening, mild afternoon.

At home, my mom surprised me with a great congratulations hug. A wonderful smell came from my aunt and uncle's kitchen. Mom had set a fine table with a white bed sheet, and all our combined dishes plus a few borrowed ones. A vase with lily of the valley flowers stood in the middle of the table, with a white candle on each side of it. This was the first time I had seen a table with a white sheet and flowers on it.

My mom busily tended several pots that were cooking at the same time on the iron stove. A few more relatives arrived with their children. I asked my mom if I could change my clothes and go outside to play with them.

She answered, "Oh, no, my child, you sit down at the head of the table with your pretty outfit on, and enjoy this evening of your great celebration."

Disappointed, I sat at the table as told. Grandma brought out her best liquor and poured everyone a drink in fine, very small, real, clear glasses. They lifted their glasses, pointed them toward me, and congratulated me. The congratulations overwhelmed me, and I wondered if it was for my outstanding report card, or for the confirmation. Then I realized that most of my relatives didn't

651

know how well I did in school, so it had to be for my confirmation.

To get confirmed in our religion was very easy. You only had to show up to the religious lessons once a week for two years and attend church twelve times each year. Singing in the choir counted as attending Sunday church service, even if I only showed up to sing the opening song and didn't stay for the service. I couldn't understand why my family made such fuss over that.

At that time, I had no idea of the meaning of this religious celebration. To me it was just something everyone did.

Before long, Mom announced, "Here comes dinner."

All the adults sat around the crowded table. My mom proudly brought a plate with a big piece of meat over to the table. To see such a big piece of meat on our table truly surprised me.

She handed Uncle Fred a big knife and asked him, "Please carve the roast."

Then my mom brought dishes filled with mashed potatoes, cooked carrots and red, sweet cabbage over to the table. The food astounded everyone and they complimented my mom. She smiled with pride, fetched the big pot of gravy, placed it on the table and sat down.

Grandma called the children inside and told them to sit on the floor, near the window. Then she lit the two white candles that stood on the table, cleared her throat and began to say thanks to her God. At the end of her prayer, she asked Him for all the help he could spare to show me to take the right path in my life. Finally, the feast began.

First, Aunt Hilde fixed the children a plate and handed the food to them. The small children ate in a hurry and finished before we even filled our plates. They looked up to us from their empty plates, but knew not to ask for seconds. Quickly, all of them ran back outside to play.

How great it smelled in this kitchen. We laughed, talked, and slowly ate our delicious meal. The pork roast had a good amount of fat on it and tasted absolutely wonderful, as did all the rest of it.

Mom must have saved up for a long time to cook such a rich meal.

Amid all the talking and eating, I smelled a sweet smell coming from the oven. My mom smelled it also, got up from the table and walked over to the stove. What a surprise. She took a big sheet cake out of my aunt's stove. It had dried plums on it and brown sugar. She placed it on the wood box by the stove, to cool down. Is all this for me? I couldn't believe all the trouble my mom went through.

When the last person finished eating their meal, my mom stood up and brought the sheet cake over to the table. While she cut it into enough pieces so all of us could have a piece, we licked our plates clean. She served the cake while my grandma filled the tiny glasses with another round of her fine liquor.

I didn't care for the brown, strong stuff, but my grandma knew that and poured my little glass full of sweet strawberry wine. After we ate our delicious piece of cake, my family passed a cup around the table and everyone dropped a coin or two inside of it.

Then my mom handed me the cup and said, "This is your present from all of us. You may keep it."

I stood up, hugged my mom and thanked her for the wonderful celebration with all the excellent food. She whispered in my ear, "That's all I can do for you, my child. Now you go on and take care of yourself." My mom's warm tears ran down my neck.

The adults called the children inside and handed them another plate of food and a piece of cake. While everyone talked, I eagerly counted the money. I had exactly three-and-a-half Marks to my name. One more round out of grandma's bottle and people said their goodbyes with hardy hugs and big promises to see each other again soon.

My mom carefully put the leftover food in suitable containers so the mice and rats couldn't get to it during storage in the cooler lean-to. Grandma washed all the dishes and pots in less than a gallon of hot, soapy water and I dried them. We didn't know then that one should rinse dishes after washing them. We stacked the dishes up, according to whom we had borrowed them from, so we could return them to the rightful owners the next morning.

Bedtime came, and together we climbed our stairs. My sister and I waited until my mom carried my little brother into her room. He slept now in a nicely decorated fish box on the floor right next to my mom's narrow couch. When my mom closed the door behind them, my sister and I took off our shoes, I took off my borrowed dress, and we crawled into our bed. I looked up at the shingles over our bed for the last time and anxiously wondered if the plan I had in my mind would work.

The house quieted. In the glow of the moon, shining through our window, I thought my plans over one more time. When I closed my eyes, I faintly saw Ola's face and fell asleep with a warm feeling inside.

No burritos, ticks or toothpicks, but we knew how to spell cheese.
It was not K.R.A.F.T!

Chapter 86

The farewell letter.

My dear Mom,

You proudly called and made me look like a grown up woman at my confirmation. So, I'll try to speak to you now as a woman and not as a child.

I absolutely will not live and work at the butcher shop. I cannot look those poor, painfully screaming animals into their pleading eyes, begging me to spare their lives, as people slaughter them Perhaps see them fighting for their lives, while their blood runs out of them. Then, before they stop moving their legs, ever so hopelessly trying to run away from death, get cut open and have their guts ripped out of them, to soon hang on the ladder and see their last warm steam rising from their still warm flesh up into the cold air.

What were you thinking, Mom? I want to become a veterinarian to help and rescue animals, not watch, or likely have to help in the torture of killing them.

I know it's customary, and time for me to leave home, or pay my own way and stay here. I don't mind working in the fields during the growing season, but fighting hunger for the rest of the year feels awfully painful. I saw you hungry so many days just so we kids had a warm meal, which I appreciated, but it made me feel sad. Mom, please understand I want more out of life than you had.

I thank you so very much for having the strength to do without so much, just to raise me. Also, many thanks for the great ceremony on my confirmation day, with all the delicious food and fun. I shall never forget that day and all the work you went through to make it happen, and most likely, all the days you saved up for this day without taking in much nourishment.

I'll walk around our island once more today, to say goodbye to all the special places that meant so much to me.

By tomorrow, when my grandma hands you this letter, I will have left our island to search for a better life.

I took the whole loaf of bread with me and left you my confirmation gift money to bake many other loaves for you, my sister and little, sweet Willie.

Oh, how I will miss all of you.

When I find work, I'll send money home, so all of you can afford to have enough to eat in the brutal winters.

I know this will make you cry, but please don't worry. Ola walks with me.

I love you, Mom, thank you for my life and how you raised me.

Edith

No nail polishes, Scotch Tape or ribbons, but on occasions we could buy oranges and bananas at our little store now.

Chapter 87

A last walk around my island.

The day after my confirmation, I awoke early.

Before my mom left that morning to work in the fields, she bid me farewell with a sad face and said, "Come home if you should get a day off from work."

I said yes, but I couldn't look into her face. After she left, I packed my bundle with the extra set of clothes I had and put the fine loaf of bread my mom just baked on top of it. Then I tied the ends of my bundle close and walked downstairs.

There I said goodbye to my smaller sister and handed her my box of all my collected treasures. She smiled at me and shyly waved goodbye. I kissed my sweet little brother and wished him well. My grandma knew my plans about leaving the island and wished me the best of luck. She handed me a long, smoked eel, wrapped up in newspapers, and a few apples for my journey. Then she hugged me for a long time.

I told her, "You're the best grandma in the whole, wide world," and clung tightly to her for a moment.

After she let loose of me, I handed her the letter addressed to my mom. She knew to wait until the next day to hand it to my mom. When I walked out of my grandma's room, I saw her wiping tears from her face with the corner of her apron. That was one of the rare times I saw my grandma's tears.

Quickly, I left our house before I changed my mind to stay. Oh, how hard it was to leave my family. With tears streaming down my face, but feeling strong and calm inside about my journey, I started to walk away from the house I had grown up in.

I looked back through my tear-filled eyes a few times, but each time I did so, I grew more confident that I needed to leave. Soon, my tears stopped, and I walked with a happy heart and excitement around our island.

First, I walked to our cemetery to say goodbye to my beloved dog, whom I buried in my grandpa's grave. I told him that, in my mind, he walked beside me on my journey. After leaving a few tears on his grave, I walked down the row where all the people I had lost over the years were buried.

I stopped at Robert's grave for a moment. Oh how I remembered his sparkling, blue eyes. Guilt over his death crept up inside of me again. With those thoughts on my mind, I walked over to Sinners' Row and bid Albert farewell. My grandma promised to take care of his grave too, after I left. On my way out of the cemetery, I stood still in front of the oldest grave with all the pretty flowers on it and wondered if our island witch's body really lay beneath the dark earth. Leaving the cemetery, I took one quick look at the old windmill, and the very scary night I spent inside it with some of my friends came to mind.

On my way down to the bay, I strolled through the small town of Burg, past my clapboard schoolhouse. Oh, how many memories flew through my mind: all the fights at my younger age; our grumpy old teacher, who didn't like me; all the days I slept away in that classroom. Then Ola reacted to so many complaints from us children and in walked our new teacher. He made school so much fun.

I stopped at our beautiful, old church and looked up at her high bell tower. One lone, black raven sat there and looked down at me. At that moment, the happy little bell began to ring to announce the birth of a child. I wished it a long, good life.

With happy feelings, I opened the huge, heavy church door and walked inside. After the little busy bell quit ringing, our old church once more stood silent. In awe, I slowly walked down the wide aisle toward the small chapel. If only these huge, thick walls could tell what they saw and heard over the many centuries they stood here. I wished they could tell me about the souls buried beneath the floor. With memories of all the fine Christmas plays I took part in, and the time the devil came to kill me, I walked inside the little chapel.

I knelt in front of the Forget Me Not boulder, touched its wet surface and asked God and Ola, "Please watch over my family."

On my way out, I looked up at the huge pipe organ and on to the pillar where our island witch often sat. My heart jumped with excitement when I saw a few black threads hanging down from that tall pillar. I lifted my head and waved at the invisible Ola sitting up there, watching over me.

On my way out of our huge church, I walked through the massive church tower, and the day I climbed to the top passed before my eyes, as if it had happened yesterday. Gently I whispered a thank you to the ghost that saved me from falling to my death.

A fresh breeze greeted me outside. The clouds had flown away and the sun had warmed up our island. I stopped in front of Ola's house to remember the fun times I had there, the day she died and took the sea away for a short time. Somehow, I knew she still lived. I felt her closeness and she assured me with different signs that she remained nearby. A few big ravens sat at her fence, as though guarding the entrance to her house. The sun shone on the black ravens, which made their feathers shimmer almost a deep purple now.

When I neared the field where they hung Albert and we found two of our neighbors dead, I hurried past to forget the shocking events.

From there, I walked along the narrow footpath toward the bay. Our favorite castle stood in the bay to my right, about half under water. How much fun my friends and I had diving down into it. To my left, I saw the carp pond with its few huge fish and many smaller ones. I could almost see my family there at harvest time. A few more steps and I could hear the ocean's gentle waves lapping onto the sandy shore.

As soon as I reached the beach, I took off my shoes and ran in the soft sand all the way to the tall stand of trees where I spent hours climbing them, or searching for treasurers. Here, I had first seen my precious dog, Harras. Then I climbed up on top of my secret boulder, where he and I often spent time hiding away and sorting out things life threw at me. I took the loaf of bread and the smoked eel from my bundle and ate just a little of each.

Walking about half-way around our island, I noticed that the sun had licked away all the low ground fog over the ocean. I could faintly see the coastline of Denmark shimmering above the silvery, calm ocean. That brought my thoughts to my little brother, whom Mom had given away to a couple in that country. I thought he must be walking and talking for some time now and calling someone else Mom. I wondered what he looked like.

After another hour, I reached the old stone mound graves. For the past two years, I could no longer crawl into my special grave to visit with the fox family. I just outgrew the entrance. Hopeful to get at least a glance at them, I climbed up the steep coast and walked over to the old burial grounds. I didn't have to watch out for the old, grumpy ghost anymore. He had finally moved on to wherever his soul needed to go. Happy for him and relieved not to have stones thrown at me anymore, I smiled and waved.

The moment I stepped into the graveyard, complete amazement ran through me. There, near the entrance to their den, sat mama fox in the sunshine, watching her four small offspring playing in the dirt. How happy that made me. Quietly, so as not to disturb them, I slipped back down the coast and walked on. By early afternoon, I reached the area where the devil's fingers tore apart the twin villages and sank the school ship Lore. I climbed back up the steep coast to see the long grave one more time. In silence, I stood at the graveside, still seeing the horrifying sight in front of me.

A gentle hand touched my arm and someone said, "Hi, Edith."

I turned around and said, "Hello, how are you?"

I saw the woman who almost gave birth inside the dugout grave. She had a milk can in her hand full of fresh, still steaming milk.

She asked, "Would you like to have a drink of this fine milk?"

Gladly I nodded and said, "Oh yes!"

She called one of her children to run and fetch the ladle. When the child handed the ladle to its mother, she filled it to the rim with fresh milk and offered it to me. Eagerly, I took the ladle and slowly enjoyed the tasty, warm milk.

She offered me another ladle full, but I politely said, "No thank you, ma'am."

She asked me where I was going and I told her my plan. She smiled, wished me good luck and left.

On my way I went, around the last bend of our island. Soon I passed by Miss Mali's, the palm reader's lighthouse. I started to laugh, thinking about that night the two of us tried to catch the flounder. She died a year ago and so did her dog. Lightning struck both of them. They lay buried together in a small plot near her lighthouse. I walked over to her grave and said my goodbye. A man moved in and took care of the important lighthouse now. I liked her and will miss her.

By the time the sun slowly wandered down to her watery bed I arrived at the ferry landing. The old man sat on his ferry, holding his fishing pole. A wet stump of a cigar hung out of the side of his mouth. His shaggy big dog lay beside him, watching me as I approached the two of them. I stopped at the strong wooden pole where the little ferry sat tethered, and said hello.

The old ferryman turned and said, "Hello Edith, what's up? Are you going to the higher school in Berlin?"

Disappointed, I said no and told him my plans. Then I told him that I had no money and asked him if I could do some work for him to pay for my way across the ocean.

He smiled and answered, "Sure girl, can you cook?"

Proudly I told him, "I'm a fine cook. My mom taught me long ago."

He smiled and said, "Great, come to my shack in the early morning and cook these fish I caught for my breakfast. After that, I'll take you across."

Ever so enthusiastic to have that problem solved, I ran toward the sand dunes and climbed on top of the highest one. Somewhat out of breath, but so excited, I sat down in the still warm sand. From up here I clearly saw my little fishing village and the sea burial grounds. I started to shake, thinking about all of us falling overboard, right into the devil's hands. A little off to the left on the tiny isle, which we children called Fillalilla, sat our ocean liner. We sure had fun traveling around our island in our small, discarded rowboat, with only one hole in its lower side. Oh, what fun we had and what danger we got into at times.

The slight breeze stopped completely, and the fiery, golden ball of the sun started to sink into the vast ocean. She lit the whole western part of the sky on fire. From her golden, hot ball emerged steaming vapor. At first, it had the same golden color of the sun, then it changed into a slight reddish color and soon it spilled its bright red flames all around over the sky. Higher up, the sky now glowed with pink and light purple colors. The narrow bands of clouds farthest from the sun slowly turned slightly reddish brown. A hint of blue green showed up in some places on the smaller clouds. In great awe, I sat watching the spectacular sunset. What a wonderful farewell concert of colors.

The moment the body of the sun sank into her watery bed, a large flock of seagulls came home from their evening dinner flight and settled down close to each other on one of the tiny islets in the bay. Twilight slowly crept over our small island. Ever so excited, I ran and stumbled down the tall sand dune. Down at the beach, I took all my clothes off, stored them and my important bundle on top of a boulder, and ran into the cold sea.

I swam way out to sea as fast as I could. It calmed me down and tired me out. When I turned around to swim back to shore, I noticed that someone, or something came swimming my way. For a moment, I worried at being caught naked, but then I noticed the head of a dog. My heart jumped with hope to see my dog, Harras, swimming toward me. To my disappointment, I soon recognized the shaggy dog of the ferryman.

When the dog reached me, he turned around and we swam back to the shore together. By the time we walked out of the cold ocean water, the first stars appeared in the sky and the silver moon started to light up the world.

Shivering, I ran over to the boulder with my clothes on it and got dressed. The shaggy dog ran next to me, shaking the water from his long, fur coat. Since I didn't have a jacket, I put my second set of clothes on over the first one to keep me warm for the night.

Without any problems, I found a soft, sandy spot in the dunes to bed down. From here, I could see the huge moon and the mighty, restless ocean. Far out in the sea I saw lights moving, most likely, a big merchant ship, traveling all over the world. For a moment, I wishfully traveled with the ship. Then hunger reminded me of the good food I had inside my bundle.

Carefully, I ripped off two small pieces of bread, bit off the head off the eel, and sucked the good stuff out of it. Then I handed the dog the eel's head and one of the small pieces of bread, which he slung down immediately. I ate the other piece of bread and packed the rest back into my bundle. Tired and a little exhausted from the long swim, I lay down in the sand. The shaggy dog crawled next to me and lay beside me. Through sleepy eyes, I watched the now slightly pinkish moon smile down at me.

It seemed as though
    The bright, close moon
        Reached down and gently kissed the weeping earth

With a soft, white
    puffy cloud
        He wiped away her running tears

In his gentle arms
    She smiled
        And forgot her painful fears

She spread her restless wings
    So wide, so pleased
        And flew away with him in joyful, soothing ease
        On this, starlit, so long wished for night.

No dog or cat food, Pepto-Bismol or, sweet sodas.
We had no idea what viruses were.

Chapter 88

Leaving my island

Though still dark, the shaggy dog woke me the next morning with a snarling growl. Another dog had tried to get close to my bundle of food and clothes. When both of us stood up, the other dog found it safer to carefully retreat. I thanked the shaggy dog with a pat on his head. Then I shook the sand from my clothes and hair and walked down to the sea to splash some cold water in my face.

Slowly, while the slightest sign of dawn appeared on the horizon, I swung my light bundle over my shoulder and walked toward the ferryman's shack. The shaggy dog followed me faithfully, as if he belonged to me. I felt nervous and excited at the prospect of leaving my island today.

Happy to see light shining through the small window of the ferryman's shack, I softly knocked on his door. I called, "Good morning."

He opened the clapboard shack's door, smiled and said, "Come on inside, girl. You'll find the fish in the bucket. I already gutted them. I keep potatoes in the wood bin and you'll see the grease in the old can next to the stove. I'll come back in a little while."

I noticed that he had already lit the little iron stove and that the fire burned well. His tiny stove had only enough room for one pan or pot at a time. I found a frying pan, with yesterday's grease inside of it, standing on the floor beneath the tiny oven. A kettle stood right next to it. I filled the kettle with water from the outside water barrel and placed it on the stove and hoped that I'd find some tea in the shack. I sliced a few potatoes, placed them on one side of the frying pan and three nice looking herrings on the other side.

Before long, I took the boiling water off the stove and searched for a lid for the pan, so the hot grease wouldn't spit all over the stove. I found it beneath his cot. A quick blow and the dust flew off the lid. Then I set the frying pan with the tightly fitting lid on the red hot stovetop.

While the food cooked, I looked around for some tea. Sure enough, dried dandelions hung down from the ceiling of the shack near the rear wall. A carved wooden spatula lay on a short shelf next to a metal mug, with one spoon in it which I placed on the makeshift table.

When the old ferryman came back, I had the frying pan with the delicious smelling food sitting on the fish box table, next to his cot. Tea steamed in his cup and since I couldn't find a plate, I laid his spoon next to the pan.

He smiled and said, "Girl, this looks great!"

When he sat in the only chair, the shaggy dog jumped up on the cot and put his nose on the shaking table and waited for his share of the food.

Just about to dig into the pan with his spoon, the old man stopped, looked at me and then at his dog and said, "My God, look at us. We have no manners."

He stood up from his chair, asked me to sit down and pulled an old bucket over to the low table for himself to sit in. He handed me his spoon and told me nicely to eat all I wanted to.

I thanked him and handed him his metal cup, but he shook his head and pushed it back to me. He took the teapot and drank out of it. Then, after I took a spoonful of potatoes out of the pan, he took a fish out of the pan with his hands, placed it in front of his dog on the makeshift table and said "Wait!" to the dog.

The dog patiently waited, with the tempting food in front of him. The smiling, old ferryman then took another fish out of the pan and placed it on the table in front of himself. He grabbed a good amount of potatoes out of the pan with his other hand. Then he nodded as his sweet shaggy dog just about slung that fried herring down in one piece. The dog then laid his head back down onto the table and kept his wishful eyes on the frying pan.

While I scraped small pieces of the fish with my spoon out of the pan and politely ate it that way, the old ferryman kept on eating his way without utensils. The grease ran down his arms to his elbows and then onto his pants, but my, did he enjoy eating and talking at the same time. The food tasted great and soon disappeared.

The friendly old man put his fish bones back into the frying pan and pushed the pan over to his shaggy dog. The dog eagerly ate the bones and licked out the frying pan. I wished my wonderful dog I loved so much could have eaten with us like this dog did.

When the big dog finished licking out the pan, I offered to wash the few dishes, but the ferryman told me, "Girl, there's no need for washing the dishes."

He stood up, took the frying pan and the wooden spatula from the table. He laid the spatula into the pan and pushed it back beneath the little stove. Then he licked the spoon off, put it inside his metal mug and set them on the short shelf.

While putting on his sailor cap, he looked at me and said, "If you still want to leave the island, girl, come along now."

I thanked him for the meal, and excitedly followed him to the little ferryboat.

Almost daylight now, a wet fog hung in the air. Droplets of water clung to the ferryboat's railings and slowly fell into the ocean. It looked as though the old, little ferry wept. When I stepped onto her, a sudden strong feeling of sadness and fear crept up from deep inside of me. What will happen to me?

After a few tries and a swift kick to awaken the sleeping ferry, its engine quit arguing, stuttered away for a brief moment, and then purred in a regular rhythm. One last look at me, to see if I changed my mind, and the friendly ferryman untied the boat from its mooring.

The grey ocean rolled calmly that morning and the seagulls still slept. The nearby lighthouse warned the sailors about the dangerous reefs with a deep sorrowful moaning sound that sounded ghostly, and I shivered with fear.

What will the future hold for me? Could I make enough money to go and study at the Berliner University? Could I fulfill my dream of coming back to my island as a veterinarian to help all the creatures in need? A slight, wet breeze touched my face and brought me out of my worries. I turned my face in the direction of my fishing village and raised my hand to bid her farewell. Into the light breeze I whispered, "I will return."

At the age of barely fifteen and scared, I leaned against the wet railing of the little ferryboat and watched my island slowly disappear in the light fog. I felt like someone stood beside me and laid a hand on my shoulder, but I could see no one.

My grandma's face shone clearly in my mind. Oh, how I missed her already. My mom should have my farewell letter by now. I could see her sitting in her small, sparsely furnished room, holding it in her shaking hand with her head hung low and the letter wet with her tears. A few tears crept up from deep inside me. How it hurt to leave.

The moment my first tear fell into the grey ocean a warm hand touched my shoulder. In surprise, I turned to see no one in sight. A warm stillness reached my heart, and I believed that Ola stood beside me.

A huge, black raven silently landed on top of the ferry's engine hut and stared at me. Droplets of water ran down from its shiny, black coat onto the hut and the raven began to drink. Then it hopped, turned its head slightly and looked toward my island. I wondered if it was the huge raven from Ola's beautiful garden and if it too decided to leave all its loved ones behind.

Soon the fog swallowed the last faded image of my island. I closed my wet eyes and watched the candle softly flicker inside our island witch's window.

To order additional copies of
Faraway...the Candle Softly Flickers

Name _____

Address _____

_____

_____

Faraway...the Candle Softly Flickers
        by Edy Elfring
$22.95 x _____ copies = _____

Sales Tax _____
(Texas residents add 8.25% sales tax)

Please add $3.00 postage and handling for the first book
and $1.25 for each additional book

_____

Total amount due: _____

Please send check or money order for books to:
Special Delivery Books
WordWright Business Park
46561 State Highway 118
Alpine, Texas 79830

We also invite you to call 877/380-3321,
our toll free number,
and order by credit card.

For a complete catalog of books,
visit our site at
http://www.SpecialDeliveryBooks.com

CPSIA information can be obtained at www.ICGtesting.com
Printed in the USA
BVOW07s0414191113

336672BV00001B/27/P